WEALTH OF NATIONS

WEALTH OF NATIONS

ADAM SMITH

GREAT MINDS SERIES

PROMETHEUS BOOKS
59 John Glenn Drive • Amherst, New York 14228-2197

Published 1991 by Prometheus Books
59 John Glenn Drive, Amherst, New York 14228–2197.
VOICE: 716–691–0133, ext. 207. FAX: 716–564–2711.
WWW.PROMETHEUSBOOKS.COM

Library of Congress Cataloging-in-Publication Data

Smith, Adam, 1727–1790.
[Inquiry into the nature and causes of the wealth of nations]
The wealth of nations / Adam Smith.
p. cm. — (Great minds series)
ISBN 0–87975–705–1 (pbk. : alk. paper)
1. Economics. I. Title. II. Series
HB161.S65 1991b
330.15'3—dc20 91–61907
CIP

Printed in the United States of America on acid-free paper

Great Minds Paperback Series
(Economics)

- ❑ Charlotte Perkins Gilman—*Women and Economics: A Study of the Economic Relation between Women and Men*
- ❑ John Maynard Keynes—*The General Theory of Employment, Interest, and Money*
- ❑ John Maynard Keynes—*A Tract on Monetary Reform*
- ❑ Thomas R. Malthus—*An Essay on the Principle of Population*
- ❑ Alfred Marshall—*Money, Credit, and Commerce*
- ❑ Alfred Marshall—*Principles of Economics*
- ❑ Karl Marx—*Theories of Surplus Value*
- ❑ John Stuart Mill—*Principles of Political Economy*
- ❑ David Ricardo—*Principles of Political Economy and Taxation*
- ❑ Adam Smith—*Wealth of Nations*
- ❑ Thorstein Veblen—*Theory of the Leisure Class*

See the back of this volume for a complete list of titles in Prometheus's Great Books in Philosophy and Great Minds series.

ADAM SMITH was born in Kirkcaldy, Scotland, on June 5, 1723. Smith's father was a lawyer and customs official, who died before his son's birth, and his mother belonged to the Scottish gentry. At fourteen, Smith began studies at the University of Glasgow, and three years later entered Balliol College, Oxford, where he remained as a scholarship student until 1746. After leaving Oxford, Smith returned to the University of Glasgow to lecture on English literature and economics. The publication, in 1759, of his *Theory of Moral Sentiments* led to Smith's appointment as tutor to the third Duke of Buccleuch. In this capacity he lived for nearly three years in France, where he made the acquaintance of several of that nation's leading intellectuals, including François Quesnay, the physician and economist, and the renowned philosopher and critic of religion, Voltaire. Returning to Britain in 1766, Smith lived mainly in Kirkcaldy and London, working on his *Wealth of Nations,* which was published to great acclaim in 1776.

Smith's advocacy of what we would call classical liberal capitalism was a radical departure from the long-standing traditions of absolutism and transcendantalism with their view of human beings as inherently wayward, sinful, and therefore in constant need of strong secular and ecclesiastical authority. Drawing on contemporary natural and political science, Smith argued that humankind ought to be left to follow its inborn inclinations, which were to sustain life and to acquire goods. Human interests are best served by a government that abstains from interference in free enterprise, putting checks only on undue strife and competition. Attracted by their own interests, individuals will do what serves the common good, for in that all will gain and prosper.

Smith based his arguments on vast historical knowledge and worked out his principles with ingenuity and reason. Despite the passage of more than two centuries, the *Wealth of Nations* still stands as the best statement and defense of capitalist economics.

Adam Smith died in Edinburgh on July 17, 1790.

CONTENTS

BOOK I

BOOK II

BOOK III

BOOK IV

BOOK V

AN INQUIRY INTO THE NATURE AND CAUSES
OF THE
WEALTH OF NATIONS

BOOK I

OF THE CAUSES OF IMPROVEMENT IN THE PRODUCTIVE POWER OF LABOUR AND OF THE ORDER ACCORDING TO WHICH ITS PRODUCE IS NATURALLY DISTRIBUTED AMONG THE DIFFERENT RANKS OF THE PEOPLE.

CHAPTER I

OF THE DIVISION OF LABOUR

THE greatest improvement in the productive powers of labour, and the greater part of the skill, dexterity, and judgment with which it is any where directed, or applied, seem to have been the effects of the division of labour.

The effects of the division of labour, in the general business of society, will be more easily understood, by considering in what manner it operates in some particular manufactures. It is commonly supposed to be carried furthest in some very trifling ones; not perhaps that it really is carried further in them than in others of more importance: but in those trifling manufactures which are destined to supply the small wants of but a small number of people, the whole number of workmen must necessarily be small; and those employed in every different branch of the work can often be collected into the same workhouse, and placed at once under the view of the spectator.

In those great manufactures, on the contrary, which are destined to supply the great wants of the great body of the people, every different branch of the work employs so great a number of workmen, that it is impossible to collect them all into the same workhouse. We can seldom see more, at one time, than those employed in one single branch. Though in such manufactures, therefore, the work may really be divided into a much greater number of parts, than in those of a more trifling nature, the division is not near so obvious, and has accordingly been much less observed.

To take an example, therefore, from a very trifling manufacture; but one in which the division of labour has been very often taken notice of, the trade of the pin-maker; a workman not educated to this business (which the division of labour has rendered a distinct trade), nor acquainted with the use of the machinery employed in it (to the invention of which the same division of labour has probably given occasion), could scarce, perhaps, with his utmost industry, make one pin in a day, and certainly could not make twenty. But in the way in which this business is now carried on, not only the whole work is a peculiar trade, but it is divided into a number of branches, of which the greater part are likewise peculiar trades. One man draws out the wire, another straights it, a third cuts it, a fourth points it, a fifth grinds it at the top for receiving the head; to make the head requires two or three distinct operations; to put it on, is a peculiar business, to whiten the pins is another; it is even a trade by itself to put them into the paper; and the important business of making a pin is, in this manner, divided into about eighteen distinct operations, which, in some manufactories, are all performed by distinct hands, though in others the same man will sometimes perform two or three of them. I have seen a small manufactory of this kind where ten men only were employed, and where some of them consequently performed two or three distinct operations. But though they were very poor, and therefore but indifferently accommodated with the necessary machinery, they could, when they exerted themselves, make among them about twelve pounds of pins in a day. There are in a pound upwards of four thousand pins of a middling size. Those ten persons, therefore, could make among them upwards of forty-eight thousand pins in a day. Each person, therefore, making a tenth part of forty-eight thousand pins, might be considered as making four thousand eight hundred pins in a day. But if they had all wrought separately and independently, and without any of them having been educated to this peculiar business, they certainly could not each of them have made twenty, perhaps not one pin in a day; that is, certainly, not the two hundred and fortieth, perhaps not the four thousand eight hundredth part of what they are at present capable of performing, in consequence of a proper division and combination of their different operations.

In every other art and manufacture, the effects of the division of labour are similar to what they are in this very trifling one; though, in many of them, the labour can neither be so much subdivided, nor reduced to so great a simplicity of operation. The division of labour, however, so far as it can be introduced, occasions, in every art, a proportionate increase of the productive powers of labour. The separation of different trades and employments from one another, seems to have taken place, in consequence of this advantage. This separation too is generally carried furthest in those countries which enjoy the highest degree of industry and improvement; what is the work of one man in a rude state of society, being generally that of several in an improved one. In every improved society, the farmer is generally nothing but a farmer; the manufacturer, nothing but a manufacturer. The labour too which is necessary to produce any one complete manufacture, is almost always divided among a great number of hands. How many different trades are employed in each branch of the linen and woollen manufacturers, from the growers of the flax and the wool, to the bleachers and smoothers of the linen, or to the dyers and dressers of the cloth! The nature of agriculture, indeed, does not admit of so many subdivisions of labour, nor of so complete a separation of one business from another, as manufactures. It is impossible to separate so entirely, the business of the grazier from that of the corn-farmer, as the trade of carpenter is commonly separated from that of the smith. The spinner is almost always a distinct person from the weaver; but the ploughman, the harrower, the sower of the seed, and the reaper of the corn, are often the same. The occasions for those different sorts of labour returning with the different seasons of the year, it is impossible that one man should be constantly employed in any one of them. This impossibility of making so complete and entire a separation of all the different branches of labour employed in agriculture, is perhaps the reason why the improvement of the productive powers of labour in this art, does not always keep pace with their improvement in manufactures. The most opulent nations, indeed, generally excel all their neighbours in agriculture as well as in manufactures; but they are commonly more distinguished by their superiority in the latter than in the former. Their lands are in general better cultivated, and having more labour and expence bestowed upon them, produce more in proportion to the extent and natural fertility of the ground. But this superiority of produce is seldom much more than in proportion to the superiority of labour and expence. In agriculture, the labour of the rich country is not always much more productive than that of the poor; or, at least, it is never so much more productive, as it commonly is in manufactures. The corn of the rich country, therefore, will not always, in the same degree of goodness, come cheaper to market than that of the poor. The corn of Poland, in the same degree of goodness, is as cheap as that of France, notwithstanding the superior opulence and improvement of the latter country. The corn of France is, in the corn provinces, fully as good, and in most years nearly about the same price with the corn of England, though, in opulence and improvement, France is perhaps inferior to England. The corn-lands of England, however, are better cultivated than those of France, and the corn-lands of France are said to be much better cultivated than those of Poland. But though the poor country, notwithstanding the inferiority of its cultivation, can, in some measure, rival the rich in the cheapness and goodness of its corn, it can pretend to no such competition in its manufactures; at least if those manufactures suit the soil, climate, and situation of the rich country. The silks of France are better and cheaper than those of England, because the silk manufacture, at least under the present high duties upon the importation of raw silk, does not so well suit the climate of England as that of France. But the hard-ware and the coarse woollens of England are beyond all comparison superior to those of France, and much cheaper too in the same degree of goodness. In Poland there are said to be scarce any manufactures of any kind, a few of those coarser household manufactures excepted, without which no country can well subsist.

This great increase of the quantity of work, which, in consequence of the division of labour, the same number of people are capable of performing, is owing to three different circumstances; first, to the increase of dexterity in every particular workman; secondly, to the saving of the time which is commonly lost in passing from one species of work to another; and lastly, to the invention of a great number of machines which facilitate and abridge labour, and enable one man to do the work of many.

First, the improvement of the dexterity of the workman necessarily increases the quantity of the work he can perform; and the division of labour, by reducing every man's business to some one simple operation, and by making this operation the sole employment of his life, necessarily increases very much the dexterity of the workman. A common smith, who, though accustomed to handle the hammer, has never been used to make nails, if upon some particular occasion he is obliged to attempt it, will scarce, I am assured, be able to make above two or three hundred nails in a day, and those too very bad ones. A smith who has been accustomed to make nails, but whose sole or principal business has not been that of a nailer, can seldom with his utmost diligence make more than eight hundred or a thousand nails in a day. I have seen several boys under twenty years of age who had never exercised any other trade but that of making nails, and who, when they exerted themselves, could make, each of them, upwards of two thousand three hundred nails in a day. The making of a nail, however, is by no means one of the simplest operations. The same person blows the bellows, stirs or mends the fire as there is occasion, heats the iron, and forges every part of the nail: In forging the head too he is obliged to change his tools. The different operations into which the making of a pin, or of a metal button, is subdivided, are all of them much more simple, and the dexterity of the person, of whose life it has been the sole business to perform them, is usually much greater. The rapidity with which some of the operations of those manufactures are performed, exceeds what the human hand could, by those who had never seen them, be supposed capable of acquiring.

Secondly, the advantage which is gained by saving the time commonly lost in passing from one sort of work to another, is much greater than we should at first view be apt to imagine it. It is impossible to pass very quickly from one kind of work to another, that is carried on in a different place, and with quite different tools. A country weaver, who cultivates a small farm, must lose a good deal of time in passing from his loom to the field, and from the field to his loom. When the two trades can be carried on in the same workhouse, the loss of time is no doubt much less. It is even in this case, however, very considerable. A man commonly saunters a little in turning his hand from one sort of employment to another. When he first begins the new work he is seldom very keen and hearty; his mind, as they say, does not go to it, and for some time he rather trifles than applies to good purpose. The habit of sauntering and of indolent careless application, which is naturally, or rather necessarily acquired by every country workman who is obliged to change his work and his tools every half hour, and to apply his hand in twenty different ways almost every day of his life; renders him almost always slothful and lazy, and incapable of any vigorous application even on the most pressing occasions. Independent, therefore, of his deficiency in point of dexterity, this cause alone must always reduce considerably the quantity of work which he is capable of performing.

Thirdly, and lastly, every body must be sensible how much labour is facilitated and abridged by the application of proper machinery. It is unnecessary to give any example. I shall only observe, therefore, that the invention of all those machines by which labour is so much facilitated and abridged, seems to have been originally owing to the division of labour. Men are much more likely to discover easier and readier methods of attaining any object, when the whole attention of their minds is directed towards that single object, than when it is dissipated among a great variety of things. But in consequence of the division of labour, the whole of every man's attention comes naturally to be directed towards some one very simple object. It is naturally to be expected, therefore, that some one or other of those who are employed in each particular branch of labour should soon find out easier and readier methods of performing their own particular work, wherever the nature of it admits of such improvement. A great part of the machines made use of in those manufactures in which labour is most subdivided, were originally the inventions of common workmen, who, being each of them employed in some very simple operation, naturally turned their thoughts towards finding out easier and readier methods of performing it. Whoever has been much accustomed to visit such manufactures, must frequently have been shewn very pretty machines, which were the inventions of such workmen, in order to facilitate and quicken their own particular part of the work. In the first fire-engines, a boy was constantly employed to open and shut alternately the communication between the boiler and the cylinder, according as the piston either ascended or descended. One of those boys, who loved to play with his companions, observed that, by tying a string from the handle of the valve which opened this communication to another part of the machine, the valve would open and shut without his assistance, and leave him at liberty to divert himself with his play-fellows. One of the greatest improvements that has been made upon this machine, since it was first invented, was in this manner the discovery of a boy who wanted to save his own labour.

All the improvements in machinery, however, have by no means been the inventions of those who had occasion to use the machines. Many improvements have been made by the ingenuity of the makers of the machines, when to make them became the business of a peculiar trade; and some by that of those who are called philosophers or men of speculation, whose trade it is not to do any thing, but to observe every thing; and who, upon that account, are often capable of combining together the powers of the most distant and dissimilar objects. In the progress of society, philosophy or speculation becomes, like every other employment, the principal or sole trade and occupation of a particular class of citizens. Like every other employment too, it is subdivided into a great number of different branches, each of which affords occupation to a peculiar tribe or class of philosophers; and this subdivision of employment in philosophy, as well as in every other business, improves dexterity, and saves time. Each individual becomes more expert in his own peculiar branch, more work is done upon the whole, and the quantity of science is considerably increased by it.

It is the great multiplication of the productions of all the different arts, in consequence of the division of labour, which occasions, in a well-governed society, that universal opulence which extends itself to the lowest ranks of the people. Every workman has a great quantity of his own work to dispose of beyond what he himself has occasion for; and every other workman being exactly in the same situation, he is enabled to exchange a great quantity of his own goods for a great quantity, or, what comes to the same thing, for the price of a great quantity of theirs. He supplies them abundantly with what they have occasion for, and they accommodate him as amply with what he has occasion for, and a general plenty diffuses itself through all the different ranks of the society.

Observe the accommodation of the most common artificer or day-labourer in a civilized and thriving country, and you will perceive that the number of people of whose industry a part, though but a small part, has been employed in procuring him this accommodation, exceeds all computation. The woollen coat, for example, which covers the day-labourer, as coarse and rough as it may appear, is the produce of the joint labour of a great multitude of workmen. The shepherd, the sorter of the wool, the wool-comber or carder, the dyer, the scribbler, the spinner, the weaver, the fuller, the dresser, with many others, must all join their different arts in order to complete even this homely production. How many merchants and carriers, besides, must have been employed in transporting the materials from some of those workmen to others who often live in a very distant part of the country! how much commerce and navigation in particular, how many ship-builders, sailors, sail-makers, rope-makers, must have been employed in order to bring together the different drugs made use of by the dyer, which often come from the remotest corners of the world! What a variety of labour too is necessary in order to produce the tools of the meanest of those workmen! To say nothing of such complicated machines as the ship of the sailor, the mill of the fuller, or even the loom of the weaver, let us consider only what a variety of labour is requisite in order to form that very simple machine, the shears with which the shepherd clips the wool. The miner, the builder of the furnace for smelting the ore, the feller of the timber, the burner of the charcoal to be made use of in the smelting-house, the brick-maker, the brick-layer, the workmen who attend the furnace, the mill-wright, the forger, the smith, must all of them join their different arts in order to produce them. Were we to examine, in the same manner, all the different parts of his dress and household furniture, the coarse linen shirt which he wears next his skin, the shoes which cover his feet, the bed which he lies on, and all the different parts which compose it, the kitchen-grate at which he prepares his victuals, the coals which he makes use of for that purpose, dug from the bowels of the earth, and brought to him perhaps by a long sea and a long land carriage, all the other utensils of his kitchen, all the furniture of his table, the knives and forks, the earthen or pewter plates upon which he serves up and divides his victuals, the different hands employed in preparing his bread and his beer, the glass window which lets in the heat and the light, and keeps out the wind and the rain, with all the knowledge and art requisite for preparing that beautiful and happy invention, without which these northern parts of the world could scarce have afforded a very comfortable habitation, together with the tools of all the different workmen employed in producing those different conveniences; if we examine, I say, all these things, and consider what a variety of labour is employed about each of them, we shall be sensible that without the assistance and co-operation of many thousands, the very meanest person in a civilized country could not be provided, even according to, what we very falsely imagine, the easy and simple manner in which he is commonly accommodated. Compared, indeed, with the more extravagant luxury of the great, his accommodation must no doubt appear extremely simple and easy; and yet it may be true, perhaps, that the accommodation of an European prince does not always so much exceed that of an industrious and frugal peasant, as the accommodation of the latter exceeds that of many an African king, the absolute master of the lives and liberties of ten thousand naked savages.

CHAPTER II

Of the Principle Which Gives Occasion to the Division of Labour

THIS division of labour, from which so many advantages are derived, is not originally the effect of any human wisdom, which foresees and intends that general opulence to which it gives occasion. It is the necessary, though very slow and gradual, consequence of a certain propensity in human nature which has in view no such extensive utility; the propensity to truck, barter, and exchange one thing for another.

Whether this propensity be one of those original principles in human nature, of which no further account can be given; or whether, as seems more probable, it be the necessary consequence of the faculties of reason and speech, it belongs not to our present subject to enquire. It is common to all men, and to be found in no other race of animals, which seem to know neither this nor any other species of contracts. Two greyhounds, in running down the same hare, have sometimes the appearance of acting in some sort of concert. Each turns her towards his companion, or endeavours to intercept her when his companion turns her toward himself. This, however, is not the effect of any contract, but of the accidental concurrence of their passions in the same object at that particular time. Nobody ever saw a dog make a fair and deliberate exchange of one bone for another with another dog. Nobody ever saw one animal by its gestures and natural cries signify to another, this is mine, that yours; I am willing to give this for that. When an animal wants to obtain something either of a man or of another animal, it has no other means of persuasion but to gain the favour of those whose service it requires. A puppy fawns upon its dam, and a spaniel endeavours by a thousand attractions to engage the attention of its master who is at dinner, when it wants to be fed by him. Man sometimes uses the same arts with his brethren, and when he has no other means of engaging them to act according to his inclinations, endeavours by every servile and fawning attention to obtain their good will. He has not time, however, to do this upon every occasion. In civilized society he stands at all times in need of the co-operation and assistance of great multitudes, while his whole life is scarce sufficient to gain the friendship of a few persons. In almost every other race of animals each individual, when it is grown up to maturity, is entirely independent, and in its natural state has occasion for the assistance of no other living creature. But man has almost constant occasion for the help of his brethren, and it is in vain for him to expect it from their benevolence only. He will be more likely to prevail if he can interest their self-love in his favour, and shew them that it is for their own advantage to do for him what he requires of them. Whoever offers to another a bargain of any kind, proposes to do this: Give me that which I want, and you shall have this which you want, is the meaning of every such offer; and it is in this manner that we obtain from one another the far greater part of those good offices which we stand in need of.

It is not from the benevolence of the butcher, the brewer, or the baker, that we expect our dinner, but from their regard to their own interest. We address ourselves, not to their humanity but to their self-love, and never talk to them of our own necessities but of their advantages. Nobody but a beggar chuses to depend chiefly upon the benevolence of his fellow-citizens. Even a beggar does not depend upon it entirely. The charity of well-disposed people, indeed, supplies him with the whole fund of his subsistence. But though this principle ultimately provides him with all the necessaries of life which he has occasion for, it neither does nor can provide him with them as he has occasion for them. The greater part of his occasional wants are supplied in the same manner as those of other people, by treaty, by barter, and by purchase. With the money which one man gives him he purchases food. The old cloaths which another bestows upon him he exchanges for other old cloaths which suit him better, or for lodging, or for food, or for money, with which he can buy either food, cloaths, or lodging, as he has occasion.

As it is by treaty, by barter, and by purchase, that we obtain from one another the greater part of those mutual good offices which we stand in need of, so it is this same trucking disposition which originally gives occasion to the division of labour. In a tribe of hunters or shepherds a particular person makes bows and arrows, for example, with more readiness and dexterity than any other. He frequently exchanges them for cattle or for venison with his companions; and he finds at last that he can in this manner get more cattle and venison, than if he himself went to the field to catch them. From a regard to his own interest, therefore, the making of bows and arrows grows to be his chief business, and he becomes a sort of armourer. Another excels in making the frames and covers of their little huts or moveable houses. He is accustomed to be of use in this way to his neighbours, who reward him in the same manner with cattle and with venison, till at last he finds it his interest to dedicate himself entirely to this employment, and to become a sort of house-carpenter. In the same manner a third becomes a smith or a brazier; a fourth a tanner or dresser of hides or skins, the principal part of the clothing of savages. And thus the certainty of being able to exchange all that surplus part of the produce of his own labour, which is over and above his own consumption, for such parts of the produce of other men's labour as he may have occasion for, encourages every man to apply himself to a particular occupation and to cultivate and bring to perfection whatever talent or genius he may possess for that particular species of business.

The difference of natural talents in different men is, in reality, much less than we are aware of; and the very different genius which appears to distinguish men of different professions, when grown up to maturity, is not upon many occasions so much the cause, as the effect of the division of labour. The difference between the most dissimilar characters, between a philosopher and a common street porter, for example, seems to arise not so much from nature, as from habit, custom, and education. When they came into the world, and for the first six or eight years of their existence, they were, perhaps, very much alike, and neither their parents nor playfellows could perceive any remarkable difference. About that age, or soon after, they come to be employed in very different occupations. The difference of talents comes then to be taken notice of, and widens by degrees, till at last the vanity of the philosopher is willing to acknowledge scarce any resemblance. But without the disposition to truck, barter, and exchange, every man must have procured to himself every necessary and conveniency of life which he wanted. All must have had the same duties to perform, and the same work to do, and there could have been no such difference of employment as could alone give occasion to any great difference of talents.

As it is this disposition which forms that difference of talents, so remarkable among men of different professions, so it is this same disposition which renders that difference useful. Many tribes of animals acknowledged to be all of the same species, derive from nature a much more remarkable distinction of genius, than what, antecedent to custom and education, appears to take place among men. By nature a philosopher is not in genius and disposition half so different from a street porter, as a mastiff is from a greyhound, or a greyhound from a spaniel, or this last from a shepherd's dog. Those different tribes of animals, however, though all of the same species, are of scarce any use to one another. The strength of the mastiff is not in the least supported either by the swiftness of the greyhound, or by the sagacity of the spaniel, or by the docility of the shepherd's dog. The effects of those different geniuses and talents, for want of the power or disposition to barter and exchange, cannot be brought into a common stock, and do not in the least contribute to the better accommodation and conveniency of the species. Each animal is still obliged to support and defend itself, separately and independently, and derives no sort of advantage from that variety of talents with which nature has distinguished its fellows. Among men, on the contrary, the most dissimilar geniuses are of use to one another; the different produces of their respective talents, by the general disposition to truck, barter, and exchange, being brought, as it were, into a common stock, where every man may purchase whatever part of the produce of other men's talents he has occasion for.

CHAPTER III

That the Division of Labour is Limited by the Extent of the Market

AS it is the power of exchanging that gives occasion to the division of labour, so the extent of this division must always be limited by the extent of that power, or, in other words, by the extent of the market. When the market is very small, no person can have any encouragement to dedicate himself entirely to one employment, for want of the power to exchange all that surplus part of the produce of his own labour, which is over and above his own consumption, for such parts of the produce of other men's labour as he has occasion for.

There are some sorts of industry, even of the lowest kind, which can be carried on no where but in a great town. A porter, for example, can find employment and subsistence in no other place. A village is by much too narrow a sphere for him; even an ordinary market town is scarce large enough to afford him constant occupation. In the lone houses and very small villages which are scattered about in so desert a country as the Highlands of Scotland, every farmer must be butcher, baker and brewer for his own family. In such situations we can scarce expect to find even a smith, a carpenter, or a mason, within less than twenty miles of another of the same trade. The scattered families that live at eight or ten miles distant from the nearest of them, must learn to perform themselves a great number of little pieces of work, for which, in more populous countries, they would call in the assistance of those workmen. Country workmen are almost everywhere obliged to apply themselves to all the different branches of industry that have so much affinity to one another as to be employed about the same sort of materials. A country carpenter deals in every sort of work that is made of wood: a country smith in every sort of work that is made of iron. The former is not only a carpenter, but a joiner, a cabinet maker, and even a carver in wood, as well as a wheelwright, a plough-wright, a cart and waggon maker. The employments of the latter are still more various. It is impossible there should be such a trade as even that of a nailer in the remote and inland parts of the Highlands of Scotland. Such a workman at the rate of a thousand nails a day, and three hundred working days in the year, will make three hundred thousand nails in the year. But in such a situation it would be impossible to dispose of one thousand, that is, of one day's work in the year.

As by means of water-carriage a more extensive market is opened to every sort of industry than what land-carriage alone can afford it, so it is upon the sea-coast, and along the banks of navigable rivers, that industry of every kind naturally begins to subdivide and improve itself, and it is frequently not till a long time after that those improvements extend themselves to the inland parts of the country. A broad-wheeled waggon, attended by two men, and drawn by eight horses, in about six weeks time carries and brings back between London and Edinburgh near four ton weight of goods. In about the same time a ship navigated by six or eight men, and sailing between the ports of London and Leith, frequently carries and brings back two hundred ton weight of goods. Six or eight men, therefore, by the help of water-carriage, can carry and bring back in the same time the same quantity of goods between London and Edinburgh, as fifty broad-wheeled waggons, attended by a hundred men, and drawn by four hundred horses. Upon two hundred tons of goods, therefore, carried by the cheapest land-carriage from London to Edinburgh, there must be charged the maintenance of a hundred men for three weeks, and both the maintenance, and, what is nearly equal to the maintenance, the wear and tear of four hundred horses as well as of fifty great waggons. Whereas, upon the same quantity of goods carried by water, there is to be charged only the maintenance of six or eight men, and the wear and tear of a ship of two hundred tons burthen, together with the value of the superior risk, or the difference of the insurance between land

and water-carriage. Were there no other communication between those two places, therefore, but by land-carriage, as no goods could be transported from the one to the other, except such whose price was very considerable in proportion to their weight, they could carry on but a small part of that commerce which at present subsists between them, and consequently could give but a small part of that encouragement which they at present mutually afford to each other's industry. There could be little or no commerce of any kind between the distant parts of the world. What goods could bear the expence of land-carriage between London and Calcutta? Or if there were any so precious as to be able to support this expence, with what safety could they be transported through the territories of so many barbarous nations? Those two cities, however, at present carry on a very considerable commerce with each other, and by mutually affording a market, give a good deal of encouragement to each other's industry.

Since such, therefore, are the advantages of water-carriage, it is natural that the first improvements of art and industry should be made where this conveniency opens the whole world for a market to the produce of every sort of labour, and that they should always be much later in extending themselves into the inland parts of the country. The inland parts of the country can for a long time have no other market for the greater part of their goods, but the country which lies round about them, and separates them from the sea-coast, and the great navigable rivers. The extent of their market, therefore, must for a long time be in proportion to the riches and populousness of that country, and consequently their improvement must always be posterior to the improvement of that country. In our North American colonies the plantations have constantly followed either the sea-coast or the banks of the navigable rivers, and have scarce any where extended themselves to any considerable distance from both.

The nations that, according to the best authenticated history, appear to have been first civilized, were those that dwelt round the coast of the Mediterranean sea. That sea, by far the greatest inlet that is known in the world, having no tides, nor consequently any waves except such as are caused by the wind only, was, by the smoothness of its surface, as well as by the multitude of its islands, and the proximity of its neighbouring shores, extremely favourable to the infant navigation of the world; when, from their ignorance of the compass, men were afraid to quit the view of the coast, and from the imperfection of the art of ship-building, to abandon themselves to the boisterous waves of the ocean. To pass beyond the pillars of Hercules, that is, to sail out of the Streights of Gibraltar, was, in the antient world, long considered as a most wonderful and dangerous exploit of navigation. It was late before even the Phenicians and Carthaginians, the most skilful navigators and ship-builders of those old times, attempted it, and they were for a long time the only nations that did attempt it.

Of all the countries on the coast of the Mediterranean sea, Egypt seems to have been the first in which either agriculture or manufactures were cultivated and improved to any considerable degree. Upper Egypt extends itself nowhere above a few miles from the Nile, and in Lower Egypt that great river breaks itself into many different canals, which, with the assistance of a little art, seem to have afforded a communication by water-carriage, not only between all the great towns, but between all the considerable villages, and even to many farm-houses in the country; nearly in the same manner as the Rhine and the Maese do in Holland at present. The extent and easiness of this inland navigation was probably one of the principal causes of the early improvement of Egypt.

The improvements in agriculture and manufactures seem likewise to have been of very great antiquity in the provinces of Bengal in the East Indies, and in some of the eastern provinces of China; though the great extent of this antiquity is not authenticated by any histories of whose authority we, in this part of the world, are well assured. In Bengal the Ganges and several other great rivers form a great number of navigable canals in the same manner as the Nile does in Egypt. In the eastern provinces of China, too, several great rivers form, by their different branches, a multitude of canals, and by communicating with one another afford an inland navigation much more extensive than that either of the Nile or the Ganges, or perhaps than both of them put together. It is remarkable that neither the antient Egyptians, nor the Indians, nor the Chinese, encouraged foreign commerce, but seem all to have derived their great opulence from this inland navigation.

All the inland parts of Africa, and all that part of Asia which lies any considerable way north of the Euxine and Caspian seas, the antient Scythia, the modern Tartary and Siberia, seem in all ages of the world to have been in the same barbarous and uncivilized state in which we find them at present. The sea of Tartary is the frozen ocean which admits of no navigation, and though some of the greatest rivers in the world run through that country, they are at too great a distance from one another to carry commerce and communication through the greater part of it. There are in Africa none of those great inlets, such as the Baltic and Adriatic seas in Europe, the Mediterranean and Euxine seas in both Europe and Asia, and the gulphs of Arabia, Persia, India, Bengal, and Siam, in Asia, to carry maritime commerce into the interior parts of that great continent: and the great rivers of Africa are at too great a distance from one another to give occasion to any considerable inland navigation. The commerce besides which any nation can carry on by means of a river which does not break itself into any great number of branches or canals, and which runs into another territory before it reaches the sea, can never be very considerable; because it is always in the power of the nations who possess that other territory to obstruct the communication between the upper country and the sea. The navigation of the Danube is of very little use to the different states of Bavaria, Austria and Hungary, in comparison of what it would be if any of them possessed the whole of its course till it falls into the Black Sea.

CHAPTER IV

Of the Origin and Use of Money

WHEN the division of labour has been once thoroughly established, it is but a very small part of a man's wants which the produce of his own labour can supply. He supplies the far greater part of them by exchanging that surplus part of the produce of his own labour, which is over and above his own consumption, for such parts of the produce of other men's labour as he has occasion for. Every man thus lives by exchanging, or becomes in some measure a merchant, and the society itself grows to be what is properly a commercial society.

But when the division of labour first began to take place, this power of exchanging must frequently have been very much clogged and embarrassed in its operations. One man, we shall suppose, has more of a certain commodity than he himself has occasion for, while another has less. The former consequently would be glad to dispose of, and the latter to purchase, a part of this superfluity. But if this latter should chance to have nothing that the former stands in need of, no exchange can be made between them. The butcher has more meat in his shop than he himself can consume, and the brewer and the baker would each of them be willing to purchase a part of it. But they have nothing to offer in exchange, except the different productions of their respective trades, and the butcher is already provided with all the bread and beer which he has immediate occasion for. No exchange can, in this case, be made between them. He cannot be their merchant, nor they his customers; and they are all of them thus mutually less serviceable to one another. In order to avoid the inconveniency of such situations, every prudent man in every period of society, after the first establishment of the division of labour, must naturally have endeavoured to manage his affairs in such a manner, as to have at all times by him, besides the peculiar produce of his own industry, a certain quantity of some one commodity or other, such as he imagined few people would be likely to refuse in exchange for the produce of their industry.

Many different commodities, it is probable, were successively both thought of and employed for this purpose. In the rude ages of society, cattle are said to have been the common instrument of commerce; and, though they must have been a most inconvenient one, yet in old times we find things were frequently valued according to the number of cattle which had been given in exchange for them. The armour of Diomede, says Homer, cost only nine oxen; but that of Glaucus cost an hundred oxen. Salt is said to be the common instrument of commerce and exchanges in Abyssinia; a species of shells in some parts of the coast of India; dried cod at Newfoundland; tobacco in Virginia; sugar in some of our West India colonies; hides or dressed leather in some other countries; and there is at this day a village in Scotland where it is not uncommon, I am told, for a workman to carry nails instead of money to the baker's shop or the ale-house.

In all countries, however, men seem at last to have been determined by irresistible reasons to give the preference, for this employment, to metals above every other commodity. Metals can not only be kept with as little loss as any other commodity, scarce any thing being less perishable than they are, but they can likewise, without any loss, be divided into any number of parts, as by fusion those parts can easily be reunited again; a quality which no other equally durable commodities possess, and which more than any other quality renders them fit to be the instruments of commerce and circulation. The man who wanted to buy salt, for example, and had nothing but cattle to give in exchange for it, must have been obliged to buy salt to the value of a whole ox, or a whole sheep, at a time. He could seldom buy less than this, because what he was to give for it could seldom be divided without loss; and if he had a mind to buy more, he must, for the same reasons, have been obliged to buy double or triple the quantity, the value, to wit, of two or three oxen, or of two or three sheep. If on the contrary, instead of sheep or oxen, he had metals to give in exchange for it, he could easily proportion the quantity of the metal to the precise quantity of the commodity which he had immediate occasion for.

Different metals have been made use of by different nations for this purpose. Iron was the common instrument of commerce among the antient Spartans; copper among the antient Romans; and gold and silver among all rich and commercial nations.

Those metals seem originally to have been made use of for this purpose in rude bars, without any stamp or coinage. Thus we are told by Pliny, upon the authority of Timæus, an antient historian, that, till the time of Servius Tullius, the Romans had no coined money, but made use of unstamped bars of copper, to purchase whatever they had occasion for. These rude bars, therefore, performed at this time the function of money.

The use of metals in this rude state was attended with two very considerable inconveniences; first with the trouble of weighing; and, secondly, with that of assaying them. In the precious metals, where a small difference in the quantity makes a great difference in the value, even the business of weighing, with proper exactness, requires at least very accurate weights and scales. The weighing of gold in particular is an operation of some nicety. In the coarser metals, indeed, where a small error would be of little consequence, less accuracy would, no doubt, be necessary. Yet we should find it excessively troublesome, if every time a poor man had occasion either to buy or sell a farthing's worth of goods, he was obliged to weigh the farthing. The operation of assaying is still more difficult, still more tedious, and, unless a part of the metal is fairly melted in the crucible, with proper dissolvents, any conclusion that can be drawn from it, is extremely uncertain. Before the institution of coined money, however, unless they went through this tedious and difficult operation, people must always have been liable to the grossest frauds and impositions, and instead of a pound weight of pure silver, or pure copper, might receive in exchange for their goods, an adulterated composition of the coarsest and cheapest materials, which had, however, in their outward appearance, been made to resemble those metals. To prevent such abuses, to facilitate exchanges, and thereby to encourage all sorts of industry and commerce, it has been found necessary, in all countries that have made any considerable advances towards improvement, to affix a public stamp upon certain quantities of such particular metals, as were in those countries commonly made use of to purchase goods. Hence the origin of coined money, and of those public offices called mints; institutions exactly of the same nature with those of the aulnagers and stampmasters of woollen and linen cloth. All of them are equally meant to ascertain, by means of a public stamp, the quantity and uniform goodness of those different commodities when brought to market.

The first public stamps of this kind that were affixed to the current metals, seem in many cases to have been intended to ascertain, what it was both most difficult and most important to ascertain, the goodness or fineness of the metal, and to have resembled the sterling mark which is at present affixed to plate and bars of silver, or the Spanish mark which is sometimes affixed to ingots of gold, and which being struck only upon one side of the piece, and not covering the whole surface, ascertains the fineness, but not the weight of the metal. Abraham weighs to Ephron the four hundred shekels of silver which he had agreed to pay for the field of Machpelah. They are said, however, to be the current money of the merchant, and yet are received by weight and not by tale, in the same manner as ingots of gold and bars of silver are at present. The revenues of the antient Saxon kings of England are said to have been paid, not in money but in kind, that is, in victuals and provisions of all sorts. William the Conqueror introduced the custom of paying them in money. This money, however, was, for a long time, received at the exchequer, by weight and not by tale.

The inconveniency and difficulty of weighing those metals with exactness gave occasion to the institution of coins, of which the stamp, covering entirely both sides of the piece and sometimes the edges too, was supposed to ascertain not only the fineness, but the weight of the metal. Such coins, therefore, were received by tale as at present, without the trouble of weighing.

The denominations of those coins seem originally to have expressed the weight or quantity of metal contained in them. In the time of Servius Tullius, who first coined money at Rome, the Roman As or Pondo contained a Roman pound of good copper. It was divided in the same manner as our Troyes pound, into twelve ounces, each of which contained a real ounce of good copper. The English pound sterling in the time of Edward I., contained a pound, Tower weight, of silver of a known fineness. The Tower pound seems to have been something more than the Roman pound, and something less than the Troyes pound. This last was not introduced into the mint of England till the 18th of Henry VIII. The French livre contained in the time of Charlemagne a pound, Troyes weight, of silver of a known fineness. The fair of Troyes in Champaign was at that time frequented by all the nations of Europe, and the weights and measures of so famous a market were generally known and esteemed. The Scots money pound contained, from the time of Alexander the First to that of Robert Bruce, a pound of silver of the same weight and fineness with the English pound sterling. English, French, and Scots pennies too, contained all of them originally a real pennyweight of silver, the twentieth part of an ounce, and the two-hundred-and-fortieth part of a pound. The shilling, too, seems originally to have been the denomination of a weight. *When wheat is at twelve shillings the quarter,* says an antient statute of Henry III., *then wastel bread of a farthing shall weigh eleven shillings and four pence.* The proportion, however, between the shilling and either the penny on the one hand, or the pound on the other, seems not to have been so constant and uniform as that between the penny and the pound. During the first race of the kings of France, the French sou or shilling appears upon different occasions to have contained five, twelve, twenty, and forty pennies. Among the antient Saxons a shilling appears at one time to have contained only five pennies, and it is not improbable that it may have been as variable among them as among their neighbours, the antient Franks. From the time of Charlemagne among the French, and from that of William the Conquerer among the English, the proportion between the pound, the shilling, and the penny, seems to have been uniformly the same as at present, though the value of each has been very different. For in every country of the world, I believe, the avarice and injustice of princes and sovereign states, abusing the confidence of their subjects, have by degrees diminished the real quantity of metal, which had been originally contained in their coins. The Roman As, in the latter ages of the Republic, was reduced to the twenty-fourth part of its original value, and, instead of weighing a pound, came to weigh only half an ounce. The English pound and penny contain at present about a third only; the Scots pound and penny about a thirty-sixth; and the French pound and penny about a sixty-sixth part of their original value. By means of those operations the princes and sovereign states which performed them were enabled, in appearance, to pay their debts and to fulfil their engagements with a smaller quantity of silver than would otherwise have been requisite. It was indeed in appearance only; for their creditors were really defrauded of a part of what was due to them. All other debtors in the state were allowed the same privilege, and might pay with the same nominal sum of the new and debased coin whatever they had borrowed in the old. Such operations, therefore, have always proved favourable to the debtor, and ruinous to the creditor, and have sometimes produced a greater and more universal revolution in the fortunes of private persons, than could have been occasioned by a very great public calamity.

It is in this manner that money has become in all civilized nations the universal instrument of commerce, by the intervention of which goods of all kinds are bought and sold, or exchanged for one another.

What are the rules which men naturally observe in exchanging them either for money or for one another, I shall now proceed to examine. These rules determine what may be called the relative or exchangeable value of goods.

The word VALUE, it is to be observed, has two different meanings, and sometimes expresses the utility of some particular object, and sometimes the power of purchasing other goods which the possession of that object conveys. The one may be called "value in use;" the other, "value in exchange." The things which have the greatest value in use have frequently little or no value in exchange; and on the contrary, those which have the greatest value in exchange have frequently little or no value in use. Nothing is more useful than water: but it will purchase scarce any thing; scarce any thing can be had in exchange for it. A diamond, on the contrary, has scarce any value in use; but a very great quantity of other goods may frequently be had in exchange for it.

In order to investigate the principles which regulate the exchangeable value of commodities, I shall endeavour to shew,

First, what is the real measure of this exchangeable value; or, wherein consists the real price of all commodities.

Secondly, what are the different parts of which this real price is composed or made up.

And, lastly, what are the different circumstances which sometimes raise some or all of these different parts of price above, and sometimes sink them below their natural or ordinary rate; or, what are the causes which sometimes hinder the market price, that is, the actual price of commodities, from coinciding exactly with what may be called their natural price.

I shall endeavour to explain, as fully and distinctly as I can, those three subjects in the three following chapters, for which I must very earnestly entreat both the patience and attention of the reader: his patience in order to examine a detail which may perhaps in some places appear unnecessarily tedious; and his attention in order to understand what may, perhaps, after the fullest explication which I am capable of giving of it, appear still in some degree obscure. I am always willing to run some hazard of being tedious in order to be sure that I am perspicuous; and after taking the utmost pains that I can to be perspicuous, some obscurity may still appear to remain upon a subject in its own nature extremely abstracted.

CHAPTER V

Of the Real and Nominal Price of Commodities, or of Their Price in Labour, and Their Price in Money

EVERY man is rich or poor according to the degree in which he can afford to enjoy the necessaries, conveniences, and amusements of human life. But after the division of labour has once thoroughly taken place, it is but a very small part of these with which a man's own labour can supply him. The far greater part of them he must derive from the labour of other people, and he must be rich or poor according to the quantity of that labour which he can command, or which he can afford to purchase. The value of any commodity, therefore, to the person who possesses it, and who means not to use or consume it himself, but to exchange it for other commodities, is equal to the quantity of labour which it enables him to purchase or command. Labour, therefore, is the real measure of the exchangeable value of all commodities.

The real price of every thing, what every thing really costs to the man who wants to acquire it, is the toil and trouble of acquiring it. What every thing is really worth to the man who has acquired it, and who wants to dispose of it or exchange it for something else, is the toil and trouble which it can save to himself, and which it can impose upon other people. What is bought with money or with goods is purchased by labour, as much as what we acquire by the toil of our own body. That money or those goods indeed save us this toil. They contain the value of a certain quantity of labour which we exchange for what is supposed at the time to contain the value of an equal quantity. Labour was the first price, the original purchase-money that was paid for all things. It was not by gold or by silver, but by labour, that all the wealth of the world was originally purchased;

and its value, to those who possess it, and who want to exchange it for some new productions, is precisely equal to the quantity of labour which it can enable them to purchase or command.

Wealth, as Mr. Hobbes says, is power. But the person who either acquires, or succeeds to a great fortune, does not necessarily acquire or succeed to any political power, either civil or military. His fortune may, perhaps, afford him the means of acquiring both, but the mere possession of that fortune does not necessarily convey to him either. The power which that possession immediately and directly conveys to him, is the power of purchasing; a certain command over all the labour, or over all the produce of labour which is then in the market. His fortune is greater or less, precisely in proportion to the extent of this power, or to the quantity either of other men's labour, or, what is the same thing, of the produce of other men's labour, which it enables him to purchase or command. The exchangeable value of every thing must always be precisely equal to the extent of this power which it conveys to its owner.

But though labour be the real measure of the exchangeable value of all commodities, it is not that by which their value is commonly estimated. It is often difficult to ascertain the proportion between two different quantities of labour. The time spent in two different sorts of work will not always alone determine this proportion. The different degrees of hardship endured, and of ingenuity exercised, must likewise be taken into account. There may be more labour in an hour's hard work than in two hours' easy business; or in an hour's application to a trade which it cost ten years' labour to learn, than in a month's industry at an ordinary and obvious employment. But it is not easy to find any accurate measure either of hardship or ingenuity. In exchanging indeed the different productions of different sorts of labour for one another, some allowance is commonly made for both. It is adjusted, however, not by any accurate measure, but by the higgling and bargaining of the market, according to that sort of rough equality which, though not exact, is sufficient for carrying on the business of common life.

Every commodity besides, is more frequently exchanged for, and thereby compared with, other commodities than with labour. It is more natural, therefore, to estimate its exchangeable value by the quantity of some other commodity than by that of the labour which it can purchase. The greater part of people, too, understand better what is meant by a quantity of a particular commodity, than by a quantity of labour. The one is a plain palpable object; the other an abstract notion, which, though it can be made sufficiently intelligible, is not altogether so natural and obvious.

But when barter ceases, and money has become the common instrument of commerce, every particular commodity is more frequently exchanged for money than for any other commodity. The butcher seldom carries his beef or his mutton to the baker, or the brewer, in order to exchange them for bread or for beer; but he carries them to the market, where he exchanges them for money, and afterwards exchanges that money for bread and for beer. The quantity of money which he gets for them regulates, too, the quantity of bread and beer which he can afterwards purchase. It is more natural and obvious to him, therefore, to estimate their value by the quantity of money, the commodity for which he immediately exchanges them, than by that of bread and beer, the commodities for which he can exchange them only by the intervention of another commodity; and rather to say that his butcher's meat is worth threepence or fourpence a pound, than that it is worth three or four pounds of bread, or three or four quarts of small beer. Hence it comes to pass, that the exchangeable value of every commodity is more frequently estimated by the quantity of money, than by the quantity either of labour or of any other commodity which can be had in exchange for it.

Gold and silver, however, like every other commodity, vary in their value, are sometimes cheaper and sometimes dearer, sometimes of easier and sometimes of more difficult purchase. The quantity of labour which any particular quantity of them can purchase or command, or the quantity of other goods which it will exchange for, depends always upon the fertility or barrenness of the mines which happen to be known about the time when such exchanges are made. The discovery of the abundant mines of America reduced, in the sixteenth century, the value of gold and silver in Europe to about a third of what it had been before. As it cost less labour to bring those metals from the mine to the market, so when they are brought thither they could purchase or command less labour; and this revolution in their value, though perhaps the greatest, is by no means the only one of which history gives some account. But as a measure of quantity, such as the natural foot, fathom, or handful, which is continually varying in its own quantity, can never be an accurate measure of the quantity of other things; so a commodity which is itself continually varying in its own value, can never be an accurate measure of the value of other commodities. Equal quantities of labour, at all times and places, may be said to be of equal value to the labourer. In his ordinary state of health, strength and spirits; in the ordinary degree of his skill and dexterity, he must always lay down the same portion of his ease, his liberty, and his happiness. The price which he pays must always be the same, whatever may be the quantity of the goods which he receives in return for it. Of these, indeed, it may sometimes purchase a greater and sometimes a smaller quantity; but it is their value which varies, not that of the labour which purchases them. At all times and places that is dear which it is difficult to come at, or which costs much labour to acquire; and that cheap which is to be had easily, or with very little labour. Labour alone, therefore, never varying in its own value, is alone the ultimate and real standard by which the value of all commodities can at all times and places be estimated and compared. It is their real price; money is their nominal price only.

But though equal quantities of labour are always of equal value to the labourer, yet to the person who employs him they appear sometimes to be of greater and sometimes of smaller value. He purchases them sometimes with a greater and sometimes with a smaller quantity of goods, and to him the price of labour seems to vary like that of all other things. It appears to him dear in the one case, and cheap in the other. In reality, however, it is the goods which are cheap in the one case, and dear in the other.

In this popular sense, therefore, labour, like commodities, may be said to have a real and a nominal price. Its real price may be said to consist in the quantity of the necessaries and conveniences of life which are given for it; its nominal price, in the quantity of money. The labourer is rich or poor, is well or ill rewarded, in proportion to the real, not to the nominal price of his labour.

The distinction between the real and the nominal price of commodities and labour, is not a matter of mere speculation, but may sometimes be of considerable use in practice. The same real price is always of the same value; but on account of the variations in the value of gold and silver, the same nominal price is sometimes of very different value. When a landed estate, therefore, is sold with a reservation of a perpetual rent, if it is intended that this rent should always be of the same value, it is of importance to the family in whose favour it is reserved, that it should not consist in a particular sum of money. Its value would in this case be liable to variations of two different kinds; first, to those which arise from the different quantities of gold and silver which are contained at different times in coin of the same denomination; and, secondly, to those which arise from the different values of equal quantities of gold and silver at different times.

Princes and sovereign states have frequently fancied that they had a temporary interest to diminish the quantity of pure metal contained in their coins; but they seldom have fancied that they had any to augment it. The quantity of metal contained in the coins, I believe of all nations, has, accordingly, been almost continually diminishing, and hardly ever augmenting. Such variations therefore tend almost always to diminish the value of a money rent.

The discovery of the mines of America diminished the value of gold and silver in Europe. This diminution, it is commonly supposed, though I apprehend without any certain proof, is still going on gradually, and is likely to continue to do so for a long time. Upon this supposition, therefore, such variations are more likely to diminish, than to augment the value of a money rent, even though it should be stipulated to be paid, not in such a quantity of coined money of such a denomination (in so many pounds sterling, for example), but in so many ounces either of pure silver, or of silver of a certain standard.

The rents which have been reserved in corn have preserved their value much better than those which have been reserved in money, even where the denomination of the coin has not been altered. By the 18th of Elizabeth it was enacted, That a third of the rent of all college leases should be reserved in corn, to be paid, either in kind, or according to the current prices at the nearest public market. The money arising from this corn rent, though originally but a third of the whole, is in the present times, according to Doctor Blackstone, commonly near double of what arises from the other two-thirds. The old money rents of colleges must, according to this account, have sunk almost to a fourth part of their antient value; or are worth little more than a fourth part of the corn which they were formerly worth. But since the reign of Philip and Mary the denomination of the English coin has undergone little or no alteration, and the same number of pounds, shillings and pence have contained very nearly the same quantity of pure silver. This degradation, therefore, in the value of the money rents of colleges, has arisen altogether from the degradation in the value of silver.

When the degradation in the value of silver is combined with the diminution of the quantity of it contained in the coin of the same denomination, the loss is frequently still greater. In Scotland, where the denomination of the coin has undergone much greater alterations than it ever did in England, and in France, where it has undergone still greater than it ever did in Scotland, some antient rents, originally of considerable value, have in this manner been reduced almost to nothing.

Equal quantities of labour will at distant times be purchased more nearly with equal quantities of corn, the subsistence of the labourer, than with equal quantities of gold and silver, or perhaps of any other commodity. Equal quantities of corn, therefore, will, at distant times, be more nearly of the same real value, or enable the possessor to purchase or command more nearly the same quantity of the labour of other people. They will do this, I say, more nearly than equal quantities of almost any other commodity; for even equal quantities of corn will not do it exactly. The subsistence of the labourer, or the real price of labour, as I shall endeavour to show hereafter, is very different upon different occasions; more liberal in a society advancing to opulence, than in one that is standing still; and in one that is standing still, than in one that is going backwards. Every other commodity, however, will at any particular time purchase a greater or smaller quantity of labour in proportion to the quantity of subsistence which it can purchase at that time. A rent therefore reserved in corn is liable only to the variations in the quantity of labour which a certain quantity of corn can purchase. But a rent reserved in any other commodity is liable, not only to the variations in the quantity of labour which any particular quantity of corn can purchase, but to the variations in the quantity of corn which can be purchased by any particular quantity of that commodity.

Though the real value of a corn rent, it is to be observed however, varies much less from century to century than that of a money rent, it varies much more from year to year. The money price of labour, as I shall endeavour to show hereafter, does not fluctuate from year to year with the money price of corn, but seems to be every where accommodated, not to the temporary or occasional, but to the average or ordinary price of that necessary of life. The average or ordinary price of corn again is regulated, as I shall likewise endeavour to show hereafter, by the value of silver, by the richness or barrenness of the mines which supply the market with that metal, or by the quantity of labour which must be employed, and consequently of corn which must be consumed, in order to bring any particular quantity of silver from the mine to the market. But the value of silver, though it sometimes varies greatly from century to century, seldom varies much from year to year, but frequently continues the same, or very nearly the same, for half a century or a century together. The ordinary or average money price of corn, therefore, may, during so long a period, continue the same or very nearly the same too, and along with it the money price of labour, provided, at least, the society continues, in other respects, in the same or nearly in the same condition. In the mean time the temporary and occasional price of corn may frequently be double, one year, of what it had been the year before, or fluctuate, for example, from five and twenty to fifty shillings the quarter. But when corn is at the latter price, not only the nominal, but the real value of a corn rent will be double of what it is when at the former, or will command double the quantity either of labour or of the greater part of other commodities; the money price of labour, and along with it that of most other things, continuing the same during all these fluctuations.

Labour, therefore, it appears evidently, is the only universal, as well as the only accurate measure of value, or the only standard by which we can compare the values of different commodities at all times and at all places. We cannot estimate, it is allowed, the real value of different commodities from century to century by the quantities of silver which were given for them. We cannot estimate it from year to year by the quantities of corn. By the quantities of labour we can, with the greatest accuracy, estimate it both from century to century and from year to year. From century to century, corn is a better measure than silver, because, from century to century, equal quantities of corn will command the same quantity of labour more nearly than equal quantities of silver. From year to year, on the contrary, silver is a better measure than corn, because equal quantities of it will more nearly command the same quantity of labour.

But though in establishing perpetual rents, or even in letting very long leases, it may be of use to distinguish between real and nominal price; it is of none in buying and selling, the more common and ordinary transactions of human life.

At the same time and place the real and the nominal price of all commodities are exactly in proportion to one another. The more or less money you get for any commodity, in the London market, for example, the more or less labour it will at that time and place enable you to purchase or command. At the same time and place, therefore, money is the exact measure of the real exchangeable value of all commodities. It is so, however, at the same time and place only.

Though at distant places, there is no regular proportion between the real and the money price of commodities, yet the merchant who carries goods from the one to the other has nothing to consider but their money price, or the difference between the quantity of silver for which he buys them, and that for which he is likely to sell them. Half an ounce of silver at Canton in China may command a greater quantity both of labour and of the necessaries and conveniencies of life, than an ounce at London. A commodity, therefore, which sells for half an ounce of silver at Canton may there be really dearer, of more real importance to the man who possesses it there, than a commodity which sells for an ounce at London is to the man who possesses it at London. If a London merchant, however, can buy at Canton for half an ounce of silver, a commodity which he can afterwards sell at London for an ounce, he gains a hundred per cent. by the bargain, just as much as if an ounce of silver was at London exactly of the same value as at Canton. It is of no importance to him that half an ounce of silver at Canton would have given him the command of more labour and of a greater quantity of the necessaries and conveniencies of life than an ounce can do at London. An ounce at London will always give him the command of double the quantity of all these, which half an ounce could have done there, and this is precisely what he wants.

As it is the nominal or money price of goods, therefore, which finally determines the prudence or imprudence of all purchases and sales, and thereby regulates almost the whole business of common life in which price is concerned, we cannot wonder that it should have been so much more attended to than the real price.

In such a work as this, however, it may sometimes be of use to compare the different real values of a particular commodity at different times and places, or the different degrees of power over the labour of other people which it may, upon different occasions, have given to those who possessed it. We must in this case compare, not so much the different quantities of silver for which it was commonly sold, as the different quantities of labour which those different quantities of silver could have purchased. But the current prices of labour at distant times and places can scarce ever be known with any degree of exactness. Those of corn, though they have in a few places been regularly recorded, are in general better known and have been more frequently taken notice of by historians and other writers. We must generally, therefore, content ourselves with them, not as being always exactly in the same proportion as the current prices of labour, but as being the nearest approximation which can commonly be had to that proportion. I shall hereafter have occasion to make several comparisons of this kind.

In the progress of industry, commercial nations have found it convenient to coin several different metals into money; gold for larger payments, silver for purchases of moderate value, and copper, or some other coarse metal, for those of still smaller consideration. They have always, however, considered one of those metals as more peculiarly the measure of value than any of the other two; and this preference seems generally to have been given to the metal which they happened first to make use of as the instrument of commerce. Having once begun to use it as their standard, which they must have done when they had no other money, they have generally continued to do so even when the necessity was not the same.

The Romans are said to have had nothing but copper money till within five years before the first Punic war, when they first began to coin silver. Copper, therefore, appears to have continued always the measure of value in that republic. At Rome all accounts appear to have been kept, and the value of all estates to have been computed, either in *Asses* or in *Sestertii.* The *As* was always the denomination of a copper coin. The word *Sestertius* signifies two *Asses* and a half. Though the *Sestertius,* therefore, was originally a silver coin, its value was estimated in copper. At Rome, one who owed a great deal of money, was said to have a great deal of other people's copper.

The northern nations who established themselves upon the ruins of the Roman empire, seem to have had silver money from the first beginning of their settlements, and not to have known either gold or copper coins for several ages thereafter. There were silver coins in England in the time of the Saxons;

but there was little gold coined till the time of Edward III. nor any copper till that of James I. of Great Britain. In England, therefore, and for the same reason, I believe, in all other modern nations of Europe, all accounts are kept, and the value of all goods and of all estates is generally computed in silver: and when we mean to express the amount of a person's fortune, we seldom mention the number of guineas, but the number of pounds sterling which we suppose would be given for it.

Originally, in all countries, I believe, a legal tender of payment could be made only in the coin of that metal, which was peculiarly considered as the standard or measure of value. In England, gold was not considered as a legal tender for a long time after it was coined into money. The proportion between the values of gold and silver money was not fixed by any public law or proclamation; but was left to be settled by the market. If a debtor offered payment in gold, the creditor might either reject such payment altogether, or accept of it at such a valuation of the gold as he and his debtor could agree upon. Copper is not at present a legal tender, except in the change of the smaller silver coins. In this state of things the distinction between the metal which was the standard, and that which was not the standard, was something more than a nominal distinction.

In process of time, and as people became gradually more familiar with the use of the different metals in coin, and consequently better acquainted with the proportion between their respective values, it has in most countries, I believe, been found convenient to ascertain this proportion, and to declare by a public law that a guinea, for example, of such a weight and fineness, should exchange for one-and-twenty shillings, or be a legal tender for a debt of that amount. In this state of things, and during the continuance of any one regulated proportion of this kind, the distinction between the metal which is the standard, and that which is not the standard, becomes little more than a nominal distinction.

In consequence of any change, however, in this regulated proportion, this distinction becomes, or at least seems to become, something more than nominal again. If the regulated value of a guinea, for example, was either reduced to twenty, or raised to two-and-twenty shillings, all accounts being kept and almost all obligations for debt being expressed in silver money, the greater part of payments could in either case be made with the same quantity of silver money as before; but would require very different quantities of gold money; a greater in the one case, and a smaller in the other. Silver would appear to be more invariable in its value than gold. Silver would appear to measure the value of gold, and gold would not appear to measure the value of silver. The value of gold would seem to depend upon the quantity of silver which it would exchange for; and the value of silver would not seem to depend upon the quantity of gold which it would exchange for. This difference, however, would be altogether owing to the custom of keeping accounts, and of expressing the amount of all great and small sums rather in silver than in gold money. One of Mr. Drummond's notes for five-and-twenty or fifty guineas would, after an alteration of this kind, be still payable with five-and-twenty or fifty guineas in the same manner as before. It would, after such an alteration, be payable with the same quantity of gold as before, but with very different quantities of silver. In the payment of such a note, gold would appear to be more invariable in its value than silver. Gold would appear to measure the value of silver, and silver would not appear to measure the value of gold. If the custom of keeping accounts, and of expressing promissory notes and other obligations for money in this manner, should ever become general, gold, and not silver, would be considered as the metal which was peculiarly the standard or measure of value.

In reality, during the continuance of any one regulated proportion between the respective values of the different metals in coin, the value of the most precious metal regulates the value of the whole coin. Twelve copper pence contain half a pound, avoirdupois, of copper, of not the best quality, which, before it is coined, is seldom worth sevenpence in silver. But as by the regulation twelve such pence are ordered to exchange for a shilling, they are in the market considered as worth a shilling, and a shilling can at any time be had for them. Even before the late reformation of the gold coin of Great Britain, the gold, that part of it at least which circulated in London and its neighbourhood, was in general less degraded below its standard weight than the greater part of the silver. One-and-twenty worn and defaced shillings, however, were considered as equivalent to a guinea, which perhaps, indeed, was worn and defaced too, but seldom so much so. The late regulations have brought the gold coin as near perhaps to its standard weight as it is possible to bring the current coin of any nation; and the order, to receive no gold at the public offices but by weight, is likely to preserve it so, as long as that order is enforced. The silver coin still continues in the same worn and degraded state as before the reformation of the gold coin. In the market, however, one-and-twenty shillings of this degraded silver coin are still considered as worth a guinea of this excellent gold coin.

The reformation of the gold coin has evidently raised the value of the silver coin which can be exchanged for it.

The occasional fluctuations in the market price of gold and silver bullion arise from the same causes as the like fluctuations in that of all other commodities. The frequent loss of those metals from various accidents by sea and by land, the continual waste of them in gilding and plating, in lace and embroidery, in the wear and tear of coin, and in that of plate; require, in all countries which possess no mines of their own, a continual importation, in order to repair this loss and this waste. The merchant importers, like all other merchants, we may believe, endeavour, as well as they can, to suit their occasional importations to what, they judge, is likely to be the immediate demand. With all their attention, however, they sometimes over-do the business, and sometimes under-do it. When they import more bullion than is wanted, rather than incur the risk and trouble of exporting it again, they are sometimes willing to sell a part of it for something less than the ordinary or average price. When, on the other hand, they import less than is wanted, they get something more than this price. But when, under all those occasional fluctuations, the market price either of gold or silver bullion continues for several years together steadily and constantly, either more or less above, or more or less below the mint price: we may be assured that this steady and constant, either superiority or inferiority of price, is the effect of something in the state of the coin, which, at that time, renders a certain quantity of coin either of more value or of less value than the precise quantity of bullion which it ought to contain. The constancy and steadiness of the effect, supposes a proportionable constancy and steadiness in the cause.

The money of any particular country is, at any particular time and place, more or less an accurate measure of value according as the current coin is more or less exactly agreeable to its standard, or contains more or less exactly the precise quantity of pure gold or pure silver which it ought to contain. If in England, for example, forty-four guineas and a half contained exactly a pound weight of standard gold, or eleven ounces of fine gold and one ounce of alloy, the gold coin of England would be as accurate a measure of the actual value of goods at any particular time and place as the nature of the thing would admit. But if, by rubbing and wearing, forty-four guineas and a half generally contain less than a pound weight of standard gold; the diminution, however, being greater in some pieces than in others; the measure of value comes to be liable to the same sort of uncertainty to which all other weights and measures are commonly exposed. As it rarely happens that these are exactly agreeable to their standard, the merchant adjusts the price of his goods, as well as he can, not to what those weights and measures ought to be, but to what, upon an average, he finds by experience they actually are. In consequence of a like disorder in the coin, the price of goods comes, in the same manner, to be adjusted, not to the quantity of pure gold or silver which the coin ought to contain, but to that which, upon an average, it is found by experience it actually does contain.

By the money-price of goods, it is to be observed, I understand always the quantity of pure gold or silver for which they are sold, without any regard to the denomination of the coin. Six shillings and eight-pence, for example, in the time of Edward I., I consider as the same money-price with a pound sterling in the present times; because it contained, as nearly as we can judge, the same quantity of pure silver.

CHAPTER VI

Of the Component Parts of the Price of Commodities

IN that early and rude state of society which precedes both the accumulation of stock and the appropriation of land, the proportion between the quantities of labour necessary for acquiring different objects seems to be the only circumstance which can afford any rule for exchanging them for one another. If among a nation of hunters, for example, it usually costs twice the labour to kill a beaver which it does to kill a deer, one beaver should naturally exchange for or be worth two deer. It is natural that what is usually the produce of two days or two hours labour, should be worth double of what is usually the produce of one day's or one hour's labour.

If the one species of labour should be more severe than the other, some allowance will naturally be made for this superior hardship; and the produce of one hour's labour in the one way may frequently exchange for that of two hours labour in the other.

Or if the one species of labour requires an uncommon degree of dexterity and ingenuity, the esteem which men have for such talents, will naturally give a value to their produce, superior to what would be due to the time employed about it. Such talents can seldom be acquired but in consequence of long application, and the superior value of their produce may frequently be no more than a reasonable compensation for the time and labour which must be spent in acquiring them. In the advanced state of society, allowances of this kind, for superior hardship and superior skill, are commonly made in the wages of labour; and something of the same kind must probably have taken place in its earliest and rudest period.

In this state of things, the whole produce of labour belongs to the labourer; and the quantity of labour commonly employed in acquiring or producing any commodity, is the only circumstance which can regulate the quantity of labour which it ought commonly to purchase, command, or exchange for.

As soon as stock has accumulated in the hands of particular persons, some of them will naturally employ it in setting to work industrious people, whom they will supply with materials and subsistence, in order to make a profit by the sale of their work, or by what their labour adds to the value of the materials. In exchanging the complete manufacture either for money, for labour, or for other goods, over and above what may be sufficient to pay the price of the materials, and the wages of the workmen, something must be given for the profits of the undertaker of the work who hazards his stock in this adventure. The value which the workmen add to the materials, therefore, resolves itself in this case into two parts, of which the one pays their wages, the other the profits of their employer upon the whole stock of materials and wages which he advanced. He could have no interest to employ them, unless he expected from the sale of their work something more than what was sufficient to replace his stock to him; and he could have no interest to employ a great stock rather than a small one, unless his profits were to bear some proportion to the extent of his stock.

The profits of stock, it may perhaps be thought, are only a different name for the wages of a particular sort of labour, the labour of inspection and direction. They are, however, altogether different, are regulated by quite different principles, and bear no proportion to the quantity, the hardship, or the ingenuity of this supposed labour of inspection and direction. They are regulated altogether by the value of the stock employed, and are greater or smaller in proportion to the extent of this stock. Let us suppose, for example, that in some particular place, where the common annual profits of manufacturing stock are ten per cent. there are two different manufactures, in each of which twenty workmen are employed at the rate of fifteen pounds a year each, or at the expence of three hundred a year in each manufactory. Let us suppose too, that the coarse materials annually wrought up in the one cost only seven hundred pounds, while the finer materials in the other cost seven thousand. The capital annually employed in the one will in this case amount only to one thousand pounds; whereas that employed in the other will amount to seven thousand three hundred pounds. At the rate of ten per cent. therefore, the undertaker of the one will expect an yearly profit of about one hundred pounds only; while that of the other will expect about seven hundred and thirty pounds. But though their profits are so very different, their labour of inspection and direction may be either altogether or very nearly the same. In many great works, almost the whole labour of this kind is committed to some principal clerk. His wages properly express the value of this labour of inspection and direction. Though in settling them some regard is had commonly, not only to his labour and skill, but to the trust which is reposed in him, yet they never bear any regular proportion to the capital of which he oversees the management; and the owner of this capital, though he is thus discharged of almost all labour, still expects that his profits should bear a regular proportion to his capital. In the price of commodities, therefore, the profits of stock constitute a component part altogether different from the wages of labour, and regulated by quite different principles.

In this state of things, the whole produce of labour does not always belong to the labourer. He must in most cases share it with the owner of the stock which employs him. Neither is the quantity of labour commonly employed in acquiring or producing any commodity, the only circumstance which can regulate the quantity which it ought commonly to purchase, command, or exchange for. An additional quantity, it is evident, must be due for the profits of the stock which advanced the wages and furnished the materials of that labour.

As soon as the land of any country has all become private property, the landlords, like all other men, love to reap where they never sowed, and demand a rent even for its natural produce. The wood of the forest, the grass of the field, and all the natural fruits of the earth, which, when land was in common, cost the labourer only the trouble of gathering them, come, even to him, to have an additional price fixed upon them. He must then pay for the licence to gather them; and must give up to the landlord a portion of what his labour either collects or produces. This portion, or, what comes to the same thing, the price of this portion, constitutes the rent of land, and in the price of the greater part of commodities makes a third component part.

The real value of all the different component parts of price, it must be observed, is measured by the quantity of labour which they can, each of them, purchase or command. Labour measures the value not only of that part of price which resolves itself into labour, but of that which resolves itself into rent, and of that which resolves itself into profit.

In every society the price of every commodity finally resolves itself into some one or other, or all of those three parts; and in every improved society, all the three enter more or less, as component parts, into the price of the far greater part of commodities.

In the price of corn, for example, one part pays the rent of the landlord, another pays the wages or maintenance of the labourers and labouring cattle employed in producing it, and the third pays the profit of the farmer. These three parts seem either immediately or ultimately to make up the whole price of corn. A fourth part, it may perhaps be thought, is necessary for replacing the stock of the farmer, or for compensating the wear and tear of his labouring cattle, and other instruments of husbandry. But it must be considered that the price of any instrument of husbandry, such as a labouring horse, is itself made up of the same three parts; the rent of the land upon which he is reared, the labour of tending and rearing him, and the profits of the farmer who advances both the rent of this land, and the wages of this labour. Though the price of the corn, therefore, may pay the price as well as the maintenance of the horse, the whole price still resolves itself either immediately or ultimately into the same three parts of rent, labour, and profit.

In the price of flour or meal, we must add to the price of

the corn, the profits of the miller, and the wages of his servants; in the price of bread, the profits of the baker, and the wages of his servants; and in the price of both, the labour of transporting the corn from the house of the farmer to that of the miller, and from that of the miller to that of the baker, together with the profits of those who advance the wages of that labour.

The price of flax resolves itself into the same three parts as that of corn. In the price of linen we must add to this price the wages of the flax-dresser, of the spinner, of the weaver, of the bleacher, &c., together with the profits of their respective employers.

As any particular commodity comes to be more manufactured, that part of the price which resolves itself into wages and profit, comes to be greater in proportion to that which resolves itself into rent. In the progress of the manufacture, not only the number of profits increase, but every subsequent profit is greater than the foregoing; because the capital from which it is derived must always be greater. The capital which employs the weavers, for example, must be greater than that which employs the spinners; because it not only replaces that capital with its profits, but pays, besides, the wages of the weavers; and the profits must always bear some proportion to the capital.

In the most improved societies, however, there are always a few commodities of which the price resolves itself into two parts only, the wages of labour, and the profits of stock; and a still smaller number, in which it consists altogether in the wages of labour. In the price of sea-fish, for example, one part pays the labour of the fishermen, and the other the profits of the capital employed in the fishery. Rent very seldom makes any part of it, though it does sometimes, as I shall shew hereafter. It is otherwise, at least through the greater part of Europe, in river fisheries. A salmon fishery pays a rent, and rent, though it cannot well be called the rent of land, makes a part of the price of a salmon as well as wages and profit. In some parts of Scotland a few poor people make a trade of gathering, along the sea-shore, those little variegated stones commonly known by the name of Scotch Pebbles. The price which is paid to them by the stone-cutter is altogether the wages of their labour; neither rent nor profit make any part of it.

But the whole price of any commodity must still finally resolve itself into some one or other, or all of those three parts; as whatever part of it remains after paying the rent of the land, and the price of the whole labour employed in raising, manufacturing, and bringing it to market, must necessarily be profit to somebody.

As the price or exchangeable value of every particular commodity, taken separately, resolves itself into some one or other, or all of those three parts; so that of all the commodities which compose the whole annual produce of the labour of every country, taken complexly, must resolve itself into the same three parts, and be parcelled out among different inhabitants of the country, either as the wages of their labour, the profits of their stock, or the rent of their land. The whole of what is annually either collected or produced by the labour of every society, or what comes to the same thing, the whole price of it, is in this manner originally distributed among some of its different members. Wages, profit, and rent, are the three original sources of all revenue as well as of all exchangeable value. All other revenue is ultimately derived from some one or other of these.

Whoever derives his revenue from a fund which is his own, must draw it either from his labour, from his stock, or from his land. The revenue derived from labour is called wages. That derived from stock, by the person who manages or employs it, is called profit. That derived from it by the person who does not employ it himself, but lends it to another, is called the interest or the use of money. It is the compensation which the borrower pays to the lender, for the profit which he has an opportunity of making by the use of the money. Part of that profit naturally belongs to the borrower, who runs the risk and takes the trouble of employing it; and part to the lender, who affords him the opportunity of making this profit. The interest of money is always a derivative revenue, which, if it is not paid from the profit which is made by the use of the money, must be paid from some other source of revenue, unless perhaps the borrower is a spendthrift, who contracts a second debt in order to pay the interest of the first. The revenue which proceeds altogether from land, is called rent, and belongs to the landlord. The revenue of the farmer is derived partly from his labour, and partly from his stock. To him, land is only the instrument which enables him to earn the wages of this labour, and to make the profits of this stock. All taxes, and all the revenue which is founded upon them, all salaries, pensions, and annuities of every kind, are ultimately derived from some one or other of those three original sources of revenue, and are paid either immediately or mediately from the wages of labour, the profits of stock, or the rent of land.

When those three different sorts of revenue belong to different persons, they are readily distinguished; but when they belong to the same they are sometimes confounded with one another, at least in common language.

A gentleman who farms a part of his own estate, after paying the expense of cultivation, should gain both the rent of the landlord and the profit of the farmer. He is apt to denominate, however, his whole gain, profit, and thus confounds rent with profit, at least in common language. The greater part of our North American and West Indian planters are in this situation. They farm, the greater part of them, their own estates, and accordingly we seldom hear of the rent of a plantation, but frequently of its profit.

Common farmers seldom employ any overseer to direct the general operations of the farm. They generally too work a good deal with their own hands, as ploughmen, harrowers, &c. What remains of the crop after paying the rent, therefore, should not only replace to them their stock employed in cultivation, together with its ordinary profits, but pay them the wages which are due to them, both as labourers and overseers. Whatever remains, however, after paying the rent and keeping up the stock, is called profit. But wages evidently make a part of it. The farmer, by saving these wages, must necessarily gain them. Wages, therefore, are in this case confounded with profit.

An independent manufacturer, who has stock enough both to purchase materials, and to maintain himself till he can carry his work to market, should gain both the wages of a journeyman who works under a master, and the profit which that master makes by the sale of the journeyman's work. His whole gains, however, are commonly called profit, and wages are, in this case too, confounded with profit.

A gardener who cultivates his own garden with his own hands, unites in his own person the three different characters, of landlord, farmer, and labourer. His produce, therefore, should pay him the rent of the first, the profit of the second, and the wages of the third. The whole, however, is commonly considered as the earnings of his labour. Both rent and profit are, in this case, confounded with wages.

As in a civilized country there are but few commodities of which the exchangeable value arises from labour only, rent and profit contributing largely to that of the far greater part of them, so the annual produce of its labour will always be sufficient to purchase or command a much greater quantity of labour than what was employed in raising, preparing, and bringing that produce to market. If the society were annually to employ all the labour which it can annually purchase, as the quantity of labour would increase greatly every year, so the produce of every succeeding year would be of vastly greater value than that of the foregoing. But there is no country in which the whole annual produce is employed in maintaining the industrious. The idle every where consume a great part of it; and according to the different proportions in which it is annually divided between those two different orders of people, its ordinary or average value must either annually increase, or diminish, or continue the same from one year to another.

CHAPTER VII

Of the Natural and Market Price of Commodities

THERE is in every society or neighbourhood an ordinary or average rate both of wages and profit in every different employment of labour and stock. This rate is naturally regulated, as I shall show hereafter, partly by the general circumstances of the society, their riches or poverty, their advancing, stationary, or declining condition; and partly by the particular nature of each employment.

There is likewise in every society or neighbourhood an ordinary or average rate of rent, which is regulated too, as I shall shew hereafter, partly by the general circumstances of the society or neighbourhood in which the land is situated, and partly by the natural or improved fertility of the land.

(These ordinary or average rates may be called the natural rates of wages, profit, and rent, at the time and place in which they commonly prevail.)

When the price of any commodity is neither more nor less than what is sufficient to pay the rent of the land, the wages of the labour, and the profits of the stock employed in raising, preparing, and bringing it to market, according to their natural rates, the commodity is then sold for what may be called its natural price.

The commodity is then sold precisely for what it is worth, or for what it really costs the person who brings it to market; for though in common language what is called the prime cost of any commodity does not comprehend the profit of the person who is to sell it again, yet if he sells it at a price which does not allow him the ordinary rate of profit in his neighbourhood, he is evidently a loser by the trade; since by employing his stock in some other way he might have made that profit. His profit, besides, is his revenue, the proper fund of his subsistence. As, while he is preparing and bringing the goods to market, he advances to his workmen their wages, or their subsistence; so he advances to himself, in the same manner, his own subsistence, which is generally suitable to the profit which he may reasonably expect from the sale of his goods. Unless they yield him this profit, therefore, they do not repay him what they may very properly be said to have really cost him.

Though the price, therefore, which leaves him this profit, is not always the lowest at which a dealer may sometimes sell his goods, it is the lowest at which he is likely to sell them for any considerable time; at least where there is perfect liberty, or where he may change his trade as often as he pleases.

The actual price at which any commodity is commonly sold is called its market price. It may either be above, or below, or exactly the same with its natural price.

The market price of every particular commodity is regulated by the proportion between the quantity which is actually brought to market, and the demand of those who are willing to pay the natural price of the commodity, or the whole value of the rent, labour, and profit, which must be paid in order to bring it thither. Such people may be called the effectual demanders, and their demand the effectual demand; since it may be sufficient to effectuate the bringing of the commodity to market. It is different from the absolute demand. A very poor man may be said in some sense to have a demand for a coach and six; he might like to have it; but his demand is not an effectual demand, as the commodity can never be brought to market in order to satisfy it.

When the quantity of any commodity which is brought to market falls short of the effectual demand, all those who are willing to pay the whole value of the rent, wages, and profit, which must be paid in order to bring it thither, cannot be supplied with the quantity which they want. Rather than want it altogether, some of them will be willing to give more. A competition will immediately begin among them, and the market price will rise more or less above the natural price, according as either the greatness of the deficiency, or the wealth and wanton luxury of the competitors, happen to animate more or less the eagerness of the competition. Among competitors of equal wealth and luxury the same deficiency will generally occasion a more or less eager competition, according as the acquisition of the commodity happens to be of more or less importance to them. Hence the exorbitant price of the necessaries of life during the blockade of a town or in a famine.

When the quantity brought to market exceeds the effectual demand, it cannot be all sold to those who are willing to pay the whole value of the rent, wages and profit, which must be paid in order to bring it thither. Some part must be sold to those who are willing to pay less, and the low price which they give for it must reduce the price of the whole. The market price will sink more or less below the natural price, according as the greatness of the excess increases more or less the competition of the sellers, or according as it happens to be more or less important to them to get immediately rid of the commodity. The same excess in the importation of perishable, will occasion a much greater competition than in that of durable commodities; in the importation of oranges, for example, than in that of old iron.

When the quantity brought to market is just sufficient to supply the effectual demand and no more, the market price naturally comes to be either exactly, or as nearly as can be judged of, the same with the natural price. The whole quantity upon hand can be disposed of for this price, and cannot be disposed of for more. The competition of the different dealers obliges them all to accept of this price, but does not oblige them to accept of less.

The quantity of every commodity brought to market naturally suits itself to the effectual demand. It is the interest of all those who employ their land, labour, or stock, in bringing any commodity to market, that the quantity never should exceed the effectual demand; and it is the interest of all other people that it never should fall short of that demand.

If at any time it exceeds the effectual demand, some of the component parts of its price must be paid below their natural rate. If it is rent, the interest of the landlords will immediately prompt them to withdraw a part of their land;

and if it is wages or profit, the interest of the labourers in the one case, and of their employers in the other, will prompt them to withdraw a part of their labour or stock from this employment. The quantity brought to market will soon be no more than sufficient to supply the effectual demand. All the different parts of its price will rise to their natural rate, and the whole price to its natural price.

If, on the contrary, the quantity brought to market should at any time fall short of the effectual demand, some of the component parts of its price must rise above their natural rate. If it is rent, the interest of all other landlords will naturally prompt them to prepare more land for the raising of this commodity; if it is wages or profit, the interest of all other labourers and dealers will soon prompt them to employ more labour and stock in preparing and bringing it to market. The quantity brought thither will soon be sufficient to supply the effectual demand. All the different parts of its price will soon sink to their natural rate, and the whole price to its natural price.

The natural price, therefore, is, as it were, the central price, to which the prices of all commodities are continually gravitating. Different accidents may sometimes keep them suspended a good deal above it, and sometimes force them down even somewhat below it. But whatever may be the obstacles which hinder them from settling in this center of repose and continuance, they are constantly tending towards it.

The whole quantity of industry annually employed in order to bring any commodity to market, naturally suits itself in this manner to the effectual demand. It naturally aims at bringing always that precise quantity thither which may be sufficient to supply, and no more than supply, that demand.

But in some employments the same quantity of industry will in different years produce very different quantities of commodities; while in others it will produce always the same, or very nearly the same. The same number of labourers in husbandry will, in different years, produce very different quantities of corn, wine, oil, hops, &c. But the same number of spinners and weavers will every year produce the same or very nearly the same quantity of linen and woollen cloth. It is only the average produce of the one species of industry which can be suited in any respect to the effectual demand; and as its actual produce is frequently much greater and frequently much less than its average produce, the quantity of the commodities brought to market will sometimes exceed a good deal, and sometimes fall short a good deal, of the effectual demand. Even though that demand therefore should continue always the same, their market price will be liable to great fluctuations, will sometimes fall a good deal below, and sometimes rise a good deal above, their natural price. In the other species of industry, the produce of equal quantities of labour being always the same, or very nearly the same, it can be more exactly suited to the effectual demand. While that demand continues the same, therefore, the market price of the commodities is likely to do so too, and to be either altogether, or as nearly as can be judged of, the same with the natural price. That the price of linen and woollen cloth is liable neither to such frequent nor to such great variations as the price of corn, every man's experience will inform him. The price of the one species of commodities varies only with the variations in the demand: That of the other varies not only with the variations in the demand, but with the much greater and more frequent variations in the quantity of what is brought to market in order to supply that demand.

The occasional and temporary fluctuations in the market price of any commodity fall chiefly upon those parts of its price which resolve themselves into wages and profit. That part which resolves itself into rent is less affected by them. A rent certain in money is not in the least affected by them either in its rate or in its value. A rent which consists either in a certain proportion or in a certain quantity of the rude produce, is no doubt affected in its yearly value by all the occasional and temporary fluctuations in the market price of that rude produce; but it is seldom affected by them in its yearly rate. In settling the terms of the lease, the landlord and farmer endeavour, according to their best judgment, to adjust that rate, not to the temporary and occasional, but to the average and ordinary price of the produce.

Such fluctuations affect both the value and the rate either

of wages or of profit, according as the market happens to be either over-stocked or under-stocked with commodities or with labour; with work done, or with work to be done. A public mourning raises the price of black cloth (with which the market is almost always under-stocked upon such occasions), and augments the profits of the merchants who possess any considerable quantity of it. It has no effect upon the wages of the weavers. The market is under-stocked with commodities, not with labour; with work done, not with work to be done. It raises the wages of journeymen taylors. The market is here under-stocked with labour. There is an effectual demand for more labour, for more work to be done than can be had. It sinks the price of coloured silks and cloths, and thereby reduces the profits of the merchants who have any considerable quantity of them upon hand. It sinks too the wages of the workmen employed in preparing such commodities, for which all demand is stopped for six months, perhaps for a twelvemonth. The market is here over-stocked both with commodities and with labour.

But though the market price of every particular commodity is in this manner continually gravitating, if one may say so, towards the natural price, yet sometimes particular accidents, sometimes natural causes, and sometimes particular regulations of police, may, in many commodities, keep up the market price, for a long time together, a good deal above the natural price.

When by an increase in the effectual demand, the market price of some particular commodity happens to rise a good deal above the natural price, those who employ their stocks in supplying that market are generally careful to conceal this change. If it was commonly known, their great profit would tempt so many new rivals to employ their stocks in the same way, that, the effectual demand being fully supplied, the market price would soon be reduced to the natural price, and perhaps for some time even below it. If the market is at a great distance from the residence of those who supply it, they may sometimes be able to keep the secret for several years together, and may so long enjoy their extraordinary profits without any new rivals. Secrets of this kind, however, it must be acknowledged, can seldom be long kept; and the extraordinary profit can last very little longer than they are kept.

Secrets in manufactures are capable of being longer kept than secrets in trade. A dyer who has found the means of producing a particular colour with materials which cost only half the price of those commonly made use of, may, with good management, enjoy the advantage of his discovery as long as he lives, and even leave it as a legacy to his posterity. His extraordinary gains arise from the high price which is paid for his private labour. They properly consist in the high wages of that labour. But as they are repeated upon every part of his stock, and as their whole amount bears, upon that account, a regular proportion to it, they are commonly considered as extraordinary profits of stock.

Such enhancements of the market price are evidently the effects of particular accidents, of which, however, the operation may sometimes last for many years together.

Some natural productions require such a singularity of soil and situation, that all the land in a great country, which is fit for producing them, may not be sufficient to supply the effectual demand. The whole quantity brought to market, therefore, may be disposed of to those who are willing to give more than what is sufficient to pay the rent of the land which produced them, together with the wages of the labour, and the profits of the stock which were employed in preparing and bringing them to market, according to their natural rates. Such commodities may continue for whole centuries together to be sold at this high price; and that part of it which resolves itself into the rent of land is in this case the part which is generally paid above its natural rate. The rent of the land which affords such singular and esteemed productions, like the rent of some vineyards in France of a peculiarly happy soil and situation, bears no regular proportion to the rent of other equally fertile and equally well-cultivated land in its neighbourhood. The wages of the labour and the profits of the stock employed in bringing such commodities to market, on the contrary, are seldom out of their natural proportion to those of the other employments of labour and stock in their neighbourhood.

Such enhancements of the market price are evidently the

effect of natural causes which may hinder the effectual demand from ever being fully supplied, and which may continue, therefore, to operate for ever.

A monopoly granted either to an individual or to a trading company has the same effect as a secret in trade or manufactures. The monopolists, by keeping the market constantly under-stocked, by never fully supplying the effectual demand, sell their commodities much above the natural price, and raise their emoluments, whether they consist in wages or profit, greatly above their natural rate.

The price of monopoly is upon every occasion the highest which can be got. The natural price, or the price of free competition, on the contrary, is the lowest which can be taken, not upon every occasion indeed, but for any considerable time together. The one is upon every occasion the highest which can be squeezed out of the buyers, or which, it is supposed, they will consent to give: The other is the lowest which the sellers can commonly afford to take, and at the same time continue their business.

The exclusive privileges of corporations, statutes of apprenticeship, and all those laws which restrain, in particular employments, the competition to a smaller number than might otherwise go into them, have the same tendency, though in a less degree. They are a sort of enlarged monopolies, and may frequently, for ages together, and in whole classes of employments, keep up the market price of particular commodities above the natural price, and maintain both the wages of the labour and the profits of the stock employed about them somewhat above their natural rate.

Such enhancements of the market price may last as long as the regulations of police which give occasion to them.

The market price of any particular commodity, though it may continue long above, can seldom continue long below, its natural price. Whatever part of it was paid below the natural rate, the persons whose interest it affected would immediately feel the loss, and would immediately withdraw either so much land, or so much labour, or so much stock, from being employed about it, that the quantity brought to market would soon be no more than sufficient to supply the effectual demand. Its market price, therefore, would soon rise to the natural price. This at least would be the case where there was perfect liberty.

The same statutes of apprenticeship and other corporation laws indeed, which, when a manufacture is in prosperity, enable the workman to raise his wages a good deal above their natural rate, sometimes oblige him, when it decays, to let them down a good deal below it. As in the one case they exclude many people from his employment, so in the other they exclude him from many employments. The effect of such regulations, however, is not near so durable in sinking the workman's wages below, as in raising them above, their natural rate. Their operation in the one way may endure for many centuries, but in the other it can last no longer than the lives of some of the workmen who were bred to the business in the time of its prosperity. When they are gone, the number of those who are afterwards educated to the trade will naturally suit itself to the effectual demand. The police must be as violent as that of Indostan or antient Egypt (where every man was bound by a principle of religion to follow the occupation of his father, and was supposed to commit the most horrid sacrilege if he changed it for another), which can in any particular employment, and for several generations together, sink either the wages of labour or the profits of stock below their natural rate.

This is all that I think necessary to be observed at present concerning the deviations, whether occasional or permanent, of the market price of commodities from the natural price.

The natural price itself varies with the natural rate of each of its component parts, of wages, profit, and rent; and in every society this rate varies according to their circumstances, according to their riches or poverty, their advancing, stationary, or declining condition. I shall, in the four following chapters, endeavour to explain, as fully and distinctly as I can, the causes of those different variations.

First, I shall endeavour to explain what are the circumstances which naturally determine the rate of wages, and in what manner those circumstances are affected by the riches or poverty, by the advancing, stationary, or declining state of the society.

Secondly, I shall endeavour to shew what are the circumstances which naturally determine the rate of profit, and in what manner too those circumstances are affected by the like variations in the state of the society.

Though pecuniary wages and profits are very different in the different employments of labour and stock; yet a certain proportion seems commonly to take place between both the pecuniary wages in all the different employments of labour, and the pecuniary profits in all the different employments of stock. This proportion, it will appear hereafter, depends partly upon the nature of the different employments, and partly upon the different laws and policy of the society in which they are carried on. But though in many respects dependent upon the laws and policy, this proportion seems to be little affected by the riches or poverty of that society; by its advancing, stationary, or declining condition; but to remain the same or very nearly the same in all those different states. I shall, in the third place, endeavour to explain all the different circumstances which regulate this proportion.

In the fourth and last place, I shall endeavor to show what are the circumstances which regulate the rent of land, and which either raise or lower the real price of all the different substances which it produces.

CHAPTER VIII

Of the Wages of Labour

THE produce of labour constitutes the natural recompence or wages of labour.

In that original state of things, which precedes both the appropriation of land and the accumulation of stock, the whole produce of labour belongs to the labourer. He has neither landlord nor master to share with him.

Had this state continued, the wages of labour would have augmented with all those improvements in its productive powers, to which the division of labour gives occasion. All things would gradually have become cheaper. They would have been produced by a smaller quantity of labour; and as the commodities produced by equal quantities of labour would naturally in this state of things be exchanged for one another, they would have been purchased likewise with the produce of a smaller quantity.

But though all things would have become cheaper in reality, in appearance many things might have become dearer than before, or have been exchanged for a greater quantity of other goods. Let us suppose, for example, that in the greater part of employments the productive powers of labour had been improved to tenfold, or that a day's labour could produce ten times the quantity of work which it had done originally; but that in a particular employment they had been improved only to double, or that a day's labour could produce only twice the quantity of work which it had done before. In exchanging the produce of a day's labour in the greater part of employments, for that of a day's labour in this particular one, ten times the original quantity of work in them would purchase only twice the original quantity in it. Any particular quantity in it, therefore, a pound weight, for example, would appear to be five times dearer than before. In reality, however, it would be twice as cheap. Though it required five times the quantity of other goods to purchase it, it would require only half the quantity of labour either to purchase or to produce it. The acquisition, therefore, would be twice as easy as before.

But this original state of things, in which the labourer enjoyed the whole produce of his own labour, could not last beyond the first introduction of the appropriation of land and the accumulation of stock. It was at an end, therefore, long before the most considerable improvements were made in the productive powers of labour, and it would be to no purpose to trace further what might have been its effects upon the recompence or wages of labour.

As soon as land becomes private property, the landlord demands a share of almost all the produce which the labourer can either raise, or collect from it. His rent makes the first deduction from the produce of the labour which is employed upon land.

It seldom happens that the person who tills the ground has wherewithal to maintain himself till he reaps the harvest. His maintenance is generally advanced to him from the stock of a master, the farmer who employs him, and who would have no interest to employ him, unless he was to share in the produce of his labour, or unless his stock was to be replaced to him with a profit. This profit makes a second deduction from the produce of the labour which is employed upon land.

The produce of almost all other labour is liable to the like deduction of profit. In all arts and manufactures the greater part of the workmen stand in need of a master to advance them the materials of their work, and their wages and maintenance till it be compleated. He shares in the produce of their labour, or in the value which it adds to the materials upon which it is bestowed; and in this share consists his profit.

It sometimes happens, indeed, that a single independent workman has stock sufficient both to purchase the materials of his work, and to maintain himself till it be compleated. He is both master and workman, and enjoys the whole produce of his own labour, or the whole value which it adds to the materials upon which it is bestowed. It includes what are usually two distinct revenues, belonging to two distinct persons, the profits of stock, and the wages of labour.

Such cases, however, are not very frequent, and in every part of Europe, twenty workmen serve under a master for one that is independent; and the wages of labour are every where understood to be, what they usually are, when the labourer is one person, and the owner of the stock which employs him another.

What are the common wages of labour, depends every where upon the contract usually made between those two parties, whose interests are by no means the same. The workmen desire to get as much, the masters to give as little as possible. The former are disposed to combine in order to raise, the latter in order to lower the wages of labour.

It is not, however, difficult to foresee which of the two parties must, upon all ordinary occasions, have the advantage in the dispute, and force the other into a compliance with their terms. The masters, being fewer in number, can combine much more easily; and the law, besides, authorises, or at least does not prohibit their combinations, while it prohibits those of the workmen. We have no acts of parliament against combining to lower the price of work; but many against combining to raise it. In all such disputes the masters can hold out much longer. A landlord, a farmer, a master manufacturer, or merchant, though they did not employ a single workman, could generally live a year or two upon the stocks which they have already acquired. Many workmen could not subsist a week, few could subsist a month, and scarce any a year without employment. In the long-run the workman may be as necessary to his master as his master is to him; but the necessity is not so immediate.

We rarely hear, it has been said, of the combinations of masters; though frequently of those of workmen. But whoever imagines, upon this account, that masters rarely combine, is as ignorant of the world as of the subject. Masters are always and every where in a sort of tacit, but constant and uniform combination, not to raise the wages of labour above their actual rate. To violate this combination is every where a most unpopular action, and a sort of reproach to a master among his neighbours and equals. We seldom, indeed, hear of this combination, because it is the usual, and one may say, the natural state of things which nobody ever hears of. Masters too sometimes enter into particular combinations to sink the wages of labour even below this rate. These are always conducted with the utmost silence and secrecy, till the moment of execution, and when the workmen yield, as they sometimes do, without resistance, though severely felt by them, they are never heard of by other people. Such combinations, however, are frequently resisted by a contrary defensive combination of the workmen; who sometimes too, without any provocation of this kind, combine of their own accord to raise the price of their labour. Their usual pretences are, sometimes the high price of provisions; sometimes the great profit which their masters make by their work. But whether their combinations be offensive or defensive, they are always abundantly heard of. In order to bring the point to a speedy decision, they have always recourse to the loudest clamour, and sometimes to the most shocking violence and outrage. They are desperate, and act with the folly and extravagance of desperate men, who must either starve, or frighten their masters into an immediate compliance with their demands. The masters upon these occasions are just as clamorous upon the other side, and never cease to call aloud for the assistance of the civil magistrate, and the rigorous execution of those laws which have been enacted with so much severity against the combinations of servants, labourers, and journeymen. The workmen, accordingly, very seldom derive any advantage from the violence of those tumultuous combinations, which, partly from the interposition of the civil magistrate, partly from the superior steadiness of the masters, partly from the necessity which the greater part of the workmen are under of submitting for the sake of present subsistence, generally end in nothing, but the punishment or ruin of the ringleaders.

But though in disputes with their workmen, masters must generally have the advantage, there is however a certain rate below which it seems impossible to reduce, for any considerable time, the ordinary wages even of the lowest species of labour.

A man must always live by his work, and his wages must at least be sufficient to maintain him. They must even upon most occasions be somewhat more; otherwise it would be impossible for him to bring up a family, and the race of such workmen could not last beyond the first generation. Mr. Cantillon seems, upon this account, to suppose that the lowest species of common labourers must every where earn at least double their own maintenance, in order that one with another they may be enabled to bring up two children; the labour of the wife, on account of her necessary attendance on the children, being supposed no more than sufficient to provide for herself. But one-half the children born, it is computed, die before the age of manhood. The poorest labourers, therefore, according to this account, must, one with another, attempt to rear at least four children, in order that two may have an equal chance of living to that age. But the necessary maintenance of four children, it is supposed, may be nearly equal to that of one man. The labour of an able-bodied slave, the same author adds, is computed to be worth double his maintenance; and that of the meanest labourer, he thinks, cannot be worth less than that of an able-bodied slave. Thus far at least seems certain, that, in order to bring up a family, the labour of the husband and wife together must, even in the lowest species of common labour, be able to earn something more than what is precisely necessary for their own maintenance; but in what proportion, whether in that above mentioned, or in any other, I shall not take upon me to determine.

There are certain circumstances, however, which sometimes give the labourers an advantage, and enable them to raise their wages considerably above this rate; evidently the lowest which is consistent with common humanity.

When in any country the demand for those who live by wages, labourers, journeymen, servants of every kind, is continually increasing; when every year furnishes employment for a greater number than had been employed the year before, the workmen have no occasion to combine in order to raise their wages. The scarcity of hands occasions a competition among masters, who bid against one another, in order to get workmen, and thus voluntarily break through the natural combination of masters not to raise wages.

The demand for those who live by wages, it is evident, cannot increase but in proportion to the increase of the funds which are destined for the payment of wages. These funds are of two kinds; first, the revenue which is over and above what is necessary for the maintenance; and, secondly, the stock which is over and above what is necessary for the employment of their masters.

When the landlord, annuitant, or monied man, has a greater revenue than what he judges sufficient to maintain his own family, he employs either the whole or a part of the surplus in maintaining one or more menial servants. Increase this surplus, and he will naturally increase the number of those servants.

When an independent workman, such as a weaver or shoemaker, has got more stock than what is sufficient to purchase the materials of his own work, and to maintain himself till he can dispose of it, he naturally employs one or more journeymen with the surplus, in order to make a profit by their work. Increase this surplus, and he will naturally increase the number of his journeymen.

The demand for those who live by wages, therefore, necessarily increases with the increase of the revenue and stock of every country, and cannot possibly increase without it. The increase of revenue and stock is the increase of national wealth. The demand for those who live by wages, therefore, naturally increases with the increase of national wealth, and cannot possibly increase without it.

It is not the actual greatness of national wealth, but its continual increase, which occasions a rise in the wages of labour. It is not, accordingly, in the richest countries, but in the most thriving, or in those which are growing rich the fastest, that the wages of labour are highest. England is certainly, in the present times, a much richer country than any part of North America. The wages of labour, however, are much higher in North America than in any part of England. In the province of New York, common labourers earn three shillings and sixpence currency, equal to two shillings sterling, a day; ship carpenters, ten shillings and sixpence currency, with a pint of rum worth sixpence sterling, equal in all to six shillings and sixpence sterling; house carpenters and bricklayers, eight shillings currency, equal to four shillings and sixpence sterling; journeymen taylors, five shillings currency, equal to about two shillings and tenpence sterling. These prices are all above the London price; and wages are said to be as high in the other colonies as in New York. The price of provisions is every where in North America much lower than in England. A dearth has never been known there. In the worst seasons, they have always had a sufficiency for themselves, though less for exportation. If the money price of labour, therefore, be higher than it is any where in the mother country, its real price, the real command of the necessaries and conveniencies of life which it conveys to the labourer, must be higher in a still greater proportion.

But though North America is not yet so rich as England, it is much more thriving, and advancing with much greater rapidity to the further acquisition of riches. The most decisive mark of the prosperity of any country is the increase of the number of its inhabitants. In Great Britain, and most other European countries, they are not supposed to double in less than five hundred years. In the British colonies in North America, it has been found, that they double in twenty or five-and-twenty years. Nor in the present times is this increase principally owing to the continual importation of new inhabitants, but to the great multiplication of the species. Those who live to old age, it is said, frequently see there from fifty to a hundred, and sometimes many more, descendants from their own body. Labour is there so well rewarded that a numerous family of children, instead of being a burthen is a source of opulence and prosperity to the parents. The labour of each child, before it can leave their house, is computed to be worth a hundred pounds clear gain to them. A young widow with four or five young children, who, among the middling or inferior ranks of people in Europe, would have so little chance for a second husband, is there frequently courted as a sort of fortune. The value of children is the greatest of all encouragements to marriage. We cannot, therefore, wonder that the people in North America should generally marry very young. Notwithstanding the great increase occasioned by such early marriages, there is a continual complaint of the scarcity of hands in North America. The demand for labourers, the funds destined for maintaining them, increase, it seems, still faster than they can find labourers to employ.

Though the wealth of a country should be very great, yet if it has been long stationary, we must not expect to find the wages of labour very high in it. The funds destined for the payment of wages, the revenue and stock of its inhabitants, may be of the greatest extent; but if they have continued for several centuries of the same, or very nearly of the same extent, the number of labourers employed every year could easily supply, and even more than supply, the number wanted the following year. There could seldom be any scarcity of hands, nor could the masters be obliged to bid against one another in order to get them. The hands, on the contrary, would, in this case, naturally multiply beyond their employment. There would be a constant scarcity of employment, and the labourers would be obliged to bid against one another in order to get it. If in such a country the wages of labour had ever been more than sufficient to maintain the labourer, and to enable him to bring up a family, the competition of the labourers and interest of the masters would soon reduce them to this lowest rate which is consistent with common humanity. China has been long one of the richest, that is, one of the most fertile, best cultivated, most industrious, and most populous countries in the world. It seems, however, to have been long stationary. Marco Polo, who visited it more than five hundred years ago, describes its cultivation, industry, and populousness, almost in the same terms in which they are described by travellers in the present times. It had perhaps, even long before his time, acquired that full complement of riches which the nature of its laws and institutions permits it to acquire. The accounts of all travellers, inconsistent in many other respects, agree in the low wages of labour, and in the difficulty which a labourer finds in bringing up a family in China. If by digging the ground a whole day he can get what will purchase a small quantity of rice in the evening, he is contented. The condition of artificers is, if possible, still worse. Instead of waiting indolently in their work-houses, for the calls of their customers, as in Europe, they are continually running about the streets with the tools of their respective trades offering their service, and as it were begging employment. The poverty of the lower ranks of people in China far surpasses that of the most beggarly nations in Europe. In the neighbourhood of Canton many hundreds, it is commonly said, many thousand families have no habitation on the land, but live constantly in little fishing boats upon the rivers and canals. The subsistence which they find there is so scanty that they are eager to fish up the nastiest garbage thrown overboard from any European ship. Any carrion, the carcase of a dead dog or cat, for example, though half putrid and stinking, is as welcome to them as the most wholesome food to the people of other countries. Marriage is encouraged in China, not by the profitableness of children, but by the liberty of destroying them. In all great towns several are every night exposed in the street, or drowned like puppies in the water. The performance of this horrid office is even said to be the avowed business by which some people earn their subsistence.

China, however, though it may perhaps stand still, does not seem to go backwards. Its towns are no-where deserted by their inhabitants. The lands which had once been cultivated are no-where neglected. The same or very nearly the same annual labour must therefore continue to be performed, and the funds destined for maintaining it must not, consequently, be sensibly diminished. The lowest class of labourers, therefore, notwithstanding their scanty subsistence, must some way or another make shift to continue their race so far as to keep up their usual numbers.

But it would be otherwise in a country where the funds destined for the maintenance of labour were sensibly decaying. Every year the demand for servants and labourers would, in all the different classes of employments, be less than it had been the year before. Many who had been bred in the superior classes, not being able to find employment in their own business, would be glad to seek it in the lowest.

The lowest class being not only overstocked with its own workmen, but with the overflowings of all the other classes, the competition for employment would be so great in it, as to reduce the wages of labour to the most miserable and scanty subsistence of the labourer. Many would not be able to find employment even upon these hard terms, but would either starve, or be driven to seek a subsistence either by begging, or by the perpetration perhaps of the greatest enormities. Want, famine, and mortality would immediately prevail in that class, and from thence extend themselves to all the superior classes, till the number of inhabitants in the country was reduced to what could easily be maintained by the revenue and stock which remained in it, and which had escaped either the tyranny or calamity which had destroyed the rest. This perhaps is nearly the present state of Bengal, and of some other of the English settlements in the East Indies. In a fertile country which had before been much depopulated, where subsistence, consequently, should not be very difficult, and where, notwithstanding, three or four hundred thousand people die of hunger in one year, we may be assured that the funds destined for the maintenance of the labouring poor are fast decaying. The difference between the genius of the British constitution which protects and governs North America, and that of the mercantile company which oppresses and domineers in the East Indies, cannot perhaps be better illustrated than by the different state of those countries.

The liberal reward of labour, therefore, as it is the necessary effect, so it is the natural symptom of increasing national wealth. The scanty maintenance of the labouring poor, on the other hand, is the natural symptom that things are at a stand, and their starving condition that they are going fast backwards.

In Great Britain the wages of labour seem, in the present times, to be evidently more than what is precisely necessary to enable the labourer to bring up a family. In order to satisfy ourselves upon this point it will not be necessary to enter into any tedious or doubtful calculation of what may be the lowest sum upon which it is possible to do this. There are many plain symptoms that the wages of labour are no-where in this country regulated by this lowest rate which is consistent with common humanity.

First, in almost every part of Great Britain there is a distinction, even in the lowest species of labour, between summer and winter wages. Summer wages are always highest. But on account of the extraordinary expence of fewel, the maintenance of a family is most expensive in winter. Wages, therefore, being highest when this expence is lowest, it seems evident that they are not regulated by what is necessary for this expence; but by the quantity and supposed value of the work. A labourer, it may be said indeed, ought to save part of his summer wages in order to defray his winter expence; and that through the whole year they do not exceed what is necessary to maintain his family through the whole year. A slave, however, or one absolutely dependent on us for immediate subsistence, would not be treated in this manner. His daily subsistence would be proportioned to his daily necessities.

Secondly, the wages of labour do not in Great Britain fluctuate with the price of provisions. These vary everywhere from year to year, frequently from month to month. But in many places the money price of labour remains uniformly the same sometimes for half a century together. If in these places, therefore, the labouring poor can maintain their families in dear years, they must be at their ease in times of moderate plenty, and in affluence in those of extraordinary cheapness. The high price of provisions during these ten years past has not in many parts of the kingdom been accompanied with any sensible rise in the money price of labour. It has, indeed, in some; owing probably more to the increase of the demand for labour than to that of the price of provisions.

Thirdly, as the price of provisions varies more from year to year than the wages of labour, so on the other hand, the wages of labour vary more from place to place than the price of provisions. The prices of bread and butcher's meat are generally the same or very nearly the same through the greater part of the united kingdom. These and most other things which are sold by retail, the way in which the labouring poor buy all things, are generally fully as cheap or cheaper in great towns than in the remoter parts of the country, for reasons which I shall have occasion to explain hereafter. But the wages of labour in a great town and its neighbourhood are frequently a fourth or a fifth part, twenty or five-and-twenty per cent. higher than at a few miles distance. Eighteen pence a day may be reckoned the common price of labour in London and its neighbourhood. At a few miles distance it falls to fourteen and fifteen pence. Ten pence may be reckoned its price in Edinburgh and its neighbourhood. At a few miles distance it falls to eight pence, the usual price of common labour through the greater part of the low country of Scotland, where it varies a good deal less than in England. Such a difference of prices, which it seems is not always sufficient to transport a man from one parish to another, would necessarily occasion so great a transportation of the most bulky commodities, not only from one parish to another, but from one end of the kingdom, almost from one end of the world to the other, as would soon reduce them more nearly to a level. After all that has been said of the levity and inconstancy of human nature, it appears evidently from experience that a man is of all sorts of luggage the most difficult to be transported. If the labouring poor, therefore, can maintain their families in those parts of the kingdom where the price of labour is lowest, they must be in affluence where it is highest.

Fourthly, the variations in the price of labour not only do not correspond either in place or time with those in the price of provisions, but they are frequently quite opposite.

Grain, the food of the common people, is dearer in Scotland than in England, whence Scotland receives almost every year very large supplies. But English corn must be sold dearer in Scotland, the country to which it is brought, than in England, the country from which it comes; and in proportion to its quality it cannot be sold dearer in Scotland than the Scotch corn that comes to the same market in competition with it. The quality of grain depends chiefly upon the quantity of flour or meal which it yields at the mill, and in this respect English grain is so much superior to the Scotch, that, though often dearer in appearance, or in proportion to the measure of its bulk, it is generally cheaper in reality, or in proportion to its quality, or even to the measure of its weight. The price of labour, on the contrary, is dearer in England than in Scotland. If the labouring poor, therefore, can maintain their families in the one part of the united kingdom, they must be in affluence in the other. Oatmeal indeed supplies the common people in Scotland with the greatest and the best part of their food, which is in general much inferior to that of their neighbours of the same rank in England. This difference, however, in the mode of their subsistence is not the cause, but the effect, of the difference in their wages; though, by a strange misapprehension, I have frequently heard it represented as the cause. It is not because one man keeps a coach while his neighbour walks a-foot, that the one is rich and the other poor; but because the one is rich he keeps a coach, and because the other is poor he walks a-foot.

During the course of the last century, taking one year with another, grain was dearer in both parts of the united kingdom than during that of the present. This is a matter of fact which cannot now admit of any reasonable doubt; and the proof of it is, if possible, still more decisive with regard to Scotland than with regard to England. It is in Scotland supported by the evidence of the public fiars, annual valuations made upon oath, according to the actual state of the markets, of all the different sorts of grain in every different county of Scotland. If such direct proof could require any collateral evidence to confirm it, I would observe that this has likewise been the case in France, and probably in most other parts of Europe. With regard to France there is the clearest proof. But though it is certain that in both parts of the united kingdom grain was somewhat dearer in the last century than in the present, it is equally certain that labour was much cheaper. If the labouring poor, therefore, could bring up their families then, they must be much more at their ease now. In the last century, the most usual day wages of common labour through the greater part of Scotland were sixpence in summer and fivepence in winter. Three shillings a week, the same price very nearly, still continues to be paid in some parts of the Highlands and Western Islands. Through the greater part of the low country the most usual wages of common labour are now eight-pence a day; ten-pence, sometimes a shilling about Edinburgh, in the counties which border upon England, probably on account of that neighbourhood, and in a few other places where there has lately been a considerable rise in the demand for labour, about Glasgow, Carron, Ayr-shire, &c. In England the improvements of agriculture, manufactures and commerce began much earlier than in Scotland. The demand for labour, and consequently its price, must necessarily have increased with those improvements. In the last century, accordingly, as well as in the present, the wages of labour were higher in England than in Scotland. They have risen too considerably since that time, though, on account of the greater variety of wages paid there in different places, it is more difficult to ascertain how much. In 1614, the pay of a foot soldier was the same as in the present times, eight-pence a day. When it was first established it would naturally be regulated by the usual wages of common labourers, the rank of people from which foot soldiers are commonly drawn. Lord Chief Justice Hales, who wrote in the time of Charles II., computes the necessary expence of a labourer's family, consisting of six persons, the father and mother, two children able to do something, and two not able, at ten shillings a week, or twenty-six pounds a year. If they cannot earn this by their labour, they must make it up, he supposes, either by begging or stealing. He appears to have enquired very carefully into this subject. In 1688, Mr. Gregory King, whose skill in political arithmetic is so much extolled by Doctor Davenant, computed the ordinary income of labourers and out-servants to be fifteen pounds a year to a family, which he supposed to consist, one with another, of three and a half persons. His calculation, therefore, though different in appearance, corresponding very nearly at bottom with that of Judge Hales. Both suppose the weekly expence of such families to be about twenty pence a head. Both the pecuniary income and expence of such families have increased considerably since that time through the greater part of the kingdom; in some places more, and in some less; though perhaps scarce any where so much as some exaggerated accounts of the present wages of labour have lately represented them to the public. The price of labour, it must be observed, cannot be ascertained very accurately any where, different prices being often paid at the same place and for the same sort of labour, not only according to the different abilities of the workmen, but according to the easiness or hardness of the masters. Where wages are not regulated by law, all that we can pretend to determine is what are the most usual; and experience seems to show that law can never regulate them properly, though it has often pretended to do so.

The real recompence of labour, the real quantity of the necessaries and conveniencies of life which it can procure to the labourer, has, during the course of the present century, increased perhaps in a still greater proportion than its money price. Not only grain has become somewhat cheaper, but many other things, from which the industrious poor derive an agreeable and wholesome variety of food, have become a great deal cheaper. Potatoes, for example, do not at present, through the greater part of the kingdom, cost half the price which they used to do thirty or forty years ago. The same thing may be said of turnips, carrots, cabbages; things which were formerly never raised but by the spade, but which are now commonly raised by the plough. All sort of garden stuff too has become cheaper. The greater part of apples and even of the onions consumed in Great Britain were in the last century imported from Flanders. The great improvements in the coarser manufactures of both linen and woolen cloth furnish the labourers with cheaper and better cloathing; and those in the manufactures of the coarser metals, with cheaper and better instruments of trade, as well as with many agreeable and convenient pieces of houshold furniture. Soap, salt, candles, leather, and fermented liquors, have, indeed, become a good deal dearer; chiefly from the taxes which have been laid upon them. The quantity of these, however, which the labouring poor are under any necessity of consuming, is so very small, that the increase in their price does not compensate the diminution in that of so many other things. The common complaint that luxury extends itself even to the lowest ranks of the people, and that the labouring poor will not now be contented with the same food, cloathing and lodging which satisfied them in former times, may convince us that it is not the money price of labour only, but its real recompence, which has augmented.

Is this improvement in the circumstances of the lower ranks of the people to be regarded as an advantage or as an inconveniency to the society? The answer seems at first sight abundantly plain. Servants, labourers and workmen of different kinds, make up the far greater part of every great political society. But what improves the circumstances of the greater part can never be regarded as an inconveniency to the whole. No society can surely be flourishing and happy, of which the far greater part of the members are poor and miserable. It is but equity, besides, that they who feed, cloath and lodge the whole body of the people, should have such a share of the produce of their own labour as to be themselves tolerably well fed, cloathed and lodged.

Poverty, though it no doubt discourages, does not always prevent marriage. It seems even to be favourable to generation. A half-starved Highland woman frequently bears more than twenty children, while a pampered fine lady is often incapable of bearing any, and is generally exhausted by two or three. Barrenness, so frequent among women of fashion, is very rare among those of inferior station. Luxury in the fair sex, while it inflames perhaps the passion for enjoyment, seems always to weaken, and frequently to destroy altogether, the powers of generation.

But poverty, though it does not prevent the generation, is extremely unfavourable to the rearing of children. The tender plant is produced, but in so cold a soil, and so severe a climate, soon withers and dies. It is not uncommon, I have been frequently told, in the Highlands of Scotland for a mother who has borne twenty children not to have two alive. Several officers of great experience have assured me, that so far from recruiting their regiment, they have never been able to supply it with drums and fifes from all the soldiers' children that were born in it. A greater number of fine children, however, is seldom seen any where than about a barrack of soldiers. Very few of them, it seems, arrive at the age of thirteen or fourteen. In some places one half the children born die before they are four years of age; in many places before they are seven; and in almost all places before they are nine or ten. This great mortality, however, will every where be found chiefly among the children of the common people, who cannot afford to tend them with the same care as those of better station. Though their marriages are generally more fruitful than those of people of fashion, a smaller proportion of their children arrive at maturity. In foundling hospitals, and among the children brought up by parish charities, the mortality is still greater than among those of the common people.

Every species of animals naturally multiplies in proportion to the means of their subsistence, and no species can ever multiply beyond it. But in civilized society it is only among the inferior ranks of people that the scantiness of subsistence can set limits to the further multiplication of the human species; and it can do so in no other way than by destroying a great part of the children which their fruitful marriages produce.

The liberal reward of labour, by enabling them to provide better for their children, and consequently to bring up a greater number, naturally tends to widen and extend those limits. It deserves to be remarked too, that it necessarily does this as nearly as possible in the proportion which the demand for labour requires. If this demand is continually increasing, the reward of labour must necessarily encourage in such a manner the marriage and multiplication of labourers, as may enable them to supply that continually increasing demand by a continually increasing population. If the reward should at any time be less than what was requisite for this purpose, the deficiency of hands would soon raise it; and if it should at any time be more, their excessive multiplication would soon lower it to this necessary rate. The market would be so much under-stocked with labour in the one case, and so much over-stocked in the other, as would soon force back its price to that proper rate which the circumstances of the society required. It is in this manner that the demand for men, like that for any other commodity, necessarily regulates the production of men; quickens it when it goes on too slowly, and stops it when it advances too fast. It is this demand which regulates and determines the state of propagation in all the different countries of the world, in North America, in Europe, and in China; which renders it rapidly progressive in the first, slow and gradual in the second, and altogether stationary in the last.

The wear and tear of a slave, it has been said, is at the expence of his master; but that of a free servant is at his own expence. The wear and tear of the latter, however, is, in reality, as much at the expence of his master as that of the former. The wages paid to journeymen and servants of every kind must be such as may enable them, one with another, to continue the race of journeymen and servants, according as the increasing, diminishing, or stationary demand of the society may happen to require. But though the wear and tear of a free servant be equally at the expence of his master, it generally costs him much less than that of a slave. The fund destined for replacing or repairing, if I may say so, the wear and tear of the slave, is commonly managed by a negligent master or careless overseer. That destined for performing the same office with regard to the free man, is managed by the free man himself. The disorders which generally prevail in the economy of the rich, naturally introduce themselves into the management of the former: The strict frugality and parsimonious attention of the poor as naturally establish themselves in that of the latter. Under such different management, the same purpose must require very different degrees of expence to execute it. It appears, accordingly, from the experience of all ages and nations, I believe, that the work done by freemen comes cheaper in the end than that performed by slaves. It is found to do so even at Boston, New York, and Philadelphia, where the wages of common labour are so very high.

The liberal reward of labour, therefore, as it is the effect of increasing wealth, so it is the cause of increasing population. To complain of it, is to lament over the necessary effect and cause of the greatest public prosperity.

It deserves to be remarked, perhaps, that it is in the progressive state, while the society is advancing to the further acquisition, rather than when it has acquired its full complement of riches, that the condition of the labouring poor, of the great body of the people, seems to be the happiest and the most comfortable. It is hard in the stationary, and miserable in the declining state. The progressive state is in reality the cheerful and the hearty state to all the different orders of the society. The stationary is dull; the declining melancholy.

The liberal reward of labour, as it encourages the propagation, so it increases the industry of the common people. The wages of labour are the encouragement of industry, which, like every other human quality, improves in proportion to the encouragement it receives. A plentiful subsistence increases the bodily strength of the labourer, and the comfortable hope of bettering his condition, and of ending his days perhaps in ease and plenty, animates him to exert that strength to the utmost. Where wages are high, accordingly, we shall always find the workmen more active, diligent, and expeditious, than where they are low; in England, for example, than in Scotland; in the neighbourhood of great towns, than in remote country places. Some workmen, indeed, when they can earn in four days what will maintain them through the week, will be idle the other three. This, however, is by no means the case with the greater part. Workmen, on the contrary, when they are liberally paid by the piece, are very apt to over-work themselves, and to ruin their health and constitution in a few years. A carpenter in London, and in some other places, is not supposed to last in his utmost vigour above eight years. Something of the same kind happens in many other trades, in which the workmen are paid by the piece; as they generally are in manufactures, and even in country labour, wherever wages are higher than ordinary. Almost every class of artificers is subject to some peculiar infirmity occasioned by excessive application to their peculiar species of work. Ramuzzini, an eminent Italian physician, has written a particular book concerning such disease. We do not reckon our soldiers the most industrious set of people among us. Yet when soldiers have been employed in some particular sorts of work, and liberally paid by the piece, their officers have frequently been obliged to stipulate with the undertaker, that they should not be allowed to earn above a certain sum every day, according to the rate at which they were paid. Till this stipulation was made, mutual emulation and the desire of greater gain, frequently prompted them to over-work themselves, and to hurt their health by excessive labour. Excessive application during four days of the week, is frequently the real cause of the idleness of the other three, so much and so loudly complained of. Great labour, either of mind or body, continued for several days together, is in most men naturally followed by a great desire of relaxation, which, if not restrained by force or by some strong necessity, is almost irresistible. It is the call of nature, which requires to be relieved by some indulgence, sometimes of ease only, but sometimes too of dissipation and diversion. If it is not complied with, the consequences are often dangerous, and sometimes fatal, and such as almost always, sooner or later, bring on the peculiar infirmity of the trade. If masters would always listen to the dictates of reason and humanity, they have frequently occasion rather to moderate, than to animate the application of many of their workmen. It will be found, I believe, in every sort of trade, that the man who works so moderately, as to be able to work constantly, not only preserves his health the longest, but, in the course of the year, executes the greatest quantity of work.

In cheap years, it is pretended, workmen are generally more idle, and in dear ones more industrious than ordinary. A plentiful subsistence therefore, it has been concluded, relaxes, and a scanty one quickens their industry. That a little more plenty than ordinary may render some workmen idle, cannot well be doubted; but that it should have this effect upon the greater part, or that men in general should work better when they are ill fed than when they are well fed, when they are disheartened than when they are in good spirits, when they are frequently sick than when they are generally in good health, seems not very probable. Years of dearth, it is to be observed, are generally among the common people years of sickness and mortality, which cannot fail to diminish the produce of their industry.

In years of plenty, servants frequently leave their masters and trust their subsistence to what they can make by their own industry. But the same cheapness of provisions, by increasing the fund which is destined for the maintenance of servants, encourages masters, farmers especially, to employ a greater number. Farmers upon such occasions expect more profit from their corn by maintaining a few more labouring servants, than by selling it at a low price in the market. The demand for servants increases, while the number of those who offer to supply that demand diminishes. The price of labour, therefore, frequently rises in cheap years.

In years of scarcity, the difficulty and uncertainty of subsistence make all such people eager to return to service. But the high price of provisions, by diminishing the funds destined for the maintenance of servants, disposes masters rather to diminish than to increase the number of those they have. In dear years too, poor independent workmen frequently consume the little stocks with which they had used to supply themselves with the materials of their work, and are obliged to become journeymen for subsistence. More people want employment than can easily get it; many are willing to take it upon lower terms than ordinary, and the wages of both servants and journeymen frequently sink in dear years.

Masters of all sorts, therefore, frequently make better bargains with their servants in dear than in cheap years, and find them more humble and dependent in the former than in the latter. They naturally, therefore, commend the former as more favourable to industry. Landlords and farmers, besides, two of the largest classes of masters, have another reason for being pleased with dear years. The rents of the one and the profits of the other depend very much upon the price of provisions. Nothing can be more absurd, however, than to imagine that men in general should work less when they work for themselves, than when they work for other people. A poor independent workman will generally be more industrious than even a journeyman who works by the piece. The one enjoys the whole produce of his own industry; the other shares it with his master. The one, in his separate independent state, is less liable to the temptations of bad company, which in large manufactories so frequently ruin the morals of the other. The superiority of the independent workman over those servants who are hired by the month or by the year, and whose wages and maintenance are the same whether they do much or do little, is likely to be still greater. Cheap years tend to increase the proportion of independent workmen to journeymen and servants of all kinds, and dear years to diminish it.

A French author of great knowledge and ingenuity, Mr. Messance, receiver of the tailles in the election of St. Etienne, endeavours to show that the poor do more work in cheap than in dear years, by comparing the quantity and value of the goods made upon those different occasions in three different manufactures; one of coarse woollens carried on at Elbeuf; one of linen, and another of silk, both which extend through the whole generality of Rouen. It appears from his account, which is copied from the registers of the public offices, that the quantity and value of the goods made in all those three manufactures has generally been greater in cheap than in dear years; and that it has always been greatest in the cheapest, and least in the dearest years. All the three seem to be stationary manufactures, or which, though their produce may vary somewhat from year to year, are upon the whole neither going backwards nor forwards.

The manufacture of linen in Scotland, and that of coarse woollens in the west riding of Yorkshire, are growing manufactures, of which the produce is generally, though with some variations, increasing both in quantity and value. Upon examining, however, the accounts which have been published of their annual produce, I have not been able to observe that its variations have had any sensible connection with the dearness or cheapness of the seasons. In 1740, a year of great scarcity, both manufactures, indeed, appear to have declined very considerably. But in 1756, another year of great scarcity, the Scotch manufacture made more than ordinary advances. The Yorkshire manufacture, indeed, declined, and its produce did not rise to what it had been in 1755 till 1766, after the repeal of the American stamp act. In that and the following year it greatly exceeded what it had ever been before, and it has continued to advance ever since.

The produce of all great manufactures for distant sale must necessarily depend, not so much upon the dearness or cheapness of the seasons in the countries where they are carried on, as upon the circumstances which affect the demand in the countries where they are consumed; upon peace or war, upon the prosperity or declension of other rival manufactures, and upon the good or bad humour of their principal customers. A great part of the extraordinary work, besides, which is probably done in cheap years, never enters the public registers of manufactures. The men servants who leave their masters become independent labourers. The women return to their parents, and commonly spin in order to make cloaths for themselves and their families. Even the independent workmen do not always work for public sale, but are employed by some of their neighbours in manufactures for family use. The produce of their labour, therefore, frequently makes no figure in those public registers of which the records are sometimes published with so much parade, and from which our merchants and manufacturers would often vainly pretend to announce the prosperity or declension of the greatest empires.

Though the variations in the price of labour, not only do not always correspond with those in the price of provisions, but are frequently quite opposite, we must not, upon this account, imagine that the price of provisions has no influence upon that of labour. The money price of labour is necessarily regulated by two circumstances: the demand for labour, and the price of the necessaries and conveniencies of life. The demand for labour, according as it happens to be increasing, stationary, or declining, or to require an increasing, stationary, or declining population, determines the quantity of the necessaries and conveniencies of life which must be given to the labourer; and the money price of labour is determined by what is requisite for purchasing this quantity. Though the money price of labour, therefore, is sometimes high where the price of provisions is low, it would be still higher, the demand continuing the same, if the price of provisions was high.

It is because the demand for labour increases in years of sudden and extraordinary plenty, and diminishes in those of sudden and extraordinary scarcity, that the money price of labour sometimes rises in the one, and sinks in the other.

In a year of sudden and extraordinary plenty, there are funds in the hands of many of the employers of industry, sufficient to maintain and employ a greater number of industrious people than had been employed the year before; and this extraordinary number cannot always be had. Those masters, therefore, who want more workmen, bid against one another, in order to get them, which sometimes raises both the real and the money price of their labour.

The contrary of this happens in a year of sudden and extraordinary scarcity. The funds destined for employing industry are less than they had been the year before. A considerable number of people are thrown out of employment, who bid against one another, in order to get it, which sometimes lowers both the real and the money price of labour. In 1740, a year of extraordinary scarcity, many people were willing to work for bare subsistence. In the succeeding years of plenty, it was more difficult to get labourers and servants.

The scarcity of a dear year, by diminishing the demand for labour, tends to lower its price, as the high price of provisions tends to raise it. The plenty of a cheap year, on the contrary, by increasing the demand, tends to raise the price of labour, as the cheapness of provisions tends to lower it. In the ordinary variations of the price of provisions, those two opposite causes seem to counterbalance one another; which is probably in part the reason why the wages of labour are every-where so much more steady and permanent than the price of provisions.

The increase in the wages of labour necessarily increases the price of many commodities, by increasing that part of it which resolves itself into wages, and so far tends to diminish their consumption both at home and abroad. The same cause, however, which raises the wages of labour, the increase of stock, tends to increase its productive powers, and to make a smaller quantity of labour produce a greater quantity of work. The owner of the stock which employs a great number of labourers, necessarily endeavours, for his own advantage, to make such a proper division and distribution of employment, that they may be enabled to produce the greatest quantity of work possible. For the same reason, he endeavours to supply them with the best machinery which either he or they can think of. What takes place among the labourers in a particular workhouse, takes place, for the same reason, among those of a great society. The greater their number, the more they naturally divide themselves into different classes and subdivisions of employment. More heads are occupied in inventing the most proper machinery for executing the work of each, and it is, therefore, more likely to be invented. There are many commodities, therefore, which, in consequence of these improvements, come to be produced by so much less labour than before, that the increase of its price is more than compensated by the diminution of its quantity.

CHAPTER IX

OF THE PROFITS OF STOCK

THE rise and fall in the profits of stock depend upon the same causes with the rise and fall in the wages of labour, the increasing or declining state of the wealth of the society; but those causes affect the one and the other very differently.

The increase of stock, which raises wages, tends to lower profit. When the stocks of many rich merchants are turned into the same trade, their mutual competition naturally tends to lower its profit; and when there is a like increase of stock in all the different trades carried on in the same society, the same competition must produce the same effect in them all.

It is not easy, it has already been observed, to ascertain what are the average wages of labour even in a particular place, and at a particular time. We can, even in this case, seldom determine more than what are the most usual wages. But even this can seldom be done with regard to the profits of stock. Profit is so very fluctuating, that the person who carries on a particular trade cannot always tell you himself what is the average of his annual profit. It is affected, not only by every variation of price in the commodities which he deals in, but by the good or bad fortune both of his rivals and of his customers, and by a thousand other accidents to which goods when carried either by sea or by land, or even when stored in a warehouse, are liable. It varies, therefore, not only from year to year, but from day to day, and almost from hour to hour. To ascertain what is the average profit of all the different trades carried on in a great kingdom, must be much more difficult; and to judge of what it may have been formerly, or in remote periods of time, with any degree of precision, must be altogether impossible.

But though it may be impossible to determine with any degree of precision, what are or were the average profits of stock, either in the present, or in ancient times, some notion may be formed of them from the interest of money. It may be laid down as a maxim, that wherever a great deal can be made by the use of money, a great deal will commonly be given for the use of it; and that wherever little can be made by it, less will commonly be given for it. According, therefore, as the usual market rate of interest varies in any country, we may be assured that the ordinary profits of stock must vary with it, must sink as it sinks, and rise as it rises. The progress of interest, therefore, may lead us to form some notion of the progress of profit.

By the 37th of Henry VIII. all interest above ten per cent. was declared unlawful. More, it seems, had sometimes been taken before that. In the reign of Edward VI. religious zeal prohibited all interest. This prohibition, however, like all others of the same kind, is said to have produced no effect, and probably rather increased than diminished the evil of usury. The statute of Henry VIII. was revived by the 13th of Elizabeth, cap. 8. and ten per cent. continued to be the legal rate of interest till the 21st of James I. when it was restricted to eight per cent. It was reduced to six per cent. soon after the restoration, and by the 12th of Queen Anne, to five per cent. All these different statutory regulations seem to have been made with great propriety. They seem to have followed and not to have gone before the market rate of interest, or the rate at which people of good credit usually borrowed. Since the time of Queen Anne, five per cent. seems to have been rather above than below the market rate. Before the late war, the government borrowed at three per cent.; and people of good credit in the capital, and in many other parts of the kingdom, at three and a half, four, and four and a half per cent.

Since the time of Henry VIII. the wealth and revenue of the country have been continually advancing, and, in the course of their progress, their pace seems rather to have been gradually accelerated than retarded. They seem, not only to have been going on, but to have been going on faster and faster. The wages of labour have been continually increasing during the same period, and in the greater part of the different branches of trade and manufacture the profits of stock have been diminishing.

It generally requires a greater stock to carry on any sort of trade in a great town than in a country village. The great stocks employed in every branch of trade, and the number of rich competitors, generally reduce the rate of profit in the former below what it is in the latter. But the wages of labour are generally higher in a great town than in a country village. In a thriving town the people who have great stocks to employ, frequently cannot get the number of workmen they want, and therefore bid against one another in order to get as many as they can, which raises the wages of labour, and lowers the profits of stock. In the remote parts of the country there is frequently not stock sufficient to employ all the people, who therefore bid against one another in order to get employment, which lowers the wages of labour, and raises the profits of stock.

In Scotland, though the legal rate of interest is the same as in England, the market rate is rather higher. People of the best credit there seldom borrow under five per cent. Even private bankers in Edinburgh give four per cent. upon their promissory notes, of which payment either in whole or in part may be demanded at pleasure. Private bankers in London give no interest for the money which is deposited with them. There are few trades which cannot be carried on with a smaller stock in Scotland than in England. The common rate of profit, therefore, must be somewhat greater. The wages of labour, it has already been observed, are lower in Scotland than in England. The country too is not only much poorer, but the steps by which it advances to a better condition, for it is evidently advancing, seem to be much slower and more tardy.

The legal rate of interest in France has not, during the course of the present century, been always regulated by the market rate. In 1720 interest was reduced from the twentieth to the fiftieth penny, or from five to two per cent. In 1724 it was raised to the thirtieth penny, or to 3 1-3 per cent. In 1725 it was again raised to the twentieth penny, or to five per cent. In 1766, during the administration of Mr. Laverdy, it was reduced to the twenty-fifth penny, or to four per cent.

The Abbe Terray raised it afterwards to the old rate of five per cent. The supposed purpose of many of those violent reductions of interest was to prepare the way for reducing that of the public debts; a purpose which has sometimes been executed. France is perhaps in the present times not so rich a country as England; and though the legal rate of interest has in France frequently been lower than in England, the market rate has generally been higher; for there, as in other countries, they have several very safe and easy methods of evading the law. The profits of trade, I have been assured by British merchants who had traded in both countries, are higher in France than in England; and it is no doubt upon this account that many British subjects chuse rather to employ their capitals in a country where trade is in disgrace, than in one where it is highly respected. The wages of labour are lower in France than in England. When you go from Scotland to England, the difference which you may remark between the dress and countenance of the common people in the one country and in the other, sufficiently indicates the difference in their condition. The contrast is still greater when you return from France. France, though no doubt a richer country than Scotland, seems not to be going forward so fast. It is a common and even a popular opinion in the country, that it is going backwards; an opinion which, I apprehend, is ill-founded even with regard to France, but which nobody can possibly entertain with regard to Scotland, who sees the country now, and who saw it twenty or thirty years ago.

The province of Holland, on the other hand, in proportion to the extent of its territory and the number of its people, is a richer country than England. The government there borrow at two per cent., and private people of good credit at three. The wages of labour are said to be higher in Holland than in England, and the Dutch, it is well known, trade upon lower profits than any people in Europe. The trade of Holland, it has been pretended by some people, is decaying, and it may perhaps be true that some particular branches of it are so. But these symptoms seem to indicate sufficiently that there is no general decay. When profit diminishes, merchants are very apt to complain that trade decays; though the diminution of profit is the natural effect of its prosperity, or of a greater stock being employed in it than before. During the late war the Dutch gained the whole carrying trade of France, of which they still retain a very large share. The great property which they possess both in the French and English funds, about forty millions, it is said, in the latter (in which I suspect, however, there is a considerable exaggeration); the great sums which they lend to private people in countries where the rate of interest is higher than in their own, are circumstances which no doubt demonstrate the redundancy of their stock, or that it has increased beyond what they can employ with tolerable profit in the proper business of their own country: but they do not demonstrate that that business has decreased. As the capital of a private man, though acquired by a particular trade, may increase beyond what he can employ in it, and yet that trade continue to increase too; so may likewise the capital of a great nation.

In our North American and West Indian colonies, not only the wages of labour, but the interest of money, and consequently the profits of stock, are higher than in England. In the different colonies both the legal and the market rate of interest run from six to eight per cent. High wages of labour and high profits of stock, however, are things, perhaps, which scarce ever go together, except in the peculiar circumstances of new colonies. A new colony must always for some time be more under-stocked in proportion to the extent of its territory, and more under-peopled in proportion to the extent of its stock, than the greater part of other countries. They have more land than they have stock to cultivate. What they have, therefore, is applied to the cultivation only of what is most fertile and most favourably situated, the land near the sea shore, and along the banks of navigable rivers. Such land too is frequently purchased at a price below the value even of its natural produce. Stock employed in the purchase and improvement of such lands must yield a very large profit, and consequently afford to pay a very large interest. Its rapid accumulation in so profitable an employment enables the planter to increase the number of his hands faster than he can find them in a new settlement. Those whom he can find, therefore, are very liberally rewarded. As the colony increases, the profits of stock gradually diminish. When the most fertile and best situated lands have been all occupied, less profit can be made by the cultivation of what is inferior both in soil and situation, and less interest can be afforded for the stock which is so employed. In the greater part of our colonies, accordingly, both the legal and the market rate of interest have been considerably reduced during the course of the present century. As riches, improvement, and population have increased, interest has declined. The wages of labour do not sink with the profits of stock. The demand for labour increases with the increase of stock whatever be its profits; and after these are diminished, stock may not only continue to increase, but to increase much faster than before. It is with industrious nations who are advancing in the acquisition of riches, as with industrious individuals. A great stock, though with small profits, generally increases faster than a small stock with great profits. Money, says the proverb, makes money. When you have got a little, it is often easy to get more. The great difficulty is to get that little. The connection between the increase of stock and that of industry, or of the demand for useful labour, has partly been explained already, but will be explained more fully hereafter in treating of the accumulation of stock.

The acquisition of new territory, or of new branches of trade, may sometimes raise the profits of stock, and with them the interest of money, even in a country which is fast advancing in the acquisition of riches. The stock of the country not being sufficient for the whole accession of business, which such acquisitions present to the different people among whom it is divided, is applied to those particular branches only which afford the greatest profit. Part of what had before been employed in other trades, is necessarily withdrawn from them, and turned into some of the new and more profitable ones. In all those old trades, therefore, the competition comes to be less than before. The market comes to be less fully supplied with many different sorts of goods. Their price necessarily rises more or less, and yields a greater profit to those who deal in them, who can, therefore, afford to borrow at a higher interest. For some time after the conclusion of the late war, not only private people of the best credit, but some of the greatest companies in London, commonly borrowed at five per cent. who before that had not been used to pay more than four, and four and a half per cent. The great accession both of territory and trade, by our acquisitions in North America and the West Indies, will sufficiently account for this, without supposing any diminution in the capital stock of the society. So great an accession of new business to be carried on by the old stock, must necessarily have diminished the quantity employed in a great number of particular branches, in which the competition being less, the profits must have been greater. I shall hereafter have occasion to mention the reasons which dispose me to believe that the capital stock of Great Britain was not diminished even by the enormous expence of the late war.

The diminution of the capital stock of the society, or of the funds destined for the maintenance of industry, however, as it lowers the wages of labour, so it raises the profits of stock, and consequently the interest of money. By the wages of labour being lowered, the owners of what stock remains in the society can bring their goods at less expence to market than before, and less stock being employed in supplying the market than before, they can sell them dearer. Their goods cost them less, and they get more for them. Their profits, therefore, being augmented at both ends, can well afford a large interest. The great fortunes so suddenly and so easily acquired in Bengal and the other British settlements in the East Indies, may satisfy us that, as the wages of labour are very low, so the profits of stock are very high in those ruined countries. The interest of money is proportionably so. In Bengal, money is frequently lent to the farmers at forty, fifty, and sixty per cent. and the succeeding crop is mortgaged for the payment. As the profits which can afford such an interest must eat up almost the whole rent of the landlord, so such enormous usury must in its turn eat up the greater part of those profits. Before the fall of the Roman republic, a usury of the same kind seems to have been common in the provinces, under the ruinous administration of their proconsuls. The virtuous Brutus lent money in

Cyprus at eight-and-forty per cent. as we learn from the letters of Cicero.

In a country which had acquired that full complement of riches which the nature of its soil and climate, and its situation with respect to other countries, allowed it to acquire; which could, therefore, advance no further, and which was not going backwards, both the wages of labour and the profits of stock would probably be very low. In a country fully peopled in proportion to what either its territory could maintain or its stock employ, the competition for employment would necessarily be so great as to reduce the wages of labour to what was barely sufficient to keep up the number of labourers, and, the country being already fully peopled, that number could never be augmented. In a country fully stocked in proportion to all the business it had to transact, as great a quantity of stock would be employed in every particular branch as the nature and extent of the trade would admit. The competition, therefore, would every-where be as great, and consequently the ordinary profit as low as possible.

But perhaps no country has ever yet arrived at this degree of opulence. China seems to have been long stationary, and had probably long ago acquired that full complement of riches which is consistent with the nature of its laws and institutions. But this complement may be much inferior to what, with other laws and institutions, the nature of its soil, climate, and situation might admit of. A country which neglects or despises foreign commerce, and which admits the vessels of foreign nations into one or two of its ports only, cannot transact the same quantity of business which it might do with different laws and institutions. In a country too, where, though the rich or the owners of large capitals enjoy a good deal of security, the poor or the owners of small capitals enjoy scarce any, but are liable, under the pretence of justice, to be pillaged and plundered at any time by the inferior mandarines, the quantity of stock employed in all the different branches of business transacted within it, can never be equal to what the nature and extent of that business might admit. In every different branch, the oppression of the poor must establish the monopoly of the rich, who, by engrossing the whole trade to themselves, will be able to make very large profits. Twelve per cent. accordingly is said to be the common interest of money in China, and the ordinary profits of stock must be sufficient to afford this large interest.

A defect in the law may sometimes raise the rate of interest considerably above what the condition of the country, as to wealth or poverty, would require. When the law does not enforce the performance of contracts, it puts all borrowers nearly upon the same footing with bankrupts or people of doubtful credit in better regulated countries. The uncertainty of recovering his money makes the lender exact the same usurious interest which is usually required from bankrupts. Among the barbarous nations who over-run the western provinces of the Roman empire, the performance of contracts was left for many ages to the faith of the contracting parties. The courts of justice of their kings seldom intermeddled in it. The high rate of interest which took place in those ancient times may perhaps be partly accounted for from this cause.

When the law prohibits interest altogether, it does not prevent it. Many people must borrow, and nobody will lend without such a consideration for the use of their money as is suitable, not only to what can be made by the use of it, but to the difficulty and danger of evading the law. The high rate of interest among all Mahometan nations is accounted for by Mr. Montesquieu, not from their poverty, but partly from this, and partly from the difficulty of recovering the money.

The lowest ordinary rate of profit must always be something more than what is sufficient to compensate the occasional losses to which every employment of stock is exposed. It is this surplus only which is neat or clear profit. What is called gross profit comprehends frequently, not only this surplus, but what is retained for compensating such extraordinary losses. The interest which the borrower can afford to pay is in proportion to the clear profit only.

The lowest ordinary rate of interest must, in the same manner, be something more than sufficient to compensate the occasional losses to which lending, even with tolerable prudence, is exposed. Were it not more, charity or friendship could be the only motives for lending.

In a country which had acquired its full complement of riches, where in every particular branch of business there was the greatest quantity of stock that could be employed in it, as the ordinary rate of clear profit would be very small, so the usual market rate of interest which could be afforded out of it, would be so low as to render it impossible for any but the very wealthiest people to live upon the interest of their money. All people of small or middling fortunes would be obliged to superintend themselves the employment of their own stocks. It would be necessary that almost every man should be a man of business, or engage in some sort of trade. The province of Holland seems to be approaching near to this state. It is there unfashionable not to be a man of business. Necessity makes it usual for almost every man to be so, and custom every where regulates fashion. As it is ridiculous not to dress, so is it, in some measure, not to be employed, like other people. As a man of a civil profession seems awkward in a camp or a garrison, and is even in some danger of being despised there, so does an idle man among men of business.

The highest ordinary rate of profit may be such as, in the price of the greater part of commodities, eats up the whole of what should go to the rent of the land, and leaves only what is sufficient to pay the labour of preparing and bringing them to market, according to the lowest rate at which labour can any-where be paid, the bare subsistence of the labourer. The workman must always have been fed in some way or other while he was about the work; but the landlord may not always have been paid. The profits of the trade which the servants of the East India Company carry on in Bengal may not perhaps be very far from this rate.

The proportion which the usual market rate of interest ought to bear to the ordinary rate of clear profit, necessarily varies as profit rises or falls. Double interest is in Great Britain reckoned, what the merchants call, a good, moderate, reasonable profit; terms which I apprehend mean no more than a common and usual profit. In a country where the ordinary rate of clear profit is eight or ten per cent., it may be reasonable that one half of it should go to interest, wherever business is carried on with borrowed money. The stock is at the risk of the borrower, who, as it were, insures it to the lender; and four or five per cent. may, in the greater part of trades, be both a sufficient profit upon the risk of this insurance, and a sufficient recompence for the trouble of employing the stock. But the proportion between interest and clear profit might not be the same in countries where the ordinary rate of profit was either a good deal lower, or a good deal higher. If it were a good deal lower, one half of it perhaps could not be afforded for interest; and more might be afforded if it were a good deal higher.

In countries which are fast advancing to riches, the low rate of profit may, in the price of many commodities, compensate the high wages of labour, and enable those countries to sell as cheap as their less thriving neighbours, among whom the wages of labour may be lower.

In reality high profits tend much more to raise the price of work than high wages. If in the linen manufacture, for example, the wages of the different working people, the flax-dressers, the spinners, the weavers, &c. should, all of them, be advanced two pence a day; it would be necessary to heighten the price of a piece of linen only by a number of two pences equal to the number of people that had been employed about it, multiplied by the number of days during which they had been so employed. That part of the price of the commodity which resolved itself into wages would, through all the different stages of the manufacture, rise only in arithmetical proportion to this rise of wages. But if the profits of all the different employers of those working people should be raised five per cent. that part of the price of the commodity which resolved itself into profit, would, through all the different stages of the manufacture, rise in geometrical proportion to this rise of profit. The employer of the flax-dressers would in selling his flax require an additional five per cent. upon the whole value of the materials and wages would be advanced to his workmen. The employer of the spinners would require an additional five per cent. both upon the advanced price of the flax and upon the wages of the spinners. And the employer of the weavers would require a like five per cent. both upon the advanced price of the linen yarn and upon the wages of the weavers. In raising the price of commodities the rise of wages operates in the same manner as simple interest does in the accumulation of debt. The rise of profit operates like compound interest. Our merchants and master-manufacturers complain much of the bad effects of high wages in raising the price, and thereby lessening the sale of their goods both at home and abroad. They say nothing concerning the bad effects of high profits. They are silent with regard to the pernicious effects of their own gains. They complain only of those of other people.

CHAPTER X

Of Wages and Profit in the Different Employments of Labour and Stock

THE whole of the advantages and disadvantages of the different employments of labour and stock must, in the same neighbourhood, be either perfectly equal or continually tending to equality. If in the same neighbourhood, there was any employment evidently either more or less advantageous than the rest, so many people would crowd into it in the one case, and so many would desert it in the other, that its advantages would soon return to the level of other employments. This at least would be the case in a society where things were left to follow their natural course, where there was perfect liberty, and where every man was perfectly free both to chuse what occupation he thought proper, and to change it as often as he thought proper. Every man's interest would prompt him to seek the advantageous, and to shun the disadvantageous employment.

Pecuniary wages and profit, indeed, are every-where in Europe extremely different according to the different employments of labour and stock. But this difference arises partly from certain circumstances in the employments themselves, which, either really, or at least in the imaginations of men, make up for a small pecuniary gain in some, and counterbalance a great one in others; and partly from the policy of Europe, which no-where leaves things at perfect liberty.

The particular consideration of those circumstances and of that policy will divide this chapter into two parts.

PART I

Inequalities arising from the Nature of the Employments themselves

The five following are the principal circumstances which, so far as I have been able to observe, make up for a small pecuniary gain in some employments, and counter-balance a great one in others; first, the agreeableness or disagreeableness of the employments themselves; secondly, the easiness and cheapness, or the difficulty and expence of learning them; thirdly, the constancy or inconstancy of employment in them; fourthly, the small or great trust which must be reposed in those who exercise them; and fifthly, the probability or improbability of success in them.

First, The wages of labour vary with the ease or hardship, the cleanliness or dirtiness, the honourableness or dishonourableness of the employment. Thus in most places, take the year round, a journeyman taylor earns less than a journeyman weaver. His work is much easier. A journeyman weaver earns less than a journeyman smith. His work is not always easier, but it is much cleanlier. A journeyman blacksmith, though an artificer, seldom earns so much in twelve hours as a collier, who is only a labourer, does in eight. His work is not quite so dirty, is less dangerous, and is carried on in day-light, and above ground. Honour makes a great part of the reward of all honourable professions. In point of pecuniary gain, all things considered, they are generally under-recompensed, as I shall endeavour to show by and by. Disgrace has the contrary effect. The trade of the butcher is a brutal and an odious business; but it is in most places more profitable than the greater part of common trades. The most detestable of all employments, that of public executioner, is, in proportion to the quantity of work done, better paid than any common trade whatever.

Hunting and fishing, the most important employments of mankind in the rude state of society, become in its advanced state their most agreeable amusements, and they pursue for pleasure what they once followed from necessity. In the advanced state of society, therefore, they are all very poor people who follow as a trade, what other people pursue as a pastime. Fishermen have been so since the time of Theocritus. A poacher is every-where a very poor man in Great Britain. In countries where the rigour of the law suffers no poachers, the licensed hunter is not in a much better condition. The natural taste for those employments makes more people follow them than can live comfortably by them, and the produce of their labour, in proportion to its quantity, comes always too cheap to market to afford anything but the most scanty subsistence to the labourers.

Disagreeableness and disgrace affect the profits of stock in the same manner as the wages of labour. The keeper of an inn or tavern, who is never master of his own house, and who is exposed to the brutality of every drunkard, exercises neither a very agreeable nor a very creditable business. But there is scarce any common trade in which a small stock yields so great a profit.

Secondly, The wages of labour vary with the easiness and cheapness, or the difficulty and expence of learning the business.

When any expensive machine is erected, the extraordinary work to be performed by it before it is worn out, it must be expected, will replace the capital laid out upon it, with at least the ordinary profits. A man educated at the expence of much labour and time to any of those employments which require extraordinary dexterity and skill, may be compared to one of those expensive machines. The work which he learns to perform, it must be expected, over and above the usual wages of common labour, will replace to him the whole expence of his education, with at least the ordinary profits of an equally valuable capital. It must do this too in a reasonable time, regard being had to the very uncertain duration of human life, in the same manner as to the more certain duration of the machine.

The difference between the wages of skilled labour and those of common labour, is founded upon this principle.

The policy of Europe considers the labour of all mechanics, artificers, and manufacturers, as skilled labour; and that of all country labourers as common labour. It seems to suppose that of the former to be of a more nice and delicate nature than that of the latter. It is so perhaps in some cases; but in the greater part it is quite otherwise, as I shall endeavour to shew by and by. The laws and customs of Europe, therefore, in order to qualify any person for exercising the one species of labour, impose the necessity of an apprenticeship, though with different degrees of rigour in different places. They leave the other free and open to every body. During the continuance of the apprenticeship, the whole labour of the apprentice belongs to his master. In the mean time he must, in many cases, be maintained by his parents or relations, and in almost all cases must be cloathed by them. Some money too is commonly given to the master for teaching him his trade. They who cannot give money, give time, or become bound for more than the usual number of years; a consideration which, though it is not always advantageous to the master, on account of the usual idleness of apprentices, is always disadvantageous to the apprentice. In country labour, on the contrary, the labourer, while he is employed about the easier, learns the more difficult parts of his business, and his own labour maintains him through all the different stages of his employment. It is reasonable, therefore, that in Europe the wages of mechanics, artificers, and manufacturers, should be somewhat higher than those of common labourers. They are so accordingly, and their superior gains make them in most places be considered as a superior rank of people. This superiority, however, is generally very small; the daily or weekly earnings of journeymen in the more common sorts of manufactures, such as those of plain linen and woollen cloth, computed at an average, are, in most places, very little more than the day wages of common labourers. Their employment, indeed, is more steady and uniform, and the superiority of their earnings, taking the whole year together, may be somewhat greater. It seems evidently, however, to be no greater than what is sufficient to compensate the superior expence of their education.

Education in the ingenious arts and in the liberal professions, is still more tedious and expensive. The pecuniary recompence, therefore, of painters and sculptors, of lawyers and physicians, ought to be much more liberal: and it is so accordingly.

The profits of stock seem to be very little affected by the

easiness or difficulty of learning the trade in which it is employed. All the different ways in which stock is commonly employed in great towns seem, in reality, to be almost equally easy and equally difficult to learn. One branch either of foreign or domestic trade, cannot well be a much more intricate business than another.

Thirdly, The wages of labour in different occupations vary with the constancy or inconstancy of employment.

Employment is much more constant in some trades than in others. In the greater part of manufactures, a journeyman may be pretty sure of employment almost every day in the year that he is able to work. A mason or bricklayer, on the contrary, can work neither in hard frost nor in foul weather, and his employment at all other times depends upon the occasional calls of his customers. He is liable, in consequence, to be frequently without any. What he earns, therefore, while he is employed, must not only maintain him while he is idle, but make him some compensation for those anxious and desponding moments which the thought of so precarious a situation must sometimes occasion. Where the computed earnings of the greater part of manufacturers, accordingly, are nearly upon a level with the day wages of common labourers, those of masons and bricklayers are generally from one half more to double those wages. Where common labourers earn four and five shillings a week, masons and bricklayers frequently earn seven and eight; where the former earn six, the latter often earn nine and ten, and where the former earn nine and ten, as in London, the latter commonly earn fifteen and eighteen. No species of skilled labour, however, seems more easy to learn than that of masons and bricklayers. Chairmen in London, during the summer season, are said sometimes to be employed as bricklayers. The high wages of those workmen, therefore, are not so much the recompence of their skill, as the compensation for the inconstancy of their employment.

A house carpenter seems to exercise rather a nicer and more ingenious trade than a mason. In most places however, for it is not universally so, his day-wages are somewhat lower. His employment, though it depends much, does not depend so entirely upon the occasional calls of his customers; and it is not liable to be interrupted by the weather.

When the trades which generally afford constant employment, happen in a particular place not to do so, the wages of the workmen always rise a good deal above their ordinary proportion to those of common labour. In London almost all journeymen artificers are liable to be called upon and dismissed by their masters from day to day, and from week to week, in the same manner as day-labourers in other places. The lowest order of artificers, journeymen taylors, accordingly, earn there half a crown a day, though eighteen pence may be reckoned the wages of common labour. In small towns and country villages, the wages of journeymen taylors frequently scarce equal those of common labour; but in London they are often many weeks without employment, particularly during the summer.

When the inconstancy of employment is combined with the hardship, disagreeableness, and dirtiness of the work, it sometimes raises the wages of the most common labour above those of the most skilful artificers. A collier working by the piece is supposed, at Newcastle, to earn commonly about double, and in many parts of Scotland about three times the wages of common labour. His high wages arise altogether from the hardship, disagreeableness, and dirtiness of his work. His employment may, upon most occasions, be as constant as he pleases. The coal-heavers in London exercise a trade which in hardship, dirtiness, and disagreeableness, almost equals that of colliers; and from the unavoidable irregularity in the arrivals of coal-ships, the employment of the greater part of them is necessarily very inconstant. If colliers, therefore, commonly earn double and triple the wages of common labour, it ought not to seem unreasonable that coal-heavers should sometimes earn four and five times those wages. In the enquiry made into their condition a few years ago, it was found that at the rate at which they were then paid, they could earn from six to ten shillings a day. Six shillings are about four times the wages of common labour in London, and in every particular trade, the lowest common earnings may always be considered as those of the far greater number. How extravagant soever those earnings may appear, if they were more than sufficient to compensate all the disagreeable circumstances of the business, there would soon be so great a number of competitors as, in a trade which has no exclusive privilege, would quickly reduce them to a lower rate.

The constancy or inconstancy of employment cannot effect the ordinary profits of stock in any particular trade. Whether the stock is or is not constantly employed depends, not upon the trade, but the trader.

Fourthly, The wages of labour vary according to the small or great trust which must be reposed in the workmen.

The wages of goldsmiths and jewellers are every-where superior to those of many other workmen, not only of equal, but of much superior ingenuity; on account of the precious materials with which they are intrusted.

We trust our health to the physician; our fortune and sometimes our life and reputation to the lawyer and attorney. Such confidence could not safely be reposed in people of a very mean or low condition. Their reward must be such, therefore, as may give them that rank in the society which so important a trust requires. The long time and the great expence which must be laid out in their education, when combined with this circumstance, necessarily enhance still further the price of their labour.

When a person employs only his own stock in trade, there is no trust; and the credit which he may get from other people, depends, not upon the nature of his trade, but upon their opinion of his fortune, probity, and prudence. The different rates of profit, therefore, in the different branches of trade, cannot arise from the different degrees of trust reposed in the traders.

Fifthly, The wages of labour in different employments vary according to the probability or improbability of success in them.

The probability that any particular person shall ever be qualified for the employment to which he is educated, is very different in different occupations. In the greater part of mechanic trades, success is almost certain; but very uncertain in the liberal professions. Put your son apprentice to a shoemaker, there is little doubt of his learning to make a pair of shoes: But send him to study law, it is at least twenty to one if ever he makes such proficiency as will enable him to live by the business. In a perfectly fair lottery, those who draw the prizes ought to gain all that is lost by those who draw the blanks. In a profession where twenty fail for one that succeeds, that one ought to gain all that should have been gained by the unsuccessful twenty. The counsellor at law who, perhaps, at near forty years of age, begins to make something by his profession, ought to receive the retribution, not only of his own so tedious and expensive education, but of that of more than twenty others who are never likely to make any thing by it. How extravagant soever the fees of counsellors at law may sometimes appear, their real retribution is never equal to this. Compute in any particular place, what is likely to be annually gained, and what is likely to be annually spent, by all the different workmen in any common trade, such as that of shoemakers or weavers, and you will find that the former sum will generally exceed the latter. But make the same computation with regard to all the counsellors and students of law, in all the different inns of court, and you will find that their annual gains bear but a very small proportion to their annual expence, even though you rate the former as high, and the latter as low, as can well be done. The lottery of the law, therefore, is very far from being a perfectly fair lottery; and that, as well as many other liberal and honorable professions, is, in point of pecuniary gain, evidently under-recompenced.

Those professions keep their level, however, with other occupations and, notwithstanding these discouragements, all the most generous and liberal spirits are eager to crowd into them. Two different causes contribute to recommend them. First, the desire of the reputation which attends upon superior excellence in any of them; and, secondly, the natural confidence which every man has more or less, not only in his own abilities, but in his own good fortune.

To excel in any profession, in which but few arrive at mediocrity, is the most decisive mark of what is called genius or superior talents. The public admiration which attends upon such distinguished abilities, makes always a part of their reward; a greater or smaller in proportion as it is higher or lower in degree. It makes a considerable part of that reward in the profession of physic; a still greater perhaps in that of law; in poetry and philosophy it makes almost the whole.

There are some very agreeable and beautiful talents of which the possession commands a certain sort of admiration; but of which the exercise for the sake of gain is considered, whether from reason or prejudice, as a sort of public prostitution. The pecuniary recompence, therefore, of those who exercise them in this manner, must be sufficient, not only to pay for the time, labour and expence of acquiring the talents, but for the discredit which attends the employment of them as a means of subsistence. The exorbitant rewards of players, opera-singers, opera-dancers, &c. are founded upon those two principles; the rarity and beauty of the talents, and the discredit of employing them in this manner. It seems absurd at first sight that we should despise their persons, and yet reward their talents with the most profuse liberality. While we do the one, however, we must of necessity do the other. Should the public opinion or prejudice ever alter with regard to such occupations, their pecuniary recompence would quickly diminish. More people would apply to them, and the competition would quickly reduce the price of their labour. Such talents, though far from being common, are by no means so rare as is imagined. Many people possess them in great perfection, who disdain to make use of them; and many more are capable of acquiring them, if any thing could be made honourably by them.

The over-weening conceit which the greater part of men have of their own abilities, is an ancient evil remarked by the philosophers and moralists of all ages. Their absurd presumption in their own good fortune, has been less taken notice of. It is, however, if possible, still more universal. There is no man living who, when in tolerable health and spirits, has not some share of it. The chance of gain is by every man more or less over-valued, and the chance of loss is by most men under-valued, and by scarce any man, who is in tolerable health and spirits, valued more than it is worth.

That the chance of gain is naturally over-valued, we may learn from the universal success of lotteries. The world neither ever saw, nor ever will see, a perfectly fair lottery; or one in which the whole gain compensated the whole loss; because the undertaker could make nothing by it. In the state lotteries the tickets are really not worth the price which is paid by the original subscribers, and yet commonly sell in the market for twenty, thirty, and sometimes forty per cent. advance. The vain hope of gaining some of the great prizes is the sole cause of this demand. The soberest people scarce look upon it as a folly to pay a small sum for the chance of gaining ten or twenty thousand pounds; though they know that even that small sum is perhaps twenty or thirty per cent. more than the chance is worth. In a lottery in which no prize exceeded twenty pounds, though in other respects it approached much nearer to a perfectly fair one than the common state lotteries, there would not be the same demand for tickets. In order to have a better chance for some of the great prizes, some people purchase several tickets, and others, small shares in a still greater number. There is not, however, a more certain proposition in mathematics, than that the more tickets you adventure upon, the more likely you are to be a loser. Adventure upon all the tickets in the lottery, and you lose for certain; and the greater the number of your tickets the nearer you approach to this certainty.

That the chance of loss is frequently undervalued, and scarce ever valued more than it is worth, we may learn from the very moderate profit of insurers. In order to make insurance, either from fire or sea-risk, a trade at all, the common premium must be sufficient to compensate the common losses, to pay the expence of management, and to afford such a profit as might have been drawn from an equal capital employed in any common trade. The person who pays no more than this, evidently pays no more than the real value of the risk, or the lowest price at which he can reasonably expect to insure it. But though many people have made a little money by insurance, very few have made a great fortune; and from this consideration alone, it seems evident enough, that the ordinary balance of profit and loss is not more advantageous in this, than in other common trades by which so many people make fortunes. Moderate, however, as the premium of insurance commonly is, many people despise the risk too much to care to pay it. Taking the whole kingdom at an average, nineteen houses in twenty, or rather, perhaps, ninety-nine in a hundred, are not insured from fire. Sea-risk is more alarming to the greater part of people, and the proportion of ships insured to those not insured is much greater. Many sail, however, at all seasons, and even in time of war, without any insurance. This may sometimes perhaps be done without any imprudence. When a great company, or even a great merchant, has twenty or thirty ships at sea, they may, as it were, insure one another. The premium saved upon them all, may more than compensate such losses as they are likely to meet with in the common course of chances. The neglect of insurance upon shipping, however, in the same manner as upon houses is, in most cases, the effect of no such nice calculation, but of mere thoughtless rashness and presumptuous contempt of the risk.

The contempt of risk and the presumptuous hope of success, are in no period of life more active than at the age at which young people chuse their professions. How little the fear of misfortune is then capable of balancing the hope of good luck, appears still more evidently in the readiness of the common people to enlist as soldiers, or to go to sea, than in the eagerness of those of better fashion to enter into what are called the liberal professions.

What a common soldier may lose is obvious enough. Without regarding the danger, however, young volunteers never enlist so readily as at the beginning of a new war; and though they have scarce any chance of preferment, they figure to themselves, in their youthful fancies, a thousand occasions of acquiring honour and distinction which never occur. These romantic hopes make the whole price of their blood. Their pay is less than that of common laborers, and in actual service their fatigues are much greater.

The lottery of the sea is not altogether so disadvantageous as that of the army. The son of a creditable labourer or artificer may frequently go to sea with his father's consent; but if he enlists as a soldier, it is always without it. Other people see some chance of his making something by the one trade; nobody but himself sees any of his making any thing by the other. The great admiral is less the object of public admiration than the great general, and the highest success in the sea service promises a less brilliant fortune and reputation than equal success in the land. The same difference runs through all the inferior degrees of preferment in both. By the rules of precedency a captain in the navy ranks with a colonel in the army: but he does not rank with him in the common estimation. As the great prizes in the lottery are less, the smaller ones must be more numerous. Common sailors, therefore, more frequently get some fortune and preferment than common soldiers; and the hope of those prizes is what principally recommends the trade. Though their skill and dexterity are much superior to that of almost any artificer's, and though their whole life is one continual scene of hardship and danger, yet for all this dexterity and skill, for all those hardships and dangers, while they remain in the condition of common sailors, they receive scarce any other recompence but the pleasure of exercising the one and of surmounting the other. Their wages are not greater than those of common laborers at the port which regulates the rate of seamen's wages. As they are continually going from port to port, the monthly pay of those who sail from all the different ports of Great Britain, is more nearly upon a level than that of any other workmen in those different places; and the rate of the port to and from which the greatest number sail, that is the port of London, regulates that of all the rest. At London the wages of the greater part of the different classes of workmen are about double those of the same classes at Edinburgh. But the sailors who sail from the port of London seldom earn above three or four shillings a month more than those who sail from the port of Leith, and the difference is frequently not so great. In time of peace, and in the merchant service, the London price is from a guinea to about seven-and-twenty shillings the calendar month. A common labourer in London, at the rate of nine or ten shillings a month, may earn in the calendar month from forty to five-and-forty shillings. The sailor, indeed, over and above his pay, is supplied with provisions. Their value, however, may not perhaps always exceed the difference between his pay and that of the common labourer; and though it sometimes should, the excess will not be clear gain to the sailor, because he cannot share it with his wife and family, whom he must maintain out of his wages at home.

The dangers and hair-breadth escapes of a life of adventures, instead of disheartening young people, seem frequently to recommend a trade to them. A tender mother, among the inferior ranks of people, is often afraid to send her son to school at a sea-port town, lest the sight of the ships and the conversation and adventures of the sailors should entice him to go to sea. The distant prospect of hazards, from which we can hope to extricate ourselves by courage and address, is not disagreeable to us, and does not raise the wages of labour in any employment. It is otherwise with those in which courage and address can be of no avail. In trades which are known to be very unwholesome, the wages of labour are always remarkably high. Unwholesomeness is a species of disagreeableness, and its effects upon the wages of labour are to be ranked under that general head.

In all the different employments of stock, the ordinary rate of profit varies more or less with the certainty or uncertainty of the returns. These are in general less uncertain in the inland than in the foreign trade, and in some branches of foreign trade than others; in the trade to North America, for example, than in that to Jamaica. The ordinary rate of profit always rises more or less with the risk. It does not, however, seem to rise in proportion to it, or so as to compensate it completely. Bankruptcies are most frequent in the most hazardous trades. The most hazardous of all trades, that of a smuggler, though when the adventure succeeds it is likewise the most profitable, is the infallible road to bankruptcy. The presumptuous hope of success seems to act here as upon all other occasions, and to entice so many adventurers into those hazardous trades, that their competition reduces the profit below what is sufficient to compensate the risk. To compensate it completely, the common returns ought, over and above the ordinary profits of stock, not only to make up for all occasional losses, but to afford a surplus profit to the adventurers of the same nature with the profit of insurers. But if the common returns were sufficient for all this, bankruptcies would not be more frequent in these than in other trades.

Of the five circumstances, therefore, which vary the wages of labour, two only affect the profits of stock; the agreeableness or disagreeableness of the business, and the risk or security with which it is attended. In point of agreeableness or disagreeableness, there is little or no difference in the far greater part of the different employments of stock; but a great deal in those of labour; and the ordinary profit of stock, though it rises with the risk, does not always seem to rise in proportion to it. It should follow from all this, that, in the same society or neighborhood, the average and ordinary rates of profit in the different employments of stock should be more nearly upon a level than the pecuniary wages of the different sorts of labour. They are so accordingly. The difference between the earnings of a common labourer and those of a well employed lawyer or physician, is evidently much greater than that between the ordinary profits in any two different branches of trade. The apparent difference, besides, in the profits of different trades, is generally a deception arising from our not always distinguishing what ought to be considered as wages, from what ought to be considered as profit.

Apothecaries' profit is become a bye-word, denoting something uncommonly extravagant. This great apparent profit, however, is frequently no more than the reasonable wages of labour. The skill of an apothecary is a much nicer and more delicate matter than that of any artificer whatever; and the trust which is reposed in him is of much greater importance. He is the physician of the poor in all cases, and of the rich when the distress or danger is not very great. His reward, therefore, ought to be suitable to his skill and his trust, and it arises generally from the price at which he sells his drugs. But the whole drugs which the best employed apothecary, in a large market town, will sell in a year, may not perhaps cost him above thirty or forty pounds. Though he should sell them, therefore, for three or four hundred, or at a thousand per cent. profit, this may frequently be no more than the reasonable wages of his labour charged, in the only way in which he can charge them, upon the price of his drugs. The greater part of the apparent profit is real wages disguised in the garb of profit.

In a small sea-port town, a little grocer will make forty or fifty per cent. upon a stock of a single hundred pounds, while a considerable wholesale merchant in the same place will scarce make eight or ten per cent. upon a stock of ten thousand. The trade of the grocer may be necessary for the conveniency of the inhabitants, and the narrowness of the market may not admit the employment of a larger capital in the business. The man, however, must not only live by his trade, but live by it suitably to the qualifications which it requires. Besides possessing a little capital, he must be able to read, write, and account, and must be a tolerable judge too of, perhaps, fifty or sixty different sorts of goods, their prices, qualities, and the markets where they are to be had cheapest. He must have all the knowledge, in short, that is necessary for a great merchant, which nothing hinders him from becoming but the want of sufficient capital. Thirty or forty pounds a year cannot be considered as too great a recompence for the labour of a person so accomplished. Deduct this from the seemingly great profits of his capital, and little more will remain, perhaps, than the ordinary profits of stock. The greater part of the apparent profit is, in this case too, real wages.

The difference between the apparent profit of the retail and that of the wholesale trade, is much less in the capital than in small towns and country villages. Where ten thousand pounds can be employed in the grocery trade, the wages of the grocer's labour make but a very trifling addition to the real profits of so great a stock. The apparent profits of the wealthy retailer, therefore, are there more nearly upon a level with those of the wholesale merchant. It is upon this account that goods sold by retail are generally as cheap and frequently much cheaper in the capital than in small towns and country villages. Grocery goods, for example, are generally much cheaper; bread and butcher's meat frequently as cheap. It costs no more to bring grocery goods to the great town than to the country village; but it costs a great deal more to bring corn and cattle, as the greater part of them must be brought from a much greater distance. The prime cost of grocery goods, therefore, being the same in both places, they are cheapest where the least profit is charged upon them. The prime cost of bread and butcher's meat is greater in the great town than in the country village; and though the profit is less, therefore they are not always cheaper there, but often equally cheap. In such articles as bread and butcher's meat, the same cause, which diminishes apparent profit, increases prime cost. The extent of the market, by giving employment to greater stocks, diminishes apparent profit; but by requiring supplies from a greater distance, it increases prime cost. This diminution of the one and increase of the other seem, in most cases, nearly to counter-balance one another; which is probably the reason that, though the prices of corn and cattle are commonly very different in different parts of the kingdom, those of bread and butcher's meat are generally very nearly the same through the greater part of it.

Though the profits of stock both in the wholesale and retail trade are generally less in the capital than in small towns and country villages, yet great fortunes are frequently acquired from small beginnings in the former, and scarce ever in the latter. In small towns and country villages, on account of the narrowness of the market, trade cannot always be extended as stock extends. In such places, therefore, though the rate of a particular person's profits may be very high, the sum or amount of them can never be very great, nor consequently that of his annual accumulation. In great towns, on the contrary, trade can be extended as stock increases, and the credit of a frugal and thriving man increases much faster than his stock. His trade is extended in proportion to the amount of both, and the sum or amount of his profits is in proportion to the extent of his trade, and his annual accumulation in proportion to the amount of his profits. It seldom happens, however, that great fortunes are made even in great towns by any one regular, established, and well-known branch of business, but in consequence of a long life of industry, frugality, and attention. Sudden fortunes, indeed, are sometimes made in such places by what is called the trade of speculation. The speculative merchant exercises no one regular, established, or well-known branch of business. He is a corn merchant this year, and a wine merchant the next, and a sugar, tobacco, or tea merchant the year after.

He enters into every trade when he foresees that it is likely to be more than commonly profitable, and he quits it when he foresees that its profits are likely to return to the level of other trades. His profits and losses, therefore, can bear no regular proportion to those of any one established and well-known branch of business. A bold adventurer may sometimes acquire a considerable fortune by two or three successful speculations; but is just as likely to lose one by two or three unsuccessful ones. This trade can be carried on no where but in great towns. It is only in places of the most extensive commerce and correspondence that the intelligence requisite for it can be had.

The five circumstances above mentioned, though they occasion considerable inequalities in the wages of labour and profits of stock, occasion none in the whole of the advantages and disadvantages, real or imaginary, of the different employments of either. The nature of those circumstances is such, that they make up for a small pecuniary gain in some, and counter-balance a great one in others.

In order, however, that this equality may take place in the whole of their advantages or disadvantages, three things are requisite even where there is the most perfect freedom. First, the employments must be well known and long established in the neighborhood; secondly, they must be in their ordinary, or what may be called their natural state; and, thirdly, they must be the sole or principal employments of those who occupy them.

First, this equality can take place only in those employments which are well known, and have been long established in the neighbourhood.

Where all other circumstances are equal, wages are generally higher in new than in old trades. When a projector attempts to establish a new manufacture, he must at first entice his workmen from other employments by higher wages than they can either earn in their own trades, or than the nature of his work would otherwise require, and a considerable time must pass away before he can venture to reduce them to the common level. Manufactures for which the demand arises altogether from fashion and fancy, are continually changing, and seldom last long enough to be considered as old established manufactures. Those, on the contrary, for which the demand arises chiefly from use or necessity, are less liable to change, and the same form or fabric may continue in demand for whole centuries together. The wages of labour, therefore, are likely to be higher in manufactures of the former, than in those of the latter kind. Birmingham deals chiefly in manufactures of the former kind; Sheffield in those of the latter; and the wages of labour in those two different places, are said to be suitable to this difference in the nature of their manufactures.

The establishment of any new manufacture, of any new branch of commerce, or of any new practice in agriculture, is always a speculation, from which the projector promises himself extraordinary profits. These profits sometimes are very great, and sometimes, more frequently, perhaps, they are quite otherwise; but in general they bear no regular proportion to those of other old trades in the neighbourhood. If the project succeeds, they are commonly at first very high. When the trade or practice becomes thoroughly established and well known, the competition reduces them to the level of other trades.

Secondly, This equality in the whole of the advantages and disadvantages of the different employments of labour and stock, can take place only in the ordinary, or what may be called the natural state of those employments.

The demand for almost every different species of labour is sometimes greater and sometimes less than usual. In the one case the advantages of the employment rise above, in the other they fall below the common level. The demand for country labour is greater at hay-time and harvest, than during the greater part of the year; and wages rise with the demand. In time of war, when forty or fifty thousand sailors are forced from the merchant service into that of the king, the demand for sailors to merchant ships necessarily rises with their scarcity, and their wages upon such occasions commonly rise from a guinea and seven-and-twenty shillings, to forty shillings and three pounds a month. In a decaying manufacture, on the contrary, many workmen, rather than quit their old trade, are contented with smaller wages than would otherwise be suitable to the nature of their employment.

The profits of stock vary with the price of the commodities in which it is employed. As the price of any commodity rises above the ordinary or average rate, the profits of at least some part of the stock that is employed in bringing it to market, rise above their proper level, and as it falls they sink below it. All commodities are more or less liable to variations of price, but some are much more so than others. In all commodities which are produced by human industry, the quantity of industry annually employed is necessarily regulated by the annual demand, in such a manner that the average annual produce may, as nearly as possible, be equal to the average annual consumption. In some employments, it has already been observed, the same quantity of industry will always produce the same, or very nearly the same quantity of commodities. In the linen or woollen manufactures, for example, the same number of hands will annually work up very nearly the same quantity of linen and woollen cloth. The variations in the market price of such commodities, therefore, can arise only from some accidental variation in the demand. A public mourning raises the price of black cloth. But as the demand for most sorts of plain linen and woollen cloth is pretty uniform, so is likewise the price. But there are other employments in which the same quality of industry will not always produce the same quantity of commodities. The same quantity of industry, for example, will, in different years, produce very different quantities of corn, wine, hops, sugar, tobacco, &c. The price of such commodities, therefore, varies not only with the variations of demand, but with the much greater and more frequent variations of quantity, and is consequently extremely fluctuating. But the profit of some of the dealers must necessarily fluctuate with the price of the commodities. The operations of the speculative merchant are principally employed about such commodities. He endeavours to buy them up when he foresees that their price is likely to rise, and to sell them when it is likely to fall.

Thirdly, This equality in the whole of the advantages and disadvantages of the different employments of labour and stock, can take place only in such as are the sole or principal employments of those who occupy them.

When a person derives his subsistence from one employment, which does not occupy the greater part of his time; in the intervals of his leisure he is often willing to work at another for less wages than would otherwise suit the nature of the employment.

There still subsists in many parts of Scotland a set of people called Cotters or Cottagers, though they were more frequent some years ago than they are now. They are a sort of out-servants of the landlords and farmers. The usual reward which they receive from their masters is a house, a small garden for pot herbs, as much grass as will feed a cow, and, perhaps, an acre or two of bad arable land. When their master has occasion for their labour, he gives them, besides, two pecks of oatmeal a week, worth about sixteen pence sterling. During a great part of the year he has little or no occasion for their labour, and the cultivation of their own little possession is not sufficient to occupy the time which is left at their own disposal. When such occupiers were more numerous than they are at present, they are said to have been willing to give their spare time for a very small recompence to any body, and to have wrought for less wages than other labourers. In ancient times they seem to have been common all over Europe. In countries ill cultivated and worse inhabited, the greater part of landlords and farmers could not otherwise provide themselves with the extraordinary number of hands, which country labour requires at certain seasons. The daily or weekly recompence which such labourers occasionally received from their masters, was evidently not the whole price of their labour. Their small tenement made a considerable part of it. This daily or weekly recompence, however, seems to have been considered as the whole of it, by many writers who have collected the prices of labour and provisions in ancient times, and who have taken pleasure in representing both as wonderfully low.

The produce of such labour comes frequently cheaper to market than would otherwise be suitable to its nature. Stockings in many parts of Scotland are knit much cheaper than they can any-where be wrought upon the loom. They are the work of servants and labourers, who derive the principal part of their subsistence from some other employment. More than a thousand pair of Shetland stockings are annually imported into Leith, of which the price is from five pence to seven pence a pair. At Learwick, the small capital of the Shetland islands, ten pence a day, I have been assured, is a common price of common labour. In the same islands they knit worsted stockings to the value of a guinea a pair and upwards.

The spinning of linen yarn is carried on in Scotland nearly in the same way as the knitting of stockings, by servants who are chiefly hired for other purposes. They earn but a very scanty subsistence, who endeavour to get their whole livelihood by either of those trades. In most parts of Scotland she is a good spinner who can earn twenty pence a week.

In opulent countries the market is generally so extensive, that any one trade is sufficient to employ the whole labour and stock of those who occupy it. Instances of people's living by one employment, and at the same time deriving some little advantage from another, occur chiefly in poor countries. The following instance, however, of something of the same kind is to be found in the capital of a very rich one. There is no city in Europe, I believe, in which house-rent is dearer than in London, and yet I know no capital in which a furnished apartment can be hired so cheap. Lodging is not only much cheaper in London than in Paris; it is much cheaper than in Edinburgh of the same degree of goodness; and what may seem extraordinary, the dearness of house-rent is the cause of the cheapness of lodging. The dearness of house-rent in London arises, not only from those causes which render it dear in all great capitals, the dearness of labour, the dearness of all the materials of building, which must generally be brought from a great distance, and above all the dearness of ground-rent, every landlord acting the part of a monopolist, and frequently exacting a higher rent for a single acre of bad land in a town, than can be had for a hundred of the best in the country; but it arises in part from the peculiar manners and customs of the people which oblige every master of a family to hire a whole house from top to bottom. A dwelling-house in England means every thing that is contained under the same roof. In France, Scotland, and many other parts of Europe, it frequently means no more than a single story. A tradesman in London is obliged to hire a whole house in that part of the town where his customers live. His shop is upon the ground-floor, and he and his family sleep in the garret; and he endeavours to pay a part of his house-rent by letting the two middle stories to lodgers. He expects to maintain his family by his trade, and not by his lodgers. Whereas, at Paris and Edinburgh, the people who let lodgings have commonly no other means of subsistence; and the price of the lodging must pay, not only the rent of the house, but the whole expence of the family.

PART II

Inequalities occasioned by the Policy of Europe

Such are the inequalities in the whole of the advantages and disadvantages of the different employments of labour and stock, which the defect of any of the three requisites above-mentioned must occasion, even where there is the most perfect liberty. But the policy of Europe, by not leaving things at perfect liberty, occasions other inequalities of much greater importance.

It does this chiefly in the three following ways. First, by restraining the competition in some employments to a smaller number than would otherwise be disposed to enter into them; secondly, by increasing it in others beyond what it naturally would be; and, thirdly, by obstructing the free circulation of labour and stock, both from employment to employment and from place to place.

First, The Policy of Europe occasions a very important inequality in the whole of the advantages and disadvantages of the different employments of labour and stock, by restraining the competition in some employments to a smaller number than might otherwise be disposed to enter into them.

The exclusive privileges of corporations are the principal means it makes use of for this purpose.

The exclusive privilege of an incorporated trade necessarily restrains the competition, in the town where it is established, to those who are free of the trade. To have served an apprenticeship in the town under a master properly qualified, is commonly the necessary requisite for obtaining this freedom. The bye-laws of the corporation regulate sometimes the number of apprentices which any master is allowed to have, and almost always the number of years which each apprentice is obliged to serve. The intention of both regulations is to restrain the competition to a much smaller number than might otherwise be disposed to enter into the trade. The limitation of the number of apprentices restrains it directly. A long term of apprenticeship restrains it more indirectly, but as effectually, by increasing the expence of education.

In Sheffield no master cutler can have more than one apprentice at a time, by a bye-law of the corporation. In Norfolk and Norwich no master weaver can have more than two apprentices, under pain of forfeiting five pounds a month to the king. No master hatter can have more than two apprentices any-where in England, or in the English plantations, under pain of forfeiting five pounds a month, half to the king, and half to him who shall sue in any court of record. Both these regulations, though they have been confirmed by a public law of the kingdom, are evidently dictated by the same corporation spirit which enacted the bye-law of Sheffield. The silk weavers in London had scarce been incorporated a year when they enacted a bye-law, restraining any master from having more than two apprentices at a time. It required a particular act of parliament to rescind this bye-law.

Seven years seem anciently to have been, all over Europe, the usual term established for the duration of apprenticeships in the greater part of incorporated trades. All such incorporations were anciently called universities; which indeed is the proper Latin name for any incorporation whatever. The university of smiths, the university of taylors, &c. are expressions which we commonly meet with in the old charters of ancient towns. When those particular incorporations which are now peculiarly called universities were first established, the term of years which it was necessary to study, in order to obtain the degree of master of arts, appears evidently to have been copied from the term of apprenticeship in common trades, of which the incorporations were much more ancient. As to have wrought seven years under a master properly qualified, was necessary, in order to entitle any person to become a master, and to have himself apprentices in a common trade; so to have studied seven years under a master properly qualified, was necessary to entitle him to become a master, teacher, or doctor (words anciently synonimous) in the liberal arts, and to have scholars or apprentices (words likewise originally synonimous) to study under him.

By the 5th of Elizabeth, commonly called the Statute of Apprenticeship, it was enacted, that no person should for the future exercise any trade, craft, or mastery at that time exercised in England, unless he had previously served to it an apprenticeship of seven years at least; and what before had been the bye-law of many particular corporations, became in England the general and public law of all trades carried on in market towns. For though the words of the statute are very general, and seem plainly to include the whole kingdom, by interpretation its operation has been limited to market towns, it having been held that in country villages a person may exercise several different trades, though he has not served a seven years' apprenticeship to each, they being necessary for the conveniency of the inhabitants, and the number of people frequently not being sufficient to supply each with a particular set of hands.

By a strict interpretation of the words, too, the operation of this statute has been limited to those trades which were established in England before the 5th of Elizabeth, and has never been extended to such as have been introduced since that time. This limitation has given occasion to several distinctions which, considered as rules of police, appear as foolish as can well be imagined. It has been adjudged, for example, that a coach-maker can neither himself make nor employ journeymen to make his coach-wheels; but must buy them of a master wheel-wright; this latter trade having been exercised in England before the 5th of Elizabeth. But a wheel-wright, though he has never served an apprenticeship to a coach-maker, may either himself make or employ journeymen to make coaches; the trade of a coach-maker not being within the statute, because not exercised in England at the time when it was made. The manufactures of Manchester, Birmingham, and Wolverhampton, are many of them, upon this account, not within the statute; not having been exercised in England before the 5th of Elizabeth.

In France, the duration of apprenticeships is different in different towns and in different trades. In Paris, five years is the term required in a great number; but before any person can be qualified to exercise the trade as a master, he must, in many of them, serve five years more as a journeyman. During this latter term he is called the companion of his master, and the term itself is called his companionship.

In Scotland there is no general law which regulates universally the duration of apprenticeships. The term is different in different corporations. Where it is long, a part of it may generally be redeemed by paying a small fine. In most towns, too, a very small fine is sufficient to purchase the freedom of any corporation. The weavers of linen and hempen cloth, the principal manufactures of the country, as well as all other artificers subservient to them, wheel-makers, reel-makers, &c. may exercise their trades in any town corporate without paying any fine. In all towns corporate all persons are free to sell butcher's meat upon any lawful day of the week. Three years is in Scotland a common term of apprenticeship, even in some very nice trades; and in general I know of no country in Europe in which corporation laws are so little oppressive.

The property which every man has in his own labour, as it is the original foundation of all other property, so it is the most sacred and inviolable. The patrimony of a poor man lies in the strength and dexterity of his hands; and to hinder him from employing this strength and dexterity in what manner he thinks proper without injury to his neighbour, is a plain violation of this most sacred property. It is a manifest encroachment upon the just liberty both of the workman, and of those who might be disposed to employ him. As it hinders the one from working at what he thinks proper, so it hinders the others from employing whom they think proper. To judge whether he is fit to be employed, may surely be trusted to the discretion of the employers whose interest it so much concerns. The affected anxiety of the law-giver lest they should employ an improper person, is evidently as impertinent as it is oppressive.

The institution of long apprenticeships can give no security that insufficient workmanship shall not frequently be exposed to public sale. When this is done it is generally the effect of fraud, and not of inability; and the longest apprenticeship can give no security against fraud. Quite different regulations are necessary to prevent this abuse. The sterling mark upon plate, and the stamps upon linen and woollen cloth, give the purchaser much greater security than any statute of apprenticeship. He generally looks at these, but never thinks it worth while to enquire whether the workmen had served a seven years' apprenticeship.

The institution of long apprenticeships has no tendency to form young people to industry. A journeyman who works by the piece is likely to be industrious, because he derives a benefit from every exertion of his industry. An apprentice is likely to be idle, and almost always is so, because he has no immediate interest to be otherwise. In the inferior employments, the sweets of labour consist altogether in the recompence of labour. They who are soonest in a condition to enjoy the sweets of it, are likely soonest to conceive a relish for it, and to acquire the early habit of industry. A young man naturally conceives an aversion to labour, when for a long time he receives no benefit from it. The boys who are put out apprentices from public charities are generally bound for more than the usual number of years, and they generally turn out very idle and worthless.

Apprenticeships were altogether unknown to the ancients. The reciprocal duties of master and apprentice make a considerable article in every modern code. The Roman law is perfectly silent with regard to them. I know no Greek or Latin word (I might venture, I believe, to assert that there is none) which expresses the idea we now annex to the word Apprentice, a servant bound to work at a particular trade for the benefit of a master, during a term of years, upon condition that the master shall teach him that trade.

Long apprenticeships are altogether unnecessary. The arts, which are much superior to common trades, such as those of making clocks and watches, contain no such mystery as to require a long course of instruction. The first invention of such beautiful machines, indeed, and even that of some of the instruments employed in making them, must, no doubt, have been the work of deep thought and long time, and may justly be considered as among the happiest efforts of human ingenuity. But when both have been fairly invented and are well understood, to explain to any young man, in the completest manner, how to apply the instruments and how to construct the machines, cannot well require more than the lessons of a few weeks: perhaps those of a few days might be sufficient. In the common mechanic trades, those of a few days might certainly be sufficient. The dexterity of hand, indeed, even in common trades, cannot be acquired without much practice and experience. But a young man would practise with much more diligence and attention, if from the beginning he wrought as a journeyman, being paid in proportion to the little work which he could execute, and paying in his turn for the materials which he might sometimes spoil through awkwardness and inexperience. His education would generally in this way be more effectual, and always less tedious and expensive. The master, indeed, would be a loser. He would lose all the wage of the apprentice, which he now saves, for seven years together. In the end, perhaps, the apprentice himself would be a loser. In a trade so easily learnt he would have more competitors, and his wages, when he came to be a complete workman, would be much less than at present. The same increase of competition would reduce the profits of the masters as well as the wages of the workmen. The trades, the crafts, the mysteries, would all be losers. But the public would be a gainer, the work of all artificers coming in this way much cheaper to market.

It is to prevent this reduction of price, and consequently of wages and profit, by restraining that free competition which would most certainly occasion it, that all corporations, and the greater part of corporation laws, have been established. In order to erect a corporation, no other authority in ancient times was requisite in many parts of Europe, but that of the town corporate in which it was established. In England, indeed, a charter from the king was likewise necessary. But this prerogative of the crown seems to have been reserved rather for extorting money from the subject, than for the defence of the common liberty against such oppressive monopolies. Upon paying a fine to the king, the charter seems generally to have been readily granted; and when any particular class of artificers or traders thought proper to act as a corporation without a charter, such adulterine guilds, as they were called, were not always disfranchised upon that account, but obliged to fine annually to the king for permission to exercise their usurped privileges. The immediate inspection of all corporations, and of the bye-laws which they might think proper to enact for their own government, belonged to the town corporate in which they were established; and whatever discipline was exercised over them, proceeded commonly, not from the king, but from that greater incorporation of which those subordinate ones were only parts or members.

The government of towns corporate was altogether in the hands of traders and artificers; and it was the manifest interest of every particular class of them, to prevent the market from being over-stocked, as they commonly express it, with their own particular species of industry; which is in reality to keep it always under-stocked. Each class was eager to establish regulations proper for this purpose, and, provided it was allowed to do so, was willing to consent that every other class should do the same. In consequence of such regulations, indeed, each class was obliged to buy the goods they had occasion for from every other within the town, somewhat dearer than they otherwise might have done. But in recompence, they were enabled to sell their own just as much dearer; so that so far it was as broad as long, as they say; and in the dealings of the different classes within the town with one another, none of them were losers by these regulations. But in their dealings with the country they were all great gainers; and in these latter dealings consists the whole trade which supports and enriches every town.

Every town draws its whole subsistence, and all the materials of its industry, from the country. It pays for these chiefly in two ways: first, by sending back to the country a part of those materials wrought up and manufactured; in which case their price is augmented by the wages of the workmen, and the profits of their masters or immediate employers: secondly, by sending to it a part both of the rude and manufactured produce, either of other countries, or of distant parts of the same country, imported into the town; in which case too the original price of those goods is augmented by the wages of the carriers or sailors, and by the profits of the merchants who employ them. In what is gained upon the first of those two branches of commerce, consists the advantage which the town makes by its manufactures; in what is gained upon the second, the advantage of its inland and foreign trade. The wages of the workmen, and the profits of their different employers, make up the whole of what is gained upon both. Whatever regulations, therefore, tend to increase those wages and profits beyond what they otherwise would be, tend to enable the town to purchase, with a smaller quantity of its labour, the produce of a greater quantity of the labour of the country. They give the traders and artificers in the town an advantage over the landlords, farmers, and labourers in the country, and break down that natural equality which would otherwise take place in the commerce which is carried on between them. The whole annual produce of the labour of the society is annually divided between those two different sets of people. By means of those regulations a greater share of it is given to the inhabitants of the town than would otherwise fall to them; and a less to those of the country.

The price which the town really pays for the provisions and materials annually imported into it, is the quantity of manufactures and other goods annually exported from it. The dearer the latter are sold, the cheaper the former are bought. The industry of the town becomes more, and that of the country less advantageous.

That the industry which is carried on in towns is, everywhere in Europe, more advantageous than that which is carried on in the country, without entering into any very nice computations, we may satisfy ourselves by one very simple and obvious observation. In every country of Europe we find, at least, a hundred people who have acquired great fortunes from small beginnings by trade and manufactures, the industry which properly belongs to towns, for one who has done so by that which properly belongs to the country, the raising of rude produce by the improvement and cultivation of land. Industry, therefore, must be better rewarded, the wages of labour and the profits of stock must evidently be greater in the one situation than in the other. But stock and labour naturally seek the most advantageous employment. They naturally, therefore, resort as much as they can to the town, and desert the country.

The inhabitants of a town, being collected into one place, can easily combine together. The most insignificant trades carried on in towns have accordingly, in some place or other, been incorporated; and even where they have never been incorporated, yet the corporation spirit, the jealousy of strangers, the aversion to take apprentices, or to communicate the secret of their trade, generally prevail in them, and often teach them, by voluntary associations and agreements, to prevent that free competition which they cannot prohibit by bye-laws. The trades which employ but a small number of hands, run most easily into such combinations. Half a dozen wool-combers, perhaps, are necessary to keep a thousand spinners and weavers at work. By combining not to take apprentices they can not only engross the employment, but reduce the whole manufacture into a sort of slavery to themselves, and raise the price of their labour above what is due to the nature of their work.

The inhabitants of the country, dispersed in distant places, cannot easily combine together. They have not only never been incorporated, but the corporation spirit never has prevailed among them. No apprenticeship has ever been thought necessary to qualify for husbandry, the great trade of the country. After what are called the fine arts, and the liberal professions, however, there is perhaps no trade which requires so great a variety of knowledge and experience. The innumerable volumes which have been written upon it in all languages, may satisfy us, that among the wisest and most learned nations, it has never been regarded as a matter very easily understood. And from all those volumes we shall in vain attempt to collect that knowledge of its various and complicated operations, which is commonly possessed even by the common farmer; how contemptuously soever the very contemptible authors of some of them may sometimes affect to speak of him. There is scarce any common mechanic trade, on the contrary, of which all the operations may not be as completely and distinctly explained in a pamphlet of a very few pages, as it is possible for words illustrated by figures to explain them. In the history of the arts, now publishing by the French academy of sciences, several of them are actually explained in this manner. The direction of operations, besides, which must be varied with every change of the weather, as well as with many other accidents, requires much more judgment and discretion, than of those which are always the same or very nearly the same.

Not only the art of the farmer, the general direction of the operations of husbandry, but many inferior branches of country labour, require much more skill and experience than the greater part of mechanic trades. The man who works upon brass and iron, works with instruments and upon materials of which the temper is always the same, or very nearly the same. But the man who ploughs the ground with a team of horses or oxen, works with instruments of which the health, strength, and temper, are very different upon different occasions. The condition of the materials which he works upon too is as variable as that of the instruments which he works with, and both require to be managed with much judgment and discretion. The common ploughman, though generally regarded as the pattern of stupidity and ignorance, is seldom defective in this judgment and discretion. He is less accustomed, indeed, to social intercourse than the mechanic who lives in a town. His voice and language are more uncouth and more difficult to be understood by those who are not used to them. His understanding, however, being accustomed to consider a greater variety of objects, is generally much superior to that of the other, whose whole attention from morning till night is commonly occupied in performing one or two very simple operations. How much the lower ranks of people in the country are really superior to those of the town, is well known to every man whom either business or curiosity has led to converse with both. In China and Indostan accordingly both the rank and the wages of country labourers are said to be superior to those of the greater part of artificers and manufacturers. They would probably be so every-where, if corporation laws and the corporation spirit did not prevent it.

The superiority which the industry of the towns has every-where in Europe over that of the country, is not altogether owing to corporations and corporation laws. It is supported by many other regulations. The high duties upon foreign manufactures and upon all goods imported by alien merchants, all tend to the same purpose. Corporation laws enable the inhabitants of towns to raise their prices, without fearing to be under-sold by the free competition of their own countrymen. Those other regulations secure them equally against that of foreigners. The enhancement of price occasioned by both is every-where finally paid by the landlords, farmers, and labourers of the country, who have seldom opposed the establishment of such monopolies. They have commonly neither inclination nor fitness to enter into combinations; and the clamour and sophistry of merchants and manufacturers easily persuade them that the private interest of a part, and of a subordinate part of the society, is the general interest of the whole.

In Great Britain the superiority of the industry of the towns over that of the country, seems to have been greater formerly than in the present times. The wages of country labour approach nearer to those of manufacturing labour, and the profits of stock employed in agriculture to those of trading and manufacturing stock, than they are said to have done in the last century, or in the beginning of the present. This change may be regarded as the necessary, though very late consequence of the extraordinary encouragement given to the industry of the towns. The stock accumulated in them comes in time to be so great, that it can no longer be employed with the ancient profit in that species of industry which is peculiar to them. That industry has its limits like every other; and the increase of stock, by increasing the competition, necessarily reduces the profit. The lowering of profit in the town forces out stock to the country, where, by creating a new demand for country labour, it necessarily raises its wages. It then spreads itself, if I may say so, over the face of the land, and by being employed in agriculture is in part restored to the country, at the expence of which, in a great measure, it had originally been accumulated in the town. That every-where in Europe the greatest improvements of the country have been owing to such overflowings of the stock originally accumulated in the towns, I shall endeavour to show hereafter; and at the same time to demonstrate, that though some countries have by this course attained to a considerable degree of opulence, it is in itself necessarily slow, uncertain, liable to be disturbed and interrupted by innumerable accidents, and in every respect contrary to the order of nature and of reason. The interests, prejudices, laws and customs which have given occasion to it, I shall endeavour to explain as fully and distinctly as I can in the third and fourth books of this inquiry.

People of the same trade seldom meet together, even for merriment and diversion, but the conversation ends in a conspiracy against the public, or in some contrivance to raise prices. It is impossible indeed to prevent such meetings, by any law which either could be executed, or would be consistent with liberty and justice. But though the law cannot hinder people of the same trade from sometimes assembling together, it ought to do nothing to facilitate such assemblies; much less to render them necessary.

A regulation which obliges all those of the same trade in a particular town to enter their names and places of abode in a public register, facilitates such assemblies. It connects individuals who might never otherwise be known to one another, and gives every man of the trade a direction where to find every other man of it.

A regulation which enables those of the same trade to tax themselves in order to provide for their poor, their sick, their widows and orphans, by giving them a common interest to manage, renders such assemblies necessary.

An incorporation not only renders them necessary, but makes the act of the majority binding upon the whole. In a free trade an effectual combination cannot be established but by the unanimous consent of every single trader, and it cannot last longer than every single trader continues of the same mind. The majority of a corporation can enact a bye-law with proper penalties, which will limit the competition more effectually and more durably than any voluntary combination whatever.

The pretence that corporations are necessary for the better government of the trade, is without any foundation. The real and effectual discipline which is exercised over a workman is not that of his corporation, but that of his customers. It is the fear of losing their employment which restrains his frauds and corrects his negligence. An exclusive corporation necessarily weakens the force of this discipline. A particular set of workmen must then be employed, let them behave well or ill. It is upon this account that in many large incorporated towns no tolerable workmen are to be found, even in some of the most necessary trades. If you would have your work tolerably executed, it must be done in the suburbs, where the workmen, having no exclusive privilege, have nothing but their character to depend upon, and you must then smuggle it into the town as well as you can.

It is in this manner that the policy of Europe, by restraining the competition in some employments to a smaller number than would otherwise be disposed to enter into them, occasions a very important inequality in the whole of the advantages and disadvantages of the different employments of labour and stock.

Secondly, The policy of Europe, by increasing the competition in some employments beyond what it naturally would be, occasions another inequality of an opposite kind in the whole of the advantages and disadvantages of the different employments of labour and stock.

It has been considered as of so much importance that a proper number of young people should be educated for certain professions, that, sometimes the public, and sometimes the piety of private founders have established many pensions, scholarships, exhibitions, bursaries, &c., for this purpose, which draw many more people into those trades than could otherwise pretend to follow them. In all christian countries, I believe, the education of the greater part of churchmen is paid for in this manner. Very few of them are educated altogether at their own expence. The long, tedious, and expensive education, therefore, of those who are, will not always procure them a suitable reward, the church being crowded with people who, in order to get employment, are willing to accept of a much smaller recompence than what such an education would otherwise have entitled them to; and in this manner the competition of the poor takes away the reward of the rich. It would be indecent, no doubt, to compare either a curate or a chaplain with a journeyman in any common trade. The pay of a curate or chaplain, however, may very properly be considered as of the same nature with the wages of a journeyman. They are, all three, paid for their work according to the contract which they may happen to make with their respective superiors. Till after the middle of the fourteenth century, five merks, containing about as much silver as ten pounds of our present money, was in England the usual pay of a curate or stipendiary parish priest, as we find it regulated by the decrees of several different national councils. At the same period four pence a day, containing the same quantity of silver as a shilling of our present money, was declared to be the pay of a master mason, and three pence a day, equal to nine pence of our present money, that of a journeyman mason. The wages of both these labourers, therefore, supposing them to have been constantly employed, were much superior to those of the curate. The wages of the master mason, supposing him to have been without employment one third of the year, would have fully equalled them. By the 12th of Queen Anne, c. 12, it is declared, "That whereas for want of sufficient maintenance and encouragement to curates, the cures have in several places been meanly supplied, the bishop is, therefore, empowered to appoint by writing under his hand and seal a sufficient certain stipend or allowance, not exceeding fifty and not less than twenty pounds a year." Forty pounds a year is reckoned at present very good pay for a curate, and notwithstanding this act of parliament, there are many curacies under twenty pounds a year. There are journeymen shoemakers in London who can earn forty pounds a year, and there is scarce an industrious workman of any kind in that metropolis who does not earn more than twenty. This last sum indeed does not exceed what is frequently earned by common labourers in many country parishes. Whenever the law has attempted to regulate the wages of workmen, it has always been rather to lower them than to raise them. But the law has upon many occasions attempted to raise the wages of curates, and for the dignity of the church, to oblige the rectors of parishes to give them more than the wretched maintenance which they themselves might be willing to accept of. And in both cases the law seems to have been equally ineffectual, and has never either been able to raise the wages of curates, or to sink those of labourers to the degree that was intended: because it has never been able to hinder either the one from being willing to accept of less than the legal allowance, on account of the indigence of their situation and the multitude of their competitors; or the other from receiving more, on account of the contrary competition of those who expected to derive either profit or pleasure from employing them.

The great benefices and other ecclesiastical dignities support the honour of the church, notwithstanding the mean circumstances of some of its inferior members. The respect paid to the profession too makes some compensation even to them for the meanness of their pecuniary recompence. In England, and in all Roman Catholic countries, the lottery of the church is in reality much more advantageous than is necessary. The example of the churches of Scotland, of Geneva, and of several other protestant churches, may satisfy us, that in so creditable a profession, in which education is so easily procured, the hopes of much more moderate benefices will draw a sufficient number of learned, decent, and respectable men into holy orders.

In professions in which there are no benefices, such as law and physic, if an equal proportion of people were educated at the public expence, the competition would soon be so great, as to sink very much their pecuniary reward. It might then not be worth any man's while to educate his son to either of those professions at his own expence. They would be entirely abandoned to such as had been educated by those public charities, whose numbers and necessities would oblige them in general to content themselves with a very miserable recompence, to the entire degradation of the now respectable professions of law and physic.

That unprosperous race of men commonly called men of letters, are pretty much in the situation which lawyers and physicians probably would be in upon the foregoing supposition. In every part of Europe the greater part of them have been educated for the church, but have been hindered by different reasons from entering into holy orders. They have generally, therefore, been educated at the public expence, and their numbers are every-where so great as commonly to reduce the price of their labour to a very paultry recompence.

Before the invention of the art of printing, the only employment by which a man of letters could make any thing by his talents, was that of a public or private teacher, or by communicating to other people the curious and useful knowledge which he had acquired himself: And this is still surely a more honourable, a more useful, and in general even a more profitable employment than that other of writing for a bookseller, to which the art of printing has given occasion. The time and study, the genius, knowledge, and application requisite to qualify an eminent teacher of the sciences, are at least equal to what is necessary for the greatest practitioners in law and physic. But the usual reward of the eminent teacher bears no proportion to that of the lawyer or physician; because the trade of the one is crowded with indigent people who have been brought up to it at the public expence; whereas those of the other two are incumbered with very few who have not been educated at their own. The usual recompence, however, of public and private teachers, small as it may appear, would undoubtedly be less than it is, if the competition of those yet more indigent men of letters who write for bread was not taken out of the market. Before the invention of the art of printing, a scholar and a beggar seem to have been terms very nearly synonymous. The different governors of the universities before that time appear to have often granted licences to their scholars to beg.

In ancient times, before any charities of this kind had been established for the education of indigent people to the learned professions, the rewards of eminent teachers appear to have been much more considerable. Isocrates, in what is called his discourse against the sophists, reproaches the teachers of his own times with inconsistency. "They make the most magnificent promises to their scholars, says he, and undertake to teach them to be wise, to be happy, and to be just, and in return for so important a service they stipulate the paultry reward of four or five minæ. They who teach wisdom, continues he, ought certainly to be wise themselves; but if any man were to sell such a bargain for such a price, he would be convicted of the most evident folly." He certainly does not mean here to exaggerate the reward, and we may be assured that it was not less than he represents it. Four minæ were equal to thirteen pounds six shillings and eight pence: five minæ to sixteen pounds thirteen shillings and four pence. Something not less than the largest of those two sums, therefore, must at that time have been usually paid to the most eminent teachers at Athens. Isocrates himself demanded ten minæ, or thirty-three pounds six shillings and eight pence, from each scholar. When he taught at Athens, he is said to have had an hundred scholars. I understand this to be the number whom he taught at one time, or who attended what we would call one course of lectures, a number which will not appear extraordinary from so great a city to so famous a teacher, who taught too what was at that time the most fashionable of all sciences, rhetoric. He must have made, therefore, by each course of lectures, a thousand minæ, or *3,333l. 6s. 8d.* A thousand minæ, accordingly, is said by Plutarch in another place, to have been his Didactron, or usual price of teaching. Many other eminent teachers in those times appear to have acquired great fortunes. Gorgias made a present to the temple of Delphi of his own statue in solid gold. We must not, I presume, suppose that it was as large as the life. His way of living, as well as that of Hippias and Protagoras, two other eminent teachers of those times, is represented by Plato as splendid even to ostentation. Plato himself is said to have lived with a good deal of magnificence. Aristotle, after having been tutor to Alexander, and most munificently rewarded, as it is universally agreed, both by him and his father Philip, thought it worth while, notwithstanding, to return to Athens, in order to resume the teaching of his school. Teachers of the sciences were probably in those times less common than they came to be in an age or two afterwards, when the competition had probably somewhat reduced both the price of their labour and the admiration for their persons. The most eminent of them, however, appear always to have enjoyed a degree of consideration much superior to any of the like profession in the present times. The Athenians sent Carneades the academic, and Diogenes the stoic, upon a solemn embassy to Rome; and though their city had then declined from its former grandeur, it was still an independent and considerable republic. Carneades too was a Babylonian by birth, and as there never was a people more jealous of admitting foreigners to public offices than the Athenians, their consideration for him must have been very great.

This inequality is upon the whole, perhaps, rather advantageous than hurtful to the public. It may somewhat degrade the profession of a public teacher; but the cheapness of literary education is surely an advantage which greatly over-balances this trifling inconveniency. The public too might derive still greater benefit from it, if the constitution of those schools and colleges, in which education is carried on, was more reasonable than it is at present through the greater part of Europe.

Thirdly, The policy of Europe, by obstructing the free circulation of labour and stock both from employment to employment, and from place to place, occasions in some cases a very inconvenient inequality in the whole of the advantages and disadvantages of their different employments.

The statute of apprenticeship obstructs the free circulation of labour from one employment to another, even in the same place. The exclusive privileges of corporations obstruct it from one place to another, even in the same employment.

It frequently happens that while high wages are given to the workmen in one manufacture, those in another are obliged to content themselves with bare subsistence. The one is in an advancing state, and has, therefore, a continual demand for new hands: The other is in a declining state, and the super-abundance of hands is continually increasing. Those two manufactures may sometimes be in the same town, and sometimes in the same neighbourhood, without being able to lend the least assistance to one another. The statute of apprenticeship may oppose it in the one case, and both that and an exclusive corporation in the other. In many different manufactures, however, the operations are so much alike, that the workmen could easily change trades with one another, if those absurd laws did not hinder them. The arts of weaving plain linen and plain silk, for example, are almost entirely the same. That of weaving plain woollen is somewhat different; but the difference is so insignificant, that either a linen or a silk weaver might become a tolerable workman in a very few days. If any of those three capital manufactures, therefore, were decaying, the workmen might find a resource in one of the other two which was in a more prosperous condition; and their wages would neither rise too high in the thriving, nor sink too low in the decaying manufacture. The linen manufacture indeed is, in England, by a particular statute, open to every body; but as it is not much cultivated through the greater part of the country, it can afford no general resource to the workmen of other decaying manufactures, who, wherever the statute of apprenticeship takes place, have no other choice but either to come upon the parish, or to work as common labourers, for which, by their habits, they are much worse qualified than for any sort of manufacture that bears any resemblance to their own. They generally, therefore, chuse to come upon the parish.

Whatever obstructs the free circulation of labour from one employment to another, obstructs that of stock likewise; the quantity of stock which can be employed in any branch of business depending very much upon that of the labour which can be employed in it. Corporation laws, however, give less obstruction to the free circulation of stock from one place to another than to that of labour. It is everywhere much easier for a wealthy merchant to obtain the privilege of trading in a town corporate, than for a poor artificer to obtain that of working in it.

The obstruction which corporation laws give to the free circulation of labour is common, I believe, to every part of Europe. That which is given to it by the poor laws is, so far as I know, peculiar to England. It consists in the difficulty which a poor man finds in obtaining a settlement, or even in being allowed to exercise his industry in any parish but that to which he belongs. It is the labour of artificers and manufacturers only of which the free circulation is obstructed by corporation laws. The difficulty of obtaining settlements obstructs even that of common labour. It may be worth while to give some account of the rise, progress, and present state of this disorder, the greatest perhaps of any in the police of England.

When by the destruction of monasteries the poor had been deprived of the charity of those religious houses, after some other ineffectual attempts for their relief, it was enacted by the 43d of Elizabeth, c. 2. that every parish should be bound to provide for its own poor; and that overseers of the poor should be annually appointed, who, with the churchwardens, should raise, by a parish rate, competent sums for this purpose.

By this statute the necessity of providing for their own poor was indispensably imposed upon every parish. Who were to be considered as the poor of each parish, became, therefore, a question of some importance. This question, after some variation, was at last determined by the 13th and 14th of Charles II. when it was enacted, that forty days undisturbed residence should gain any person a settlement in any parish; but that within that time it should be lawful for two justices of the peace, upon complaint made by the churchwardens or overseers of the poor, to remove any new inhabitant to the parish where he was last legally settled; unless he either rented a tenement of ten pounds a year, or could give such security for the discharge of the parish where he was then living, as those justices should judge sufficient.

Some frauds, it is said, were committed in consequence of this statute; parish officers sometimes bribing their own poor to go clandestinely to another parish, and by keeping themselves concealed for forty days to gain a settlement there, to the discharge of that to which they properly belonged. It was enacted, therefore, by the 1st of James II. that the forty days undisturbed residence of any person necessary to gain a settlement, should be accounted only from the time of his delivering notice in writing, of the place of his abode and the number of his family, to one of the churchwardens or overseers of the parish where he came to dwell.

But parish officers, it seems, were not always more honest with regard to their own, than they had been with regard to other parishes, and sometimes connived at such intrusions, receiving the notice, and taking no proper steps in consequence of it. As every person in a parish, therefore, was supposed to have an interest to prevent as much as possible their being burdened by such intruders, it was further enacted by the 3d of William III. that the forty days residence should be accounted only from the publication of such notice in writing on Sunday in the church, immediately after divine service.

"After all," says Doctor Burn, "this kind of settlement, by continuing forty days after publication of notice in writing, is very seldom obtained; and the design of the acts is not so much for gaining of settlements, as for the avoiding of them by persons coming into a parish clandestinely: for the giving of notice is only putting a force upon the parish to remove. But if a person's situation is such, that it is doubtful whether he is actually removeable or not, he shall by giving of notice compel the parish either to allow him a settlement uncontested, by suffering him to continue forty days; or, by removing him, to try the right."

This statute, therefore, rendered it almost impracticable for a poor man to gain a new settlement in the old way, by forty days inhabitancy. But that it might not appear to preclude altogether the common people of one parish from ever establishing themselves with security in another, it appointed four other ways by which a settlement might be gained without any notice delivered or published. The first was, by being taxed to parish rates and paying them; the second by being elected into an annual parish office, and serving in it a year; the third, by serving an apprenticeship in the parish; the fourth, by being hired into service there for a year, and continuing in the same service during the whole of it.

Nobody can gain a settlement by either of the two first ways, but by the public deed of the whole parish, who are too well aware of the consequences to adopt any new-comer who has nothing but his labour to support him, either by taxing him to parish rates, or by electing him into a parish office.

No married man can well gain any settlement in either of the two last ways. An apprentice is scarce ever married; and it is expressly enacted, that no married servant shall gain any settlement by being hired for a year. The principal effect of introducing settlement by service, has been to put out in a great measure the old fashion of hiring for a year, which before had been so customary in England, that even at this day, if no particular term is agreed upon, the law intends that every servant is hired for a year. But masters are not always willing to give their servants a settlement by hiring them in this manner; and servants are not always willing to be so hired, because, as every last settlement discharges all the foregoing, they might thereby lose their original settlement in the places of their nativity, the habitation of their parents and relations.

No independent workman, it is evident, whether labourer or artificer, is likely to gain any new settlement either by apprenticeship or by service. When such a person, therefore, carried his industry to a new parish, he was liable to be removed, how healthy and industrious soever, at the caprice of any churchwarden or overseer, unless he either rented a tenement of ten pounds a year, a thing impossible for one who has nothing but his labour to live by; or could give such security for the discharge of the parish as two justices of the peace should judge sufficient. What security they shall require, indeed, is left altogether to their discretion; but they cannot well require less than thirty pounds, it having been enacted, that the purchase even of a freehold estate of less than thirty pounds value, shall not gain any person a settlement, as not being sufficient for the discharge of the parish. But this is a security which scarce any man who lives by labour can give; and much greater security is frequently demanded.

In order to restore in some measure that free circulation of labour which those different statutes had almost entirely taken away, the invention of certificates was fallen upon. By the 8th or 9th of William III. it was enacted, that if any person should bring a certificate from the parish where he was at last legally settled, subscribed by the churchwardens and overseers of the poor, and allowed by two justices of the peace, that every other parish should be obliged to receive him; that he should not be removeable merely upon account of his being likely to become chargeable, but only upon his becoming actually chargeable, and that then the parish which granted the certificate should be obliged to pay the expence both of his maintenance and of his removal. And in order to give the most perfect security to the parish where such certificated man should come to reside, it was further enacted by the same statute, that he should gain no settlement there by any means whatever, except either by renting a tenement of ten pounds a year, or by serving upon his own account in an annual parish office for one whole year; and consequently neither by notice, nor by service, nor by apprenticeship, nor by paying parish rates. By the 12th of Queen Anne too, stat. l. c. 18. it was further enacted, that neither the servants nor apprentices of such certificated man should gain any settlement in the parish where he resided under such certificate.

How far this invention has restored that free circulation of labour which the preceding statutes had almost entirely taken away, we may learn from the following very judicious observation of Doctor Burn. "It is obvious," says he, "that there are divers good reasons for requiring certificates with persons coming to settle in any place; namely, that persons residing under them can gain no settlement, neither by apprenticeship, nor by service, nor by giving notice, nor by paying parish rates; that they can settle neither apprentices nor servants; that if they become chargeable, it is certainly known whither to remove them, and the parish shall be paid for the removal, and for their maintenance in the mean time; and that if they fall sick, and cannot be removed, the parish which gave the certificate must maintain them: none of which can be without a certificate. Which reasons will hold proportionably for parishes not granting certificates in ordinary cases; for it is far more than an equal chance, but that they will have the certificated persons again, and in a worse condition." The moral of this observation seems to be, that certificates ought always to be required by the parish where any poor man comes to reside, and that they ought very seldom to be granted by that which he proposes to leave. "There is somewhat of hardship in this matter of certificates," says the same very intelligent Author, in his History of the Poor Laws, "by putting it in the power of a parish officer, to imprison a man as it were for life; however inconvenient it may be for him to continue at that place where he has had the misfortune to acquire what is called a settlement, or whatever advantage he may propose to himself by living elsewhere."

Though a certificate carries along with it no testimonial of good behaviour, and certifies nothing but that the person belongs to the parish to which he really does belong, it is altogether discretionary in the parish officers either to grant or to refuse it. A mandamus was once moved for, says Doctor Burn, to compel the churchwardens and overseers to sign a certificate; but the court of King's Bench rejected the motion as a very strange attempt.

The very unequal price of labour which we frequently find in England in places at no great distance from one another, is probably owing to the obstruction which the law of settlements gives to a poor man who would carry his industry from one parish to another without a certificate. A single man, indeed, who is healthy and industrious, may sometimes reside by sufferance without one; but a man with a wife and family who should attempt to do so, would in most parishes be sure of being removed, and if the single man should afterwards marry, he would generally be removed likewise. The scarcity of hands in one parish, therefore, cannot always be relieved by their super-abundance in another, as it is constantly in Scotland, and, I believe, in all other countries where there is no difficulty of settlement. In such countries, though wages may sometimes rise a little in the neighbourhood of a great town, or wherever else there is an extraordinary demand for labour, and sink gradually as the distance from such places increases, till they fall back to the common rate of the country; yet we never meet with those sudden and unaccountable differences in the wages of neighbouring places which we sometimes find in England, where it is often more difficult for a poor man to pass the artificial boundary of a parish, than an arm of the sea or a ridge of high mountains, natural boundaries which sometimes separate very distinctly different rates of wages in other countries.

To remove a man who has committed no misdemeanour from the parish where he chuses to reside, is an evident violation of natural liberty and justice. The common people of England, however, so jealous of their liberty, but like the common people of most other countries never rightly understanding wherein it consists, have now for more than a century together suffered themselves to be exposed to this oppression without a remedy. Though men of reflection too have sometimes complained of the law of settlements as a public grievance; yet it has never been the object of any general popular clamour, such as that against general warrants, an abusive practice undoubtedly, but such a one as was not likely to occasion any general oppression. There is scarce a poor man in England of forty years of age, I will venture to say, who has not in some part of his life felt himself most cruelly oppressed by this ill-contrived law of settlements.

I shall conclude this long chapter with observing, that though anciently it was usual to rate wages, first by general laws extending over the whole kingdom, and afterwards by particular orders of the justices of peace in every particular county, both these practices have now gone entirely into disuse. "By the experience of above four hundred years," says Doctor Burn, "it seems time to lay aside all endeavours to bring under strict regulations, what in its own nature seems incapable of minute limitation: for if all persons in the same kind of work were to receive equal wages, there would be no emulation, and no room left for industry or ingenuity."

Particular acts of parliament, however, still attempt sometimes to regulate wages in particular trades and in particular places. Thus the 8th of George III. prohibits under heavy penalties all master taylors in London, and five miles round it, from giving, and their workmen from accepting, more than two shillings and sevenpence halfpenny a day, except in the case of a general mourning. Whenever the legislature attempts to regulate the differences between masters and their workmen, its counsellors are always the masters. When the regulation, therefore, is in favour of the workmen, it is always just and equitable; but it is sometimes otherwise when in favour of the masters. Thus the law which obliges the masters in several different trades to pay their workmen in money and not in goods, is quite just and equitable. It imposes no real hardship upon the masters. It only obliges them to pay that value in money, which they pretended to pay, but did not always really pay, in goods. This law is in favour of the workmen; but the 8th of George III. is in favour of the masters. When masters combine together in order to reduce the wages of their workmen, they commonly enter into a private bond or agreement, not to give more than a certain wage under a certain penalty. Were the workmen to enter into a contrary combination of the same kind, not to accept of a certain wage under a certain penalty, the law would punish them very severely; and if it dealt impartially, it would treat the masters in the same manner. But the 8th of George III. enforces by law that very regulation which masters sometimes attempt to establish by such combinations. The complaint of the workmen, that it puts the ablest and most industrious upon the same footing with an ordinary workman, seems perfectly well founded.

In ancient times too it was usual to attempt to regulate the profits of merchants and other dealers, by rating the price both of provisions and other goods. The assize of bread is, so far as I know, the only remnant of this ancient usage. Where there is an exclusive corporation, it may perhaps be proper to regulate the price for the first necessary of life. But where there is none, the competition will regulate it much better than any assize. The method of fixing the assize of bread established by the 31st of George II. could not be put in practice in Scotland, on account of a defect in the law; its execution depending upon the office of clerk of the market, which does not exist there. This defect was not remedied till the 3d of George III. The want of an assize occasioned no sensible inconveniency, and the establishment of one in the few places where it has yet taken place, has produced no sensible advantage. In the greater part of the towns of Scotland, however, there is an incorporation of bakers who claim exclusive privileges, though they are not very strictly guarded.

The proportion between the different rates both of wages and profit in the different employments of labour and stock, seems not to be much affected, as has already been observed, by the riches or poverty, the advancing, stationary, or declining state of the society. Such revolutions in the public welfare, though they affect the general rates both of wages and profit, must in the end affect them equally in all different employments. The proportion between them, therefore, must remain the same, and cannot well be altered, at least for any considerable time, by any such revolutions.

CHAPTER XI

Of the Rent of Land

RENT, considered as the price paid for the use of land, is naturally the highest which the tenant can afford to pay in the actual circumstances of the land. In adjusting the terms of the lease, the landlord endeavours to leave him no greater share of the produce than what is sufficient to keep up the stock from which he furnishes the seed, pays the labour, and purchases and maintains the cattle and other instruments of husbandry, together with the ordinary profits of farming stock in the neighbourhood. This is evidently the smallest share with which the tenant can content himself without being a loser, and the landlord seldom means to leave him any more. Whatever part of the produce, or, what is the same thing, whatever part of its price, is over and above this share, he naturally endeavours to reserve to himself as the rent of his land, which is evidently the highest the tenant can afford to pay in the actual circumstances of the land. Sometimes, indeed, the liberality, more frequently the ignorance of the landlord, makes him accept of somewhat less than this portion; and sometimes too, though more rarely, the ignorance of the tenant makes him undertake to pay somewhat more, or to content himself with somewhat less, than the ordinary profits of farming stock in the neighbourhood. This portion, however, may still be considered as the natural rent of land, or the rent for which it is naturally meant that land should for the most part be let.

The rent of land, it may be thought, is frequently no more than a reasonable profit or interest for the stock laid out by the landlord upon its improvement. This, no doubt, may be partly the case upon some occasions; for it can scarce ever be more than partly the case. The landlord demands a rent even for unimproved land, and the supposed interest or profit upon the expence of improvement is generally an addition to this original rent. Those improvements, besides, are not always made by the stock of the landlord, but sometimes by that of the tenant. When the lease comes to be renewed, however, the landlord commonly demands the same augmentation of rent, as if they had been all made by his own.

He sometimes demands rent for what is altogether incapable of human improvement. Kelp is a species of sea-weed, which, when burnt, yields an alkaline salt, useful for making glass, soap, and for several other purposes. It grows in several parts of Great Britain, particularly in Scotland, upon such rocks only as lie within the high water mark, which are twice every day covered with the sea, and of which the produce, therefore, was never augmented by human industry. The landlord, however, whose estate is bounded by a kelp shore of this kind, demands a rent for it as much as for his corn fields.

The sea in the neighbourhood of the islands of Shetland is more than commonly abundant in fish, which makes a great part of the subsistence of their inhabitants. But in order to profit by the produce of the water, they must have a habitation upon the neighbouring land. The rent of the landlord is in proportion, not to what the farmer can make by the land, but to what he can make both by the land and by the water. It is partly paid in sea-fish; and one of the very few instances in which rent makes a part of the price, of that commodity, is to be found in that country.

The rent of land, therefore, considered as the price paid for the use of the land, is naturally a monopoly price. It is not at all proportioned to what the landlord may have laid out upon the improvement of the land, or to what he can afford to take; but to what the farmer can afford to give.

Such parts only of the produce of land can commonly be brought to market of which the ordinary price is sufficient to replace the stock which must be employed in bringing them thither, together with its ordinary profits. If the ordinary price is more than this, the surplus part of it will naturally go to the rent of the land. If it is not more, though the commodity may be brought to market, it can afford no rent to the landlord. Whether the price is, or is not more, depends upon the demand.

There are some parts of the produce of land for which the demand must always be such as to afford a greater price than what is sufficient to bring them to market; and there are others for which it either may or may not be such as to afford this greater price. The former must always afford a rent to the landlord. The latter sometimes may, and sometimes may not, according to different circumstances.

Rent, it is to be observed, therefore, enters into the composition of the price of commodities in a different way from wages and profit. High or low wages and profit, are the causes of high or low price; high or low rent is the effect of it. It is because high or low wages and profit must be paid, in order to bring a particular commodity to market, that its price is high or low. But it is because its price is high or low; a great deal more, or very little more, or no more, than what is sufficient to pay those wages and profit, that it affords a high rent, or a low rent, or no rent at all.

The particular consideration, first, of those parts of the produce of land which always afford some rent; secondly, of those which sometimes may and sometimes may not afford rent; and, thirdly, of the variations which, in the different periods of improvement, naturally take place, in the relative value of those two different sorts of rude produce, when compared both with one another and with manufactured commodities, will divide this chapter into three parts.

PART I

Of the Produce of Land which Always Affords Rent

As men, like all other animals, naturally multiply in proportion to the means of their subsistence, food is always, more or less, in demand. It can always purchase or command a greater or smaller quantity of labour, and somebody can always be found who is willing to do something in order to obtain it. The quantity of labour, indeed, which it can purchase, is not always equal to what it could maintain, if managed in the most œconomical manner, on account of the high wages which are sometimes given to labour. But it can always purchase such a quantity of labour as it can maintain, according to the rate at which that sort of labour is commonly maintained in the neighbourhood.

But land, in almost any situation, produces a greater quantity of food than what is sufficient to maintain all the labour necessary for bringing it to market, in the most liberal way in which that labour is ever maintained. The surplus too is always more than sufficient to replace the stock which employed that labour, together with its profits. Something, therefore, always remains for a rent to the landlord.

The most desert moors in Norway and Scotland produce some sort of pasture for cattle, of which the milk and the increase are always more than sufficient, not only to maintain all the labour necessary for tending them, and to pay the ordinary profit to the farmer or owner of the herd or flock; but to afford some small rent to the landlord. The rent increases in proportion to the goodness of the pasture. The same extent of ground not only maintains a greater number of cattle, but as they are brought within a smaller compass, less labour becomes requisite to tend them, and to collect their produce. The landlord gains both ways; by the increase of the produce, and by the diminution of the labour which must be maintained out of it.

The rent of land not only varies with its fertility, whatever be its produce, but with its situation, whatever be its fertility. Land in the neighbourhood of a town gives a greater rent than land equally fertile in a distant part of the country. Though it may cost no more labour to cultivate the one than the other, it must always cost more to bring the produce of the distant land to market. A greater quantity of labour, therefore, must be maintained out of it; and the surplus, from which are drawn both the profit of the farmer and the rent of the landlord, must be diminished. But in remote parts of the country the rate of profits, as has already been shown, is generally higher than in the neighbourhood of a large town. A smaller proportion of this diminished surplus, therefore, must belong to the landlord.

Good roads, canals, and navigable rivers, by diminishing the expence of carriage, put the remote parts of the country more nearly upon a level with those in the neighbourhood of the town. They are upon that account the greatest of all improvements. They encourage the cultivation of the remote, which must always be the most extensive circle of the country. They are advantageous to the town, by breaking down the monopoly of the country in its neighbourhood. They are advantageous even to that part of the country. Though they introduce some rival commodities into the old market, they open many new markets to its produce. Monopoly, besides, is a great enemy to good management, which can never be universally established but in consequence of that free and universal competition which forces everybody to have recourse to it for the sake of self-defence. It is not more than fifty years ago, that some of the counties in the neighbourhood of London petitioned the parliament against the extension of the turnpike roads into the remoter counties. Those remote counties, they pretended, from the cheapness of labour, would be able to sell their grass and corn cheaper in the London market than themselves, and would thereby reduce their rents, and ruin their cultivation. Their rents, however, have risen, and their cultivation has been improved since that time.

A corn field of moderate fertility produces a much greater quantity of food for man, than the best pasture of equal extent. Though its cultivation requires much more labour, yet the surplus which remains after replacing the seed and maintaining all that labour, is likewise much greater. If a pound of butcher's-meat, therefore, was never supposed to be worth more than a pound of bread, this greater surplus would every-where be of greater value, and constitute a greater fund both for the profit of the farmer and the rent of the landlord. It seems to have done so universally in the rude beginnings of agriculture.

But the relative values of those two different species of food, bread, and butcher's-meat, are very different in the different periods of agriculture. In its rude beginnings, the unimproved wilds, which then occupy the far greater part of the country, are all abandoned to cattle. There is more butcher's-meat than bread, and bread, therefore, is the food for which there is the greatest competition, and which consequently brings the greatest price. At Buenos Ayres, we are told by Ulloa, four reals, one-and-twenty pence halfpenny sterling, was, forty or fifty years ago, the ordinary price of an ox, chosen from a herd of two or three hundred. He says nothing of the price of bread, probably because he found nothing remarkable about it. An ox there, he says, costs little more than the labour of catching him. But corn can no-where be raised without a great deal of labour, and in a country which lies upon the river Plate, at that time the direct road from Europe to the silver mines of Potosi, the money price of labour could not be very cheap. It is otherwise when cultivation is extended over the greater part of the country. There is then more bread than butcher's-meat. The competition changes its direction, and the price of butcher's-meat becomes greater than the price of bread.

By the extension besides of cultivation the unimproved wilds become insufficient to supply the demand for butcher's-meat. A great part of the cultivated lands must be employed in rearing and fattening cattle, of which the price, therefore, must be sufficient to pay, not only the labour necessary for tending them, but the rent which the landlord and the profit which the farmer could have drawn from such land employed in tillage. The cattle bred upon the most uncultivated moors, when brought to the same market, are, in proportion to their weight or goodness, sold at the same price as those which are reared upon the most improved land. The proprietors of those moors profit by it, and raise the rent of their land in proportion to the price of their cattle. It is not more than a century ago that in many parts of the highlands of Scotland, butcher's-meat was as cheap or cheaper than even bread made of oat-meal. The union opened the market of England to the highland cattle. Their ordinary price is at present about three times greater than at the beginning of the century, and the rents of many highland estates have been tripled and quadrupled in the same time. In almost every part of Great Britain a pound of the best butcher's-meat is, in the present times, generally worth more than two pounds of the best white bread; and in plentiful years it is sometimes worth three or four pounds.

It is thus that in the progress of improvement the rent and

profit of unimproved pasture come to be regulated in some measure by the rent and profit of what is improved, and these again by the rent and profit of corn. Corn is an annual crop. Butcher's-meat, a crop which requires four or five years to grow. As an acre of land, therefore, will produce a much smaller quantity of the one species of food than of the other, the inferiority of the quantity must be compensated by the superiority of the price. If it was more than compensated, more corn land would be turned into pasture; and if it was not compensated, part of what was in pasture would be brought back into corn.

This equality, however, between the rent and profit of grass and those of corn; of the land of which the immediate produce is food for cattle, and of that of which the immediate produce is food for men; must be understood to take place only through the greater part of the improved lands of a great country. In some particular local situations it is quite otherwise, and the rent and profit of grass are much superior to what can be made by corn.

Thus in the neighbourhood of a great town, the demand for milk and for forage to horses, frequently contribute, together with the high price of butcher's-meat, to raise the value of grass above what may be called its natural proportion to that of corn. This local advantage, it is evident, cannot be communicated to the lands at a distance.

Particular circumstances have sometimes rendered some countries so populous, that the whole territory, like the lands in the neighbourhood of a great town, has not been sufficient to produce both the grass and the corn necessary for the subsistence of their inhabitants. Their lands, therefore, have been principally employed in the production of grass, the more bulky commodity, and which cannot be so easily brought from a great distance; and corn, the food of the great body of the people, has been chiefly imported from foreign countries. Holland is at present in this situation, and a considerable part of ancient Italy seems to have been so during the prosperity of the Romans. To feed well, old Cato said, as we are told by Cicero, was the first and most profitable thing in the management of a private estate; to feed tolerably well, the second; and to feed ill, the third. To plough, he ranked only in the fourth place of profit and advantage Tillage, indeed, in that part of ancient Italy which lay in the neighbourhood of Rome, must have been very much discouraged by the distributions of corn which were frequently made to the people, either gratuitously, or at a very low price. This corn was brought from the conquered provinces, of which several, instead of taxes, were obliged to furnish a tenth part of their produce at a stated price, about sixpence a peck, to the republic. The low price at which this corn was distributed to the people, must necessarily have sunk the price of what could be brought to the Roman market from Latium, or the ancient territory of Rome, and must have discouraged its cultivation in that country.

In an open country too, of which the principal produce is corn, a well-enclosed piece of grass will frequently rent higher than any corn field in its neighbourhood. It is convenient for the maintenance of the cattle employed in the cultivation of the corn, and its high rent is, in this case, not so properly paid from the value of its own produce, as from that of the corn lands which are cultivated by means of it. It is likely to fall, if ever the neighbouring lands are completely enclosed. The present high rent of enclosed land in Scotland seems owing to the scarcity of enclosure, and will probably last no longer than that scarcity. The advantage of enclosure is greater for pasture than for corn. It saves the labour of guarding the cattle, which feed better too when they are not liable to be disturbed by their keeper or his dog.

But where there is no local advantage of this kind, the rent and profit of corn, or whatever else is the common vegetable food of the people, must naturally regulate, upon the land which is fit for producing it, the rent and profit of pasture.

The use of the artificial grasses, of turnips, carrots, cabbages, and the other expedients which have been fallen upon to make an equal quantity of land feed a greater number of cattle than when in natural grass, should somewhat reduce, it might be expected, the superiority which, in an improved country, the price of butcher's-meat naturally has over that of bread. It seems accordingly to have done so; and there is some reason for believing that, at least in the London market, the price of butcher's-meat in proportion to the price of bread, is a good deal lower in the present times than it was in the beginning of the last century.

In the appendix to the Life of Prince Henry, Doctor Birch has given us an account of the prices of butcher's-meat as commonly paid by that prince. It is there said that the four quarters of an ox weighing six hundred pounds usually cost him nine pounds ten shillings, or thereabouts; that is, thirty-one shillings and eight pence per hundred pounds weight. Prince Henry died on the 6th of November 1612, in the nineteenth year of his age.

In March 1764, there was a parliamentary inquiry into the causes of the high price of provisions at that time. It was then, among other proof to the same purpose, given in evidence by a Virginia merchant, that in March 1763, he had victualled his ships for twenty-four or twenty-five shillings the hundred weight of beef, which he considered as the ordinary price; whereas, in that dear year, he had paid twenty-seven shillings for the same weight and sort. This high price in 1764 is, however, four shillings and eight pence cheaper than the ordinary price paid by prince Henry; and it is the best beef only, it must be observed, which is fit to be salted for those distant voyages.

The price paid by prince Henry amounts to 3 4-5*d.* per pound weight of the whole carcase, coarse and choice pieces taken together; and at that rate the choice pieces could not have been sold by retail for less than 4½*d.* or 5*d.* the pound.

In the parliamentary inquiry in 1764, the witnesses stated the price of the choice pieces of the best beef to be to the consumer 4*d.* and 4¼*d.* the pound; and the coarse pieces in general to be from seven farthings to 2½*d.* and 2¾*d.*; and this they said was in general one half-penny dearer than the same sort of pieces had usually been sold in the month of March. But even this high price is still a good deal cheaper than what we can well suppose the ordinary retail price to have been in the time of prince Henry.

During the twelve first years of the last century, the average price of the best wheat at the Windsor market was 1*l.* 18*s.* 3 1-6*d.* the quarter of nine Winchester bushels.

But in the twelve years preceding 1764, including that year, the average price of the same measure of the best wheat at the same market was *2l. 1s. 9½d.*

In the twelve first years of the last century, therefore, wheat appears to have been a good deal cheaper, and butcher's-meat a good deal dearer, than in the twelve years preceding 1764, including that year.

In all great countries the greater part of the cultivated lands are employed in producing either food for men or food for cattle. The rent and profit of these regulate the rent and profit of all other cultivated land. If any particular produce afforded less, the land would soon be turned into corn or pasture; and if any afforded more, some part of the lands in corn and pasture would soon be turned to that produce.

Those productions, indeed, which require either a greater original expence of improvement, or a greater annual expence of cultivation, in order to fit the land for them, appear commonly to afford, the one a greater rent, the other a greater profit than corn or pasture. This superiority, however, will seldom be found to amount to more than a reasonable interest or compensation for this superior expence.

In a hop garden, a fruit garden, a kitchen garden, both the rent of the landlord, and the profit of the farmer, are generally greater than in a corn or grass field. But to bring the ground into this condition requires more expence. Hence a greater rent becomes due to the landlord. It requires too a more attentive and skilful management. Hence a greater profit becomes due to the farmer. The crop too, at least in the hop and fruit garden, is more precarious. Its price, therefore, besides compensating all occasional losses, must afford something like the profit of insurance. The circumstances of gardeners, generally mean, and always moderate, may satisfy us that their great ingenuity is not commonly over-recompenced. Their delightful art is practised by so many rich people for amusement, that little advantage is to be made by those who practise it for profit; because the persons who should naturally be their best customers, supply themselves with all their most precious productions.

The advantage which the landlord derives from such improvements seems at no time to have been greater than what was sufficient to compensate the original expence of making them. In the ancient husbandry, after the vineyard, a well-watered kitchen garden seems to have been the part of the farm which was supposed to yield the most valuable produce. But Democritus, who wrote upon husbandry about two thousand years ago, and who was regarded by the ancients as one of the fathers of art, thought they did not act wisely who enclosed a kitchen garden. The profit, he said, would not compensate the expence of a stone wall; and bricks (he meant, I suppose, bricks baked in the sun) mouldered with the rain, and the winter storm, and required continual repairs. Columella, who reports this judgment of Democritus, does not controvert it, but proposes a very frugal method of enclosing with a hedge of brambles and briars, which, he says, he had found by experience to be both a lasting and an impenetrable fence; but which, it seems, was not commonly known in the time of Democritus. Palladius adopts the opinion of Columella, which had before been recommended by Varro. In the judgment of those ancient improvers, the produce of a kitchen garden had, it seems, been little more than sufficient to pay the extraordinary culture and the expence of watering; for in countries so near the sun, it was thought proper, in those times as in the present, to have the command of a stream of water, which could be conducted to every bed in the garden. Through the greater part of Europe, a kitchen garden is not at present supposed to deserve a better enclosure than that recommended by Columella. In Great Britain, and some other northern countries, the finer fruits cannot be brought to perfection but by the assistance of a vall. Their price, therefore, in such countries, must be sufficient to pay the expence of building and maintaining what they cannot be had without. The fruit-wall frequently surrounds the kitchen garden, which thus enjoys the benefit of an enclosure which its own produce could seldom pay for.

That the vineyard, when properly planted and brought to perfection, was the most valuable part of the farm, seems to have been an undoubted maxim in the ancient agriculture, as it is in the modern through all the wine countries. But whether it was advantageous to plant a new vineyard, was a matter of dispute among the ancient Italian husbandmen, as we learn from Columella. He decides, like a true lover of all curious cultivation, in favour of the vineyard, and endeavours to show, by a comparison of the profit and expense, that it was a most advantageous improvement. Such comparisons, however, between the profit and expense of new projects, are commonly very fallacious; and in nothing more so than in agriculture. Had the gain actually made by such plantations been commonly as great as he imagined it might have been, there could have been no dispute about it. The same point is frequently at this day a matter of controversy in the wine countries. Their writers on agriculture, indeed, the lovers and promoters of high cultivation, seem generally disposed to decide with Columella in favour of the vineyard. In France the anxiety of the proprietors of the old vineyards to prevent the planting of any new ones, seems to favour their opinion, and to indicate a consciousness in those who must have the experience, that this species of cultivation is at present in that country more profitable than any other. It seems at the same time, however, to indicate another opinion, that this superior profit can last no longer than the laws which at present restrain the free cultivation of the vine. In 1731, they obtained an order of council, prohibiting both the planting of new vineyards, and the renewal of those old ones, of which the cultivation had been interrupted for two years, without a particular permission from the king, to be granted only in consequence of an information from the intendant of the province, certifying that he had examined the land, and that it was incapable of any other culture. The pretence of this order was the scarcity of corn and pasture, and the super-abundance of wine. But had this super-abundance been real, it would, without any order of council, have effectually prevented the plantation of new vineyards, by reducing the profits of this species of cultivation below their natural proportion to those of corn and pasture. With regard to the supposed scarcity of corn occasioned by the multiplication of vineyards, corn is nowhere in France more carefully cultivated than in the wine provinces, where the land is fit for producing it; as in Burgundy, Guienne, and the Upper Languedoc. The numerous hands employed in the one species of cultivation necessarily encourage the other, by affording a ready market for its produce. To diminish the number of those who are capable of paying for it, is surely a most unpromising expedient for encouraging the cultivation of corn. It is like the policy which would promote agriculture by discouraging manufactures.

The rent and profit of those productions, therefore, which require either a greater original annual expence of improvement in order to fit the land for them, or a greater annual expence of cultivation, though often much superior to those of corn and pasture, yet when they do no more than compensate such extraordinary expence, are in reality regulated by the rent and profit of those common crops.

It sometimes happens, indeed, that the quantity of land which can be fitted for some particular produce, is too small to supply the effectual demand. The whole produce can be disposed of to those who are willing to give somewhat more than what is sufficient to pay the whole rent, wages and profit necessary for raising and bringing it to market, according to their natural rates, or according to the rates at which they are paid in the greater part of other cultivated land. The surplus part of the price which remains after defraying the whole expence of improvement and cultivation may commonly, in this case, and in this case only, bear no regular proportion to the like surplus in corn or pasture, but may exceed it in almost any degree; and the greater part of this excess naturally goes to the rent of the landlord.

The usual and natural proportion, for example, between the rent and profit of wine and those of corn and pasture, must be understood to take place only with regard to those vineyards which produce nothing but good common wine, such as can be raised almost any-where, upon any light, gravelly, or sandy soil, and which has nothing to recommend it but its strength and wholesomeness. It is with such vineyards only that the common land of the country can be brought into competition; for with those of a peculiar quality it is evident that it cannot.

The vine is more affected by the difference of soils than any other fruit tree. From some it derives a flavour which no culture or management can equal, it is supposed, upon any other. This flavour, real or imaginary, is sometimes peculiar to the produce of a few vineyards; sometimes it extends through the greater part of a small district, and sometimes through a considerable part of a large province. The whole quantity of such wines that is brought to market falls short of the effectual demand, or the demand of those who would be willing to pay the whole rent, profit and wages necessary for preparing and bringing them thither, according to the ordinary rate, or according to the rate at which they are paid in common vineyards. The whole quantity, therefore, can be disposed of to those who are willing to pay more, which necessarily raises the price above that of common wine. The difference is greater or less, according as the fashionableness and scarcity of the wine render the competition of the buyers more or less eager. Whatever it be, the greater part of it goes to the rent of the landlord. For though such vineyards are in general more carefully cultivated than most others, the high price of the wine seems to be, not so much the effect, as the cause of this careful cultivation. In so valuable a produce the loss occasioned by negligence is so great as to force even the most careless to attention. A small part of this high price, therefore, is sufficient to pay the wages of the extraordinary labour bestowed upon their cultivation, and the profits of the extraordinary stock which puts that labour into motion.

The sugar colonies possessed by the European nations in the West Indies, may be compared to those precious vineyards. Their whole produce falls short of the effectual demand of Europe, and can be disposed of to those who are willing to give more than what is sufficient to pay the whole rent, profit and wages necessary for preparing and bringing it to market, according to the rate at which they are commonly paid by any other produce. In Cochin-china the finest white sugar commonly sells for three piastres the quintal, about thirteen shillings and sixpence of our money, as we are told by Mr. Poivre, a very careful observer of the agriculture of that country. What is there called the quintal weighs from a hundred and fifty to two hundred Paris pounds, or a hundred and seventy-five Paris pounds at a medium, which reduces the price of the hundred weight English to about eight shillings sterling, not a fourth part of what is commonly paid for the brown or muskavada sugars imported from our colonies, and not a sixth part of what is paid for the finest white sugar. The greater part of the cultivated lands in Cochin-china are employed in producing corn and rice, the food of the great body of the people. The respective prices of corn, rice, and sugar, are there probably in the natural proportion, or in that which naturally takes place in the different crops of the greater part of cultivated land, and which recompences the landlord and farmer, as nearly as can be computed, according to what is usually the original expence of improvement and the annual expence of cultivation. But in our sugar colonies the price of sugar bears no such proportion to that of the produce of a rice or corn field either in Europe or in America. It is commonly said, that a sugar planter expects that the rum and the molasses should defray the whole expence of his cultivation, and that his sugar should be all clear profit. If this be true, for I pretend not to affirm it, it is as if a corn farmer expected to defray the expence of his cultivation with the chaff and the straw, and that the grain should be all clear profit. We see frequently societies of merchants in London and other trading towns, purchase waste lands in our sugar colonies, which they expect to improve and cultivate with profit by means of factors and agents; notwithstanding the great distance and the uncertain returns, from the defective administration of justice in those countries. Nobody will attempt to improve and cultivate in the same manner the most fertile lands of Scotland, Ireland, or the corn provinces of North America, though from the more exact administration of justice in these countries, more regular returns might be expected.

In Virginia and Maryland the cultivation of tobacco is preferred, as more profitable, to that of corn. Tobacco might be cultivated with advantage through the greater part of Europe; but in almost every part of Europe it has become a principal subject of taxation, and to collect a tax from every different farm in the country where this plant might happen to be cultivated, would be more difficult, it has been supposed, than to levy one upon its importation at the custom-house. The cultivation of tobacco has upon this account been most absurdly prohibited through the greater part of Europe, which necessarily gives a sort of monopoly to the countries where it is allowed; and as Virginia and Maryland produce the greatest quantity of it, they share largely, though with some competitors, in the advantage of this monopoly. The cultivation of tobacco, however, seems not to be so advantageous as that of sugar. I have never even heard of any tobacco plantation that was improved and cultivated by the capital of merchants who resided in Great Britain, and our tobacco colonies send us home no such wealthy planters as we see frequently arrive from our sugar islands. Though from the preference given in those colonies to the cultivation of tobacco above that of corn, it would appear that the effectual demand of Europe for tobacco is not completely supplied, it probably is more nearly so than that for sugar: And though the present price of tobacco is probably more than sufficient to pay the whole rent, wages and profit necessary for preparing and bringing it to market, according to the rate at which they are commonly paid in corn land; it must not be so much more as the present price of sugar. Our tobacco planters, accordingly, have shewn the same fear of the super-abundance of tobacco, which the proprietors of the old vineyards in France have of the super-abundance of wine. By act of assembly they have restrained its cultivation to six thousand plants, supposed to yield a thousand weight of tobacco, for every negro between sixteen and sixty years of age. Such a negro, over and above this quantity of tobacco, can manage, they reckon, four acres of Indian corn. To prevent the market from being overstocked too, they have sometimes, in plentiful years, we are told by Dr. Douglas, (I suspect he has been ill informed) burnt a certain quantity of tobacco for every negro, in the same manner as the Dutch are said to do of spices. If such violent methods are necessary to keep up the present price of tobacco, the superior advantage of its culture over that of corn, if it still has any, will not probably be of long continuance.

It is in this manner that the rent of the cultivated land, of which the produce is human food, regulates the rent of the greater part of other cultivated land. No particular produce can long afford less; because the land would immediately be turned to another use: And if any particular produce commonly affords more, it is because the quantity of land which can be fitted for it is too small to supply the effectual demand.

In Europe corn is the principal produce of land which serves immediately for human food. Except in particular situations, therefore, the rent of corn land regulates in Europe that of all other cultivated land. Britain need envy neither the vineyards of France nor the olive plantations of Italy. Except in particular situations, the value of these is regulated by that of corn, in which the fertility of Britain is not much inferior to that of either of those two countries.

If in any country the common and favorite vegetable food of the people should be drawn from a plant of which the most common land, with the same or nearly the same culture, produced a much greater quantity than the most fertile does of corn, the rent of the landlord, or the surplus quantity of food which would remain to him, after paying the labour and replacing the stock of the farmer together with its ordinary profits, would necessarily be much greater. Whatever was the rate at which labour was commonly maintained in that country, this greater surplus could always maintain a greater quantity of it, and consequently enable the landlord to purchase or command a greater quantity of it. The real value of his rent, his real power and authority, his command of the necessaries and conveniencies of life with which the labor of other people could supply him, would necessarily be much greater.

A rice field produces a much greater quantity of food than the most fertile corn field. Two crops in the year from thirty to sixty bushels each, are said to be the ordinary produce of an acre. Though its cultivation, therefore, requires more labour, a much greater surplus remains after maintaining all that labour. In those rice countries, therefore, where rice is the common and favourite vegetable food of the people, and where the cultivators are chiefly maintained with it, a greater share of this greater surplus should belong to the landlord than in corn countries. In Carolina, where the planters, as in other British colonies, are generally both farmers and landlords, and where rent consequently is confounded with profit, the cultivation of rice is found to be more profitable than that of corn, though their fields produce only one crop in the year, and though, from the prevalence of the customs of Europe, rice is not there the common and favourite vegetable food of the people.

A good rice field is a bog at all seasons, and at one season a bog covered with water. It is unfit either for corn, or pasture, or vineyard, or, indeed, for any other vegetable produce that is very useful to men: And the lands which are fit for those purposes, are not fit for rice. Even in the rice countries, therefore, the rent of rice lands cannot regulate the rent of the other cultivated land which can never be turned to that produce.

The food produced by a field of potatoes is not inferior in quantity to that produced by a field of rice, and much superior to what is produced by a field of wheat. Twelve thousand weight of potatoes from an acre of land is not a greater produce than two thousand weight of wheat. The food or solid nourishment, indeed, which can be drawn from each of those two plants, is not altogether in proportion to their weight, on account of the watery nature of potatoes. Allowing, however, half the weight of this root to go to water, a very large allowance, such an acre of potatoes will still produce six thousand weight of solid nourishment, three times the quantity produced by the acre of wheat. An acre of potatoes is cultivated with less expence than an acre of wheat; the fallow, which generally precedes the sowing of wheat, more than compensating the hoeing and other extraordinary culture which is always given to potatoes. Should this root ever become in any part of Europe, like rice in some rice countries, the common and favourite vegetable food of the people, so as to occupy the same proportion of the land in tillage which wheat and other sorts of grain for human food do at present, the same quantity of cultivated land would maintain a much greater number of people, and the labourers being generally fed with potatoes, a greater surplus would remain after replacing all the stock and maintaining all the labour employed in cultivation. A greater share of this surplus too would belong to the landlord. Population would increase, and rents would rise much beyond what they are at present.

The land which is fit for potatoes, is fit for almost every other useful vegetable. If they occupied the same proportion of cultivated land which corn does at present, they would regulate, in the same manner, the rent of the greater part of other cultivated land.

In some parts of Lancashire it is pretended, I have been told, that bread of oatmeal is a heartier food for labouring people than wheaten bread, and I have frequently heard the same doctrine held in Scotland. I am, however, somewhat doubtful of the truth of it. The common people in Scotland, who are fed with oatmeal, are in general neither so strong nor so handsome as the same rank of people in England, who are fed with wheaten bread. They neither work so well, nor look so well; and as there is not the same difference between the people of fashion in the two countries, experience would seem to show, that the food of the common people in Scotland is not so suitable to the human constitution as that of their neighbours of the same rank in England. But it seems to be otherwise with potatoes. The chairmen, porters, and coal-heavers in London, and those unfortunate women who live by prostitution, the strongest men and the most beautiful women perhaps in the British dominions, are said to be, the greater part of them, from the lowest rank of people in Ireland, who are generally fed with this root. No food can afford a more decisive proof of its nourishing quality, or of its being peculiarly suitable to the health of the human constitution.

It is difficult to preserve potatoes through the year, and impossible to store them like corn, for two or three years together. The fear of not being able to sell them before they rot, discourages their cultivation, and is, perhaps, the chief obstacle to their ever becoming in any great country, like bread, the principal vegetable food of all the different ranks of the people.

PART II

Of the Produce of Land which sometimes does and sometimes does not, afford Rent

Human food seems to be the only produce of land which always and necessarily affords some rent to the landlord. Other sorts of produce sometimes may and sometimes may not, according to different circumstances.

After food, cloathing and lodging are the two great wants of mankind.

Land in its original rude state can afford the materials of cloathing and lodging to a much greater number of people than it can feed. In its improved state it can sometimes feed a greater number of people than it can supply with those materials; at least in the way in which they require them, and are willing to pay for them. In the one state, therefore, there is always a super-abundance of those materials, which are frequently, upon that account, of little or no value. In the other there is often a scarcity, which necessarily augments their value. In the one state a great part of them is thrown away as useless, and the price of what is used is considered as equal only to the labour and expence of fitting it for use, and can, therefore, afford no rent to the landlord. In the other they are all made use of, and there is frequently a demand for more than can be had. Somebody is always willing to give more for every part of them than what is sufficient to pay the expence of bringing them to market. Their price, therefore, can always afford some rent to the landlord.

The skins of the larger animals were the original materials of cloathing. Among nations of hunters and shepherds, therefore, whose food consists chiefly in the flesh of those animals, every man, by providing himself with food, provides himself with the materials of more cloathing than he can wear. If there was no foreign commerce, the greater part of them would be thrown away as things of no value. This was probably the case among the hunting nations of North America, before their country was discovered by the Europeans, with whom they now exchange their surplus peltry, for blankets, fire-arms, and brandy, which gives it some value. In the present commercial state of the known world, the most barbarous nations, I believe, among whom land property is established, have some foreign commerce of this kind, and find among their wealthier neighbours such a demand for all the materials of cloathing, which their land produces, and which can neither be wrought up nor consumed at home, as raises their price above what it costs to send them to those wealthier neighbours. It affords, therefore, some rent to the landlord. When the greater part of the highland cattle were consumed on their own hills, the exportation of their hides made the most considerable article of the commerce of that country, and what they were exchanged for afforded some addition to the rent of the highland estates. The wool of England, which in old times could neither be consumed nor wrought up at home, found a market in the then wealthier and more industrious country of Flanders, and its price afforded something to the rent of the land which produced it. In countries not better cultivated than England was then, or than the highlands of Scotland are now, and which had no foreign commerce, the materials of cloathing would evidently be so super-abundant, that a great part of them would be thrown away as useless, and no part could afford any rent to the landlord.

The materials of lodging cannot always be transported to so great a distance as those of cloathing, and do not so readily become an object of foreign commerce. When they are super-abundant in the country which produces them, it frequently happens, even in the present commercial state of the world, that they are of no value to the landlord. A good stone quarry in the neighbourhood of London would afford a considerable rent. In many parts of Scotland and Wales it affords none. Barren timber for building is of great value in a populous and well-cultivated country, and the land which produces it affords a considerable rent. But in many parts of North America the landlord would be much obliged to any body who would carry away the greater part of his large trees. In some parts of the highlands of Scotland the bark is the only part of the wood which, for want of roads and water-carriage, can be sent to market. The timber is left to rot upon the ground. When the materials of lodging are so super-abundant, the part made use of is worth only the labour and expence of fitting it for that use. It affords no rent to the landlord, who generally grants the use of it to whoever takes the trouble of asking it. The demand of wealthier nations, however, sometimes enables him to get a rent for it. The paving of the streets of London has enabled the owners of some barren rocks on the coast of Scotland to draw a rent from what never afforded any before. The woods of Norway and of the coasts of the Baltic, find a market in many parts of Great Britain which they could not find at home, and thereby afford some rent to their proprietors.

Countries are populous, not in proportion to the number of people whom their produce can cloath and lodge, but in proportion to that of those whom it can feed. When food is provided, it is easy to find the necessary cloathing and lodging. But though these are at hand, it may often be difficult to find food. In some parts even of the British dominions what is called A House, may be built by one day's labour of one man. The simplest species of cloathing, the skins of animals, require somewhat more labour to dress and prepare them for use. They do not, however, require a great deal. Among savages and barbarous nations, a hundredth or little more than a hundredth part of the labour of the whole year, will be sufficient to provide them with such cloathing and lodging as satisfy the greater part of the people. All the other ninety-nine parts are frequently no more than enough to provide them with food.

But when by the improvement and cultivation of land the labour of one family can provide food for two, the labour of half the society becomes sufficient to provide food for the whole. The other half, therefore, or at least the greater part of them, can be employed in providing other things, or in satisfying the other wants and fancies of mankind. Cloathing and lodging, houshold furniture, and what is called Equipage, are the principal objects of the greater part of those wants and fancies. The rich man consumes no more food than his poor neighbour. In quality it may be very different, and to select and prepare it may require more labour and art; but in quantity it is very nearly the same. But compare the spacious palace and great wardrobe of the one, with the hovel and the few rags of the other, and you will be sensible that the difference between their cloathing, lodging, and houshold furniture, is almost as great in quantity as it is in quality. The desire of food is limited in every man by the narrow capacity of the human stomach; but the desire of the conveniencies and ornaments of building, dress, equipage, and houshold furniture, seems to have no limit or certain boundary. Those, therefore, who have the command of more food than they themselves can consume, are always willing to exchange the surplus, or, what is the same thing, the price of it, for gratifications of this other kind. What is over and above satisfying the limited desire, is given for the amusement of those desires which cannot be satisfied, but seem to be altogether endless. The poor, in order to obtain food, exert themselves to gratify those fancies of the rich, and to obtain it more certainly, they vie with one another in the cheapness and perfection of their work. The number of workmen increases with the increasing quantity of food, or with the growing improvement and cultivation of the lands and as the nature of their business admits of the utmost subdivisions of labour, the quantity of materials which they can work up, increases in a much greater proportion than their numbers. Hence arises a demand for every sort of material which human invention can employ, either usefully or ornamentally, in building, dress, equipage, or houshold furniture; for the fossils and minerals contained in the bowels of the earth, the precious metals, and the precious stones.

Food is in this manner, not only the original source of rent, but every other part of the produce of land which afterwards affords rent, derives that part of its value from the improvement of the powers of labour in producing food by means of the improvement and cultivation of land.

Those other parts of the produce of land, however, which afterwards afford rent, do not afford it always. Even in improved and cultivated countries, the demand for them is not always such as to afford a greater price than what is sufficient to pay the labour, and replace, together with its ordinary profits, the stock which must be employed in bringing them to market. Whether it is or is not such, depends upon different circumstances.

Whether a coal-mine, for example, can afford any rent, depends partly upon its fertility, and partly upon its situation.

A mine of any kind may be said to be either fertile or barren, according as the quantity of mineral which can be brought from it by a certain quantity of labour, is greater or less than what can be brought by an equal quantity from the greater part of other mines of the same kind.

Some coal-mines advantageously situated, cannot be wrought on account of their barrenness. The produce does not pay the expence. They can afford neither profit nor rent.

There are some of which the produce is barely sufficient to pay the labour, and replace, together with its ordinary profits, the stock employed in working them. They afford some profit to the undertaker of the work, but no rent to the landlord. They can be wrought advantageously by nobody but the landlord, who being himself undertaker of the work, gets the ordinary profit of the capital which he employs in it. Many coal-mines in Scotland are wrought in this manner, and can be wrought in no other. The landlord will allow nobody else to work them without paying some rent, and nobody can afford to pay any.

Other coal-mines in the same country sufficiently fertile, cannot be wrought on account of their situation. A quantity of mineral sufficient to defray the expence of working, could be brought from the mine by the ordinary, or even less than the ordinary quantity of labour: But in an inland country, thinly inhabited, and without either good roads or water-carriage, this quantity could not be sold.

Coals are a less agreeable fewel than wood: they are said too to be less wholesome. The expence of coals, therefore, at the place where they are consumed, must generally be somewhat less than that of wood.

The price of wood again varies with the state of agriculture, nearly in the same manner, and exactly for the same reason, as the price of cattle. In its rude beginnings the greater part of every country is covered with wood, which is then a mere incumbrance of no value to the landlord, who would gladly give it to any body for the cutting. As agriculture advances, the woods are partly cleared by the progress of tillage, and partly go to decay in consequence of the increased number of cattle. These, though they do not increase in the same proportion as corn, which is altogther the acquisition of human industry, yet multiply under the care and protection of men; who store up in the season of plenty what may maintain them in that of scarcity, who through the whole year furnish them with a greater quantity of food than uncultivated nature provides for them, and who by destroying and extirpating their enemies, secure them in the free enjoyment of all that she provides. Numerous herds of cattle, when allowed to wander through the woods, though they do not destroy the old trees, hinder any young ones from coming up, so that in the course of a century or two the whole forest goes to ruin. The scarcity of wood then raises its price. It affords a good rent, and the landlord sometimes finds that he can scarce employ his best lands more advantageously than in growing barren timber, of which the greatness of the profit often compensates the lateness of the returns. This seems in the present times to be nearly the state of things in several parts of Great Britain, where the profit of planting is found to be equal to that of either corn or pasture. The advantage which the landlord derives from planting, can no-where exceed, at least for any considerable time, the rent which these could afford him; and in an inland country which is highly cultivated, it will frequently not fall much short of this rent Upon the sea-coast of a well-improved country, indeed, if coals can conveniently be had for fewel, it may sometimes be cheaper to bring barren timber for building from less cultivated foreign countries, than to raise it at home. In the new town of Edinburgh, built within these few years, there is not, perhaps, a single stick of Scotch timber.

Whatever may be the price of wood, if that of coals is such that the expence of a coal-fire is nearly equal to that of a wood one, we may be assured, that at that place, and in these circumstances, the price of coals is as high as it can be. It seems to be so in some of the inland parts of England, particularly in Oxfordshire, where it is usual, even in the fires of the common people, to mix coals and wood together, and where the difference in the expence of those two sorts of fewel cannot, therefore, be very great.

Coals, in the coal countries, are every-where much below this highest price. If they were not, they could not bear the expence of a distant carriage, either by land or by water. A small quantity only could be sold, and the coal masters and coal proprietors find it more for their interest to sell a great quantity at a price somewhat above the lowest, than a small quantity at the highest. The most fertile coal-mine too, regulates the price of coals at all the other mines in its neighbourhood. Both the proprietor and the undertaker of the work find, the one that he can get a greater rent, the other that he can get a greater profit, by somewhat underselling all their neighbours. Their neighbours are soon obliged to sell at the same price, though they cannot so well afford it, and though it always diminishes, and sometimes takes away altogether both their rent and their profit. Some works are abandoned altogether; others can afford no rent, and can be wrought only by the proprietor.

The lowest price at which coals can be sold for any considerable time, is, like that of all other commodities, the price which is barely sufficient to replace, together with its ordinary profits, the stock which must be employed in bringing them to market. At a coal-mine for which the landlord can get no rent, but which he must either work himself or let it alone altogether, the price of coals must generally be nearly about this price.

Rent, even where coals afford one, has generally a smaller share in their price than in that of most other parts of the rude produce of land. The rent of an estate above ground, commonly amounts to what is supposed to be a third of the gross produce; and it is generally a rent certain and independent of the occasional variations in the crop. In coal-mines a fifth of the gross produce is a very great rent; a tenth the common rent, and it is seldom a rent certain, but depends upon the occasional variations in the produce. These are so great, that in a country where thirty years purchase is considered as a moderate price for the property for a landed estate, ten years purchase is regarded as a good price for that of a coal-mine.

The value of a coal-mine to the proprietor frequently depends as much upon its situation as upon its fertility. That of a metallic mine depends more upon its fertility, and less upon its situation. The coarse, and still more the precious metals, when separated from the ore, are so valuable that they can generally bear the expence of a very long land, and of the most distant sea carriage. Their market is not confined to the countries in the neighbourhood of the mine, but extends to the whole world. The copper of Japan makes an article of commerce in Europe; the iron of Spain in that of Chili and Peru. The silver of Peru finds its way, not only to Europe, but from Europe to China.

The price of coals in Westmorland or Shropshire can have little effect on their price at Newcastle; and their price in the Lionnois can have none at all. The productions of such distant coal-mines can never be brought into competition with one another. But the productions of the most distant metallic mines frequently may, and in fact commonly are. The price, therefore, of the coarse, and still more that of the precious metals, at the most fertile mines in the world, must necessarily more or less affect their price at every other in it. The price of copper in Japan must have some influence upon its price at the copper mines in Europe. The price of silver in Peru, or the quantity either of labour or of other goods which it will purchase there, must have some influence on its price, not only at the silver mines of Europe, but at those of China. After the discovery of the mines of Peru, the silver mines of Europe were, the greater part of them, abandoned. The value of silver was so much reduced that their produce could no longer pay the expence of working them, or replace, with a profit, the food, cloaths, lodging and other necessaries which were consumed in that operation. This was the case too with the mines of Cuba and St. Domingo, and even with the ancient mines of Peru, after the discovery of those of Potosi.

The price of every metal at every mine, therefore, being regulated in some measure by its price at the most fertile mine in the world that is actually wrought, it can at the greater part of mines do very little more than pay the expence of working, and can seldom afford a very high rent to the landlord. Rent, accordingly, seems at the greater part of mines to have but a small share in the price of the coarse, and a still smaller in that of the precious metals. Labour and profit make up the greater part of both.

A sixth part of the gross produce may be reckoned the average rent of the tin mines of Cornwall, the most fertile that are known in the world, as we are told by the Rev. Mr. Borlace, vice-warden of the stannaries. Some, he says, afford more, and some do not afford so much. A sixth part of the gross produce is the rent too of several very fertile lead mines in Scotland.

In the silver mines of Peru, we are told by Frezier and Ulloa, the proprietor frequently exacts no other acknowledgment from the undertaker of the mine, but that he will grind the ore at his mill, paying him the ordinary multure or price of grinding. Till 1736, indeed, the tax of the king of Spain amounted to one-fifth of the standard silver, which till then might be considered as the real rent of the greater part of the silver mines of Peru, the richest which have been known in the world. If there had been no tax, this fifth would naturally have belonged to the landlord, and many mines might have been wrought which could not then be wrought, because they could not afford this tax. The tax of the duke of Cornwall upon tin is supposed to amount to more than five per cent. or one-twentieth part of the value; and whatever may be his proportion, it would naturally too belong to the proprietor of the mine, if tin was duty free. But if you add one-twentieth to one-sixth, you will find that the whole average rent of the tin mines of Cornwall, was to the whole average rent of the silver mines of Peru, as thirteen to twelve. But the silver mines of Peru are not now able to pay even this low rent, and the tax upon silver was, in 1736, reduced from one-fifth to one-tenth. Even this tax upon silver too gives more temptation to smuggling than the tax of one-twentieth upon tin; and smuggling must be much easier in the precious than in the bulky commodity. The tax of the king of Spain accordingly is said to be very ill paid, and that of the duke of Cornwall very well. Rent, therefore, it is probable, makes a greater part of the price of tin at the most fertile tin mines, than it does of silver at the most fertile silver mines in the world. After replacing the stock employed in working those different mines, together with its ordinary profits, the residue which remains to the proprietor, is greater it seems in the coarse, than in the precious metal.

Neither are the profits of the undertakers of silver mines commonly very great in Peru. The same most respectable and well informed authors acquaint us, that when any person undertakes to work a new mine in Peru, he is universally looked upon as a man destined to bankruptcy and ruin, and is upon that account shunned and avoided by every body. Mining, it seems, is considered there in the same light as here, as a lottery, in which the prizes do not compensate the blanks, though the greatness of some tempts many adventurers to throw away their fortunes in such unprosperous projects.

As the sovereign, however, derives a considerable part of his revenue from the produce of silver mines, the law in Peru gives every possible encouragement to the discovery and working of new ones. Whoever discovers a new mine, is entitled to measure off two hundred and forty-six feet in length, according to what he supposes to be the direction of the vein, and half as much in breadth. He becomes proprietor of this portion of the mine, and can work it without paying any acknowledgment to the landlord. The interest of the duke of Cornwall has given occasion to a regulation nearly of the same kind in that ancient duchy. In waste and uninclosed lands any person who discovers a tin mine, may mark out its limits to a certain extent, which is called bounding a mine. The bounder becomes the real proprietor of the mine, and may either work it himself, or give it in lease to another, without the consent of the owner of the land, to whom, however, a very small acknowledgment must be paid upon working it. In both regulations the sacred rights of private property are sacrificed to the supposed interests of public revenue.

The same encouragement is given in Peru to the discovery and working of new gold mines; and in gold the king's tax amounts only to a twentieth part of the standard metal. It was once a fifth, and afterwards a tenth, as in silver; but it was found that the work could not bear even the lowest of these two taxes. If it is rare, however, say the same authors, Frezier and Ulloa, to find a person who has made his fortune by a silver, it is still much rarer to find one who has done so by a gold mine. This twentieth part seems to be the whole rent which is paid by the greater part of the gold mines in Chili and Peru. Gold too is much more liable to be smuggled than even silver; not only on account of the superior value of the metal in proportion to its bulk, but on account of the peculiar way in which nature produces it. Silver is very seldom found virgin, but, like most other metals, is generally mineralized with some other body, from which it is impossible to separate it in such quantities as will pay for the expence, but by a very laborious and tedious operation, which cannot well be carried on but in work-houses erected for the purpose, and therefore exposed to the inspection of the king's officers. Gold, on the contrary, is almost always found virgin. It is sometimes found in pieces of some bulk; and even when mixed in small and almost insensible particles with sand, earth, and other extraneous bodies, it can be separated from them by a very short and simple operation, which can be carried on in any private house by any body who is possessed of a small quantity of mercury. If the king's tax, therefore, is but ill paid upon silver, it is likely to be much worse paid upon gold; and rent must make a much smaller part of the price of gold, than even of that of silver.

The lowest price at which the precious metals can be sold, or the smallest quantity of other goods for which they can be exchanged during any considerable time, is regulated by the same principles which fix the lowest ordinary price of all other goods. The stock which must commonly be employed, the food, cloaths, and lodging which must commonly be consumed in bringing them from the mine to the market, determine it. It must at least be sufficient to replace that stock, with the ordinary profits.

Their highest price, however, seems not to be necessarily determined by any thing but the actual scarcity or plenty of those metals themselves. It is not determined by that of any other commodity, in the same manner as the price of coals is by that of wood, beyond which no scarcity can ever raise it. Increase the scarcity of gold to a certain degree, and the smallest bit of it may become more precious than a diamond, and exchange for a greater quantity of other goods.

The demand for those metals arises partly from their utility, and partly from their beauty. If you except iron, they are more useful, perhaps, than any other metal. As they are less liable to rust and impurity, they can more easily be kept clean; and the utensils either of the table or the kitchen are often upon that account more agreeable when made of them. A silver boiler is more cleanly than a lead, copper, or tin one; and the same quality would render a gold boiler still better than a silver one. Their principal merit, however, arises from their beauty, which renders them peculiarly fit for the ornaments of dress and furniture. No paint or dye can give so splendid a colour as gilding. The merit of their beauty is greatly enhanced by their scarcity. With the greater part of rich people, the chief enjoyment of riches consists in the parade of riches, which in their eye is never so complete as when they appear to possess those decisive marks of opulence which nobody can possess but themselves. In their eyes the merit of an object which is in any degree either useful or beautiful, is greatly enhanced by its scarcity, or by the great labour which it requires to collect any considerable quantity of it, a labour which nobody can afford to pay but themselves. Such objects they are willing to purchase at a higher price than things much more beautiful and useful, but more common. These qualities of utility, beauty, and scarcity, are the original foundation of the high price of those metals, or of the great quantity of other goods for which they can everywhere be exchanged. This value was antecedent to and independent of their being employed as coin, and was the quality which fitted them for that employment. That employment, however, by occasioning a new demand, and by diminishing the quantity which could be employed in any other way, may have afterwards contributed to keep up or increase their value.

The demand for the precious stones arises altogether from their beauty. They are of no use, but as ornaments; and the merit of their beauty is greatly enhanced by their scarcity, or by the difficulty and expence of getting them from the mine. Wages and profit accordingly make up, upon most occasions, almost the whole of their high price. Rent comes in but for a very small share; frequently for no share; and the most fertile mines only afford any considerable rent. When Tavernier, a jeweller, visited the diamond mines of Golconda and Visiapour, he was informed that the sovereign of the country, for whose benefit they were wrought, had ordered all of them to be shut up, except those which yielded the largest and finest stones. The others, it seems, were to the proprietor not worth the working.

As the price both of the precious metals and of the precious stones is regulated all over the world by their price at the most fertile mine in it, the rent which a mine of either can afford to its proprietor is in proportion, not to its absolute, but to what may be called its relative fertility, or to its superiority over other mines of the same kind. If new mines were discovered as much superior to those of Potosi as they were superior to those of Europe, the value of silver might be so much degraded as to render even the mines of Potosi not worth the working. Before the discovery of the Spanish West Indies, the most fertile mines in Europe may have afforded as great a rent to their proprietor as the richest mines in Peru do at present. Though the quantity of silver was much less, it might have exchanged for an equal quantity of other goods, and the proprietor's share might have enabled him to purchase or command an equal quantity either of labour or of commodities. The value both of the produce and of the rent, the real revenue which they afforded both to the public and to the proprietor, might have been the same.

The most abundant mines either of the precious metals or of the precious stones could add little to the wealth of the world. A produce of which the value is principally derived from its scarcity, is necessarily degraded by its abundance. A service of plate, and the other frivolous ornaments of dress and furniture, could be purchased for a smaller quantity of labour, or for a smaller quantity of commodities; and in this would consist the sole advantage which the world could derive from that abundance.

It is otherwise in estates above ground. The value both of their produce and of their rent is in proportion to their absolute, and not to their relative fertility. The land which produces a certain quantity of foods, cloaths, and lodging, can always feed, cloath, and lodge a certain number of people; and whatever may be the proportion of the landlord, it will always give him a proportionable command of the labour of those people, and of the commodities with which that labour can supply him. The value of the most barren lands is not diminished by the neighbourhood of the most fertile. On the contrary, it is generally increased by it. The great number of people maintained by the fertile lands afford a market to many parts of the produce of the barren, which they could never have found among those whom their own produce could maintain.

Whatever increases the fertility of land in producing food, increases not only the value of the lands upon which the improvement is bestowed, but contributes likewise to increase that of many other lands, by creating a new demand for their produce. That abundance of food, of which, in consequence of the improvement of land, many people have the disposal beyond what they themselves can consume, is the great cause of the demand both for the precious metals and the precious stones, as well as for every other conveniency and ornament of dress, lodging, household furniture, and equipage. Food not only constitutes the principal part of the riches of the world, but it is the abundance of food which gives the principal part of their value to many other sorts of riches. The poor inhabitants of Cuba and St. Domingo, when they were first discovered by the Spaniards, used to wear little bits of gold as ornaments in their hair and other parts of their dress. They seemed to value them as we would do any little pebbles of somewhat more than ordinary beauty, and to consider them as just worth the picking up, but not worth the refusing to anybody who asked them. They gave them to their new guests at the first request, without seeming to think that they had made them any very valuable present. They were astonished to observe the rage of the Spaniards to obtain them; and had no notion that there could any-where be a country in which many people had the disposal of so great a superfluity of food, so scanty always among themselves, that for a very small quantity of those glittering baubles they would willingly give as much as might maintain a whole family for many years. Could they have been made to understand this, the passion of the Spaniards would not have surprised them.

PART III

Of the Variations in the Proportion between the respective Values of that Sort of Produce which always affords Rent, and of that which sometimes does and sometimes does not afford Rent

The increasing abundance of food, in consequence of increasing improvement and cultivation, must necessarily increase the demand for every part of the produce of land which is not food, and which can be applied either to use or to ornament. In the whole progress of improvement, it might therefore be expected, there should be only one variation in the comparative values of those two different sorts of produce. The value of that sort which sometimes does and sometimes does not afford rent, should constantly rise in proportion to that which always affords some rent. As art and industry advance, the materials of cloathing and lodging, the useful fossils and minerals of the earth, the precious metals and the precious stones should gradually come to be more and more in demand, should gradually exchange for a greater and a greater quantity of food, or in other words, should gradually become dearer and dearer. This accordingly has been the case with most of these things upon most occasions, and would have been the case with all of them upon all occasions, if particular accidents had not upon some occasions increased the supply of some of them in a still greater proportion than the demand.

The value of a free-stone quarry, for example, will necessarily increase with the increasing improvement and population of the country round about it; especially if it should be the only one in the neighbourhood. But the value of a silver mine, even though there should not be another within a thousand miles of it, will not necessarily increase with the improvement of the country in which it is situated. The market for the produce of a free-stone quarry can seldom extend more than a few miles round about it, and the demand must generally be in proportion to the improvement and population of that small district. But the market for the produce of a silver mine may extend over the whole known world. Unless the world in general, therefore, be advancing in improvement and population, the demand for silver might not be at all increased by the improvement even of a large country in the neighbourhood of the mine. Even though the world in general were improving, yet, if, in the course of its improvement, new mines should be discovered, much more fertile than any which had been known before, though the demand for silver would necessarily increase, yet the supply might increase in so much a greater proportion, that the real price of that metal might gradually fall; that is, any given quantity, a pound weight of it, for example, might gradually purchase or command a smaller and a smaller quantity of labour, or exchange for a smaller and a smaller quantity of corn, the principal part of the subsistence of the labourer.

The great market for silver is the commercial and civilized part of the world.

If by the general progress of improvement the demand of this market should increase, while at the same time the supply did not increase in the same proportion, the value of silver would gradually rise in proportion to that of corn. Any given quantity of silver would exchange for a greater and a greater quantity of corn; or, in other words, the average money price of corn would gradually become cheaper and cheaper.

If, on the contrary, the supply by some accident should increase for many years together in a greater proportion than the demand, that metal would gradually become cheaper and cheaper; or, in other words, the average money price of corn would, in spite of all improvements, gradually become dearer and dearer.

But if, on the other hand, the supply of the metal should increase nearly in the same proportion as the demand, it would continue to purchase or exchange for nearly the same quantity of corn, and the average money price of corn would, in spite of all improvements, continue very nearly the same.

These three seem to exhaust all the possible combinations of events which can happen in the progress of improvement; and during the course of the four centuries preceding the present, if we may judge by what has happened both in

France and Great Britain, each of those three different combinations seem to have taken place in the European market, and nearly in the same order too in which I have here set them down.

DIFFERENT EFFECTS OF THE PROGRESS OF IMPROVEMENT UPON THREE DIFFERENT SORTS OF RUDE PRODUCE

These different sorts of rude produce may be divided into three classes. The first comprehends those which it is scarce in the power of human industry to multiply at all. The second, those which it can multiply in proportion to the demand. The third, those in which the efficacy of industry is either limited or uncertain. In the progress of wealth and improvement, the real price of the first may rise to any degree of extravagance, and seems not to be limited by any certain boundary. That of the second, though it may rise greatly, has, however, a certain boundary beyond which it cannot well pass for any considerable time together. That of the third, though its natural tendency is to rise in the progress of improvement, yet in the same degree of improvement it may sometimes happen even to fall, sometimes to continue the same, and sometimes to rise more or less, according as different accidents render the efforts of human industry, in multiplying this sort of rude produce, more or less successful.

FIRST SORT

The first sort of rude produce of which the price rises in the progress of improvement, is that which it is scarce in the power of human industry to multiply at all. It consists in those things which nature produces only in certain quantities, and which being of a very perishable nature, it is impossible to accumulate together the produce of many different seasons. Such are the greater part of rare and singular birds and fishes, many different sorts of game, almost all wild-fowl, all birds of passage in particular, as well as many other things. When wealth and the luxury which accompanies it increase, the demand for those is likely to increase with them, and no effort of human industry may be able to increase the supply much beyond what it was before this increase of the demand. The quantity of such commodities, therefore, remaining the same, or nearly the same, while the competition to purchase them is continually increasing, their price may rise to any degree of extravagance, and seems not to be limited by any certain boundary. If woodcocks should become so fashionable as to sell for twenty guineas a-piece, no effort of human industry could increase the number of those brought to market, much beyond what it is at present. The high price paid by the Romans, in the time of their greatest grandeur, for rare birds and fishes, may in this manner easily be accounted for. These prices were not the effects of the low value of silver in those times, but of the high value of such rarities and curiosities as human industry could not multiply at pleasure. The real value of silver was higher at Rome, for some time before and after the fall of the republic, than it is through the great part of Europe at present. Three sestertii, equal to about sixpence sterling, was the price which the republic paid for the modius or peck of the tithe wheat of Sicily. This price, however, was probably below the average market price, the obligation to deliver their wheat at this rate being considered as a tax upon the Sicilian farmers. When the Romans, therefore, had occasion to order more corn than the tithe of wheat amounted to, they were bound by capitulation to pay for the surplus at the rate of four sestertii, or eight-pence sterling, the peck; and this had probably been reckoned the moderate and reasonable, that is, the ordinary or average contract price of those times; it is equal to about one-and-twenty shillings the quarter. Eight-and-twenty shillings the quarter was, before the late years of scarcity, the ordinary contract price of English wheat, which in quality is inferior to the Sicilian, and generally sells for a lower price in the European market. The value of silver, therefore, in those ancient times, must have been to its value in the present, as three to four inversely; that is, three ounces of silver would then have purchased the same quantity of labour and commodities which four ounces will do at present. When we read in Pliny, therefore, that Seius bought a white nightingale, as a present for the empress Agrippina, at the price of six thousand sestertii, equal to about fifty pounds of our present money; and that Asinius Celer purchased a surmullet at the price of eight thousand sestertii, equal to about sixty-six pounds thirteen shillings and fourpence of our present money; the extravagance of those prices, how much soever it may surprise us, is apt, nothwithstanding, to appear to us about one-third less than it really was. Their real price, the quantity of labour and subsistence which was given away for them, was about one-third more than their nominal price is apt to express to us in the present times. Seius gave for the nightingale the command of a quantity of labour and subsistence equal to what 66*l.* 13*s.* 4*d.* would purchase in the present times, and Asinius Celer gave for the surmullet the command of a quantity equal to what 88*l.* 17*s.* 9*d.* ⅓ would purchase. What occasioned the extravagance of those high prices was, not so much the abundance of silver, as the abundance of labour and subsistence, of which those Romans had the disposal, beyond what was necessary for their own use. The quantity of silver, of which they had the disposal was a good deal less than what the command of the same quantity of labour and subsistence would have procured to them in the present times.

SECOND SORT

The second sort of rude produce of which the price rises in the progress of improvement, is that which human industry can multiply in proportion to the demand. It consists in those useful plants and animals, which, in uncultivated countries, nature produces with such profuse abundance, that they are of little or no value, and which, as cultivation advances, are therefore forced to give place to some more profitable produce. During a long period in the progress of improvement, the quantity of these is continually diminishing, while at the same time the demand for them is continually increasing. Their real value, therefore, the real quantity of labour which they will purchase or command, gradually rises, till at last it gets so high as to render them as profitable a produce as any thing else which human industry can raise upon the most fertile and best cultivated land. When it has got so high it cannot well go higher. If it did, more land and more industry would soon be employed to increase their quantity.

When the price of cattle, for example, rises so high that it is as profitable to cultivate land in order to raise food for them, as in order to raise food for man, it cannot well go higher. If it did, more corn land would soon be turned into pasture. The extension of tillage, by diminishing the quantity of wild pasture, diminishes the quantity of butcher's-meat which the country naturally produces without labour or cultivation, and by increasing the number of those who have either corn, or, what comes to the same thing, the price of corn, to give in exchange for it, increases the demand. The price of butcher's-meat, therefore, and consequently of cattle, must gradually rise till it gets so high, that it becomes as profitable to employ the most fertile and best cultivated lands in raising food for them as in raising corn. But it must always be late in the progress of improvement before tillage can be so far extended as to raise the price of cattle to this height; and till it has got to this height, if the country is advancing at all, their price must be continually rising. There are, perhaps, some parts of Europe in which the price of cattle has not yet got to this height. It had not got to this height in any part of Scotland before the union. Had the Scotch cattle been always confined to the market of Scotland, in a country in which the quantity of land, which can be applied to no other purpose but the feeding of cattle, is so great in proportion to what can be applied to other purposes, it is scarce possible, perhaps, that their price could ever have risen so high as to render it profitable to cultivate land for the sake of feeding them. In England, the price of cattle, it has already been observed, seems, in the neighbourhood of London, to have got to this height about the beginning of the last century; but it was much later probably before it got to it through the greater part of the remoter counties; in some of which, perhaps, it may scarce yet have got to it. Of all the different substances, however, which compose this second sort of rude produce, cattle is, perhaps, that of which the price, in the progress of improvement, first rises to this height.

Till the price of cattle, indeed, has got to this height, it seems scarce possible that the greater part, even of those lands which are capable of the highest cultivation, can be completely cultivated. In all farms too distant from any town to carry manure from it, that is, in the far greater part of those of every extensive country, the quantity of well-cultivated land must be in proportion to the quantity of manure which the farm itself produces; and this again must be in proportion to the stock of cattle which are maintained upon it. The land is manured either by pasturing the cattle upon it, or by feeding them in the stable, and from thence carrying out their dung to it. But unless the price of the cattle be sufficient to pay both the rent and profit of cultivated land, the farmer cannot afford to pasture them upon it; and he can still less afford to feed them in the stable. It is with the produce of improved and cultivated land only, that cattle can be fed in the stable; because to collect the scanty and scattered produce of waste and unimproved lands would require too much labour and be too expensive. If the price of the cattle, therefore, is not sufficient to pay for the produce of improved and cultivated land, when they are allowed to pasture it, that price will be still less sufficient to pay for that produce when it must be collected with a good deal of additional labour, and brought into the stable to them. In these circumstances, therefore, no more cattle can, with profit, be fed in the stable than what are necessary for tillage. But these can never afford manure enough for keeping constantly in good condition, all the lands which they are capable of cultivating. What they afford being insufficient for the whole farm, will naturally be reserved for the lands to which it can be most advantageously or conveniently applied; the most fertile, or those, perhaps, in the neighbourhood of the farm-yard. These, therefore, will be kept constantly in good condition and fit for tillage. The rest will, the greater part of them, be allowed to lie waste, producing scarce any thing but some miserable pasture, just sufficient to keep alive a few straggling, half-starved cattle; the farm, though much under-stocked in proportion to what would be necessary for its complete cultivation, being very frequently overstocked in proportion to its actual produce. A portion of this waste land, however, after having been pastured in this wretched manner for six or seven years together, may be ploughed up, when it will yield, perhaps, a poor crop or two of bad oats, or of some other coarse grain, and then, being entirely exhausted, it must be rested and pastured again as before, and another portion ploughed up to be in the same manner exhausted and rested again in its turn. Such accordingly was the general system of management all over the low country of Scotland before the union. The lands which were kept constantly well manured and in good condition, seldom exceeded a third or a fourth part of the whole farm, and sometimes did not amount to a fifth or a sixth part of it. The rest were never manured, but a certain portion of them was in its turn, notwithstanding, regularly cultivated and exhausted. Under this system of management, it is evident, even that part of the lands of Scotland which is capable of good cultivation, could produce but little in comparison of what it may be capable of producing. But how disadvantageous soever this system may appear, yet before the union the low price of cattle seems to have rendered it almost unavoidable. If, notwithstanding a great rise in their price, it still continues to prevail through a considerable part of the country, it is owing, in many places, no doubt, to ignorance and attachment to old customs, but in most places to the unavoidable obstructions which the natural course of things opposes to the immediate or speedy establishment of a better system: first, to the poverty of the tenants, to their not having yet had time to acquire a stock of cattle sufficient to cultivate their lands more completely, the same rise of price which would render it advantageous for them to maintain a greater stock, rendering it more difficult for them to acquire it; and, secondly, to their not having yet had time to put their lands in condition to maintain this greater stock properly, supposing they were capable of acquiring it. The increase of stock and the improvement of land are two events which must go hand in hand, and of which the one can no-where much out-run the other. Without some increase of stock, there can be scarce any improvement of land, but there can be no considerable increase of stock but in consequence of a considerable improvement of land; because otherwise the land could not maintain it.

These natural obstructions to the establishment of a better system, cannot be removed but by a long course of frugality and industry; and half a century or a century more, perhaps, must pass away before the old system, which is wearing out gradually, can be completely abolished through all the different parts of the country. Of all the commercial advantages, however, which Scotland has derived from the union with England, this rise in the price of cattle is, perhaps, the greatest. It has not only raised the value of all highland estates, but it has, perhaps, been the principal cause of the improvement of the low country.

In all new colonies the great quantity of waste land, which can for many years be applied to no other purpose but the feeding of cattle, soon renders them extremely abundant, and in every thing great cheapness is the necessary consequence of great abundance. Though all the cattle of the European colonies in America were originally carried from Europe, they soon multiplied so much there, and became of so little value, that even horses were allowed to run wild in the woods without any owner thinking it worth while to claim them. It must be a long time after the first establishment of such colonies, before it can become profitable to feed cattle upon the produce of cultivated land. The same causes, therefore, the want of manure, and the disproportion between the stock employed in cultivation, and the land which it is destined to cultivate, are likely to introduce there a system of husbandry not unlike that which still continues to take place in so many parts of Scotland. Mr. Kalm, the Swedish traveller, when he gives an account of the husbandry of some of the English colonies in North America, as he found it in 1749, observes, accordingly, that he can with difficulty discover there the character of the English nation, so well skilled in all the different branches of agriculture. They make scarce any manure for their corn fields, he says; but when one piece of ground has been exhausted by continual cropping, they clear and cultivate another piece of fresh land; and when that is exhausted, proceed to a third. Their cattle are allowed to wander through the woods and other uncultivated grounds, where they are half-starved; having long ago extirpated almost all the annual grasses by cropping them too early in the spring, before they had time to form their flowers, or to shed their seeds. The annual grasses were, it seems, the best natural grasses in that part of North America; and when the Europeans first settled there, they used to grow very thick, and to rise three or four feet high. A piece of ground which, when he wrote, could not maintain one cow, would in former times, he was assured, have maintained four, each of which would have given four times the quantity of milk that one was capable of giving. The poorness of the pasture had, in his opinion, occasioned the degradation of their cattle, which degenerated sensibly from one generation to another. They were probably not unlike that stunted breed which was common all over Scotland thirty or forty years ago, and which is now so much mended through the greater part of the low country, not so much by a change of the breed, though that expedient has been employed in some places, as by a more plentiful method of feeding them.

Though it is late, therefore, in the progress of improvement before cattle can bring such a price as to render it profitable to cultivate land for the sake of feeding them; yet of all the different parts which compose this second sort of rude produce, they are perhaps the first which bring this price; because till they bring it, it seems impossible that improvement can be brought near even to that degree of perfection to which it has arrived in many parts of Europe.

As cattle are among the first, so perhaps venison is among the last parts of this sort of rude produce which bring this price. The price of venison in Great Britain, how extravagant soever it may appear, is not near sufficient to compensate the expence of a deer park, as is well known to all those who have had any experience in the feeding of deer. If it was otherwise, the feeding of deer would soon become an article of common farming; in the same manner as the feeding of those small birds called Turdi was among the ancient Romans. Varro and Columella assure us that it was a most profitable article. The fattening of ortolans, birds of passage which arrive lean in the country, is said to be so in some parts of France. If venison continues in fashion, and the wealth and luxury of Great Britain increase as they have done for some time past, its price may very probably rise still higher than it is at present.

Between that period in the progress of improvement which brings to its height the price of so necessary an article as cattle, and that which brings to it the price of such a superfluity as venison, there is a very long interval, in the course of which many other sorts of rude produce gradually arrive at their highest price, some sooner and some later, according to different circumstances.

Thus in every form the offals of the barn and stables will maintain a certain number of poultry. These, as they are fed with what would otherwise be lost, are a mere save-all; and as they cost the farmer scarce any thing, so he can afford to sell them for very little. Almost all that he gets is pure gain, and their price can scarce be so low as to discourage him from feeding this number. But in countries ill cultivated, and, therefore, but thinly inhabited, the poultry, which are thus raised without expence, are often fully sufficient to supply the whole demand. In this state of things, therefore, they are often as cheap as butcher's-meat, or any other sort of animal food. But the whole quantity of poultry, which the farm in this manner produces without expence, must always be much smaller than the whole quantity of butcher's-meat which is reared upon it; and in times of wealth and luxury what is rare, with only nearly equal merit, is always preferred to what is common. As wealth and luxury increase, therefore, in consequence of improvement and cultivation, the price of poultry gradually rises above that of butcher's-meat, till at last it gets so high that it becomes profitable to cultivate land for the sake of feeding them. When it has got to this height, it cannot well go higher. If it did, more land would soon be turned to this purpose. In several provinces of France, the feeding of poultry is considered as a very important article in rural economy, and sufficiently profitable to encourage the farmer to raise a considerable quantity of Indian corn and buck-wheat for this purpose. A middling farmer will there sometimes have four hundred fowls in his yard. The feeding of poultry seems scarce yet to be generally considered as a matter of so much importance in England. They are certainly, however, dearer in England than in France, as England receives considerable supplies from France. In the progress of improvement, the period at which every particular sort of animal food is dearest, must naturally be that which immediately precedes the general practice of cultivating land for the sake of raising it. For some time before this practice becomes general, the scarcity must necessarily raise the price. After it has become general, new methods of feeding are commonly fallen upon, which enable the farmer to raise upon the same quantity of ground a much greater quantity of that particular sort of animal food. The plenty not only obliges him to sell cheaper, but in consequence of these improvements he can afford to sell cheaper; for if he could not afford it, the plenty would not be of long continuance. It has been probably in this manner that the introduction of clover, turnips, carrots, cabbages, &c., has contributed to sink the common price of butcher's-meat in the London market somewhat below what it was about the beginning of the last century.

The hog, that finds his food among ordure, and greedily devours many things rejected by every other useful animal, is, like poultry, originally kept as a save-all. As long as the number of such animals, which can thus be reared at little or no expence, is fully sufficient to supply the demand, this sort of butcher's-meat comes to market at a much lower price than any other. But when the demand rises beyond what this quantity can supply, when it becomes necessary to raise food on purpose for feeding and fattening hogs, in the same manner as for feeding and fattening other cattle, the price necessarily rises, and becomes proportionably either higher or lower than that of other butcher's-meat, according as the nature of the country, and the state of its agriculture, happen to render the feeding of hogs more or less expensive than that of other cattle. In France, according to Mr. Buffon, the price of pork is nearly equal to that of beef. In most parts of Great Britain it is at present somewhat higher.

The great rise in the price of both hogs and poultry has in Great Britain been frequently imputed to the diminution of the number of cottagers and other small occupiers of land; an event which has in every part of Europe been the immediate forerunner of improvement and better cultivation, but which at the same time may have contributed to raise the price of those articles, both somewhat sooner and somewhat faster than it would otherwise have risen. As the poorest family can often maintain a cat or a dog, without any expence, so the poorest occupiers of land can commonly maintain a few poultry, or a sow and a few pigs, at very little. The little offals of their own table, their whey, skimmed milk and butter-milk, supply those animals with a part of their food, and they find the rest in the neighbouring fields without doing any sensible damage to any body. By diminishing the number of those small occupiers, therefore, the quantity of this sort of provisions which is thus produced at little or no expence, must certainly have been a good deal diminished, and their price must consequently have been raised both sooner and faster than it would otherwise have risen. Sooner or later, however, in the progress of improvement, it must at any rate have risen to the utmost height to which it is capable of rising; or to the price which pays the labour and expence of cultivating the land which furnishes them with food as well as these are paid upon the greater part of other cultivated land.

The business of the dairy, like the feeding of hogs and poultry, is originally carried on as a save-all. The cattle necessarily kept upon the farm, produce more milk than either the rearing of their own young, or the consumption of the farmer's family requires; and they produce most at one particular season. But of all the productions of land, milk is perhaps the most perishable. In the warm season, when it is most abundant, it will scarce keep four-and-twenty hours. The farmer, by making it into fresh butter, stores a small part of it for a week: by making it into salt butter, for a year: and by making it into cheese, he stores a much greater part of it for several years. Part of all these is reserved for the use of his own family. The rest goes to market, in order to find the best price which is to be had, and which can scarce be so low as to discourage him from sending thither whatever is over and above the use of his own family. If it is very low, indeed, he will be likely to manage his dairy in a very slovenly and dirty manner, and will scarce perhaps think it worth while to have a particular room or building on purpose for it, but will suffer the business to be carried on amidst the smoke, filth, and nastiness of his own kitchen; as was the case of almost all the farmers dairies in Scotland thirty or forty years ago, and as is the case of many of them still. The same causes which gradually raise the price of butcher's-meat, the increase of the demand, and, in consequence of the improvement of the country, the diminution of the quantity which can be fed at little or no expence, raise, in the same manner, that of the produce of the dairy, of which the price naturally connects with that of butcher's-meat, or with the expence of feeding cattle. The increase of price pays for more labour, care, and cleanliness. The dairy becomes more worthy of the farmer's attention, and the quality of its produce gradually improves. The price at last gets so high that it becomes worth while to employ some of the most fertile and best cultivated lands in feeding cattle merely for the purpose of the dairy; and when it has got to this height, it cannot well go higher. If it did, more land would soon be turned to this purpose. It seems to have got to this height through the greater part of England, where much good land is commonly employed in this manner. If you except the neighbourhood of a few considerable towns, it seems not yet to have got to this height anywhere in Scotland, where common farmers seldom employ much good land in raising food for cattle merely for the purpose of the dairy. The price of the produce, though it has risen very considerably within these few years, is probably still too low to admit of it. The inferiority of the quality, indeed, compared with that of the produce of English dairies, is fully equal to that of the price. But this inferiority of quality is, perhaps, rather the effect of this lowness of price than the cause of it. Though the quality was much better, the greater part of what is brought to market could not, I apprehend, in the present circumstances of the country, be disposed of at a much better price; and the present price, it is probable, would not pay the expence of the land and labour necessary for producing a much better quality. Through the greater part of England, notwithstanding the superiority of price, the dairy is not reckoned a more profitable employment of land than the raising of corn, or the fattening of cattle, the two great objects of agriculture. Through the greater part of Scotland, therefore, it cannot yet be even so profitable.

The lands of no country, it is evident, can ever be completely cultivated and improved, till once the price of every produce, which human industry is obliged to raise upon them, has got so high as to pay for the expence of complete improvement and cultivation. In order to do this, the price of each particular produce must be sufficient, first, to pay the rent of good corn land, as it is that which regulates the rent of the greater part of other cultivated land; and secondly, to pay the labour and expence of the farmer as well as they are commonly paid upon good corn-land; or, in other words, to replace with the ordinary profits the stock which he employs about it. This rise in the price of each particular produce, must evidently be previous to the improvement and cultivation of the land which is destined for raising it. Gain is the end of all improvement, and nothing could deserve that name of which loss was to be the necessary consequence. But loss must be the necessary consequence of improving land for the sake of a produce of which the price could never bring back the expence. If the complete improvement and cultivation of the country be, as it most certainly is, the greatest of all public advantages, this rise in the price of all those different sorts of rude produce, instead of being considered as a public calamity, ought to be regarded as the necessary forerunner and attendant of the greatest of all public advantages.

This rise too in the nominal or money-price of all those different sorts of rude produce has been the effect, not of any degradation in the value of silver, but of a rise in their real price. They have become worth, not only a greater quantity of silver, but a greater quantity of labour and subsistence than before. As it costs a greater quantity of labour and subsistence to bring them to market, so when they are brought thither, they represent or are equivalent to a greater quantity.

THIRD SORT

The third and last sort of rude produce, of which the price naturally rises in the progress of improvement, is that in which the efficacy of human industry, in augmenting the quantity, is either limited or uncertain. Though the real price of this sort of rude produce, therefore, naturally tends to rise in the progress of improvement, yet, according as different accidents happen to render the efforts of human industry more or less successful in augmenting the quantity, it may happen sometimes even to fall, sometimes to continue the same in very different periods of improvement, and sometimes to rise more or less in the same period.

There are some sorts of rude produce which nature has rendered a kind of appendages to other sorts; so that the quantity of the one which any country can afford, is necessarily limited by that of the other. The quantity of wool or of raw hides, for example, which any country can afford, is necessarily limited by the number of great and small cattle that are kept in it. The state of its improvement, and the nature of its agriculture, again necessarily determine this number.

The same causes, which, in the progress of improvement, gradually raise the price of butcher's-meat, should have the same effect, it may be thought, upon the prices of wool and raw hides, and raise them too nearly in the same proportion. It probably would be so, if in the rude beginnings of improvement the market for the latter commodities was confined within as narrow bounds as that for the former. But the extent of their respective markets is commonly extremely different.

The market for butcher's-meat is almost every-where confined to the country which produces it. Ireland, and some part of British America indeed, carry on a considerable trade in salt provisions; but they are, I believe, the only countries in the commercial world which do so, or which export to other countries any considerable part of their butcher's-meat.

The market for wool and raw hides, on the contrary, is in the rude beginnings of improvement very seldom confined to the country which produces them. They can easily be transported to distant countries, wool without any preparation, and raw hides with very little: and as they are the materials of many manufactures, the industry of other countries may occasion a demand for them, though that of the country which produces them might not occasion any.

In countries ill cultivated, and therefore but thinly inhabited, the price of the wool and the hide bears always a much greater proportion to that of the whole beast, than in countries where, improvement and population being further advanced, there is more demand for butcher's-meat. Mr. Hume observes, that in the Saxon times, the fleece was estimated at two-fifths of the value of the whole sheep, and that this was much above the proportion of its present estimation. In some provinces of Spain, I have been assured, the sheep is frequently killed merely for the sake of the fleece and the tallow. The carcase is often left to rot upon the ground, or to be devoured by beasts and birds of prey. If this sometimes happens even in Spain, it happens almost constantly in Chili, at Buenos Ayres, and in many other parts of Spanish America, where the horned cattle are almost constantly killed merely for the sake of the hide and the tallow. This too used to happen almost constantly in Hispaniola, while it was infested by the Buccaneers, and before the settlement, improvement, and populousness of the French plantations (which now extend round the coast of almost the whole western half of the island) had given some value to the cattle of the Spaniards, who still continue to possess, not only the eastern part of the coast, but the whole inland and mountainous part of the country.

Though in the progress of improvement and population, the price of the whole beast necessarily rises, yet the price of the carcase is likely to be much more affected by this rise than that of the wool and the hide. The market for the carcase, being in the rude state of society confined always to the country which produces it, must necessarily be extended in proportion to the improvement and population of that country. But the market for the wool and the hides even of a barbarous country often extending to the whole commercial world, it can very seldom be enlarged in the same proportion. The state of the whole commercial world can seldom be much affected by the improvement of any particular country; and the market for such commodities may remain the same, or very nearly the same, after such improvements, as before. It should, however, in the natural course of things rather upon the whole be somewhat extended in consequence of them. If the manufactures, especially, of which those commodities are the materials, should ever come to flourish in the country, the market, though it might not be much enlarged, would at least be brought much nearer to the place of growth than before; and the price of those materials might at least be increased by what had usually been the expence of transporting them to distant countries. Though it might not rise therefore in the same proportion as that of butcher's-meat, it ought naturally to rise somewhat, and it ought certainly not to fall.

In England, however, notwithstanding the flourishing state of its woollen manufacture, the price of English wool has fallen very considerably since the time of Edward III. There are many authentic records which demonstrate that during the reign of that prince (towards the middle of the fourteenth century, or about 1339) what was reckoned the moderate and reasonable price of the tod or twenty-eight pounds of English wool was not less than ten shillings of the money of those times, containing, at the rate of twenty-pence the ounce, six ounces of silver Tower-weight, equal to about thirty shillings of our present money. In the present times, one-and-twenty shillings the tod may be reckoned a good price for very good English wool. The money-price of wool, therefore, in the time of Edward III, was to its money-price in the present times as ten to seven. The superiority of its real price was still greater. At the rate of six shillings and eight-pence the quarter, ten shillings was in those ancient times the price of twelve bushels of wheat. At the rate of twenty-eight shillings the quarter, one-and-twenty shillings is in the present time the price of six bushels only. The proportion between the real prices of ancient and modern times, therefore, is as twelve to six, or as two to one. In those ancient times a tod of wool would have purchased twice the quantity of subsistence which it will purchase at present; and consequently twice the quantity of labour, if the real recompence of labour had been the same in both periods.

This degradation both in the real and nominal value of wool, could never have happened in consequence of the natural course of things. It has accordingly been the effect of violence and artifice: First, of the absolute prohibition of exporting wool from England; Secondly, of the permission of importing it from Spain duty free; Thirdly, of the prohibition of exporting it from Ireland to any other country but England. In consequence of these regulations, the market for English wool, instead of being somewhat extended in consequence of the improvement of England, has been confined to the home market, where the wool of several other countries is allowed to come into competition with it, and where that of Ireland is forced into competition with it. As the woollen manufactures too of Ireland are fully as much discouraged as is consistent with justice and fair dealing, the Irish can work up but a small part of their own wool at home, and are, therefore, obliged to send a greater proportion of it to Great Britain, the only market they are allowed.

I have not been able to find any such authentic records concerning the price of raw hides in ancient times. Wool was commonly paid as a subsidy to the king, and its valuation in that subsidy ascertains, at least in some degree, what was its ordinary price. But this seems not to have been the case with raw hides. Fleetwood, however, from an account in 1425, between the prior of Burcester Oxford and one of his canons, gives us their price, at least as it was stated, upon that particular occasion; viz. five ox hides at twelve shillings; five cow hides at seven shillings and three pence; thirty-six sheep skins of two years old at nine shillings; sixteen calves skins at two shillings. In 1425, twelve shillings contained about the same squantity of silver as four-and-twenty shillings of our present money. An ox hide, therefore, was in this account valued at the same quantity of silver at 4s. 4-5ths of our present money. Its nominal price was a good deal lower than at present. But at the rate of six shillings and eight-pence the quarter, twelve shillings would in those times have purchased fourteen bushels and four-fifths of a bushel of wheat, which, at three and six-pence the bushel, would in the present times cost 51*s.* 4*d.* An ox hide, therefore, would in those times have purchased as much corn as ten shillings and three-pence would purchase at present. Its real value was equal to ten shillings and three-pence of our present money. In those ancient times, when the cattle were half starved during the greater part of the winter, we cannot suppose that they were of a very large size. An ox hide which weighs four stone of sixteen pounds averdupois, is not in the present times reckoned a bad one; and in those ancient times would probably have been reckoned a very good one. But at half a crown the stone, which at this moment (February 1773) I understand to be the common price, such a hide would at present cost only ten shillings. Though its nominal price, therefore, is higher in the present than it was in those ancient times, its real price, the real quantity of subsistence which it will purchase or command, is rather somewhat lower. The price of cow hides, as stated in the above account, is nearly in the common proportion to that of ox hides. That of sheep skins is a good deal above it. They had probably been sold with the wool. That of calves skins, on the contrary, is greatly below it. In countries where the price of cattle is very low, the calves, which are not intended to be reared in order to keep up the stock, are generally killed very young; as was the case in Scotland twenty or thirty years ago. It saves the milk, which their price would not pay for. Their skins, therefore, are commonly good for little.

The price of raw hides is a good deal lower at present than it was a few years ago; owing probably to the taking off the duty upon seal skins, and to the allowing, for a limited time, the importation of raw hides from Ireland and from the plantations duty free, which was done in 1769. Take the whole of the present century at an average, their real price has probably been somewhat higher than it was in those ancient times. The nature of the commodity renders it not quite so proper for being transported to distant markets as wool. It suffers more by keeping. A salted hide is reckoned inferior to a fresh one, and sells for a lower price. This circumstance must necessarily have some tendency to sink the price of raw hides produced in a country which does not manufacture them, but is obliged to export them; and comparatively to raise that of those produced in a country which does manufacture them. It must have some tendency to sink their price in a barbarous, and to raise it in an improved and manufacturing country. It must have had some tendency therefore to sink it in ancient, and to raise it in modern times. Our tanners besides have not been quite so successful as our clothiers, in convincing the wisdom of the nation, that the safety of the commonwealth depends upon the prosperity of their particular manufacture. They have accordingly been much less favoured. The exportation of raw hides has, indeed, been prohibited, and declared a nuisance: but their importation from foreign countries has been subjected to a duty; and though this duty has been taken off from those of Ireland and the plantations (for the limited time of five years only), yet Ireland has not been confined to the market of Great Britain for the sale of its surplus hides, or of those which are not manufactured at home. The hides of common cattle have but within these few years been put among the enumerated commodities which the plantations can send no-where but to the mother country; neither has the commerce of Ireland been in this case oppressed hitherto, in order to support the manufactures of Great Britain.

Whatever regulations tend to sink the price either of wool or of raw hides below what it naturally would be, must, in an improved and cultivated country, have some tendency to raise the price of butcher's-meat. The price both of the great and small cattle, which are fed on improved and cultivated land, must be sufficient to pay the rent which the landlord, and the profit which the farmer has reason to expect from improved and cultivated land. If it is not, they will soon cease to feed them. Whatever part of this price, therefore, is not paid by the wool and the hide, must be paid by the carcase. The less there is paid for the one, the more must be paid for the other. In what manner this price is to be divided upon the different parts of the beast, is indifferent to the landlords and farmers, provided it is all paid to them. In an improved and cultivated country, therefore, their interest as landlords and farmers cannot be much affected by such regulations, though their interest as consumers may, by the rise in the price of provisions. It would be quite otherwise, however, in an unimproved and uncultivated country, where the greater part of the lands could be applied to no other purpose but the feeding of cattle, and where the wool and the hide made the principal part of the value of those cattle. Their interest as landlords and farmers would in this case be very deeply affected by such regulations, and their interest as consumers very little. The fall in the price of the wool and the hide, would not in this case raise the price of the carcase; because the greater part of the lands of the country being applicable to no other purpose but the feeding of cattle, the same number would still continue to be fed. The same quantity of butcher's-meat would still come to market. The demand for it would be no greater than before. Its price, therefore, would be the same as before. The whole price of cattle would fall, and along with it both the rent and the profit of all those lands of which cattle was the principal produce, that is, of the greater part of the lands of the country. The perpetual prohibition of the exportation of wool, which is commonly, but very falsely, ascribed to Edward III, would, in the then circumstances of the country, have been the most destructive regulation which could well have been thought of. It would not only have reduced the actual value of the greater part of the lands of the kingdom, but by reducing the price of the most important species of small cattle, it would have retarded very much its subsequent improvement.

The wool of Scotland fell very considerably in its price in consequence of the union with England, by which it was excluded from the great market of Europe, and confined to the narrow one of Great Britain. The value of the greater part of the lands in the southern counties of Scotland, which are chiefly a sheep country, would have been very deeply affected by this event, had not the rise in the price of butcher's-meat fully compensated the fall in the price of wool.

As the efficacy of human industry, in increasing the quantity either of wool or of raw hides, is limited, so far as it depends upon the produce of the country where it is exerted; so it is uncertain as far as it depends upon the produce of other countries. It so far depends, not so much upon the quantity which they produce, as upon that which they do not manufacture; and upon the restraints which they may or may not think proper to impose upon the exportation of this sort of rude produce. These circumstances, as they are altogether independent of domestic industry, so they necessarily render the efficacy of its efforts more or less uncertain. In multiplying this sort of rude produce, therefore, the efficacy of human industry is not only limited, but uncertain.

In multiplying another very important sort of rude produce, the quantity of fish that is brought to market, it is likewise both limited and uncertain. It is limited by the local situation of the country, by the proximity or distance of its different provinces from the sea, by the number of its lakes and rivers, and by what may be called the fertility or barrenness of those seas, lakes and rivers, as to this sort of rude produce. As population increases, as the annual produce of the land and labour of the country grows greater and greater, there come to be more buyers of fish, and those buyers too have a greater quantity and variety of other goods, or, what is the same thing, the price of a greater quantity and variety of other goods, to buy with. But it will generally be impossible to supply the great and extended market without employing a quantity of labour greater than in proportion to what had been requisite for supplying the narrow and confined one. A market which, from requiring only one thousand, comes to require annually ten thousand ton of fish, can seldom be supplied without employing more than ten times the quantity of labour which had before been sufficient to supply it. The fish must generally be sought for at a greater distance, larger vessels must be employed, and more expensive machinery of every kind made use of. The real price of this commodity, therefore, naturally rises in the progress of improvement. It has accordingly done so, I believe, more or less in every country.

Though the success of a particular day's fishing may be a very uncertain matter, yet, the local situation of the country being supposed, the general efficacy of industry in bringing a certain quantity of fish to market, taking the course of a year, or of several years together, it may perhaps be thought, is certain enough; and it, no doubt, is so. As it depends more, however, upon the local situation of the country, than upon the state of its wealth and industry; as upon this account it may in different countries be the same in very different periods of improvement, and very different in the same period; its connection with the state of improvement is uncertain, and it is of this sort of uncertainty that I am here speaking.

In increasing the quantity of the different minerals and metals which are drawn from the bowels of the earth, that of the more precious ones particularly, the efficacy of human industry seems not to be limited, but to be altogether uncertain.

The quantity of the precious metals which is to be found in any country is not limited by any thing in its local situation, such as the fertility or barrenness of its own mines. Those metals frequently abound in countries which possess no mines. Their quantity in every particular country seems to depend upon two different circumstances; first, upon its power of purchasing, upon the state of its industry, upon the annual produce of its land and labour, in consequence of which it can afford to employ a greater or a smaller quantity of labour and subsistence in bringing or purchasing such superfluities as gold and silver, either from its own mines or from those of other countries; and, secondly, upon the fertility or barrenness of the mines which may happen at any particular time to supply the commercial world with those metals. The quantity of those metals in the countries most remote from the mines, must be more or less affected by this fertility or barrenness, on account of the easy and cheap transportation of those metals, of their small bulk and great value. Their quantity in China and Indostan must have been more or less affected by the abundance of the mines of America.

So far as their quantity in any particular country depends upon the former of those two circumstances (the power of purchasing), their real price, like that of all other luxuries and superfluities, is likely to rise with the wealth and improvement of the country, and to fall with its poverty and depression. Countries which have a great quantity of labour and subsistence to spare, can afford to purchase any particular quantity of those metals at the expence of a greater quantity of labour and subsistence, than countries which have less to spare.

So far as their quantity in any particular country depends upon the latter of those two circumstances (the fertility or barrenness of the mines which happen to supply the commercial world), their real price, the real quantity of labour and subsistence which they will purchase or exchange for, will, no doubt, sink more or less in proportion to the fertility, and rise in proportion to the barrenness, of those mines.

The fertility or barrenness of the mines, however, which may happen at any particular time to supply the commercial world, is a circumstance which, it is evident, may have no sort of connection with the state of industry in a particular country. It seems even to have no very necessary connection with that of the world in general. As arts and commerce, indeed, gradually spread themselves over a greater and a greater part of the earth, the search for new mines, being extended over a wider surface, may have somewhat a better chance for being successful, than when confined within narrower bounds. The discovery of new mines, however, as the old ones come to be gradually exhausted, is a matter of the greatest uncertainty, and such as no human skill or industry can ensure. All indications, it is acknowledged, are doubtful, and the actual discovery and successful working of a new mine can alone ascertain the reality of its value, or even of its existence. In this search there seem to be no certain limits either to the possible success, or to the possible disappointment of human industry. In the course of a century or two, it is possible that new mines may be discovered more fertile than any that have ever yet been known; and it is just equally possible that the most fertile mine then known may be more barren than any that was wrought before the discovery of the mines of America. Whether the one or the other of those two events may happen to take place, is of very little importance to the real wealth and prosperity of the world, to the real value of the annual produce of the land and labour of mankind. Its nominal value, the quantity of gold and silver by which this annual produce could be expressed or represented, would, no doubt, be very different; but its real value, the real quantity of labour which it could purchase or command, would be precisely the same. A shilling might in the one case represent no more labour than a penny does at present; and a penny in the other might represent as much as a shilling does now. But in the one case he who had a shilling in his pocket, would be no richer than he who has a penny at present; and in the other he who had a penny would be just as rich as he who has a shilling now. The cheapness and abundance of gold and silver plate, would be the sole advantage which the world could derive from the one event, and the dearness and scarcity of those trifling superfluities the only inconveniency it could suffer from the other.

EFFECTS OF THE PROGRESS OF IMPROVEMENT UPON THE REAL PRICE OF MANUFACTURES

It is the natural effect of improvement, however, to diminish gradually the real price of almost all manufactures. That of the manufacturing workmanship diminishes, perhaps, in all of them without exception. In consequence of better machinery, of greater dexterity, and of a more proper division and distribution of work, all of which are the natural effects of improvement, a much smaller quantity of labour becomes requisite for executing any particular piece of work; and though, in consequence of the flourishing circumstances of the society, the real price of labour should rise very considerably, yet the great diminution of the quantity will generally much more than compensate the greatest rise which can happen in the price.

There are, indeed, a few manufactures, in which the necessary rise in the real price of the rude materials will more than compensate all the advantages which improvement can introduce into the execution of the work. In carpenters and joiners work, and in the coarser sort of cabinet work, the necessary rise in the real price of barren timber, in consequence of the improvement of land, will more than compensate all the advantages which can be derived from the best machinery, the greatest dexterity, and the most proper division and distribution of work.

But in all cases in which the real price of the rude materials either does not rise at all, or does not rise very much, that of the manufactured commodity sinks very considerably.

This diminution of price has, in the course of the present and preceding century, been most remarkable in those manufactures of which the materials are the coarser metals. A better movement of a watch, than about the middle of the last century could have been bought for twenty pounds, may now perhaps be had for twenty shillings. In the work of cutlers and locksmiths, in all the toys which are made of the coarser metals, and in all those goods which are commonly known by the name of Birmingham and Sheffield ware, there has been, during the same period, a very great reduction of price, though not altogether so great as in watch-work. It has, however, been sufficient to astonish the workmen of every other part of Europe, who in many cases acknowledge that they can produce no work of equal goodness for double, or even for triple the price. There are perhaps no manufactures in which the division of labour can be carried further, or in which the machinery employed admits of a greater variety of improvements, than those of which the materials are the coarser metals.

In the clothing manufacture there has, during the same period, been no such sensible reduction of price. The price of superfine cloth, I have been assured, on the contrary, has, within these five-and-twenty or thirty years, risen somewhat in proportion to its quality; owing, it was said, to a considerable rise in the price of the material, which consists altogether of Spanish wool. That of the Yorkshire cloth, which is made altogether of English wool, is said indeed, during the course of the present century, to have fallen a good deal in proportion to its quality. Quality, however, is so very disputable a matter, that I look upon all information of this kind as somewhat uncertain. In the clothing manufacture, the division of labour is nearly the same now as it was a century ago, and the machinery employed is not very different. There may, however, have been some small improvement in both, which may have occasioned some reduction of price.

But the reduction will appear much more sensible and undeniable, if we compare the price of this manufacture in the present times with what it was in a much remoter period, towards the end of the fifteenth century, when the labour was probably much less subdivided, and the machinery employed much more imperfect, than it is at present.

In 1487, being the 4th of Henry VII. it was enacted, that "whosoever shall sell by retail a broad yard of the finest scarlet grained, or of other grained cloth of the finest making, above sixteen shillings, shall forfeit forty shillings for every yard so sold." Sixteen shillings, therefore, containing about the same quantity of silver as four-and-twenty shillings of our present money, was, at that time, reckoned not an unreasonable price for a yard of the finest cloth; and as this is a sumptuary law, such cloth, it is probable, had usually been sold somewhat dearer. A guinea may be reckoned the highest price in the present times. Even though the quality of the cloths, therefore, should be supposed equal, and that of the present times is most probably much superior, yet, even upon this supposition, the money price of the finest cloth appears to have been considerably reduced since the end of the fifteenth century. But its real price has been much more reduced. Six shillings and eight-pence was then, and long afterwards, reckoned the average price of a quarter of wheat. Sixteen shillings, therefore, was the price of two quarters and more than three bushels of wheat. Valuing a quarter of wheat in the present times at eight-and-twenty shillings, the real price of a yard of fine cloth must, in those times, have been equal to at least three pounds six shillings and sixpence of our present money. The man who bought it must have parted with the command of a quantity of labour and subsistence equal to what that sum would purchase in the present times.

The reduction in the real price of the coarse manufacture, though considerable, has not been so great as in that of the fine.

In 1463, being the 3d of Edward IV., it was enacted, that "no servant in husbandry, nor common labourer, nor servant to any artificer inhabiting out of a city or burgh, shall use or wear in their clothing any cloth above two shillings the broad yard." In the 3d of Edward IV. two shillings contained very nearly the same quantity of silver as four of our present money. But the Yorkshire cloth which is now sold at four shillings the yard, is probably much superior to any that was then made for the wearing of the very poorest order of common servants. Even the money price of their clothing, therefore, may, in proportion to the quality, be somewhat cheaper in the present than it was in those ancient times. The real price is certainly a good deal cheaper. Tenpence was then reckoned what is called the moderate and reasonable price of a bushel of wheat. Two shillings, therefore, was the price of two bushels and near two pecks of wheat, which in the present times, at three shillings and sixpence the bushel, would be worth eight shillings and ninepence. For a yard of this cloth the poor servant must have parted with the power of purchasing a quantity of subsistence equal to what eight shillings and nine-pence would purchase in the present times. This is a sumptuary law too, restraining the luxury and extravagance of the poor. Their clothing, therefore, had commonly been much more expensive.

The same order of people are, by the same law, prohibited from wearing hose, of which the price should exceed fourteen-pence the pair, equal to about eight-and-twenty pence of our present money. But fourteen-pence was in those times the price of a bushel and near two pecks of wheat; which, in the present times, at three and sixpence the bushel, would cost five shillings and three-pence. We should in the present times consider this as a very high price for a pair of stockings to a servant of the poorest and lowest order. He must, however, in those times have paid what was really equivalent to this price for them.

In the time of Edward IV. the art of knitting stockings was probably not known in any part of Europe. Their hose were made of common cloth, which may have been one of the causes of their dearness. The first person that wore stockings in England is said to have been Queen Elizabeth. She received them as a present from the Spanish ambassador.

Both in the coarse and in the fine woollen manufacture, the machinery employed was much more imperfect in those ancient, than it is in the present times. It has since received three very capital improvements, besides, probably, many smaller ones of which it may be difficult to ascertain either the number or the importance. The three capital improvements are: first, The exchange of the rock and spindle for the spinning-wheel, which, with the same quantity of labour, will perform more than double the quantity of work. Secondly, the use of several very ingenious machines which facilitate and abridge in a still greater proportion the winding of the worsted and woollen yarn, or the proper arrangement of the warp and woof before they are put into the loom; an operation which, previous to the inventions of those machines, must have been extremely tedious and troublesome. Thirdly, the employment of the fulling mill for thickening the cloth, instead of treading it in water. Neither wind nor water mills of any kind were known in England so early as the beginning of the sixteenth century, nor, so far as I know, in any other part of Europe north of the Alps. They had been introduced into Italy some time before.

The consideration of these circumstances may, perhaps, in some measure explain to us why the real price both of the coarse and of the fine manufacture, was so much higher in those ancient, than it is in the present times. It cost a greater quantity of labour to bring the goods to market. When they were brought thither, therefore, they must have purchased or exchanged for the price of a greater quantity.

The coarse manufacture probably was, in those ancient times, carried on in England, in the same manner as it always has been in countries where arts and manufactures are in their infancy. It was probably a houshold manufacture, in which every different part of the work was occasionally performed by all the different members of almost every private family; but so as to be their work only when they had nothing else to do, and not to be the principal business from which any of them derived the greater part of their subsistence. The work which is performed in this manner, it has already been observed, comes always much cheaper to market than that which is the principal or sole fund of the workman's subsistence. The fine manufacture, on the other hand, was not in those times carried on in England, but in the rich and commercial country of Flanders; and it was probably conducted then, in the same manner as now, by people who derived the whole, or the principal part of their subsistence from it. It was besides a foreign manufacture, and must have paid some duty, the ancient custom of tonnage and poundage at least, to the king. This duty, indeed, would not probably be very great. It was not then the policy of Europe to restrain, by high duties, the importation of foreign manufactures, but rather to encourage it, in order that merchants might be enabled to supply, at as easy a rate as possible, the great men with the conveniencies and luxuries which they wanted, and which the industry of their own country could not afford them.

The consideration of these circumstances may perhaps in some measure explain to us why, in those ancient times, the real price of the coarse manufacture was, in proportion to that of the fine, so much lower than in the present times.

CONCLUSION OF THE CHAPTER

I shall conclude this very long chapter with observing that every improvement in the circumstances of the society tends either directly or indirectly to raise the real rent of land, to increase the real wealth of the landlord, his power of purchasing the labour, or the produce of the labour of other people.

The extension of improvement and cultivation tends to raise it directly. The landlord's share of the produce necessarily increases with the increase of the produce.

That rise in the real price of those parts of the rude produce of land, which is first the effect of extended improvement and cultivation, and afterwards the cause of their being still further extended, the rise in the price of cattle, for example, tends too to raise the rent of land directly, and in a still greater proportion. The real value of the landlord's share, his real command of the labour of other people, not only rises with the real value of the produce, but the proportion of his share to the whole produce rises with it. That produce, after the rise in its real price, requires no more labour to collect it than before. A smaller proportion of it will, therefore, be sufficient to replace, with the ordinary profit, the stock which employs that labour. A greater proportion of it must, consequently, belong to the landlord.

All those improvements in the productive powers of labour, which tend directly to reduce the real price of manufactures, tend indirectly to raise the real rent of land. The landlord exchanges that part of his rude produce, which is over and above his own consumption, or what comes to the same thing, the price of that part of it, for manufactured produce. Whatever reduces the real price of the latter, raises that of the former. An equal quantity of the former becomes thereby equivalent to a greater quantity of the latter; and the landlord is enabled to purchase a greater quantity of the conveniencies, ornaments, or luxuries, which he has occasion for.

Every increase in the real wealth of the society, every increase in the quantity of useful labour employed within it, tends indirectly to raise the real rent of land. A certain proportion of this labour naturally goes to the land. A greater number of men and cattle are employed in its cultivation, the produce increases with the increase of the stock which is thus employed in raising it, and the rent increases with the produce.

The contrary circumstances, the neglect of cultivation and improvement, the fall in the real price of any part of the rude produce of land; the rise in the real price of manufactures from the decay of manufacturing art and industry, the declension of the real wealth of the society, all tend, on the other hand, to lower the real rent of land, to reduce the real wealth of the landlord, to diminish his power of purchasing either the labour, or the produce of the labour of other people.

The whole annual produce of the land and labour of every country, or what comes to the same thing, the whole price of that annual produce, naturally divides itself, it has already been observed, into three parts; the rent of land, the wages of labour, and the profits of stock; and constitutes a revenue to three different orders of people; to those who live by rent, to those who live by wages, and to those who live by profit. These are the three great, original and constituent orders of every civilized society, from whose revenue that of every other order is ultimately derived.

The interest of the first of those three great orders, it appears from what has been just now said, is strictly and inseparably connected with the general interest of the society.

Whatever either promotes or obstructs the one, necessarily promotes or obstructs the other. When the public deliberates concerning any regulation of commerce or police, the proprietor of land never can mislead it, with a view to promote the interest of their own particular order; at least, if they have any tolerable knowledge of that interest. They are, indeed, too often defective in this tolerable knowledge. They are the only one of the three orders whose revenue costs them neither labour nor care, but comes to them, as it were, of its own accord, and independent of any plan or project of their own. That indolence, which is the natural effect of the ease and security of their situation, renders them too often, not only ignorant, but incapable of that application of mind which is necessary in order to foresee and understand the consequences of any public regulation.

The interest of the second order, that of those who live by wages, is as strictly connected with the interest of the society as that of the first. The wages of the labourer, it has already been shewn, are never so high as when the demand for labour is continually rising, or when the quantity employed is every year increasing considerably. When this real wealth of the society becomes stationary, his wages are soon reduced to what is barely enough to enable him to bring up a family, or to continue the race of labourers. When the society declines, they fall even below this. The order of proprietors may, perhaps, gain more by the prosperity of the society, than that of labourers: but there is no order that suffers so cruelly from its decline. But though the interest of the labourer is strictly connected with that of the society, he is incapable either of comprehending that interest, or of understanding its connexion with his own. His condition leaves him no time to receive the necessary information, and his education and habits are commonly such as to render him unfit to judge even though he was fully informed. In the public deliberations, therefore, his voice is little heard and less regarded, except upon some particular occasions, when his clamour is animated, set on, and supported by his employers, not for his, but their own particular purposes.

His employers constitute the third order, that of those who

live by profit. It is the stock that is employed for the sake of profit, which puts into motion the greater part of the useful labour of every society. The plans and projects of the employers of stock regulate and direct all the most important operations of labour, and profit is the end proposed by all those plans and projects. But the rate of profit does not, like rent and wages, rise with the prosperity, and fall with the declension, of the society. On the contrary, it is naturally low in rich, and high in poor countries, and it is always highest in the countries which are going fastest to ruin. The interest of this third order, therefore, has not the same connexion with the general interest of the society as that of the other two. Merchants and master manufacturers are, in this order, the two classes of people who commonly employ the largest capitals, and who by their wealth draw to themselves the greatest share of the public consideration. As during their whole lives they are engaged in plans and projects, they have frequently more acuteness of understanding than the greater part of country gentlemen. As their thoughts, however, are commonly exercised rather about the interest of their own particular branch of business, than about that of the society, their judgment, even when given with the greatest candour (which it has not been upon every occasion), is much more to be depended upon with regard to the former of those two objects, than with regard to the latter. Their superiority over the country gentleman is, not so much in their knowledge of the public interest, as in their having a better knowledge of their own interest than he has of his. It is by this superior knowledge of their own interest that they have frequently imposed upon his generosity, and persuaded him to give up both his own interest and that of the public, from a very simple but honest conviction, that their interest, and not his, was the interest of the public. The interest of the dealers, however, in any particular branch of trade or manufacture, is always in some respects different from, and even opposite to, that of the public. To widen the market and to narrow the competition, is always the interest of the dealers. To widen the market may frequently be agreeable enough to the interest of the public; but to narrow the competition must always be against it, and can serve only to enable the dealers, by raising their profits above what they naturally would be, to levy, for their own benefit, an absurd tax upon the rest of their fellow-citizens. The proposal of any new law or regulation of commerce which comes from this order, ought always to be listened to with great precaution, and ought never to be adopted till after having been long and carefully examined, not only with the most scrupulous, but with the most suspicious attention. It comes from an order of men, whose interest is never exactly the same with that of the public, who have generally an interest to deceive and even to oppress the public, and who accordingly have, upon many occasions, both deceived and oppressed it.

BOOK II

Of the Nature, Accumulation, and Employment of Stock

INTRODUCTION

IN that rude state of society in which there is no division of labour, in which exchanges are seldom made, and in which every man provides every thing for himself, it is not necessary that any stock should be accumulated or stored up beforehand, in order to carry on the business of the society. Every man endeavours to supply by his own industry his own occasional wants as they occur. When he is hungry, he goes to the forest to hunt; when his coat is worn out, he clothes himself with the skin of the first large animal he kills: and when his hut begins to go to ruin, he repairs it, as well as he can, with the trees and the turf that are nearest it.

But when the division of labour has once been thoroughly introduced, the produce of a man's own labour can supply but a very small part of his occasional wants. The far greater part of them are supplied by the produce of other men's labour, which he purchases with the produce, or, what is the same thing, with the price of the produce of his own. But this purchase cannot be made till such time as the produce of his own labour has not only been completed, but sold. A stock of goods of different kinds, therefore, must be stored up somewhere sufficient to maintain him, and to supply him with the materials and tools of his work, till such time, at least, as both these events can be brought about. A weaver cannot apply himself entirely to his peculiar business, unless there is beforehand stored up somewhere, either in his own possession or in that of some other person, a stock sufficient to maintain him, and to supply him with the materials and tools of his work, till he has not only completed but sold his web. This accumulation must, evidently, be previous to his applying his industry for so long a time to such a peculiar business.

As the accumulation of stock must, in the nature of things, be previous to the division of labour, so labour can be more and more subdivided in proportion only as stock is previously more and more accumulated. The quantity of materials which the same number of people can work up, increases in a great proportion as labour comes to be more and more subdivided; and as the operations of each workman are gradually reduced to a greater degree of simplicity, a variety of new machines come to be invented for facilitating and abridging those operations. As the division of labour advances, therefore, in order to give constant employment to an equal number of workmen, an equal stock of provisions, and a greater stock of materials and tools than what would have been necessary in a ruder state of things, must be accumulated beforehand. But the number of workmen in every branch of business generally increases with the division of labour in that branch, or rather it is the increase of their number which enables them to class and subdivide themselves in this manner.

As the accumulation of stock is previously necessary for carrying on this great improvement in the productive powers of labour, so that accumulation naturally leads to this improvement. The person who employs his stock in maintaining labour, necessarily wishes to employ it in such a manner as to produce as great a quantity of work as possible. He endeavours, therefore, both to make among his workmen the most proper distribution of employment, and to furnish them with the best machines which he can either invent or afford to purchase. His abilities in both these respects are generally in proportion to the extent of his stock, or to the number of people whom it can employ. The quantity of industry, therefore, not only increases in every country with the increase of the stock which employs it, but, in consequence of that increase, the same quantity of industry produces a much greater quantity of work.

Such are in general the effects of the increase of stock upon industry and its productive powers.

In the following book I have endeavoured to explain the nature of stock, the effects of its accumulation into capitals of different kinds, and the effects of the different employments of those capitals. This book is divided into five chapters. In the first chapter, I have endeavoured to show what are the different parts or branches into which the stock, either of an individual, or of a great society, naturally divides itself. In the second, I have endeavoured to explain the nature and operation of money considered as a particular branch of the general stock of the society. The stock which is accumulated into a capital, may either be employed by the person to whom it belongs, or it may be lent to some other person. In the third and fourth chapters, I have endeavoured to examine the manner in which it operates in both these situations. The fifth and last chapter treats of the different effects which the different employments of capital immediately produce upon the quantity both of national industry, and of the annual produce of land and labour.

CHAPTER I

Of the Division of Stock

When the stock which a man possesses is no more than sufficient to maintain him for a few days or a few weeks, he seldom thinks of deriving any revenue from it. He consumes it as sparingly as he can, and endeavours by his labour to acquire something which may supply its place before it be consumed altogether. His revenue is, in this case, derived from his labour only. This is the state of the greater part of the labouring poor in all countries.

But when he possesses stock sufficient to maintain him for months or years, he naturally endeavours to derive a revenue from the greater part of it; reserving only so much for his immediate consumption as may maintain him till this revenue begins to come in. His whole stock, therefore, is distinguished into two parts. That part which, he expects, is to afford him this revenue, is called his capital. The other is that which supplies his immediate consumption; and which consists either, first, in that portion of his whole stock which was originally reserved for this purpose; or, secondly, in his revenue, from whatever source derived, as it gradually comes in; or, thirdly, in such things as had been purchased by either of these in former years, and which are not yet entirely consumed; such as a stock of clothes, household furniture, and the like. In one, or other, or all of these three articles, consists the stock which men commonly reserve for their own immediate consumption.

There are two different ways in which a capital may be employed so as to yield a revenue or profit to its employer.

First, it may be employed in raising, manufacturing, or purchasing goods, and selling them again with a profit. The capital employed in this manner yields no revenue or profit to its employer, while it either remains in his possession, or continues in the same shape. The goods of the merchant yield him no revenue or profit till he sells them for money, and the money yields him as little till it is again exchanged for goods. His capital is continually going from him in one shape, and returning to him in another, and it is only by means of such circulation, or successive exchanges, that it can yield him any profit. Such capitals, therefore, may very properly be called circulating capitals.

Secondly, it may be employed in the improvement of land, in the purchase of useful machines and instruments of trade, or in such-like things as yield a revenue or profit without changing masters, or circulating any further. Such capitals, therefore, may very properly be called fixed capitals.

Different occupations require very different proportions between the fixed and circulating capitals employed in them.

The capital of a merchant, for example, is altogether a circulating capital. He has occasion for no machines or instruments of trade, unless his shop, or warehouse, be considered as such.

Some part of the capital of every master artificer or manufacturer must be fixed in the instruments of his trade. This part, however, is very small in some, and very great in others. A master taylor requires no other instruments of trade but a parcel of needles. Those of the master shoemaker are a little, though but a very little, more expensive. Those of the weaver rise a good deal above those of the shoemaker. The far greater part of the capital of all such master artificers, however, is circulated, either in the wages of their workmen, or in the price of their materials, and repaid with a profit by the price of the work.

In other works a much greater fixed capital is required. In a great iron-work, for example, the furnace for melting the ore, the forge, the slitt-mill, are instruments of trade which cannot be erected without a very great expence. In coal-works, and mines of every kind, the machinery necessary both for drawing out the water and for other purposes, is frequently still more expensive.

That part of the capital of the farmer which is employed

in the instruments of agriculture is a fixed; that which is employed in the wages and maintenance of his labouring servants, is a circulating capital. He makes a profit of the one by keeping it in his own possession, and of the other by parting with it. The price or value of his labouring cattle is a fixed capital in the same manner as that of the instruments of husbandry: Their maintenance is a circulating capital in the same manner as that of the labouring servants. The farmer makes his profit by keeping the labouring cattle, and by parting with their maintenance. Both the price and the maintenance of the cattle which are bought in and fattened, not for labour, but for sale, are a circulating capital. The farmer makes his profit by parting with them. A flock of sheep or a herd of cattle that, in a breeding country, is bought in, neither for labour, nor for sale, but in order to make a profit by their wool, by their milk, and by their increase, is a fixed capital. The profit is made by keeping them. Their maintenance is a circulating capital. The profit is made by parting with it; and it comes back with both its own profit, and the profit upon the whole price of the cattle, in the price of the wool, the milk, and the increase. The whole value of the seed too is properly a fixed capital. Though it goes backwards and forwards between the ground and the granary, it never changes masters, and therefore does not properly circulate. The farmer makes his profit, not by its sale, but by its increase.

The general stock of any country or society is the same with that of all its inhabitants or members, and therefore naturally divides itself into the same three portions, each of which has a distinct function or office.

The First, is that portion which is reserved for immediate consumption, and of which the characteristic is, that it affords no revenue or profit. It consists in the stock of food, clothes, household furniture, &c., which have been purchased by their proper consumers, but which are not yet entirely consumed. The whole stock of mere dwelling-houses too subsisting at any one time in the country, make a part of this first portion. The stock that is laid out in a house, if it is to be the dwelling-house of the proprietor, ceases from that moment to serve in the function of a capital, or to afford any revenue to its owner. A dwelling-house, as such, contributes nothing to the revenue of its inhabitant; and though it is, no doubt, extremely useful to him, it is as his clothes and household furniture are useful to him, which, however, make a part of his expence, and not of his revenue. If it is to be let to a tenant for rent, as the house itself can produce nothing, the tenant must always pay the rent out of some other revenue which he derives either from labour, or stock, or land. Though a house, therefore, may yield a revenue to its proprietor, and thereby serve in the function of a capital to him, it cannot yield any to the public, nor serve in the function of a capital to it, and the revenue of the whole body of the people can never be in the smallest degree increased by it. Clothes, and household furniture, in the same manner, sometimes yield a revenue, and thereby serve in the function of a capital to particular persons. In countries where masquerades are common, it is a trade to let out masquerade dresses for a night. Upholsterers frequently let furniture by the month or by the year. Undertakers let the furniture of funerals by the day and by the week. Many people let furnished houses, and get a rent, not only for the use of the house, but for that of the furniture. The revenue, however, which is derived from such things, must always be ultimately drawn from some other source of revenue. Of all parts of the stock, either of an individual, or of a society, reserved for immediate consumption, what is laid out in houses is most slowly consumed. A stock of clothes may last several years: a stock of furniture half a century or a century: but a stock of houses, well built and properly taken care of, may last many centuries. Though the period of their total consumption, however, is more distant, they are still as really a stock reserved for immediate consumption as either clothes or household furniture.

The Second of the three portions into which the general stock of the society divides itself, is the fixed capital; of which the charactertistic is, that it affords a revenue or profit without circulating or changing masters. It consists chiefly of the four following articles:

First, of all useful machines and instruments of trade which facilitate and abridge labour:

Secondly, of all those profitable buildings which are the means of procuring a revenue, not only to their proprietor who lets them for a rent, but to the person who possesses them and pays that rent for them; such as shops, warehouses, workhouses, farmhouses, with all their necessary buildings, stables, granaries, &c. These are very different from mere dwelling houses. They are a sort of instruments of trade, and may be considered in the same light:

Thirdly, of the improvements of land, of what has been profitably laid out in clearing, draining, enclosing, manuring, and reducing it into the condition most proper for tillage and culture. An improved farm may very justly be regarded in the same light as those useful machines which facilitate and abridge labour, and by means of which, an equal circulating capital can afford a much greater revenue to its employer. An improved farm is equally advantageous and more durable than any of those machines, frequently requiring no other repairs than the most profitable application of the farmer's capital employed in cultivating it:

Fourthly, of the acquired and useful abilities of all the inhabitants or members of the society. The acquisition of such talents, by the maintenance of the acquirer during his education, study, or apprenticeship, always costs a real expence, which is a capital fixed and realized, as it were, in his person. Those talents, as they make a part of his fortune, so do they likewise of that of the society to which he belongs. The improved dexterity of a workman may be considered in the same light as a machine or instrument of trade which facilitates and abridges labour, and which, though it costs a certain expence, repays that expence with a profit.

The Third and last of the three portions into which the general stock of the society naturally divides itself, is the circulating capital; of which the characteristic is, that it affords a revenue only by circulating or changing masters. It is composed likewise of four parts:

First, of the money by means of which all the other three are circulated and distributed to their proper consumers:

Secondly, of the stock of provisions which are in the possession of the butcher, the grazier, the farmer, the corn-merchant, the brewer, &c. and from the sale of which they expect to derive a profit:

Thirdly, of the materials, whether altogether rude, or more or less manufactured, of clothes, furniture and building, which are not yet made up into any of those three shapes, but which remain in the hands of the growers, the manufacturers, the mercers, and drapers, the timber-merchants, the carpenters and joiners, the brick-makers, &c.

Fourthly, and lastly, of the work which is made up and completed, but which is still in the hands of the merchant or manufacturer, and not yet disposed of or distributed to the proper consumers; such as the finished work which we frequently find ready-made in the shops of the smith, the cabinet-maker, the goldsmith, the jeweller, the china-merchant, &c. The circulating capital consists in this manner, of the provisions, materials, and finished work of all kinds that are in the hands of their respective dealers, and of the money that is necessary for circulating and distributing them to those who are finally to use, or to consume them.

Of these four parts three, provisions, materials, and finished work, are, either annually, or in a longer or shorter period, regularly withdrawn from it, and placed either in the fixed capital or in the stock reserved for immediate consumption.

Every fixed capital is both originally derived from, and requires to be continually supported by a circulating capital. All useful machines and instruments of trade are originally derived from a circulating capital, which furnishes the materials of which they are made, and the maintenance of the workmen who make them. They require too a capital of the same kind to keep them in constant repair.

No fixed capital can yield any revenue but by means of a circulating capital. The most useful machines and instruments of trade will produce nothing without the circulating capital which affords the materials they are employed upon, and the maintenance of the workmen who employ them. Land, however improved, will yield no revenue without a circulating capital, which maintains the labourers who cultivate and collect its produce.

To maintain and augment the stock which may be reserved

for immediate consumption, is the sole end and purpose both of the fixed and circulating capitals. It is this stock which feeds, clothes, and lodges the people. Their riches or poverty depends upon the abundant or sparing supplies which those two capitals can afford to the stock reserved for immediate consumption.

So great a part of the circulating capital being continually withdrawn from it, in order to be placed in the other two branches of the general stock of the society; it must in its turn require continual supplies, without which it would soon cease to exist. These supplies are principally drawn from three sources, the produce of land, of mines, and of fisheries. These afford continual supplies of provisions and materials, of which part is afterwards wrought up into finished work, and by which are replaced the provisions, materials, and finished work continually withdrawn from the circulating capital. From mines too is drawn what is necessary for maintaining and augmenting that part of it which consists in money. For though, in the ordinary course of business, this part is not, like the other three, necessarily withdrawn from it, in order to be placed in the other two branches of the general stock of the society, it must, however, like all other things, be wasted and worn out at last, and sometimes too be either lost or sent abroad, and must, therefore, require continual, though, no doubt, much smaller supplies.

Land, mines, and fisheries, require all both a fixed and a circulating capital to cultivate them: and their produce replaces with a profit, not only those capitals, but all the others in the society. Thus the farmer annually replaces to the manufacturer the provisions which he had consumed and the materials which he had wrought up the year before; and the manufacturer replaces to the farmer the finished work which he had wasted and worn out in the same time. This is the real exchange that is annually made between those two orders of people, though it seldom happens that the rude produce of the one and the manufactured produce of the other, are directly bartered for one another; because it seldom happens that the farmer sells his corn and his cattle, his flax and his wool, to the very same person of whom he chuses to purchase the clothes, furniture, and instruments of trade which he wants. He sells, therefore, his rude produce for money, with which he can purchase, wherever it is to be had, the manufactured produce he has occasion for. Land even replaces, in part at least, the capitals with which fisheries and mines are cultivated. It is the produce of land which draws the fish from the waters; and it is the produce of the surface of the earth which extracts the minerals from its bowels.

The produce of land, mines, and fisheries, when their natural fertility is equal, is in proportion to the extent and proper application of the capitals employed about them. When the capitals are equal and equally well applied, it is in proportion to their natural fertility.

In all countries where there is tolerable security, every man of common understanding will endeavour to employ whatever stock he can command, in procuring either present enjoyment or future profit. If it is employed in procuring present enjoyment, it is a stock reserved for immediate consumption. If it is employed in procuring future profit, it must procure this profit either by staying with him, or by going from him. In the one case it is a fixed, in the other it is a circulating capital. A man must be perfectly crazy who, where there is tolerable security, does not employ all the stock which he commands, whether it be his own or borrowed of other people, in some one or other of those three ways.

In those unfortunate countries, indeed, where men are continually afraid of the violence of their superiors, they frequently bury and conceal a great part of their stock, in order to have it always at hand to carry with them to some place of safety, in case of their being threatened with any of these disasters to which they consider themselves as at all times exposed. This is said to be a common practice in Turkey, in Indostan, and, I believe, in most other governments of Asia. It seems to have been a common practice among our ancestors during the violence of the feudal government. Treasure-trove was in those times considered as no contemptible part of the revenue of the greatest sovereigns in Europe. It consisted in such treasure as was found concealed in the earth, and to which no particular person could prove any right. This was regarded in those times as so important an object, that it was always considered as belonging to the sovereign, and neither to the finder nor to the proprietor of the land, unless the right to it had been conveyed to the latter by an express clause in his charter. It was put upon the same footing with gold and silver mines, which, without a special clause in the charter, were never supposed to be comprehended in the general grant of the lands, though mines of lead, copper, tin, and coal were, as things of smaller consequence.

CHAPTER II

Of Money Considered as a Particular Branch of the General Stock of the Society, or of the Expence of Maintaining the National Capital

IT has been shewn in the First Book, that the price of the greater part of commodities resolves itself into three parts, of which one pays the wages of the labour, another the profits of the stock, and a third the rent of the land which had been employed in producing and bringing them to market: that there are, indeed, some commodities of which the price is made up of two of those parts only, the wages of labour, and the profits of stock: and a very few in which it consists altogether in one, the wages of labour: but that the price of every commodity necessarily resolves itself into some one, or other, or all of these three parts; every part of it which goes neither to rent nor to wages, being necessarily profit to somebody.

Since this is the case, it has been observed, with regard to every particular commodity, taken separately; it must be so with regard to all the commodities which compose the whole annual produce of the land and labour of every country, taken complexly. The whole price or exchangeable value of that annual produce, must resolve itself into the same three parts, and be parcelled out among the different inhabitants of the country, either as the wages of their labour, the profits of their stock, or the rent of their land.

But though the whole value of the annual produce of the land and labour of every country is thus divided among and constitutes a revenue to its different inhabitants; yet as in the rent of a private estate we distinguish between the gross rent and the neat rent, so may we likewise in the revenue of all the inhabitants of a great country.

The gross rent of a private estate comprehends whatever

is paid by the farmer; the neat rent, what remains free to the landlord, after deducting the expence of management, of repairs, and all other necessary charges; or what, without hurting his estate, he can afford to place in his stock reserved for immediate consumption, or to spend upon his table, equipage, the ornaments of his house and furniture, his private enjoyments and amusements. His real wealth is in proportion, not to his gross, but to his neat rent.

The gross revenue of all the inhabitants of a great country, comprehends the whole annual produce of their land and labour; the neat revenue, what remains free to them after deducting the expence of maintaining; first, their fixed; and, secondly, their circulating capital; or what, without encroaching upon their capital, they can place in their stock reserved for immediate consumption, or spend upon their subsistence, conveniencies, and amusements. Their real wealth too is in proportion, not to their gross, but to their neat revenue.

The whole expence of maintaining the fixed capital, must evidently be excluded from the neat revenue of the society. Neither the materials necessary for supporting their useful machines and instruments of trade, their profitable buildings, &c. nor the product of the labour necessary for fashioning those materials into the proper form, can ever make any part of it. The price of that labour may indeed make a part of it; as the workmen so employed may place the whole value of their wages in their stock reserved for immediate consumption. But in other sorts of labour, both the price and the produce go to this stock, the price to that of the workmen, the produce to that of other people, whose subsistence, conveniencies, and amusements, are augmented by the labour of those workmen.

The intention of the fixed capital is to increase the productive powers of labour, or to enable the same number of labourers to perform a much greater quantity of work. In a farm where all the necessary buildings, fences, drains, communications, &c. are in the most perfect good order, the same number of labourers and labouring cattle will raise a much greater produce, than in one of equal extent and equally good ground, but not furnished with equal conveniencies. In manufactures the same number of hands, assisted with the best machinery, will work up a much greater quantity of goods than with more imperfect instruments of trade. The expence which is properly laid out upon a fixed capital of any kind, is always repaid with great profit, and increases the annual produce by a much greater value than that of the support which such improvements require. This support, however, still requires a certain portion of that produce. A certain quantity of materials, and the labour of a certain number of workmen, both of which might have been immediately employed to augment the food, clothing and lodging, the subsistence and conveniencies of the society, are thus diverted to another employment, highly advantageous indeed, but still different from this one. It is upon this account that all such improvements in mechanics, as enable the same number of workmen to perform an equal quantity of work with cheaper and simpler machinery than had been usual before, are always regarded as advantageous to every society. A certain quantity of materials, and the labour of a certain number of workmen, which had before been employed in supporting a more complex and expensive machinery, can afterwards be applied to augment the quantity of work which that or any other machinery is useful only for performing. The undertaker of some great manufactory who employs a thousand a-year in the maintenance of his machinery, if he can reduce this expence to five hundred, will naturally employ the other five hundred in purchasing an additional quantity of materials to be wrought up by an additional number of workmen. The quantity of that work, therefore, which his machinery was useful only for performing, will naturally be augmented, and with it all the advantage and conveniency which the society can derive from that work.

The expence of maintaining the fixed capital in a great country, may very properly be compared to that of repairs in a private estate. The expense of repairs may frequently be necessary for supporting the produce of the estate, and consequently both the gross and the neat rent of the landlord. When by a more proper direction, however, it can be diminished without occasioning any diminution of produce, the gross rent remains at least the same as before, and the neat rent is necessarily augmented.

But though the whole expence of maintaining the fixed capital is thus necessarily excluded from the neat revenue of the society, it is not the same case with that of maintaining the circulating capital. Of the four parts of which this latter capital is composed, money, provisions, materials, and finished work, the three last, it has already been observed, are regularly withdrawn from it, and placed either in the fixed capital of the society, or in their stock reserved for immediate consumption. Whatever portion of those consumable goods is not employed in maintaining the former, goes all to the latter, and makes a part of the neat revenue of the society. The maintenance of those three parts of the circulating capital, therefore, withdraws no portion of the annual produce from the neat revenue of the society, besides what is necessary for maintaining the fixed capital.

The circulating capital of a society is in this respect different from that of an individual. That of an individual is totally excluded from making any part of his neat revenue, which must consist altogether in his profits. But though the circulating capital of every individual makes a part of that of the society to which he belongs, it is not upon that account totally excluded from making a part likewise of their neat revenue. Though the whole goods in a merchant's shop must by no means be placed in his own stock reserved for immediate consumption, they may in that of other people, who, from a revenue derived from other funds, may regularly replace their value to him, together with its profits, without occasioning any diminution either of his capital or of theirs.

Money, therefore, is the only part of the circulating capital of a society, of which the maintenance can occasion any diminution in their neat revenue.

The fixed capital, and that part of the circulating capital which consists in money, so far as they affect the revenue of the society, bear a very great resemblance to one another.

First, as those machines and instruments of trade, &c., require a certain expence, first to erect them, and afterwards to support them, both which expences, though they make a part of the gross, are deductions from the neat revenue of the society; so the stock of money which circulates in any country must require a certain expence, first to collect it, and afterwards to support it, both which expences, though they make a part of the gross, are, in the same manner, deductions from the neat revenue of the society. A certain quantity of very valuable materials, gold and silver, and of very curious labour, instead of augmenting the stock reserved for immediate consumption, the subsistence, conveniencies, and amusements of individuals, is employed in supporting that great but expensive instrument of commerce, by means of which every individual in the society has his subsistence, conveniencies, and amusements, regularly distributed to him in their proper proportion.

Secondly, as the machines and instruments of trade, &c. which compose the fixed capital either of an individual or of a society, make no part either of the gross or of the neat revenue of either; so money, by means of which the whole revenue of the society is regularly distributed among all its different members, makes itself no part of that revenue. The great wheel of circulation is altogether different from the goods which are circulated by means of it. The revenue of the society consists altogether in those goods, and not in the wheel which circulates them. In computing either the gross or the neat revenue of any society, we must always, from their whole annual circulation of money and goods, deduct the whole value of the money, of which not a single farthing can ever make any part of either.

It is the ambiguity of language only which can make this proposition appear either doubtful or paradoxical. When properly explained and understood, it is almost self-evident.

When we talk of any particular sum of money, we sometimes mean nothing but the metal pieces of which it is composed; and sometimes we include in our meaning some obscure reference to the goods which can be had in exchange for it, or to the power of purchasing which the possession of it conveys. Thus when we say, that the circulating money of England has been computed at eighteen millions, we mean only to express the amount of the metal pieces, which some writers have computed, or rather have supposed to circulate in that country. But when we say that a man is worth fifty or a hundred pounds a-year, we mean commonly to express not only the amount of the metal pieces which are annually paid to him, but the value of the goods which he can annually purchase or consume. We mean commonly to ascertain what is or ought to be his way of living, or the quantity and quality of the necessaries and conveniencies of life in which he can with propriety indulge himself.

When, by any particular sum of money, we mean not only to express the amount of the metal pieces of which it is composed, but to include in its signification some obscure reference to the goods which can be had in exchange for them, the wealth or revenue which it in this case denotes, is equal only to one of the two values which are thus intimated somewhat ambiguously by the same word, and to the latter more properly than to the former, to the money's worth more properly than to the money.

Thus if a guinea be the weekly pension of a particular person, he can in the course of the week purchase with it a certain quantity of subsistence, conveniencies, and amusements. In proportion as this quantity is great or small, so are his real riches, his real weekly revenue. His weekly revenue is certainly not equal both to the guinea, and to what can be purchased with it, but only to one or other of those two equal values; and to the latter more properly than to the former, to the guinea's worth rather than to the guinea.

If the pension of such a person was paid to him, not in gold, but in a weekly bill for a guinea, his revenue surely would not so properly consist in the piece of paper, as in what he could get for it. A guinea may be considered as a bill for a certain quantity of necessaries and conveniencies upon all the tradesmen in the neighbourhood. The revenue of the person to whom it is paid, does not so properly consist in the piece of gold, as in what he can get for it, or in what he can exchange it for. If it could be exchanged for nothing, it would, like a bill upon a bankrupt, be of no more value than the most useless piece of paper.

Though the weekly or yearly revenue of all the different inhabitants of any country, in the same manner, may be, and in reality frequently is paid to them in money, their real riches, however, the real weekly or yearly revenue of all of them taken together, must always be great or small in proportion to the quantity of consumable goods which they can all of them purchase with this money. The whole revenue of all of them taken together is evidently not equal to both the money and the consumable goods; but only to one or other of those two values, and to the latter more properly than to the former.

Though we frequently, therefore, express a person's revenue by the metal pieces which are annually paid to him, it is because the amount of those pieces regulates the extent of his power of purchasing, or the value of the goods which he can annually afford to consume. We still consider his revenue as consisting in this power of purchasing or consuming, and not in the pieces which convey it.

But if this is sufficiently evident even with regard to an individual, it is still more so with regard to a society. The amount of the metal pieces which are annually paid to an individual, is often precisely equal to his revenue, and is upon that account the shortest and best expression of its value. But the amount of the metal pieces which circulate in a society, can never be equal to the revenue of all its members. As the same guinea which pays the weekly pension of one man to-day, may pay that of another to-morrow, and that of a third the day thereafter, the amount of the metal pieces which annually circulate in any country, must always be of much less value than the whole money pensions annually paid with them. But the power of purchasing, or the goods which can successively be bought with the whole of those money pensions as they are successively paid, must always be precisely of the same value with those pensions; as must likewise be the revenue of the different persons to whom they are paid. That revenue, therefore, cannot consist in those metal pieces, of which the amount is so much inferior to its value, but in the power of purchasing, in the goods which can successively be bought with them as they circulate from hand to hand.

Money, therefore, the great wheel of circulation, the great instrument of commerce, like all other instruments of trade, though it makes a part and a very valuable part of the capital, makes no part of the revenue of the society to which it belongs; and though the metal pieces of which it is composed, in the course of their annual circulation, distribute to every man the revenue which properly belongs to him, they make themselves no part of that revenue.

Thirdly, and lastly, the machines and instruments of trade, &c. which compose the fixed capital, bear this further resemblance to that part of the circulating capital which consists in money; that as every saving in the expence of erecting and supporting those machines, which does not diminish the productive powers of labour, is an improvement of the neat revenue of the society; so every saving in the expence of collecting and supporting that part of the circulating capital which consists in money, is an improvement of exactly the same kind.

It is sufficiently obvious, and it has partly too been explained already, in what manner every saving in the expence of supporting the fixed capital is an improvement of the neat revenue of the society. The whole capital of the undertaker of every work is necessarily divided between his fixed and his circulating capital. While his whole capital remains the same, the smaller the one part, the greater must necessarily be the other. It is the circulating capital which furnishes the materials and wages of labour, and puts industry into motion. Every saving, therefore, in the expence of maintaining the fixed capital, which does not diminish the productive powers of labour, must increase the fund which puts industry into motion, and consequently the annual produce of land and labour, the real revenue of every society.

The substitution of paper in the room of gold and silver money, replaces a very expensive instrument of commerce with one much less costly, and sometimes equally convenient. Circulation comes to be carried on by a new wheel, which it costs less both to erect and to maintain than the old one. But in what manner this operation is performed, and in what manner it tends to increase either the gross or the neat revenue of the society, is not altogether so obvious, and may therefore require some further explication.

There are several different sorts of paper money; but the circulating notes of banks and bankers are the species which is best known, and which seems best adapted for this purpose. When the people of any particular country have such confidence in the fortune, probity, and prudence of a particular banker, as to believe that he is always ready to pay upon demand such of his promissory notes as are likely to be at any time presented to him; those notes come to have the same currency as gold and silver money, from the confidence that such money can at any time be had for them.

A particular banker lends among his customers his own promissory notes, to the extent, we shall suppose, of a hundred thousand pounds. As those notes serve all the purposes of money, his debtors pay him the same interest as if he had lent them so much money. This interest is the source of his gain. Though some of those notes are continually coming back upon him for payment, part of them continue to circulate for months and years together. Though he has generally in circulation, therefore, notes to the extent of a hundred thousand pounds, twenty thousand pounds in gold and silver may, frequently, be a sufficient provision for answering occasional demands. By this operation, therefore, twenty thousand pounds in gold and silver perform all the functions which a hundred thousand could otherwise have performed. The same exchanges may be made, the same quantity of consumable goods may be circulated and distributed to their proper consumers, by means of his promissory notes, to the value of a hundred thousand pounds, as by an equal value of gold and silver money. Eighty thousand pounds of gold and silver, therefore, can, in this manner, be spared from the circulation of the country; and if different operations of the same kind should, at the same time, be carried on by many different banks and bankers, the whole circulation may thus be conducted with a fifth part only of the gold and silver which would otherwise have been requisite.

Let us suppose, for example, that the whole circulating money of some particular country amounted, at a particular time, to one million sterling, that sum being then sufficient for circulating the whole annual produce of their land and labour. Let us suppose too, that some time thereafter, different banks and bankers issued promissory notes, payable to the bearer, to the extent of one million, reserving in their different coffers two hundred thousand pounds for answering occasional demands. There would remain, therefore, in circulation, eight hundred thousand pounds in gold and silver, and a million of bank notes, or eighteen hundred thousand pounds of paper and money together. But the annual produce of the land and labour of the country had before required only one million to circulate and distribute it to its proper consumers, and that annual produce cannot be immediately augmented by those operations of banking. One million, therefore, will be sufficient to circulate it after them. The goods to be bought and sold being precisely the same as before, the same quantity of money will be sufficient for buying and selling them. The channel of circulation, if I may be allowed such an expression, will remain precisely the same as before. One million we have supposed sufficient to fill that channel. Whatever, therefore, is poured into it beyond this sum, cannot run in it, but must overflow. One million eight hundred thousand pounds are poured into it. Eight hundred thousand pounds, therefore, must overflow, that sum being over and above what can be employed in the circulation of the country. But though this sum cannot be employed at home, it is too valuable to be allowed to lie idle. It will, therefore, be sent abroad, in order to seek that profitable employment which it cannot find at home. But the paper cannot go abroad; because at a distance from the banks which issue it, and from the country in which payment of it can be exacted by law, it will not be received in common payments. Gold and silver, therefore, to the amount of eight hundred thousand pounds will be sent abroad, and the channel of home circulation will remain filled with a million of paper, instead of the million of those metals which filled it before.

But though so great a quantity of gold and silver is thus sent abroad, we must not imagine that it is sent abroad for nothing, or that its proprietors make a present of it to foreign nations. They will exchange it for foreign goods of some kind or another, in order to supply the consumption either of some other foreign country, or of their own.

If they employ it in purchasing goods in one foreign country in order to supply the consumption of another, or in what is called the carrying trade, whatever profit they make will be an addition to the neat revenue of their own country. It is like a new fund, created for carrying on a new trade; domestic business being now transacted by paper, and the gold and silver being converted into a fund for this new trade.

If they employ it in purchasing foreign goods for home consumption, they may either, first, purchase such goods as are likely to be consumed by idle people who produce nothing, such as foreign wines, foreign silks, &c.; or, secondly, they may purchase an additional stock of materials, tools, and provisions, in order to maintain and employ an additional number of industrious people, who re-produce, with a profit, the value of their annual consumption.

So far as it is employed in the first way, it promotes prodigality, increases expence and consumption without increasing production, or establishing any permanent fund for supporting that expence, and is in every respect hurtful to the society.

So far as it is employed in the second way, it promotes industry; and though it increases the consumption of the society, it provides a permanent fund for supporting that consumption, the people who consume re-producing, with a profit, the whole value of their annual consumption. The gross revenue of the society, the annual produce of their land and labour, is increased by the whole value which the labour of those workmen adds to the materials upon which they are employed; and their neat revenue by what remains of this value, after deducting what is necessary for supporting the tools and instruments of their trade.

That the greater part of the gold and silver which, being forced abroad by those operations of banking, is employed in purchasing foreign goods for home consumption, is and must be employed in purchasing those of this second kind, seems not only probable but almost unavoidable. Though some particular men may sometimes increase their expence very considerably though their revenue does not increase at all, we may be assured that no class or order of men ever does so; because, though the principles of common prudence do not always govern the conduct of every individual, they always influence that of the majority of every class or order. But the revenue of idle people, considered as a class or order, cannot, in the smallest degree, be increased by those operations of banking. Their expence in general, therefore, cannot be much increased by them, though that of a few individuals among them may, and in reality sometimes is. The demand of idle people, therefore, for foreign goods, being the same, or very nearly the same, as before, a very small part of the money, which being forced abroad by those operations of banking, is employed in purchasing foreign goods for home consumption, is likely to be employed in purchasing those for their use. The greater part of it will naturally be destined for the employment of industry, and not for the maintenance of idleness.

When we compute the quantity of industry which the circulating capital of any society can employ, we must always have regard to those parts of it only, which consist in provisions, materials, and finished work: the other, which consists in money, and which serves only to circulate those three, must always be deducted. In order to put industry into motion, three things are requisite; materials to work upon, tools to work with, and the wages or recompence for the sake of which the work is done. Money is neither a material to work upon, nor a tool to work with; and though the wages of the workman are commonly paid to him in money, his real revenue, like that of all other men, consists, not in the money, but in the money's worth; not in the metal pieces, but in what can be got for them.

The quantity of industry which any capital can employ, must, evidently, be equal to the number of workmen whom it can supply with materials, tools, and a maintenance suitable to the nature of the work. Money may be requisite for purchasing the materials and tools of the work, as well as the maintenance of the workmen. But the quantity of industry which the whole capital can employ, is certainly not equal both to the money which purchases, and to the materials, tools, and maintenance, which are purchased with it; but only to one or other of those two values, and to the latter more properly than to the former.

When paper is substituted in the room of gold and silver money, the quantity of the materials, tools, and maintenance, which the whole circulating capital can supply, may be increased by the whole value of gold and silver which used to be employed in purchasing them. The whole value of the great wheel of circulation and distribution, is added to the goods which are circulated and distributed by means of it. The operation, in some measure, resembles that of the undertaker of some great work, who, in consequence of some improvement in mechanics, takes down his old machinery, and adds the difference between its price and that of the new to his circulating capital, to the fund from which he furnishes materials and wages to his workmen.

What is the proportion which the circulating money of any country bears to the whole value of the annual produce circulated by means of it, it is, perhaps, impossible to determine. It has been computed by different authors at a fifth, at a tenth, at a twentieth, and at a thirtieth part of that value. But how small soever the proportion which the circulating money may bear to the whole value of the annual produce, as but a part, and frequently but a small part, of that produce, is ever destined for the maintenance of industry, it must always bear a very considerable proportion to that part. When, therefore, by the substitution of paper, the gold and silver necessary for circulation is reduced to, perhaps, a fifth part of the former quantity, if the value of only the greater part of the other four-fifths be added to the funds which are destined for the maintenance of industry, it must make a very considerable addition to the quantity of that industry, and, consequently, to the value of the annual produce of land and labour.

An operation of this kind has, within these five-and-twenty or thirty years, been performed in Scotland, by the erection of new banking companies in almost every considerable town, and even in some country villages. The effects of it have been precisely those above described. The business of the country is almost entirely carried on by means of the paper of those different banking companies, with which purchases and payments of all kinds are commonly made. Silver very seldom appears except in the change of a twenty shillings bank note, and gold still seldomer. But though the conduct of all those different companies has not been unexceptionable, and has accordingly required an act of parliament to regulate it; the country, notwithstanding, has evidently derived great benefit from their trade. I have heard it asserted, that the trade of the city of Glasgow, doubled in about fifteen years after the first erection of the banks there; and that the trade of Scotland has more than quadrupled since the first erection of the two public banks at Edinburgh, of which the one, called The Bank of Scotland, was established by act of parliament in 1695; the other, called The Royal Bank, by royal charter in 1727. Whether the trade, either of Scotland in general, or of the city of Glasgow in particular, has really increased in so great a proportion, during so short a period, I do not pretend to know. If either of them has increased in this proportion, it seems to be an effect too great to be accounted for by the sole operation of this cause. That the trade and industry of Scotland, however, have increased very considerably during this period, and that the banks have contributed a good deal to this increase, cannot be doubted.

The value of the silver money which circulated in Scotland before the union, in 1707, and which, immediately after it, was brought into the bank of Scotland in order to be recoined, amounted to 411,117*l.* 10*s.* 9*d.* sterling. No account has been got of the gold coin; but it appears from the ancient accounts of the mint of Scotland, that the value of the gold annually coined somewhat exceeded that of the silver. There were a good many people too upon this occasion, who, from a diffidence of repayment, did not bring their silver into the bank of Scotland: and there was, besides, some English coin, which was not called in. The whole value of the gold and silver, therefore, which circulated in Scotland before the union, cannot be estimated at less than a million sterling. It seems to have constituted almost the whole circulation of that country; for though the circulation of the bank of Scotland, which had then no rival, was considerable, it seems to have made but a very small part of the whole. In the present times the whole circulation of Scotland cannot be estimated at less than two millions, of which that part which consists in gold and silver, most probably, does not amount to half a million. But though the circulating gold and silver of Scotland have suffered so great a diminution during this period, its real riches and prosperity do not appear to have suffered any. Its agriculture, manufactures, and trade, on the contrary, the annual produce of its land and labour, have evidently been augmented.

It is chiefly by discounting bills of exchange, that is, by advancing money upon them before they are due, that the greater part of banks and bankers issue their promissory notes. They deduct always, upon whatever sum they advance, the legal interest till the bill shall become due. The payment of the bill, when it becomes due, replaces to the bank the value of what had been advanced, together with a clear profit of the interest. The banker who advances to the merchant whose bill he discounts, not gold and silver, but his own promissory notes, has the advantage of being able to discount to a greater amount by the whole value of his promissory notes, which he finds by experience, are commonly in circulation. He is thereby enabled to make his clear gain of interest on so much a larger sum.

The commerce of Scotland, which at present is not very great, was still more inconsiderable when the two first banking companies were established; and those companies would have had but little trade, had they confined their business to the discounting of bills of exchange. They invented, therefore, another method of issuing their promissory notes; by granting, what they called, cash accounts, that is by giving credit to the extent of a certain sum (two or three thousand pounds, for example), to any individual who could procure two persons of undoubted credit and good landed estate to become surety for him, that whatever money should be advanced to him, within the sum for which the credit had been given, should be repaid upon demand, together with the legal interest. Credits of this kind are, I believe, commonly granted by banks and bankers in all different parts of the world. But the easy terms upon which the Scotch banking companies accept of re-payment are, so far as I know, peculiar to them, and have, perhaps, been the principal cause, both of the great trade of those companies, and of the benefit which the country has received from it.

Whoever has a credit of this kind with one of those companies, and borrows a thousand pounds upon it, for example, may repay this sum piece-meal, by twenty and thirty pounds at a time, the company discounting a proportionable part of the interest of the great sum from the day on which each of those small sums is paid in, till the whole be in this manner repaid. All merchants, therefore, and almost all men of business, find it convenient to keep such cash accounts with them, and are thereby interested to promote the trade of those companies, by readily receiving their notes in all payments, and by encouraging all those with whom they have any influence to do the same. The banks, when their customers apply to them for money, generally advance it to them in their own promissory notes. These the merchants pay away to the manufacturers for goods, the manufacturers to the farmers for materials and provisions, the farmers to their landlords for rent, the landlords repay them to the merchants for the conveniencies and luxuries with which they supply them, and the merchants again return them to the banks in order to balance their cash accounts, or to replace what they may have borrowed of them; and thus almost the whole money business of the country is transacted by means of them. Hence the great trade of those companies.

By means of those cash accounts every merchant can, without imprudence, carry on a greater trade than he otherwise could do. If there are two merchants, one in London, and the other in Edinburgh, who employ equal stocks in the same branch of trade, the Edinburgh merchant can, without imprudence, carry on a greater trade, and give employment to a greater number of people than the London merchant. The London merchant must always keep by him a considerable sum of money, either in his own coffers, or in those of his banker, who gives him no interest for it, in order to answer the demands continually coming upon him for payment of the goods which he purchases upon credit. Let the ordinary amount of this sum be supposed five hundred pounds. The value of the goods in his warehouse must always be less by five hundred pounds than it would have been, had he not been obliged to keep such a sum unemployed.

Let us suppose that he generally disposes of his whole stock upon hand, or of goods to the value of his whole stock upon hand, once in the year. By being obliged to keep so great a sum unemployed, he must sell in a year five hundred pounds worth less goods than he might otherwise have done. His annual profits must be less by all that he could have made by the sale of five hundred pounds worth more goods; and the number of people employed in preparing his goods for the market, must be less by all those that five hundred pounds more stock could have employed. The merchant in Edinburgh, on the other hand, keeps no money unemployed for answering such occasional demands. When they actually come upon him, he satisfies them from his cash account with the bank, and gradually replaces the sum borrowed with the money or paper which comes in from the occasional sales of his goods. With the same stock, therefore, he can, without imprudence, have at all times in his warehouse a larger quantity of goods than the London merchant; and can thereby both make a greater profit himself, and give constant employment to a greater number of industrious people who prepare those goods for the market. Hence the great benefit which the country has derived from this trade.

The facility of discounting bills of exchange, it may be thought, indeed, gives the English merchants a conveniency equivalent to the cash accounts of the Scotch merchants. But the Scotch merchants, it must be remembered, can discount their bills of exchange as easily as the English merchants; and have, besides, the additional conveniency of their cash accounts.

The whole paper money of every kind which can easily circulate in any country never can exceed the value of the gold and silver, of which it supplies the place, or which (the commerce being supposed the same) would circulate there, if there was no paper money. If twenty shilling notes, for example, are the lowest paper money current in Scotland, the whole of that currency which can easily circulate there cannot exceed the sum of gold and silver which would be necessary for transacting the annual exchange of twenty shillings value and upwards usually transacted within that country. Should the circulating paper at any time exceed that sum, as the excess could neither be sent abroad nor be employed in the circulation of the country, it must immediately return upon the banks to be exchanged for gold and silver. Many people would immediately perceive that they had more of this paper than was necessary for transacting their business at home, and as they could not send it abroad, they would immediately demand payment of it from the banks. When this superfluous paper was converted into gold and silver, they could easily find a use for it by sending it abroad; but they could find none while it remained in the shape of paper. There would immediately, therefore, be a run upon the banks to the whole extent of this superfluous paper, and, if they shewed any difficulty or backwardness in payment, to a much greater extent; the alarm, which this would occasion, necessarily increasing the run.

Over and above the expences which are common to every branch of trade; such as the expence of house-rent, the wages of servants, clerks, accountants, &c.; the expences peculiar to a bank consist chiefly in two articles: First, in the expence of keeping at all times in its coffers, for answering the occasional demands of the holders of its notes, a large sum of money, of which it loses the interest: And, secondly, in the expence of replenishing those coffers as fast as they are emptied by answering such occasional demands.

A banking company, which issues more paper than can be employed in the circulation of the country, and of which the excess is continually returning upon them for payment, ought to increase the quantity of gold and silver, which they keep at all times in their coffers, not only in proportion to this excessive increase of their circulation, but in a much greater proportion; their notes returning upon them much faster than in proportion to the excess of their quantity. Such a company, therefore, ought to increase the first article of their expence, not only in proportion to this forced increase of their business, but in a much greater proportion.

The coffers of such a company too, though they ought to be filled much fuller, yet must empty themselves much faster than if their business was confined within more reasonable bounds, and must require, not only a more violent, but a more constant and uninterrupted exertion of expence in order to replenish them. The coin too, which is thus continually drawn in such large quantities from their coffers, cannot be employed in the circulation of the country. It comes in place of a paper which is over and above what can be employed in that circulation, and is therefore over and above what can be employed in it too. But as that coin will not be allowed to lie idle, it must, in one shape or another, be sent abroad, in order to find that profitable employment which it cannot find at home; and this continual exportation of gold and silver, by enhancing the difficulty, must necessarily enhance still further the expence of the bank, in finding new gold and silver in order to replenish those coffers, which empty themselves so very rapidly. Such a company, therefore, must, in proportion to this forced increase of their business, increase the second article of their expence still more than the first.

Let us suppose that all the paper of a particular bank, which the circulation of the country can easily absorb and employ, amounts exactly to forty thousand pounds; and that for answering occasional demands, this bank is obliged to keep at all times in its coffers ten thousand pounds in gold and silver. Should this bank attempt to circulate forty-four thousand pounds, the four thousand pounds which are over and above what the circulation can easily absorb and employ, will return upon it almost as fast as they are issued. For answering occasional demands, therefore, this bank ought to keep at all times in its coffers, not eleven thousand pounds only, but fourteen thousand pounds. It will thus gain nothing by the interest of the four thousand pounds excessive circulation; and it will lose the whole expence of continually collecting four thousand pounds in gold and silver, which will be continually going out of its coffers as fast as they are brought into them.

Had every particular banking company always understood and attended to its own particular interest, the circulation never could have been overstocked with paper money. But every particular banking company has not always understood or attended to its own particular interest, and the circulation has frequently been overstocked with paper money.

By issuing too great a quantity of paper, of which the excess was continually returning, in order to be exchanged for gold and silver, the bank of England was for many years together obliged to coin gold to the extent of between eight hundred thousand pounds and a million a year; or at an average, about eight hundred and fifty thousand pounds. For this great coinage the bank (in consequence of the worn and degraded state into which the gold coin had fallen a few years ago) was frequently obliged to purchase gold bullion at the high price of four pounds an ounce, which it soon after issued in coin at 3*l.* 17*s.* 10½*d.* an ounce, losing in this manner between two and a half and three per cent. upon the coinage of so very large a sum. Though the bank therefore paid no seignorage, though the government was properly at the expence of the coinage, this liberality of government did not prevent altogether the expence of the bank.

The Scotch banks, in consequence of an excess of the same kind, were all obliged to employ constantly agents at London to collect money for them, at an expence which was seldom below one and a half or two per cent. This money was sent down by the waggon, and insured by the carriers at an additional expence of three quarters per cent. or fifteen shillings on the hundred pounds. Those agents were not always able to replenish the coffers of their employers so fast as they were emptied. In this case the resource of the banks was, to draw upon their correspondents in London bills of exchange to the extent of the sum which they wanted. When those correspondents afterwards drew upon them for the payment of this sum, together with the interest and a commission, some of those banks, from the distress into which their excessive circulation had thrown them, had sometimes no other means of satisfying this draught but by drawing a second set of bills either upon the same, or upon some other correspondents in London; and the same sum, or rather bills for the same sum, would in this manner make sometimes more than two or three journies: the debtor bank, paying always the interest and commission upon the whole accumulated sum. Even those Scotch banks which never distinguished themselves by their extreme imprudence, were sometimes obliged to employ this ruinous resource.

The gold coin which was paid out either by the bank of England, or by the Scotch banks, in exchange for that part of their paper which was over and above what could be employed in the circulation of the country, being likewise over and above what could be employed in that circulation, was sometimes sent abroad in the shape of coin, sometimes melted down and sent abroad in the shape of bullion, and sometimes melted down and sold to the bank of England at the high price of four pounds an ounce. It was the newest, the heaviest, and the best pieces only which were carefully picked out of the whole coin, and either sent abroad or melted down. At home, and while they remained in the shape of coin, those heavy pieces were of no more value than the light: But they were of more value abroad, or when melted down into bullion, at home. The bank of England, notwithstanding their great annual coinage, found to their astonishment, that there was every year the same scarcity of coin as there had been the year before; and that notwithstanding the great quantity of good and new coin which was every year issued from the bank, the state of the coin, instead of growing better and better, became every year worse and worse. Every year they found themselves under the necessity of coining nearly the same quantity of gold as they had coined the year before, and from the continual rise in the price of gold bullion, in consequence of the continual wearing and clipping of the coin, the expence of this great annual coinage became every year greater and greater. The bank of England, it is to be observed, by supplying its own coffers with coin, is indirectly obliged to supply the whole kingdom, into which coin is continually flowing from those coffers in a great variety of ways. Whatever coin therefore was wanted to support this excessive circulation both of Scotch and English paper money, whatever vacuities this excessive circulation occasioned in the necessary coin of the kingdom, the bank of England was obliged to supply them. The Scotch banks, no doubt, paid all of them very dearly for their own imprudence and inattention. But the bank of England paid very dearly, not only for its own imprudence, but for the much greater imprudence of almost all the Scotch banks.

The over-trading of some bold projectors in both parts

of the united kingdom, was the original cause of this excessive circulation of paper money.

What a bank can with propriety advance to a merchant or undertaker of any kind, is not either the whole capital with which he trades, or even any considerable part of that capital; but that part of it only, which he would otherwise be obliged to keep by him unemployed, and in ready money for answering occasional demands. If the paper money which the bank advances never exceeds this value, it can never exceed the value of the gold and silver, which would necessarily circulate in the country if there was no paper money; it can never exceed the quantity which the circulation of the country can easily absorb and employ.

When a bank discounts to a merchant a real bill of exchange drawn by a real creditor upon a real debtor, and which, as soon as it becomes due, is really paid by that debtor; it only advances to him a part of the value which he would otherwise be obliged to keep by him unemployed and in ready money for answering occasional demands. The payment of the bill, when it becomes due, replaces to the bank the value of what it had advanced, together with the interest. The coffers of the bank, so far as its dealings are confined to such customers, resemble a water pond, from which, though a stream is continually running out, yet another is continually running in, fully equal to that which runs out; so that, without any further care or attention, the pond keeps always equally, or very near equally full. Little or no expence can ever be necessary for replenishing the coffers of such a bank.

A merchant, without over-trading, may frequently have occasion for a sum of ready money, even when he has no bills to discount. When a bank, besides discounting his bills, advances him likewise upon such occasions, such sums upon his cash account, and accepts of a piece meal repayment as the money comes in from the occasional sale of his goods, upon the easy terms of the banking companies of Scotland; it dispenses him entirely from the necessity of keeping any part of his stock by him unemployed and in ready money for answering occasional demands. When such demands actually come upon him, he can answer them sufficiently from his cash account. The bank, however, in dealing with such customers, ought to observe with great attention, whether in the course of some short period (of four, five, six, or eight months, for example) the sum of the repayments which it commonly receives from them, is, or is not, fully equal to that of the advances which it commonly makes to them. If, within the course of such short periods, the sum of the repayments from certain customers is, upon most occasions, fully equal to that of the advances, it may safely continue to deal with such customers. Though the stream which is in this case continually running out from its coffers may be very large, that which is continually running into them must be at least equally large; so that without any further care or attention those coffers are likely to be always equally or very nearly equally full; and scarce ever to require any extraordinary expence to replenish them. If, on the contrary, the sum of the repayments from certain other customers falls commonly very much short of the advances which it makes to them, it cannot with any safety continue to deal with such customers, at least if they continue to deal with it in this manner. The stream which is in this case continually running out from its coffers is necessarily much larger than that which is continually running in; so that, unless they are replenished by some great and continual effort of expence, those coffers must soon be exhausted altogether.

The banking companies of Scotland, accordingly, were for a long time very careful to require frequent and regular repayments from all their customers, and did not care to deal with any person, whatever might be his fortune or credit, who did not make, what they called, frequent and regular operations with them. By this attention, besides saving almost entirely the extraordinary expence of replenishing their coffers, they gained two other very considerable advantages.

First, by this attention they were enabled to make some tolerable judgment concerning the thriving or declining circumstances of their debtors, without being obliged to look out for any other evidence besides what their own books afforded them; men being for the most part either regular or irregular in their repayments, according as their circumstances are either thriving or declining. A private man who lends out his money to perhaps half a dozen or a dozen of debtors, may, either by himself or his agents, observe and enquire both constantly and carefully into the conduct and situation of each of them. But a banking company, which lends money to perhaps five hundred different people, and of which the attention is continually occupied by objects of a very different kind, can have no regular information concerning the conduct and circumstances of the greater part of its debtors beyond what its own books afford it. In requiring frequent and regular repayments from all their customers, the banking companies of Scotland had probably this advantage in view.

Secondly, by this attention they secured themselves from the possibility of issuing more paper money than what the circulation of the country could easily absorb and employ. When they observed, that within moderate periods of time the repayments of a particular customer were upon most occasions fully equal to the advances which they had made to him, they might be assured that the paper money which they had advanced to him, had not at any time exceeded the quantity of gold and silver which he would otherwise have been obliged to keep by him for answering occasional demands; and that, consequently, the paper money, which they had circulated by this means, had not at any time exceeded the quantity of gold and silver which would have circulated in the country, had there been no paper money. The frequency, regularity and amounts of his repayments would sufficiently demonstrate that the amount of their advances had at no time exceeded that part of his capital which he would otherwise have been obliged to keep by him unemployed and in ready money for answering occasional demands; that is, for the purpose of keeping the rest of his capital in constant employment. It is this part of his capital only which, within moderate periods of time, is continually returning to every dealer in the shape of money, whether paper or coin, and continually going from him in the same shape. If the advances of the bank had commonly exceeded this part of his capital, the ordinary amount of his repayments could not, within moderate periods of time, have equalled the ordinary amount of its advances. The stream which, by means of his dealings, was continually running into the coffers of the bank, could not have been equal to the stream which, by means of the same dealings, was continually running out. The advances of the bank paper, by exceeding the quantity of gold and silver which, had there been no such advances, he would have been obliged to keep by him for answering occasional demands, might soon come to exceed the whole quantity of gold and silver which (the commerce being supposed the same) would have circulated in the country had there been no paper money; and consequently to exceed the quantity which the circulation of the country could easily absorb and employ; and the excess of this paper money would immediately have returned upon the bank in order to be exchanged for gold and silver. This second advantage, though equally real, was not perhaps so well understood by all the different banking companies of Scotland as the first.

When, partly by the conveniency of discounting bills, and partly by that of cash accounts, the creditable traders of any country can be dispensed from the necessity of keeping any part of their stock by them unemployed and in ready money for answering occasional demands, they can reasonably expect no farther assistance from banks and bankers, who, when they have gone thus far, cannot, consistently with their own interest and safety, go farther. A bank cannot, consistently with its own interest, advance to a trader the whole or even the greater part of the circulating capital with which he trades; because, though that capital is continually returning to him in the shape of money, and going from him in the same shape, yet the whole of the returns is too distant from the whole of the outgoings, and the sum of his repayments could not equal the sum of its advances within such moderate periods of time as suit the conveniency of a bank. Still less could a bank afford to advance him any considerable part of his fixed capital; of the capital which the undertaker of an iron forge, for example, employs in erecting his forge and dwelling-house, his work-houses and ware-houses, the dwelling-house of his workman, &c.; of the capital which the undertaker of a mine employs in sinking his shafts, in erecting engines for drawing out the water, in making roads and waggon-ways, &c.; of the capital which the person who undertakes to improve land employs in clearing, draining, enclosing, manuring and ploughing waste and uncultivated fields, in building farm-houses, with all their necessary appendages of stables, granaries, &c. The returns of the fixed capital are in almost all cases much slower than those of the circulating capital; and such expences, even when laid out with the greatest prudence and judgment, very seldom return to the undertaker till after a period of many years, a period by far too distant to suit the conveniency of a bank. Traders and other undertakers may, no doubt, with great propriety, carry on a very considerable part of their projects with borrowed money. In justice to their creditors, however, their own capital ought, in this case, to be sufficient to ensure, if I may say so, the capital of those creditors; or to render it extremely improbable that those creditors should incur any loss, even though the success of the project should fall very much short of the expectation of the projectors. Even with this precaution too, the money which is borrowed, and which it is meant should not be repaid till after a period of several years, ought not to be borrowed of a bank, but ought to be borrowed upon bond or mortgage, of such private people as propose to live upon the interest of their money, without taking the trouble themselves to employ the capital; and who are upon that account willing to lend that capital to such people of good credit as are likely to keep it for several years. A bank, indeed, which lends its money without the expence of stampt paper, or of attornies fees for drawing bonds and mortgages, and which accepts of repayment upon the easy terms of the banking companies of Scotland; would, no doubt, be a very convenient creditor to such traders and undertakers. But such traders and undertakers would, surely, be most inconvenient debtors to such a bank.

* * * * * * * *

It is not by augmenting the capital of the country, but by rendering a greater part of that capital active and productive than would otherwise be so, that the most judicious operations of banking can increase the industry of the country. That part of his capital which a dealer is obliged to keep by him unemployed, and in ready money for answering occasional demands, is so much dead stock, which, so long as it remains in this situation, produces nothing either to him or to his country. The judicious operations of banking enable him to convert this dead stock into active and productive stock; into materials to work upon, into tools to work with, and into provisions and subsistence to work for; into stock which produces something both to himself and to his country. The gold and silver money which circulates in any country, and by means of which the produce of its land and labour is annually circulated and distributed to the proper consumers, is, in the same manner as the ready money of the dealer, all dead stock. It is a very valuable part of the capital of the country, which produces nothing to the country. The judicious operations of banking, by substituting paper in the room of a great part of this gold and silver, enables the country to convert a great part of this dead stock into active and productive stock; into stock which produces something to the country. The gold and silver money which circulates in any country may very properly be compared to a highway, which, while it circulates and carries to market all the grass and corn of the country, produces itself not a single pile of either. The judicious operations of banking, by providing, if I may be allowed so violent a metaphor, a sort of waggon-way through the air: enable the country to convert, as it were, a great part of its highways into good pastures and corn-fields, and thereby to increase very considerably the annual produce of its land and labour. The commerce and industry of the country, however, it must be acknowledged, though they may be somewhat augmented, cannot be altogether so secure, when they are thus, as it were, suspended upon the Dædalian wings of paper money, as when they travel about upon the solid ground of gold and silver. Over and above the accidents to which they are exposed from the unskilfulness of the conductors of this paper money, they are liable to several others, from which no prudence of will of those conductors can guard them.

An unsuccessful war, for example, in which the enemy got possession of the capital, and consequently of that treasure which supported the credit of the paper money, would occasion a much greater confusion in a country where the whole circulation was carried on by paper, than in one where the greater part of it was carried on by gold and silver. The usual instrument of commerce having lost its value, no exchanges could be made but either by barter or upon credit. All taxes having been usually paid in paper money, the prince would not have wherewithal either to pay his troops, or to furnish his magazines; and the state of the country would be much more irretrievable than if the greater part of its circulation had consisted in gold and silver. A prince, anxious to maintain his dominions at all times in the state in which he can most easily defend them, ought, upon this account, to guard, not only against that excessive multiplication of paper money which ruins the very banks which issue it; but even against that multiplication of it, which enables them to fill the greater part of the circulation of the country with it.

The circulation of every country may be considered as divided into two different branches; the circulation of the dealers with one another, and the circulation between the dealers and the consumers. Though the same pieces of money, whether paper or metal, may be employed sometimes in the one circulation and sometimes in the other; yet as both are constantly going on at the same time, each requires a certain stock of money of one kind or another, to carry it on. The value of the goods circulated between the different dealers, never can exceed the value of those circulated between the dealers and the consumers; whatever is bought by the dealers, being ultimately destined to be sold to the consumers. The circulation between the dealers, as it is carried on by wholesale, requires generally a pretty large sum for every particular transaction. That between the dealers and the consumers, on the contrary, as it is generally carried on by retail, frequently requires but very small ones, a shilling, or even a halfpenny, being often sufficient. But small sums circulate much faster than large ones. A shilling changes masters more frequently than a guinea, and a halfpenny more frequently than a shilling. Though the annual purchases of all the consumers, therefore, are at least equal in value to those of all the dealers, they can generally be transacted with a much smaller quantity of money; the same pieces, by a more rapid circulation, serving as the instrument of many more purchases of the one kind than of the other.

Paper money may be so regulated, as either to confine itself very much to the circulation between the different dealers, or to extend itself likewise to a great part of that between the dealers and the consumers. Where no bank notes are circulated under ten pounds value, as in London, paper money confines itself very much to the circulation between the dealers. When a ten pound bank note comes into the hands of a consumer, he is generally obliged to change it at the first shop where he has occasion to purchase five shillings worth of goods; so that it often returns into the hands of a dealer, before the consumer has spent the fortieth part of the money. Where bank notes are issued for so small sums as twenty shillings, as in Scotland, paper money extends itself to a considerable part of the circulation between dealers and consumers. Before the act of parliament, which put a stop to the circulation of ten and five shilling notes, it filled a still greater part of that circulation. In the currencies of North America, paper was commonly issued for so small a sum as a shilling, and filled almost the whole of that circulation. In some paper currencies of Yorkshire, it was issued even for so small a sum as a sixpence.

Where the issuing of bank notes for such very small sums is allowed and commonly practised, many mean people are both enabled and encouraged to become bankers. A person whose promissory note for five pounds, or even for twenty shillings, would be rejected by every body, will get it to be received without scruple when it is issued for so small a sum as a sixpence. But the frequent bankruptcies to which such beggarly bankers must be liable, may occasion a very considerable inconveniency, and sometimes even a very great calamity, to many poor people who had received their notes in payment.

It were better, perhaps, that no bank notes were issued in any part of the kindom for a smaller sum than five pounds. Paper money would then, probably, confine itself, in every part of the kindom, to the circulation between the different dealers, as much as it does at present in London, where no bank notes are issued under ten pounds value; five pounds being, in most parts of the kingdom, a sum which, though it will purchase, perhaps, little more than half the quantity of goods, is as much considered, and is as seldom spent all at once, as ten pounds are amidst the profuse expence of London.

Where paper money, it is to be observed, is pretty much confined to the circulation between dealers and dealers, as at London, there is always plenty of gold and silver. Where it extends itself to a considerable part of the circulation between dealers and consumers, as in Scotland, and still more in North America, it banishes gold and silver almost entirely from the country; almost all the ordinary transactions of its interior commerce being thus carried on by paper. The suppression of ten and five shilling bank notes, somewhat relieved the scarcity of gold and silver in Scotland; and the suppression of twenty shilling notes, would probably relieve it still more. Those metals are said to have become more abundant in America, since the suppression of some of their paper currencies. They are said, likewise, to have been more abundant before the institution of those currencies.

Though paper money should be pretty much confined to the circulation between dealers and dealers, yet banks and bankers might still be able to give nearly the same assistance to the industry and commerce of the country, as they had done when paper money filled almost the whole circulation. The ready money which a dealer is obliged to keep by him, for answering occasional demands, is destined altogether for the circulation between himself and other dealers, of whom he buys goods. He has no occasion to keep any by him for the circulation between himself and the consumers, who are his customers, and who bring ready money to him, instead of taking any from him. Though no paper money, therefore, was allowed to be issued, for such sums as would confine it pretty much to the circulation between dealers and dealers; yet, partly by discounting real bills of exchange, and partly by lending upon cash accounts, banks and bankers, might still be able to relieve the greater part of those dealers from the necessity of keeping any considerable part of their stock by them, unemployed and in ready money, for answering occasional demands. They might still be able to give the utmost assistance which banks and bankers can, with propriety, give to traders of every kind.

To restrain private people, it may be said, from receiving in payment the promissory notes of a banker, for any sum whether great or small, when they themselves are willing to receive them; or, to restrain a banker from issuing such notes, when all his neighbours are willing to accept of them, is a manifest violation of that natural liberty which it is the proper business of law, not to infringe, but to support. Such regulations may, no doubt, be considered as in some respect a violation of natural liberty. But those exertions of the natural liberty of a few individuals, which might endanger the security of the whole society, are, and ought to be, restrained by the laws of all governments; of the most free, as well as of the most despotical. The obligation of building party walls, in order to prevent the communication of fire, is a violation of natural liberty, exactly of the same kind with the regulations of the banking trade which are here proposed.

A paper money consisting in bank notes, issued by people of undoubted credit, payable upon demand without any condition, and in fact always readily paid as soon as presented, is, in every respect, equal in value to gold and silver money; since gold and silver money can at any time be had for it. Whatever is either bought or sold for such paper, must necessarily be bought or sold as cheap as it could have been for gold and silver.

The increase of paper money, it has been said, by augmenting the quantity, and consequently diminishing the value of the whole currency, necessarily augments the money price of commodities. But as the quantity of gold and silver, which is taken from the currency, is always equal to the quantity of paper which is added to it, paper money does not necessarily increase the quantity of the whole currency. From the beginning of the last century to the present time, provisions never were cheaper in Scotland than in 1759, though, from the circulation of ten and five shilling bank notes, there was then more paper money in the country than at present. The proportion between the prices of provisions in Scotland and that in England, is the same now as before the great multiplication of banking companies in Scotland. Corn is, upon most occasions, fully as cheap in England as in France; though there is a great deal of paper money in England and scarce any in France. In 1751 and in 1752, when Mr. Hume published his Political Discourses, and soon after the great multiplication of paper money in Scotland, there was a very sensible rise in the price of provisions, owing, probably to the badness of the seasons, and not to the multiplication of paper money.

It would be otherwise, indeed, with a paper money consisting in promissory notes, of which the immediate payment depended, in any respect, either upon the good will of those who issued them; or upon a condition which the holder of the notes might not always have it in his power to fulfil; or of which the payment was not exigible till after a certain number of years, and which in the meantime bore no interest. Such a paper money would, no doubt, fall more or less below the value of gold and silver, according as the difficulty or uncertainty of obtaining immediate payment was supposed to be greater or less; or according to the greater or less distance of time at which payment was exigible.

Some years ago the different banking companies of Scotland were in the practice of inserting into their bank notes, what they called an Optional Clause, by which they promised payment to the bearer, either as soon as the note should be presented, or, in the option of the directors, six months after such presentment, together with the legal interest for the said six months. The directors of some of those banks sometimes took advantage of this optional clause, and sometimes threatened those who demanded gold and silver in exchange for a considerable number of their notes, that they would take advantage of it, unless such demanders would content themselves with a part of what they demanded. The promissory notes of those banking companies constituted at that time the far greater part of the currency of Scotland, which this uncertainty of payment necessarily degraded below the value of gold and silver money. During the continuance of this abuse (which prevailed chiefly in 1762, 1763 and 1764), while the exchange between London and Carlisle was at par, that between London and Dumfries would sometimes be four per cent. against Dumfries, though this town is not thirty miles distant from Carlisle. But at Carlisle, bills were paid in gold and silver; whereas at Dumfries they were paid in Scotch bank notes, and the uncertainty of getting those bank notes exchanged for gold and silver coin had thus degraded them four per cent. below the value of that coin. The same act of parliament which suppressed ten and five shilling bank notes, suppressed likewise this optional clause, and thereby restored the exchange between England and Scotland to its natural rate, or to what the course of trade and remittances might happen to make it.

In the paper currencies of Yorkshire, the payment of so small a sum as a sixpence sometimes depended upon the condition that the holder of the note should bring the change of a guinea to the person who issued it; a condition, which the holders of such notes might frequently find it very difficult to fulfil, and which must have degraded this currency below the value of gold and silver money. An act of parliament, accordingly, declared all such clauses unlawful, and suppressed, in the same manner as in Scotland, all promissory notes, payable to the bearer, under twenty shillings value.

The paper currencies of North America consisted, not in bank notes payable to the bearer on demand, but in a government paper, of which the payment was not exigible till several years after it was issued: And though the colony governments paid no interest to the holders of this paper, they declared it to be, and in fact rendered it, a legal tender of payment for the full value for which it was issued. But allowing the colony security to be perfectly good, a hundred pounds payable fifteen years hence, for example, in a country where interest is at six per cent. is worth little more than forty pounds ready money. To oblige a creditor, therefore, to accept of this as full payment for a debt of a hundred pounds actually paid down in ready money, was an act of such violent injustice, as has scarce, perhaps, been attempted by the government of any other country which pretended to be free. It bears the evident marks of having originally been, what the honest and downright Doctor Douglas assures us it was, a scheme of fraudulent debtors to cheat their creditors, The government of Pensylvania, indeed, pretended, upon their first emission of paper money, in 1722, to render their paper of equal value with gold and silver, by enacting penalties against all those who made any difference in the price of their goods when they sold them for a colony paper, and when they sold them for gold and silver; a regulation equally tyrannical, but much less effectual than that which it was meant to support. A positive law may render a shilling a legal tender for a guinea; because it may direct the courts of justice to discharge the debtor who has made that tender. But no positive law can oblige a person who sells goods, and who is at liberty to sell or not to sell, as he pleases, to accept of a shilling as equivalent to a guinea in the price of them. Notwithstanding any regulation of this kind, it appeared by the course of exchange with Great Britain, that a hundred pounds sterling was occasionally considered as equivalent, in some of the colonies, to a hundred and thirty pounds, and in others to so great a sum as eleven hundred pounds currency; this difference in the value arising from the difference in the quantity of paper emitted in the different colonies, and in the distance and probability of the term of its final discharge and redemption.

No law, therefore, could be more equitable than the act of parliament, so unjustly complained of in the colonies, which declared that no paper currency to be emitted there in time coming should be a legal tender of payment.

Pensylvania was always more moderate in its emissions of paper money than any other of our colonies. Its paper currency accordingly is said never to have sunk below the value of the gold and silver which was current in the colony before the first emission of its paper money. Before that emission, the colony had raised the denomination of its coin, and had, by act of assembly, ordered five shillings sterling to pass in the colony for six and three-pence, and afterwards for six and eight-pence. A pound colony currency, therefore, even when that currency was gold and silver, was more than thirty per cent. below the value of a pound sterling, and when that currency was turned into paper, it was seldom much more than thirty per cent. below that value. The pretence for raising the denomination of the coin was to prevent the exportation of gold and silver, by making equal quantities of those metals pass for greater sums in the colony than they did in the mother country. It was found, however, that the price of all goods from the mother country rose exactly in proportion as they raised the denomination of their coin, so that their gold and silver were exported as fast as ever.

The paper of each colony being received in the payment of the provincial taxes, for the full value for which it had been issued, it necessarily derived from this use some additional value, over and above what it would have had, from the real or supposed distance of the term of its final discharge and redemption. This additional value was greater or less, according as the quantity of paper issued was more or less above what could be employed in the payment of the taxes of the particular colony which issued it. It was in all the colonies very much above what could be employed in this manner.

A prince, who should enact that a certain proportion of his taxes should be paid in a paper money of a certain kind, might thereby give a certain value to this paper money; even though the term of its final discharge and redemption should depend altogether upon the will of the prince. If the bank which issued this paper was careful to keep the quantity of it always somewhat below what could easily be employed in this manner, the demand for it might be such as to make it even bear a premium, or sell for somewhat more in the market than the quantity of gold or silver currency for which it was issued.

Some people account in this manner for what is called the Agio of the bank of Amsterdam, or for the superiority of bank money over current money, though this bank money, as they pretend, cannot be taken out of the bank at the will of the owner. The greater part of foreign bills of exchange must be paid in bank money, that is, by a transfer in the books of the bank; and the directors of the bank, they allege, are careful to keep the whole quantity of bank money always below what this use occasions a demand for. It is upon this account, they say, that bank money sells for a premium, or bears an agio of four or five per cent. above the same nominal sum of the gold and silver currency of the country. This account of the bank of Amsterdam, however, it will appear hereafter, is in a great measure chimerical.

A paper currency which falls below the value of gold and silver coin, does not thereby sink the value of those metals, or occasion equal quantities of them to exchange for a smaller quantity of goods of any other kind. The proportion between the value of gold and silver and that of goods of any other kind, depends in all cases, not upon the nature or quantity of any particular paper money, which may be current in any particular country, but upon the richness or poverty of the mines, which happen at any particular time to supply the great market of the commercial world with those metals. It depends upon the proportion between the quantity of labour which is necessary in order to bring a certain quantity of gold and silver to market, and that which is necessary in order to bring thither a certain quantity of any other sort of goods.

If bankers are restrained from issuing any circulating bank notes, or notes payable to the bearer, for less than a certain sum; and if they are subjected to the obligation of an immediate and unconditional payment of such bank notes as soon as presented, their trade may, with safety to the public, be rendered in all other respects perfectly free. The late multiplication of banking companies in both parts of the united kingdom, an event by which many people have been much alarmed, instead of diminishing, increases the security of the public. It obliges all of them to be more circumspect in their conduct, and, by not extending their currency beyond its due proportion to their cash, to guard themselves against those malicious runs, which the rivalship of so many competitors is always ready to bring upon them. It restrains the circulation of each particular company within a narrower circle, and reduces their circulating notes to a smaller number. By dividing the whole circulation into a greater number of parts, the failure of any one company, an accident which, in the course of things, must sometimes happen, becomes of less consequence to the public. This free competition too obliges all bankers to be more liberal in their dealings with their customers, lest their rivals should carry them away. In general, if any branch of trade, or any division of labour, be advantageous to the public, the freer and more general the competition, it will always be the more so.

CHAPTER III

Of the Accumulation of Capital, or of Productive and Unproductive Labour

THERE is one sort of labour which adds to the value of the subject upon which it is bestowed: there is another which has no such effect. The former, as it produces a value, may be called productive; the latter, unproductive labour. Thus the labour of a manufacturer adds, generally, to the value of the materials which he works upon, that of his own maintenance, and of his master's profit. The labour of a menial servant, on the contrary, adds to the value of nothing. Though the manufacturer has his wages advanced to him by his master, he, in reality, costs him no expense, the value of those wages being generally restored, together with a profit, in the improved value of the subject upon which his labour is bestowed. But the maintenance of a menial servant never is restored. A man grows rich by employing a multitude of manufacturers: he grows poor, by maintaining a multitude of menial servants. The labour of the latter, however, has its value, and deserves its reward as well as that of the former. But the labour of the manufacturer fixes and realizes itself in some particular subject or vendible commodity, which lasts for some time at least after that labour is past. It is, as it were, a certain quantity of labour stocked and stored up to be employed, if necessary, upon some other occasion. That subject, or what is the same thing, the price of that subject, can afterwards, if necessary, put into motion a quantity of labour equal to that which had originally produced it. The labour of the menial servant, on the contrary, does not fix or realize itself in any particular subject or vendible commodity. His services generally perish in the very instant of their performance, and seldom leave any trace or value behind them, for which an equal quantity of service could afterwards be procured.

The labour of some of the most respectable orders in the society is, like that of menial servants, unproductive of any value, and does not fix or realize itself in any permanent subject, or vendible commodity, which endures after that labour is past and for which an equal quantity of labour could afterwards be procured. The sovereign, for example, with all the officers both of justice and war who serve under him, the whole army and navy, are unproductive labourers. They are the servants of the public, and are maintained by a part of the annual produce of the industry of other people. Their service, how honourable, how useful, or how necessary soever, produces nothing for which an equal quantity of service can afterwards be procured. The protection, security, and defence of the commonwealth, the effect of their labour this year, will not purchase its protection, security, and defence for the year to come. In the same class must be ranked, some both of the gravest and most important, and some of the most frivolous professions: churchmen, lawyers, physicians, men of letters of all kinds; players, buffoons, musicians, opera-singers, opera-dancers, &c. The labour of the meanest of these has a certain value, regulated by the very same principles which regulate that of every sort of labour; and that of the noblest and most useful, produces nothing which could afterwards purchase or procure an equal quantity of labour. Like the declamation of the actor, the harangue of the orator, or the tune of the musician, the work of all of them perishes in the very instant of its production.

Both productive and unproductive labourers, and those who do not labour at all, are all equally maintained by the annual produce of the land and labour of the country. This produce, how great soever, can never be infinite, but must have certain limits. According, therefore, as a smaller or greater proportion of it is in any one year employed in maintaining unproductive hands, the more in the one case and the less in the other will remain for the productive, and the next year's produce will be greater or smaller accordingly; the whole annual produce, if we except the spontaneous productions of the earth, being the effect of productive labour. Though the whole annual produce of the land and labour of every country, is, no doubt, ultimately destined for supplying the consumption of its inhabitants, and for procuring a revenue to them; yet when it first comes either from the ground, or from the hands of the productive labourers, it naturally divides itself into two parts. One of them, and frequently the largest, is, in the first place, destined for replacing a capital, or for renewing the provisions, materials, and finished work, which had been withdrawn from a capital; the other for constituting a revenue either to the owner of this capital, as the profit of his stock; or to some other person, as the rent of his land. Thus, of the produce of land, one part replaces the capital of the farmer; the other pays his profit and the rent of the landlord; and thus constitutes a revenue both to the owner of this capital, as the profits of his stock; and to some other person, as the rent of his land. Of the produce of a great manufactory, in the same manner, one part, and that always the largest, replaces the capital of the undertaker of the work; the other pays his profit, and thus constitutes a revenue to the owner of this capital.

That part of the annual produce of the land and labour of any country which replaces a capital, never is immediately employed to maintain any but productive hands. It pays the wages of productive labour only. That which is immediately destined for constituting a revenue either as profit or as rent, may maintain indifferently either productive or unproductive hands.

Whatever part of his stock a man employs as a capital, he always expects is to be replaced to him with a profit. He employs it, therefore, in maintaining productive hands only; and after having served in the function of a capital to him, it constitutes a revenue to them. Whenever he employs any part of it in maintaining unproductive hands of any kind, that part is, from that moment, withdrawn from his capital, and placed in his stock reserved for immediate consumption.

Unproductive labourers, and those who do not labour at all, are all maintained by revenue; either, first, by that part of the annual produce which is originally destined for constituting a revenue to some particular persons, either as the rent of land or as the profits of stock; or, secondly, by that part which, though orginally destined for replacing a capital and for maintaining productive labourers only, yet when it comes into their hands, whatever part of it is over and above their necessary subsistence, may be employed in maintaining indifferently either productive or unproductive hands. Thus, not only the great landlord or the rich merchant, but even the common workman, if his wages are considerable, may maintain a menial servant; or he may sometimes go to a play or a puppet-show, and so contribute his share towards maintaining one set of unproductive labourers; or he may pay some taxes, and thus help to maintain another set, more honourable and useful, indeed, but equally unproductive. No part of the annual produce, however, which had been originally destined to replace a capital, is ever directed towards maintaining unproductive hands, till after it has put into motion its full complement of productive labour, or all that it could put into motion in the way in which it was employed. The workman must have earned his wages by work done, before he can employ any part of them in this manner. That part too is generally but a small one. It is his spare revenue only, of which productive labourers have seldom a great deal. They generally have some, however; and in the payment of taxes the greatness of their number may compensate, in some measure, the smallness of their contribution. The rent of land and the profits of stock are everywhere, therefore, the principal sources from which unproductive hands derive their subsistence. These are the two sorts of revenue of which the owners have generally most to spare. They might both maintain indifferently either productive or unproductive hands. They seem, however, to have some predilection for the latter. The expence of a great lord feeds generally more idle than industrious people. The rich merchant, though with his capital he maintains industrious people only, yet by his expence, that is, by the employment of his revenue, he feeds commonly the very same sort as the great lord.

The proportion, therefore, between the productive and unproductive hands, depends very much in every country upon the proportion between that part of the annual produce, which, as soon as it comes either from the ground or from the hands of the productive labourers, is destined for replacing a capital, and that which is destined for constituting a revenue, either as rent, or as profit. This proportion is very different in rich from what it is in poor countries.

Thus, at present, in the opulent countries of Europe, a very large, frequently the largest portion of the produce of the land, is destined for replacing the capital of the rich and independent farmer; the other for paying his profits, and the rent of the landlord. But anciently, during the prevalency of the feudal government, a very small portion of the produce was sufficient to replace the capital employed in cultivation. It consisted commonly in a few wretched cattle, maintained altogether by the spontaneous produce of uncultivated land, and which might, therefore, be considered as a part of that spontaneous produce. It generally too belonged to the landlord, and was by him advanced to the occupiers of the land. All the rest of the produce properly belonged to him too, either as rent for his land, or as profit upon this paultry capital. The occupiers of land were generally bondmen, whose persons and effects were equally his property. Those who were not bondmen were tenants at will, and though the rent which they paid was often nominally little more than a quit-rent, it really amounted to the whole produce of the land. Their lord could at all times command their labour in peace, and their service in war. Though they lived at a distance from his house, they were equally dependent upon him as his retainers who lived in it.

But the whole produce of the land undoubtedly belongs to him, who can dispose of the labour and service of all those whom it maintains. In the present state of Europe, the share of the landlord seldom exceeds a third, sometimes not a fourth part of the whole produce of the land. The rent of land, however, in all the improved parts of the country, has been tripled and quadrupled since those ancient times; and this third or fourth part of the annual produce is, it seems, three or four times greater than the whole had been before. In the progress of improvement, rent, though it increases in proportion to the extent, diminishes in proportion to the produce of the land.

In the opulent countries of Europe, great capitals are at present employed in trade and manufactures. In the ancient state, the little trade that was stirring, and the few homely and coarse manufactures that were carried on, required but very small capitals. These, however, must have yielded very large profits. The rate of interest was nowhere less than ten per cent. and their profits must have been sufficient to afford this great interest. At present the rate of interest, in the improved parts of Europe, is no-where higher than six per cent. and in some of the most improved it is so low as four, three, and two per cent. Though that part of the revenue of the inhabitants which is derived from the profits of stock is always much greater in rich than in poor countries, it is because the stock is much greater: in proportion to the stock the profits are generally much less.

That part of the annual produce, therefore, which, as soon as it comes either from the ground, or from the hands of the productive labourers, is destined for replacing a capital, is not only much greater in rich than in poor countries, but bears a much greater proportion to that which is immediately destined for constituting a revenue either as rent or as profit. The funds destined for the maintenance of productive labour, are not only much greater in the former than in the latter, but bear a much greater proportion to those which, though they may be employed to maintain either productive or unproductive hands, have generally a predilection for the latter.

The proportion between those different funds necessarily determines in every country the general character of the inhabitants as to industry or idleness. We are more industrious than our forefathers; because in the present times the funds destined for the maintenance of industry, are much greater in proportion to those which are likely to be employed in the maintenance of idleness, than they were two or three centuries ago. Our ancestors were idle for want of a sufficient encouragement to industry. It is better, says the proverb, to play for nothing, than to work for nothing. In mercantile and manufacturing towns, where the inferior ranks of people are chiefly maintained by the employment of capital, they are in general industrious, sober, and thriving; as in many English, and in most Dutch towns. In those towns which are principally supported by the constant or occasional residence of a court, and in which the inferior ranks of people are chiefly maintained by the spending of revenue, they are in general idle, dissolute, and poor; as at Rome, Versailles, Compiegne, and Fontainbleau. If you except Rouen and Bourdeaux, there is little trade or industry in any of the parliament towns of France; and the inferior ranks of people, being chiefly maintained by the expence of the members of the courts of justice, and of those who come to plead before them, are in general idle and poor. The great trade of Rouen and Bourdeaux seems to be altogether the effect of their situation. Rouen is necessarily the entrepôt of almost all the goods which are brought either from foreign countries, or from the maritime provinces of France, for the consumption of the great city of Paris. Bourdeaux is in the same manner the entrepôt of the wines which grow upon the banks of the Garonne, and of the rivers which run into it, one of the richest wine countries in the world, and which seems to produce the wine fittest for exportation, or best suited to the taste of foreign nations. Such advantageous situations necessarily attract a great capital by the great employment which they afford it; and the employment of this capital is the cause of the industry of those two cities. In the other parliament towns of France, very little more capital seems to be employed than what is necessary for supplying their own consumption; that is, little more than the smallest capital which can be employed in them. The same thing may be said of Paris, Madrid, and Vienna. Of those three cities, Paris is by far the most industrious: but Paris itself is the principal market of all the manufactures established at Paris, and its own consumption is the principal object of all the trade which it carries on. London, Lisbon, and Copenhagen, are, perhaps, the only three cities in Europe, which are both the constant residence of a court, and can at the same time be considered as trading cities, or as cities which trade not only for their own consumption, but for that of other cities and countries. The situation of all the three is extremely advantageous, and naturally fits them to be the entrepôts of a great part of the goods destined for the consumption of distant places. In a city where a great revenue is spent, to employ with advantage a capital for any other purpose than for supplying the consumption of that city, is probably more difficult than in one in which the inferior ranks of people have no other maintenance but what they derive from the employment of such a capital. The idleness of the greater part of the people who are maintained by the expence of revenue, corrupts, it is probable, the industry of those who ought to be maintained by the employment of capital, and renders it less advantageous to employ a capital there than in other places. There was little trade or industry in Edinburgh before the Union. When the Scotch parliament was no longer to be assembled in it, when it ceased to be the necessary residence of the principal nobility and gentry of Scotland, it became a city of some trade and industry. It still continues, however, to be the residence of the principal courts of justice in Scotland, of the boards of customs and excise, &c. A considerable revenue, therefore, still continues to be spent in it. In trade and industry it is much inferior to Glasgow, of which the inhabitants are chiefly maintained by the employment of capital. The inhabitants of a large village, it has sometimes been observed, after having made considerable progress in manufactures, have become idle and poor, in consequence of a great lord's having taken up his residence in their neighbourhood.

The proportion between capital and revenue, therefore, seems everywhere to regulate the proportion between industry and idleness. Wherever capital predominates, industry prevails; wherever revenue, idleness. Every increase or diminution of capital, therefore, naturally tends to increase or diminish the real quantity of industry, the number of productive hands, and consequently, the exchangeable value of the annual produce of the land and labour of the country, the real wealth and revenue of all its inhabitants.

Capitals are increased by parsimony, and diminished by prodigality and misconduct.

Whatever a person saves from his revenue he adds to his

capital, and either employs it himself in maintaining an additional number of productive hands, or enables some other person to do so, by lending it to him for an interest, that is, for a share of the profits. As the capital of an individual can be increased only by what he saves from his annual revenue or his annual gains, so the capital of a society, which is the same with that of all the individuals who compose it, can be increased only in the same manner.

Parsimony, and not industry, is the immediate cause of the increase of capital. Industry, indeed, provides the subject which parsimony accumulates. But whatever industry might acquire, if parsimony did not save and store up, the capital would never be the greater.

Parsimony, by increasing the fund which is destined for the maintenance of productive hands, tends to increase the number of those hands whose labour adds to the value of the subject upon which it is bestowed. It tends therefore to increase the exchangeable value of the annual produce of the land and labour of the country. It puts into motion an additional quantity of industry, which gives an additional value to the annual produce.

What is annually saved is as regularly consumed as what is annually spent, and nearly in the same time too; but it is consumed by a different set of people. That portion of his revenue which a rich man annually spends, is in most cases consumed by idle guests, and menial servants, who leave nothing behind them in return for their consumption. That portion which he annually saves, as for the sake of the profit it is immediately employed as a capital, is consumed in the same manner, and nearly in the same time too, but by a different set of people, by labourers, manufacturers, and artificers, who re-produce with a profit the value of their annual consumption. His revenue, we shall suppose, is paid him in money. Had he spent the whole, the food, clothing, and lodging, which the whole could have purchased, would have been distributed among the former set of people. By saving a part of it, as that part is for the sake of the profit immediately employed as a capital either by himself or by some other person, the food, clothing, and lodging, which may be purchased with it, are necessarily reserved for the latter.

The consumption is the same, but the consumers are different.

By what a frugal man annually saves, he not only affords maintenance to an additional number of productive hands, for that or the ensuing year, but, like the founder of a public workhouse, he establishes as it were a perpetual fund for the maintenance of an equal number in all times to come. The perpetual allotment and destination of this fund, indeed, is not always guarded by any positive law, by any trust-right or deed of mortmain. It is always guarded, however, by a very powerful principle, the plain and evident interest of every individual to whom any share of it shall ever belong. No part of it can ever afterwards be employed to maintain any but productive hands, without an evident loss to the person who thus perverts it from its proper destination.

The prodigal perverts it in this manner. By not confining his expence within his income, he encroaches upon his capital. Like him who perverts the revenues of some pious foundation to profane purposes, he pays the wages of idleness with those funds which the frugality of his forefathers had, as it were, consecrated to the maintenance of industry. By diminishing the funds destined for the employment of productive labour, he necessarily diminishes, so far as it depends upon him, the quantity of that labour which adds a value to the subject upon which it is bestowed, and, consequently, the value of the annual produce of the land and labour of the whole country, the real wealth and revenue of its inhabitants. If the prodigality of some was not compensated by the frugality of others, the conduct of every prodigal, by feeding the idle with the bread of the industrious, tends not only to beggar himself, but to impoverish his country.

Though the expence of the prodigal should be altogether in home-made, and no part of it in foreign commodities, its effect upon the productive funds of the society would still be the same. Every year there would still be a certain quantity of food and clothing, which ought to have maintained productive, employed in maintaining unproductive hands. Every year, therefore, there would still be some diminution in what would otherwise have been the value of the annual produce of the land and labour of the country.

This expence, it may be said indeed, not being in foreign goods, and not occasioning any exportation of gold and silver, the same quantity of money would remain in the country as before. But if the quantity of food and clothing, which were thus consumed by unproductive, had been distributed among productive hands, they would have re-produced, together with a profit, the full value of their consumption. The same quantity of money would in this case equally have remained in the country, and there would besides have been a reproduction of an equal value of consumable goods. There would have been two values instead of one.

The same quantity of money, besides, cannot long remain in any country in which the value of the annual produce diminishes. The sole use of money is to circulate consumable goods. By means of it, provisions, materials, and finished work, are bought and sold, and distributed to their proper consumers. The quantity of money, therefore, which can be annually employed in any country, must be determined by the value of the consumable goods annually circulated within it. These must consist either in the immediate produce of the land and labour of the country itself, or in something which had been purchased with some part of that produce. Their value, therefore, must diminish as the value of that produce diminishes, and along with it the quantity of money which can be employed in circulating them. But the money which by this annual diminution of produce is annually thrown out of domestic circulation, will not be allowed to lie idle. The interest of whoever possesses it, requires that it should be employed. But having no employment at home, it will, in spite of all laws and prohibitions, be sent abroad, and employed in purchasing consumable goods which may be of some use at home. Its annual exportation will in this manner continue for some time to add something to the annual consumption of the country beyond the value of its own annual produce. What in the days of its prosperity had been saved from that annual produce, and employed in purchasing gold and silver, will contribute for some little time to support its consumption in adversity. The exportation of gold and silver is, in this case, not the cause, but the effect of its declension, and may even, for some little time, alleviate the misery of that declension.

The quantity of money, on the contrary, must in every country naturally increase as the value of the annual produce increases. The value of the consumable goods annually circulated within the society being greater, will require a greater quantity of money to circulate them. A part of the increased produce, therefore, will naturally be employed in purchasing, wherever it is to be had, the additional quantity of gold and silver necessary for circulating the rest. The increase of those metals will in this case be the effect, not the cause, of the public prosperity. Gold and silver are purchased every-where in the same manner. The food, clothing, and lodging, the revenue and maintenance of all those whose labour or stock is employed in bringing them from the mine to the market, is the price paid for them in Peru as well as in England. The country which has this price to pay, will never be long without the quantity of those metals which it has occasion for; and no country will ever long retain a quantity which it has no occasion for.

Whatever, therefore, we may imagine the real wealth and revenue of a country to consist in, whether in the value of the annual produce of its land and labour, as plain reason seems to dictate; or in the quantity of the precious metals which circulate within it, as vulgar prejudices suppose; in either view of the matter, every prodigal appears to be a public enemy, and every frugal man a public benefactor.

The effects of misconduct are often the same as those of prodigality. Every injudicious and unsuccessful project in agriculture, mines, fisheries, trade, or manufactures, tends in the same manner to diminish the funds destined for the maintenance of productive labour. In every such project, though the capital is consumed by productive hands only, yet, as by the injudicious manner in which they are employed, they do not reproduce the full value of their consumption, there must always be some diminution in what would otherwise have been the productive funds of the society.

It can seldom happen, indeed, that the circumstances of a great nation can be much affected either by the prodigality or misconduct of individuals; the profusion or imprudence of some, being always more than compensated by the frugality and good conduct of others.

With regard to profusion, the principle which prompts to expence, is the passion for present enjoyment; which, though sometimes violent and very difficult to be restrained, is in general only momentary and occasional. But the principle which prompts to save, is the desire of bettering our condition, a desire which, though generally calm and dispassionate, comes with us from the womb, and never leaves us till we go into the grave. In the whole interval which separates those two moments, there is scarce perhaps a single instant in which any man is so perfectly and completely satisfied with his situation, as to be without any wish of alteration or improvement of any kind. An augmentation of fortune is the means by which the greater part of men propose and wish to better their condition. It is the means the most vulgar and the most obvious; and the most likely way of augmenting their fortune, is to save and accumulate some part of what they acquire, either regularly and annually, or upon some extraordinary occasions. Though the principle of expence, therefore, prevails in almost all men upon some occasions, and in some men upon almost all occasions, yet in the greater part of men, taking the whole course of their life at an average, the principle of frugality seems not only to predominate but to predominate very greatly.

With regard to misconduct, the number of prudent and successful undertakings is every-where much greater than that of injudicious and unsuccessful ones. After all our complaints of the frequency of bankruptcies, the unhappy men who fall into this misfortune make but a very small part of the whole number engaged in trade, and all other sorts of business; not much more perhaps than one in a thousand. Bankruptcy is perhaps the greatest and most humiliating calamity which can befal an innocent man. The greater part of men, therefore, are sufficiently careful to avoid it. Some, indeed, do not avoid it; as some do not avoid the gallows.

Great nations are never impoverished by private, though they sometimes are by public prodigality and misconduct. The whole, or almost the whole public revenue, is in most countries employed in maintaining unproductive hands. Such are the people who compose a numerous and splendid court, a great eccleciastical establishment, great fleets and armies, who in time of peace produce nothing, and in time of war acquire nothing which can compensate the expence of maintaining them, even while the war lasts. Such people, as they themselves produce nothing, are all maintained by the produce of other men's labour. When multiplied, therefore, to an unnecessary number, they may in a particular year consume so great a share of this produce, as not to leave a sufficiency for maintaining the productive labourers, who should reproduce it next year. The next year's produce, therefore, will be less than that of the foregoing, and if the same disorder should continue, that of the third year will be still less than that of the second. Those unproductive hands, who should be maintained by a part only of the spare revenue of the people, may consume so great a share of their whole revenue, and thereby oblige so great a number to encroach upon their capitals, upon the funds destined for the maintenance of productive labour, that all the frugality and good conduct of individuals may not be able to compensate the waste and degradation of produce occasioned by this violent and forced encroachment.

This frugality and good conduct, however, is upon most occasions, it appears from experience, sufficient to compensate, not only the private prodigality and misconduct of individuals, but the public extravagance of government. The uniform, constant, and uninterrupted effort of every man to better his condition, the principle from which the public and national, as well as private opulence is originally derived, is frequently powerful enough to maintain the natural progress of things toward improvement, in spite both of the extravagance of government, and of the greatest errors of administration. Like the unknown principle of animal life, it frequently restores health and vigour to the constitution, in spite, not only of the disease, but of the absurd prescriptions of the doctor.

The annual produce of the land and labour of any nation can be increased in its value by no other means, but by increasing either the number of its productive labourers, or the productive powers of those labourers who had before been employed. The number of its productive labourers, it is evident, can never be much increased, but in consequence of an increase of capital, or of the funds destined for maintaining them. The productive powers of the same number of labourers cannot be increased, but in consequence either of some addition and improvement to those machines and instruments which facilitate and abridge labour; or of a more proper division and distribution of employment. In either case an additional capital is almost always required. It is by means of an additional capital only, that the undertaker of any work can either provide his workmen with better machinery, or make a more proper distribution of employment among them. When the work to be done consists of a number of parts, to keep every man constantly employed in one way, requires a much greater capital than where every man is occasionally employed in every different part of the work. When we compare, therefore, the state of a nation at two different periods, and find, that the annual produce of its land and labour is evidently greater at the latter than at the former, that its lands are better cultivated, its manufactures more numerous and more flourishing, and its trade more extensive, we may be assured that its capital must have increased during the interval between those two periods, and that more must have been added to it by the good conduct of some, than had been taken from it either by the private misconduct of others, or by the public extravagance of government. But we shall find this to have been the case of almost all nations, in all tolerably quiet and peaceable times, even of those who have not enjoyed the most prudent and parsimonious governments. To form a right judgment of it, indeed, we must compare the state of the country at periods somewhat distant from one another. The progress is frequently so gradual, that, at near periods, the improvement is not only not sensible, but from the declension either of certain branches of industry, or of certain districts of the country, things which sometimes happen though the country in general be in great prosperity, there frequently arises a suspicion, that the riches and industry of the whole are decaying.

The annual produce of the land and labour of England, for example, is certainly much greater than it was, a little more than a century ago, at the restoration of Charles II. Though, at present, few people, I believe, doubt of this, yet during this period, five years have seldom passed away in which some book or pamphlet has not been published, written too with such abilities as to gain some authority with the public, and pretending to demonstrate that the wealth of the nation was fast declining, that the country was depopulated, agriculture neglected, manufactures decaying, and trade undone. Nor have these publications been all party pamphlets, the wretched offspring of falsehood and venality. Many of them have been written by very candid and very intelligent people; who wrote nothing but what they believed, and for no other reason but because they believed it.

The annual produce of the land and labour of England again, was certainly much greater at the restoration, than we can suppose it to have been about an hundred years before, at the accession of Elizabeth. At this period, too, we have all reason to believe, the country was much more advanced in improvement, than it had been about a century before, towards the close of the dissensions between the houses of York and Lancaster. Even then it was, probably, in a better condition than it had been at the Norman conquest, and at the Norman conquest, than during the confusion of the Saxon Heptarchy. Even at this early period, it was certainly a more improved country than at the invasion of Julius Cæsar, when its inhabitants were nearly in the same state with the savages in North America.

In each of those periods, however, there was, not only much private and public profusion, many expensive and unnecessary wars, great perversion of the annual produce from maintaining productive to maintain unproductive hands; but sometimes, in the confusion of civil discord, such absolute waste and destruction of stock, as might be supposed, not only to retard, as it certainly did, the natural accumulation of riches, but to have left the country, at the end of the period, poorer than at the beginning. Thus, in the happiest and most fortunate period of them all, that which has passed since the restoration, how many disorders and misfortunes have occurred, which, could they have been foreseen, not only the impoverishment, but the total ruin of the country would have been expected from them? The fire and the plague of London, the two Dutch wars, the disorders of the revolution, the war in Ireland, the four expensive French wars of 1688, 1702, 1742, and 1756, together with the two rebellions of 1715 and 1745. In the course of the four French wars, the nation has contracted more than a hundred and forty-five millions of debt, over and above all the other extraordinary annual expence which they occasioned, so that the whole cannot be computed at less than two hundred millions. So great a share of the annual produce of the land and labour of the country, has, since the revolution, been employed upon different occasions, in maintaining an extraordinary number of unproductive hands. But had not those wars given this particular direction to so large a capital, the greater part of it would naturally have been employed in maintaining productive hands, whose labour would have replaced, with a profit, the whole value of their consumption. The value of the annual produce of the land and labour of the country, would have been considerably increased by it every year, and every year's increase would have augmented still more that of the following year. More houses would have been built, more lands would have been improved, and those which had been improved before would have been better cultivated, more manufactures would have been established, and those which had been established before would have been more extended; and to what height the real wealth and revenue of the country might, by this time, have been raised, it is not perhaps very easy even to imagine.

But though the profusion of government must, undoubtedly, have retarded the natural progress of England towards wealth and improvement, it has not been able to stop it. The annual produce of its land and labour is, undoubtedly, much greater at present than it was either at the restoration or at the revolution. The capital, therefore, annually employed in cultivating this land, and in maintaining this labour, must likewise be much greater. In the midst of all the exactions of government, this capital has been silently and gradually accumulated by the private frugality and good conduct of individuals, by their universal, continual, and uninterrupted effort to better their own condition. It is this effort, protected by law and allowed by liberty to exert itself in the manner that is most advantageous, which has maintained the progress of England towards opulence and improvement in almost all former times, and which, it is to be hoped, will do so in all future times. England, however, as it has never been blessed with a very parsimonious government, so parsimony has at no time been the characteristical virtue of its inhabitants. It is the highest impertinence and presumption, therefore, in kings and ministers to pretend to watch over the economy of private people, and to restrain their expence, either by sumptuary laws, or by prohibiting the importation of foreign luxuries. They are themselves always, and without any exception, the greatest spendthrifts in the society. Let them look well after their own expence, and they may safely trust private people with theirs. If their own extravagance does not ruin the state, that of their subjects never will.

As frugality increases, and prodigality diminishes the public capital, so the conduct of those whose expence just equals their revenue, without either accumulating or encroaching, neither increases nor diminishes it. Some modes of expence, however, seem to contribute more to the growth of public opulence than others.

The revenue of an individual may be spent, either in things which are consumed immediately, and in which one day's expence can neither alleviate nor support that of another; or it may be spent in things more durable, which can therefore be accumulated, and in which every day's expence may, as he chuses, either alleviate or support and heighten the effect of that of the following day. A man of fortune, for example, may either spend his revenue in a profuse and sumptuous table, and in maintaining a great number of menial servants, and a multitude of dogs and horses; or contenting himself with a frugal table and few attendants, he may lay out the greater part of it in adorning his house or his country villa, in useful or ornamental buildings, in useful or ornamental furniture, in collecting books, statues, pictures; or in things more frivolous, jewels, baubles, ingenious trinkets of different kinds; or, what is most trifling of all, in amassing a great wardrobe of fine clothes, like the favourite and minister of a great prince who died a few years ago. Were two men of equal fortune to spend their revenue, the one chiefly in the one way, the other in the other, the magnificence of the person whose expence had been chiefly in durable commodities, would be continually increasing, every day's expence contributing something to support and heighten the effect of that of the following day: that of the other, on the contrary, would be no greater at the end of the period than at the beginning. The former too would, at the end of the period, be the richer man of the two. He would have a stock of goods of some kind or other, which, though it might not be worth all that it cost, would always be worth something. No trace or vestige of the expence of the latter would remain, and the effects of ten or twenty years profusion would be as completely annihilated as if they had never existed.

As the one mode of expence is more favourable than the other to the opulence of an individual, so is it likewise to that of a nation. The houses, the furniture, the clothing of the rich, in a little time, become useful to the inferior and middling ranks of people. They are able to purchase them when their superiors grow weary of them, and the general accommodation of the whole people is thus gradually improved, when this mode of expence becomes universal among men of fortune. In countries which have long been rich, you will frequently find the inferior ranks of people in possession both of houses and furniture perfectly good and entire, but of which neither the one could have been built, nor the other have been made for their use. What was formerly a seat of the family of Seymour, is now an inn upon the Bath road. The marriage-bed of James the First of Great Britain, which his Queen brought with her from Denmark, as a present fit for a sovereign to make to a sovereign, was, a few years ago, the ornament of an ale-house at Dunfermline. In some ancient cities, which either have been long stationary, or have gone somewhat to decay, you will sometimes scarce find a single house which could have been built for its present inhabitants. If you go into those houses too, you will frequently find many excellent, though antiquated pieces of furniture, which are still very fit for use, and which could as little have been made for them. Noble palaces, magnificent villas, great collections of books, statues, pictures, and other curiosities, are frequently both an ornament and an honour, not only to the neighbourhood, but to the whole country to which they belong. Versailles is an ornament and an honour to France, Stowe and Wilton to England. Italy still continues to command some sort of veneration by the number of monuments of this kind which it possesses, though the wealth which produced them has decayed, and though the genius which planned them seems to be extinguished, perhaps, from not having the same employment.

The expence too, which is laid out in durable commodities, is favourable, not only to accumulation, but to frugality. If a person should at any time exceed in it, he can easily reform without exposing himself to the censure of the public. To reduce very much the number of his servants, to reform his table from great profusion to great frugality, to lay down his equipage after he has once set it up, are changes which cannot escape the observation of his neighbours, and which are supposed to imply some acknowledgment of preceding bad conduct Few, therefore, of those who have once been so unfortunate as to launch out too far into this sort of expence, have afterwards the courage to reform, till ruin and bankruptcy oblige them. But if a person has, at any time, been at too great an expence in building, in furniture, in books or pictures, no imprudence can be inferred from his changing his conduct. These are things in which further expence is frequently rendered unnecessary by former expence; and when a person stops short, he appears to do so, not because he has exceeded his fortune, but because he has satisfied his fancy.

The expence, besides, that is laid out in durable commodities, gives maintenance, commonly, to a greater number of people, than that which is employed in the most profuse hospitality. Of two or three hundred weight of provisions, which may sometimes be served up at a great festival, one-half, perhaps, is thrown to the dunghill, and there is always a great deal wasted and abused. But if the expense of this entertainment had been employed in setting to work masons, carpenters, upholsterers, mechanics, &c. a quantity of provisions, of equal value, would have been distributed among a still greater number of people, who would have bought them in penny-worths and pound weights, and not have lost or thrown away a single ounce of them. In the one way, besides, this expense maintains productive, in the other unproductive hands. In the one way, therefore, it increases, in the other, it does not increase, the exchangeable value of the annual produce of the land and labour of the country.

I would not, however, by all this be understood to mean, that the one species of expence always betokens a more liberal or generous spirit than the other. When a man of fortune spends his revenue chiefly in hospitality, he shares the greater part of it with his friends and companions; but when he employs it in purchasing such durable commodities, he often spends the whole upon his own person, and gives nothing to any body without an equivalent. The latter species of expence, therefore, especially when directed towards frivolous objects, the little ornaments of dress and furniture, jewels, trinkets, gewgaws, frequently indicates, not only a trifling, but a base and selfish disposition. All that I mean is, that the one sort of expence, as it always occasions some accumulation of valuable commodities, as it is more favourable to private frugality, and, consequently, to the increase of the public capital, and as it maintains productive, rather than unproductive hands, conduces more than the other to the growth of public opulence.

CHAPTER IV

Of Stock Lent at Interest

THE stock which is lent at interest is always considered as a capital by the lender. He expects that in due time it is to be restored to him, and that in the mean time the borrower is to pay him a certain annual rent for the use of it. The borrower may use it either as a capital, or as a stock reserved for immediate consumption. If he uses it as a capital, he employs it in the maintenance of productive labourers, who reproduce the value with a profit. He can, in this case, both restore the capital and pay the interest without alienating or encroaching upon any other source of revenue. If he uses it as a stock reserved for immediate consumption, he acts the part of a prodigal, and dissipates in the maintenance of the idle, what was destined for the support of the industrious. He can, in this case, neither restore the capital nor pay the interest, without either alienating or encroaching upon some other source of revenue, such as the property or the rent of land.

The stock which is lent at interest is, no doubt, occasionally employed in both these ways, but in the former much more frequently than in the latter. The man who borrows in order to spend will soon be ruined, and he who lends to him will generally have occasion to repent of his folly. To borrow or to lend for such a purpose, therefore, is in all cases, where gross usury is out of the question, contrary to the interest of both parties; and though it no doubt happens sometimes that people do both the one and the other; yet, from the regard that all men have for their own interest, we may be assured, that it cannot happen so very frequently as we are sometimes apt to imagine. Ask any rich man of common prudence, to which of the two sorts of people he has lent the greater part of his stock, to those who, he thinks, will employ it profitably, or to those who will spend it idly, and he will laugh at you for proposing the question. Even among borrowers, therefore, not the people in the world most famous for frugality, the number of the frugal and industrious surpasses considerably that of the prodigal and idle.

The only people to whom stock is commonly lent, without their being expected to make any very profitable use of it, are country gentlemen who borrow upon mortgage. Even they scarce ever borrow merely to spend. What they borrow, one may say, is commonly spent before they borrow it. They have generally consumed so great a quantity of goods, advanced to them upon credit by shopkeepers and tradesmen, that they find it necessary to borrow at interest in order to pay the debt. The capital borrowed replaces the capitals of those shopkeepers and tradesmen, which the country gentlemen could not have replaced from the rents of their estates. It is not properly borrowed in order to be spent, but in order to replace a capital which had been spent before.

Almost all loans at interest are made in money, either of paper, or of gold and silver. But what the borrower really wants, and what the lender really supplies him with, is not the money, but the money's worth, or the goods which it can purchase. If he wants it as a stock for immediate consumption, it is those goods only which he can place in that stock. If he wants it as a capital for employing industry, it is from those goods only that the industrious can be furnished with the tools, materials, and maintenance, necessary for carrying on their work. By means of the loan, the lender, as it were, assigns to the borrower his right to a certain portion of the annual produce of the land and labour of the country, to be employed as the borrower pleases.

The quantity of stock, therefore, or, as it is commonly expressed, of money which can be lent at interest in any country, is not regulated by the value of the money, whether paper or coin, which serves as the instrument of the different loans made in that country, but by the value of that part of the annual produce which, as soon as it comes either from the ground, or from the hands of the productive labourers, is destined not only for replacing a capital, but such a capital as the owner does not care to be at the trouble of employing himself. As such capitals are commonly lent out and paid back in money, they constitute what is called the monied interest. It is distinct, not only from the landed, but from the trading and manufacturing interests, as in these last the owners themselves employ their own capitals. Even in the monied interest, however, the money is, as it were, but the deed of assignment, which conveys from one hand to another those capitals which the owners do not care to employ themselves. Those capitals may be greater in almost any proportion, than the amount of the money which serves as the instrument of their conveyance; the same pieces of money successively serving for many different loans, as well as for many different purchases. A, for example, lends to W a thousand pounds, with which W immediately purchases of B a thousand pounds worth of goods. B having no occasion for the money himself, lends the identical pieces to X, with which X immediately purchases of C another thousand pounds worth of goods. C in the same manner, and for the same reason, lends them to Y, who again purchases goods with them of D. In this manner the same pieces, either of coin or of paper, may, in the course of a few days, serve as the instrument of three different loans, and of three different purchases, each of which is, in value, equal to the whole amount of those pieces. What the three monied men, A, B, and C, assign to the three borrowers, W, X, Y, is the power of making those purchases. In this power consist both the value and the use of the loans. The stock lent by the three monied men, is equal to the value of the goods which can be purchased with it, and is three times greater than that of the money with which the purchases are made. Those loans, however, may be all perfectly well secured, the goods purchased by the different debtors being so employed, as, in due time, to bring back, with a profit, an equal value either of coin or of paper. And as the same pieces of money can thus serve as the instrument of different loans to three, or for the same reason, to thirty times their value, so they may likewise successively serve as the instrument of repayment.

A capital lent at interest may, in this manner, be considered as an assignment from the lender to the borrower of a certain considerable portion of the annual produce; upon condition that the borrower in return shall, during the continuance of the loan, annually assign to the lender a smaller portion, called the interest; and at the end of it, a portion equally considerable with that which had originally been assigned to him, called the repayment. Though money, either coin or paper, serves generally as the deed of assignment both to the smaller, and to the more considerable portion, it is itself altogether different from what is assigned by it.

In proportion as that share of the annual produce which, as soon as it comes either from the ground, or from the hands of the productive labourers, is destined for replacing a capital, increases in any country, what is called the monied interest naturally increases with it. The increase of those particular capitals from which the owners wish to derive a revenue, without being at the trouble of employing them themselves, naturally accompanies the general increase of capitals; or, in other words, as stock increases, the quantity of stock to be lent at interest grows gradually greater and greater.

As the quantity of stock to be lent at interest increases, the interest, or the price which must be paid for the use of that stock, necessarily diminishes, not only from those general causes which make the market price of things commonly diminish as their quantity increases, but from other causes which are peculiar to this particular case. As capitals increase in any country, the profits which can be made by employing them necessarily diminish. It becomes gradually more and more difficult to find within the country a profitable method of employing any new capital. There arises in consequence a competition between different capitals, the owner of one endeavouring to get possession of that employment which is occupied by another. But upon most occasions he can hope to justle that other out of this employment, by no other means but by dealing upon more reasonable terms. He must not only sell what he deals in somewhat cheaper, but in order to get it to sell, he must sometimes too buy it dearer.

The demand for productive labour, by the increase of the funds which are destined for maintaining it, grows every day greater and greater. Labourers easily find employment, but the owners of capitals find it difficult to get labourers to employ. Their competition raises the wages of labour, and sinks the profits of stock. But when the profits which can be made by the use of a capital are in this manner diminished, as it were, at both ends, the price which can be paid for the use of it, that is, the rate of interest, must necessarily be diminished with them.

Mr. Locke, Mr. Law, and Mr. Montesquieu, as well as many other writers, seem to have imagined that the increase of the quantity of gold and silver, in consequence of the discovery of the Spanish West Indies, was the real cause of the lowering of the rate of interest through the greater part of Europe. Those metals, they say, having become of less value themselves, the use of any particular portion of them necessarily became of less value too, and consequently the price which could be paid for it. This notion, which at first sight seems so plausible, has been so fully exposed by Mr. Hume, that it is perhaps, unnecessary to say any thing more about it. The following very short and plain argument, however, may serve to explain more distinctly the fallacy which seems to have misled those gentlemen.

Before the discovery of the Spanish West Indies, ten per cent. seems to have been the common rate of interest through the greater part of Europe. It has since that time in different countries sunk to six, five, four, and three per cent. Let us suppose that in every particular country the value of silver has sunk precisely in the same proportion as the rate of interest; and that in those countries, for example, where interest has been reduced from ten to five per cent., the same quantity of silver can now purchase just half the quantity of goods which it could have purchased before. This supposition will not, I believe, be found any-where agreeable to the truth; but it is the most favourable to the opinion which we are going to examine; and even upon this supposition it is utterly impossible that the lowering of the value of silver could have the smallest tendency to lower the rate of interest. If a hundred pounds are in those countries now of no more value than fifty pounds were then, ten pounds must now be of no more value than five pounds were then. Whatever were the causes which lowered the value of the capital, the same must necessarily have lowered that of the interest, and exactly in the same proportion. The proportion between the value of the capital and that of the interest, must have remained the same, though the rate had never been altered. By altering the rate, on the contrary, the proportion between those two values is necessarily altered. If a hundred pounds now are worth no more than fifty were then, five pounds now can be worth no more than two pounds ten shillings were then. By reducing the rate of interest, therefore, from ten to five per cent., we give for the use of a capital, which is supposed to be equal to one-half of its former value, an interest which is equal to one-fourth only of the value of the former interest.

Any increase in the quantity of silver, while that of the commodities circulated by means of it remained the same, could have no other effect than to diminish the value of that metal. The nominal value of all sorts of goods would be greater, but their real value would be precisely the same as before. They would be exchanged for a greater number of pieces of silver; but the quantity of labour which they could command, the number of people whom they could maintain and employ, would be precisely the same. The capital of the country would be the same, though a greater number of pieces might be requisite for conveying any equal portion of it from one hand to another. The deeds of assignment, like the conveyances of a verbose attorney, would be more cumbersome, but the thing assigned would be precisely the same as before, and could produce only the same effects. The funds for maintaining productive labour being the same, the demand for it would be the same. Its price or wages, therefore, though nominally greater, would really be the same. They would be paid in a greater number of pieces of silver; but they would purchase only the same quantity of goods. The profits of stock would be the same both nominally and really. The wages of labour are commonly computed by the quantity of silver which is paid to the labourer. When that is increased, therefore, his wages appear to be increased, though they may sometimes be no greater than before. But the profits of stock are not computed by the number of pieces of silver with which they are paid, but by the proportion which those pieces bear to the whole capital employed. Thus in a particular country five shillings a week are said to be the common wages of labour, and ten per cent. the common profits of stock. But the whole capital of the country being the same as before, the competition between the different capitals of individuals into which it was divided would likewise be the same. They would all trade with the same advantages and disadvantages. The common proportion between capital and profit, therefore, would be the same, and consequently the common interest of money; what can commonly be given for the use of money being necessarily regulated by what can commonly be made by the use of it.

Any increase in the quantity of commodities annually circulated within the country, while that of the money which circulated them remained the same, would, on the contrary, produce many other important effects, besides that of raising the value of the money. The capital of the country, though it might nominally be the same, would really be augmented. It might continue to be expressed by the same quantity of money, but it would command a greater quantity of labour. The quantity of productive labour which it could maintain and employ would be increased, and consequently the demand for that labour. Its wages would naturally rise with the demand, and yet might appear to sink. They might be paid with a smaller quantity of money, but that smaller quantity might purchase a greater quantity of goods than a greater had done before. The profits of stock would be diminished both really and in appearance. The whole capital of the country being augmented, the competition between the different capitals of which it was composed, would naturally be augmented along with it. The owners of those particular capitals would be obliged to content themselves with a smaller proportion of the produce of that labour which their respective capitals employed. The interest of money, keeping pace always with the profits of stock, might, in this manner, be greatly diminished, though the value of money, or the quantity of goods which any particular sum could purchase, was greatly augmented.

In some countries the interest of money has been prohibited by law. But as something can every-where be made by the use of money, something ought every-where to be paid for the use of it. This regulation, instead of preventing, has been found from experience to increase the evil of usury; the debtor being obliged to pay, not only for the use of the money, but for the risk which his creditor runs by accepting a compensation for that use. He is obliged, if one may say so, to insure his creditor from the penalties of usury.

In countries where interest is permitted, the law, in order to prevent the extortion of usury, generally fixes the highest rate which can be taken without incurring a penalty. This rate ought always to be somewhat above the lowest market price, or the price which is commonly paid for the use of money by those who can give the most undoubted security. If this legal rate should be fixed below the lowest market rate, the effects of this fixation must be nearly the same as those of a total prohibition of interest. The creditor will not lend his money for less than the use of it is worth, and the debtor must pay him for the risk which he runs by accepting the full value of that use. If it is fixed precisely at the lowest market price, it ruins with honest people, who respect the laws of their country, the credit of all those who cannot give the very best security, and obliges them to have recourse to exorbitant usurers. In a country, such as Great Britain, where money is lent to government at three per cent. and to private people upon good security at four, and four and a half, the present legal rate, five per cent., is perhaps, as proper as any.

The legal rate, it is to be observed, though it ought to be somewhat above, ought not to be much above the lowest market rate. If the legal rate of interest in Great Britain, for example, was fixed so high as eight or ten per cent., the greater part of the money which was to be lent, would be lent to prodigals and projectors, who alone would be willing to give this high interest. Sober people, who will give for the use of money no more than a part of what they they are likely to make by the use of it, would not venture into the competition. A great part of the capital of the country would thus be kept out of the hands which were most likely to make a profitable and advantageous use of it, and thrown into those which were most likely to waste and destroy it. Where the legal rate of interest, on the contrary, is fixed but a very little above the lowest market rate, sober people are universally preferred, as borrowers, to prodigals and projectors. The person who lends money gets nearly as much interest from the former as he dares to take from the latter, and his money is much safer in the hands of the one set of people, than in those of the other. A great part of the capital of the country is thus thrown into the hands in which it is most likely to be employed with advantage.

No law can reduce the common rate of interest below the lowest ordinary market rate at the time when that law is made. Notwithstanding the edict of 1766, by which the French king attempted to reduce the rate of interest from five to four per cent., money continued to be lent in France at five per cent., the law being evaded in several different ways.

The ordinary market price of land, it is to be observed, depends every-where upon the ordinary market rate of interest. The person who has a capital from which he wishes to derive a revenue, without taking the trouble to employ it himself, deliberates whether he should buy land with it, or lend it out at interest. The superior security of land, together with some other advantages which almost every-where attend upon this species of property, will generally dispose him to content himself with a smaller revenue from land, than what he might have by lending out his money at interest. These advantages are sufficient to compensate a certain difference of revenue; but they will compensate a certain difference only; and if the rent of land should fall short of the interest of money by a greater difference, nobody would buy land, which would soon reduce its ordinary price. On the contrary, if the advantages should much more than compensate the difference, every body would buy land, which again would soon raise its ordinary price. When interest was at ten per cent., land was commonly sold for ten and twelve years purchase. As interest sunk to six, five, and four per cent., the price of land rose to twenty, five and twenty, and thirty years purchase. The market rate of interest is higher in France than in England; and the common price of land is lower. In England it commonly sells at thirty; in France at twenty years purchase.

CHAPTER V

Of the Different Employment of Capitals

THOUGH all capitals are destined for the maintenance of productive labour only, yet the quantity of that labour, which equal capitals are capable of putting into motion, varies extremely according to the diversity of their employment; as does likewise the value which that employment adds to the annual produce of the land and labour of the country.

A capital may be employed in four different ways: either, first, in procuring the rude produce annually required for the use and consumption of the society; or, secondly, in manufacturing and preparing that rude produce for immediate use and consumption; or, thirdly, in transporting either the rude or manufactured produce from the places where they abound to those where they are wanted; or, lastly, in dividing particular portions of either into such small parcels as suit the occasional demands of those who want them. In the first way are employed the capitals of all those who undertake the improvement or cultivation of lands, mines, or fisheries; in the second, those of all master manufacturers; in the third, those of all wholesale merchants; and in the fourth, those of all retailers. It is difficult to conceive that a capital should be employed in any way which may not be classed under some one or other of those four.

Each of those four methods of employing a capital is essentially necessary either to the existence or extension of the other three, or to the general conveniency of the society.

Unless a capital was employed in furnishing rude produce to a certain degree of abundance, neither manufactures nor trade of any kind could exist.

Unless a capital was employed in manufacturing that part

of the rude produce which requires a good deal of preparation before it can be fit for use and consumption, it either would never be produced, because there could be no demand for it; or if it was produced spontaneously, it would be of no value in exchange, and could add nothing to the wealth of the society.

Unless a capital was employed in transporting, either the rude or manufactured produce, from the places where it abounds to those where it is wanted, no more of either could be produced than was necessary for the consumption of the neighbourhood. The capital of the merchant exchanges the surplus produce of one place for that of another, and thus encourages the industry and increases the enjoyments of both.

Unless a capital was employed in breaking and dividing certain portions either of the rude or manufactured produce, into such small parcels as suit the occasional demands of those who want them, every man would be obliged to purchase a greater quantity of the goods he wanted, than his immediate occasions required. If there was no such trade as a butcher, for example, every man would be obliged to purchase a whole ox or a whole sheep at a time. This would generally be inconvenient to the rich, and much more so to the poor. If a poor workman was obliged to purchase a month's or six months' provisions at a time, a great part of the stock which he employs as a capital in the instruments of his trade, or in the furniture of his shop, and which yields him a revenue, he would be forced to place in that part of his stock which is reserved for immediate consumption, and which yields him no revenue. Nothing can be more convenient for such a person than to be able to purchase his subsistence from day to day, or even from hour to hour, as he wants it. He is thereby enabled to employ almost his whole stock as a capital. He is thus enabled to furnish work to a greater value, and the profit, which he makes by it in this way, much more than compensates the additional price which the profit of the retailer imposes upon the goods. The prejudices of some political writers against shopkeepers and tradesmen, are altogether without foundation. So far is it from being necessary, either to tax them, or to restrict their numbers, that they can never be multiplied so as to hurt the publick, though they may so as to hurt one another. The quantity of grocery goods, for example, which can be sold in a particular town, is limited by the demand of that town and its neighbourhood. The capital, therefore, which can be employed in the grocery trade cannot exceed what is sufficient to purchase that quantity. If this capital is divided between two different grocers, their competition will tend to make both of them sell cheaper, than if it were in the hands of one only; and if it were divided among twenty, their competition would be just so much the greater, and the chance of their combining together, in order to raise the price, just so much the less. Their competition might perhaps ruin some of themselves; but to take care of this is the business of the parties concerned, and it may safely be trusted to their discretion. It can never hurt either the consumer, or the producer; on the contrary, it must tend to make the retailers both sell cheaper and buy dearer, than if the whole trade was monopolized by one or two persons. Some of them, perhaps, may sometimes decoy a weak customer to buy what he has no occasion for. This evil, however, is of too little importance to deserve the publick attention, nor would it necessarily be prevented by restricting their numbers. It is not the multitude of ale-houses, to give the most suspicious example, that occasions a general disposition to drunkenness among the common people; but that disposition arising from other causes necessarily gives employment to a multitude of ale-houses.

The persons whose capitals are employed in any of those four ways are themselves productive labourers. Their labour, when properly directed, fixes and realizes itself in the subject or vendible commodity upon which it is bestowed, and generally adds to its price the value at least of their own maintenance and consumption. The profits of the farmer, of the manufacturer, of the merchant, and retailer, are all drawn from the price of the goods which the two first produce, and the two last buy and sell. Equal capitals, however, employed in each of these four different ways, will immediately put into motion very different quantities of productive labour, and augment too in very different proportions the value of the annual produce of the land and labour of the society to which they belong.

The capital of the retailer replaces, together with its profits, that of the merchant of whom he purchases goods, and thereby enables him to continue his business. The retailer himself is the only productive labourer whom it immediately employs. In his profits, consists the whole value which its employment adds to the annual produce of the land and labour of the society.

The capital of the wholesale merchant replaces, together with their profits, the capitals of the farmers and manufacturers of whom he purchases the rude and manufactured produce which he deals in, and thereby enables them to continue their respective trades. It is by this service chiefly that he contributes indirectly to support the productive labour of the society, and to increase the value of its annual produce. His capital employs too the sailors and carriers who transport his goods from one place to another, and it augments the price of those goods by the value, not only of his profits, but of their wages. This is all the productive labour which it immediately puts into motion, and all the value which it immediately adds to the annual produce. Its operation in both these respects is a good deal superior to that of the capital of the retailer.

Part of the capital of the master manufacturer is employed as a fixed capital in the instruments of his trade, and replaces, together with its profits, that of some other artificer of whom he purchases them. Part of his circulating capital is employed in purchasing materials, and replaces, with their profits, the capitals of the farmers and miners of whom he purchases them. But a great part of it is always, either annually, or in a much shorter period, distributed among the different workmen whom he employs. It augments the value of those materials by their wages, and by their masters profits upon the whole stock of wages, materials, and instruments of trade employed in the business. It puts immediately into motion, therefore, a much greater quantity of productive labour, and adds a much greater value to the annual produce of the land and labour of the society, than an equal capital in the hands of any wholesale merchant.

No equal capital puts into motion a greater quantity of productive labour than that of the farmer. Not only his labouring servants, but his labouring cattle, are productive labourers. In agriculture too nature labours along with man; and though her labour costs no expence, its produce has its value, as well as that of the most expensive workmen. The most important operations of agriculture seem intended, not so much to increase, though they do that too, as to direct the fertility of nature towards the production of the plants most profitable to man. A field overgrown with briars and brambles may frequently produce as great a quantity of vegetables as the best cultivated vineyard or corn field. Planting and tillage frequently regulate more than they animate the active fertility of nature; and after all their labour, a great part of the work always remains to be done by her. The labourers and labouring cattle, therefore, employed in agriculture, not only occasion, like the workmen in manufactures, the reproduction of a value equal to their own consumption, or to the capital which employs them, together with its owners profits; but of a much greater value. Over and above the capital of the farmer and all its profits, they regularly occasion the reproduction of the rent of the landlord. This rent may be considered as the produce of those powers of nature, the use of which the landlord lends to the farmer. It is greater or smaller according to the supposed extent of those powers, or in other words, according to the supposed natural or improved fertility of the land. It is the work of nature which remains after deducting or compensating every thing which can be regarded as the work of man. It is seldom less than a fourth, and frequently more than a third of the whole produce. No equal quantity of productive labour employed in manufactures can ever occasion so great a reproduction. In them nature does nothing; man does all; and the reproduction must always be in proportion to the strength of the agents that occasion it. The capital employed in agriculture, therefore, not only puts into motion a greater quantity of productive labour than any equal capital employed in manufactures, but in proportion too to the quantity of productive labour which it employs, it adds a much greater value to the annual produce of the land and labour of the country, to the real wealth and revenue of its inhabitants. Of all the ways in which a capital can be employed, it is by far the most advantageous to the society.

The capitals employed in the agriculture and in the retail trade of any society, must always reside within that society. Their employment is confined almost to a precise spot, to the farm, and to the shop of the retailer. They must generally too, though there are some exceptions to this, belong to resident members of the society.

The capital of a wholesale merchant, on the contrary, seems to have no fixed or necessary residence anywhere, but may wander about from place to place, according as it can either buy cheap or sell dear.

The capital of the manufacturer must no doubt reside where the manufacture is carried on; but where this shall be is not alway necessarily determined. It may frequently be at a great distance both from the place where the materials grow, and from that where the complete manufacture is consumed. Lyons is very distant both from the places which afford the materials of its manufactures, and from those which consume them. The people of fashion of Sicily are cloathed in silks made in other countries, from the materials which their own produces. Part of the wool of Spain is manufactured in Great Britain, and some part of that cloth is afterwards sent back to Spain.

Whether the merchant whose capital exports the surplus produce of any society be a native or a foreigner, is of very little importance. If he is a foreigner, the number of their productive labourers is necessarily less than if he had been a native by one man only; and the value of their annual produce, by the profits of that one man. The sailors or carriers whom he employs may still belong indifferently either to his country, or to their country, or to some third country, in the same manner as if he had been a native. The capital of a foreigner gives a value to their surplus produce equally with that of a native, by exchanging it for something for which there is a demand at home. It as effectually replaces the capital of the person who produces that surplus, and as effectually enables him to continue his business; the service by which the capital of a wholesale merchant chiefly contributes to support the productive labour, and to augment the value of the annual produce of the society to which he belongs.

It is of more consequence that the capital of the manufacturer should reside within the country. It necessarily puts into motion a greater quantity of productive labour, and adds a greater value to the annual produce of the land and labour of the society. It may, however, be very useful to the country, though it should not reside within it. The capitals of the British manufacturers who work up the flax and hemp annually imported from the coasts of the Baltic, are surely very useful to the countries which produce them. Those materials are a part of the surplus produce of those countries which, unless it was annually exchanged for something which is in demand there, would be of no value, and would soon cease to be produced. The merchants who export it, replace the capitals of the people who produce it, and thereby encourage them to continue the production; and the British manufacturers replace the capitals of those merchants.

A particular country, in the same manner as a particular person, may frequently not have capital sufficient both to improve and cultivate all its lands, to manufacture and prepare their whole rude produce for immediate use and consumption, and to transport the surplus part either of the rude or manufactured produce to those distant markets where it can be exchanged for something for which there is a demand at home. The inhabitants of many different parts of Great Britain have not capital sufficient to improve and cultivate all their lands. The wool of the southern counties of Scotland is, a great part of it, after a long land carriage through very bad roads, manufactured in Yorkshire, for want of a capital to manufacture it at home. There are many little manufacturing towns in Great Britain, of which the inhabitants have not capital sufficient to transport the produce of their own industry to those distant markets where there is demand and consumption for it. If there are any merchants among them, they are properly only the agents of wealthier merchants who reside in some of the greater commercial cities.

When the capital of any country is not sufficient for all

those three purposes, in proportion as a greater share of it is employed in agriculture, the greater will be the quantity of productive labour which it puts into motion within the country; as will likewise be the value which its employment adds to the annual produce of the land and labour of the society. After agriculture, the capital employed in manufactures puts into motion the greatest quantity of productive labour, and adds the greatest value to the annual produce. That which is employed in the trade of exportation, has the least effect of any of the three.

The country, indeed, which has not capital sufficient for all those three purposes, has not arrived at that degree of opulence for which it seems naturally destined. To attempt, however, prematurely and with an insufficient capital, to do all the three, is certainly not the shortest way for a society, no more than it would be for an individual, to acquire a sufficient one. The capital of all the individuals of a nation, has its limits in the same manner as that of a single individual, and is capable of executing only certain purposes. The capital of all the individuals of a nation is increased in the same manner as that of a single individual, by their continually accumulating and adding to it whatever they save out of their revenue. It is likely to increase the fastest, therefore, when it is employed in the way that affords the greatest revenue to all the inhabitants of the country, as they will thus be enabled to make the greatest savings. But the revenue of all the inhabitants of the country is necessarily in proportion to the value of the annual produce of their land and labour.

It has been the principal cause of the rapid progress of our American colonies towards wealth and greatness, that almost their whole capitals have hitherto been employed in agriculture. They have no manufactures, those houshold and coarser manufactures excepted which necessarily accompany the progress of agriculture, and which are the work of the women and children in every private family. The greater part both of the exportation and coasting trade of America, is carried on by the capitals of merchants who reside in Great Britain. Even the stores and warehouses from which goods are retailed in some provinces, particularly in

Virginia and Maryland, belong many of them to merchants who reside in the mother country, and afford one of the few instances of the retail trade of a society being carried on by the capitals of those who are not resident members of it. Were the Americans, either by combination or by any other sort of violence, to stop the importation of European manufactures, and, by thus giving a monopoly to such of their own countrymen as could manufacture the like goods, divert any considerable part of their capital into this employment, they would retard instead of accelerating the further increase in the value of their annual produce, and would obstruct instead of promoting the progress of their country towards real wealth and greatness. This would be still more the case, were they to attempt, in the same manner, to monopolize to themselves their whole exportation trade.

The course of human prosperity, indeed, seems scarce ever to have been of so long continuance as to enable any great country to acquire capital sufficient for all those three purposes; unless, perhaps, we give credit to the wonderful accounts of the wealth and cultivation of China, of those of antient Egypt, and of the antient state of Indostan. Even those three countries, the wealthiest, according to all accounts, that ever were in the world, are chiefly renowned for their superiority in agriculture and manufactures. They do not appear to have been eminent for foreign trade. The antient Egyptians had a superstitious antipathy to the sea; a superstition nearly of the same kind prevails among the Indians; and the Chinese have never excelled in foreign commerce. The greater part of the surplus produce of all those three countries seems to have been always exported by foreigners, who gave in exchange for it something else for which they found a demand there, frequently gold and silver.

It is thus that the same capital will in any country put into motion a greater or smaller quantity of productive labour, and add a greater or smaller value to the annual produce of its land and labour, according to the different proportions in which it is employed in agriculture, manufactures, and wholesale trade. The difference too is very great, according to the different sorts of wholesale trade in which any part of it is employed

All wholesale trade, all buying in order to sell again by wholesale, may be reduced to three different sorts. The home trade, the foreign trade of consumption, and the carrying trade. The home trade is employed in purchasing in one part of the same country, and selling in another, the produce of the industry of that country. It comprehends both the inland and the coasting trade. The foreign trade of consumption is employed in purchasing foreign goods for home consumption. The carrying trade is employed in transacting the commerce of foreign countries, or in carrying the surplus produce of one to another.

The capital which is employed in purchasing in one part of the country in order to sell in another the produce of the industry of that country, generally replaces by every such operation two distinct capitals that had both been employed in the agriculture or manufactures of that country, and thereby enables them to continue that employment. When it sends out from the residence of the merchant a certain value of commodities, it generally brings back in return at least an equal value of other commodities. When both are the produce of domestick industry, it necessarily replaces by every such operation two distinct capitals, which had both been employed in supporting productive labour, and thereby enables them to continue that support. The capital which sends Scotch manufactures to London, and brings back English corn and manufactures to Edinburgh, necessarily replaces, by every such operation, two British capitals which had both been employed in the agriculture or manufactures of Great Britain.

The capital employed in purchasing foreign goods for home-consumption, when this purchase is made with the produce of domestick industry, replaces too, by every such operation, two distinct capitals; but one of them only is employed in supporting domestick industry. The capital which sends British goods to Portugal, and brings back Portuguese goods to Great Britain, replaces by every such operation only one British capital. The other is a Portuguese one. Though the returns, therefore, of the foreign trade of consumption should be as quick as those of the home-trade, the capital employed in it will give but one-half the encouragement to the industry or productive labour of the country.

But the returns of the foreign trade of consumption are very seldom so quick as those of the home-trade. The returns of the home-trade generally come in before the end of the year, and sometimes three or four times in the year. The returns of the foreign trade of consumption seldom come in before the end of the year, and sometimes not till after two or three years. A capital, therefore, employed in the home-trade will sometimes make twelve operations, or be sent out and returned twelve times, before a capital employed in the foreign trade of consumption has made one. If the capitals are equal, therefore, the one will give four and twenty times more encouragement and support to the industry of the country than the other.

The foreign goods for home-consumption may sometimes be purchased, not with the produce of domestick industry, but with some other foreign goods. These last, however, must have been purchased either immediately with the produce of domestick industry, or with something else that had been purchased with it; for the case of war and conquest excepted, foreign goods can never be acquired, but in exchange for something that had been produced at home, either immediately, or after two or more different exchanges. The effects, therefore, of a capital employed in such a round-about foreign trade of consumption, are, in every respect, the same as those of one employed in the most direct trade of the same kind, except that the final returns are likely to be still more distant, as they must depend upon the returns of two or three distinct foreign trades. If the flax and hemp of Riga are purchased with the tobacco of Virginia, which had been purchased with British manufactures, the merchant must wait for the returns of two distinct foreign trades before he can employ the same capital in re-purchasing a like quantity of British manufactures. If the tobacco of Virginia had been purchased, not with British manufactures, but with the sugar and rum of Jamaica which had been purchased with those manufactures, he must wait for the returns of three. If those two or three distinct foreign trades should happen to be carried on by two or three distinct merchants, of whom the second buys the goods imported by the first, and the third buys those imported by the second, in order to export them again, each merchant indeed will in this case receive the returns of his own capital more quickly; but the final returns of the whole capital employed in the trade will be just as slow as ever. Whether the whole capital employed in such a round-about trade belong to one merchant or to three, can make no difference with regard to the country, though it may with regard to the particular merchants. Three times a greater capital must in both cases be employed, in order to exchange a certain value of British manufactures for a certain quantity of flax and hemp, than would have been necessary, had the manufactures and the flax and hemp been directly exchanged for one another. The whole capital employed, therefore, in such a round-about foreign trade of consumption, will generally give less encouragement and support to the productive labour of the country, than an equal capital employed in a more direct trade of the same kind.

Whatever be the foreign commodity with which the foreign goods for home-consumption are purchased, it can occasion no essential difference either in the nature of the trade, or in the encouragement and support which it can give to the productive labour of the country from which it is carried on. If they are purchased with the gold of Brazil, for example, or with the silver of Peru, this gold and silver, like the tobacco of Virginia, must have been purchased with something that either was the produce of the industry of the country, or that had been purchased with something else that was so. So far, therefore, as the productive labour of the country is concerned, the foreign trade of consumption which is carried on by means of gold and silver, has all the advantages and all the inconveniencies of any other equally round-about foreign trade of consumption, and will replace just as fast or just as slow the capital which is immediately employed in supporting that productive labour. It seems even to have one advantage over any other equally round-about foreign trade. The transportation of those metals from one place to another, on account of their small bulk and great value, is less expensive than that of almost any other foreign goods of equal value. Their freight is much less, and their insurance not greater; and no goods, besides, are less liable to suffer by the carriage. An equal quantity of foreign goods, therefore, may frequently be purchased with a smaller quantity of the produce of domestick industry, by the intervention of gold and silver, than by that of any other foreign goods. The demand of the country may frequently, in this manner, be supplied more completely and at a smaller expence than in any other. Whether, by the continual exportation of those metals, a trade of this kind is likely to impoverish the country from which it is carried on, in any other way, I shall have occasion to examine at great length hereafter.

That part of the capital of any country which is employed in the carrying trade, is altogether withdrawn from supporting the productive labour of that particular country, to support that of some foreign countries. Though it may replace by every operation two distinct capitals, yet neither of them belongs to that particular country. The capital of the Dutch merchant, which carries the corn of Poland to Portugal, and brings back the fruits and wines of Portugal to Poland, replaces by every such operation two capitals, neither of which had been employed in supporting the productive labour of Holland; but one of them in supporting that of Poland, and the other that of Portugal. The profits only return regularly to Holland, and constitute the whole addition which this trade necessarily makes to the annual produce of the land and labour of that country. When, indeed, the carrying trade of any particular country is carried on with the ships and sailors of that country, that part of the capital employed in it which pays the freight, is distributed among, and puts into motion, a certain number of productive labourers of that country. Almost all nations that have had any considerable share of the carrying trade have, in fact, carried it on in this manner. The trade itself has probably derived its name from it, the people of such countries being the carriers to other countries. It does not, however, seem essential to the nature of the trade that it should be so. A Dutch merchant may, for example, employ his capital in transacting the commerce of Poland and Portugal, by carrying part of the surplus produce of the one to the other, not in Dutch, but in British bottoms. It may be presumed, that he actually does so upon some particular occasions. It is upon this account, however, that the carrying trade has been supposed peculiarly advantageous to such a country as Great Britain, of which the defence and security depend upon the number of its sailors and shipping. But the same capital may employ as many sailors and shipping, either in the foreign trade of consumption, or even in the home-trade, when carried on by coasting vessels, as it could in the carrying trade. The number of sailors and shipping which any particular capital can employ, does not depend upon the nature of the trade, but partly upon the bulk of the goods in proportion to their value, and partly upon the distance of the ports between which they are to be carried; chiefly upon the former of those two circumstances. The coal-trade from Newcastle to London, for example, employs more shipping than all the carrying trade of England, though the ports are at no great distance. To force, therefore, by extraordinary encouragements, a larger share of the capital of any country into the carrying trade, than what would naturally go to it, will not always necessarily increase the shipping of that country.

The capital, therefore, employed in the home-trade of any country will generally give encouragement and support to a greater quantity of productive labour in that country, and increase the value of its annual produce more than an equal capital employed in the foreign trade of consumption: and the capital employed in this latter trade has in both these respects a still greater advantage over an equal capital employed in the carrying trade. The riches, and so far as power depends upon riches, the power of every country, must always be in proportion to the value of its annual produce, the fund from which all taxes must ultimately be paid. But the great object of the political economy of every country, is to increase the riches and power of that country. It ought, therefore, to give no preference nor superior encouragement to the foreign trade of consumption above the home-trade, nor to the carrying trade above either of the other two. It ought neither to force nor to allure into either of those two channels, a greater share of the capital of the country than what would naturally flow into them of its own accord.

Each of those different branches of trade, however, is not only advantageous, but necessary and unavoidable, when the course of things, without any constraint or violence, naturally introduces it.

When the produce of any particular branch of industry exceeds what the demand of the country requires, the surplus must be sent abroad, and exchanged for something for which there is a demand at home. Without such exportation, a part of the productive labour of the country must cease, and the value of its annual produce diminish. The land and labour of Great Britain produce generally more corn, woollens, and hard ware, than the demand of the home-market requires. The surplus part of them, therefore, must be sent abroad, and exchanged for something for which there is a demand at home. It is only by means of such exportation, that this surplus can acquire a value sufficient to compensate the labour and expence of producing it. The neighbourhood of the sea coast, and the banks of all navigable rivers are advantageous situations for industry, only because they facilitate the exportation and exchange of such surplus produce for something else which is more in demand there.

When the foreign goods which are thus purchased with the surplus produce of domestic industry exceed the demand of the home-market, the surplus part of them must be sent abroad again, and exchanged for something more in demand at home. About ninety-six thousand hogsheads of tobacco are annually purchased in Virginia and Maryland, with a part of the surplus produce of British industry. But the demand of Great Britain does not require, perhaps, more than fourteen thousand. If the remaining eighty-two thousand, therefore, could not be sent abroad and exchanged for something more in demand at home, the importation of them must cease immediately, and with it the productive labour of all those inhabitants of Great Britain, who are at present employed in preparing the goods with which these eighty-two thousand hogsheads are annually purchased. Those goods, which are part of the produce of the land and labour of Great Britain, having no market at home, and being deprived of that which they had abroad, must cease to be produced. The most round-about foreign trade of consumption, therefore, may, upon some occasions, be as necessary for supporting the productive labour of the country, and the value of its annual produce, as the most direct.

When the capital stock of any country is increased to such a degree, that it cannot be all employed in supplying the consumption, and supporting the productive labour of that particular country, the surplus part of it naturally disgorges itself into the carrying trade, and is employed in performing the same offices to other countries. The carrying trade is the natural effect and symptom of great national wealth; but it does not seem to be the natural cause of it. Those statesmen who have been disposed to favour it with particular encouragements, seem to have mistaken the effect and symptom for the cause. Holland, in proportion to the extent of the land and the number of its inhabitants, by far the richest country in Europe, has, accordingly, the greatest share of the carrying trade of Europe. England, perhaps the second richest country of Europe, is likewise supposed to have a considerable share of it; though what commonly passes for the carrying trade of England, will frequently, perhaps, be found to be no more than a round-about foreign trade of consumption. Such are, in a great measure, the trades which carry the goods of the East and West Indies, and of America, to different European markets. Those goods are generally purchased either immediately with the produce of British industry, or with something else which had been purchased with that produce, and the final returns of those trades are generally used or consumed in Great Britain. The trade which is carried on in British bottoms between the different ports of the Mediterranean, and some trade of the same kind carried on by British merchants between the different ports of India, make, perhaps, the principal branches of what is properly the carrying trade of Great Britain.

The extent of the home-trade and of the capital which can be employed in it, is necessarily limited by the value of the surplus produce of all those distant places within the country which have occasion to exchange their respective productions with one another. That of the foreign trade of consumption, by the value of the surplus produce of the whole country and of what can be purchased with it. That of the carrying trade, by the value of the surplus produce of all the different countries in the world. Its possible extent, therefore, is in a manner infinite in comparison of that of the other two, and is capable of absorbing the greatest capitals.

The consideration of his own private profit, is the sole motive which determines the owner of any capital to employ it either in agriculture, in manufactures, or in some particular branch of the wholesale or retail trade. The different quantities of productive labour which it may put into motion, and the different values which it may add to the annual produce of the land and labour of the society, according as it is employed in one or other of those different ways, never enter into his thoughts. In countries, therefore, where agriculture is the most profitable of all employments, and farming and improving the most direct roads to a splendid fortune, the capitals of individuals will naturally be employed in the manner most advantageous to the whole society. The profits of agriculture, however, seem to have no superiority over those of other employments in any part of Europe. Projectors, indeed, in every corner of it, have within these few years amused the public with most magnificent accounts of the profits to be made by the cultivation and improvement of land. Without entering into any particular discussion of their calculations, a very simple observation may satisfy us that the result of them must be false. We see every day the most splendid fortunes that have been acquired in the course of a single life by trade and manufactures, frequently from a very small capital, sometimes from no capital. A single instance of such a fortune acquired by agriculture in the same time, and from such a capital, has not, perhaps, occurred in Europe during the course of the present century. In all the great countries of Europe, however, much good land still remains uncultivated, and the greater part of what is cultivated, is far from being improved to the degree of which it is capable. Agriculture, therefore, is almost every-where capable of absorbing a much greater capital than has ever yet been employed in it. What circumstances in the policy of Europe have given the trades which are carried on in towns so great an advantage over that which is carried on in the country, that private persons frequently find it more for their advantage to employ their capitals in the most distant carrying trades of Asia and America, than in the improvement and cultivation of the most fertile fields in their own neighbourhood, I shall endeavour to explain at full length in the two following books.

BOOK III

Of the Different Progress of Opulence in Different Nations

CHAPTER I

Of the Natural Progress of Opulence

THE great commerce of every civilized society, is that carried on between the inhabitants of the town and those of the country. It consists in the exchange of rude for manufactured produce, either immediately, or by the intervention of money, or of some sort of paper which represents money. The country supplies the town with the means of subsistence, and the materials of manufacture. The town repays this supply by sending back a part of the manufactured produce to the inhabitants of the country. The town, in which there neither is nor can be any reproduction of substances, may very properly be said to gain its whole wealth and subsistence from the country. We must not, however, upon this account, imagine that the gain of the town is the loss of the country. The gains of both are mutual and reciprocal, and the division of labour is in this, as in all other cases, advantageous to all the different persons employed in the various occupations into which it is subdivided. The inhabitants of the country purchase of the town a greater quantity of manufactured goods, with the produce of a much smaller quantity of their own labour, than they must have employed had they attempted to prepare them themselves. The town affords a market for the surplus produce of the country, or what is over and above the maintenance of the cultivators, and it is there that the inhabitants of the country exchange it for something else which is in demand among them. The greater the number and revenue of the inhabitants of the town, the more extensive is the market which it affords to those of the country; and the more extensive that market, it is always the more advantageous to a great number. The corn which grows within a mile of the town, sells there for the same price with that which comes from twenty miles distance. But the price of the latter must generally, not only pay the expence of raising and bringing it to market, but afford too the ordinary profits of agriculture to the farmer. The proprietors and cultivators of the country, therefore, which lies in the neighbourhood of the town, over and above the ordinary profits of agriculture, gain, in the price of what they sell, the whole value of the carriage of the like produce that is brought from more distant parts, and they save, besides, the whole value of this carriage in the price of what they buy. Compare the cultivation of the lands in the neighbourhood of any considerable town, with that of those which lie at some distance from it, and you will easily satisfy yourself how much the country is benefited by the commerce of the town. Among all the absurd speculations that have been propagated concerning the balance of trade, it has never been pretended that either the country loses by its commerce with the town, or the town by that with the country which maintains it.

As subsistence is, in the nature of things, prior to conveniency and luxury, so the industry which procures the former, must necessarily be prior to that which ministers to the latter. The cultivation and improvement of the country, therefore, which affords subsistence, must, necessarily, be prior to the increase of the town, which furnishes only the means of conveniency and luxury. It is the surplus produce of the country only, or what is over and above the maintenance of the cultivators, that constitutes the subsistence of the town, which can therefore increase only with the increase of this surplus produce. The town, indeed, may not always derive its whole subsistence from the country in its neighbourhood, or even from the territory to which it belongs, but from very distant countries; and this, though it forms no exception from the general rule, has occasioned considerable variations in the progress of opulence in different ages and nations.

That order of things which necessity imposes in general, though not in every particular country, is, in every particular country, promoted by the natural inclinations of man. If human institutions had never thwarted those natural inclinations, the towns could no-where have increased beyond what the improvement and cultivation of the territory in which they were situated could support; till such time, at least, as the whole of that territory was completely cultivated and improved. Upon equal, or nearly equal profits, most men will chuse to employ their capitals rather in the improvement and cultivation of land, than either in manufactures or in foreign trade. The man who employs his capital in land, has it more under his view and command, and his fortune is much less liable to accident, than that of the trader, who is obliged frequently to commit it, not only to the winds and the waves, but to the more uncertain elements of human folly and injustice, by giving great credits in distant countries to men, with whose character and situation he can seldom be thoroughly acquainted. The capital of the landlord, on the contrary, which is fixed in the improvement of his land, seems to be as well secured as the nature of human affairs can admit of. The beauty of the country besides, the pleasure of a country life, the tranquillity of mind which it promises, and wherever the injustice of human laws does not disturb it, the independency which it really affords, have charms that more or less attract every body; and as to cultivate the ground was the original destination of man, so in every stage of his existence he seems to retain a predilection for this primitive employment.

Without the assistance of some artificers, indeed, the cultivation of land cannot be carried on, but with great inconveniency and continual interruption. Smiths, carpenters, wheel-wrights, and plough-wrights, masons, and bricklayers, tanners, shoemakers, and taylors, are people, whose service the farmer has frequent occasion for. Such artificers too stand, occasionally, in need of the assistance of one another; and as their residence is not, like that of the farmer, necessarily tied down to a precise spot, they naturally settle in the neighbourhood of one another, and thus form a small town or village. The butcher, the brewer, and the baker, soon join them, together with many other artificers and retailers, necessary or useful for supplying their occasional wants, and who contribute still further to augment the town. The inhabitants of the town and those of the country are mutually the servants of one another. The town is a continual fair or market, to which the inhabitants of the country resort, in order to exchange their rude for manufactured produce. It is this commerce which supplies the inhabitants of the town both with the materials of their work, and the means of their subsistence. The quantity of the finished work which they sell to the inhabitants of the country, necessarily regulates the quantity of the materials and provisions which they buy. Neither their employment nor subsistence, therefore, can augment, but in proportion to the augmentation of the demand from the country for finished work; and this demand can augment only in proportion to the extension of improvement and cultivation. Had human institutions, therefore, never disturbed the natural course of things, the progressive wealth and increase of the towns would, in every political society, be consequential, and in proportion to the improvement and cultivation of the territory or country.

In our North American colonies, where uncultivated land is still to be had upon easy terms, no manufactures for distant sale have ever yet been established in any of their towns. When an artificer has acquired a little more stock than is necessary for carrying on his own business in supplying the neighbouring country, he does not, in North America, attempt to establish with it a manufacture for more distant sale, but employs it in the purchase and improvement of uncultivated land. From artificer he becomes planter, and neither the large wages nor the easy subsistence which that country affords to artificers, can bribe him rather to work for other people than for himself. He feels that an artificer is the servant of his customers, from whom he derives his subsistence; but that a planter who cultivates his own land, and derives his necessary subsistence from the labour of his own family, is really a master, and independent of all the world.

In countries, on the contrary, where there is either no uncultivated land, or none that can be had upon easy terms, every artificer who has acquired more stock than he can employ in the occasional jobs of the neighbourhood, endeavours to prepare work for more distant sale. The smith erects some sort of iron, the weaver some sort of linen or woollen manufactory. Those different manufactures come, in process of time, to be gradually subdivided, and thereby improved and refined in a great variety of ways, which may easily be conceived, and which it is therefore unnecessary to explain any further.

In seeking for employment to a capital, manufactures are, upon equal or nearly equal profits, naturally preferred to foreign commerce, for the same reason that agriculture is naturally preferred to manufactures. As the capital of the landlord or farmer is more secure than that of the manufacturer, so the capital of the manufacturer, being at all times more within his view and command, is more secure than that of the foreign merchant. In every period, indeed, of every society, the surplus part both of the rude and manufactured produce, or that for which there is no demand at home, must be sent abroad in order to be exchanged for something for which there is some demand at home. But whether the capital, which carries this surplus produce abroad, be a foreign or a domestic one, is of very little importance. If the society has not acquired sufficient capital both to cultivate all its lands, and to manufacture in the completest manner the whole of its rude produce, there is even a considerable advantage that that rude produce should be exported by a foreign capital, in order that the whole stock of the society may be employed in more useful purposes. The wealth of ancient Egypt, that of China and Indostan, sufficiently demonstrate that a nation may attain a very high degree of opulence, though the greater part of its exportation trade be carried on by foreigners. The progress of our North American and West Indian colonies would have been much less rapid, had no capital but what belonged to themselves been employed in exporting their surplus produce.

According to the natural course of things, therefore, the greater part of the capital of every growing society is, first, directed to agriculture, afterwards to manufactures, and last of all to foreign commerce. This order of things is so very natural, that in every society that had any territory, it has always, I believe, been in some degree observed. Some of their lands must have been cultivated before any considerable towns could be established, and some sort of coarse industry of the manufacturing kind must have been carried on in those towns, before they could well think of employing themselves in foreign commerce.

But though this natural order of things must have taken place in some degree in every such society, it has, in all the modern states of Europe, been, in many respects, entirely inverted. The foreign commerce of some of their cities has introduced all their finer manufactures, or such as were fit for distant sale; and manufactures and foreign commerce together, have given birth to the principal improvements of agriculture. The manners and customs which the nature of their original government introduced, and which remained after that government was greatly altered, necessarily forced them into this unnatural and retrograde order.

BOOK IV

Of Systems of Political Œconomy

INTRODUCTION

POLITICAL œconomy, considered as a branch of the science of a statesman or legislator, proposes two distinct objects: first, to provide a plentiful revenue or subsistence for the people, or more properly to enable them to provide such a revenue or subsistence for themselves; and secondly, to supply the state or commonwealth with a revenue sufficient for the public services. It proposes to enrich both the people and the sovereign.

The different progress of opulence in different ages and nations, has given occasion to two different systems of political œconomy, with regard to enriching the people. The one may be called the system of commerce, the other that of agriculture. I shall endeavour to explain both as fully and distinctly as I can, and shall begin with the system of commerce. It is the modern system, and is best understood in our own country and in our own times.

CHAPTER I

Of the Principle of the Commercial or Mercantile System

THAT wealth consists in money, or in gold and silver, is a popular notion which naturally arises from the double function of money, as the instrument of commerce, and as the measure of value. In consequence of its being the instrument of commerce, when we have money we can more readily obtain whatever else we have occasion for, than by means of any other commodity. The great affair, we always find, is to get money. When that is obtained, there is no difficulty in making any subsequent purchase. In consequence of its being the measure of value, we estimate that of all other commodities by the quantity of money which they will exchange for. We say of a rich man that he is worth a great deal, and of a poor man that he is worth very little money. A frugal man, or a man eager to be rich, is said to love money; and a careless, a generous, or a profuse man, is said to be indifferent about it. To grow rich is to get money; and wealth and money, in short, are, in common language, considered as in every respect synonymous.

A rich country, in the same manner as a rich man, is supposed to be a country abounding in money; and to heap up gold and silver in any country is supposed to be the readiest way to enrich it. For some time after the discovery of America, the first enquiry of the Spaniards, when they arrived upon any unknown coast, used to be, if there was any gold or silver to be found in the neighbourhood? By the information which they received, they judged whether it was worth while to make a settlement there, or if the country was worth the conquering. Plano Carpino, a monk sent ambassador from the king of France to one of the sons of the famous Gengis Khan, says that the Tartars used frequently to ask him, if there was plenty of sheep and oxen in the kingdom of France? Their enquiry had the same object with that of the Spaniards. They wanted to know if the country was rich enough to be worth the conquering. Among the Tartars, as among all other nations of shepherds, who are generally ignorant of the use of money, cattle are the instruments of commerce and the measures of value. Wealth, therefore, according to them, consisted in cattle, as according to the Spaniards it consisted in gold and silver. Of the two, the Tartar notion, perhaps, was the nearest to the truth.

Mr. Locke remarks a distinction between money and other moveable goods. All other moveable goods, he says, are of so consumable a nature that the wealth which consists in them cannot be much depended on, and a nation which abounds in them one year may, without any exportation, but merely by their own waste and extravagance, be in great want of them the next. Money, on the contrary, is a steady friend, which, though it may travel about from hand to hand, yet if it can be kept from going out of the country, is not very liable to be wasted and consumed. Gold and silver, therefore, are, according to him, the most solid and substantial part of the moveable wealth of a nation, and to multiply those metals ought, he thinks, upon that account, to be the great object of its political œconomy.

Others admit that if a nation could be separated from all the world, it would be of no consequence how much, or how little money circulated in it. The consumable goods which were circulated by means of this money, would only be exchanged for a greater or a smaller number of pieces; but the real wealth or poverty of the country, they allow, would depend altogether upon the abundance or scarcity of those consumable goods. But it is otherwise, they think, with countries which have connections with foreign nations, and which are obliged to carry on foreign wars, and to maintain fleets and armies in distant countries. This, they say, cannot be done, but by sending abroad money to pay them with; and a nation cannot send much money abroad, unless it has a good deal at home. Every such nation, therefore, must endeavour in time of peace to accumulate gold and silver, that, when occasion requires, it may have wherewithal to carry on foreign wars.

In consequence of these popular notions, all the different nations of Europe have studied, though to little purpose, every possible means of accumulating gold and silver in their respective countries. Spain and Portugal, the proprietors of the principal mines which supply Europe with those metals, have either prohibited their exportation under the severest penalties, or subjected it to a considerable duty. The like prohibition seems anciently to have made a part of the policy of most other European nations. It is even to be found, where we should least of all expect to find it, in some old Scotch acts of parliament, which forbid under heavy penalties the carrying gold or silver *forth of the kingdom.* The like policy anciently took place both in France and England.

When those countries became commercial, the merchants found this prohibition, upon many occasions, extremely inconvenient. They could frequently buy more advantageously with gold and silver than with any other commodity, the foreign goods which they wanted, either to import into their own, or to carry to some other foreign country. They remonstrated, therefore, against this prohibition as hurtful to trade.

They represented, first, that the exportation of gold and silver in order to purchase foreign goods, did not always diminish the quantity of those metals in the kingdom. That, on the contrary, it might frequently increase that quantity; because, if the consumption of foreign goods was not thereby increased in the country, those goods might be re-exported to foreign countries, and, being there sold for a large profit, might bring back much more treasure than was originally sent out to purchase them. Mr. Mun compares this operation of foreign trade to the seed-time and harvest of agriculture. "If we only behold," says he, "the actions of the husbandman in the seed-time, when he casteth away much good corn into the ground, we shall account him rather a madman than a husbandman. But when we consider his labours in the harvest, which is the end of his endeavours, we shall find the worth and plentiful increase of his actions."

They represented, secondly, that this prohibition could not

hinder the exportation of gold and silver, which, on account of the smallness of their bulk in proportion to their value, could easily be smuggled abroad. That this exportation could only be prevented by a proper attention to, what they called, the balance of trade. That when the country exported to a greater value than it imported, a balance became due to it from foreign nations, which was necessarily paid to it in gold and silver, and thereby increased the quantity of those metals in the kingdom. But that when it imported to a greater value than it exported, a contrary balance became due to foreign nations, which was necessarily paid to them in the same manner, and thereby diminished that quantity. That in this case to prohibit the exportation of those metals could not prevent it, but only by making it more dangerous, render it more expensive. That the exchange was thereby turned more against the country which owed the balance, than it otherwise might have been; the merchant who purchased a bill upon the foreign country being obliged to pay the banker who sold it, not only for the natural risk, trouble and expence of sending the money thither, but for the extraordinary risk arising from the prohibition. But that the more the exchange was against any country, the more the balance of trade became necessarily against it; the money of that country becoming necessarily of so much less value, in comparison with that of the country to which the balance was due. That if the exchange between England and Holland, for example, was five per cent. against England, it would require a hundred and five ounces of silver in England to purchase a bill for a hundred ounces of silver in Holland: that a hundred and five ounces of silver in England, therefore, would be worth only a hundred ounces of silver in Holland, and would purchase only a proportionable quantity of Dutch goods: but that a hundred ounces of silver in Holland, on the contrary, would be worth a hundred and five ounces in England, and would purchase a proportionable quantity of English goods: that the English goods which were sold to Holland would be sold so much cheaper; and the Dutch goods which were sold to England, so much dearer, by the difference of the exchange; that the one would draw so much less Dutch money to England, and the other so much more English money to Holland, as this difference amounted to: and that the balance of trade, therefore, would necessarily be so much more against England, and would require a greater balance of gold and silver to be exported to Holland.

Those arguments were partly solid and partly sophistical. They were solid so far as they asserted that the exportation of gold and silver in trade might frequently be advantageous to the country. They were solid too, in asserting that no prohibition could prevent their exportation, when private people found any advantage in exporting them. But they were sophistical in supposing, that either to preserve or to augment the quantity of those metals required more the attention of government, than to preserve or to augment the quantity of any other useful commodities, which the freedom of trade, without any such attention, never fails to supply in the proper quantity. They were sophistical too, perhaps, in asserting that the high price of exchange necessarily increased, what they called, the unfavourable balance of trade, or occasioned the exportation of a greater quantity of gold and silver. That high price, indeed, was extremely disadvantageous to the merchants who had any money to pay in foreign countries. They paid so much dearer for the bills which their bankers granted them upon those countries. But though the risk arising from the prohibition might occasion some extraordinary expence to the bankers, it would not necessarily carry any more money out of the country. This expence would generally be all laid out in the country, in smuggling the money out of it, and could seldom occasion the exportation of a single six-pence beyond the precise sum drawn for. The high price of exchange too would naturally dispose the merchants to endeavour to make their exports nearly balance their imports, in order that they might have this high exchange to pay upon as small a sum as possible. The high price of exchange, besides, must necessarily have operated as a tax, in raising the price of foreign goods, and thereby diminishing their consumption. It would tend, therefore, not to increase, but to diminish, what they called, the unfavourable balance of trade, and consequently the exportation of gold and silver.

Such as they were, however, those arguments convinced the people to whom they were addressed. They were addressed by merchants to parliaments, and to the councils of princes, to nobles, and to country gentlemen; by those who were supposed to understand trade, to those who were conscious to themselves that they knew nothing about the matter. That foreign trade enriched the country, experience demonstrated to the nobles and country gentlemen, as well as to the merchants; but how, or in what manner, none of them well knew. The merchants knew perfectly in what manner it enriched themselves. It was their business to know it. But to know in what manner it enriched the country, was no part of their business. This subject never came into their consideration, but when they had occasion to apply to their country for some change in the laws relating to foreign trade. It then became necessary to say something about the beneficial effects of foreign trade, and the manner in which those effects were obstructed by the laws as they then stood. To the judges who were to decide the business, it appeared a most satisfactory account of the matter, when they were told that foreign trade brought money into the country, but that the laws in question hindered it from bringing so much as it otherwise would do. Those arguments therefore produced the wished-for effect. The prohibition of exporting gold and silver was in France and England confined to the coin of those respective countries. The exportation of foreign coin and of bullion was made free. In Holland, and in some other places, this liberty was extended even to the coin of the country. The attention of government was turned away from guarding against the exportation of gold and silver, to watch over the balance of trade, as the only cause which could occasion any augmentation or diminution of those metals. From one fruitless care it was turned away to another care much more intricate, much more embarrassing, and just equally fruitless. The title of Mun's book, England's Treasure in Foreign Trade, became a fundamental maxim in the political œconomy, not of England only, but of all other commercial countries. The inland or home trade, the most important of all, the trade in which an equal capital affords the greatest revenue, and creates the greatest employment to the people of the country, was considered as subsidiary only to foreign trade. It neither brought money into the country, it was said, nor carried any out of it. The country therefore could never become either richer or poorer by means of it, except so far as its prosperity or decay might indirectly influence the state of foreign trade.

A country that has no mines of its own must undoubtedly draw its gold and silver from foreign countries, in the same manner as one that has no vineyards of its own must draw its wines. It does not seem necessary, however, that the attention of government should be more turned towards the one than towards the other object. A country that has wherewithal to buy wine, will always get the wine which it has occasion for; and a country that has wherewithal to buy gold and silver, will never be in want of those metals. They are to be bought for a certain price like all other commodities, and as they are the price of all other commodities, so all other commodities are the price of those metals. We trust with perfect security that the freedom of trade, without any attention of government, will always supply us with the wine which we have occasion for: and we may trust with equal security that it will always supply us with all the gold and silver which we can afford to purchase or to employ, either in circulating our commodities, or in other uses.

The quantity of every commodity which human industry can either purchase or produce, naturally regulates itself in every country according to the effectual demand, or according to the demand of those who are willing to pay the whole rent, labour and profits which must be paid in order to prepare and bring it to market. But no commodities regulate themselves more easily or more exactly according to this effectual demand than gold and silver; because, on account of the small bulk and great value of those metals, no commodities can be more easily transported from one place to another, from the places where they are cheap, to those where they are dear, from the places where they exceed, to those where they fall short of this effectual demand. If there were in England, for example, an effectual demand for an additional quantity of gold, a packet-boat could bring from

Lisbon, or from wherever else it was to be had, fifty tuns of gold, which could be coined into more than five millions of guineas. But if there were an effectual demand for grain to the same value, to import it would require, at five guineas a tun, a million of tuns of shipping, or a thousand ships of a thousand tuns each. The navy of England would not be sufficient.

When the quantity of gold and silver imported into any country exceeds the effectual demand, no vigilance of government can prevent their exportation. All the sanguinary laws of Spain and Portugal are not able to keep their gold and silver at home. The continual importations from Peru and Brazil exceed the effectual demand of those countries, and sink the price of those metals there below that in the neighbouring countries. If, on the contrary, in any particular country their quantity fell short of the effectual demand, so as to raise their price above that of neighbouring countries, the government would have no occasion to take any pains to import them. If it were even to take pains to prevent their importation, it would not be able to effectuate it. Those metals, when the Spartans had got wherewithal to purchase them, broke through all the barriers which the laws of Lycurgus opposed to their entrance into Lacedemon. All the sanguinary laws of the customs are not able to prevent the importation of the teas of the Dutch and Gottenburgh East India companies; because somewhat cheaper than those of the British company. A pound of tea, however, is about a hundred times the bulk of one of the highest prices, sixteen shillings, that is commonly paid for it in silver, and more than two thousand times the bulk of the same price in gold, and consequently just so many times more difficult to smuggle.

It is partly owing to the easy transportation of gold and silver from the places where they abound to those where they are wanted, that the price of those metals does not fluctuate continually like that of the greater part of other commodities, which are hindered by their bulk from shifting their situation, when the market happens to be either over or under-stocked with them. The price of those metals, indeed, is not altogether exempted from variation, but the changes to which it is liable are generally slow, gradual, and uniform. In Europe, for example, it is supposed, without much foundation, perhaps, that, during the course of the present and preceding century, they have been constantly, but gradually, sinking in their value, on account of the continual importations from the Spanish West Indies. But to make any sudden change in the price of gold and silver, so as to raise or lower at once, sensibly and remarkably, the money price of all other commodities, requires such a revolution in commerce as that occasioned by the discovery of America.

If, notwithstanding all this, gold and silver should at any time fall short in a country which has wherewithal to purchase them, there are more expedients for supplying their place, than that of almost any other commodity. If the materials of manufacture are wanted, industry must stop. If provisions are wanted, the people must starve. But if money is wanted, barter will supply its place, though with a good deal of inconveniency. Buying and selling upon credit, and the different dealers compensating their credits with one another, once a month or once a year, will supply it with less inconveniency. A well-regulated paper money will supply it, not only without any inconveniency, but, in some cases, with some advantages. Upon every account, therefore, the attention of government never was so unnecessarily employed, as when directed to watch over the preservation or increase of the quantity of money in any country.

No complaint, however, is more common than that of a scarcity of money. Money, like wine, must always be scarce with those who have neither wherewithal to buy it, nor credit to borrow it. Those who have either, will seldom be in want either of the money, or of the wine which they have occasion for. This complaint, however, of the scarcity of money, is not always confined to improvident spendthrifts. It is sometimes general through a whole mercantile town, and the country in its neighbourhood. Over-trading is the common cause of it. Sober men, whose projects have been disproportioned to their capitals, are as likely to have neither wherewithal to buy money, nor credit to borrow it, as prodigals whose expence has been disproportioned to their revenue. Before their projects can be brought to bear, their stock is gone, and their credit with it. They run about everywhere to borrow money, and every body tells them that they have none to lend. Even such general complaints of the scarcity of money do not always prove that the usual number of gold and silver pieces are not circulating in the country, but that many people want those pieces who have nothing to give for them. When the profits of trade happen to be greater than ordinary, over-trading becomes a general error both among great and small dealers. They do not always send more money abroad than usual, but they buy upon credit both at home and abroad, an unusual quantity of goods, which they send to some distant market, in hopes that the returns will come in before the demand for payment. The demand comes before the returns, and they have nothing at hand, with which they can either purchase money, or give solid security for borrowing. It is not any scarcity of gold and silver, but the difficulty which such people find in borrowing, and which their creditors find in getting payment, that occasions the general complaint of the scarcity of money.

It would be too ridiculous to go about seriously to prove, that wealth does not consist in money, or in gold and silver; but in what money purchases, and is valuable only for purchasing. Money, no doubt, makes always a part of the national capital; but it has already been shown that it generally makes but a small part, and always the most unprofitable part of it.

It is not because wealth consists more essentially in money than in goods, that the merchant finds it generally more easy to buy goods with money, than to buy money with goods; but because money is the known and established instrument of commerce, for which every thing is readily given in exchange, but which is not always with equal readiness to be got in exchange for every thing. The greater part of goods besides are more perishable than money, and he may frequently sustain a much greater loss by keeping them. When his goods are upon hand too, he is more liable to such demands for money as he may not be able to answer, than when he has got their price in his coffers. Over and above all this, his profit arises more directly from selling than from buying, and he is upon all these accounts generally much more anxious to exchange his goods for money, than his money for goods. But though a particular merchant, with abundance of goods in his warehouse, may sometimes be ruined by not being able to sell them in time, a nation or country is not liable to the same accident. The whole capital of a merchant frequently consists in perishable goods destined for purchasing money. But it is but a very small part of the annual produce of the land and labour of a country which can ever be destined for purchasing gold and silver from their neighbours. The far greater part is circulated and consumed among themselves; and even of the surplus which is sent abroad, the greater part is generally destined for the purchase of other foreign goods. Though gold and silver, therefore, could not be had in exchange for the goods destined to purchase them, the nation would not be ruined. It might, indeed, suffer some loss and inconveniency, and be forced upon some of those expedients which are necessary for supplying the place of money. The annual produce of its land and labour, however, would be the same, or very nearly the same, as usual, because the same, or very nearly the same consumable capital would be employed in maintaining it. And though goods do not always draw money so readily as money draws goods, in the long-run they draw it more necessarily than even it draws them. Goods can serve many other purposes besides purchasing money, but money can serve no other purpose besides purchasing goods. Money, therefore, necessarily runs after goods, but goods do not always or necessarily run after money. The man who buys, does not always mean to sell again, but frequently to use or to consume; whereas he who sells, always means to buy again. The one may frequently have done the whole, but the other can never have done more than the one-half of his business. It is not for its own sake that men desire money, but for the sake of what they can purchase with it.

Consumable commodities, it is said, are soon destroyed; whereas gold and silver are of a more durable nature, and, were it not for this continual exportation, might be accumulated for ages together, to the incredible augmentation of the real wealth of the country. Nothing, therefore, it is pretended, can be more disadvantageous to any country, than the trade which consists in the exchange of such lasting for such perishable commodities. We do not, however, reckon that trade disadvantageous which consists in the exchange of the hard-ware of England for the wines of France; and yet hard-ware is a very durable commodity, and were it not for this continual exportation, might too be accumulated for ages together, to the incredible augmentation of the pots and pans of the country. But it readily occurs that the number of such utensils is in every country necessarily limited by the use which there is for them; that it would be absurd to have more pots and pans than were necessary for cooking the victuals usually consumed there; and that if the quantity of victuals were to increase, the number of pots and pans would readily increase along with it, a part of the increased quantity of victuals being employed in purchasing them, or in maintaining an additional number of workmen whose business it was to make them. It should as readily occur that the quantity of gold and silver is in every country limited by the use which there is for those metals; that their use consists in circulating commodities as coin, and in affording a species of household furniture as plate; that the quantity of coin in every country is regulated by the value of the commodities which are to be circulated by it: increase that value, and immediately a part of it will be sent abroad to purchase wherever it is to be had, the additional quantity of coin requisite for circulating them: that the quantity of plate is regulated by the number and wealth of those private families who chuse to indulge themselves in that sort of magnificence: increase the number and wealth of such families, and a part of this increased wealth will most probably be employed in purchasing, wherever it is to be found, an additional quantity of plate: that to attempt to increase the wealth of any country, either by introducing or by detaining in it an unnecessary quantity of gold and silver, is as absurd as it would be to attempt to increase the good cheer of private families, by obliging them to keep an unnecessary number of kitchen utensils. As the expence of purchasing those unnecessary utensils would diminish instead of increasing either the quantity or goodness of the family provisions; so the expence of purchasing an unnecessary quantity of gold and silver must, in every country, as necessarily diminish the wealth which feeds, clothes, and lodges, which maintains and employs the people. Gold and silver, whether in the shape of coin or of plate, are utensils, it must be remembered, as much as the furniture of the kitchen. Increase the use for them, increase the consumable commodities which are to be circulated, managed, and prepared by means of them, and you will infallibly increase the quantity; but if you attempt, by extraordinary means, to increase the quantity, you will as infallibly diminish the use and even the quantity too, which in those metals can never be greater than what the use requires. Were they ever to be accumulated beyond this quantity, their transportation is so easy, and the loss which attends their lying idle and unemployed so great, that no law could prevent their being immediately sent out of the country.

It is not always necessary to accumulate gold and silver, in order to enable a country to carry on foreign wars, and to maintain fleets and armies in distant countries. Fleets and armies are maintained, not with gold and silver, but with consumable goods. The nation which, from the annual produce of its domestic industry, from the annual revenue arising out of its lands, labour, and consumable stock, has wherewithal to purchase those consumable goods in distant countries, can maintain foreign wars there.

A nation may purchase the pay and provisions of an army in a distant country three different ways; by sending abroad either, first, some part of its accumulated gold and silver; or secondly, some part of the annual produce of its manufactures; or last of all, some part of its annual rude produce.

The gold and silver which can properly be considered as accumulated or stored up in any country, may be distinguished into three parts; first, the circulating money; secondly, the plate of private families; and last of all, the money which may have been collected by many years parsimony, and laid up in the treasury of the prince.

It can seldom happen that much can be spared from the circulating money of the country; because in that there can seldom be much redundancy. The value of goods annually bought and sold in any country requires a certain quantity of money to circulate and distribute them to their proper consumers, and can give employment to no more. The channel of circulation necessarily draws to itself a sum sufficient to fill it, and never admits any more. Something, however, is generally withdrawn from this channel in the case of foreign war. By the great number of people who are maintained abroad, fewer are maintained at home. Fewer goods are circulated there, and less money becomes necessary to circulate them. An extraordinary quantity of paper money, of some sort or other too, such as exchequer notes, navy bills, and bank bills in England, is generally issued upon such occasions, and by supplying the place of circulating gold and silver, gives an opportunity of sending a greater quantity of it abroad. All this, however, could afford but a poor resource for maintaining a foreign war, of great expence and several years duration.

The melting down the plate of private families, has upon every occasion been found a still more insignificant one. The French, in the beginning of the last war, did not derive so much advantage from this expedient as to compensate the loss of the fashion.

The accumulated treasures of the prince have, in former times, afforded a much greater and more lasting resource. In the present times, if you except the king of Prussia, to accumulate treasure seems to be no part of the policy of European princes.

The funds which maintained the foreign wars of the present century, the most expensive perhaps which history records, seem to have had little dependency upon the exportation either of the circulating money, or of the plate of private families, or of the treasure of the prince. The last French war cost Great Britain upwards of ninety millions, including not only the seventy-five millions of new debt that was contracted, but the additional two shillings in the pound land tax, and what was annually borrowed of the sinking fund. More than two-thirds of this expence were laid out in distant countries; in Germany, Portugal, America, in the ports of the Mediterranean, in the East and West Indies. The kings of England had no accumulated treasure. We never heard of any extraordinary quantity of plate being melted down. The circulating gold and silver of the country had not been supposed to exceed eighteen millions. Since the late recoinage of the gold, however, it is believed to have been a good deal under-rated. Let us suppose, therefore, according to the most exaggerated computation which I remember to have either seen or heard of, that, gold and silver together, it amounted to thirty millions. Had the war been carried on, by means of our money, the whole of it must, even according to this computation, have been sent out and returned again at least twice, in a period of between six and seven years. Should this be supposed, it would afford the most decisive argument to demonstrate how unnecessary it is for government to watch over the preservation of money, since upon this supposition the whole money of the country must have gone from it and returned to it again, two different times in so short a period, without any body's knowing any thing of the matter. The channel of circulation, however, never appeared more empty than usual during any part of this period. Few people wanted money who had wherewithal to pay for it. The profits of foreign trade, indeed, were greater than usual during the whole war; but especially towards the end of it. This occasioned, what it always occasions, a general over-trading in all the ports of Great Britain; and this again occasioned the usual complaint of the scarcity of money, which always follows over-trading. Many people wanted it, who had neither wherewithal to buy it, nor credit to borrow it; and because the debtors found it difficult to borrow, the creditors found it difficult to get payment. Gold and silver, however, were generally to be had for their value, by those who had that value to give for them.

The enormous expense of the late war, therefore, must have been chiefly defrayed, not by the exportation of gold and silver, but by that of British commodities of some kind or other. When the government, or those who acted under them, contracted with a merchant for a remittance to some foreign country, he would naturally endeavour to pay his foreign correspondent, upon whom he had granted a bill, by sending abroad rather commodities than gold and silver. If the commodities of Great Britain were not in demand in that country, he would endeavour to send them to some other country, in which he could purchase a bill upon that country. The transportation of commodities, when properly suited to the market, is always attended with a considerable profit; whereas that of gold and silver is scarce ever attended with any. When those metals are sent abroad in order to purchase foreign commodities, the merchant's profit arises, not from the purchase, but from the sale of the returns. But when they are sent abroad merely to pay a debt, he gets no returns, and consequently no profit. He naturally, therefore, exerts his invention to find out a way of paying his foreign debts, rather by the exportation of commodities than by that of gold and silver. The great quantity of British goods exported during the course of the late war, without bringing back any returns, is accordingly remarked by the author of The Present State of the Nation.

Besides the three sorts of gold and silver above mentioned, there is in all great commercial countries a good deal of bullion alternately imported and exported for the purposes of foreign trade. This bullion, as it circulates among different commercial countries in the same manner as the national coin circulates in every particular country, may be considered as the money of the great mercantile republic. The national coin receives its movement and direction from the commodities circulated within the precincts of each particular country: the money of the mercantile republic, from those circulated between different countries. Both are employed in facilitating exchanges, the one between different individuals of the same, the other between those of different nations. Part of this money of the great mercantile republic may have been, and probably was, employed in carrying on the late war. In time of a general war, it is natural to suppose that a movement and direction should be impressed upon it, different from what it usually follows in profound peace; that it should circulate more about the seat of the war, and be more employed in purchasing there, and in the neighbouring countries, the pay and provisions of the different armies. But whatever part of this money of the mercantile republic, Great Britain may have annually employed in this manner, it must have been annually purchased, either with British commodities, or with something else that had been purchased with them; which still brings us back to commodities, to the annual produce of the land and labour of the country, as the ultimate resources which enabled us to carry on the war. It is natural indeed to suppose, that so great an annual expence must have been defrayed from a great annual produce. The expence of 1761, for example, amounted to more than nineteen millions. No accumulation could have supported so great an annual profusion. There is no annual produce even of gold and silver which could have supported it. The whole gold and silver annually imported into both Spain and Portugal, according to the best accounts, does not commonly much exceed six millions sterling, which, in some years, would scarce have paid four months expence of the late war.

* * * * * * * *

The importation of gold and silver is not the principal, much less the sole benefit which a nation derives from its foreign trade. Between whatever places foreign trade is carried on, they all of them derive two distinct benefits from it. It carries out that surplus part of the produce of their land and labour for which there is no demand among them, and brings back in return for it something else for which there is a demand. It gives a value to their superfluities, by exchanging them for something else, which may satisfy a part of their wants, and increase their enjoyments. By means of it, the narrowness of the home market does not hinder the division of labour in any particular branch of art or manufacture from being carried to the highest perfection. By opening a more extensive market for whatever part of the produce of their labour may exceed the home consumption, it encourages them to improve its productive powers, and to augment its annual produce to the utmost, and thereby to increase the real revenue and wealth of the society. These great and important services foreign trade is continually occupied in performing, to all the different countries between which it is carried on. They all derive great benefit from it, though that in which the merchant resides generally derives the greatest, as he is generally more employed in supplying the wants, and carrying out the superfluities of his own, than of any other particular country. To import the gold and silver which may be wanted, into the countries which have no mines, is, no doubt, a part of the business of foreign commerce. It is, however, a most insignificant part of it. A country which carried on foreign trade merely upon this account, could scarce have occasion to freight a ship in a century.

It is not by the importation of gold and silver, that the discovery of America has enriched Europe. By the abundance of the American mines, those metals have become cheaper. A service of plate can now be purchased for about a third part of the corn, or a third part of the labour, which it would have cost in the fifteenth century. With the same annual expence of labour and commodities, Europe can annually purchase about three times the quantity of plate which it could have purchased at that time. But when a commodity comes to be sold for a third part of what had been its usual price, not only those who purchased it before can purchase three times their former quantity, but it is brought down to the level of a much greater number of purchasers, perhaps to more than ten, perhaps to more than twenty times the former number. So that there may be in Europe at present not only more than three times, but more than twenty or thirty times the quantity of plate which would have been in it, even in its present state of improvement, had the discovery of the American mines never been made. So far Europe has, no doubt, gained a real conveniency, though surely a very trifling one. The cheapness of gold and silver renders those metals rather less fit for the purposes of money than they were before. In order to make the same purchases, we must load ourselves with a greater quantity of them, and carry about a shilling in our pocket where a groat would have done before. It is difficult to say which is most trifling, this inconveniency, or the opposite conveniency. Neither the one nor the other could have made any very essential change in the state of Europe. The discovery of America, however, certainly made a most essential one. By opening a new and inexhaustible market to all the commodities of Europe, it gave occasion to new divisions of labour and improvements of art, which, in the narrow circle of the ancient commerce, could never have taken place for want of a market to take off the greater part of their produce. The productive powers of labour were improved, and its produce increased in all the different countries of Europe, and together with it the real revenue and wealth of the inhabitants. The commodities of Europe were almost all new to America, and many of those of America were new to Europe. A new set of exchanges, therefore, began to take place which had never been thought of before, and which should naturally have proved as advantageous to the new, as it certainly did to the old continent. The savage injustice of the Europeans rendered an event, which ought to have been beneficial to all, ruinous and destructive to several of those unfortunate countries.

The discovery of a passage to the East Indies, by the Cape of Good Hope, which happened much about the same time, opened, perhaps, a still more extensive range to foreign commerce than even that of America, notwithstanding the greater distance. There were but two nations in America, in any respect superior to savages, and these were destroyed almost as soon as discovered. The rest were mere savages. But the empires of China, Indostan, Japan, as well as several others in the East Indies, without having richer mines of gold or silver, were in every other respect much richer, better cultivated, and more advanced in all arts and manufactures than either Mexico or Peru, even though we should credit, what plainly deserves no credit, the exaggerated accounts of the Spanish writers, concerning the ancient state of those empires. But rich and civilized nations can always exchange to a much greater value with one another, than with savages and barbarians. Europe, however, has hitherto derived much less advantage from its commerce with the East Indies, than from that with America. The Portuguese monopolized the East India trade to themselves for about a century, and it was only indirectly and through them, that the other nations of Europe could either send out or receive any goods from that country. When the Dutch, in the beginning of the last century, began to encroach upon them, they vested their whole East India commerce in an exclusive company. The English, French, Swedes, and Danes, have all followed their example, so that no great nation in Europe has ever yet had the benefit of a free commerce to the East

Indies. No other reason need be assigned why it has never been so advantageous as the trade to America, which, between almost every nation of Europe and its own colonies, is free to all its subjects. The exclusive privileges of those East India companies, their great riches, the great favour and protection which these have procured them from their respective governments, have excited much envy against them. This envy has frequently represented their trade as altogether pernicious, on account of the great quantities of silver, which it every year exports from the countries from which it is carried on. The parties concerned have replied, that their trade, by this continual exportation of silver, might, indeed, tend to impoverish Europe in general, but not the particular country from which it was carried on; because, by the exportation of a part of the returns to other European countries, it annually brought home a much greater quantity of that metal than it carried out. Both the objection and the reply are founded in the popular notion which I have been just now examining. It is, therefore, unnecessary to say any thing further about either. By the annual exportation of silver to the East Indies, plate is probably somewhat dearer in Europe than it otherwise might have been; and coined silver probably purchases a larger quantity both of labour and commodities. The former of these two effects is a very small loss, the latter a very small advantage; both too insignificant to deserve any part of the public attention. The trade to the East Indies, by opening a market to the commodities of Europe, or, what comes nearly to the same thing, to the gold and silver which is purchased with those commodities, must necessarily tend to increase the annual production of European commodities, and consequently the real wealth and revenue of Europe. That it has hitherto increased them so little, is probably owing to the restraints which it every-where labours under.

I thought it necessary, though at the hazard of being tedious, to examine at full length this popular notion that wealth consists in money, or in gold and silver. Money in common language, as I have already observed, frequently signifies wealth; and this ambiguity of expression has rendered this popular notion so familiar to us, that even they, who are convinced of its absurdity, are very apt to forget their own principles, and in the course of their reasonings to take it for granted as a certain and undeniable truth. Some of the best English writers upon commerce set out with observing, that the wealth of a country consists, not in its gold and silver only, but in its lands, houses, and consumable goods of all different kinds. In the course of their reasonings, however, the lands, houses, and consumable goods seem to slip out of their memory, and the strain of their argument frequently supposes that all wealth consists in gold and silver, and that to multiply those metals is the great object of national industry and commerce.

The two principles being established, however, that wealth consisted in gold and silver, and that those metals could be brought into a country which had no mines only by the balance of trade, or by exporting to a greater value than it imported; it necessarily became the great object of political œconomy to diminish as much as possible the importation of foreign goods for home consumption, and to increase as much as possible the exportation of the produce of domestic industry. Its two great engines for enriching the country, therefore, were restraints upon importation, and encouragements to exportation.

The restraints upon importation were of two kinds.

First, Restraints upon the importation of such foreign goods for home consumption as could be produced at home, from whatever country they were imported.

Secondly, Restraints upon the importation of goods of almost all kinds from those particular countries with which the balance of trade was supposed to be disadvantageous.

Those different restraints consisted sometimes in high duties, and sometimes in absolute prohibitions.

Exportation was encouraged sometimes by drawbacks, sometimes by bounties, sometimes by advantageous treaties of commerce with foreign states, and sometimes by the establishment of colonies in distant countries.

Drawbacks were given upon two different occasions. When the home manufacturers were subject to any duty or excise either the whole or a part of it was frequently drawn back upon their exportation; and when foreign goods liable to a duty were imported in order to be exported again, either the whole or a part of this duty was sometimes given back upon such exportation.

Bounties were given for the encouragement either of some beginning manufactures, or of such sorts of industry of other kinds as were supposed to deserve particular favour.

By advantageous treaties of commerce, particular privileges were procured in some foreign state for the goods and merchants of the country, beyond what were granted to those of other countries.

By the establishment of colonies in distant countries, not only particular privileges, but a monopoly was frequently procured for the goods and merchants of the country which established them.

The two sorts of restraints upon importation above-mentioned, together with these four encouragements to exportation, constitute the six principal means by which the commercial system proposes to increase the quantity of gold and silver in any country by turning the balance of trade in its favour. I shall consider each of them in a particular chapter, and without taking much further notice of their supposed tendency to bring money into the country, I shall examine chiefly what are likely to be the effects of each of them upon the annual produce of its industry. According as they tend either to increase or diminish the value of this annual produce, they must evidently tend either to increase or diminish the real wealth and revenue of the country.

CHAPTER II

Of Restraints Upon the Importation from Foreign Countries of Such Goods as Can Be Produced at Home

BY restraining, either by high duties, or by absolute prohibitions, the importation of such goods from foreign countries as can be produced at home, the monopoly of the home market is more or less secured to the domestic industry employed in producing them. Thus the prohibition of importing either live cattle or salt provisions from foreign countries secures to the graziers of Great Britain the monopoly of the home market for butcher's meat. The high duties upon the importation of corn, which in times of moderate plenty amount to a prohibition, give a like advantage to the growers of that commodity. The prohibition of the importation of foreign woollens is equally favourable to the woollen manufacturers. The silk manufacture, though altogether employed upon foreign materials, has lately obtained the same advantage. The linen manufacture has not yet obtained it, but is making great strides towards it. Many other sorts of manufacturers have, in the same manner, obtained in Great Britain, either altogether, or very nearly a monopoly against their countrymen. The variety of goods of which the importation into Great Britain is prohibited, either absolutely, or under certain circumstances, greatly exceeds what can easily be suspected by those who are not well acquainted with the laws of the customs.

That this monopoly of the home-market frequently gives great encouragement to that particular species of industry which enjoys it, and frequently turns towards that employment a greater share of both the labour and stock of the society than would otherwise have gone to it, cannot be doubted. But whether it tends either to increase the general industry of the society, or to give it the most advantageous direction, is not, perhaps, altogether so evident.

The general industry of the society never can exceed what the capital of the society can employ. As the number of workmen that can be kept in employment by any particular person must bear a certain proportion to his capital, so the number of those that can be continually employed by all the members of a great society, must bear a certain proportion to the whole capital of that society, and never can exceed that proportion. No regulation of commerce can increase the quantity of industry in any society beyond what its capital can maintain. It can only divert a part of it into a direction into which it might not otherwise have gone; and it is by no means certain that this artificial direction is likely to be more advantageous to the society than that into which it would have gone of its own accord.

Every individual is continually exerting himself to find out the most advantageous employment for whatever capital he can command. It is his own advantage, indeed, and not that of the society, which he has in view. But the study of his own advantage naturally, or rather necessarily leads him to prefer that employment which is most advantageous to the society.

First, every individual endeavours to employ his capital as near home as he can, and consequently as much as he can in the support of domestic industry; provided always that he can thereby obtain the ordinary, or not a great deal less than the ordinary profits of stock.

Thus, upon equal or nearly equal profits, every wholesale merchant naturally prefers the home-trade to the foreign trade of consumption, and the foreign trade of consumption to the carrying trade. In the home-trade his capital is never so long out of his sight as it frequently is in the foreign trade of consumption. He can know better the character and situation of the person whom he trusts, and if he should happen to be deceived, he knows better the laws of the country from which he must seek redress. In the carrying trade, the capital of the merchant is, as it were, divided between two foreign countries, and no part of it is ever necessarily brought home, or placed under his own immediate view and command. The capital which an Amsterdam merchant employs in carrying corn from Konnigsberg to Lisbon, and fruit and wine from Lisbon to Konnigsberg, must generally be the one-half of it at Konnigsberg and the other half at Lisbon. No part of it need ever come to Amsterdam. The natural residence of such a merchant should either be at Konnigsberg or Lisbon, and it can only be some very particular circumstances which can make him prefer the residence of Amsterdam. The uneasiness, however, which he feels at being separated so far from his capital, generally determines him to bring part both of the Konnigsberg goods which he destines for the market of Lisbon, and of the Lisbon goods which he destines for that of Konnigsberg, to Amsterdam; and though this necessarily subjects him to a double charge of loading and unloading, as well as to the payment of some duties and customs, yet for the sake of having some part of his capital always under his own view and command, he willingly submits to this extraordinary charge; and it is in this manner that every country which has any considerable share of the carrying trade, becomes always the emporium, or general market, for the goods of all the different countries whose trade it carries on. The merchant, in order to save a second loading and unloading, endeavors always to sell in the home-market as much of the goods of all those different countries as he can, and thus, so far as he can, to convert his carrying trade into a foreign trade of consumption. A merchant, in the same manner, who is engaged in the foreign trade of consumption, when he collects goods for foreign markets, will always be glad, upon equal or nearly equal profits, to sell as great a part of them at home as he can. He saves himself the risk and trouble of exportation, when, so far as he can, he thus converts his foreign trade of consumption into a home-trade. Home is in this manner the center, if I may say so, round which the capitals of the inhabitants of every country are continually circulating, and towards which they are always tending, though by particular causes they may sometimes be driven off and repelled from it towards more distant employments. But a capital employed in the home-trade, it has already been shown, necessarily puts into motion a greater quantity of domestic industry, and gives revenue and employment to a greater number of the inhabitants of the country, than an equal capital employed in the foreign trade of consumption: and one employed in the foreign trade of consumption has the same advantage over an equal capital employed in the carrying trade. Upon equal, or only nearly equal profits, therefore, every individual naturally inclines to employ his capital in the manner in which it is likely to afford the greatest support to domestic industry, and to give revenue and employment to the greatest number of people of his own country.

Secondly, every individual who employs his capital in the support of domestic industry, necessarily endeavours so to direct that industry, that its produce may be of the greatest possible value.

The produce of industry is what it adds to the subject or materials upon which it is employed. In proportion as the value of this produce is great or small, so will likewise be the profits of the employer. But it is only for the sake of profit that any man employs a capital in the support of industry; and he will always, therefore, endeavour to employ it in the support of that industry of which the produce is likely to be of the greatest value, or to exchange for the greatest quantity either of money or of other goods.

But the annual revenue of every society is always precisely equal to the exchangeable value of the whole annual produce of its industry, or rather is precisely the same thing with that exchangeable value. As every individual, therefore, endeavours as much as he can both to employ his capital in the support of domestic industry, and so to direct that industry that its produce may be of the greatest value; every individual necessarily labours to render the annual revenue of the society as great as he can. He generally, indeed, neither intends to promote the public interest, nor knows how much he is promoting it. By preferring the support of domestic to that of foreign industry, he intends only his own security; and by directing that industry in such a manner as its produce may be of the greatest value, he intends only his own gain, and he is in this, as in many other cases, led by an invisible hand to promote an end which was no part of his intention. Nor is it always the worse for the society that it was no part of it. By pursuing his own interest he frequently promotes that of the society more effectually than when he really intends to promote it. I have never known much good done by those who affected to trade for the public good. It is an affectation, indeed, not very common among merchants, and very few words need be employed in dissuading them from it.

What is the species of domestic industry which his capital can employ, and of which the produce is likely to be of the greatest value, every individual, it is evident, can, in his local situation, judge much better than any statesman or lawgiver can do for him. The statesman, who should attempt to direct private people in what manner they ought to employ their capitals, would not only load himself with a most unnecessary attention, but assume an authority which could safely be trusted, not only to no single person, but to no council or senate whatever, and which would no-where be so dangerous as in the hands of a man who had folly and presumption enough to fancy himself fit to exercise it.

To give the monopoly of the home-market to the produce of domestic industry, in any particular art or manufacture, is in some measure to direct private people in what manner they ought to employ their capitals, and must, in almost all cases, be either a useless or a hurtful regulation. If the produce of domestic can be brought there as cheap as that of foreign industry, the regulation is evidently useless. If it cannot, it must generally be hurtful. It is the maxim of every prudent master of a family, never to attempt to make at home what it will cost him more to make than to buy. The taylor does not attempt to make his own shoes, but buys them of the shoemaker. The shoemaker does not attempt to make his own clothes, but employs a taylor. The farmer attempts to make neither the one nor the other, but employs those different artificers. All of them find it for their interest to employ their whole industry in a way in which they have some advantage over their neighbours, and to purchase with a part of its produce, or what is the same thing, with the price of a part of it, whatever else they have occasion for.

What is prudence in the conduct of every private family, can scarce be folly in that of a great kingdom. If a foreign country can supply us with a commodity cheaper than we ourselves can make it, better buy it of them with some part of the produce of our own industry, employed in a way in which we have some advantage. The general industry of the country, being always in proportion to the capital which employs it, will not thereby be diminished, no more than that of the above-mentioned artificers; but only left to find out the way in which it can be employed with the greatest advantage. It is certainly not employed to the greatest advantage, when it is thus directed towards an object which it can buy cheaper than it can make. The value of its annual produce is certainly more or less diminished, when it is thus turned away from producing commodities evidently of more value than the commodity which it is directed to produce. According to the supposition, that commodity could be purchased from foreign countries cheaper than it can be made at home. It could, therefore, have been purchased with a part only of the commodities, or, what is the same thing, with a part only of the price of the commodities, which the industry employed by an equal capital would have produced at home, had it been left to follow its natural course. The industry of the country, therefore, is thus turned away from a more, to a less advantageous employment, and the exchangeable value of its annual produce, instead of being increased, according to the intention of the lawgiver, must necessarily be diminished by every such regulation.

By means of such regulations, indeed, a particular manufacture may sometimes be acquired sooner than it could have been otherwise, and after a certain time may be made at home as cheap or cheaper than in the foreign country. But though the industry of the society may be thus carried with advantage into a particular channel sooner than it could have been otherwise, it will by no means follow that the sum total, either of its industry, or of its revenue, can ever be augmented by any such regulation. The industry of the society can augment only in proportion as its capital augments, and its capital can augment only in proportion to what can be gradually saved out of its revenue. But the immediate effect of every such regulation is to diminish its revenue, and what diminishes its revenue is certainly not very likely to augment its capital faster than it would have augmented of its own accord, had both capital and industry been left to find out their natural employments.

Though for want of such regulations the society should never acquire the proposed manufacture, it would not, upon that account, necessarily be the poorer in any one period of its duration. In every period of its duration its whole capital and industry might still have been employed, though upon different objects, in the manner that was most advantageous at the time. In every period its revenue might have been the greatest which its capital could afford, and both capital and revenue might have been augmented with the greatest possible rapidity.

The natural advantages which one country has over another in producing particular commodities are sometimes so great that it is acknowledged by all the world to be in vain to struggle with them. By means of glasses, hotbeds, and hotwalls, very good grapes can be raised in Scotland, and very good wine too can be made of them at about thirty times the expence for which at least equally good can be brought from foreign countries. Would it be a reasonable law to prohibit the importation of all foreign wines, merely to encourage the making of claret and burgundy in Scotland? But if there would be a manifest absurdity in turning towards any employment, thirty times more of the capital and industry of the country, than would be necessary to purchase from foreign countries an equal quantity of the commodities wanted, there must be an absurdity, though not altogether so glaring, yet exactly of the same kind, in turning towards any such employment a thirtieth, or even a three hundredth part more of either. Whether the advantages which one country has over another, be natural or acquired, is in this respect of no consequence. As long as the one country has those advantages, and the other wants them, it will always be more advantageous for the latter, rather to buy of the former than to make. It is an acquired advantage only, which one artificer has over his neighbour, who exercises another trade; and yet they both find it more advantageous to buy of one another, than to make what does not belong to their particular trades.

Merchants and manufacturers are the people who derive the greatest advantage from this monopoly of the home-market. The prohibition of the importation of foreign cattle, and of salt provisions, together with the high duties upon foreign corn, which in times of moderate plenty amount to a prohibition, are not near so advantageous to the graziers and farmers of Great Britain, as other regulations of the same kind are to its merchants and manufacturers. Manufactures, those of the finer kind especially, are more easily transported from one country to another than corn or cattle. It is in the fetching and carrying manufactures, accordingly, that foreign trade is chiefly employed. In manufactures, a very small advantage will enable foreigners to undersell our own workmen, even in the home market. It will require a very great one to enable them to do so in the rude produce of the soil. If the free importation of foreign manufactures were permitted, several of the home manufactures would probably suffer, and some of them, perhaps, go to ruin altogether, and a considerable part of the stock and industry at present employed in them, would be forced to find out some other employment. But the freest importation of the rude produce of the soil could have no such effect upon the agriculture of the country.

If the importation of foreign cattle, for example, were made ever so free, so few could be imported, that the grazing trade of Great Britain could be little affected by it. Live cattle are, perhaps, the only commodity of which the transportation is more expensive by sea than by land. By land they carry themselves to market. By sea, not only the cattle, but their food and water too, must be carried at no small expence and inconveniency. The short sea between Ireland and Great Britain, indeed, renders the importation of Irish cattle more easy. But though the free importation of them, which was lately permitted only for a limited time, were rendered perpetual, it could have no considerable effect upon the interest of the graziers of Great Britain. Those parts of Great Britain which border upon the Irish sea are all grazing countries. Irish cattle could never be imported for their use, but must be drove through those very extensive countries, at no small expence and inconveniency, before they could arrive at their proper market. Fat cattle could not be drove so far. Lean cattle, therefore, only could be imported, and such importation could interfere, not with the interest of the feeding or fattening countries, to which, by reducing the price of lean cattle, it would rather be advantageous, but with that of the breeding countries only. The small number of Irish cattle imported since their importation was permitted, together with the good price at which lean cattle still continue to sell, seem to demonstrate that even the breeding countries of Great Britain are never likely to be much affected by the free importation of Irish cattle. The common people of Ireland, indeed, are said to have sometimes opposed with violence the exportation of their cattle. But if the exporters had found any great advantage in continuing the trade, they could easily, when the law was on their side, have conquered this mobbish opposition.

Feeding and fattening countries, besides, must always be highly improved, whereas breeding countries are generally uncultivated. The high price of lean cattle, by augmenting the value of uncultivated land, is like a bounty against improvement. To any country which was highly improved throughout, it would be more advantageous to import its lean cattle than to breed them. The province of Holland, accordingly, is said to follow this maxim at present. The mountains of Scotland, Wales and Northumberland, indeed, are countries not capable of much improvement, and seem destined by nature to be the breeding countries of Great Britain. The freest importation of foreign cattle could have no other effect than to hinder those breeding countries from taking advantage of the increasing population and improvement of the rest of the kingdom from raising their price to an exorbitant height, and from laying a real tax upon all the more improved and cultivated parts of the country.

The freest importation of salt provisions, in the same manner, could have as little effect upon the interest of the graziers of Great Britain as that of live cattle. Salt provisions are not only a very bulky commodity, but when compared with fresh meat, they are a commodity both of worse quality, and as they cost more labour and expence, of higher price. They could never, therefore, come into competition with the fresh meat, though they might with the salt provisions of the country. They might be used for victualling ships for distant voyages, and such like uses, but could never make any considerable part of the food of the people. The small quantity of salt provisions imported from Ireland since their importation was rendered free, is an experimental proof that our graziers have nothing to apprehend from it. It does not appear that the price of butcher's-meat has ever been sensibly affected by it.

Even the free importation of foreign corn could very little affect the interest of the farmers of Great Britain. Corn is a much more bulky commodity than butcher's-meat. A pound of wheat at a penny is as dear as a pound of butcher's-meat at fourpence. The small quantity of foreign corn imported even in times of the greatest scarcity, may satisfy our farmers that they can have nothing to fear from the freest importation. The average quantity imported one year with another, amounts only, according to the very well informed author of the tracts upon the corn trade, to twenty-three thousand seven hundred and twenty-eight quarters of all sorts of grain, and does not exceed the five hundredth and seventy-one part of the annual consumption. But as the bounty upon corn occasions a greater exportation in years of plenty, so it must of consequence occasion a greater importation in years of scarcity, than in the actual state of tillage would otherwise take place. By means of it, the plenty of one year does not compensate the scarcity of another, and as the average quantity exported is necessarily augmented by it, so must likewise, in the actual state of tillage, the average quantity imported. If there were no bounty, as less corn would be exported, so it is probable that, one year with another, less would be imported than at present. The corn merchants, the fetchers and carriers of corn between Great Britain and foreign countries, would have much less employment, and might suffer considerably; but the country gentlemen and farmers could suffer very little. It is in the corn merchants accordingly, rather than in the country gentlemen and farmers, that I have observed the greatest anxiety for the renewal and continuation of the bounty.

Country gentlemen and farmers are, to their great honour, of all people, the least subject to the wretched spirit of monopoly. The undertaker of a great manufactory is sometimes alarmed if another work of the same kind is established within twenty miles of him. The Dutch undertaker of the woollen manufacture at Abbeville stipulated, that no work of the same kind should be established within thirty leagues of that city. Farmers and country gentlemen, on the contrary, are generally disposed rather to promote than to obstruct the cultivation and improvement of their neighbours' farms and estates. They have no secrets, such as those of the greater part of manufacturers, but are generally rather fond of communicating to their neighbours, and of extending as far as possible any new practice which they have found to be advantageous. *Pius Questus,* says old Cato, *stabilissimusque, minimeque invidiosus; minimeque male cogitantes sunt, qui in eo studio occupati sunt.* Country gentlemen and farmers, dispersed in different parts of the country, cannot so easily combine as merchants and manufacturers, who being collected into towns, and accustomed to that exclusive corporation spirit which prevails in them, naturally endeavour to obtain against all their countrymen, the same exclusive privilege which they generally possess against the inhabitants of their respective towns. They accordingly seem to have been the original inventors of those restraints upon the importation of foreign goods, which secure to them the monopoly of the home-market. It was probably in imitation of them, and to put themselves upon a level with those who, they found, were disposed to oppress them, that the country gentlemen and farmers of Great Britain so far forgot the generosity which is natural to their station, as to demand the exclusive privilege of supplying their countrymen with corn and butcher's-meat. They did not perhaps take time to consider, how much less their interest could be affected by the freedom of trade, than that of the people whose example they followed.

To prohibit by a perpetual law the importation of foreign corn and cattle, is in reality to enact, that the population and industry of the country shall at no time exceed what the rude produce of its own soil can maintain.

There seem, however, to be two cases in which it will generally be advantageous to lay some burden upon foreign, for the encouragement of domestic industry.

The first, is, when some particular sort of industry is necessary for the defence of the country. The defence of Great Britain, for example, depends very much upon the number of its sailors and shipping. The act of navigation, therefore, very properly endeavours to give the sailors and shipping of Great Britain the monopoly of the trade of their own country, in some cases, by absolute prohibitions, and in others by heavy burdens upon the shipping of foreign countries. The following are the principal dispositions of this act.

First, all ships, of which the owners, masters, and three-fourths of the mariners are not British subjects, are prohibited, upon pain of forfeiting ship and cargo, from trading to the British settlements and plantations, or from being employed in the coasting trade of Great Britain.

Secondly, a great variety of the most bulky articles of importation can be brought into Great Britain only, either in such ships as are above described, or in ships of the country where those goods are produced, and of which the owners, masters, and three-fourths of the mariners, are of that particular country; and when imported even in ships of this latter kind, they are subject to double aliens duty. If imported in ships of any other country, the penalty is forfeiture of ship and goods. When this act was made, the Dutch were, what they still are, the great carriers of Europe, and by this regulation they were entirely excluded from being the carriers to Great Britain, or from importing to us the goods of any other European country.

Thirdly, a great variety of the most bulky articles of importation are prohibited from being imported, even in British ships, from any country but that in which they are produced; under pain of forfeiting ship and cargo. This regulation too was probably intended against the Dutch. Holland was then, as now, the great emporium for all European goods, and by this regulation, British ships were hindered from loading in Holland the goods of any other European country.

Fourthly, salt fish of all kinds, whale-fins, whale-bone, oil, and blubber, not caught by and cured on board British vessels, when imported into Great Britain, are subjected to double aliens duty. The Dutch, as they are still the principal, were then the only fishers in Europe that attempted to supply foreign nations with fish. By this regulation, a very heavy burden was laid upon their supplying Great Britain.

When the act of navigation was made, though England and Holland were not actually at war, the most violent animosity subsisted between the two nations. It had begun during the government of the long parliament, which first framed this act, and it broke out soon after in the Dutch wars during that of the Protector and of Charles the Second. It is not impossible, therefore, that some of the regulations of this famous act may have proceeded from national animosity. They are as wise, however, as if they had all been dictated by the most deliberate wisdom. National animosity at that particular time aimed at the very same object which the most deliberate wisdom could have recommended, the diminution of the naval power of Holland, the only naval power which could endanger the security of England.

The act of navigation is not favourable to foreign commerce, or to the growth of that opulence which can arise from it. The interest of a nation in its commercial relations to foreign nations is, like that of a merchant with regard to the different people with whom he deals, to buy as cheap and to sell as dear as possible. But it will be most likely to buy cheap, when by the most perfect freedom of trade it encourages all nations to bring to it the goods which it has occasion to purchase; and, for the same reason, it will be most likely to sell dear, when its markets are thus filled with the greatest number of buyers. The act of navigation, it is true, lays no burden upon foreign ships that come to export the produce of British industry. Even the ancient aliens duty, which used to be paid on all goods exported as well as imported, has, by several subsequent acts, been taken off from the greater part of the articles of exportation. But if foreigners, either by prohibitions or high duties, are hindered from coming to sell, they cannot always afford to come to buy; because coming without a cargo, they must lose the freight from their own country to Great Britain. By diminishing the number of sellers, therefore, we necessarily diminish that of buyers, and are thus likely not only to buy foreign goods dearer, but to sell our own cheaper, than if there was a more perfect freedom of trade. As defence, however, is of much more importance than opulence, the act of navigation is, perhaps, the wisest of all the commercial regulations of England.

The second case, in which it will generally be advantageous to lay some burden upon foreign for the encouragement of domestic industry, is, when some tax is imposed at home upon the produce of the latter. In this case, it seems reasonable that an equal tax should be imposed upon the like produce of the former. This would not give the monopoly of the home market to domestic industry, nor turn towards a particular employment a greater share of the stock and labour of the country, than what would naturally go to it. It would only hinder any part of what would naturally go to it from being turned away by the tax, into a less natural direction, and would leave the competition between foreign and domestic industry, after the tax, as nearly as possible upon the same footing as before it. In Great Britain, when any such tax is laid upon the produce of domestic industry, it is usual at the same time, in order to stop the clamorous complaints of our merchants and manufacturers, that they will be undersold at home, to lay a much heavier duty upon the importation of all foreign goods of the same kind.

This second limitation of the freedom of trade according to some people should, upon some occasions, be extended much farther than to the precise foreign commodities which could come into competition with those which had been taxed at home. When the necessaries of life have been taxed in any country, it becomes proper, they pretend, to tax not only the like necessaries of life imported from other countries, but all sorts of foreign goods which can come into competition with any thing that is the produce of domestic industry. Subsistence, they say, becomes necessarily dearer in consequence of such taxes; and the price of labour must always rise with the price of the labourers subsistence. Every commodity, therefore, which is the produce of domestic industry, though not immediately taxed itself, becomes dearer in consequence of such taxes, because the labour which produces it becomes so. Such taxes, therefore, are really equivalent, they say, to a tax upon every particular commodity produced at home. In order to put domestic upon the same footing with foreign industry, therefore, it becomes necessary, they think, to lay some duty upon every foreign commodity, equal to this enhancement of the price of the home commodities with which it can come into competition.

Whether taxes upon the necessaries of life, such as those in Great Britain upon soap, salt, leather, candles, &c. necessarily raise the price of labour, and consequently that of all other commodities, I shall consider hereafter, when I come to treat of taxes. Supposing, however, in the mean time, that they have this effect, and they have it undoubtedly, this general enhancement of the price of all commodities, in consequence of that of labour, is a case which differs in the two following respects from that of a particular commodity, of which the price was enhanced by a particular tax immediately imposed upon it.

First, it might always be known with great exactness how far the price of such a commodity could be enhanced by such a tax: but how far the general enhancement of the price of labour might affect that of every different commodity about which labour was employed, could never be known with any tolerable exactness. It would be impossible, therefore, to proportion with any tolerable exactness the tax upon every foreign, to this enhancement of the price of every home commodity.

Secondly, taxes upon the necessaries of life have nearly the same effect upon the circumstances of the people as a poor soil and a bad climate. Provisions are thereby rendered dearer in the same manner as if it required extraordinary labour and expence to raise them. As in the natural scarcity arising from soil and climate, it would be absurd to direct the people in what manner they ought to employ their capitals and industry, so is it likewise in the artificial scarcity arising from such taxes. To be left to accommodate, as well as they could, their industry to their situation, and to find out those employments in which, notwithstanding their unfavourable circumstances, they might have some advantage either in the home or in the foreign market, is what in both cases would evidently be most for their advantage. To lay a new tax upon them, because they are already overburdened with taxes, and because they already pay too dear for the necessaries of life, to make them likewise pay too dear for the greater part of other commodities, is certainly a most absurd way of making amends.

Such taxes, when they have grown up to a certain height, are a curse equal to the barrenness of the earth and the inclemency of the heavens; and yet it is in the richest and most industrious countries that they have been most generally imposed. No other countries could support so great a disorder. As the strongest bodies only can live and enjoy health, under an unwholesome regimen; so the nations only, that in every sort of industry have the greatest natural and acquired advantages, can subsist and prosper under such taxes. Holland is the country in Europe in which they abound most, and which from peculiar circumstances continues to prosper, not by means of them, as has been most absurdly supposed, but in spite of them.

As there are two cases in which it will generally be advantageous to lay some burden upon foreign, for the encouragement of domestic industry; so there are two others in which it may sometimes be a matter of deliberation; in the one, how far it is proper to continue the free importation of certain foreign goods; and in the other, how far, or in what manner, it may be proper to restore that free importation after it has been for some time interrupted.

The case in which it may sometimes be a matter of deliberation how far it is proper to continue the free importation of certain foreign goods, is, when some foreign nation restrains by high duties or prohibitions the importation of some of our manufactures into their country. Revenge in this case naturally dictates retaliation, and that we should impose the like duties and prohibitions upon the importation of some or all of their manufactures into ours. Nations accordingly seldom fail to retaliate in this manner. The French have been particularly forward to favour their own manufactures by restraining the importation of such foreign goods as could come into competition with them. In this consisted a great part of the policy of Mr. Colbert, who, notwithstanding his great abilities, seems in this case to have been imposed upon by the sophistry of merchants and manufacturers, who are always demanding a monopoly against their countrymen. It is at present the opinion of the most intelligent men in France that his operations of this kind have not been beneficial to his country. That minister, by the tarif of 1667, imposed very high duties upon a great number of foreign manufactures. Upon his refusing to moderate them in favour of the Dutch, they in 1671 prohibited the importation of the wines, brandies and manufactures of France. The war of 1672 seems to have been in part occasioned by this commercial dispute. The peace of Nimeguen put an end to it in 1678, by moderating some of those duties in favour of the Dutch, who in consequence took off their prohibition. It was about the same time that the French and English began mutually to oppress each other's industry, by the like duties and prohibitions, of which the French, however, seem to have set the first example. The spirit of hostility which has subsisted between the two nations ever since, has hitherto hindered them from being moderated on either side. In 1697 the English prohibited the importation of bonelace, the manufacture of Flanders. The government of that country, at that time under the dominion of Spain, prohibited in return the importation of English woollens. In 1700, the prohibition of importing bonelace into England, was taken off upon condition that the importation of English woollens into Flanders should be put on the same footing as before.

There may be good policy in retaliations of this kind, when there is a probability that they will procure the repeal of the high duties or prohibitions complained of. The recovery of a great foreign market will generally more than compensate the transitory inconveniency of paying dearer during a short time for some sorts of goods. To judge whether such retaliations are likely to produce such an effect, does not, perhaps, belong so much to the science of a legislator, whose deliberations ought to be governed by general principles which are always the same, as to the skill of that insidious and crafty animal, vulgarly called a statesman or politician, whose councils are directed by the momentary fluctuations of affairs. When there is no probability that any such repeal can be procured, it seems a bad method of compensating the injury done to certain classes of our people, to do another injury ourselves, not only to those classes, but to almost all the other classes of them. When our neighbours prohibit some manufacture of ours, we generally prohibit, not only the same, for that alone would seldom affect them considerably, but some other manufacture of theirs. This may no doubt give encouragement to some particular class of workmen among ourselves, and by excluding some of their rivals, may enable them to raise their price in the home-market. Those workmen, however, who suffered by our neighbours prohibition will not be benefited by ours. On the contrary, they and almost all the other classes of our citizens will thereby be obliged to pay dearer than before for certain goods. Every such law, therefore, imposes a real tax upon the whole country, not in favour of that particular class of workmen who were injured by our neighbours prohibition, but of some other class.

The case in which it may sometimes be a matter of deliberation, how far, or in what manner, it is proper to restore the free importation of foreign goods, after it has been for some time interrupted, is, when particular manufactures, by means of high duties or prohibitions upon all foreign goods which can come into competition with them, have been so far extended as to employ a great multitude of hands. Humanity may in this case require that the freedom of trade should be restored only by slow gradations, and with a good deal of reserve and circumspection. Were those high duties and prohibitions taken away all at once, cheaper foreign goods of the same kind might be poured so fast into the home market, as to deprive all at once many thousands of our people of their ordinary employment and means of subsistence. The disorder which this would occasion might no doubt be very considerable. It would in all probability, however, be much less than is commonly imagined, for the two following reasons:

First, all those manufactures, of which any part is commonly exports to other European countries without a bounty, could be very little affected by the freest importation of foreign goods. Such manufactures must be sold as cheap abroad as any other foreign goods of the same quality and kind, and consequently must be sold cheaper at home. They would still, therefore, keep possession of the home market, and though a capricious man of fashion might sometimes prefer foreign wares, merely because they were foreign, to cheaper and better goods of the same kind that were made at home, this folly could, from the nature of things, extend to so few, that it could make no sensible impression upon the general employment of the people. But a great part of all the different branches of our woollen manufacture, of our tanned leather, and of our hard-ware, are annually exported to other European countries without any bounty, and these are the manufactures which employ the greatest number of hands. The silk, perhaps, is the manufacture which would suffer the most by this freedom of trade, and after it the linen, though the latter much less than the former.

Secondly, though a great number of people should, by thus restoring the freedom of trade, be thrown all at once out of their ordinary employment and common method of subsistence, it would by no means follow that they would thereby be deprived either of employment or subsistence. By the reduction of the army and navy at the end of the late war, more than a hundred thousand soldiers and seamen, a number equal to what is employed in the greatest manufactures, were all at once thrown out of their ordinary employment; but, though they no doubt suffered some inconveniency, they were not thereby deprived of all employment and subsistence. The greater part of the seamen, it is probable, gradually betook themselves to the merchant-service as they could find occasion, and in the meantime both they and the soldiers were absorbed in the great mass of the people, and employed in a great variety of occupations. Not only no great convulsion, but no sensible disorder arose from so great a change in the situation of more than a hundred thousand men, all accustomed to the use of arms, and many of them to rapine and plunder. The number of vagrants was scarce anywhere sensibly increased by it, even the wages of labour were not reduced by it in any occupation, so far as I have been able to learn, except in that of seamen in the merchant-service. But if we compare together the habits of a soldier and of any sort of manufacturer, we shall find that those of the latter do not tend so much to disqualify him from being employed in a new trade, as those of the former from being employed in any. The manufacturer has always been accustomed to look for his subsistence from his labour only: the soldier to expect it from his pay. Application and industry have been familiar to the one; idleness and dissipation to the other. But it is surely much easier to change the direction of industry from one sort of labour to another, than to turn idleness and dissipation to any. To the greater part of manufactures besides, it has already been observed, there are other collateral manufactures of so similar a nature, that a workman can easily transfer his industry from one of them to another. The greater part of such workmen, too, are occasionally employed in country labour. The stock which employed them in a particular manufacture before, will still remain in the country to employ an equal number of people in some other way. The capital of the country remaining the same, the demand for labour will likewise be the same, or very nearly the same, though it may be exerted in different places and for different occupations. Soldiers and seamen, indeed, when discharged from the king's service, are at liberty to exercise any trade, within any town or place of Great Britain or Ireland. Let the same natural liberty of exercising what species of industry they please, be restored to all his majesty's subjects, in the same manner as to soldiers and seamen; that is, break down the exclusive privileges of corporations, and repeal the statute of apprenticeship, both which are real encroachments upon natural liberty, and add to these the repeal of the law of settlements, so that a poor workman, when thrown out of employment either in one trade or in one place, may seek for it in another trade or in another place, without the fear either of a prosecution or of a removal, and neither the public nor the individuals will suffer much more from the occasional disbanding some particular classes of manufacturers, than from that of soldiers. Our manufacturers have no doubt great merit with their country, but they cannot have more than those who defend it with their blood, nor deserve to be treated with more delicacy.

To expect, indeed, that the freedom of trade should ever be entirely restored in Great Britain, is as absurd as to expect that an Oceana or Utopia should ever be established in it. Not only the prejudices of the public, but what is much more unconquerable, the private interests of many individuals, irresistibly oppose it. Were the officers of the army to oppose with the same zeal and unanimity any reduction in the number of forces, with which master manufacturers set themselves against every law that is likely to increase the number of their rivals in the home market; were the former to animate their soldiers, in the same manner as the latter enflame their workmen, to attack with violence and outrage the proposers of any such regulation; to attempt to reduce the army would be as dangerous as it has now become to attempt to diminish in any respect the monopoly which our manufacturers have obtained against us. This monopoly has so much increased the number of some particular tribes of them, that, like an overgrown standing army, they have become formidable to the government, and upon many occasions intimidate the legislature. The member of parliament who supports every proposal for strengthening this monopoly, is sure to acquire not only the reputation of understanding trade, but great popularity and influence with an order of men whose numbers and wealth render them of great importance. If he opposes them, on the contrary, and still more if he has authority enough to be able to thwart them, neither the most acknowledged probity, nor the highest rank, nor the greatest public services, can protect him from the most infamous abuse and detraction, from personal insults, nor sometimes from real danger, arising from the insolent outrage of furious and disappointed monopolists.

The undertaker of a great manufacture, who, by the home markets being suddenly laid open to the competition of foreigners, should be obliged to abandon his trade, would no doubt suffer very considerably. That part of his capital which had usually been employed in purchasing materials and in paying his workmen, might, without much difficulty, perhaps, find another employment. But that part of it which was fixed in workhouses, and in the instruments of trade, could scarce be disposed of without considerable loss. The equitable regard, therefore, to his interest requires that changes of this kind should never be introduced suddenly, but slowly, gradually, and after a very long warning. The legislature, were it possible that its deliberations could be always directed, not by the clamorous importunity of partial interests, but by an extensive view of the general good, ought upon this very account, perhaps, to be particularly careful neither to establish any new monopolies of this kind, nor to extend further those which are already established. Every such regulation introduces some degree of real disorder into the constitution of the state, which it will be difficult afterwards to cure without occasioning another disorder.

How far it may be proper to impose taxes upon the importation of foreign goods, in order, not to prevent their importation, but to raise a revenue for government, I shall consider hereafter when I come to treat of taxes. Taxes imposed with a view to prevent, or even to diminish importation, are evidently as destructive of the revenue of the customs as of the freedom of trade.

CHAPTER III

Of the Extraordinary Restraints upon the Importation of Goods of Almost All Kinds, from Those Countries with Which the Balance Is Supposed to Be Disadvantageous.

PART I

Of the Unreasonableness of those Restraints even upon the Principles of the Commercial System

TO lay extraordinary restraints upon the importation of goods of almost all kinds, from those particular countries with which the balance of trade is supposed to be disadvantageous, is the second expedient by which the commercial system proposes to increase the quantity of gold and silver. Thus in Great Britain, Silesia lawns may be imported for home consumption, upon paying certain duties. But French cambrics and lawns are prohibited to be imported, except into the port of London, there to be warehoused for exportation. Higher duties are imposed upon the wines of France than upon those of Portugal, or indeed of any other country. By what is called the impost 1692, a duty of five and twenty per cent., of the rate or value, was laid upon all French goods; while the goods of other nations were, the greater part of them, subjected to much lighter duties, seldom exceeding five per cent. The wine, brandy, salt and vinegar of France were indeed excepted; these commodities being subjected to other heavy duties, either by other laws, or by particular clauses of the same law. In 1696, a second duty of twenty-five per cent., the first not having been thought a sufficient discouragement, was imposed upon all French goods, except brandy; together with a new duty of five and twenty pounds upon the ton of

French wine, and another of fifteen pounds upon the ton of French vinegar. French goods have never been omitted in any of those general subsidies, or duties of five per cent., which have been imposed upon all, or the greater part of the goods enumerated in the book of rates. If we count the one-third and two-third subsidies as making a complete subsidy between them, there have been five of these general subsidies; so that before the commencement of the present war seventy-five per cent. may be considered as the lowest duty, to which the greater part of the goods of the growth, produce, or manufacture of France were liable. But upon the greater part of goods, those duties are equivalent to a prohibition. The French in their turn have, I believe, treated our goods and manufactures just as hardly; though I am not so well acquainted with the particular hardships which they have imposed upon them. Those mutual restraints have put an end to almost all fair commerce between the two nations, and smugglers are now the principal importers, either of British goods into France, or of French goods into Great Britain. The principles which I have been examining in the foregoing chapter took their origin from private interest and the spirit of monopoly; those which I am going to examine in this, from national prejudice and animosity. They are, accordingly, as might well be expected, still more unreasonable. They are so, even upon the principles of the commercial system.

First, though it were certain that in the case of a free trade between France and England, for example, the balance would be in favour of France, it would by no means follow that such a trade would be disadvantageous to England, or that the general balance of its whole trade would thereby be turned more against it. If the wines of France are better and cheaper than those of Portugal, or its linens than those of Germany, it would be more advantageous for Great Britain to purchase both the wine and the foreign linen which it had occasion for of France, than of Portugal and Germany. Though the value of the annual importations from France would thereby be greatly augmented, the value of the whole annual importations would be diminished, in proportion as the French goods of the same quality were cheaper than those of the other two countries. This would be the case, even upon the supposition that the whole French goods imported were to be consumed in Great Britain.

But, secondly, a great part of them might be re-exported to other countries, where, being sold with profit, they might bring back a return equal in value, perhaps, to the prime cost of the whole French goods imported. What has frequently been said of the East India trade might possibly be true of the French; that though the greater part of East India goods were bought with gold and silver, the re-exportation of a part of them to other countries, brought back more gold and silver to that which carried on the trade than the prime cost of the whole amounted to. One of the most important branches of the Dutch trade, at present, consists in the carriage of French goods to other European countries. Some part even of the French wine drank in Great Britain is clandestinely imported from Holland and Zealand. If there was either a free trade between France and England, or if French goods could be imported upon paying only the same duties as those of other European nations, to be drawn back upon exportation. England might have some share of a trade which is founa so advantageous to Holland.

Thirdly, and lastly, there is no certain criterion by which we can determine on which side what is called the balance between any two countries lies, or which of them exports to the greatest value. National prejudice and animosity, prompted always by the private interest of particular traders, are the principles which generally direct our judgment upon all questions concerning it. There are two criterions, however, which have frequently been appealed to upon such occasions, the custom-house books and the course of exchange. The custom-house books, I think, it is now generally acknowledged, are a very uncertain criterion, on account of the inaccuracy of the valuation at which the greater part of goods are rated in them. The course of exchange is, perhaps, almost equally so.

When the exchange between two places, such as London and Paris, is at par, it is said to be a sign that the debts due from London to Paris are compensated by those due from Paris to London. On the contrary, when a premium is paid at London for a bill upon Paris, it is said to be a sign that the debts due from London to Paris are not compensated by those due from Paris to London, but that a balance in money must be sent out from the latter place; for the risk, trouble, and expence of exporting which, the premium is both demanded and given. But the ordinary state of debt and credit between those two cities must necessarily be regulated, it is said, by the ordinary course of their dealings with one another. When neither of them imports from the other to a greater amount than it exports to that other, the debts and credits of each may compensate one another. But when one of them imports from the other to a greater value than it exports to that other, the former necessarily becomes indebted to the latter in a greater sum than the latter becomes indebted to it: the debts and credits of each do not compensate one another, and money must be sent out from that place of which the debts over-balance the credits. The ordinary course of exchange, therefore, being an indication of the ordinary state of debt and credit between two places, must likewise be an indication of the ordinary course of their exports and imports, as these necessarily regulate that state.

But though the ordinary course of exchange should be allowed to be a sufficient indication of the ordinary state of debt and credit between any two places, it would not from thence follow, that the balance of trade was in favour of that place which had the ordinary state of debt and credit in its favour. The ordinary state of debt and credit between any two places is not always entirely regulated by the ordinary course of their dealings with one another; but is often influenced by that of the dealings of either with many other places. If it is usual, for example, for the merchants of England to pay for the goods which they buy of Hamburgh, Dantzic, Riga, &c. by bills upon Holland, the ordinary state of debt and credit between England and Holland will not be regulated entirely by the ordinary course of the dealings of those two countries with one another, but will be influenced by that of the dealings of England with those other places. England may be obliged to send out every year money to Holland, though its annual exports to that country may exceed very much the annual value of its imports from thence; and though what is called the balance of trade may be very much in favour of England.

In the way, besides, in which the par of exchange has hitherto been computed, the ordinary course of exchange can afford no sufficient indication that the ordinary state of debt and credit is in favour of that country which seems to have, or which is supposed to have, the ordinary course of exchange in its favour: or, in other words, the real exchange may be, and, in fact, often is so very different from the computed one, that from the course of the latter, no certain conclusion can, upon many occasions, be drawn concerning that of the former.

When for a sum of money paid in England, containing, according to the standard of the English mint, a certain number of ounces of pure silver, you receive a bill for a sum of money to be paid in France, containing, according to the standard of the French mint, an equal number of ounces of pure silver, exchange is said to be at par between England and France. When you pay more, you are supposed to give a premium, and exchange is said to be against England, and in favour of France. When you pay less, you are supposed to get a premium, and exchange is said to be against France, and in favour of England.

But, first, we cannot always judge of the value of the current money of different countries by the standard of their respective mints. In some it is more, in others it is less worn, clipt, and otherwise degenerated from that standard. But the value of the current coin of every country, compared with that of any other country, is in proportion not to the quantity of pure silver which it ought to contain, but to that which it actually does contain. Before the reformation of the silver coin in King William's time, exchange between England and Holland, computed, in the usual manner, according to the standard of their respective mints, was five and twenty per cent. against England. But the value of the current coin of England, as we learn from Mr. Lowndes, was at that time rather more than five and twenty per cent. below its standard value. The real exchange, therefore, may even at that time have been in favour of England, notwithstanding the computed exchange was so much against it; a smaller number of ounces of pure silver, actually paid in England, may have purchased a bill for a greater number of ounces of pure silver to be paid in Holland, and the man who was supposed to give, may in reality have got the premium. The French coin was, before the late reformation of the English gold coin, much less worn than the English, and was, perhaps, two or three per cent. nearer its standard. If the computed exchange with France, therefore, was not more than two or three per cent. against England, the real exchange might have been in its favour. Since the reformation of the gold coin, the exchange has been constantly in favour of England, and against France.

Secondly, in some countries, the expence of coinage is defrayed by the government; in others, it is defrayed by the private people who carry their bullion to the mint, and the government even derives some revenue from the coinage. In England, it is defrayed by the government, and if you carry a pound weight of standard silver to the mint, you get back sixty-two shillings, containing a pound weight of the like standard silver. In France, a duty of eight per cent. is deducted for the coinage, which not only defrays the expence of it, but affords a small revenue to the government. In England, as the coinage costs nothing, the current coin can never be much more valuable than the quantity of bullion which it actually contains. In France, the workmanship, as you pay for it, adds to the value, in the same manner as to that of wrought plate. A sum of French money, therefore, containing a certain weight of pure silver, is more valuable than a sum of English money containing an equal weight of pure silver, and must require more bullion, or other commodities, to purchase it. Though the current coin of the two countries, therefore, were equally near the standards of their respective mints, a sum of English money could not well purchase a sum of French money, containing an equal number of ounces of pure silver, nor consequently a bill upon France for such a sum. If for such a bill no more additional money was paid than what was sufficient to compensate the expence of the French coinage, the real exchange might be at par between the two countries, their debts and credits might mutually compensate one another, while the computed exchange was considerably in favour of France. If less than this was paid, the real exchange might be in favour of England, while the computed was in favour of France.

Thirdly, and lastly, in some places, as at Amsterdam, Hamburg, Venice, &c. foreign bills of exchange are paid in what they call bank money; while in others, as at London, Lisbon, Antwerp, Leghorn, &c., they are paid in the common currency of the country. What is called bank money is always of more value than the same nominal sum of common currency. A thousand guilders in the bank of Amsterdam, for example, are of more value than a thousand guilders of Amsterdam currency. The difference between them is called the agio of the bank, which, at Amsterdam, is generally about five per cent. Supposing the current money of two countries equally near to the standard of their respective mints, and that the one pays foreign bills in this common currency, while the other pays them in bank money, it is evident that the computed exchange may be in favour of that which pays in bank money, though the real exchange should be in favour of that which pays in current money; for the same reason that the computed exchange may be in favour of that which pays in better money, or in money nearer to its own standard, though the real exchange should be in favour of that which pays in worse. The computed exchange, before the late reformation of the gold coin, was generally against London, with Amsterdam, Hamburgh, Venice, and, I believe, with all other places which pay in what is called bank money. It will by no means follow, however, that the real exchange was against it. Since the reformation of the gold coin, it has been in favour of London even with those places. The computed exchange has generally been in favour of London with Lisbon, Antwerp, Leghorn, and, if you except France, I believe, with most other parts of Europe that pay in common currency; and it is not improbable that the real exchange was so too.

PART II

Of the Unreasonableness of those Extraordinary Restraints Upon Other Principles

In the foregoing Part of this Chapter I have endeavoured to shew, even upon the principles of the commercial system, how unnecessary it is to lay extraordinary restraints upon the importation of goods from those countries with which the balance of trade is supposed to be disadvantageous.

Nothing, however, can be more absurd than this whole doctrine of the balance of trade, upon which, not only these restraints, but almost all the other regulations of commerce are founded. When two places trade with one another, this doctrine supposes that, if the balance be even, neither of them either loses or gains; but if it leans in any degree to one side, that one of them loses, and the other gains in proportion to its declension from the exact equilibrium. Both suppositions are false. A trade which is forced by means of bounties and monopolies, may be, and commonly is disadvantageous to the country in whose favour it is meant to be established, as I shall endeavour to show hereafter. But that trade which, without force or constraint, is naturally and regularly carried on between any two places, is always advantageous, though not always equally so, to both.

By advantage or gain, I understand, not the increase of the quantity of gold and silver, but that of the exchangeable value of the annual produce of the land and labour of the country, or the increase of the annual revenue of its inhabitants.

If the balance be even, and if the trade between the two places consist altogether in the exchange of their native commodities, they will, upon most occasions, not only both gain, but they will gain equally, or very near equally: each will in this case afford a market for a part of the surplus produce of the other: each will replace a capital which had been employed in raising and preparing for the market this part of the surplus produce of the other, and which had been distributed among, and given revenue and maintenance to a certain number of its inhabitants. Some part of the inhabitants of each, therefore, will indirectly derive their revenue and maintenance from the other. As the commodities exchanged too are supposed to be of equal value, so the two capitals employed in the trade will, upon most occasions, be equal, or very nearly equal; and both being employed in raising the native commodities of the two countries, the revenue and maintenance which their distribution will afford to the inhabitants of each will be equal, or very nearly equal. This revenue and maintenance, thus mutually afforded, will be greater or smaller in proportion to the extent of their dealings. If these should annually amount to an hundred thousand pounds, for example, or to a million on each side, each of them would afford an annual revenue in the one case of an hundred thousand pounds, in the other, of a million, to the inhabitants of the other.

If their trade should be of such a nature that one of them exported to the other nothing but native commodities, while the returns of that other consisted altogether in foreign goods; the balance, in this case, would still be supposed even, commodities being paid for with commodities. They would, in this case too, both gain, but they would not gain equally; and the inhabitants of the country which exported nothing but native commodities would derive the greatest revenue from the trade. If England, for example, should import from France nothing but the native commodities of that country, and, not having such commodities of its own as were in demand there, should annually repay them by sending thither a large quantity of foreign goods, tobacco, we shall suppose, and East India goods; this trade, though it would give some revenue to the inhabitants of both countries, would give more to those of France than to those of England. The whole French capital annually employed in it would annually be distributed among the people of France. But that part of the English capital only which was employed in producing the English commodities with which those foreign goods were purchased, would be annually distributed among the people of England. The greater part of it would replace the capitals which had been employed in Virginia, Indostan, and China, and which had given revenue and maintenance to the inhabitants of those distant countries. If the capitals were equal, or nearly equal, therefore, this employment of the French capital would augment much more the revenue of the people of France, than that of the English capital would the revenue of the people of England. France would in this case carry on a direct foreign trade of consumption with England; whereas England would carry on a round-about trade of the same kind with France. The different effects of a capital employed in the direct, and of one employed in the round-about foreign trade of consumption, have already been fully explained.

There is not, probably, between any two countries, a trade which consists altogether in the exchange either of native commodities on both sides, or of native commodities on one side and of foreign goods on the other. Almost all countries exchange with one another partly native and partly foreign goods. That country, however, in whose cargoes there is the greatest proportion of native, and the least of foreign goods, will always be the principal gainer.

If it was not with tobacco and East India goods, but with gold and silver, that England paid for the commodities annually imported from France, the balance, in this case, would be supposed uneven, commodities not being paid for with commodities, but with gold and silver. The trade, however, would, in this case, as in the foregoing, give some revenue to the inhabitants of both countries, but more to those of France than to those of England. It would give some revenue to those of England. The capital which had been employed in producing the English goods that purchased this gold and silver, the capital which had been distributed among, and given revenue to, certain inhabitants of England, would thereby be replaced, and enabled to continue that employment. The whole capital of England would no more be diminished by this exportation of gold and silver, than by the exportation of an equal value of any other goods. On the contrary, it would, in most cases, be augmented. No goods are sent abroad but those for which the demand is supposed to be greater abroad than at home, and of which the returns consequently, it is expected, will be of more value at home than the commodities exported. If the tobacco which, in England, is worth only a hundred thousand pounds, when sent to France will purchase wine which is, in England, worth a hundred and ten thousand pounds, the exchange will augment the capital of England by ten thousand pounds. If a hundred thousand pounds of English gold, in the same manner, purchase French wine, which, in England, is worth a hundred and ten thousand, this exchange will equally augment the capital of England by ten thousand pounds. As a merchant who has a hundred and ten thousand pounds worth of wine in his cellar, is a richer man than he who has only a hundred thousand pounds worth of tobacco in his warehouse, so is he likewise a richer man than he who has only a hundred thousand pounds worth of gold in his coffers. He can put into motion a greater quantity of industry, and give revenue, maintenance, and employment, to a greater number of people than either of the other two. But the capital of the country is equal to the capitals of all its different inhabitants, and the quantity of industry which can be annually maintained in it, is equal to what all those different capitals can maintain. Both the capital of the country, therefore, and the quantity of industry which can be annually maintained in it, must generally be augmented by this exchange. It would, indeed, be more advantageous for England that it could purchase the wines of France with its own hard-ware and broad-cloth, than with either the tobacco of Virginia, or the gold and silver of Brazil and Peru. A direct foreign trade of consumption is always more advantageous than a round-about one. But a round-about foreign trade of consumption, which is carried on with gold and silver, does not seem to be less advantageous than any other equally round-about one. Neither is a country which has no mines, more likely to be exhausted of gold and silver by this annual exportation of those metals, than one which does not grow tobacco by the like annual exportation of that plant. As a country which has wherewithal to buy tobacco will never be long in want of it, so neither will one be long in want of gold and silver which has wherewithal to purchase those metals.

It is a losing trade, it is said, which a workman carries on with the alehouse; and the trade which a manufacturing nation would naturally carry on with a wine country, may be considered as a trade of the same nature. I answer, that the trade with the alehouse is not necessarily a losing trade. In its own nature it is just as advantageous as any other, though, perhaps, somewhat more liable to be abused. The employment of a brewer, and even that of a retailer of fermented liquors, are as necessary divisions of labour as any other. It will generally be more advantageous for a workman to buy of the brewer the quantity he has occasion for, than to brew it himself, and if he is a poor workman, it will generally be more advantageous for him to buy it, by little and little, of the retailer, than a large quantity of the brewer. He may no doubt buy too much of either, as he may of any other dealers in his neighbourhood, of the butcher, if he is a glutton, or of the draper, if he affects to be a beau among his companions. It is advantageous to the great body of workmen, notwithstanding, that all these trades should be free, though this freedom may be abused in all of them, and is more likely to be so, perhaps, in some than in others. Though individuals, besides, may sometimes ruin their fortunes by an excessive consumption of fermented liquors, there seems to be no risk that a nation should do so. Though in every country there are many people who spend upon such liquors more than they can afford, there are always many more who spend less. It deserves to be remarked too, that, if we consult experience, the cheapness of wine seems to be a cause, not of drunkenness, but of sobriety. The inhabitants of the wine countries are in general the soberest people in Europe; witness the Spaniards, the Italians, and the inhabitants of the southern provinces of France. People are seldom guilty of excess in what is their daily fare. Nobody affects the character of liberality and good fellowship, by being profuse of a liquor which is as cheap as small beer. On the contrary, in the countries which, either from excessive heat or cold, produce no grapes, and where wine consequently is dear and a rarity, drunkenness is a common vice, as among the northern nations, and all those who live between the tropics, the negroes, for example, on the coast of Guinea. When a French regiment comes from some of the northern provinces of France, where wine is somewhat dear, to be quartered in the southern, where it is very cheap, the soldiers, I have frequently heard it observed, are at first debauched by the cheapness and novelty of good wine; but after a few months residence, the greater part of them become as sober as the rest of the inhabitants. Were the duties upon foreign wines, and the excises upon malt, beer, and ale, to be taken away all at once, it might, in the same manner, occasion in Great Britain a pretty general and temporary drunkenness among the middling and inferior ranks of people, which would probably be soon followed by a permanent and almost universal sobriety. At present drunkenness is by no means the vice of people of fashion, or of those who can easily afford the most expensive liquors. A gentleman drunk with ale, has scarce ever been seen among us. The restraints upon the wine trade in Great Britain, besides, do not so much seem calculated to hinder the people from going, if I may say so, to the alehouse, as from going where they can buy the best and cheapest liquor. They favour the wine trade of Portugal, and discourage that of France. The Portuguese, it is said, indeed, are better customers for our manufactures than the French, and should therefore be encouraged in preference to them. As they give us their custom, it is pretended, we should give them ours. The sneaking arts of underling tradesmen are thus erected into political maxims for the conduct of a great empire; for it is the most underling tradesmen only who make it a rule to employ chiefly their own customers. A great trader purchases his goods always where they are cheapest and best, without regard to any little interest of this kind.

By such maxims as these, however, nations have been taught that their interest consisted in beggaring all their neighbours. Each nation has been made to look with an invidious eye upon the prosperity of all the nations with which it trades, and to consider their gain as its own loss. Commerce, which ought naturally to be, among nations, as among individuals, a bond of union and friendship, has become the most fertile source of discord and animosity. The capricious ambition of kings and ministers has not, during the present and the preceding century, been more fatal to the repose of Europe, than the impertinent jealousy of merchants and manufacturers. The violence and injustice of the rulers of mankind is an ancient evil, for which, I am afraid, the nature of human affairs can scarce admit of a remedy. But the mean rapacity, the monopolizing spirit of merchants and manufacturers, who neither are, nor ought to be, the rulers of mankind, though it cannot perhaps be corrected, may very easily be prevented from disturbing the tranquillity of any body but themselves.

That it was the spirit of monopoly which originally both invented and propagated this doctrine, cannot be doubted; and they who first taught it were by no means such fools as they who believed it. In every country it always is and must be the interest of the great body of the people to buy whatever they want of those who sell it cheapest. The proposition is so very manifest, that it seems ridiculous to take any pains to prove it; nor could it ever have been called in question, had not the interested sophistry of merchants and manufacturers confounded the common sense of mankind. Their interest is, in this respect, directly opposite to that of the great body of the people. As it is the interest of the freemen of a corporation to hinder the rest of the inhabitants from employing any workmen but themselves, so it is the interest of the merchants and manufacturers of every country to secure to themselves the monopoly of the home market. Hence in Great Britain, and in most other European countries, the extraordinary duties upon almost all goods imported by alien merchants. Hence the high duties and prohibitions upon all those foreign manufactures which can come into competition with our own. Hence too the extraordinary restraints upon the importation of almost all sorts of goods from those countries with which the balance of trade is supposed to be disadvantageous; that is, from those against whom national animosity happens to be most violently inflamed.

The wealth of a neighbouring nation, however, though dangerous in war and politics, is certainly advantageous in trade. In a state of hostility it may enable our enemies to maintain fleets and armies superior to our own; but in a state of peace and commerce it must likewise enable them to exchange with us to a greater value, and to afford a better market, either for the immediate produce of our own industry, or for whatever is purchased with that produce. As a rich man is likely to be a better customer to the industrious people in his neighbourhood, than a poor, so is likewise a rich nation. A rich man, indeed, who is himself a manufacturer, is a very dangerous neighbour to all those who deal in the same way. All the rest of the neighbourhood, however, by far the greatest number, profit by the good market which his expence affords them. They even profit by his underselling the poorer workmen who deal in the same way with him. The manufacturers of a rich nation, in the same manner, may no doubt be very dangerous rivals to those of their neighbours. This very competition, however, is advantageous to the great body of the people, who profit greatly besides by the good market which the great expence of such a nation affords them in every other way. Private people who want to make a fortune, never think of retiring to the remote and poor provinces of the country, but resort either to the capital, or to some of the great commercial towns. They know, that, where little wealth circulates, there is little to be got, but that where a great deal is in motion, some shares of it may fall to them. The same maxims which would in this manner direct the common sense of one, or ten, or twenty individuals, should regulate the judgment of one, or ten, or twenty millions, and should make a whole nation regard the riches of its neighbours, as a probable cause and occasion for itself to acquire riches. A nation that would enrich itself by foreign trade, is certainly most likely to do so when its neighbours are all rich, industrious, and commercial nations. A great nation surrounded on all sides by wandering savages and poor barbarians might, no doubt, acquire riches by the cultivation of its own lands, and by its own interior commerce, but not by foreign trade. It seems to have been in this manner that the ancient Egyptians and the modern Chinese acquired their great wealth. The ancient Egyptians, it is said, neglected foreign commerce, and the modern Chinese, it is known, hold it in the utmost contempt, and scarce deign to afford it the decent protection of the laws. The modern maxims of foreign commerce, by aiming at the impoverishment of all our neighbours, so far as they are capable of producing their intended effect, tend to render that very commerce insignificant and contemptible.

It is in consequence of these maxims that the commerce between France and England has in both countries been subjected to so many discouragements and restraints. If those two countries, however, were to consider their real interest, without either mercantile jealousy or national animosity, the commerce of France might be more advantageous to Great Britain than that of any other country, and for the same reason that of Great Britain to France. France is the nearest neighbour to Great Britain. In the trade between the southern coast of England and the northern and north-western coasts of France, the returns might be expected, in the same manner as in the inland trade, four, five, or six times in the year. The capital, therefore, employed in this trade, could in each of the two countries keep in motion four, five, or six times the quantity of industry, and afford employment and subsistence to four, five, or six times the number of people, which an equal capital could do in the greater part of the other branches of foreign trade. Between the parts of France and Great Britain most remote from one another, the returns might be expected, at least, once in the year, and even this trade would so far be at least equally advantageous as the greater part of the other branches of our foreign European trade. It would be, at least, three times more advantageous, than the boasted trade with our North American colonies, in which the returns were seldom made in less than three years, frequently not in less than four or five years. France, besides, is supposed to contain twenty-four millions of inhabitants. Our North American colonies were never supposed to contain more than three millions: And France is a much richer country than North America; though, on account of the more unequal distribution of riches, there is much more poverty and beggary in the one country, than in the other. France therefore could afford a market at least eight times more extensive, and, on account of the superior frequency of the returns, four and twenty times more advantageous, than that which our North

American colonies ever afforded. The trade of Great Britain would be just as advantageous to France, and, in proportion to the wealth, population and proximity of the respective countries, would have the same superiority over that which France carries on with her own colonies. Such is the very great difference between that trade which the wisdom of both nations has thought proper to discourage, and that which it has favoured the most.

But the very same circumstances which would have rendered an open and free commerce between the two countries so advantageous to both, have occasioned the principal obstructions to that commerce. Being neighbours, they are necessarily enemies, and the wealth and power of each becomes, upon that account, more formidable to the other; and what would increase the advantage of national friendship, serves only to inflame the violence of national animosity. They are both rich and industrious nations; and the merchants and manufacturers of each, dread the competition of the skill and activity of those of the other. Mercantile jealousy is excited, and both inflames, and is itself inflamed, by the violence of national animosity: And the traders of both countries have announced, with all the passionate confidence of interested falsehood, the certain ruin of each, in consequence of that unfavourable balance of trade, which, they pretend, would be the infallible effect of an unrestrained commerce with the other.

There is no commercial country in Europe of which the approaching ruin has not frequently been foretold by the pretended doctors of this system, from an unfavourable balance of trade. After all the anxiety, however, which they have excited about this, after all the vain attempts of almost all trading nations to turn that balance in their own favour and against their neighbours, it does not appear that any one nation in Europe has been in any respect impoverished by this cause. Every town and country, on the contrary, in proportion as they have opened their ports to all nations, instead of being ruined by this free trade, as the principles of the commercial system would lead us to expect, have been enriched by it. Though there are in Europe, indeed, a few towns which in some respects deserve the name of free ports, there is no country which does so. Holland, perhaps, approaches the nearest to this character of any, though still very remote from it; and Holland, it is acknowledged, not only derives its whole wealth, but a great part of its necessary subsistence, from foreign trade.

There is another balance, indeed, which has already been explained, very different from the balance of trade, and which, according as it happens to be either favourable or unfavourable, necessarily occasions the prosperity or decay of every nation. This is the balance of the annual produce and consumption. If the exchangeable value of the annual produce, it has already been observed, exceeds that of the annual consumption, the capital of the society must annually increase in proportion to this excess. The society in this case lives within its revenue, and what is annually saved out of its revenue, is naturally added to its capital, and employed so as to increase still further the annual produce. If the exchangeable value of the annual produce, on the contrary, fall short of the annual consumption, the capital of the society must annually decay in proportion to this deficiency. The expence of the society in this case exceeds its revenue, and necessarily encroaches upon its capital. Its capital, therefore, must necessarily decay, and, together with it, the exchangeable value of the annual produce of its industry.

This balance of produce and consumption is entirely different from, what is called, the balance of trade. It might take place in a nation which had no foreign trade, but which was entirely separated from all the world. It may take place in the whole globe of the earth, of which the wealth, population, and improvement may be either gradually increasing or gradually decaying.

The balance of produce and consumption may be constantly in favour of a nation, though what is called the balance of trade be generally against it. A nation may import to a greater value than it exports for half a century, perhaps, together; the gold and silver which comes into it during all this time may be all immediately sent out of it; its circulating coin may gradually decay, different sorts of paper money being substituted in its place, and even the debts too which it contracts in the principal nations with whom it deals, may be gradually increasing; and yet its real wealth, the exchangeable value of the annual produce of its lands and labour, may, during the same period, have been increasing in a much greater proportion. The state of our North American colonies, and of the trade which they carried on with Great Britain, before the commencement of the present disturbances, may serve as a proof that this is by no means an impossible supposition.

CHAPTER IV

Of Drawbacks

MERCHANTS and manufacturers are not contented with the monopoly of the home market, but desire likewise the most extensive foreign sale for their goods. Their country has no jurisdiction in foreign nations, and therefore can seldom procure them any monopoly there. They are generally obliged, therefore, to content themselves with petitioning for certain encouragements to exportation.

Of these encouragements what are called Drawbacks seem to be the most reasonable. To allow the merchant to draw back upon exportation, either the whole or a part of whatever excise or inland duty is imposed upon domestic industry, can never occasion the exportation of a greater quantity of goods than what would have been exported had no duty been imposed. Such encouragements do not tend to turn towards any particular employment a greater share of the capital of the country, than what would go to that employment of its own accord, but only to hinder the duty from driving away any part of that share to other employments. They tend not to overturn that balance which naturally establishes itself among all the various employments of the society; but to hinder it from being overturned by the duty. They tend not to destroy, but to preserve, what it is in most cases advantageous to preserve, the natural division and distribution of labour in the society.

The same thing may be said of the drawbacks upon the re-exportation of foreign goods imported; which in Great Britain generally amount to by much the largest part of the duty upon importation.

Drawbacks were, perhaps, originally granted for the encouragement of the carrying trade, which, as the freight of the ships is frequently paid by foreigners in money, was supposed to be peculiarly fitted for bringing gold and silver into the country. But though the carrying trade certainly deserves no peculiar encouragement, though the motive of the institution was, perhaps, abundantly foolish, the institution itself seems reasonable enough. Such drawbacks cannot force into this trade a greater share of the capital of the country than what would have gone to it of its own accord, had there been no duties upon importation. They only prevent its being excluded altogether by those duties. The carrying trade, though it deserves no preference, ought not to be precluded, but to be left free like all other trades. It is a necessary resource for those capitals which cannot find employment either in the agriculture or in the manufactures of the country, either in its home trade or in its foreign trade of consumption.

The revenue of the customs, instead of suffering, profits from such drawbacks, by that part of the duty which is retained. If the whole duties had been retained, the foreign goods upon which they are paid, could seldom have been exported, nor consequently imported, for want of a market. The duties, therefore, of which a part is retained, would never have been paid.

These reasons seem sufficiently to justify drawbacks, and would justify them, though the whole duties, whether upon the produce of domestic industry, or upon foreign goods, were always drawn back upon exportation. The revenue of excise would in this case, indeed, suffer a little, and that of the customs a good deal more; but the natural balance of industry, the natural division and distribution of labour, which is always more or less disturbed by such duties, would be more nearly re-established by such a regulation.

These reasons, however, will justify drawbacks only upon exporting goods to those countries which are altogether foreign and independent, not to those in which our merchants and manufacturers enjoy a monopoly. A drawback, for example, upon the exportation of European goods to our American colonies, will not always occasion a greater exportation than what would have taken place without it. By means of the monopoly which our merchants and manufacturers enjoy there, the same quantity might frequently, perhaps, be sent thither, though the whole duties were retained. The drawback, therefore, may frequently be pure loss to the revenue of excise and customs, without altering the state of the trade, or rendering it in any respect more extensive. How far such drawbacks can be justified, as a proper encouragement to the industry of our colonies, or how far it is advantageous to the mother-country, that they should be exempted from taxes which are paid by all the rest of their fellow-subjects, will appear hereafter when I come to treat of colonies.

Drawbacks, however, it must always be understood, are useful only in those cases in which the goods for the exportation of which they are given, are really exported to some foreign country; and not clandestinely re-imported into our own. That some drawbacks, particularly those upon tobacco, have frequently been abused in this manner, and have given occasion to many frauds equally hurtful both to the revenue and to the fair trader, is well known.

CHAPTER V

OF BOUNTIES

BOUNTIES upon exportation are, in Great Britain, frequently petitioned for, and sometimes granted to the produce of particular branches of domestic industry. By means of them our merchants and manufacturers, it is pretended, will be enabled to sell their goods as cheap or cheaper than their rivals in the foreign market. A greater quantity, it is said, will thus be exported, and the balance of trade consequently turned more in favour of our own country. We cannot give our workmen a monopoly in the foreign, as we have done in the home market. We cannot force foreigners to buy their goods, as we have done our own countrymen. The next best expedient, it has been thought, therefore, is to pay them for buying. It is in this manner that the mercantile system proposes to enrich the whole country, and to put money into all our pockets by means of the balance of trade.

Bounties, it is allowed, ought to be given to those branches of trade only which cannot be carried on without them. But every branch of trade in which the merchant can sell his goods for a price which replaces to him, with the ordinary profits of stock, the whole capital employed in preparing and sending them to market, can be carried on without a bounty. Every such branch is evidently upon a level with all the other branches of trade which are carried on without bounties, and cannot therefore require one more than they. Those trades only require bounties in which the merchant is obliged to sell his goods for a price which does not replace to him his capital, together with the ordinary profit; or in which he is obliged to sell them for less than it really costs him to send them to market. The bounty is given in order to make up this loss, and to encourage him to continue, or perhaps to begin, a trade of which the expence is supposed to be greater than the returns, of which every operation eats up a part of the capital employed in it, and which is of such a nature, that, if all other trades resembled it, there would soon be no capital left in the country.

The trades, it is to be observed, which are carried on by means of bounties, are the only ones which can be carried on between two nations for any considerable time together, in such a manner as that one of them shall always and regularly lose, or sell its goods for less than it really costs to send them to market. But if the bounty did not repay to the merchant what he would otherwise lose upon the price of his goods, his own interest would soon oblige him to employ his stock in another way, or to find out a trade in which the price of the goods would replace to him, with the ordinary profit, the capital employed in sending them to market. The effect of bounties, like that of all the other expedients of the mercantile system, can only be to force the trade of a country into a channel much less advantageous than that in which it would naturally run of its own accord.

The ingenious and well-informed author of the tracts upon the corn-trade has shown very clearly, that since the bounty upon the exportation of corn was first established, the price of the corn exported, valued moderately enough, has exceeded that of the corn imported, valued very high, by a much greater sum than the amount of the whole bounties which have been paid during that period. This, he imagines, upon the true principles of the mercantile system, is a clear proof that this forced corn trade is beneficial to the nation; the value of the exportation exceeding that of the importation by a much greater sum than the whole extraordinary expence which the public has been at in order to get it exported. He does not consider that this extraordinary expence, or the bounty, is the smallest part of the expence which the exportation of corn really costs the society. The capital which the farmer employed in raising it, must likewise be taken into the account. Unless the price of the corn when sold in the foreign markets replaces, not only the bounty, but this capital, together with the ordinary profits of stock, the society is a loser by the difference, or the national stock is so much diminished. But the very reason for which it has been thought necessary to grant a bounty, is the supposed insufficiency of the price to do this.

The average price of corn, it has been said, has fallen considerably since the establishment of the bounty. That the average price of corn began to fall somewhat towards the end of the last century, and has continued to do so during the course of the sixty-four first years of the present, I have already endeavoured to show. But this event, supposing it to be as real as I believe it to be, must have happened in spite of the bounty, and cannot possibly have happened in consequence of it. It has happened in France, as well as in England, though in France there was, not only no bounty, but, till 1764, the exportation of corn was subjected to a general prohibition. This gradual fall in the average price of grain, it is probable, therefore, is ultimately owing neither to the one regulation nor to the other, but to that gradual and insensible rise in the real value of silver, which, in the first book of this discourse, I have endeavoured to show has taken place in the general market of France, during the course of the present century. It seems to be altogether impossible that the bounty could ever contribute to lower the price of grain.

In years of plenty, it has already been observed, the bounty, by occasioning an extraordinary exportation, necessarily keeps up the price of corn in the home market above what it would naturally fall to. To do so was the avowed purpose of the institution. In years of scarcity, though the bounty is frequently suspended, yet the great exportation which it occasions in years of plenty, must frequently hinder more or less the plenty of one year from relieving the scarcity of another. Both in years of plenty, and in years of scarcity, therefore, the bounty necessarily tends to raise the money price of corn somewhat higher than it otherwise would be in the home market.

That, in the actual state of tillage, the bounty must necessarily have this tendency, will not, I apprehend, be disputed by any reasonable person. But it has been thought by many people that it tends to encourage tillage, and that in two different ways; first, by opening a more extensive foreign market to the corn of the farmer, it tends, they imagine, to increase the demand for, and consequently the production of that commodity; and secondly, by securing to him a better price than he could otherwise expect in the actual state of tillage, it tends, they suppose, to encourage tillage. This double encouragement must, they imagine, in a long period of years, occasion such an increase in the production of corn, as may lower its price in the home market, much more than the bounty can raise it, in the actual state which tillage may, at the end of that period, happen to be in.

I answer, that whatever extension of the foreign market can be occasioned by the bounty, must, in every particular year, be altogether at the expence of the home market; as every bushel of corn which is exported by means of the bounty, and which would not have been exported without the bounty, would have remained in the home market to increase the consumption, and to lower the price of that commodity. The corn bounty, it is to be observed, as well as every other bounty upon exportation, imposes two different taxes upon the people; first, the tax which they are obliged to contribute, in order to pay the bounty; and secondly, the tax which arises from the advanced price of the commodity in the home market, and which, as the whole body of the people are purchasers of corn, must, in this particular commodity, be paid by the whole body of the people. In this particular commodity, therefore, this second tax is by much the heaviest of the two. Let us suppose that, taking one year with another, the bounty of five shillings upon the exportation of the quarter of wheat, raises the price of that commodity in the home market only sixpence the bushel, or four shillings the quarter, higher than it otherways would have been in the actual state of the crop. Even upon this very moderate supposition, the great body of the people, over and above contributing the tax which pays the bounty of five shillings upon every quarter of wheat exported, must pay another of four shillings upon every quarter which they themselves consume. But, according to the very well informed author of the tracts upon the corn-trade, the average proportion of the corn exported to that consumed at home, is not more than that of one to thirty-one. For every five shillings, therefore, which they contribute to the payment of the first tax, they must contribute six pounds four shillings to the payment of the second. So very heavy a tax upon the first necessary of life, must either reduce the subsistence of the labouring poor, or it must occasion some augmentation in their pecuniary wages, proportionable to that in the pecuniary price of their subsistence. So far as it operates in the one way, it must reduce the ability of the labouring poor to educate and bring up their children, and must, so far, tend to restrain the population of the country. So far as it operates in the other, it must reduce the ability of the employers of the poor, to employ so great a number as they otherwise might do, and must, so far, tend to restrain the industry of the country. The extraordinary exportation of corn, therefore, occasioned by the bounty, not only, in every particular year, diminishes the home, just as much as it extends the foreign market and consumption, but, by restraining the population and industry of the country, its final tendency is to stunt and restrain the gradual extension of the home market; and thereby, in the long run, rather to diminish, than to augment, the whole market and consumption of corn.

This enhancement of the money price of corn, however, it has been thought, by rendering that commodity more profitable to the farmer, must necessarily encourage its production.

I answer, that this might be the case if the effect of the bounty was to raise the real price of corn, or to enable the farmer, with an equal quantity of it, to maintain a greater number of labourers in the same manner, whether liberal, moderate, or scanty, that other labourers are commonly maintained in his neighbourhood. But neither the bounty, it is evident, nor any other human institution, can have any such effect. It is not the real, but the nominal price of corn, which can in any considerable degree be affected by the bounty. And though the tax, which that institution imposes upon the whole body of the people, may be very burdensome to those who pay it, it is of very little advantage to those who receive it.

The real effect of the bounty is not so much to raise the real value of corn, as to degrade the real value of silver; or to make an equal quantity of it exchange for a smaller quantity, not only of corn, but of all other home-made commodities: for the money price of corn regulates that of all other home-made commodities.

It regulates the money price of labour, which must always be such as to enable the labourer to purchase a quantity of corn sufficient to maintain him and his family either in the liberal, moderate, or scanty manner in which the advancing, stationary or declining circumstances of the society oblige his employers to maintain him.

It regulates the money price of all the other parts of the rude produce of land, which, in every period of improvement, must bear a certain proportion to that of corn, though this proportion is different in different periods. It regulates, for example, the money price of grass and hay, of butcher's meat, of horses, and the maintenance of horses, of land carriage consequently, or of the greater part of the inland commerce of the country.

By regulating the money price of all the other parts of the rude produce of land, it regulates that of the materials of almost all manufactures. By regulating the money price of labour, it regulates that of manufacturing art and industry. And by regulating both, it regulates that of the complete manufacture. The money price of labour, and of every thing that is the produce either of land or labour, must necessarily either rise or fall in proportion to the money price of corn.

Though in consequence of the bounty, therefore, the farmer should be enabled to sell his corn for four shillings the bushel instead of three and sixpence, and to pay his landlord a money rent proportionable to this rise in the money price of his produce; yet if, in consequence of this rise in the price of corn, four shillings will purchase no more home-made goods of any other kind than three and sixpence would have done before, neither the circumstances of the farmer, nor those of the landlord, will be much mended by this change. The farmer will not be able to cultivate much better: the landlord will not be able to live much better. In the purchase of foreign commodities this enhancement in the price of corn may give them some little advantage. In that of home-made commodities it can give them none at all. And almost the whole expence of the farmer, and the far greater part even of that of the landlord, is in home-made commodities.

That degradation in the value of silver which is the effect of the fertility of the mines, and which operates equally, or very near equally, through the greater part of the commercial world, is a matter of very little consequence to any particular country. The consequent rise of all money prices, though it does not make those who receive them really richer, does not make them really poorer. A service of plate becomes really cheaper, and every thing else remains precisely of the same real value as before.

But that degradation in the value of silver which, being the effect either of the peculiar situation, or of the political institutions of a particular country, takes place only in that country, is a matter of very great consequence, which, far from tending to make any body really richer, tends to make every body really poorer. The rise in the money price of all commodities, which is in this case peculiar to that country, tends to discourage more or less every sort of industry which is carried on within it, and to enable foreign nations, by furnishing almost all sorts of goods for a smaller quantity of silver than its own workmen can afford to do, to undersell them, not only in the foreign, but even in the home market.

It is the peculiar situation of Spain and Portugal as proprietors of the mines, to be the distributors of gold and silver to all the other countries of Europe. Those metals ought naturally, therefore, to be somewhat cheaper in Spain and Portugal than in any other part of Europe. The difference, however, should be no more than the amount of the freight and insurance; and, on account of the great value and small bulk of those metals, their freight is no great matter, and their insurance is the same as that of any other goods of equal value. Spain and Portugal, therefore, could suffer very little from their peculiar situation, if they did not aggravate its disadvantages by their political institutions.

Spain by taxing, and Portugal by prohibiting the exportation of gold and silver, load that exportation with the expence of smuggling, and raise the value of those metals in other countries so much more above what it is in their own, by the whole amount of this expence. When you dam up a stream of water, as soon as the dam is full, as much water must run over the dam-head as if there was no dam at all. The prohibition of exportation cannot detain a greater quantity of gold and silver in Spain and Portugal than what they can afford to employ, than what the annual produce of their land and labour will allow them to employ, in coin, plate, gilding, and other ornaments of gold and silver. When they have got this quantity the dam is full, and the whole stream which flows in afterwards must run over. The annual exportation of gold and silver from Spain and Portugal accordingly is, by all accounts, notwithstanding these restraints, very near equal to the whole annual importation. As the water, however, must always be deeper behind the dam-head than before it, so the quantity of gold and silver which these restraints detain in Spain and Portugal must, in proportion to the annual produce of their land and labour, be greater than what is to be found in other countries. The higher and stronger the dam-head, the greater must be the difference in the depth of water behind and before it. The higher the tax, the higher the penalties with which the prohibition is guarded, the more vigilant and severe the police which looks after the execution of the law, the greater must be the difference in the proportion of gold and silver to the annual produce of the land and labour of Spain and Portugal, and to that of other countries. It is said accordingly to be very considerable, and that you frequently find there a profusion of plate in houses, where there is nothing else which would, in other countries, be thought suitable or correspondent to this sort of magnificence. The cheapness of gold and silver, or what is the same thing, the dearness of all commodities, which is the necessary effect of this redundancy of the precious metals, discourages both the agriculture and manufactures of Spain and Portugal, and enables foreign nations to supply them with many sorts of rude, and with almost all sorts of manufactured produce, for a smaller quantity of gold and silver than what they themselves can either raise or make them for at home. The tax and prohibition operate in two different ways. They not only lower very much the value of the precious metals in Spain and Portugal, but by detaining there a certain quantity of those metals which would otherwise flow over other countries, they keep up their value in those other countries somewhat above what it otherwise would be, and thereby give those countries a double advantage in their commerce with Spain and Portugal. Open the flood-gates, and there will presently be less water above, and more below, the dam-head, and it will soon come to a level in both places. Remove the tax and the prohibition, and as the quantity of gold and silver will diminish considerably in Spain and Portugal, so it will increase somewhat in other countries, and the value of those metals, their proportion to the annual produce of land and labour, will soon come to a level, or very near to a level, in all. The loss which Spain and Portugal could sustain by this exportation of their gold and silver would be altogether nominal and imaginary. The nominal value of their goods, and of the annual produce of their land and labour, would fall, and would be expressed or represented by a smaller quantity of silver than before: but their real value would be the same as before, and would be sufficient to maintain, command, and employ, the same quantity of labour. As the nominal value of their goods would fall, the real value of what remained of their gold and silver would rise, and a smaller quantity of those metals would answer all the same purposes of commerce and circulation which had employed a greater quantity before. The gold and silver which would go abroad would not go abroad for nothing, but would bring back an equal value of goods of some kind or another. Those goods too would not be all matters of mere luxury and expence, to be consumed by idle people who produce nothing in return for their consumption. As the real wealth and revenue of idle people would not be augmented by this extraordinary exportation of gold and silver, so neither would their consumption be much augmented by it. Those goods would, probably, the greater part of them, and certainly some part of them, consist in materials, tools, and provisions, for the employment and maintenance of industrious people, who would reproduce, with a profit, the full value of their consumption. A part of the dead stock of the society would thus be turned into active stock, and would put into motion a greater quantity of industry than had been employed before. The annual produce of their land and labour would immediately be augmented a little, and in a few years would, probably, be augmented a great deal; their industry being thus relieved from one of the most oppressive burdens which it at present labours under.

The bounty upon the exportation of corn necessarily operates exactly in the same way as this absurd policy of Spain and Portugal. Whatever be the actual state of tillage, it renders our corn somewhat dearer in the home market than it otherwise would be in that state, and somewhat cheaper in the foreign; and as the average money price of corn regulates more or less that of all other commodities, it lowers the value of silver considerably in the one, and tends to raise it a little in the other. It enables foreigners, the Dutch in particular, not only to eat our corn cheaper than they otherwise could do, but sometimes to eat it cheaper than even our own people can do upon the same occasions; as we are assured by an excellent authority, that of Sir Matthew Decker. It hinders our own workmen from furnishing their goods for so small a quantity of silver as they otherwise might do; and enables the Dutch to furnish their's for a smaller. It tends to render our manufactures somewhat dearer in every market, and their's somewhat cheaper than they otherwise would be, and consequently to give their industry a double advantage over our own.

The bounty, as it raises in the home market, not so much the real, as the nominal price of our corn, as it augments, not the quantity of labour which a certain quantity of corn can maintain and employ, but only the quantity of silver which it will exchange for, it discourages our manufactures, without rendering any considerable service either to our farmers or country gentlemen. It puts, indeed, a little more money into the pockets of both, and it will perhaps be somewhat difficult to persuade the greater part of them that this is not rendering them a very considerable service. But if this money sinks in its value, in the quantity of labour, provisions, and home-made commodities of all different kinds which it is capable of purchasing, as much as it rises in its quantity, the service will be little more than nominal and imaginary.

There is, perhaps, but one set of men in the whole commonwealth to whom the bounty either was or could be essentially serviceable. These were the corn merchants, the exporters and importers of corn. In years of plenty the bounty necessarily occasioned a greater exportation than would otherwise have taken place; and by hindering the plenty of one year from relieving the scarcity of another, it occasioned in years of scarcity a greater importation than would otherwise have been necessary. It increased the business of the corn merchant in both; and in years of scarcity, it not only enabled him to import a greater quantity, but to sell it for a better price, and consequently with a greater profit than he could otherwise have made, if the plenty of one year had not been more or less hindered from relieving the scarcity of another. It is in this set of men, accordingly, that I have observed the greatest zeal for the continuance or renewal of the bounty.

Our country gentlemen, when they imposed the high duties upon the importation of foreign corn, which in times of moderate plenty amount to a prohibition, and when they established the bounty, seem to have imitated the conduct of our manufacturers. By the one institution, they secured to themselves the monopoly of the home market, and by the other they endeavoured to prevent that market from ever being overstocked with their commodity. By both they endeavoured to raise its real value, in the same manner as our manufacturers had, by the like institutions, raised the real value of many different sorts of manufactured goods. They did not perhaps attend to the great and essential difference which nature has established between corn and almost every other sort of goods. When, either by the monoply of the home market, or by a bounty upon exportation, you enable our woollen or linen manufacturers to sell their goods for somewhat a better price than they otherwise could get for them, you raise, not only the nominal, but the real price of those goods. You render them equivalent to a greater quantity of labour and subsistence, you encrease not only the nominal, but the real profit, the real wealth and revenue of those manufacturers, and you enable them either to live better themselves, or to employ a greater quantity of labour in those particular manufactures. You really encourage those manufactures, and direct towards them a greater quantity of the industry of the country, than what would probably go to them of its own accord. But when by the like institutions you raise the nominal or money-price of corn, you do not raise its real value. You do not increase the real wealth, the real revenue either of our farmers or country gentlemen. You do not encourage the growth of corn, because you do not enable them to maintain and employ more labourers in raising it. The nature of things has stamped upon corn a real value which cannot be altered by merely altering its money price. No bounty upon exportation, no monopoly of the home market, can raise that value. The freest competition cannot lower it. Through the world in general that value is equal to the quantity of labour which it can maintain, and in every particular place it is equal to the quantity of labour which it can maintain in the way, whether liberal, moderate, or scanty, in which labour is commonly maintained in that place. Woollen or linen cloth are not the regulating commodities by which the real value of all other commodities must be finally measured and determined; corn is. The real value of every other commodity is finally measured and determined by the proportion which its average money price bears to the average money price of corn. The real value of corn does not vary with those variations in its average money price, which sometimes occur from one century to another. It is the real value of silver which varies with them.

Bounties upon the exportation of any home-made commodity are liable, first, to that general objection which may be made to all the different expedients of the mercantile system; the objection of forcing some part of the industry of the country into a channel less advantageous than that in which it would run of its own accord: and, secondly, to the particular objection of forcing it, not only into a channel that is less advantageous, but into one that is actually disadvantageous; the trade which cannot be carried on but by means of a bounty being necessarily a losing trade. The bounty upon the exportation of corn is liable to this further objection, that it can in no respect promote the raising of that particular commodity of which it was meant to encourage the production. When our country gentlemen, therefore, demanded the establishment of the bounty, though they acted in imitation of our merchants and manufacturers, they did not act with that complete comprehension of their own interest which commonly directs the conduct of those two other orders of people. They loaded the public revenue with a very considerable expence; they imposed a very heavy tax upon the whole body of the people; but they did not, in any sensible degree, increase the real value of their own commodity; and by lowering somewhat the real value of silver, they discouraged, in some degree, the general industry of the country, and, instead of advancing, retarded more or less the improvement of their own lands, which necessarily depends upon the general industry of the country.

To encourage the production of any commodity, a bounty upon production, one should imagine, would have a more direct operation, than one upon exportation. It would, besides, impose only one tax upon the people, that which they must contribute in order to pay the bounty. Instead of raising, it would tend to lower the price of the commodity in the home market; and thereby, instead of imposing a second tax upon the people, it might at least in part, repay them for what they had contributed to the first. Bounties upon production, however, have been very rarely granted. The prejudices established by the commercial system have taught us to believe, that nominal wealth arises more immediately from exportation than from production. It has been more favoured accordingly, as the more immediate means of bringing money into the country. Bounties upon production, it has been said too, have been found by experience more liable to frauds than those upon exportation. How far this is true, I know not. That bounties upon exportation have been abused to many fraudulent purposes, is very well known. But it is not the interest of merchants and manufacturers, the great inventors of all these expedients, that the home market should be overstocked with their goods, an event which a bounty upon production might sometimes occasion.

A bounty upon exportation, by enabling them to send abroad the surplus part, and to keep up the price of what remains in the home market, effectually prevents this. Of all the expedients of the mercantile system, accordingly, it is the one of which they are the fondest. I have known the different undertakers of some particular works agree privately among themselves to give a bounty out of their own pockets upon the exportation of a certain proportion of the goods which they dealt in. This expedient succeeded so well, that it more than doubled the price of their goods in the home market, notwithstanding a very considerable increase in the produce. The operation of the bounty upon corn must have been wonderfully different, if it has lowered the money price of that commodity.

Something like a bounty upon production, however, has been granted upon some particular occasions. The tonnage bounties given to the white-herring and whale-fisheries may, perhaps, be considered as somewhat of this nature. They tend directly, it may be supposed, to render the goods cheaper in the home market than they otherwise would be. In other respects their effects, it must be acknowledged, are the same as those of bounties upon exportation. By means of them a part of the capital of the country is employed in bringing goods to market, of which the price does not repay the cost, together with the ordinary profits of stock.

If any particular manufacture was necessary, indeed, for the defence of the society, it might not always be prudent to depend upon our neighbours for the supply; and if such manufacture could not otherwise be supported at home, it might not be unreasonable that all the other branches of industry should be taxed in order to support it. The bounties upon the exportation of British-made sail-cloth, and British-made gun-powder, may, perhaps, both be vindicated upon this principle.

But though it can very seldom be reasonable to tax the industry of the great body of the people, in order to support that of some particular class of manufacturers; yet in the wantonness of great prosperity, when the public enjoys a greater revenue than it knows well what to do with, to give such bounties to favourite manufacturers, may, perhaps, be as natural, as to incur any other idle expence. In public, as well as in private expences, great wealth may, perhaps, frequently be admitted as an apology for great folly. But there must surely be something more than ordinary absurdity, in continuing such profusion in times of general difficulty and distress.

What is called a bounty is sometimes no more than a drawback, and consequently is not liable to the same objections as what is properly a bounty. The bounty, for example, upon refined sugar exported, may be considered as a drawback of the duties upon the brown and muscovado sugars from which it is made. The bounty upon wrought silk exported, a drawback of the duties upon raw and thrown silk imported. The bounty upon gunpowder exported, a drawback of the duties upon brimstone and saltpetre imported. In the language of the customs those allowances only are called drawbacks, which are given upon goods exported in the same form in which they are imported. When that form has been so altered by manufacture of any kind, as to come under a new denomination, they are called bounties.

Premiums given by the public to artists and manufacturers who excel in their particular occupations, are not liable to the same objections as bounties. By encouraging extraordinary dexterity and ingenuity, they serve to keep up the emulation of the workmen actually employed in those respective occupations, and are not considerable enough to turn towards any one of them a greater share of the capital of the country than what would go to it of its own accord. Their tendency is not to overturn the natural balance of employments, but to render the work which is done in each as perfect and complete as possible. The expence of premiums, besides, is very trifling; that of bounties very great. The bounty upon corn alone has sometimes cost the public in one year more than three hundred thousand pounds.

Bounties are sometimes called premiums, as drawbacks are sometimes called bounties. But we must in all cases attend to the nature of the thing, without paying any regard to the word.

CHAPTER VI

Of Treaties of Commerce

WHEN a nation binds itself by treaty either to permit the entry of certain goods from one foreign country which it prohibits from all others, or to exempt the goods of one country from duties to which it subjects those of all others, the country, or at least the merchants and manufacturers of the country, whose commerce is so favoured, must necessarily derive great advantage from the treaty. Those merchants and manufacturers enjoy a sort of monopoly in the country which is so indulgent to them. That country becomes a market both more extensive and more advantageous for their goods; more extensive, because the goods of other nations being either excluded or subjected to heavier duties, it takes off a greater quantity of theirs: more advantageous, because the merchants of the favoured country, enjoying a sort of monopoly there, will often sell their goods for a better price than if exposed to the free competition of all other nations.

Such treaties, however, though they may be advantageous to the merchants and manufacturers of the favoured, are necessarily disadvantageous to those of the favouring country. A monopoly is thus granted against them to a foreign nation; and they must frequently buy the foreign goods they have occasion for, dearer than if the free competition of other nations was admitted. That part of its own produce with which such a nation purchases foreign goods, must consequently be sold cheaper, because when two things are exchanged for one another, the cheapness of the one is a necessary consequence, or rather is the same thing with the dearness of the other. The exchangeable value of its annual produce, therefore, is likely to be diminished by every such treaty. This diminution, however, can scarce amount to any positive loss, but only to a lessening of the gain which it might otherwise make. Though it sells its goods cheaper than it otherwise might do, it will not probably sell them for less than they cost; nor, as in the case of bounties, for a price which will not replace the capital employed in bringing them to market, together with the ordinary profits of stock. The trade could not go on long if it did. Even the favouring country, therefore, may still gain by the trade, though less than if there was a free competition.

Some treaties of commerce, however, have been supposed advantageous upon principles very different from these; and a commercial country has sometimes granted a monopoly of this kind against itself to certain goods of a foreign nation, because it expected that in the whole commerce between them, it would annually sell more than it would buy, and that a balance in gold and silver would be annually returned to it. It is upon this principle that the treaty of commerce between England and Portugal, concluded in 1703, by Mr. Methuen, has been so much commended. The following is a literal translation of that treaty, which consists of three articles only.

ART. I

His sacred royal majesty of Portugal promises, both in his own name, and that of his successors, to admit, for ever hereafter, into Portugal, the woollen cloths, and the rest of the woollen manufactures of the British, as was accustomed, till they were prohibited by the law; nevertheless upon this condition:

ART. II

That is to say, that her sacred royal majesty of Great Britain shall, in her own name, and that of her successors, be obliged, for ever hereafter, to admit the wines of the growth of Portugal into Britain: so that at no time, whether there shall be peace or war between the kingdoms of Britain and France, any thing more shall be demanded for these wines by the name of custom or duty, or by whatsoever other title, directly or indirectly, whether they shall be imported into Great Britain in pipes or hogsheads, or other casks, than what shall be demanded for the like quantity or measure of French wine, deducting or abating a third part of the custom or duty. But if at any time this deduction or abatement of customs, which is to be made as aforesaid, shall in any manner be attempted and prejudiced, it shall be just and lawful for his sacred royal majesty of Portugal, again to prohibit the woollen cloths, and the rest of the British woollen manufactures.

ART. III

The most excellent lords the plenipotentiaries promise and take upon themselves that their above-named masters shall ratify this treaty; and within the space of two months the ratifications shall be exchanged.

By this treaty the crown of Portugal becomes bound to admit the English woollens upon the same footing as before the prohibition; that is, not to raise the duties which had been paid before that time. But it does not become bound to admit them upon any better terms than those of any other nation, of France or Holland for example. The crown of Great Britain, on the contrary, becomes bound to admit the wines of Portugal, upon paying only two-thirds of the duty, which is paid for those of France, the wines most likely to come into competition with them. So far this treaty, therefore, is evidently advantageous to Portugal, and disadvantageous to Great Britain.

It has been celebrated, however, as a masterpiece of the commercial policy of England. Portugal receives annually from the Brazils a greater quantity of gold than can be employed in its domestic commerce, whether in the shape of coin or of plate. The surplus is too valuable to be allowed to lie idle and locked up in coffers, and as it can find no advantageous market at home, it must, notwithstanding any prohibition, be sent abroad, and exchanged for something for which there is a more advantageous market at home. A large share of it comes annually to England, in return either for English goods, or for those of other European nations that receive their returns through England. Mr. Baretti was informed that the weekly packet-boat from Lisbon brings, one week with another, more than fifty thousand pounds in gold to England. The sum had probably been exaggerated. It would amount to more than two millions six hundred thousand pounds a year, which is more than the Brazils are supposed to afford.

Our merchants were some years ago out of humour with the crown of Portugal. Some privileges which had been granted them, not by treaty, but by the free grace of that crown, at the solicitation, indeed, it is probable, and in return for much greater favours, defence and protection, from the crown of Great Britain, had been either infringed or revoked. The people, therefore, usually most interested in celebrating the Portugal trade, were then rather disposed to represent it as less advantageous than it had commonly been imagined. The far greater part, almost the whole, they pretended, of this annual importation of gold, was not on account of Great Britain, but of other European nations; the fruits and wines of Portugal annually imported into Great Britain nearly compensating the value of the British goods sent thither.

Let us suppose, however, that the whole was on account of Great Britain, and that it amounted to a still greater sum than Mr. Baretti seems to imagine: this trade would not, upon that account, be more advantageous than any other in which, for the same value sent out, we received an equal value of consumable goods in return.

It is but a very small part of this importation which, it can be supposed, is employed as an annual addition either to the plate or to the coin of the kingdom. The rest must all be sent abroad and exchanged for consumable goods of some kind or other. But if those consumable goods were purchased directly with the produce of English industry, it would be more for the advantage of England, than first to purchase with that produce the gold of Portugal, and afterwards to purchase with that gold those consumable goods. A direct foreign trade of consumption is always more advantageous than a round-about one; and to bring the same value of foreign goods to the home market, requires a much smaller capital in the one way than in the other. If a smaller share of its industry, therefore, had been employed in producing goods fit for the Portugal market, and a greater in producing those fit for the other markets, where those consumable goods for which there is a demand in Great Britain are to be had, it would have been more for the advantage of England. To procure both the gold, which it wants for its own use, and the consumable goods, would, in this way, employ a much smaller capital than at present. There would be a spare capital, therefore, to be employed for other purposes, in exciting an additional quantity of industry, and in raising a greater annual produce.

Though Britain were entirely excluded from the Portugal trade, it could find very little difficulty in procuring all the annual supplies of gold which it wants, either for the purposes of plate, or of coin, or of foreign trade. Gold, like every other commodity, is always somewhere or another to be got for its value by those who have that value to give for it.

The annual surplus of gold in Portugal, besides, would still be sent abroad, and though not carried away by Great Britain, would be carried away by some other nation, which would be glad to sell it again for its price, in the same manner as Great Britain does at present. In buying gold of Portugal, indeed, we buy it at the first hand; whereas, in buying it of any other nation, except Spain, we should buy it at the second, and might pay somewhat dearer. This difference, however, would surely be too insignificant to deserve the public attention.

Almost all our gold, it is said, comes from Portugal. With other nations the balance of trade is either against us, or not much in our favour. But we should remember, that the more gold we import from one country, the less we must necessarily import from all others. The effectual demand for gold, like that for every other commodity, is in every country limited to a certain quantity. If nine-tenths of this quantity are imported from one country, there remains a tenth only to be imported from all others. The more gold besides that is annually imported from some particular countries, over and above what is requisite for plate and for coin, the more must necessarily be exported to some others; and the more that most insignificant object of modern policy, the balance of trade, appears to be in our favour with some particular countries, the more it must necessarily appear to be against us with many others.

It was upon this silly notion, however, that England could not subsist without the Portugal trade, that, towards the end of the late war, France and Spain, without pretending either offence or provocation, required the king of Portugal to exclude all British ships from his ports, and for the security of this exclusion, to receive into them French or Spanish garrisons. Had the king of Portgual submitted to those ignominious terms which his brother-in-law the king of Spain proposed to him, Britain would have been freed from a much greater inconveniency than the loss of the Portugal trade, the burden of supporting a very weak ally, so unprovided of every thing for his own defence, that the whole power of England, had it been directed to that single purpose, could scarce perhaps have defended him for another campaign.

The loss of the Portugal trade would, no doubt, have occasioned a considerable embarrassment to the merchants at that time engaged in it, who might not, perhaps, have found out, for a year or two, any other equally advantageous method of employing their capitals; and in this would probably have consisted all the inconveniency which England could have suffered from this notable piece of commercial policy.

The great annual importation of gold and silver is neither for the purpose of plate nor of coin, but of foreign trade. A round-about foreign trade of consumption can be carried on more advantageously by means of these metals than of almost any other goods. As they are the universal instruments of commerce, they are more readily received in return for all commodities than any other goods; and on account of their small bulk and great value, it costs less to transport them backward and forward from one place to another than almost any other sort of merchandize, and they lose less of their value by being so transported. Of all the commodities, therefore, which are bought in one foreign country, for no other purpose but to be sold or exchanged again for some other goods in another, there are none so convenient as gold and silver. In facilitating all the different round-about foreign trades of consumption which are carried on in Great Britain, consists the principal advantage of the Portugal trade; and though it is not a capital advantage, it is, no doubt, a considerable one.

CHAPTER VII

Of Colonies

PART I

Of the Motives for Establishing new Colonies

THE interest which occasioned the first settlement of the different European colonies in America and the West Indies, was not altogether so plain and distinct as that which directed the establishment of those of ancient Greece and Rome.

All the different states of ancient Greece possessed, each of them, but a very small territory, and when the people in any one of them multiplied beyond what that territory could easily maintain, a part of them were sent in quest of a new habitation in some remote and distant part of the world; the warlike neighbours who surrounded them on all sides, rendering it difficult for any of them to enlarge very much its territory at home. The colonies of the Dorians resorted chiefly to Italy and Sicily, which, in the times preceding the foundation of Rome, were inhabited by barbarous and uncivilized nations: those of the Ionians and Eolians, the two other great tribes of the Greeks, to Asia Minor and the islands of the Egean Sea, of which the inhabitants seem at that time to have been pretty much in the same state as those of Sicily and Italy. The mother city, though she considered the colony as a child, at all times entitled to great favour and assistance, and owing in return much gratitude and respect, yet considered it as an emancipated child, over whom she pretended to claim no direct authority or jurisdiction. The colony settled its own form of government, enacted its own laws, elected its own magistrates, and made peace or war with its neighbours as an independent state, which had no occasion to wait for the approbation or consent of the mother city. Nothing can be more plain and distinct than the interest which directed every such establishment.

Rome, like most of the other ancient republics, was originally founded upon an Agrarian law, which divided the public territory in a certain proportion among the different citizens who composed the state. The course of human affairs, by marriage, by succession, and by alienation, necessarily deranged this original division, and frequently threw the lands, which had been allotted for the maintenance of many different families into the possession of a single person. To remedy this disorder, for such it was supposed to be, a law was made, restricting the quantity of land which any citizen could possess to five hundred jugera, about three hundred and fifty English acres. This law, however, though we read of its having been executed upon one or two occasions, was either neglected or evaded, and the inequality of fortunes went on continually increasing. The greater part of the citizens had no land, and without it the manners and customs of those times rendered it difficult for a freeman to maintain his independency. In the present times, though a poor man has no land of his own, if he has a little stock, he may either farm the lands of another, or he may carry on some little retail trade; and if he has no stock, he may find employment either as a country labourer, or as an artificer. But, among the ancient Romans, the lands of the rich were all cultivated by slaves, who wrought under an overseer, who was likewise a slave; so that a poor freeman had little chance of being employed either as a farmer or as a labourer. All trades and manufactures too, even the retail trade, were carried on by the slaves of the rich for the benefit of their masters, whose wealth, authority, and protection made it difficult for a poor freeman to maintain the competition against them. The citizens, therefore, who had no land, had scarce any other means of subsistence but the bounties of the candidates at the annual elections. The tribunes, when they had a mind to animate the people against the rich and the great, put them in mind of the ancient division of lands, and represented that law which restricted this sort of private property as the fundamental law of the republic. The people became clamorous to get land, and the rich and the great, we may believe, were perfectly determined not to give them any part of theirs. To satisfy them in some measure, therefore, they frequently proposed to send out a new colony. But conquering Rome was, even upon such occasions, under no necessity of turning out her citizens to seek their fortune, if one may say so, through the wide world, without knowing where they were to settle. She assigned them lands generally in the conquered provinces of Italy, where, being within the dominions of the republic, they could never form any independent state; but were at best but a sort of corporation, which, though it had the power of enacting bye-laws for its own government, was at all times subject to the correction, jurisdiction, and legislative authority of the mother city. The sending out a colony of this kind, not only gave some satisfaction to the people, but often established a sort of garrison too in a newly conquered province, of which the obedience might otherwise have been doubtful. A Roman colony, therefore, whether we consider the nature of the establishment itself, or the motives for making it, was altogether different from a Greek one. The words accordingly, which in the original languages denote those different establishments, have very different meanings. The Latin word (*Colonia*) signifies simply a plantation. The Greek word (*ἀποικία*), on the contrary, signifies a separation of dwelling, a departure from home, a going out of the house. But, though the Roman colonies were in many respects different from the Greek ones, the interest which prompted to establish them was equally plain and distinct. Both institutions derived their origin either from irresistible necessity, or from clear and evident utility.

The establishment of the European colonies in America and the West Indies arose from no necessity: and though the utility which has resulted from them has been very great, it is not altogether so clear and evident. It was not understood at their first establishment, and was not the motive either of that establishment or of the discoveries which gave occasion to it; and the nature, extent, and limits of that utility are not, perhaps, well understood at this day.

The Venetians, during the fourteenth and fifteenth centuries, carried on a very advantageous commerce in spiceries, and other East India goods, which they distributed among the other nations of Europe. They purchased them chiefly in Egypt, at that time under the dominion of the Mammeluks, the enemies of the Turks, of whom the Venetians were the enemies; and this union of interest, assisted by the money of Venice, formed such a connection as gave the Venetians almost a monopoly of the trade.

The great profits of the Venetians tempted the avidity of the Portuguese. They had been endeavouring, during the course of the fifteenth century, to find out by sea a way to the countries from which the Moors brought them ivory and gold dust across the Desart. They discovered the Madeiras, the Canaries, the Azores, the Cape de Verd islands, the coast of Guinea, that of Loango, Congo, Angola, and Benguela, and finally, the Cape of Good Hope. They had long wished to share in the profitable traffic of the Venetians, and this last discovery opened to them a probable prospect of doing so. In 1497, Vasco de Gama sailed from the port of Lisbon with a fleet of four ships, and, after a navigation of eleven months, arrived upon the coast of Indostan, and thus completed a course of discoveries which had been pursued with great steadiness, and with very little interruption, for near a century together.

Some years before this, while the expectations of Europe were in suspense about the projects of the Portuguese, of which the success appeared yet to be doubtful, a Genoese pilot formed the yet more daring project of sailing to the East Indies by the West. The situation of those countries was at that time very imperfectly known in Europe. The few European travellers who had been there had magnified the distance; perhaps through simplicity and ignorance, what was really very great, appearing almost infinite to those who could not measure it; or, perhaps, in order to increase somewhat more the marvellous of their own adventures in visiting regions so immensely remote from Europe. The longer the way was by the East, Columbus very justly concluded, the shorter it would be by the West. He proposed, therefore, to take that way, as both the shortest and the surest, and he had the good fortune to convince Isabella of Castile of the probability of his project. He sailed from the port of Palos in August, 1492, near five years before the expedition of Vasco de Gama set out from Portugal, and, after a voyage of between two and three months, discovered first some of the small Bahama or Lucayan islands, and afterwards the great island of St. Domingo.

But the countries which Columbus discovered, either in this or in any of his subsequent voyages, had no resemblance to those which he had gone in quest of. Instead of the wealth, cultivation and populousness of China and Indostan, he found, in St. Domingo, and in all the other parts of the new world which he ever visited, nothing but a country quite covered with wood, uncultivated, and inhabited only by some tribes of naked and miserable savages. He was not very willing, however, to believe that they were not the same with some of the countries described by Marco Polo, the first European who had visited, or at least had left behind him any description of China or the East Indies; and a very slight resemblance, such as that which he found between the name of Cibao, a mountain in St. Domingo, and that of Cipango, mentioned by Marco Polo, was frequently sufficient to make him return to this favourite prepossession, though contrary to the clearest evidence. In his letters to Ferdinand and Isabella he called the countries which he had discovered, the Indies. He entertained no doubt but that they were the extremity of those which had been described by Marco Polo, and that they were not very distant from the Ganges, or from the countries which had been conquered by Alexander. Even when at last convinced that they were different, he still flattered himself that those rich countries were at no great distance, and in a subsequent voyage, accordingly, went in quest of them along the coast of Terra Firma, and towards the isthmus of Darien.

In consequence of this mistake of Columbus, the name of the Indies has stuck to those unfortunate countries ever since; and when it was at last clearly discovered that the new were altogether different from the old Indies, the former were called the West, in contradistinction to the latter, which were called the East Indies.

It was of importance to Columbus, however, that the countries which he had discovered, whatever they were, should be represented to the court of Spain as of very great consequence; and, in what constitutes the real riches of every country, the animal and vegetable productions of the soil, there was at that time nothing which could well justify such a representation of them.

The Cori, something between a rat and a rabbit, and supposed by Mr. Buffon to be the same with the Aperea of Brazil, was the largest viviparous quadruped in St. Domingo. This species seems never to have been very numerous, and the dogs and cats of the Spaniards are said to have long ago almost entirely extirpated it, as well as some other tribes of a still smaller size. These, however, together with a pretty large lizard, called the Ivana or Iguana, constituted the principal part of the animal food which the land afforded.

The vegetable food of the inhabitants, though from their want of industry not very abundant, was not altogether so scanty. It consisted in Indian corn, yams, potatoes, bananas, &c. plants which were then altogether unknown in Europe, and which have never since been very much esteemed in it, or supposed to yield a sustenance equal to what is drawn from the common sorts of grain and pulse, which have been cultivated in this part of the world time out of mind.

The cotton plant indeed afforded the material of a very important manufacture, and was at that time to Europeans undoubtedly the most valuable of all the vegetable productions of those islands. But though in the end of the fifteenth century the muslins and other cotton goods of the East Indies were much esteemed in every part of Europe, the cotton manufacture itself was not cultivated in any part of it. Even this production, therefore, could not at that time appear in the eyes of Europeans to be of very great consequence.

Finding nothing either in the animals or vegetables of the newly discovered countries, which could justify a very advantageous representation of them, Columbus turned his view towards their minerals; and in the richness of the production of this third kingdom, he flattered himself, he had found a full compensation for the insignificancy of those of the other two. The little bits of gold with which the inhabitants ornamented their dress, and which, he was informed, they frequently found in the rivulets and torrents that fell from the mountains, were sufficient to satisfy him that those mountains abounded with the richest gold mines. St. Domingo, therefore, was represented as a country abounding with gold, and, upon that account (according to the prejudices not only of the present times, but of those times), an inexhaustible source of real wealth to the crown and kindom of Spain. When Columbus, upon his return from his first voyage, was introduced with a sort of triumphal honours to the sovereigns of Castile and Arragon, the principal productions of the countries which he had discovered were carried in solemn procession before him. The only valuable part of them consisted in some little fillets, bracelets, and other ornaments of gold, and in some bales of cotton. The rest were mere objects of vulgar wonder and curiosity; some reeds of an extraordinary size, some birds of a very beautiful plumage, and some stuffed skins of the huge alligator and manati; all of which were preceded by six or seven of the wretched natives, whose singular colour and appearance added greatly to the novelty of the shew.

In consequence of the representations of Columbus, the council of Castile determined to take possession of countries of which the inhabitants were plainly incapable of defending themselves. The pious purpose of converting them to Christianity sanctified the injustice of the project. But the hope of finding treasures of gold there, was the sole motive which prompted to undertake it; and to give this motive the greater weight, it was proposed by Côlumbus that the half of all the gold and silver that should be found there should belong to the crown. This proposal was approved of by the council.

As long as the whole or the far greater part of the gold, which the first adventurers imported into Europe, was got by so very easy a method as the plundering of the defenceless natives, it was not perhaps very difficult to pay even this heavy tax. But when the natives were once fairly stript of all that they had, which, in St. Domingo, and in all the other countries discovered by Columbus, was done completely in six or eight years, and when in order to find more it had become necessary to dig for it in the mines, there was no longer any possibility of paying this tax. The rigorous exaction of it, accordingly, first occasioned, it is said, the total abandoning of the mines of St. Domingo, which have never been wrought since. It was soon reduced therefore to a third; then to a fifth; afterwards to a tenth; and at last to a twentieth part of the gross produce of the gold mines. The tax upon silver continued for a long time to be a fifth of the gross produce. It was reduced to a tenth only in the course of the present century. But the first adventurers do not appear to have been much interested about silver. Nothing less precious than gold seemed worthy of their attention.

All the other enterprises of the Spaniards in the new world, subsequent to those of Columbus, seem to have been prompted by the same motive. It was the sacred thirst of gold that carried Oieda, Nicuessa, and Vasco Nugnes de Balboa, to the isthmus of Darien, that carried Cortez to Mexico, and Almagro and Pizzarro to Chili and Peru. When those adventurers arrived upon any unknown coast, their first enquiry was always if there was any gold to be found there; and according to the information which they received concerning this particular, they determined either to quit the country or to settle in it.

Of all those expensive and uncertain projects, however, which bring bankruptcy upon the greater part of the people who engage in them, there is none perhaps more perfectly ruinous than the search after new silver and gold mines. It is perhaps the most disadvantageous lottery in the world, or the one in which the gain of those who draw the prizes bears the least proportion to the loss of those who draw the blanks; for though the prizes are few and the blanks many, the common price of a ticket is the whole fortune of a very rich man. Projects of mining, instead of replacing the capital employed in them, together with the ordinary profits of stock, commonly absorb both capital and profit. They are the projects, therefore, to which of all others a prudent law-giver, who desired to increase the capital of his nation, would least chuse to give any extraordinary encouragement, or to turn towards them a greater share of that capital than what would go to them of its own accord. Such in reality is the absurd confidence which almost all men have in their own good fortune, that wherever there is the least probability of success, too great a share of it is apt to go to them of its own accord.

But though the judgment of sober reason and experience concerning such projects has always been extremely unfavourable, that of human avidity has commonly been quite otherwise. The same passion which has suggested to so many people the absurd idea of the philosopher's stone, has suggested to others the equally absurd one of immense rich mines of gold and silver. They did not consider that the value of those metals has, in all ages and nations, arisen chiefly from their scarcity, and that their scarcity has arisen from the very small quantities of them which nature has any where deposited in one place, from the hard and intractable substances with which she has almost every where surrounded those small quantities, and consequently from the labour and expence which are every where necessary in order to penetrate to and get at them. They flattered themselves that veins of those metals might in many places be found as large and as abundant as those which are commonly found of lead, or copper, or tin, or iron. The dream of Sir Walter Raleigh concerning the golden city and country of Eldorado, may satisfy us, that even wise men are not always exempt from such strange delusions. More than a hundred years after the death of that great man, the Jesuit Gumila was still convinced of the reality of that wonderful country, and expressed with great warmth, and I dare to say, with great sincerity, how happy he should be to carry the light of the gospel to a people who could so well reward the pious labours of their missionary.

In the countries first discovered by the Spaniards, no gold or silver mines are at present known which are supposed to be worth the working. The quantities of those metals which the first adventurers are said to have found there, had probably been very much magnified, as well as the fertility of the mines which were wrought immediately after the first discovery. What those adventurers were reported to have found, however, was sufficient to inflame the avidity of all their countrymen. Every Spaniard who sailed to America expected to find an Eldorado. Fortune too did upon this what she has done upon very few other occasions. She realized in some measure the extravagant hopes of her votaries, and in the discovery and conquest of Mexico and Peru (of which the one happened about thirty, the other about forty years after the first expedition of Columbus), she presented them with something not very unlike that profusion of the precious metals which they sought for.

A project of commerce to the East Indies, therefore, gave occasion to the first discovery of the West. A project of conquest gave occasion to all the establishments of the Spaniards in those newly discovered countries. The motive which excited them to this conquest was a project of gold and silver mines; and a course of accidents, which no human wisdom could foresee, rendered this project much more successful than the undertakers had any reasonable grounds for expecting.

The first adventurers of all the other nations of Europe, who attempted to make settlements in America, were animated by the like chimerical views; but they were not equally successful. It was more than a hundred years after the first settlement of the Brazils, before any silver, gold, or diamond mines were discovered there. In the English, French, Dutch, and Danish colonies, none have ever yet been discovered; at least none that are at present supposed to be worth the working. The first English settlers in North America, however, offered a fifth of all the gold and silver which should be found there to the king, as a motive for granting them their patents. In the patents to Sir Walter Raleigh, to the London and Plymouth companies, to the council of Plymouth, &c. this fifth was accordingly reserved to the crown. To the expectation of finding gold and silver mines, those first settlers too joined that of discovering a north-west passage to the East Indies. They have hitherto been disappointed in both.

CHAPTER VIII

Conclusion of the Mercantile System

THOUGH the encouragement of exportation, and the discouragement of importation, are the two great engines by which the mercantile system proposes to enrich every country, yet with regard to some particular commodities, it seems to follow an opposite plan: to discourage exportation and to encourage importation. Its ultimate object, however, it pretends, is always the same, to enrich the country by an advantageous balance of trade. It discourages the exportation of the materials of manufacture, and of the instruments of trade, in order to give our own workmen an advantage, and to enable them to undersell those of other nations in all foreign markets; and by restraining, in this manner, the exportation of a few commodities, of no great price, it proposes to occasion a much greater and more valuable exportation of others. It encourages the importation of the materials of manufacture, in order that our own people may be enabled to work them up more cheaply, and thereby prevent a greater and more valuable importation of the manufactured commodities. I do not observe, at least in our Statute Book, any encouragement given to the importation of the instruments of trade. When manufactures have advanced to a certain pitch of greatness, the fabrication of the instruments of trade becomes itself the object of a great number of very important manufactures. To give any particular encouragement to the importation of such instruments, would interfere too much with the interest of those manufactures. Such importation, therefore, instead of being encouraged, has frequently been prohibited. Thus the importation of wool cards, except from Ireland, or when brought in as wreck or prize goods, was prohibited by the 3d of Edward IV., which prohibition was renewed by the 39th of Elizabeth, and has been continued and rendered perpetual by subsequent laws.

The importation of the materials of manufacture has sometimes been encouraged by an exemption from the duties to which other goods are subject, and sometimes by bounties.

The importation of sheep's wool from several different countries, of cotton wool from all countries, of undressed flax, of the greater part of dying drugs, of the greater part of undressed hides from Ireland or the British colonies, of seal skins from the British Greenland fishery, of pig and bar iron from the British colonies, as well as of several other materials of manufacture, has been encouraged by an exemption from all duties, if properly entered at the custom-house. The private interest of our merchants and manufacturers may, perhaps, have extorted from the legislature these exemptions, as well as the greater part of our other commercial regulations. They are, however, perfectly just and reasonable, and if, consistently with the necessities of the state, they could be extended to all the other materials of manufacture, the public would certainly be a gainer.

The avidity of our great manufacturers, however, has in some cases extended these exemptions a good deal beyond what can justly be considered as the rude materials of their work. By the 24 Geo. II. chap 46, a small duty of only one penny the pound was imposed upon the importation of foreign brown linen yarn, instead of much higher duties to which it had been subjected before, viz. of sixpence the pound upon sail yarn, of one shilling the pound upon all French and Dutch yarn, and of two pounds thirteen shillings and fourpence upon the hundred weight of all spruce or Muscovia yarn. But our manufacturers were not long satisfied with this reduction. By the 29th of the same king, chap. 15, the same law which gave a bounty upon the exportation of British and Irish linen of which the price did not exceed eighteen pence the yard, even this small duty upon the importation of brown linen yarn was taken away. In the different operations, however, which are necessary for the preparation of linen yarn, a good deal more industry is employed, than in the subsequent operation of preparing linen cloth from linen yarn. To say nothing of the industry of the flax-growers and flax-dressers, three or four spinners, at least, are necessary, in order to keep one weaver in constant employment; and more than four-fifths of the whole quantity of labour, necessary for the preparation of linen cloth, is employed in that of linen yarn; but our spinners are poor people, women commonly, scattered about in all different parts of the country, without support or protection. It is not by the sale of their work, but by that of the complete work of the weavers, that our great master manufacturers make their profits. As it is their interest to sell the complete manufacture as dear, so is it to buy the materials as cheap as possible. By extorting from the legislature bounties upon the exportation of their own linen, high duties upon the importation of all foreign linen, and a total prohibition of the home consumption of some sorts of French linen, they endeavour to sell their own goods as dear as possible. By encouraging the importation of foreign linen yarn, and thereby bringing it into competition with that which is made by our own people, they endeavour to buy the work of the poor spinners as cheap as possible. They are as intent to keep down the wages of their own weavers, as the earnings of the poor spinners, and it is by no means for the benefit of the workman, that they endeavour either to raise the price of the complete work, or to lower that of the rude materials. It is the industry which is carried on for the benefit of the rich and the powerful, that is principally encouraged by our mercantile system. That which is carried on for the benefit of the poor and the indigent, is too often, either neglected, or oppressed.

Both the bounty upon the exportation of linen, and the exemption from duty upon the importation of foreign yarn, which were granted only for fifteen years, but continued by two different prolongations, expire with the end of the session of parliament which shall immediately follow the 24th of June 1786.

The encouragement given to the importation of the materials of manufacture by bounties, has been principally confined to such as were imported from our American plantations.

The first bounties of this kind were those granted, about the beginning of the present century, upon the importation of naval stores from America. Under this denomination were comprehended timber fit for masts, yards, and bowsprits; hemp; tar, pitch, and turpentine. The bounty, however, of one pound the ton upon masting-timber, and that of six pounds the ton upon hemp, were extended to such as should be imported into England from Scotland. Both these bounties continued without any variation, at the same rate, till they were severally allowed to expire; that upon hemp on the 1st of January 1741, and that upon masting-timber at the end of the session of parliament immediately following the 24th June 1781.

The bounties upon the importation of tar, pitch, and turpentine underwent, during their continuance, several alterations. Originally that upon tar was four pounds the ton; that upon pitch the same; and that upon turpentine, three pounds the ton. The bounty of four pounds the ton upon tar was afterwards confined to such as had been prepared in a particular manner; that upon other good, clean, and merchantable tar was reduced to two pounds four shillings the ton. The bounty upon pitch was likewise reduced to one pound; and that upon turpentine to one pound ten shillings the ton.

The second bounty upon the importation of any of the materials of manufacture, according to the order of time, was that granted by the 21 Geo. II. chap 30. upon the importation of indigo from the British plantations. When the plantation indigo was worth three-fourths of the price of the best French indigo, it was by this act entitled to a bounty of sixpence the pound. This bounty, which, like most others, was granted only for a limited time, was continued by several prolongations, but was reduced to four pence the pound. It was allowed to expire with the end of the session of parliament which followed the 25th March 1781.

The third bounty of this kind was that granted (much about the time that we were beginning sometimes to court and sometimes to quarrel with our American colonies) by the 4 Geo. III. chap. 26. upon the importation of hemp, or undressed flax, from the British plantations. This bounty was granted for twenty-one years, from the 24th June 1764, to the 24th June 1785. For the first seven years it was to be at the rate of eight pounds the ton, for the second at six pounds, and for the third at four pounds. It was not extended to Scotland, of which the climate (although hemp is sometimes raised there, in small quantities and of an inferior quality) is not very fit for that produce. Such a bounty upon the importation of Scotch flax into England would have been too great a discouragement to the native produce of the southern part of the united kingdom.

The fourth bounty of this kind, was that granted by the 5 Geo. III. chap. 45. upon the importation of wood from America. It was granted for nine years, from the 1st January 1766, to the 1st January 1775. During the first three years, it was to be for every hundred and twenty good deals, at the rate of one pound; and for every load containing fifty cubic feet of other squared timber at the rate of twelve shillings. For the second three years, it was for deals to be at the rate of fifteen shillings, and for other squared timber, at the rate of eight shillings; and for the third three years, it was for deals, to be at the rate of ten shillings, and for other squared timber, at the rate of five shillings.

The fifth bounty of this kind, was that granted by the 9 Geo. III. chap. 38. upon the importation of raw silk from the British plantations. It was granted for twenty-one years, from the 1st January 1770, to the 1st January 1791. For the first seven years it was to be at the rate of twenty-five pounds for every hundred pounds value; for the second, at twenty pounds; and for the third at fifteen pounds. The management of the silk-worm, and the preparation of silk, requires so much hand labour; and labour is so very dear in America, that even this great bounty, I have been informed, was not likely to produce any considerable effect.

The sixth bounty of this kind, was that granted by 11 Geo. III. chap. 50. for the importation of pipe, hogshead, and barrel staves and heading from the British plantations. It was granted for nine years, from 1st January 1772, to the 1st January 1781. For the first three years, it was for a certain quantity of each, to be at the rate of six pounds; for the second three years, at four pounds; and for the third three years, at two pounds.

The seventh and last bounty of this kind, was that granted

by the 19 Geo. III. chap. 37. upon the importation of hemp from Ireland. It was granted in the same manner as that for the importation of hemp and undressed flax from America, for twenty-one years, from the 24th June 1779, to the 24th June 1800. This term is divided, likewise, into three periods of seven years each; and in each of those periods, the rate of the Irish bounty is the same with that of the American. It does not, however, like the American bounty, extend to the importation of undressed flax. It would have been too great a discouragement to the cultivation of that plant in Great Britain. When this last bounty was granted, the British and Irish legislatures were not in much better humour with one another, than the British and American had been before. But this boon to Ireland, it is to be hoped, has been granted under more fortunate auspices, than all those to America.

The same commodities upon which we thus gave bounties, when imported from America, were subjected to considerable duties when imported from any other country. The interest of our American colonies was regarded as the same with that of the mother country. Their wealth was considered as our wealth. Whatever money was sent out to them, it was said, came all back to us by the balance of trade, and we could never become a farthing the poorer, by any expence which we could lay out upon them. They were our own in every respect, and it was an expence laid out upon the improvement of our own property, and for the profitable employment of our own people. It is unnecessary, I apprehend, at present to say any thing further, in order to expose the folly of a system, which fatal experience has now sufficiently exposed. Had our American colonies really been a part of Great Britain, those bounties might have been considered as bounties upon production, and would still have been liable to all the objections to which such bounties are liable, but to no other.

The exportation of the materials of manufacture is sometimes discouraged by absolute prohibitions, and sometimes by high duties.

Our woollen manufacturers have been more successful than any other class of workmen, in persuading the legislature that the prosperity of the nation depended upon the success and extension of their particular business. They have not only obtained a monopoly against the consumers by an absolute prohibition of importing woollen cloths from any foreign country; but they have likewise obtained another monopoly against the sheep farmers and growers of wool, by a similar prohibition of the exportation of live sheep and wool. The severity of many of the laws which have been enacted for the security of the revenue is very justly complained of, as imposing heavy penalties upon actions which, antecedent to the statutes that declared them to be crimes, had always been understood to be innocent. But the cruellest of our revenue laws, I will venture to affirm, are mild and gentle, in comparison of some of those which the clamour of our merchants and manufacturers have extorted from the legislature, for the support of their own absurd and oppressive monopolies. Like the laws of Draco, these laws may be said to be all written in blood.

By the 8th of Elizabeth, chap. 3. the exporter of sheep, lambs or rams, was for the first offence to forfeit all his goods for ever, to suffer a year's imprisonment, and then to have his left hand cut off in a market town upon a market day, to be there nailed up; and for the second offence to be adjudged a felon, and to suffer death accordingly. To prevent the breed of our sheep from being propagated in foreign countries, seems to have been the object of this law. By the 13th and 14th of Charles II. chap. 18. the exportation of wool was made felony, and the exporter subjected to the same penalties and forfeitures as a felon.

For the honour of the national humanity, it is to be hoped that neither of these statutes were ever executed. The first of them, however, so far as I know, has never been directly repealed, and Serjeant Hawkins seems to consider it as still in force. It may however, perhaps, be considered as virtually repealed by the 12th of Charles II. chap. 32. sect. 3. which, without expressly taking away the penalties imposed by former statutes, imposes a new penalty, viz. That of twenty shillings for every sheep exported, or attempted to be exported, together with the forfeiture of the sheep and of the owner's share of the ship. The second of them was expressly repealed by the 7th and 8th of William III. chap. 28. sect. 4. By which it is declared that, "Whereas the statute of the 13th and 14th of King Charles II. made against the exportation of wool, among other things in the said act mentioned, doth enact the same to be deemed felony; by the severity of which penalty the prosecution of offenders hath not been so effectually put in execution: Be it, therefore, enacted by the authority foresaid, that so much of the said act, which relates to the making the said offence felony, be repealed and made void."

The penalties, however, which are either imposed by this milder statute, or which, though imposed by former statutes, are not repealed by this one, are still sufficiently severe. Besides the forfeiture of the goods, the exporter incurs the penalty of three shillings for every pound weight of wool either exported or attempted to be exported, that is about four or five times the value. Any merchant or other person convicted of this offence is disabled from requiring any debt or account belonging to him from any factor or other person. Let his fortune be what it will, whether he is, or is not able to pay those heavy penalties, the law means to ruin him completely. But as the morals of the great body of the people are not yet so corrupt as those of the contrivers of this statute, I have not heard that any advantage has ever been taken of this clause. If the person convicted of this offence is not able to pay the penalties within three months after judgment, he is to be transported for seven years, and if he returns before the expiration of that term, he is liable to the pains of felony, without benefit of clergy. The owner of the ship knowing this offence forfeits all his interest in the ship and furniture. The master and mariners knowing this offence forfeit all their goods and chattels, and suffer three months imprisonment. By a subsequent statute the master suffers six months imprisonment.

In order to prevent exportation, the whole inland commerce of wool is laid under very burdensome and oppressive restrictions. It cannot be packed in any box, barrel, cask, case, chest, or any other package, but only in packs of leather or pack-cloth, on which must be marked on the outside the words *wool* or *yarn,* in large letters not less than three inches long, on pain of forfeiting the same and the package, and three shillings for every pound weight, to be paid by the owner or packer. It cannot be loaden on any horse or cart, or carried by land within five miles of the coast, but between sun-rising and sun-setting, on pain of forfeiting the same, the horses and carriages. The hundred next adjoining to the sea coast, out of or through which the wool is carried or exported, forfeits twenty pounds, if the wool is under the value of ten pounds; and if of greater value, then treble that value, together with treble costs, to be sued for within the year. The execution to be against any two of the inhabitants, whom the sessions must reimburse, by an assessment on the other inhabitants, as in the cases of robbery. And if any person compounds with the hundred for less than this penalty, he is to be imprisoned for five years; and any other person may prosecute. These regulations take place through the whole kingdom.

But in the particular counties of Kent and Sussex the restrictions are still more troublesome. Every owner of wool within ten miles of the sea-coast must give an account in writing, three days after shearing, to the next officer of the customs, of the number of his fleeces, and of the places where they are lodged. And before he removes any part of them he must give the like notice of the number and weight of the fleeces, and of the name and abode of the person to whom they are sold, and of the place to which it is intended they should be carried. No person within fifteen miles of the sea, in the said counties, can buy any wool, before he enters into bond to the king, that no part of the wool which he shall so buy shall be sold by him to any other person within fifteen miles of the sea. If any wool is found carrying towards the sea-side in the said counties, unless it has been entered and security given as aforesaid, it is forfeited, and the offender also forfeits three shillings for every pound weight. If any person lays any wool, not entered as aforesaid, within fifteen miles of the sea, it must be seized and forfeited; and if, after such seizure, any person shall claim the same, he must give security to the Exchequer, that if he is cast upon trial he shall pay treble costs, besides all other penalties.

When such restrictions are imposed upon the inland trade,

the coasting trade, we may believe, cannot be left very free. Every owner of wool who carrieth or causeth to be carried any wool to any port or place on the sea-coast, in order to be from thence transported by sea to any other place or port on the coast, must first cause an entry thereof to be made at the port from whence it is intended to be conveyed, containing the weight, marks, and number of the packages before he brings the same within five miles of that port; on pain of forfeiting the same, and also the horses, carts, and other carriages; and also of suffering and forfeiting, as by the other laws in force against the exportation of wool. This law, however, (1 Will. III. chap. 32.) is so very indulgent as to declare, that "this shall not hinder any person "from carrying his wool home from the place of shearing, "though it be within five miles of the sea, provided that in "ten days after shearing, and before he remove the wool, he "do under his hand certify to the next officer of the customs, "the true number of fleeces, and where it is housed; and do "not remove the same, without certifying to such officer, "under his hand, his intention so to do, three days before." Bond must be given that the wool to be carried coast-ways is to be landed at the particular port for which it is entered outwards; and if any part of it is landed without the presence of an officer, not only the forfeiture of the wool is incurred as in other goods, but the usual additional penalty of three shillings for every pound weight is likewise incurred.

Our woollen manufacturers, in order to justify their demand of such extraordinary restrictions and regulations, confidently asserted, that English wool was of a peculiar quality, superior to that of any other country; that the wool of other countries could not, without some mixture of it, be wrought up into any tolerable manufacture; that fine cloth could not be made without it; that England, therefore, if the exportation of it could be totally prevented, could monopolize to herself almost the whole wollen trade of the world; and thus, having no rivals, could sell at what price she pleased, and in a short time acquire the most incredible degree of wealth by the most advantageous balance of trade. This doctrine, like most other doctrines which are confidently asserted by any considerable number of people, was, and still continues to be, most implicitly believed by a much greater number; by almost all those who are either unacquainted with the woollen trade, or who have not made particular enquiries. It is, however, so perfectly false, that English wool is in any respect necessary for the making of fine cloth, that it is altogether unfit for it. Fine cloth is made altogether of Spanish wool. English wool cannot be even so mixed with Spanish wool as to enter into the composition without spoiling and degrading, in some degree, the fabric of the cloth.

It has been shown in the foregoing part of this work, that the effect of these regulations has been to depress the price of English wool, not only below what it naturally would be in the present times, but very much below what it actually was in the time of Edward III. The price of Scots wool, when in consequence of the union it became subject to the same regulations, is said to have fallen about one half. It is observed by the very accurate and intelligent author of the Memoirs of Wool, the Reverend Mr. John Smith, that the price of the best English wool in England is generally below what wool of a very inferior quality commonly sells for in the market of Amsterdam. To depress the price of this commodity below what may be called its natural and proper price, was the avowed purpose of those regulations; and there seems to be no doubt of their having produced the effect that was expected from them.

This reduction of price, it may perhaps be thought, by discouraging the growing of wool, must have reduced very much the annual produce of that commodity, though not below what it formerly was, yet below what, in the present state of things, it probably would have been, had it, in consequence of an open and free market, been allowed to rise to the natural and proper price. I am, however, disposed to believe, that the quantity of the annual produce cannot have been much, though it may perhaps have been a little, affected by these regulations. The growing of wool is not the chief purpose for which the sheep farmer employs his industry and stock. He expects his profit, not so much from the price of the fleece, as from that of the carcase; and the average or ordinary price of the latter, must even, in many cases, make up to him whatever deficiency there may be in the average or ordinary price of the former. It has been observed in the foregoing part of this work, that "What-"ever regulations tend to sink the price, either of wool or "raw hides, below what it naturally would be, must, in an "improved and cultivated country, have some tendency to "raise the price of butchers meat. The price both of the "great and small cattle which are fed on improved and cul-"tivated land, must be sufficient to pay the rent which the "landlord, and the profit which the farmer has reason to "expect from improved and cultivated land. If it is not, they "will soon cease to feed them. Whatever part of this price, "therefore, is not paid by the wool and the hide, must be "paid by the carcase. The less there is paid for the one, "the more must be paid for the other. In what manner this "price is to be divided upon the different parts of the beast, "is indifferent to the landlords and farmers, provided it is "all paid to them. In an improved and cultivated country, "therefore, their interest as landlords and farmers cannot be "much affected by such regulations, though their interest as "consumers may, by the rise in the price of provisions." According to this reasoning, therefore, this degradation in the price of wool is not likely, in an improved and cultivated country, to occasion any diminution in the annual produce of that commodity; except so far as by raising the price of mutton, it may somewhat diminish the demand for, and consequently the production of, that particular species of butchers meat. Its effect, however, even in this way, it is probable, is not very considerable.

But though its effect upon the quantity of the annual produce may not have been very considerable, its effect upon the quality, it may perhaps be thought, must necessarily have been very great. The degradation in the quality of English wool, if not below what it was in former times, yet below what it naturally would have been in the present state of improvement and cultivation, must have been, it may perhaps be supposed, very nearly in proportion to the degradation of price. As the quality depends upon the breed, upon the pasture, and upon the management and cleanliness of the sheep, during the whole progress of the growth of the fleece, the attention to these circumstances, it may naturally enough be imagined, can never be greater than in proportion to the recompence which the price of the fleece is likely to make for the labour and expence which that attention requires. It happens, however, that the goodness of the fleece depends, in a great measure, upon the health, growth, and bulk of the animal; the same attention which is necessary for the improvement of the carcase, is, in some respects, sufficient for that of the fleece. Notwithstanding the degradation of price, English wool is said to have been improved considerably during the course even of the present century. The improvement might perhaps have been greater if the price had been better; but the lowness of price, though it may have obstructed, yet certainly it has not altogether prevented that improvement.

The violence of these regulations, therefore, seems to have affected neither the quantity nor the quality of the annual produce of wool so much as it might have been expected to do (though I think it probable that it may have affected the latter a good deal more than the former); and the interest of the growers of wool, though it must have been hurt in some degree, seems, upon the whole, to have been much less hurt than could well have been imagined.

These considerations, however, will not justify the absolute prohibition of the exportation of wool. But they will fully justify the imposition of a considerable tax upon that exportation.

To hurt in any degree the interest of any one order of citizens, for no other purpose but to promote that of some other, is evidently contrary to that justice and equality of treatment which the sovereign owes to all the different orders of his subjects. But the prohibition certainly hurts, in some degree, the interest of the growers of wool, for no other purpose but to promote that of the manufacturers.

Every different order of citizens is bound to contribute to the support of the sovereign or commonwealth. A tax of five, or even of ten shillings upon the exportation of every tod of wool, would produce a very considerable revenue to the sovereign. It would hurt the interest of the growers somewhat less than the prohibition, because it would not probably lower the price of wool quite so much. It would afford a sufficient advantage to the manufacturer, because, though he might not buy his wool altogether so cheap as under the prohibition, he would still buy it, at least, five or ten shillings cheaper than any foreign manufacturer could buy it, besides saving the freight and insurance, which the other would be obliged to pay. It is scarce possible to devise a tax which could produce any considerable revenue to the sovereign, and at the same time occasion so little inconveniency to any body.

The prohibition, notwithstanding all the penalties which guard it, does not prevent the exportation of wool. It is exported, it is well known, in great quantities. The great difference between the price in the home and that in the foreign market, presents such a temptation to smuggling, that all the rigour of the law cannot prevent it. This illegal exportation is advantageous to nobody but the smuggler. A legal exportation subject to a tax, by affording a revenue to the sovereign, and thereby saving the imposition of some other, perhaps, more burdensome and inconvenient taxes, might prove advantageous to all the different subjects of the state.

The exportation of fuller's earth, or fuller's clay, supposed to be necessary for preparing and cleansing the woollen manufactures, has been subjected to nearly the same penalties as the exportation of wool. Even tobacco-pipe clay, though acknowledged to be different from fuller's clay, yet, on account of their resemblance, and because fuller's clay might sometimes be exported as tobacco-pipe clay, has been laid under the same prohibitions and penalties.

By the 13th and 14th of Charles II. chap. 7. the exportation, not only of raw hides, but of tanned leather, except in the shape of boots, shoes, or slippers, was prohibited; and the law gave a monopoly to our boot-makers and shoe-makers, not only against our graziers, but against our tanners. By subsequent statutes, our tanners have got themselves exempted from this monopoly, upon paying a small tax of only one shilling on the hundred weight of tanned leather, weighing one hundred and twelve pounds. They have obtained likewise the drawback of two-thirds of the excise duties imposed upon their commodity, even when exported without further manufacture. All manufactures of leather may be exported duty free; and the exporter is besides entitled to the drawback of the whole duties of excise. Our graziers still continue subject to the old monopoly. Graziers separated from one another, and dispersed through all the different corners of the country, cannot, without great difficulty, combine together for the purpose either of imposing monopolies upon their fellow-citizens, or of exempting themselves from such as may have been imposed upon them by other people. Manufacturers of all kinds, collected together in numerous bodies in all great cities, easily can. Even the horns of cattle are prohibited to be exported; and the two insignificant trades of the horner and combmaker enjoy, in this respect, a monopoly against the graziers.

Restraints, either by prohibitions or by taxes, upon the exportation of goods which are partially, but not completely manufactured, are not peculiar to the manufacture of leather. As long as any thing remains to be done, in order to fit any commodity for immediate use and consumption, our manufacturers think that they themselves ought to have the doing of it. Woollen yarn and worsted are prohibited to be exported under the same penalties as wool. Even while cloths are subject to a duty upon exportation, and our dyers have so far obtained a monopoly against our clothiers. Our clothiers would probably have been able to defend themselves against it, but it happens that the greater part of our principal clothiers are themselves likewise dyers. Watch-cases, clock-cases, and dial-plates for clocks and watches have been prohibited to be exported. Our clock-makers and watch-makers are, it seems, unwilling that the price of this sort of workmanship should be raised upon them by the competition of foreigners.

By some old statutes of Edward III., Henry VIII., and Edward VI., the exportation of all metals was prohibited. Lead and tin were alone excepted; probably on account of the great abundance of those metals; in the exportation of which, a considerable part of the trade of the kingdom in those days consisted. For the encouragement of the mining trade, the 5th of William and Mary, chap 17, exempted from this prohibition, iron, copper, and mundic metal made from British ore. The exportation of all sorts of copper bars, foreign as well as British, was afterwards permitted by the 9th and 10th of William III., chap. 26. The exportation of unmanufactured brass, of what is called gun-metal, bell-metal, and shroff-metal, still continues to be prohibited. Brass manufactures of all sorts may be exported duty free.

The exportation of the materials of manufacture, where it is not altogether prohibited, is in many cases subjected to considerable duties.

By the 8th George I., chap. 15, the exportation of all goods, the produce or manufacture of Great Britain, upon which any duties had been imposed by former statutes, was rendered duty free. The following goods, however, were excepted: Alum, lead, lead ore, tin, tanned leather, copperas, coals, wool cards, white woollen cloths, lapis calaminaris, skins of all sorts, glue, coney hair or wool, hares wool, hair of all sorts, horses, and litharge of lead. If you except horses, all these are either materials of manufacture, or incomplete manufactures (which may be considered as materials for still further manufacture), or instruments of trade. This statute leaves them subject to all the old duties which had ever been imposed upon them, the old subsidy and one per cent. outwards.

By the same statute a great number of foreign drugs for dyers use, are exempted from all duties upon importation. Each of them, however, is afterwards subjected to a certain duty, not indeed a very heavy one, upon exportation. Our dyers, it seems, while they thought it for their interest to encourage the importation of those drugs, by an exemption from all duties, thought it likewise for their interest to throw some small discouragement upon their exportation. The avidity, however, which suggested this notable piece of mercantile ingenuity, most probably disappointed itself of its object. It necessarily taught the importers to be more careful than they might otherwise have been, that their importation should not exceed what was necessary for the supply of the home market. The home market was at all times likely to be more scantily supplied; the commodities were at all times likely to be somewhat dearer there than they would have been, had the exportation been rendered as free as the importation.

By the above-mentioned statute, gum senega, or gum arabic, being among the enumerated dying drugs, might be imported duty free. They were subjected, indeed, to a small poundage duty, amounting only to three pence in the hundred weight upon their re-exportation. France enjoyed, at that time, an exclusive trade to the country most productive of those drugs, that which lies in the neighbourhood of the Senegal; and the British market could not be easily supplied by the immediate importation of them from the place of growth. By the 25th Geo. II. therefore, gum senega was allowed to be imported (contrary to the general dispositions of the act of navigation), from any part of Europe. As the law, however, did not mean to encourage this species of trade, so contrary to the general principles of the mercantile policy of England, it imposed a duty of ten shillings the hundred weight upon such importation, and no part of this duty was to be afterwards drawn back upon its exportation. The successful war which began in 1755 gave Great Britain the same exclusive trade to those countries which France had enjoyed before. Our manufacturers, as soon as the peace was made, endeavoured to avail themselves of this advantage, and to establish a monopoly in their own favour, both against the growers, and against the importers of this commodity. By the 5th Geo. III. therefore, chap. 37. the exportation of gum senega from his majesty's dominions in Africa was confined to Great Britain, and was subjected to all the same restrictions, regulations, forfeitures, and penalties, as that of the enumerated commodities of the British colonies in America and the West Indies. Its importation, indeed, was subjected to a small duty of six-pence the hundred weight, but its re-exportation was subjected to the enormous duty of one pound ten shillings the hundred weight. It was the intention of our manufacturers that the whole produce of those countries should be imported into Great Britain, and in order that they themselves might be enabled to buy it at their own price, that no part of it should be exported again, but at such an expence as would sufficiently discourage that exportation. Their avidity, however, upon this, as well as upon many other occasions, disappointed itself of its object. This enormous duty presented such a temptation to smuggling, that great quantities of this commodity were clandestinely exported, probably to all the manufacturing countries of Europe, but particularly to Holland, not only from Great Britain but from Africa. Upon this account, by the 14 Geo. III. chap. 10. this duty upon exportation was reduced to five shillings the hundred weight.

In the book of rates, according to which the old subsidy was levied, beaver skins were estimated at six shillings and eight-pence a-piece, and the different subsidies and imposts, which before the year 1722 had been laid upon their importation, amounted to one-fifth part of the rate, or to sixteen-pence upon each skin; all of which, except half the old subsidy, amounting only to two-pence, was drawn back upon exportation. This duty upon the importation of so important a material of manufacture had been thought too high, and, in the year 1722, the rate was reduced to two shillings and six-pence, which reduced the duty upon importation to six-pence, and of this only one half was to be drawn back upon exportation. The same successful war put the country most productive of beaver under the dominion of Great Britain, and beaver skins being among the enumerated commodities, their exportation from America was consequently confined to the market of Great Britain. Our manufacturers soon bethought themselves of the advantage which they might make of this circumstance, and in the year 1764, the duty upon the importation of beaver-skin was reduced to one penny, but the duty upon exportation was raised to seven-pence each skin, without any drawback of the duty upon importation. By the same law, a duty of eighteen pence the pound was imposed upon the exportation of beaver-wool or wombs, without making any alteration in the duty upon the importation of that commodity, which when imported by British and in British shipping, amounted at that time to between four-pence and five-pence the piece.

Coals may be considered both as a material of manufacture

and as an instrument of trade. Heavy duties, accordingly, have been imposed upon their exportation, amounting at present (1783) to more than five shillings the ton, or to more than fifteen shillings the chaldron, Newcastle measure; which is in most cases more than the original value of the commodity at the coal pit, or even at the shipping port for exportation.

The exportation, however, of the instruments of trade, properly so called, is commonly restrained, not by high duties, but by absolute prohibitions. Thus by the 7th and 8th of William III. chap. 20. sect. 8. the exportation of frames or engines for knitting gloves or stockings is prohibited under the penalty, not only of the forfeiture of such frames or engines, so exported, or attempted to be exported, but of forty pounds, one half to the king, the other to the person who shall inform or sue for the same. In the same manner by the 14th Geo. III. chap. 71, the exportation to foreign parts, of any utensils made use of in the cotton, linen, woollen and silk manufactures, is prohibited under the penalty, not only of the forfeiture of such utensils, but of two hundred pounds, to be paid by the person who shall offend in this manner, and likewise of two hundred pounds to be paid by the master of the ship who shall knowingly suffer such utensils to be loaded on board his ship.

When such heavy penalties were imposed upon the exportation of the dead instruments of trade, it could not well be expected that the living instrument, the artificer, should be allowed to go free. Accordingly, by the 5 Geo. I. chap. 27. the person who shall be convicted of enticing any artificer of, or in any of the manufactures of Great Britain, to go into any foreign parts, in order to practise or teach his trade, is liable for the first offence to be fined in any sum not exceeding one hundred pounds, and to three months imprisonment, and until the fine shall be paid; and for the second offence, to be fined in any sum at the discretion of the court, and to imprisonment for twelve months, and until the fine shall be paid. By the 23 Geo. II. chap. 13. this penalty is increased for the first offence to five hundred pounds for every artificer so enticed, and to twelve months imprisonment, and until the fine shall be paid; and for the second offence, to one thousand pounds, and to two years imprisonment, and until the fine shall be paid.

By the former of those two statutes, upon proof that any person has been enticing any artificer, or that any artificer has promised or contracted to go into foreign parts for the purposes aforesaid, such artificer may be obliged to give security at the discretion of the court, that he shall not go beyond the seas, and may be committed to prison until he give such security.

If any artificer has gone beyond the seas, and is exercising or teaching his trade in any foreign country, upon warning being given to him by any of his majesty's ministers or consuls abroad, or by one of his majesty's secretaries of state for the time being, if he does not, within six months after such warning, return into this realm, and from thenceforth abide and inhabit continually within the same, he is from thenceforth declared incapable of taking any legacy devised to him within this kingdom, or of being executor or administrator to any person, or of taking any lands within this kingdom by descent, device, or purchase. He likewise forfeits to the king, all his lands, goods and chattels, is declared an alien in every respect, and is put out of the king's protection.

It is unnecessary, I imagine, to observe, how contrary such regulations are to the boasted liberty of the subject, of which we affect to be so very jealous; but which, in this case, is so plainly sacrificed to the futile interests of our merchants and manufacturers.

The laudable motive of all these regulations, is to extend our own manufactures, not by their own improvement, but by the depression of those of all our neighbours, and by putting an end, as much as possible, to the troublesome competition of such odious and disagreeable rivals. Our master manufacturers think it reasonable, that they themselves should have the monopoly of the ingenuity of all their countrymen. Though by restraining, in some trades, the number of apprentices which can be employed at one time, and by imposing the necessity of a long apprenticeship in all trades, they endeavour, all of them, to confine the knowledge of their respective employments to as small a number as possible; they are unwilling, however, that any part of this small number should go abroad to instruct foreigners.

Consumption is the sole end and purpose of all production; and the interest of the producer ought to be attended to, only so far as it may be necessary for promoting that of the consumer. The maxim is so perfectly self-evident, that it would be absurd to attempt to prove it. But in the mercantile stystem, the interest of the consumer is almost constantly sacrificed to that of the producer; and it seems to consider production, and not consumption, as the ultimate end and object of all industry and commerce.

In the restraints upon the importation of all foreign commodities which can come into competition with those of our own growth, or manufacture, the interest of the home-consumer is evidently sacrificed to that of the producer. It is altogether for the benefit of the latter, that the former is obliged to pay that enhancement of price which this monopoly almost always occasions.

It is altogether for the benefit of the producer that bounties are granted upon the exportation of some of his productions. The home-consumer is obliged to pay, first, the tax which is necessary for paying the bounty, and secondly, the still greater tax which necessarily arises from the enhancement of the price of the commodity in the home market.

By the famous treaty of commerce with Portugal, the consumer is prevented by high duties from purchasing of a neighbouring country, a commodity which our own climate does not produce, but is obliged to purchase it of a distant country, though it is acknowledged, that the commodity of the distant country is of a worse quality than that of the near one. The home-consumer is obliged to submit to this inconveniency, in order that the producer may import into the distant country some of his productions upon more advantageous terms than he would otherwise have been allowed to do. The consumer, too, is obliged to pay, whatever enhancement in the price of those very productions, this forced exportation may occasion in the home market.

But in the system of laws which has been established for the management of our American and West Indian colonies, the interest of the home-consumer has been sacrificed to that of the producer with a more extravagant profusion than in all our other commercial regulations. A great empire has been established for the sole purpose of raising up a nation of customers who should be obliged to buy from the shops of our different producers, all the goods with which these could supply them. For the sake of that little enhancement of price which this monopoly might afford our producers, the home-consumers have been burdened with the whole expence of maintaining and defending that empire. For this purpose, and for this purpose only, in the two last wars, more than two hundred millions have been spent, and a new debt of more than a hundred and seventy millions has been contracted over and above all that had been expended for the same purpose in former wars. The interest of this debt alone is not only greater than the whole extraordinary profit, which, it ever could be pretended, was made by the monopoly of the colony trade, but than the whole value of that trade, or than the whole value of the goods, which at an average have been annually exported to the colonies.

It cannot be very difficult to determine who have been the contrivers of this whole mercantile system; not the consumers, we may believe, whose interest has been entirely neglected; but the producers, whose interest has been so carefully attended to; and among this latter class our merchants and manufacturers have been by far the principal architects. In the mercantile regulations, which have been taken notice of in this chapter, the interest of our manufacturers has been most peculiarly attended to; and the interest, not so much of the consumers, as that of some other sets of producers, has been sacrificed to it.

CHAPTER IX

Of the Agricultural Systems, or of the Systems of Political Œconomy, Which Represents the Produce of Land as Either the Sole or the Principal Source of the Revenue and Wealth of Every Country

THE agricultural systems of political œconomy will not require so long an explanation as that which I have thought it necessary to bestow upon the mercantile or commercial system.

That system which represents the produce of land as the sole source of the revenue and wealth of every country has, so far as I know, never been adopted by any nation, and it at present exists only in the speculation of a few men of great learning and ingenuity in France. It would not, surely, be worth while to examine at great length the errors of a system which never has done, and probably never will do any harm in any part of the world. I shall endeavour to explain, however, as distinctly as I can, the great outlines of this very ingenious system.

Mr. Colbert, the famous minister of Lewis XIV., was a man of probity, of great industry and knowledge of detail; of great experience and acuteness in the examination of public accounts, and of abilities, in short, every way fitted for introducing method and good order into the collection and expenditure of the public revenue. That minister had unfortunately embraced all the prejudices of the mercantile system, in its nature and essence a system of restraint and regulation, and such as could scarce fail to be agreeable to a laborious and plodding man of business, who had been accustomed to regulate the different departments of public offices, and to establish the necessary checks and controls for confining each to its proper sphere. The industry and commerce of a great country he endeavoured to regulate upon the same model as the departments of a public office; and instead of allowing every man to pursue his own interest his own way, upon the liberal plan of equality, liberty, and justice, he bestowed upon certain branches of industry extraordinary privileges, which he laid others under as extraordinary restraints. He was not only disposed, like other European ministers, to encourage more the industry of the towns than that of the country; but, in order to support the industry of the towns, he was willing even to depress and keep down that of the country. In order to render provisions cheap to the inhabitants of the towns, and thereby to encourage manufactures and foreign commerce, he prohibited altogether the exportation of corn, and thus excluded the inhabitants of the country from every foreign market for by far the most important part of the produce of their industry. This prohibition, joined to the restraints imposed by the ancient provincial laws of France upon the transportation of corn from one province to another, and to the arbitrary and degrading taxes which are levied upon the cultivators in almost all the provinces, discouraged and kept down the agriculture of that country very much below the state to which it would naturally have risen in so very fertile a soil and so very happy a climate. This state of discouragement and depression was felt more or less in every different part of the country, and many different inquiries were set on foot concerning the causes of it. One of those causes appeared to be the preference given, by the institutions of Mr. Colbert, to the industry of the towns above that of the country.

If the rod be bent too much one way, says the proverb, in order to make it straight you must bend it as much the other. The French philosophers, who have proposed the system which represents agriculture as the sole source of the revenue and wealth of every country, seem to have adopted this proverbial maxim; and as in the plan of Mr. Colbert the industry of the towns was certainly over-valued in comparison with that of the country; so in their system it seems to be as certainly undervalued.

The different orders of people who have ever been supposed to contribute in any respect towards the annual produce of the land and labour of the country, they divide into three classes. The first is the class of the proprietors of land. The second is the class of the cultivators, of farmers and country labourers, whom they honor with the peculiar appellation of the productive class. The third is the class of artificers, manufacturers and merchants, whom they endeavour to degrade by the humiliating appellation of the barren or unproductive class.

The class of proprietors contributes to the annual produce by the expence which they may occasionally lay out upon the improvement of the land, upon the buildings, drains, enclosures and other ameliorations, which they may either make or maintain upon it, and by means of which the cultivators are enabled, with the same capital, to raise a greater produce, and consequently to pay a greater rent. This advanced rent may be considered as the interest or profit due to the proprietor upon the expence or capital which he thus employs in the improvement of his land. Such expences are in this system called ground expences (depenses foncieres).

The cultivators or farmers contribute to the annual produce by what are in this system called the original and annual expences (depenses primitives et depenses annuelles) which they lay out upon the cultivation of the land. The original expences consist in the instruments of husbandry, in the stock of cattle, in the seed, and in the maintenance of the farmer's family, servants and cattle, during at least a great part of the first year of his occupancy, or till he can receive some return from the land. The annual expences consist in the seed, in the wear and tear of the instruments of husbandry, and in the annual maintenance of the farmer's servants and cattle, and of his family too, so far as any part of them can be considered as servants employed in cultivation. That part of the produce of the land which remains to him after paying the rent, ought to be sufficient, first, to replace to him within a reasonable time, at least during the term of his occupancy, the whole of his original expences, together with the ordinary profits of stock; and, secondly, to replace to him annually the whole of his annual expences, together likewise with the ordinary profits of stock. Those two sorts of expences are two capitals which the farmer employs in cultivation; and unless they are regularly restored to him, together with a reasonable profit, he cannot carry on his employment upon a level with other employments; but, from a regard to his own interest, must desert it as soon as possible, and seek some other. That part of the produce of the land which is thus necessary for enabling the farmer to continue his business, ought to be considered as a fund sacred to cultivation, which if the landlord violates, he necessarily reduces the produce of his own land, and in a few years not only disables the farmer from paying this racked rent, but from paying the reasonable rent which he might otherwise have got for his land. The rent which properly belongs to the landlord, is no more than the neat produce which remains after paying in the completest manner all the necessary expences which must be previously laid out in order to raise the gross, or the whole produce. It is because the labour of the cultivators, over and above paying completely all those necessary expences, affords a neat produce of this kind, that this class of people are in this system peculiarly distinguished by the honourable appellation of the productive class. Their original and annual expences are for the same reason called, in this system, productive expences, because, over and above replacing their own value, they occasion the annual reproduction of this neat produce.

The ground expences, as they are called, or what the landlord lays out upon the improvement of his land, are in this system too honoured with the appellation of productive expences. Till the whole of those expences, together with the ordinary profits of stock, have been completely repaid to him by the advanced rent which he gets from his land, that advanced rent ought to be regarded as sacred and inviolable, both by the church and by the king; ought to be subject neither to tithe nor to taxation. If it is otherwise, by discouraging the improvement of land, the church discourages the future increase of her own tithes, and the king the future increase of his own taxes. As in a well-ordered state of things, therefore, those ground expences, over and above reproducing in the completest manner their own value, occasion likewise after a certain time a reproduction of a neat produce, they are in this system considered as productive expences.

The ground expences of the landlord, however, together with the original and the annual expences of the farmer, are the only three sorts of expences which in this system are considered as productive. All other expences and all other orders of people, even those who in the common apprehensions of men are regarded as the most productive, are in this account of things represented as altogether barren and unproductive.

Artificers and manufacturers, in particular, whose industry, in the common apprehensions of men, increases so much the value of the rude produce of land, are in this system represented as a class of people altogether barren and unproductive. Their labour, it is said, replaces only the stock which employs them, together with its ordinary profits. That stock consists in the materials, tools, and wages, advanced to them by their employer; and is the fund destined for their employment and maintenance. Its profits are the fund destined for the maintenance of their employer. Their employer, as he advances to them the stock of materials, tools and wages necessary for their employment, so he advances to himself what is necessary for his own maintenance, and this maintenance he generally proportions to the profit which he expects to make by the price of their work. Unless its price repays to him the maintenance which he advances to himself, as well as the materials, tools and wages which he advances to his workmen, it evidently does not repay to him the whole expence which he lays out upon it. The profits of manufacturing stock, therefore, are not, like the rent of land, a neat produce which remains after completely repaying the whole expence which must be laid out in order to obtain them. The stock of the farmer yields him a profit as well as that of the master manufacturer; and it yields a rent likewise to another person, which that of the master manufacturer does not. The expence, therefore, laid out in employing and maintaining artificers and manufacturers, does no more than continue, if one may say so, the existence of its own value, and does not produce any new value. It is therefore altogether a barren and unproductive expence. The expence, on the contrary, laid out in employing farmers and country labourers, over and above continuing the existence of its own value, produces a new value, the rent of the landlord. It is therefore a productive expence.

Mercantile stock is equally barren and unproductive with manufacturing stock. It only continues the existence of its own value, without producing any new value. Its profits are only the repayment of the maintenance which its employer advances to himself during the time that he employs it, or till he receives the returns of it. They are only the repayment of a part of the expence which must be laid out in employing it.

The labour of artificers and manufacturers never adds any thing to the value of the whole annual amount of the rude produce of the land. It adds indeed greatly to the value of some particular parts of it. But the consumption which in the mean time it occasions of other parts, is precisely equal to the value which it adds to those parts; so that the value of the whole amount is not, at any one moment of time, in the least augmented by it. The person who works the lace of a pair of fine ruffles, for example, will sometimes raise the value of perhaps a pennyworth of flax to thirty pounds sterling. But though at first sight he appears thereby to multiply the value of a part of the rude produce about seven thousand and two hundred times, he in reality adds nothing to the value of the whole annual amount of the rude produce. The working of that lace costs him perhaps two years' labour. The thirty pounds which he gets for it when it is finished, is no more than the repayment of the subsistence which he advances to himself during the two years that he is employed about it. The value which, by every day's, month's, or year's labour, he adds to the flax, does no more than replace the value of his own consumption during that day, month, or year. At no moment of time, therefore, does he add any thing to the value of the whole annual amount of the rude produce of the land: the portion of that produce which he is continually consuming, being always equal to the value which he is continually producing. The extreme poverty of the greater part of the persons employed in this expensive, though trifling manufacture, may satisfy us that the price of their work does not in ordinary cases exceed the value of their subsistence. It is otherwise with the work of farmers and country labourers. The rent of the landlord is a value, which, in ordinary cases, it is continually producing, over and above replacing, in the most complete manner, the whole consumption, the whole expence laid out upon the employment and maintenance both of the workmen and of their employer.

Artificers, manufacturers and merchants, can augment the revenue and wealth of their society, by parsimony only; or, as it is expressed in this system, by privation, that is, by depriving themselves of a part of the funds destined for their own subsistence. They annually reproduce nothing but those funds. Unless, therefore, they annually save some part of them, unless they annually deprive themselves of the enjoyment of some part of them, the revenue and wealth of their society can never be in the smallest degree augmented by means of their industry. Farmers and country labourers, on the contrary, may enjoy completely the whole funds destined for their own subsistence, and yet augment at the same time the revenue and wealth of their society. Over and above what is destined for their own subsistence, their industry annually affords a neat produce, of which the augmentation necessarily augments the revenue and wealth of their society. Nations, therefore, which, like France or England, consist in a great measure of proprietors and cultivators, can be enriched by industry and enjoyment. Nations, on the contrary, which, like Holland and Hamburgh, are composed chiefly of merchants, artificers and manufacturers, can grow rich only through parsimony and privation. As the interest of nations so differently circumstanced, is very different, so is likewise the common character of the people. In those of the former kind, liberality, frankness, and good fellowship, naturally make a part of that common character. In the latter, narrowness, meanness, and a selfish disposition, averse to all social pleasure and enjoyment.

The unproductive class, that of merchants, artificers and manufacturers, is maintained and employed altogether at the expence of the two other classes, of that of proprietors, and of that of cultivators. They furnish it both with the materials of its work and with the fund of its subsistence, with the corn and cattle which it consumes while it is employed about that work. The proprietors and cultivators finally pay both the wages of all the workmen of the unproductive class, and the profits of all their employers. Those workmen and their employers are properly the servants of the proprietors and cultivators. They are only servants who work without doors, as menial servants work within. Both the one and the other, however, are equally maintained at the expence of the same masters. The labour of both is equally unproductive. It adds nothing to the value of the sum total of the rude produce of the land. Instead of increasing the value of that sum total, it is a charge and expence which must be paid out of it.

The unproductive class, however, is not only useful, but greatly useful to the other two classes. By means of the industry of merchants, artificers and manufacturers, the proprietors and cultivators can purchase both the foreign goods and the manufactured produce of their own country which they have occasion for, with the produce of a much smaller quantity of their own labour, than what they would be obliged to employ, if they were to attempt, in an awkward and unskilful manner, either to import the one, or to make the other for their own use. By means of the unproductive class, the cultivators are delivered from many cares which would otherwise distract their attention from the cultivation of land. The superiority of produce, which, in consequence of this undivided attention, they are enabled to raise, is fully sufficient to pay the whole expence which the maintenance and employment of the unproductive class costs either the proprietors, or themselves. The industry of merchants, artificers and manufacturers, though in its own nature altogether unproductive, yet contributes in this manner indirectly to increase the produce of the land. It increases the productive powers of productive labour, by leaving it at liberty to confine itself to its proper employment, the cultivation of land; and the plough goes frequently the easier and the better by means of the labour of the man whose business is most remote from the plough.

It can never be the interest of the proprietors and cultivators to restrain or to discourage in any respect the industry of merchants, artificers and manufacturers. The greater the liberty which this unproductive class enjoys, the greater will be the competition in all the different trades which compose it, and the cheaper will the other two classes be supplied, both with foreign goods and with the manufactured produce of their own country.

It can never be the interest of the unproductive class to oppress the other two classes. It is the surplus produce of the land, or what remains after deducting the maintenance, first, of the cultivators, and afterwards, of the proprietors, that maintains and employs the unproductive class. The greater this surplus, the greater must likewise be the maintenance and employment of that class. The establishment of perfect justice, of perfect liberty, and of perfect equality, is the very simple secret which most effectually secures the highest degree of prosperity to all the three classes.

The merchants, artificers and manufacturers of those mercantile states which, like Holland and Hamburgh, consist chiefly of this unproductive class, are in the same manner maintained and employed altogether at the expence of the proprietors and cultivators of land. The only difference is, that those proprietors and cultivators are, the greater part of them, placed at a most inconvenient distance from the merchants, artificers and manufacturers whom they supply with the materials of their work and the fund of their subsistence, are the inhabitants of other countries, and the subjects of other governments.

Such mercantile states, however, are not only useful, but greatly useful to the inhabitants of those other countries. They fill up, in some measure, a very important void, and supply the place of the merchants, artificers and manufacturers, whom the inhabitants of those countries ought to find at home, but whom, from some defect in their policy, they do not find at home.

It can never be the interest of those landed nations, if I may call them so, to discourage or distress the industry of such mercantile states, by imposing high duties upon their trade, or upon the commodities which they furnish. Such duties, by rendering those commodities dearer, could serve only to sink the real value of the surplus produce of their own land, with which, or, what comes to the same thing, with the price of which, those commodities are purchased. Such duties could serve only to discourage the increase of that surplus produce, and consequently the improvement and cultivation of their own land. The most effectual expedient, on the contrary, for raising the value of that surplus produce, for encouraging its increase, and consequently the improvement and cultivation of their own land, would be to allow the most perfect freedom to the trade of all such mercantile nations.

This perfect freedom of trade would even be the most effectual expedient for supplying them, in due time, with all the artificers, manufacturers and merchants, whom they wanted at home, and for filling up in the properest and most advantageous manner that very important void which they felt there.

The continual increase of the surplus produce of their land, would, in due time, create a greater capital than what could be employed with the ordinary rate of profit in the improvement and cultivation of land; and the surplus part of it would naturally turn itself to the employment of artificers and manufacturers at home. But those artificers and manufacturers, finding at home both the materials of their work and the fund of their subsistence, might immediately, even with much less art and skill, be able to work as cheap as the like artificers and manufacturers of such mercantile states, who had both to bring from a great distance. Even though, from want of art and skill, they might not for some time be able to work as cheap, yet, finding a market at home, they might be able to sell their work there as cheap as that of the artificers and manufacturers of such mercantile states, which could not be brought to that market but from so great a distance; and as their art and skill improved, they would soon be able to sell it cheaper. The artificers and manufacturers of such mercantile states, therefore, would immediately be rivalled in the market of those landed nations, and soon after undersold and justled out of it altogether. The cheapness of the manufactures of those landed nations, in consequence of the gradual improvements of art and skill, would, in due time, extend their sale beyond the home market, and carry them to many foreign markets, from which they would in the same manner gradually justle out many of the manufactures of such mercantile nations.

This continual increase both of the rude and manufactured produce of those landed nations would in due time create a greater capital than could, with the ordinary rate of profit, be employed either in agriculture or in manufactures. The surplus of this capital would naturally turn itself to foreign trade, and be employed in exporting, to foreign countries, such parts of the rude and manufactured produce of its own country, as exceeded the demand of the home market. In the exportation of the produce of their own country, the merchants of a landed nation would have an advantage of the same kind over those of mercantile nations, which its artificers and manufacturers had over the artificers and manufacturers of such nations; the advantage of finding at home that cargo, and those stores and provisions, which the others were obliged to seek for at a distance. With inferior art and skill in navigation, therefore, they would be able to sell that cargo as cheap in foreign markets as the merchants of such mercantile nations; and with equal art and skill they would be able to sell it cheaper. They would soon, therefore, rival those mercantile nations in this branch of foreign trade, and in due time would justle them out of it altogether.

According to this liberal and generous system, therefore, the most advantageous method in which a landed nation can raise up artificers, manufacturers and merchants of its own, is to grant the most perfect freedom of trade to the artificers, manufacturers and merchants of all other nations. It thereby raises the value of the surplus produce of its own land, of which the continual increase gradually establishes a fund, which in due time necessarily raises up all the artificers, manufactures and merchants whom it has occasion for.

When a landed nation, on the contrary, oppresses either by high duties or by prohibitions the trade of foreign nations, it necessarily hurts its own interest in two different ways. First, by raising the price of all foreign goods and of all sorts of manufactures, it necessarily sinks the real value of the surplus produce of its own land, with which, or, what comes to the same thing, with the price of which, it purchases those foreign goods and manufactures. Secondly, by giving a sort of monopoly of the home market to its own merchants, artificers and manufacturers, it raises the rate of mercantile and manufacturing profit in proportion to that of agricultural profit, and consequently either draws from agriculture a part of the capital which had before been employed in it, or hinders from going to it a part of what would otherwise have gone to it. This policy, therefore, discourages agriculture in two different ways; first, by sinking the real value of its produce, and thereby lowering the rate of its profit; and, secondly, by raising the rate of profit in all other employments. Agriculture is rendered less advantageous, and trade and manufactures more advantageous than they otherwise would be; and every man is tempted by his own interest to turn, as much as he can, both his capital and his industry from the former to the latter employments.

Though, by this oppressive policy, a landed nation should be able to raise up artificers, manufacturers and merchants of its own, somewhat sooner than it could do by the freedom of trade; a matter, however, which is not a little doubtful; yet it would raise them up, if one may say so, prematurely, and before it was perfectly ripe for them. By raising up too hastily one species of industry, it would depress another more valuable species of industry. By raising up too hastily a species of industry which only replaces the stock which employs it, together with the ordinary profit, it would depress a species of industry which, over and above replacing that stock with its profit, affords likewise a neat produce, a free rent to the landlord. It would depress productive labour, by encouraging too hastily that labour which is altogether barren and unproductive.

In what manner, according to this system, the sum total of the annual produce of the land is distributed among the three classes above mentioned, and in what manner the labour of the unproductive class does no more than replace the value of its own consumption, without increasing in any respect the value of that sum total, is represented by Mr. Quesnai, the very ingenious and profound author of this system, in some arithmetical formularies. The first of these formularies, which by way of eminence he peculiarly distinguishes by the name of the Economical Table, represents the manner in which he supposes this distribution takes place, in a state of the most perfect liberty, and therefore of the highest prosperity; in a state where the annual produce is such as to afford the greatest possible neat produce, and where each class enjoys its proper share of the whole annual produce. Some subsequent formularies represent the manner, in which, he supposes, this distribution is made in different states of restraint and regulation; in which, either the class of proprietors, or the barren and unproductive class, is more favoured than the class of cultivators, and in which, either the one or the other encroaches more or less upon the share which ought properly to belong to this productive class. Every such encroachment, every violation of that natural distribution, which the most perfect liberty would establish, must, according to this system, necessarily degrade more or less, from one year to another, the value and sum total of the annual produce, and must necessarily occasion a gradual declension in the real wealth and revenue of the society; a declension of which the progress must be quicker or slower, according to the degree of this encroachment, according as that natural distribution, which the most perfect liberty would establish, is more or less violated. Those subsequent formularies represent the different degrees of declension, which, according to this system, correspond to the different degrees in which this natural distribution of things is violated.

Some speculative physicians seem to have imagined that the health of the human body could be preserved only by a certain precise regimen of diet and exercise, of which every, the smallest, violation necessarily occasioned some degree of disease or disorder proportioned to the degree of the violation. Experience, however, would seem to show, that the human body frequently preserves, to all appearance at least, the most perfect state of health under a vast variety of different regimens; even under some which are generally believed to be very far from being perfectly wholesome. But the healthful state of the human body, it would seem, contains in itself some unknown principle of preservation, capable either of preventing or of correcting, in many respects, the bad effects even of a very faulty regimen. Mr. Quesnai, who was himself a physician, and a very speculative physician, seems to have entertained a notion of the same kind concerning the political body, and to have imagined that it would thrive and prosper only under a certain precise regimen, the exact regimen of perfect liberty and perfect justice. He seems not to have considered that in the political body, the natural effort which every man is continually making to better his own condition, is a principle of preservation capable of preventing and correcting, in many respects, the bad effects of a political œconomy, in some degree both partial and oppressive. Such a political œconomy, though it no doubt retards more or less, is not always capable of stopping altogether the natural progress of a nation towards wealth and prosperity, and still less of making it go backwards. If a nation could not prosper without the enjoyment of perfect liberty and perfect justice, there is not in the world a nation which could ever have prospered. In the political body, however, the wisdom of nature has fortunately made ample provision for remedying many of the bad effects of the folly and injustice of man; in the same manner as it has done in the natural body, for remedying those of his sloth and intemperance.

The capital error of this system, however, seems to lie in its representing the class of artificers, manufacturers and merchants, as altogether barren and unproductive. The following observations may serve to show the impropriety of this representation.

First, this class, it is acknowledged, reproduces annually the value of its own annual consumption, and continues, at least, the existence of the stock or capital which maintains and employs it. But upon this account alone the denomination of barren or unproductive should seem to be very improperly applied to it. We should not call a marriage barren or unproductive, though it produced only a son and a daughter, to replace the father and mother, and though it did not increase the number of the human species, but only continued it as it was before. Farmers and country labourers, indeed, over and above the stock which maintains and employs them, reproduce annually a neat produce, a free rent to the landlord. As a marriage which affords three children is certainly more productive than one which affords only two; so the labour of farmers and country labourers is certainly more productive than that of merchants, artificers and manufacturers. The superior produce of the one class, however, does not render the other barren or unproductive.

Secondly, it seems, upon this account, altogether improper to consider artificers, manufacturers and merchants, in the same light as menial servants. The labour of menial servants does not continue the existence of the fund which maintains and employs them. Their maintenance and employment is altogether at the expence of their masters, and the work which they perform is not of a nature to repay that expence. That work consists in services which perish generally in the very instant of their performance, and does not fix or realize itself in any vendible commodity which can replace the value of their wages and maintenance. The labour, on the contrary, of artificers, manufacturers and merchants, naturally does fix and realize itself in some such vendible commodity. It is upon this account that, in the chapter in which I treat of productive and unproductive labour, I have classed artificers, manufacturers and merchants, among the productive labourers, and menial servants among the barren or unproductive.

Thirdly, it seems, upon every supposition, improper to say, that the labour of artificers, manufacturers and merchants, does not increase the real revenue of the society. Though we should suppose, for example, as it seems to be supposed in this system, that the value of the daily, monthly, and yearly consumption of this class was exactly equal to that of its daily, monthly, and yearly production; yet it would not from thence follow that its labour added nothing to the real revenue, to the real value of the annual produce of the land and labour of the society. An artificer, for example, who in the first six months after harvest, executes ten pounds worth of work, though he should in the same time consume ten pounds worth of corn and other necessaries, yet really adds the value of ten pounds to the annual produce of the land and labour of the society. While he has been consuming a half yearly revenue of ten pounds worth of corn and other necessaries, he has produced an equal value of work capable of purchasing, either to himself or to some other person, an equal half yearly revenue. The value, therefore, of what has been consumed and produced during these six months is equal, not to ten, but to twenty pounds. It is possible, indeed, that no more than ten pounds worth of this value, may ever have existed at any one moment of time. But if the ten pounds worth of corn and other necessaries, which were consumed by the artificer, had been consumed by a soldier or by a menial servant, the value of that part of the annual produce which existed at the end of the six months, would have been ten pounds less than it actually is in consequence of the labour of the artificer. Though the value of what the artificer produces, therefore, should not at any one moment of time be supposed greater than the value he consumes, yet at every moment of time the actually existing value of goods in the market is, in consequence of what he produces, greater than it otherwise would be.

When the patrons of this system assert, that the consumption of artificers, manufacturers and merchants, is equal to the value of what they produce, they probably mean no more than that their revenue, or the fund destined for their consumption, is equal to it. But if they had expressed themselves more accurately, and only asserted, that the revenue of this class was equal to the value of what they produced, it might readily have occurred to the reader, that what would naturally be saved out of this revenue, must necessarily increase more or less, the real wealth of the society. In order, therefore, to make out something like an argument, it was necessary that they should express themselves as they have done; and this argument, even supposing things actually were as it seems to presume them to be, turns out to be a very inconclusive one.

Fourthly, farmers and country labourers can no more augment, without parsimony, the real revenue, the annual produce of the land and labour of their society, than artificers, manufacturers and merchants. The annual produce of the land and labour of any society can be augmented only in two ways; either, first, by some improvement in the productive powers of the useful labour actually maintained within it; or, secondly, by some increase in the quantity of that labour.

The improvement in the productive powers of useful labour depend, first, upon the improvement in the ability of the workman; and, secondly, upon that of the machinery with which he works. But the labour of artificers and manufacturers, as it is capable of being more subdivided, and the labour of each workman reduced to a greater simplicity of operation, than that of farmers and country labourers, so it is likewise capable of both these sorts of improvement in a much higher degree. In this respect, therefore, the class of cultivators can have no sort of advantage over that of artificers and manufacturers.

The increase in the quantity of useful labour actually employed within any society, must depend altogether upon the increase of the capital which employs it; and the increase of that capital again must be exactly equal to the amount of the savings from the revenue, either of the particular persons who manage and direct the employment of that capital, or of some other persons who lend it to them. If merchants, artificers and manufacturers are, as this system seems to suppose, naturally more inclined to parsimony and saving than proprietors and cultivators, they are, so far, more likely to augment the quantity of useful labour employed within their society, and consequently to increase its real revenue, the annual produce of its land and labour.

Fifthly and lastly, though the revenue of the inhabitants of every country was supposed to consist altogether, as this system seems to suppose, in the quantity of subsistence which their industry could procure to them; yet, even upon this supposition, the revenue of a trading and manufacturing country must, other things being equal, always be much greater than that of one without trade or manufactures. By means of trade and manufactures, a greater quantity of subsistence can be annually imported into a particular country than what its own lands, in the actual state of their cultivation, could afford. The inhabitants of a town, though they frequently possess no lands of their own, yet draw to themselves by their industry such a quantity of the rude produce of the lands of other people as supplies them, not only with the materials of their work, but with the fund of their subsistence. What a town always is with regard to the country in its neighbourhood, one independent state or country may frequently be with regard to other independent states or countries. It is thus that Holland draws a great part of its subsistence from other countries; live cattle from Holstein and Jutland, and corn from almost all the different countries of Europe. A small quantity of manufactured produce purchases a great quantity of rude produce. A trading and manufacturing country, therefore, naturally purchases with a small part of its manufactured produce a great part of the rude produce of other countries; while, on the contrary, a country without trade and manufactures is generally obliged to purchase, at the expense of a great part of its rude produce, a very small part of the manufactured produce of other countries. The one exports what can subsist and accommodate but a very few, and imports the subsistence and accommodation of a great number. The other exports the accommodation and subsistence of a great number, and imports that of a very few only. The inhabitants of the one must always enjoy a much greater quantity of subsistence than what their own lands, in the actual state of their cultivation, could afford. The inhabitants of the other must always enjoy a much smaller quantity.

This system, however, with all its imperfections, is, perhaps, the nearest approximation to the truth that has yet been published upon the subject of political œconomy, and is upon that account well worth the consideration of every man who wishes to examine with attention the principles of that very important science. Though in representing the labour which is employed upon land as the only productive labour, the notions which it inculcates are perhaps too narrow and confined; yet in representing the wealth of nations as consisting, not in the unconsumable riches of money, but in the consumable goods annually reproduced by the labour of the society; and in representing perfect liberty as the only effectual expedient for rendering this annual reproduction the greatest possible, its doctrine seems to be in every respect as just as it is generous and liberal. Its followers are very numerous; and as men are fond of paradoxes, and of appearing to understand what surpasses the comprehension of ordinary people, the paradox which it maintains, concerning the unproductive nature of manufacturing labour, has not perhaps contributed a little to increase the number of its admirers. They have for some years past made a pretty considerable sect, distinguished in the French republic of letters by the name of, The Œconomists. Their works have certainly been of some service to their country; not only by bringing into general discussion, many subjects which had never been well examined before, but by influencing in some measure the public administration in favour of agriculture. It has been in consequence of their representations, accordingly, that the agriculture of France has been delivered from several of the oppressions which it before laboured under. The term during which such a lease can be granted, as will be valid against every future purchaser or proprietor of the land, has been prolonged from nine to twenty-seven years. The ancient provincial restraints upon the transportation of corn from one province of the kingdom to another, have been entirely taken away, and the liberty of exporting it to all foreign countries, has been established as the common law of the kingdom in all ordinary cases. This sect, in their works, which are very numerous, and which treat not only of what is properly called Political Œconomy, or of the nature and causes of the wealth of nations, but of every other branch of the system of civil government, all follow implicitly, and without any sensible variation, the doctrine of Mr. Quesnai. There is upon this account little variety in the greater part of their works. The most distinct and best connected account of this doctrine is to be found in a little book written by Mr. Mercier de la Riviere, sometime Intendant of Martinico, intitled, The natural and essential Order of Political Societies. The admiration of this whole sect for their master, who was himself a man of the greatest modesty and simplicity, is not inferior to that of any of the ancient philosophers for the founders of their respective systems. "There have been, since the world began," says a very diligent and respectable author, the Marquis de Mirabeau, "three "great inventions which have principally given stability to "political societies, independent of many other inventions "which have enriched and adorned them. The first, is the "invention of writing, which alone gives human nature the "power of transmitting, without alteration, its laws, its con- "tracts, its annals, and its discoveries. The second, is the "invention of money, which binds together all the relations "between civilized societies. The third, is the Œconomical "Table, the result of the other two, which completes them "both by perfecting their object; the great discovery of our "age, but of which our posterity will reap the benefit."

The greatest and most important branch of the commerce of every nation, it has already been observed, is that which is carried on between the inhabitants of the town and those of the country. The inhabitants of the town draw from the country the rude produce which constitutes both the materials of their work and the fund of their subsistence; and they pay for this rude produce by sending back to the country a certain portion of it manufactured and prepared for immediate use. The trade which is carried on between those two different sets of people, consists ultimately in a certain quantity of rude produce exchanged for a certain quantity of manufactured produce. The dearer the latter, therefore, the cheaper the former; and whatever tends in any country to raise the price of manufactured produce, tends to lower that of the rude produce of the land, and thereby to discourage agriculture. The smaller the quantity of manufactured produce which any given quantity of rude produce, or, what comes to the same thing, which the price of any given quantity of rude produce is capable of purchasing, the smaller the exchangeable value of that given quantity of rude produce; the smaller the encouragement which either the landlord has to increase its quantity by improving, or the farmer by cultivating the land. Whatever, besides, tends to diminish in any country the number of artificers and manufacturers, tends to diminish the home market, the most important of all markets for the rude produce of the land, and thereby still further to discourage agriculture.

Those systems, therefore, which preferring agriculture to all other employments, in order to promote it, impose restraints upon manufactures and foreign trade, act contrary to the very end which they propose, and directly discourage that very species of industry which they mean to promote. They are so far, perhaps, more inconsistent than even the mercantile system. That system, by encouraging manufactures and foreign trade more than agriculture, turns a certain portion of the capital of the society from supporting a more advantageous, to support a less advantageous species of industry. But still it really and in the end encourages that species of industry which it means to promote. Those agricultural systems, on the contrary, really and in the end discourage their own favourite species of industry.

It is thus that every system which endeavours, either, by extraordinary encouragements, to draw towards a particular species of industry a greater share of the capital of the society than what would naturally go to it; or, by extraordinary restraints, to force from a particular species of industry some share of the capital which would otherwise be employed in it; is in reality subversive of the great purpose which it means to promote. It retards, instead of accelerating, the progress of the society towards real wealth and greatness: and diminishes, instead of increasing, the real value of the annual produce of its land and labour.

All systems either of preference or of restraint, therefore, being thus completely taken away, the obvious and simple system of natural liberty, establishes itself of its own accord. Every man, as long as he does not violate the laws of justice, is left perfectly free to pursue his own interest his own way, and to bring both his industry and capital into competition with those of any other man, or order of men. The sovereign is completely discharged from a duty, in the attempting to perform which he must always be exposed to innumerable delusions, and for the proper performance of which no human wisdom or knowledge could ever be sufficient; the duty of superintending the industry of private people, and of directing it towards the employments most suitable to the interest of the society. According to the system of natural liberty, the sovereign has only three duties to attend to; three duties of great importance, indeed, but plain and intelligible to common understandings; first, the duty of protecting the society from the violence and invasion of other independent societies; secondly, the duty of protecting, as far as possible, every member of the society from the injustice or oppression of every other member of it, or the duty of establishing an exact administration of justice; and, thirdly, the duty of erecting and maintaining certain public works and certain public institutions, which it can never be for the interest of any individual, or small number of individuals, to erect and maintain; because the profit could never repay the expence to any individual or small number of individuals, though it may frequently do much more than repay it to a great society.

The proper performance of those several duties of the sovereign necessarily supposes a certain expence; and this expence again necessarily requires a certain revenue to support it. In the following book, therefore, I shall endeavour to explain; first, what are the necessary expences of the sovereign or commonwealth; and which of those expences ought to be defrayed by the general contribution of the whole society; and which of them, by that of some particular part only, or of some particular members of the society: secondly, what are the different methods in which the whole society may be made to contribute towards defraying the expences incumbent on the whole society, and what are the principal advantages and inconveniences of each of those methods: and, thirdly, what are the reasons and causes which have induced almost all modern governments to mortgage some part of this revenue, or to contract debts, and what have been the effects of those debts upon the real wealth, the annual produce of the land and labour of the society. The following book, therefore, will naturally be divided into three chapters.

BOOK V

Of the Revenue of the Sovereign or Commonwealth

CHAPTER I

Of the Expences of the Sovereign or Commonwealth

PART I

Of the Expence of Defence

THE first duty of the sovereign, that of protecting the society from the violence and invasion of other independent societies, can be performed only by means of a military force. But the expence both of preparing this military force in time of peace, and of employing it in time of war, is very different in the different states of society, in the different periods of improvement.

Among nations of hunters, the lowest and rudest state of society, such as we find it among the native tribes of North America, every man is a warrior as well as a hunter. When he goes to war, either to defend his society, or to revenge the injuries which have been done to it by other societies, he maintains himself by his own labour, in the same manner as when he lives at home. His society, for in this state of things there is properly neither sovereign nor commonwealth, is at no sort of expence, either to prepare him for the field, or to maintain him while he is in it.

* * * * * * * * * *

When a civilized nation depends for its defence upon a militia, it is at all times exposed to be conquered by any barbarous nation which happens to be in its neighbourhood. The frequent conquests of all the civilized countries in Asia by the Tartars, sufficiently demonstrates the natural superiority, which the militia of a barbarous, has over that of a civilized nation. A well-regulated standing army is superior to every militia. Such an army, as it can best be maintained by an opulent and civilized nation, so it can alone defend such a nation against the invasion of a poor and barbarous neighbour. It is only by means of a standing army, therefore, that the civilization of any country can be perpetuated, or even preserved for any considerable time.

As it is only by means of a well-regulated standing army that a civilized country can be defended; so it is only by means of it, that a barbarous country can be suddenly and tolerably civilized. A standing army establishes, with an irresistible force, the law of the sovereign through the remotest provinces of the empire, and maintains some degree of regular government in countries which could not otherwise admit of any. Whoever examines, with attention, the improvements which Peter the Great introduced into the Russian empire, will find that they almost all resolve themselves into the establishment of a well-regulated standing army. It is the instrument which executes and maintains all his other regulations. That degree of order and internal peace, which that empire has ever since enjoyed, is altogether owing to the influence of that army.

Men of republican principles have been jealous of a standing army as dangerous to liberty. It certainly is so, wherever the interest of the general and that of the principal officers are not necessarily connected with the support of the constitution of the state. The standing army of Cæsar destroyed the Roman republic. The standing army of Cromwel turned the long parliament out of doors. But where the sovereign is himself the general, and the principal nobility and gentry of the country the chief officers of the army; where the military force is placed under the command of those who have the greatest interest in the support of the civil authority, because they have themselves the greatest share of that authority, a standing army can never be dangerous to liberty. On the contrary, it may in some cases be favourable to liberty. The security which it gives to the sovereign renders unnecessary that troublessome jealousy, which, in some modern republics, seems to watch over the minutest actions, and to be at all times ready to disturb the peace of every citizen. Where the security of the magistrate, though supported by the principal people of the country, is endangered by every popular discontent; where a small tumult is capable of bringing about in a few hours a great revolution, the whole authority of government must be employed to suppress and punish every murmur and complaint against it. To a sovereign, on the contrary, who feels himself supported, not only by the natural aristocracy of the country, but by a well-regulated standing army, the rudest, the most groundless, and the most licentious remonstrances can give little disturbance. He can safely pardon or neglect them, and his consciousness of his own superiority naturally disposes him to do so. That degree of liberty which approaches to licentiousness can be tolerated only in countries where the sovereign is secured by a well-regulated standing army. It is in such countries only, that the public safety does not require, that the sovereign should be trusted with any discretionary power, for suppressing even the impertinent wantonness of this licentious liberty.

The first duty of the sovereign, therefore, that of defending the society from the violence and injustice of other independent societies, grows gradually more and more expensive, as the society advances in civilization. The military force of the society, which originally cost the sovereign no expence either in time of peace or in time of war, must, in the progress of improvement, first be maintained by him in time of war, and afterwards even in time of peace.

The great change introduced into the art of war by the invention of fire-arms, has enhanced still further both the expence of exercising and disciplining any particular number of soldiers in time of peace, and that of employing them in time of war. Both their arms and their ammunition are become more expensive. A musquet is a more expensive machine that a javelin or a bow and arrows; a cannon or a mortar than a balista or a catapulta. The powder, which is spent in a modern review, is lost irrevocably, and occasions a very considerable expence. The javelins and arrows which were thrown or shot in an ancient one, could easily be picked up again, and were besides of very little value. The cannon and the mortar are, not only much dearer, but much heavier machines than the balista or catapulta, and require a greater expence, not only to prepare them for the field, but to carry them to it. As the superiority of the modern artillery too, over that of the ancients is very great; it has become much more difficult, and consequently much more expensive, to fortify a town so as to resist even for a few weeks the attack of that superior artillery. In modern times many different causes contribute to render the defence of the society more expensive. The unavoidable effects of the natural progress of improvement have, in this respect, been a good deal enhanced by a great revolution in the art of war, to which a mere accident, the invention of gunpowder, seems to have given occasion.

In modern war the great expence of fire-arms gives an evident advantage to the nation which can best afford that expence; and consequently, to an opulent and civilized, over a poor and barbarous nation. In ancient times the opulent and civilized found it difficult to defend themselves against the poor and barbarous nations. In modern times the poor and barbarous find it difficult to defend themselves against the opulent and civilized. The invention of fire-arms, an invention which at first sight appears to be so pernicious, is certainly favourable both to the permanency and to the extension of civilization.

PART II

Of the Expence of Justice

The second duty of the sovereign, that of protecting, as far as possible, every member of the society from the injustice or oppression of every other member of it, or the duty of establishing an exact administration of justice requires too very different degrees of expence in the different periods of society.

* * * * * * * * * *

Justice, however, never was in reality administered gratis in any country. Lawyers and attornies, at least, must always be paid by the parties; and, if they were not, they would perform their duty still worse than they actually perform it. The fees annually paid to lawyers and attornies amount, in every court, to a much greater sum than the salaries of the judges. The circumstance of those salaries being paid by the crown, can no-where much diminish the necessary expence of a law-suit. But it was not so much to diminish the expence, as to prevent the corruption of justice, that the judges were prohibited from receiving any present or fee from the parties.

The office of judge is in itself so very honourable, that men are willing to accept of it, though accompanied with very small emoluments. The inferior office of justice of peace, though attended with a good deal of trouble, and in most cases with no emoluments at all, is an object of ambition to the greater part of our country gentlemen. The salaries of all the different judges, high and low, together with the whole expence of the administration and execution of justice, even where it is not managed with very good œconomy, makes, in any civilized country, but a very inconsiderable part of the whole expence of government.

The whole expence of justice too might easily be defrayed by the fees of court; and, without exposing the administration of justice to any real hazard of corruption, the public revenue might thus be entirely discharged from a certain, though, perhaps, but a small incumbrance. It is difficult to regulate the fees of court effectually, where a person so powerful as the sovereign is to share in them, and to derive any considerable part of his revenue from them. It is very easy, where the judge is the principal person who can reap any benefit from them. The law can very easily oblige the judge to respect the regulation, though it might not always be able to make the sovereign respect it. Where the fees of court are precisely regulated and ascertained, where they are paid all at once, at a certain period of every process, into the hands of a cashier or receiver, to be by him distributed in certain known proportions among the different judges after the process is decided, and not till it is decided, there seems to be no more danger of corruption than where such fees are prohibited altogether. Those fees, without occasioning any considerable increase in the expence of a law-suit, might be rendered fully sufficient for defraying the whole expence of justice. By not being paid to the judges till the process was determined, they might be some incitement to the diligence of the court in examining and deciding it. In courts which consisted of a considerable number of judges, by proportioning the share of each judge to the number of hours and days which he had employed in examining the process, either in the court or in a committee by order of the court, those fees might give some encouragement to the diligence of each particular judge. Public services are never better performed than when their reward comes only in consequence of their being performed, and is proportioned to the diligence employed in performing them. . . .

A stamp-duty upon the law proceedings of each particular court, to be levied by that court, and applied towards the maintenance of the judges and other officers belonging to it, might, in the same manner, afford a revenue sufficient for defraying the expence of the administration of justice, without bringing any burden upon the general revenue of the society. The judges indeed might, in this case, be under the temptation of multiplying unnecessarily the proceedings upon every cause, in order to increase, as much as possible, the produce of such a stamp-duty. It has been the custom in modern Europe to regulate, upon most occasions, the payment of the attornies and clerks of court, according to the number of pages which they had occasion to write; the court, however, requiring that each page should contain so many lines, and each line so many words. In order to increase their payment, the attornies and clerks have contrived to multiply words beyond all necessity, to the corruption of the law language of, I believe, every court of justice in Europe. A like temptation might perhaps occasion a like corruption in the form of law proceedings.

PART III

Of the Expence of Public Works and Public Institutions

The third and last duty of the sovereign or commonwealth is that of erecting and maintaining those public institutions and those public works, which, though they may be in the highest degree advantageous to a great society, are, however, of such a nature, that the profit could never repay the expence to any individual or small number of individuals, and which it therefore cannot be expected that any individual or small number of individuals should erect or maintain. The performance of this duty requires too very different degrees of expence in the different periods of society.

After the public institutions and public works necessary for the defence of the society, and for the administration of justice, both of which have already been mentioned, the other works and institutions of this kind are chiefly those for facilitating the commerce of the society, and those for promoting the instruction of the people. The institutions for instruction are of two kinds; those for the education of the youth, and those for the instruction of people of all ages. The consideration of the manner in which the expence of those different sorts of public works and institutions may be most properly defrayed, will divide this third part of the present chapter into three different articles.

ARTICLE I

Of the Public Works and Institutions for Facilitating the Commerce of the Society

And, First, of Those Which are Necessary for Facilitating Commerce in General

That the erection and maintenance of the public works which facilitate the commerce of any country, such as good roads, bridges, navigable canals, harbours, &c. must require very different degrees of expence in the different periods of society, is evident without any proof. The expence of making and maintaining the public roads of any country must evidently increase with the annual produce of the land and labour of that country, or with the quantity and weight of the goods which it becomes necessary to fetch and carry upon those roads. The strength of a bridge must be suited to the number and weight of the carriages which are likely to pass over it. The depth and the supply of water for a navigable canal must be proportioned to the number and tunnage of the lighters, which are likely to carry goods upon it; the extent of a harbour to the number of the shipping which are likely to take shelter in it.

It does not seem necessary that the expence of those public works should be defrayed from that public revenue, as it is commonly called, of which the collection and application are in most countries assigned to the executive power. The greater part of such public works may easily be so managed, as to afford a particular revenue sufficient for defraying their own expence, without bringing any burden upon the general revenue of the society.

A highway, a bridge, a navigable canal, for example, may in most cases be both made and maintained by a small toll upon the carriages which make use of them: a harbour, by a moderate port-duty upon the tunnage of the shipping which load or unload in it. The coinage, another institution for facilitating commerce, in many countries, not only defrays its own expence, but affords a small revenue or seignorage to the sovereign. The post-office, another institution for the same purpose, over and above defraying its own expence, affords in almost all countries a very considerable revenue to the sovereign.

When the carriages which pass over a highway or a bridge, and the lighters which sail upon a navigable canal, pay toll in proportion to their weight or their tunnage, they pay for the maintenance of those public works exactly in proportion to the wear and tear which they occasion of them. It seems scarce possible to invent a more equitable way of maintaining such works. This tax or toll too, though it is advanced by the carrier, is finally paid by the consumer, to whom it must always be charged in the price of the goods. As the expence of carriage, however, is very much reduced by means of such public works, the goods, notwithstanding the toll, come cheaper to the consumer than they could otherwise have done; their price not being so much raised by the toll, as it is lowered by the cheapness of the carriage. The person who finally pays this tax, therefore, gains by the application, more than he loses by the payment of it. His payment is exactly in proportion to his gain. It is in reality no more than a part of that gain which he is obliged to give up in order to get the rest. It seems impossible to imagine a more equitable method of raising a tax.

When the toll upon carriages of luxury, upon coaches, post-chaises, &c. is made somewhat higher in proportion to their weight, than upon carriages of necessary use, such as carts, waggons, &c. the indolence and vanity of the rich is made to contribute in a very easy manner to the relief of the poor, by rendering cheaper the transportation of heavy goods to all the different parts of the country.

When high roads, bridges, canals, &c. are in this manner made and supported by the commerce which is carried on by means of them, they can be made only where that commerce requires them, and consequently where it is proper to make them. Their expence too, their grandeur and magnificence, must be suited to what that commerce can afford to pay. They must be made consequently as it is proper to make them. A magnificent high road cannot be made through a desart country where there is little or no commerce, or merely because it happens to lead to the country villa of the intendant of the province, or to that of some great lord to whom the intendant finds it convenient to make his court. A great bridge cannot be thrown over a river at a place where nobody passes, or merely to embellish the view from the windows of a neighbouring palace: things which sometimes happen, in countries where works of this kind are carried on by any other revenue than that which they themselves are capable of affording.

In several different parts of Europe the toll or lock-duty upon a canal is the property of private persons, whose private interest obliges them to keep up the canal. If it is not kept in tolerable order, the navigation necessarily ceases altogether, and along with it the whole profit which they can make by the tolls. If those tolls were put under the management of commissioners, who had themselves no interest in them, they might be less attentive to the maintenance of the works which produced them. The canal of Languedoc cost the king of France and the province upwards of thirteen millions of livres, which (at twenty-eight livres the mark of silver, the value of French money in the end of the last century) amounted to upwards of nine hundred thousand pounds sterling. When that great work was finished, the most likely method, it was found, of keeping it in constant repair was to make a present of the tolls to Riquet the engineer, who planned and conducted the work. Those tolls constitute at present a very large estate to the different branches of the family of that gentleman, who have, therefore, a great interest to keep the work in constant repair. But had those tolls been put under the management of commissioners, who had no such interest, they might perhaps have been dissipated in ornamental and unnecessary expences, while the most essential parts of the work were allowed to go to ruin.

The tolls for the maintenance of a high road, cannot with any safety be made the property of private persons. A high road, though entirely neglected, does not become altogether impassable, though a canal does. The proprietors of the tolls upon a high road, therefore, might neglect altogether the repair of the road, and yet continue to levy very nearly the same tolls. It is proper, therefore, that the tolls for the maintenance of such work should be put under the management of commissioners or trustees.

* * * * * * * * * *

Even those public works which are of such a nature that they cannot afford any revenue for maintaining themselves, but of which the conveniency is nearly confined to some particular place or district, are always better maintained by a local or provincial revenue, under the management of a local and provincial administration, than by the general revenue of the state, of which the executive power must always have the management. Were the streets of London to be lighted and paved at the expense of the treasury, is there any probability that they would be so well lighted and paved as they are at present, or even at so small an expence? The expence, besides, instead of being raised by a local tax upon the inhabitants of each particular street, parish, or district in London, would, in this case, be defrayed out of the general revenue of the state, and would consequently be raised by a tax upon all the inhabitants of the kingdom, of whom the greater part derive no sort of benefit from the lighting and paving of the streets of London.

The abuses which sometimes creep into the local and provincial administration of a local and provincial revenue, how enormous soever they may appear, are in reality, however, almost always very trifling, in comparison of those which commonly take place in the administration and expenditure of the revenue of a great empire. They are, besides, much more easily corrected. Under the local or provincial administration of the justices of the peace in Great Britain, the six days labour which the country people are obliged to give to the reparation of the highways, is not always perhaps very judiciously applied, but it is scarce ever exacted with any circumstance of cruelty or oppression. In France, under the administration of the intendants, the application is not always more judicious, and the exaction is frequently the most cruel and oppressive. Such Corvées, as they are called, make one of the principal instruments of tyranny by which those officers chastise any parish or communeauté which has had the misfortune to fall under their displeasure.

OF THE PUBLIC WORKS AND INSTITUTIONS WHICH ARE NECESSARY FOR FACILITATING PARTICULAR BRANCHES OF COMMERCE

The object of the public works and institutions above mentioned is to facilitate commerce in general. But in order to facilitate some particular branches of it, particular institutions are necessary, which again require a particular and extraordinary expence.

Some particular branches of commerce, which are carried on with barbarous and uncivilized nations, require extraordinary protection. An ordinary store or counting-house could give little security to the goods of the merchants who trade to the western coast of Africa. To defend them from the barbarous natives, it is necessary that the place where they are deposited, should be, in some measure, fortified. The disorders in the government of Indostan have been supposed to render a like precaution necessary even among that mild and gentle people; and it was under pretence of securing their persons and property from violence, that both the English and French East India Companies were allowed to erect the first forts which they possessed in that country. Among other nations, whose vigorous government will suffer no strangers to possess any fortified place within their territory, it may be necessary to maintain some ambassador, minister, or consul, who may both decide, according to their own customs, the differences arising among his own countrymen; and, in their disputes with the natives, may, by means of his public character, interfere with more authority, and afford them a more powerful protection, than they could expect from any private man. The interests of commerce have frequently made it necessary to maintain ministers in foreign countries, where the purposes, either of war or alliance, would not have required any. The commerce of the Turkey Company first occasioned the establishment of an ordinary ambassador at Constantinople. The first English embassies to Russia arose altogether from commercial interests. The constant interference, which those interests necessarily occasioned between the subjects of the different states of Europe, has probably introduced the custom of keeping, in all neighbouring countries, ambassadors or ministers constantly resident even in the time of peace. This custom, unknown to ancient times, seems not to be older than the end of the fifteenth or beginning of the sixteenth century; that is, than the time when commerce first began to extend itself to the greater part of the nations of Europe, and when they first began to attend to its interests.

It seems not unreasonable, that the extraordinary expence, which the protection of any particular branch of commerce may occasion, should be defrayed by a moderate tax upon that particular branch; by a moderate fine, for example, to be paid by the traders when they first enter into it, or, what is more equal, by a particular duty of so much per cent. upon the goods which they either import into, or export out of, the particular countries with which it is carried on. The protection of trade in general, from pirates and free-booters, is said to have given occasion to the first institution of the duties of customs. But, if it was thought reasonable to lay a general tax upon trade, in order to defray the expence of protecting trade in general, it should seem equally reasonable to lay a particular tax upon a particular branch of trade, in order to defray the extraordinary expence of protecting that branch.

The protection of trade in general has always been considered as essential to the defence of the commonwealth, and, upon that account, a necessary part of the duty of the executive power. The collection and application of the general duties of customs, therefore, have always been left to that power. But the protection of any particular branch of trade is a part of the general protection of trade; a part, therefore, of the duty of that power; and if nations always acted consistently, the particular duties levied for the purposes of such particular protection, should always have been left equally to its disposal. But in this respect, as well as in many others, nations have not always acted consistently; and in the greater part of the commercial states of Europe, particular companies of merchants have had the address to persuade the legislature to entrust to them the performance of this part of the duty of the sovereign, together with all the powers which are necessarily connected with it.

These companies, though they may, perhaps, have been useful for the first introduction of some branches of commerce, by making, at their own expence, an experiment which the state might not think it prudent to make, have in the long-run proved, universally, either burdensome or useless, and have either mismanaged or confined the trade.

When those companies do not trade upon a joint stock, but are obliged to admit any person, properly qualified, upon paying a certain fine, and agreeing to submit to the regulations of the company, each member trading upon his own stock, and at his own risk, they are called regulated companies. When they trade upon a joint stock, each member sharing in the common profit or loss in proportion to his share in this stock, they are called joint stock companies. Such companies, whether regulated or joint stock, sometimes have, and sometimes have not, exclusive privileges.

* * * * * * * * * *

When a company of merchants undertake, at their own risk and expence, to establish a new trade with some remote and barbarous nation, it may not be unreasonable to incorporate them into a joint stock company, and to grant them, in case of their success, a monopoly of the trade for a certain number of years. It is the easiest and most natural way in which the state can recompense them for hazarding a dangerous and expensive experiment, of which the public is afterwards to reap the benefit. A temporary monopoly of this kind may be vindicated upon the same principles upon which a like monopoly of a new machine is granted to its inventor, and that of a new book to its author. But upon the expiration of the term, the monopoly ought certainly to determine; the forts and garrisons, if it was found necessary to establish any, to be taken into the hands of government, their value to be paid to the company, and the trade to be laid open to all the subjects of the state. By a perpetual monopoly, all the other subjects of the state are taxed very absurdly in two different ways; first, by the high price of goods, which, in the case of a free-trade, they could buy much cheaper; and, secondly, by their total exclusion from a branch of business, which it might be both convenient and profitable for many of them to carry on. It is for the most worthless of all purposes too that they are taxed in this manner. It is merely to enable the company to support the negligence, profusion, and malversation of their own servants, whose disorderly conduct seldom allows the dividend of the company to exceed the ordinary rate of profit in trades which are altogether free, and very frequently makes it fall even a good deal short of that rate. Without a monopoly, however, a joint stock company, it would appear from experience, cannot long carry on any branch of foreign trade. To buy in one market, in order to sell, with profit, in another, when there are many competitors in both; to watch over, not only the occasional variations in the demand, but the much greater and more frequent variations in the competition, or in the supply which that demand is likely to get from other people, and to suit with dexterity and judgment both the quantity and quality of each assortment of goods to all these circumstances, is a species of warfare of which the operations are continually changing, and which can scarce ever be conducted successfully, without such an unremitting exertion of vigilance and attention, as cannot long be expected from the directors of a joint stock company. The East India Company, upon the redemption of their funds, and the expiration of their exclusive privilege, have a right, by act of parliament, to continue a corporation with a joint stock, and to trade in their corporate capacity to the East Indies in common with the rest of their fellow-subjects. But in this situation, the superior vigilance and attention of private adventurers would, in all probability, soon make them weary of the trade.

An eminent French author, of great knowledge in matters of political œconomy, the Abbé Morellet, gives a list of fifty-five joint stock companies for foreign trade, which have been established in different parts of Europe since the year 1600, and which, according to him, have all failed from mismanagement, notwithstanding they had exclusive privileges. He has been misinformed with regard to the history of two or three of them, which were not joint stock companies and have not failed. But, in compensation, there have been several joint stock companies which have failed, and which he has omitted.

The only trades which it seems possible for a joint stock company to carry on successfully, without an exclusive privilege, are those, of which all the operations are capable of being reduced to what is called a routine, or to such a uniformity of method as admits of little or no variation. Of this kind is, first, the banking trade; secondly, the trade of insurance from fire, and from sea risk and capture in time of war; thirdly, the trade of making and maintaining a navigable cut or canal; and, fourthly, the similar trade of bringing water for the supply of a great city.

Though the principles of the banking trade may appear somewhat abstruse, the practice is capable of being reduced to strict rules. To depart upon any occasion from those rules, in consequence of some flattering speculation of extraordinary gain, is almost always extremely dangerous, and frequently fatal to the banking company which attempts it. But the constitution of joint stock companies renders them in general more tenacious of established rules than any private copartnery. Such companies, therefore, seem extremely well fitted for this trade. The principal banking companies in Europe, accordingly, are joint stock companies, many of which manage their trade very successfully without any exclusive privilege. The Bank of England has no other exclusive privilege, except that no other banking company in England shall consist of more than six persons. The two banks of Edinburgh are joint stock companies without any exclusive privilege.

The value of the risk, either from fire, or from loss by sea, or by capture, though it cannot, perhaps, be calculated very exactly, admits, however, of such a gross estimation as renders it, in some degree, reducible to strict rule and method. The trade of insurance, therefore, may be carried on successfully by a joint stock company, without any exclusive privilege. Neither the London Assurance, nor the Royal Exchange Assurance companies, have any such privilege.

When a navigable cut or canal has been once made, the management of it becomes quite simple and easy, and is reducible to strict rule and method. Even the making of it is so, as it may be contracted for with undertakers at so much a mile, and so much a lock. The same thing may be said of a canal, an aqueduct, or a great pipe for bringing water to supply a great city. Such undertakings, therefore, may be, and accordingly frequently are, very successfully managed by joint stock companies without any exclusive privilege.

To establish a joint stock company, however, for any undertaking, merely because such a company might be capable of managing it successfully; or to exempt a particular set of dealers from some of the general laws which take place with regard to all their neighbours, merely because they might be capable of thriving if they had such an exemption, would certainly not be reasonable. To render such an establishment perfectly reasonable, with the circumstance of being reducible to strict rule and method, two other circumstances ought to concur. First, it ought to appear with the clearest evidence, that the undertaking is of greater and more general utility than the greater part of common trades; and secondly, that it requires a greater capital than can easily be collected into a private copartnery. If a moderate capital were sufficient, the great utility of the undertaking would not be a sufficient reason for establishing a joint stock company; because, in this case, the demand for what it was to produce, would readily and easily be supplied by private adventurers. In the four trades above mentioned, both those circumstances concur.

The great and general utility of the banking trade when prudently managed, has been fully explained in the second book of this inquiry. But a public bank which is to support public credit, and upon particular emergencies to advance to government the whole produce of a tax, to the amount, perhaps, of several millions, a year or two before it comes in, requires a greater capital than can easily be collected into any private copartnery.

The trade of insurance gives great security to the fortunes of private people, and by dividing among a great many that loss which would ruin an individual, makes it fall light and easy upon the whole society. In order to give this security, however, it is necessary that the insurers should have a very large capital. Before the establishment of the two joint stock companies for insurance in London, a list, it is said, was laid before the attorney-general, of one hundred and fifty private insurers who had failed in the course of a few years.

That navigable cuts and canals, and the works which are sometimes necessary for supplying a great city with water, are of great and general utility; while at the same time they frequently require a greater expence than suits the fortunes of private people, is sufficiently obvious.

Except the four trades above mentioned, I have not been able to recollect any other in which all the three circumstances, requisite for rendering reasonable the establishment of a joint stock company, concur. The English copper company of London, the lead smelting company, the glass grinding company, have not even the pretext of any great or singular utility in the object which they pursue; nor does the pursuit of that object seem to require any expence unsuitable to the fortunes of many private men. Whether the trade which those companies carry on, is reducible to such strict rule and method as to render it fit for the management of a joint stock company, or whether they have any reason to boast of their extraordinary profits, I do not pretend to know. The mine-adventurers company has been long ago bankrupt. A share in the stock of the British Linen Company of Edinburgh sells, at present, very much below par, though less so than it did some years ago. The joint stock companies, which are established for the public-spirited purpose of promoting some particular manufacture, over and above managing their own affairs ill, to the diminution of the general stock of the society, can in other respects scarce ever fail to do more harm than good. Notwithstanding the most upright intentions, the unavoidable partiality of their directors to particular branches of the manufacture, of which the undertakers mislead and impose upon them, is a real discouragement to the rest, and necessarily breaks, more or less, that natural proportion which would otherwise establish itself between judicious industry and profit, and which, to the general industry of the country, is of all encouragements the greatest and the most effectual.

ARTICLE II

Of the Expence of the Institutions for the Education of Youth

The institutions for the education of the youth may, in the same manner, furnish a revenue sufficient for defraying their own expence. The fee or honorary which the scholar pays to the master naturally constitutes a revenue of this kind.

Even where the reward of the master does not arise altogether from this natural revenue, it still is not necessary that it should be derived from that general revenue of the society, of which the collection and application are, in most countries, assigned to the executive power. Through the greater part of Europe, accordingly, the endowment of schools and colleges makes either no charge upon that general revenue, or but a very small one. It every where arises chiefly from some local or provincial revenue, from the rent of some landed estate, or from the interest of some sum of money allotted and put under the management of trustees for this particular purpose, sometimes by the sovereign himself, and sometimes by some private donor.

ARTICLE III

Of the Expence of the Institutions for the Instruction of People of all Ages

The institutions for the instruction of people of all ages are chiefly those for religious instruction. This is a species of instruction of which the object is not so much to render the people good citizens in this world, as to prepare them for another and a better world in a life to come. The teachers of the doctrine which contains this instruction, in the same manner as other teachers, may either depend altogether for their subsistence upon the voluntary contributions of their hearers; or they may derive it from some other fund to which the law of their country may entitle them; such as a landed estate, a tythe or land tax, an established salary or stipend. Their exertion, their zeal and industry, are likely to be much greater in the former situation than in the latter. In this respect the teachers of new religions have always had a considerable advantage in attacking those ancient and established systems of which the clergy, reposing themselves upon their benefices, had neglected to keep up the fervour of faith and devotion in the great body of the people; and having given themselves up to indolence, were become altogether incapable of making any vigorous exertion in defence even of their own establishment.

PART IV

Of the Expence of Supporting the Dignity of the Sovereign

Over and above the expence necessary for enabling the sovereign to perform his several duties, a certain expence is requisite for the support of his dignity. This expence varies both with the different periods of improvement, and with the different forms of government.

In an opulent and improved society, where all the different orders of people are growing every day more expensive in their houses, in their furniture, in their tables, in their dress, and in their equipage; it cannot well be expected that the sovereign should alone hold out against the fashion. He naturally, therefore, or rather necessarily becomes more expensive in all those different articles too. His dignity even seems to require that he should become so.

As in point of dignity, a monarch is more raised above his subjects than the chief magistrate of any republic is ever supposed to be above his fellow-citizens; so a greater expence is necessary for supporting that higher dignity. We naturally expect more splendor in the court of a king, than in the mansion-house of a doge or burgo-master.

CONCLUSION

THE expence of defending the society, and that of supporting the dignity of the chief magistrate, are both laid out for the general benefit of the whole society. It is reasonable, therefore, that they should be defrayed by the general contribution of the whole society, all the different members contributing, as nearly as possible, in proportion to their respective abilities.

The expence of the administration of justice too, may, no doubt, be considered as laid out for the benefit of the whole society. There is no impropriety, therefore, in its being defrayed by the general contribution of the whole society. The persons, however, who give occasion to this expence are those who, by their injustice in one way or another, make it necessary to seek redress or protection from the courts of justice. The persons again most immediately benefited by this expence, are those whom the courts of justice either restore to their rights, or maintain in their rights. The expence of the administration of justice, therefore, may very properly be defrayed by the particular contribution of one or other, or both of those two different sets of persons, according as different occasions may require, that is, by the fees of court. It cannot be necessary to have recourse to the general contribution of the whole society, except for the conviction of those criminals who have not themselves any estate or fund sufficient for paying those fees.

Those local or provincial expences of which the benefit is

local or provincial (what is laid out, for example, upon the police of a particular town or district) ought to be defrayed by a local or provincial revenue, and ought to be no burden upon the general revenue of the society. It is unjust that the whole society should contribute towards an expence of which the benefit is confined to a part of the society.

The expence of maintaining good roads and communications is, no doubt, beneficial to the whole society, and may, therefore, without any injustice, be defrayed by the general contribution of the whole society. This expence, however, is most immediately and directly beneficial to those who travel or carry goods from one place to another, and to those who consume such goods. The turnpike tolls in England, and the duties called peages in other countries, lay it altogether upon those two different sets of people, and thereby discharge the general revenue of the society from a very considerable burden.

The expence of the institutions for education and religious instruction, is likewise, no doubt, beneficial to the whole society, and may, therefore, without injustice, be defrayed by the general contribution of the whole society. This expence, however, might perhaps with equal propriety, and even with some advantage, be defrayed altogether by those who receive the immediate benefit of such education and instruction, or by the voluntary contribution of those who think they have occasion for either the one or the other.

When the institutions or public works which are beneficial to the whole society, either cannot be maintained altogether, or are not maintained altogether by the contribution of such particular members of the society as are most immediately benefited by them, the deficiency must in most cases be made up by the general contribution of the whole society. The general revenue of the society, over and above defraying the expence of defending the society, and of supporting the dignity of the chief magistrate, must make up for the deficiency of many particular branches of revenue. The sources of this general or public revenue, I shall endeavour to explain in the following chapter.

CHAPTER II

Of the Sources of the General or Public Revenue of the Society

THE revenue which must defray, not only the expence of defending the society and of supporting the dignity of the chief magistrate, but all the other necessary expences of government, for which the constitution of the state has not provided any particular revenue, may be drawn, either, first, from some fund which peculiarly belongs to the sovereign or commonwealth, and which is independent of the revenue of the people; or, secondly, from the revenue of the people.

PART I

Of the Funds or Sources of Revenue Which May Peculiarly Belong to the Sovereign or Commonwealth

THE funds or sources of revenue which may peculiarly belong to the sovereign or commonwealth must consist, either in stock, or in land.

The sovereign, like any other owner of stock, may derive a revenue from it, either by employing it himself, or by lending it. His revenue is in the one case profit, in the other interest.

The revenue of a Tartar or Arabian chief consists in profit. It arises principally from the milk and increase of his own herds and flocks, of which he himself superintends the management, and is the principal shepherd or herdsman of his own horde or tribe. It is, however, in this earliest and rudest state of civil government only that profit has ever made the principal part of the public revenue of a monarchical state.

Small republics have sometimes derived a considerable

revenue from the profit of mercantile projects. The republic of Hamburgh is said to do so from the profits of a public wine cellar and apothecary's shop. The state cannot be very great of which the sovereign has leisure to carry on the trade of a wine merchant or apothecary. The profit of a public bank has been a source of revenue to more considerable states. It has been so not only to Hamburgh, but to Venice and Amsterdam. A revenue of this kind has even by some people been thought not below the attention of so great an empire as that of Great Britain. Reckoning the ordinary dividend of the bank of England at five and a half per cent., and its capital at ten millions seven hundred and eighty thousand pounds, the neat annual profit, after paying the expence of management, must amount, it is said, to five hundred and ninety-two thousand nine hundred pounds. Government, it is pretended, could borrow this capital at three per cent. interest, and by taking the management of the bank into its own hands, might make a clear profit of two hundred and sixty-nine thousand five hundred pounds a year. The orderly, vigilant, and parsimonious administration of such aristocracies as those of Venice and Amsterdam, is extremely proper, it appears from experience, for the management of a mercantile project of this kind. But whether such a government as that of England; which, whatever may be its virtues, has never been famous for good œconomy; which, in time of peace, has generally conducted itself with the slothful and negligent profusion that is perhaps natural to monarchies; and in time of war has constantly acted with all the thoughtless extravagance that democracies are apt to fall into; could be safely trusted with the management of such a project, must at least be a good deal more doubtful.

The post office is properly a mercantile project. The government advances the expence of establishing the different offices, and of buying or hiring the necessary horses or carriages, and is repaid with a large profit by the duties upon what is carried. It is perhaps the only mercantile project which has been successfully managed by, I believe, every sort of government. The capital to be advanced is not very considerable. There is no mystery in the business. The returns are not only certain, but immediate.

Princes, however, have frequently engaged in many other mercantile projects, and have been willing, like private persons, to mend their fortunes by becoming adventurers in the common branches of trade. They have scarce ever succeeded. The profusion with which the affairs of princes are always managed, renders it almost impossible that they should. The agents of a prince regard the wealth of their master as inexhaustible; are careless at what price they buy; are careless at what price they sell; are careless at what expence they transport his goods from one place to another. Those agents frequently live with the profusion of princes, and sometimes too, in spite of that profusion, and by a proper method of making up their accounts, acquire the fortunes of princes. It was thus, as we are told by Machiavel, that the agents of Lorenzo of Medicis, not a prince of mean abilities, carried on his trade. The republic of Florence was several times obliged to pay the debt into which their extravagance had involved him. He found it convenient, accordingly, to give up the business of merchant, the business to which his family had originally owed their fortune, and in the latter part of his life to employ both what remained of that fortune, and the revenue of the state of which he had the disposal, in projects and expences more suitable to his station.

No two characters seem more inconsistent than those of trader and sovereign. If the trading spirit of the English East India company renders them very bad sovereigns; the spirit of sovereignty seems to have rendered them equally bad traders. While they were traders only, they managed their trade successfully, and were able to pay from their profits a moderate dividend to the proprietors of their stock. Since they became sovereigns, with a revenue which, it is said, was originally more than three millions sterling, they have been obliged to beg the extraordinary assistance of government in order to avoid immediate bankruptcy. In their former situation, their servants in India considered themselves as the clerks of merchants: in their present situation, those servants consider themselves as the ministers of sovereigns.

A state may sometimes derive some part of its public revenue from the interest of money, as well as from the profits of stock. If it has amassed a treasure, it may lend a part of that treasure, either to foreign states, or to its own subjects. The canton of Berne derives a considerable revenue by lending a part of its treasure to foreign states; that is, by placing it in the public funds of the different indebted nations of Europe, chiefly in those of France and England. The security of this revenue must depend, first, upon the security of the funds in which it is placed, or upon the good faith of the government which has the management of them; and, secondly, upon the certainty or probability of the continuance of peace with the debtor nation. In the case of a war, the very first act of hostility, on the part of the debtor nation, might be the forfeiture of the funds of its creditor. This policy of lending money to foreign states is, so far as I know, peculiar to the canton of Berne.

The city of Hamburgh has established a sort of public pawn-shop, which lends money to the subjects of the state upon pledges at six per cent. interest. This pawn-shop or Lombard, as it is called, affords a revenue, it is pretended, to the state of a hundred and fifty thousand crowns, which, at four-and-sixpence the crown, amounts to 33,750*l* sterling.

The government of Pensylvania, without amassing any treasure, invented a method of lending, not money indeed, but what is equivalent to money, to its subjects. By advancing to private people, at interest, and upon land security to double the value, paper bills of credit to be redeemed fifteen years after their date, and in the mean time made transferrable from hand to hand like bank notes, and declared by act of assembly to be a legal tender in all payments from one inhabitant of the province to another, it raised a moderate revenue, which went a considerable way towards defraying an annual expence of about 4,500*l*. the whole ordinary expence of that frugal and orderly government. The success of an expedient of this kind must have depended upon three different circumstances; first, upon the demand for some other instrument of commerce, besides gold and silver money; or upon the demand for such a quantity of consumable stock, as could not be had without sending abroad the greater part of their gold and silver money, in order to purchase it; secondly, upon the good credit of the government which made use of this expedient; and, thirdly, upon the moderation with which it was used, the whole value of the paper bills of credit never exceeding that of the gold and silver money which would have been necessary for carrying on their circulation, had there been no paper bills of credit. The same expedient was upon different occasions adopted by several other American colonies: but, from want of this moderation, it produced, in the greater part of them, much more disorder than conveniency.

The unstable and perishable nature of stock and credit, however, render them unfit to be trusted to, as the principal funds of that sure, steady and permanent revenue, which can alone give security and dignity to government. The government of no great nation, that was advanced beyond the shepherd state, seems ever to have derived the greater part of its public revenue from such sources.

Land is a fund of a more stable and permanent nature: and the rent of public lands, accordingly, has been the principal source of the public revenue of many a great nation that was much advanced beyond the shepherd state. From the produce or rent of the public lands, the ancient republics of Greece and Italy derived, for a long time, the greater part of that revenue which defrayed the necessary expences of the commonwealth. The rent of the crown lands constituted for a long time the greater part of the revenue of the ancient sovereigns of Europe.

War and the preparation for war, are the two circumstances which in modern times occasion the greater part of the necessary expence of all great states. But in the ancient republics of Greece and Italy every citizen was a soldier, who both served and prepared himself for service at his own expence. Neither of those two circumstances, therefore, could occasion any very considerable expence to the state. The rent of a very moderate landed estate might be fully sufficient for defraying all the other necessary expences of government.

In the ancient monarchies of Europe, the manners and customs of the times sufficiently prepared the great body of the people for war; and when they took the field, they were, by the condition of their feudal tenures, to be maintained, either at their own expence, or at that of their immediate lords, without bringing any new charge upon the sovereign. The other expences of government were, the greater part of them, very moderate. The administration of justice, it has been shown, instead of being a cause of expence, was a source of revenue. The labour of the country people, for three days before and for three days after harvest, was thought a fund sufficient for making and maintaining all the bridges, highways, and other public works which the commerce of the country was supposed to require. In those days the principal expence of the sovereign seems to have consisted in the maintenance of his own family and household. The officers of his household, accordingly, were then the great officers of state. The lord treasurer received his rents. The lord steward and lord chamberlain looked after the expence of his family. The care of his stables was committed to the lord constable and the lord marshal. His houses were all built in the form of castles, and seem to have been the principal fortresses which he possessed. The keepers of those houses or castles might be considered as a sort of military governors. They seem to have been the only military officers whom it was necessary to maintain in time of peace. In these circumstances the rent of a great landed estate might, upon ordinary occasions, very well defray all the necessary expences of government.

In the present state of the greater part of the civilized monarchies of Europe, the rent of all the lands in the country, managed as they probably would be if they all belonged to one proprietor, would scarce perhaps amount to the ordinary revenue which they levy upon the people even in peaceable times. The ordinary revenue of Great Britain, for example, including not only what is necessary for defraying the current expence of the year, but for paying the interest of the public debts, and for sinking a part of the capital of those debts, amounts to upwards of ten millions a year. But the land tax, at four shillings in the pound, falls short of two millions a year. This land tax, as it is called, however, is supposed to be one-fifth, not only of the rent of all the land, but of that of all the houses, and of the interest of all the capital stock of Great Britain, that part of it only excepted which is either lent to the public, or employed as farming stock in the cultivation of land. A very considerable part of the produce of this tax arises from the rent of houses, and the interest of capital stock. The land-tax of the city of London, for example, at four shillings in the pound, amounts to 123,399*l.* 6*s.* 7*d.* That of the city of Westminster, to 63,092*l.* 1*s.* 5*d.* That of the palaces of Whitehall and St. James's, to 30,754*l.* 6*s.* 3*d.* A certain proportion of the land-tax is in the same manner assessed upon all the other cities and towns corporate in the kingdom, and arises almost altogether, either from the rent of houses, or from what is supposed to be the interest of trading and capital stock. According to the estimation, therefore, by which Great Britain is rated to the land-tax, the whole mass of revenue arising from the rent of all the lands, from that of all the houses, and from the interest of all the capital stock, that part of it only excepted which is either lent to the public, or employed in the cultivation of land, does not exceed ten millions sterling a year, the ordinary revenue which government levies upon the people even in peaceable times. The estimation by which Great Britain is rated to the land-tax is, no doubt, taking the whole kingdom at an average, very much below the real value; though in several particular counties and districts it is said to be nearly equal to that value. The rent of the lands alone, exclusive of that of houses, and of the interest of stock, has by many people been estimated at twenty millions, an estimation made in a great measure at random, and which, I apprehend, is as likely to be above as below the truth. But if the lands of Great Britain, in the present state of their cultivation, do not afford a rent of more than twenty millions a year, they could not well afford the half, most probably not the fourth part of that rent, if they all belonged to a single proprietor, and were put under the negligent, expensive, and oppressive management of his factors and agents. The crown lands of Great Britain do not at present afford the fourth part of the rent, which could probably be drawn from them if they were the property of private persons. If the crown lands were more extensive, it is probable they would be still worse managed.

The revenue which the great body of the people derives from land is in proportion, not to the rent, but to the produce of the land. The whole annual produce of the land of every country, if we except what is reserved for seed, is either annually consumed by the great body of the people, or exchanged for something else that is consumed by them. Whatever keeps down the produce of the land below what it would otherwise rise to, keeps down the revenue of the great body of the people, still more than it does that of the proprietors of land. The rent of land, that portion of the produce which belongs to the proprietors, is scarce anywhere in Great Britain supposed to be more than a third part of the whole produce. If the land, which in one state of cultivation affords a rent of ten millions sterling a year, would in another afford a rent of twenty millions; the rent being, in both cases, supposed a third part of the produce; the revenue of the proprietors would be less than it otherwise might be by ten millions a year only; but the revenue of the great body of the people would be less than it otherwise might be by thirty millions a year, deducting only what would be necessary for seed. The population of the country would be less by the number of people which thirty millions a year, deducting always the seed, could maintain, according to the particular mode of living and expence which might take place in the different ranks of men among whom the remainder was distributed.

Though there is not at present, in Europe, any civilized state of any kind which derives the greater part of its public revenue from the rent of lands which are the property of the state; yet, in all the great monarchies of Europe, there are still many large tracts of land which belong to the crown. They are generally forest; and sometimes forest where, after travelling several miles, you will scarce find a single tree; a mere waste and loss of country in respect both of produce and population. In every great monarchy of Europe the sale of the crown lands would produce a very large sum of money, which, if applied to the payment of the public debts, would deliver from mortgage a much greater revenue than any which those lands have ever afforded to the crown. In countries where lands, improved and cultivated very highly, and yielding at the time of sale as great a rent as can easily be got from them, commonly sell at thirty years purchase; the unimproved, uncultivated, and low-rented crown lands might well be expected to sell at forty, fifty, or sixty years purchase. The crown might immediately enjoy the revenue which this great price would redeem from mortgage. In the course of a few years it would probably enjoy another revenue. When the crown lands had become private property, they would, in the course of a few years, become well improved and well cultivated. The increase of their produce would increase the population of the country, by augmenting the revenue and consumption of the people. But the revenue which the crown derives from the duties of customs and excise, would necessarily increase with the revenue and consumption of the people.

The revenue which, in any civilized monarchy, the crown derives from the crown lands, though it appears to cost nothing to individuals, in reality costs more to the society than perhaps any other equal revenue which the crown enjoys. It would, in all cases, be for the interest of the society to replace this revenue to the crown by some other equal revenue, and to divide the lands among the people, which could not well be done better, perhaps, than by exposing them to public sale.

Lands, for the purposes of pleasure and magnificence, parks, gardens, public walks, &c., possessions which are every where considered as causes of expence, not as sources of revenue, seem to be the only lands which, in a great and civilized monarchy, ought to belong to the crown.

Public stock and public lands, therefore, the two sources of revenue which may peculiarly belong to the sovereign or commonwealth, being both improper and insufficient funds for defraying the necessary expence of any great and civilized state; it remains that this expence must, the greater part of it, be defrayed by taxes of one kind or another; the people contributing a part of their own private revenue in order to make up a public revenue to the sovereign or commonwealth.

PART I

Of Taxes

The private revenue of individuals, it has been shewn in the first book of this Inquiry, arises ultimately from three different sources: Rent, Profit, and Wages. Every tax must finally be paid from some one or other of those three different sorts of revenue, or from all of them indifferently. I shall endeavour to give the best account I can, first, of those taxes which, it is intended, should fall upon rent; secondly, of those which, it is intended, should fall upon profit; thirdly, of those which, it is intended, should fall upon wages; and, fourthly, of those which, it is intended, should fall indifferently upon all those three different sources of private revenue. The particular consideration of each of these four different sorts of taxes will divide the second part of the present chapter into four articles, three of which will require several other subdivisions. Many of those taxes, it will appear from the following review, are not finally paid from the fund, or source of revenue, upon which it was intended they should fall.

Before I enter upon the examination of particular taxes, it is necessary to premise the four following maxims with regard to taxes in general.

I. The subjects of every state ought to contribute towards the support of the government, as nearly as possible, in proportion to their respective abilities; that is, in proportion to the revenue which they respectively enjoy under the protection of the state. The expence of government to the individuals of a great nation, is like the expence of management to the joint tenants of a great estate, who are all obliged to contribute in proportion to their respective interests in the estate. In the observation or neglect of this maxim consists, what is called the equality or inequality of taxation. Every tax, it must be observed once for all, which falls finally upon one only of the three sorts of revenue above mentioned, is necessarily unequal, in so far as it does not affect the other two. In the following examination of different taxes I shall seldom take much further notice of this sort of inequality, but shall, in most cases, confine my observations to that inequality which is occasioned by a particular tax falling unequally even upon that particular sort of private revenue which is affected by it.

II. The tax which each individual is bound to pay ought to be certain, and not arbitrary. The time of payment, the manner of payment, the quantity to be paid, ought all to be clear and plain to the contributor, and to every other person. Where it is otherwise, every person subject to the tax is put more or less in the power of the tax-gatherer, who can either aggravate the tax upon any obnoxious contributor, or extort, by the terror of such aggravation, some present or perquisite to himself. The uncertainty of taxation encourages the insolence and favours the corruption of an order of men who are naturally unpopular, even where they are neither insolent nor corrupt. The certainty of what each individual ought to pay is, in taxation, a matter of so great importance, that a very considerable degree of inequality, it appears, I believe, from the experience of all nations, is not near so great an evil as a very small degree of uncertainty.

III. Every tax ought to be levied at the time, or in the manner, in which it is most likely to be convenient for the contributor to pay it. A tax upon the rent of land or of houses, payable at the same term at which such rents are usually paid, is levied at the time when it is most likely to be convenient for the contributor to pay; or, when he is most likely to have wherewithal to pay. Taxes upon such consumable goods as are articles of luxury, are all finally paid by the consumer, and generally in a manner that is very convenient for him. He pays them by little and little, as he has occasion to buy the goods. As he is at liberty too, either to buy, or not to buy, as he pleases, it must be his own fault if he ever suffers any considerable inconveniency from such taxes.

IV. Every tax ought to be so contrived as both to take out and to keep out of the pockets of the people as little as possible, over and above what it brings into the public treasury of the state. A tax may either take out or keep out of the pockets of the people a great deal more than it brings into the public treasury, in the four following ways. First, the levying of it may require a great number of officers, whose salaries may eat up the greater part of the produce of the tax, and whose perquisites may impose another additional tax upon the people. Secondly, it may obstruct the industry of the people, and discourage them from applying to certain branches of business which might give maintenance and employment to great multitudes. While it obliges the people to pay, it may thus diminish, or perhaps destroy, some of the funds which might enable them more easily to do so. Thirdly, by the forfeitures and other penalties which those unfortunate individuals incur who attempt unsuccessfully to evade the tax, it may frequently ruin them, and thereby put an end to the benefit which the community might have received from the employment of their capitals. An injudicious tax offers a great temptation to smuggling. But the penalties of smuggling must rise in proportion to the temptation. The law, contrary to all the ordinary principles of justice, first creates the temptation, and then punishes those who yield to it; and it commonly enhances the punishment too in proportion to the very circumstance which ought certainly to alleviate it, the temptation to commit the crime. Fourthly, by subjecting the people to the frequent visits and the odious examination of the tax-gatherers, it may expose them to much unnecessary trouble, vexation, and oppression; and though vexation is not, strictly speaking, expence, it is certainly equivalent to the expence at which every man would be willing to redeem himself from it. It is in some one or other of these four different ways that taxes are frequently so much more burdensome to the people than they are beneficial to the sovereign.

The evident justice and utility of the foregoing maxims have recommended them more or less to the attention of all nations. All nations have endeavoured, to the best of their judgment, to render their taxes as equal as they could contrive; as certain, as convenient to the contributor, both in the time and in the mode of payment, and in proportion to the revenue which they brought to the prince, as little burdensome to the people. The following short review of some of the principal taxes which have taken place in different ages and countries will show, that the endeavours of all nations have not in this respect been equally successful.

ARTICLE I

Taxes upon Rent. Taxes upon the Rent of Land.

A tax upon the rent of land may either be imposed according to a certain canon, every district being valued at a certain rent, which valuation is not afterwards to be altered; or it may be imposed in such a manner as to vary with every variation in the real rent of the land, and to rise or fall with the improvement or declension of its cultivation.

A land-tax, which, like that of Great Britain, is assessed upon each district according to a certain invariable canon, though it should be equal at the time of its first establishment, necessarily becomes unequal in process of time, according to the unequal degrees of improvement or neglect in the cultivation of the different parts of the country. In England, the valuation according to which the different counties and parishes were assessed to the land-tax by the 4th of William and Mary was very unequal even at its first establishment. This tax, therefore, so far offends against the first of the four maxims above-mentioned. It is perfectly agreeable to the other three. It is perfectly certain. The time of payment for the tax, being the same as that for the rent, is as convenient as it can be to the contributor. Though the landlord is in all cases the real contributor, the tax is commonly advanced by the tenant, to whom the landlord is obliged to allow it in the payment of the rent. This tax is levied by a much smaller number of officers than any other which affords nearly the same revenue. As the tax upon each district does not rise with the rise of the rent, the sovereign does not share in the profits of the landlord's improvements. Those improvements sometimes contribute, indeed, to the discharge of the other landlords of the district. But the aggravation of the tax, which this may sometimes occasion upon a particular estate, is always so very small, that it never can discourage those improvements, nor keep down the produce of the land below what it would otherwise rise to. As it has no tendency to diminish the quantity, it can have none to raise the price of that produce. It does not obstruct the industry of the people. It subjects the landlord to no other inconveniency besides the unavoidable one of paying the tax.

The advantage, however, which the landlord has derived from the invariable constancy of the valuation by which all the lands of Great Britain are rated to the land-tax, has been principally owing to some circumstances altogether extraneous to the nature of the tax.

It has been owing in part to the great prosperity of almost every part of the country, the rents of almost all the estates of Great Britain having, since the time when this valuation was first established, been continually rising, and scarce any of them having fallen. The landlords, therefore, have almost all gained the difference between the tax which they would have paid, according to the present rent of their estates, and that which they actually pay according to the ancient valuation. Had the state of the country been different, had rents been gradually falling in consequence of the declension of cultivation, the landlords would almost all have lost this difference. In the state of things which has happened to take place since the revolution, the constancy of the valuation has been advantageous to the landlord and hurtful to the sovereign. In a different state of things it might have been advantageous to the sovereign and hurtful to the landlord.

As the tax is made payable in money, so the valuation of the land is expressed in money. Since the establishment of this valuation the value of silver has been pretty uniform, and there has been no alteration in the standard of the coin either as to weight or fineness. Had silver risen considerably in its value, as it seems to have done in the course of the two centuries which preceded the discovery of the mines of America, the constancy of the valuation might have proved very oppressive to the landlord. Had silver fallen considerably in its value, as it certainly did for about a century at least after the discovery of those mines, the same constancy of valuation would have reduced very much this branch of the revenue of the sovereign. Had any considerable alteration been made in the standard of the money, either by sinking the same quantity of silver to a lower denomination, or by raising it to a higher; had an ounce of silver, for example, instead of being coined into five shillings and twopence, been coined, either into pieces which bore so low a denomination as two shillings and seven-pence, or into pieces which bore so high a one as ten shillings and four-pence, it would in the one case have hurt the revenue of the proprietor, in the other that of the sovereign.

In circumstances, therefore, somewhat different from those which have actually taken place, this constancy of valuation might have been a very great inconveniency, either to the contributors, or to the commonwealth. In the course of ages such circumstances, however, must, at some time or other, happen. But though empires, like all the other works of men, have all hitherto proved mortal, yet every empire aims at immortality. Every constitution, therefore, which it is meant should be as permanent as the empire itself, ought to be convenient, not in certain circumstances only, but in all circumstances; or ought to be suited, not to those circumstances which are transitory, occasional, or accidental, but to those which are necessary and therefore always the same.

A tax upon the rent of land which varies with every variation of the rent, or which rises and falls according to the improvement or neglect of cultivation, is recommended by that sect of men of letters in France, who call themselves the œconomists, as the most equitable of all taxes. All taxes, they pretend, fall ultimately upon the rent of land, and ought therefore to be imposed equally upon the fund which must finally pay them. That all taxes ought to fall as equally as possible upon the fund which must finally pay them, is certainly true. But without entering into the disagreeable discussion of the metaphysical arguments by which they support their very ingenious theory, it will sufficiently appear, from the following review, what are the taxes which fall finally upon the rent of the land, and what are those which fall finally upon some other fund.

In the Venetian territory all the arable lands which are

given in lease to farmers are taxed at a tenth of the rent. The leases are recorded in a public register which is kept by the officers of revenue in each province or district. When the proprietor cultivates his own lands, they are valued according to an equitable estimation, and he is allowed a deduction of one-fifth of the tax, so that for such lands he pays only eight instead of ten per cent. of the supposed rent.

A land-tax of this kind is certainly more equal than the land-tax of England. It might not, perhaps, be altogether so certain, and the assessment of the tax might frequently occasion a good deal more trouble to the landlord. It might too be a good deal more expensive in the levying.

Such a system of administration, however, might perhaps be contrived as would, in a great measure, both prevent this uncertainty and moderate this expence.

The landlord and tenant, for example, might jointly be obliged to record their lease in a public register. Proper penalties might be enacted against concealing or misrepresenting any of the conditions; and if part of those penalties were to be paid to either of the two parties who informed against and convicted the other of such concealment or misrepresentation, it would effectually deter them from combining together in order to defraud the public revenue. All the conditions of the lease might be sufficiently known from such a record.

Some landlords, instead of raising the rent, take a fine for the renewal of the lease. This practice is in most cases the expedient of a spendthrift, who for a sum of ready money sells a future revenue of much greater value. It is in most cases, therefore, hurtful to the landlord. It is frequently hurtful to the tenant, and it is always hurtful to the community. It frequently takes from the tenant so great a part of his capital, and thereby diminishes so much his ability to cultivate the land, that he finds it more difficult to pay a small rent than it would otherwise have been to pay a great one. Whatever diminishes his ability to cultivate, necessarily keeps down, below what it would otherwise have been, the most important part of the revenue of the community. By rendering the tax upon such fines a good deal heavier than upon the ordinary rent, this hurtful practice might be discouraged, to the no small advantage of all the different parties concerned, of the landlord, of the tenant, of the sovereign, and of the whole community.

Such a system of administration might, perhaps, free a tax of this kind from any degree of uncertainty which could occasion either oppression or inconveniency to the contributor; and might at the same time serve to introduce into the common management of land such a plan or policy, as might contribute a good deal to the general improvement and good cultivation of the country.

The expence of levying a land-tax, which varied with every variation of the rent, would no doubt be somewhat greater than that of levying one which was always rated according to a fixed valuation. Some additional expence would necessarily be incurred both by the different register offices which it would be proper to establish in the different districts of the country, and by the different valuations which might occasionally be made of the lands which the proprietor chose to occupy himself. The expence of all this, however, might be very moderate, and much below what is incurred in the levying of many other taxes, which afford a very inconsiderable revenue in comparison of what might easily be drawn from a tax of this kind.

The discouragement which a variable land-tax of this kind might give to the improvement of land, seems to be the most important objection which can be made to it. The landlord would certainly be less disposed to improve, when the sovereign, who contributed nothing to the expence, was to share in the profit of the improvement. Even this objection might perhaps be obviated by allowing the landlord, before he began his improvement, to ascertain, in conjunction with the officers of revenue, the actual value of his lands, according to the equitable arbitration of a certain number of landlords and farmers in the neighbourhood, equally chosen by both parties; and by rating him according to this valuation for such a number of years, as might be fully sufficient for his complete indemnification. To draw the attention of the sovereign towards the improvement of the land, from a regard to the increase of his own revenue, is one of the principal advantages proposed by this species of land-tax.

The term, therefore, allowed for the indemnification of the landlord, ought not to be a great deal longer than what was necessary for that purpose; lest the remoteness of the interest should discourage too much this attention. It had better, however, be somewhat too long than in any respect too short. No incitement to the attention of the sovereign can ever counterbalance the smallest discouragement to that of the landlord. The attention of the sovereign can be at best but a very general and vague consideration of what is likely to contribute to the better cultivation of the greater part of his dominions. The attention of the landlord is a particular and minute consideration of what is likely to be the most advantageous application of every inch of ground upon his estate. The principal attention of the sovereign ought to be to encourage, by every means in his power, the attention both of the landlord and of the farmer; by allowing both to pursue their own interest in their own way, and accordingly to their own judgment; by giving to both the most perfect security that they shall enjoy the full recompence of their own industry; and by procuring to both the most extensive market for every part of their produce, in consequence of establishing the easiest and safest communications both by land and by water, through every part of his own dominions, as well as the most unbounded freedom of exportation to the dominions of all other princes.

If by such a system of administration a tax of this kind could be so managed as to give, not only no discouragement, but, on the contrary, some encouragement to the improvement of land, it does not appear likely to occasion any other inconveniency to the landlord, except always the unavoidable one of being obliged to pay the tax.

In all the variations of the state of the society, in the improvement and in the declension of agriculture; in all the variations in the value of silver, and in all those in the standard of the coin, a tax of this kind would, of its own accord and without any attention of government, readily suit itself to the actual situation of things, and would be equally just and equitable in all those different changes. It would, therefore, be much more proper to be established as a perpetual and unalterable regulation, or as what is called a fundamental law of the commonwealth, than any tax which was always to be levied according to a certain valuation.

Some states, instead of the simple and obvious expedient of a register of leases, have had recourse to the laborious and expensive one of an actual survey and valuation of all the lands in the country. They have suspected, probably, that the lessor and lessee, in order to defraud the public revenue, might combine to conceal the real terms of the lease. Doomsday-book seems to have been the result of a very accurate survey of this kind.

In the ancient dominions of the king of Prussia, the land-tax is assessed according to an actual survey and valuation, which is reviewed and altered from time to time. According to that valuation, the lay proprietors pay from twenty to twenty-five per cent. of their revenue. Ecclesiastics from forty to forty-five per cent. The survey and valuation of Silesia was made by order of the present king; it is said with great accuracy. According to that valuation, the lands belonging to the bishop of Breslaw are taxed at twenty-five per cent. of their rent. The other revenues of the ecclesiastics of both religions at fifty per cent. The commanderies of the Teutonic order, and of that of Malta, at forty per cent. Lands held by a noble tenure, at thirty-eight and one-third per cent. Lands held by a base tenure, at thirty-five and one-third per cent.

A land-tax assessed according to a general survey and valuation, how equal soever it may be at first, must, in the course of a very moderate period of time, become unequal. To prevent its becoming so would require the continual and painful attention of government to all the variations in the state and produce of every different farm in the country. The governments of Prussia, of Bohemia, of Sardinia, and of the dutchy of Milan, actually exert an attention of this kind; an attention so unsuitable to the nature of government, that it is not likely to be of long continuance, and which, if it is continued, will probably in the long-run occasion much more trouble and vexation than it can possibly bring relief to the contributors.

In 1666, the generality of Montauban was assessed to the Real or predial taille according, it is said, to a very exact survey and valuation. By 1727, this assessment had become altogether unequal. In order to remedy this inconveniency, government has found no better expedient than to impose upon the whole generality an additional tax of a hundred and twenty thousand livres. This additional tax is rated upon all the different districts subject to the taille according to the old assessment. But it is levied only upon those which in the actual state of things are by that assessment under-taxed, and it is applied to the relief of those which by the same assessment are over-taxed. Two districts, for example, one of which ought in the actual state of things to be taxed at nine hundred, the other at eleven hundred livres, are by the old assessment both taxed at a thousand livres. Both these districts are by the additional tax rated at eleven hundred livres each. But this additional tax is levied only upon the district under-charged, and it is applied altogether to the relief of that over-charged, which consequently pays only nine hundred livres. The government neither gains nor loses by the additional tax, which is applied altogether to remedy the inequalities arising from the old assessment. The application is pretty much regulated according to the discretion of the intendant of the generality, and must, therefore, be in a great measure arbitrary.

TAXES WHICH ARE PROPORTIONED, NOT TO THE RENT, BUT TO THE PRODUCE OF LAND

Taxes upon the produce of land are in reality taxes upon the rent; and though they may be originally advanced by the farmer, are finally paid by the landlord. When a certain portion of the produce is to be paid away for a tax, the farmer computes, as well as he can, what the value of this portion is, one year with another, likely to amount to, and he makes a proportionable abatement in the rent which he agrees to pay to the landlord. There is no farmer who does not compute beforehand what the church tythe, which is a land-tax of this kind, is, one year with another, likely to amount to.

The tythe, and every other land-tax of this kind, under the appearance of perfect equality, are very unequal taxes;

a certain portion of the produce being, in different situations, equivalent to a very different portion of the rent. In some very rich lands the produce is so great, that the one half of it is fully sufficient to replace the farmer his capital employed in cultivation, together with the ordinary profits of farming stock in the neighbourhood. The other half, or what comes to the same thing, the value of the other half, he could afford to pay as rent to the landlord, if there was no tythe. But if a tenth of the produce is taken from him in the way of tythe, he must require an abatement of the fifth part of his rent, otherwise he cannot get back his capital with the ordinary profit. In this case the rent of the landlord, instead of amounting to a half, or five-tenths of the whole produce, will amount only to four-tenths of it. In poorer lands, on the contrary, the produce is sometimes so small, and the expence of cultivation so great, that it requires four-fifths of the whole produce to replace to the farmer his capital with the ordinary profit. In this case, though there was no tythe, the rent of the landlord could amount to no more than one-fifth or two-tenths of the whole produce. But if the farmer pays one-tenth of the produce in the way of tythe, he must require an equal abatement of the rent of the landlord, which will thus be reduced to one-tenth only of the whole produce. Upon the rent of rich lands, the tythe may sometimes be a tax of no more than one-fifth part, or four shillings in the pound; whereas upon that of poorer lands, it may sometimes be a tax of one-half, or of ten shillings in the pound.

The tythe, as it is frequently a very unequal tax upon the rent, so it is always a great discouragement both to the improvements of the landlord and to the cultivation of the farmer. The one cannot venture to make the most important, which are generally the most expensive improvements; nor the other to raise the most valuable, which are generally too the most expensive crops; when the church, which lays out no part of the expence, is to share so very largely in the profit. The cultivation of madder was for a long time confined by the tythe to the United Provinces, which, being presbyterian countries, and upon that account exempted from this destructive tax, enjoyed a sort of monopoly of that useful dying drug against the rest of Europe.

The late attempts to introduce the culture of this plant into England, have been made only in consequence of the statute which enacted that five shillings an acre should be received in lieu of all manner of tythe upon madder.

As through the greater part of Europe, the church, so in many different countries of Asia, the state, is principally supported by a land-tax, proportioned, not to the rent, but to the produce of the land. In China, the principal revenue of the sovereign consists in a tenth part of the produce of all the lands of the empire. This tenth part, however, is estimated so very moderately, that, in many provinces, it is said not to exceed a thirtieth part of the ordinary produce. The land-tax or land-rent which used to be paid to the Mahometan government of Bengal, before that country fell into the hands of the English East India company, is said to have amounted to about a fifth part of the produce. The land-tax of ancient Egypt is said likewise to have amounted to a fifth part. . . .

TAXES UPON THE RENT OF HOUSES

The rent of a house may be distinguished into two parts, of which the one may very properly be called the Building rent; the other is commonly called the Ground rent.

The building rent is the interest or profit of the capital expended in building the house. In order to put the trade of a builder upon a level with other trades, it is necessary that this rent should be sufficient, first, to pay him the same interest which he would have got for his capital if he had lent it upon good security; and, secondly, to keep the house in constant repair, or, what comes to the same thing, to replace, within a certain term of years, the capital which had been employed in building it. The building rent, or the ordinary profit of building, is, therefore, every where regulated by the ordinary interest of money. Where the market rate of interest is four per cent. the rent of a house which, over and above paying the ground rent, affords six, or six and a half per cent. upon the whole expence of building, may perhaps afford a sufficient profit to the builder. Where the market rate of interest is five per cent., it may perhaps require seven or seven and a half per cent. If, in proportion to the interest of money, the trade of the builder affords at any time a much greater profit than this, it will soon draw so much capital from other trades as will reduce the profit to its proper level. If it affords at any time much less than this, other trades will soon draw so much capital from it as will again raise that profit.

Whatever part of the whole rent of a house is over and above what is sufficient for affording this reasonable profit, naturally goes to the ground-rent; and where the owner of the ground and the owner of the building are two different persons, is, in most cases, completely paid to the former. This surplus rent is the price which the inhabitant of the house pays for some real or supposed advantage of the situation. In country houses, at a distance from any great town, where there is plenty of ground to chuse upon, the ground-rent is scarce any thing, or no more than what the ground which the house stands upon would pay if employed in agriculture. In country villas in the neighbourhood of some great town, it is sometimes a good deal higher; and the peculiar conveniency or beauty of situation is there frequently very well paid for. Ground-rents are generally highest in the capital, and in those particular parts of it where there happens to be the greatest demand for houses, whatever be the reason of that demand, whether for trade and business, for pleasure and society, or for mere vanity and fashion.

A tax upon house-rent, payable by the tenant and proportioned to the whole rent of each house, could not, for any considerable time at least, affect the building rent. If the builder did not get his reasonable profit, he would be obliged to quit the trade; which, by raising the demand for building, would in a short time bring back his profit to its proper level with that of other trades. Neither would such a tax fall altogether upon the ground-rent; but it would divide itself in such a manner as to fall, partly upon the inhabitants of the house, and partly upon the owner of the ground.

Let us suppose, for example, that a particular person judges that he can afford for house-rent an expence of sixty pounds a year; and let us suppose too that a tax of four shillings in the pound, or of one-fifth, payable by the inhabitant, is laid upon house-rent. A house of sixty pounds rent will in this case cost him seventy-two pounds a year, which is twelve pounds more than he thinks he can afford. He will, therefore, content himself with a worse house, or a house of fifty pounds rent, which, with the additional ten pounds that he must pay for the tax, will make up the sum of sixty pounds a year, the expence which he judges he can afford; and in order to pay the tax he will give up a part of the additional conveniency which he might have had from a house of ten pounds a year more rent. He will give up, I say, a part of this additional conveniency; for he will seldom be obliged to give up the whole, but will, in consequence of the tax, get a better house for fifty pounds a year, than he could have got if there had been no tax. For as a tax of this kind, by taking away this particular competitor, must diminish the competition for houses of sixty pounds rent, so it must likewise diminish it for those of fifty pounds rent, and in the same manner for those of all other rents, except the lowest rent, for which it would for some time increase the competition. But the rents of every class of houses for which the competition was diminished, would necessarily be more or less reduced. As no part of this reduction, however, could for any considerable time at least, affect the building rent; the whole of it must in the long-run necessarily fall upon the ground-rent. The final payment of this tax, therefore, would fall, partly upon the inhabitant of the house, who, in order to pay his share, would be obliged to give up a part of his conveniency; and partly upon the owner of the ground, who, in order to pay his share, would be obliged to give up a part of his revenue. In what proportion this final payment would be divided between them, it is not perhaps very easy to ascertain. The division would probably be very different in different circumstances, and a tax of this kind might, according to those different circumstances, affect very unequally both the inhabitant of the house and the owner of the ground.

The inequality with which a tax of this kind might fall upon the owners of different ground-rents, would arise altogether from the accidental inequality of this division. But the inequality with which it might fall upon the inhabitants of different houses would arise, not only from this, but from another cause. The proportion of the expence of house-rent to the whole expence of living, is different in the different degrees of fortune. It is perhaps highest in the highest degree, and it diminishes gradually through the inferior degrees, so as in general to be lowest in the lowest degree. The necessities of life occasion the great expence of the poor. Thy find it difficult to get food, and the greater part of their little revenue is spent in getting it. The luxuries and vanities of life occasion the principal expence of the rich; and a magnificent house embellishes and sets off to the best advantage all the other luxuries and vanities which they possess. A tax upon house-rents, therefore, would in general fall heaviest upon the rich; and in this sort of inequality there would not, perhaps, be any thing very unreasonable. It is not very unreasonable that the rich should contribute to the public expence, not only in proportion to their revenue, but something more than in that proportion.

The rent of houses, though it in some respects resembles the rent of land, is in one respect essentially different from it. The rent of land is paid for the use of a productive subject. The land which pays it produces it. The rent of houses is paid for the use of an unproductive subject. Neither the house nor the ground which it stands upon produce any thing. The person who pays the rent, therefore, must draw it from some other source of revenue, distinct from and independent of this subject. A tax upon the rent of houses, so far as it falls upon the inhabitants, must be drawn from the same source as the rent itself, and must be paid from their revenue, whether derived from the wages of labour, the profits of stock, or the rent of land. So far as it falls upon the inhabitants, it is one of those taxes which fall, not upon one only, but indifferently upon all the three different sources of revenue; and is in every respect of the same nature as a tax upon any other sort of consumable commodities. In general there is not, perhaps, any one article of expence or consumption by which the liberality or narrowness of a man's whole expence can be better judged of, than by his house-rent. A proportional tax upon this particular article of expence might, perhaps, produce a more considerable revenue than any which has hitherto been drawn from it in any part of Europe. If the tax indeed was very high, the greater part of people would endeavour to evade it, as much as they could, by contenting themselves with smaller houses, and by turning the greater part of their expence into some other channel.

The rent of houses might easily be ascertained with sufficient accuracy, by a policy of the same kind with that which would be necessary for ascertaining the ordinary rent of land. Houses not inhabited ought to pay no tax. A tax upon them would fall altogether upon the proprietor, who would thus be taxed for a subject which afforded him neither conveniency nor revenue. Houses inhabited by the proprietor ought to be rated, not according to the expence which they might have cost in building, but according to the rent which an equitable arbitration might judge them likely to bring, if leased to a tenant. If rated according to the expence which they may have cost in building, a tax of three or four shillings in the pound, joined with other taxes, would ruin almost all the rich and great families of this, and, I believe, of every other civilized country. Whoever will examine, with attention, the different town and country houses of some of the richest and greatest families in this country, will find that, at the rate of only six and a half, or seven per cent. upon the original expence of building, their house-rent is nearly equal to the whole neat rent of their estates. It is the accumulated expence of several successive generations, laid out upon objects of great beauty and magnificence, indeed; but, in proportion to what they cost, of very small exchangeable value.

Ground-rents are a still more proper subject of taxation than the rent of houses. A tax upon ground-rents would not raise the rents of houses. It would fall altogether upon the owner of the ground-rent, who acts always as a monopolist, and exacts the greatest rent which can be got for the use of his ground. More or less can be got for it according as the competitors happen to be richer or poorer, or can afford to gratify their fancy for a particular spot of ground at a greater or smaller expence. In every country the greatest number of rich competitors is in the capital, and it is there accordingly that the highest ground-rents are always to be found. As the wealth of those competitors would in no respect be increased by a tax upon ground-rents, they would not probably be disposed to pay more for the use of the ground. Whether the tax was to be advanced by the inhabitant, or by the owner of the ground, would be of little importance. The more the inhabitant was obliged to pay for the tax, the less he would incline to pay for the ground; so that the final payment of the tax would fall altogether upon the owner of the ground-rent. The ground-rents of uninhabited houses ought to pay no tax.

Both ground-rents and the ordinary rent of land are a species of revenue which the owner, in many cases, enjoys without any care or attention of his own. Though a part of this revenue should be taken from him in order to defray the expences of the state, no discouragement will thereby be given to any sort of industry. The annual produce of the land and labour of the society, the real wealth and revenue of the great body of the people, might be the same after such a tax as before. Ground-rents, and the ordinary rent of land, are, therefore, perhaps, the species of revenue which can best bear to have a peculiar tax imposed upon them.

Ground-rents seem, in this respect, a more proper subject of peculiar taxation than even the ordinary rent of land. The ordinary rent of land is, in many cases, owing partly at least to the attention and good management of the landlord. A very heavy tax might discourage too much this attention and good management. Ground-rents, so far as they exceed the ordinary rent of land, are altogether owing to the good government of the sovereign, which, by protecting the industry either of the whole people, or of the inhabitants of some particular place, enables them to pay so much more than its real value for the ground which they build their houses upon; or to make to its owner so much more than compensation for the loss which he might sustain by this use of it. Nothing can be more reasonable than that a fund which owes its existence to the good government of the state, should be taxed peculiarly, or should contribute something more than the greater part of other funds, towards the support of that government.

Though, in many different countries of Europe, taxes have been imposed upon the rent of houses, I do not know of any in which ground-rents have been considered as a separate subject of taxation. The contrivers of taxes have, probably, found some difficulty in ascertaining what part of the rent ought to be considered as ground-rent, and what part ought to be considered as building-rent. It should not, however, seem very difficult to distinguish those two parts of the rent from one another.

In Great Britain the rent of houses is supposed to be taxed in the same proportion as the rent of land, by what is called the annual land-tax. The valuation, according to which each different parish and district is assessed to this tax, is always the same. It was originally extremely unequal, and it still continues to be so. Through the greater part of the kingdom this tax falls still more lightly upon the rent of houses than upon that of land. In some few districts only, which were originally rated high, and in which the rents of houses have fallen considerably, the land-tax of three or four shillings in the pound, is said to amount to an equal proportion of the real rent of houses. Untenanted houses, though by law subject to the tax, are, in most districts, exempted from it by the favour of the assessors; and this exemption sometimes occasions some little variation in the rate of particular houses, though that of the district is always the same. Improvements of rent, by new buildings, repairs, &c.; go to the discharge of the district, which occasions still further variations in the rate of particular houses.

In the province of Holland every house is taxed at two and a half per cent. of its value, without any regard either to the rent which it actually pays, or to the circumstance of its being tenanted or untenanted. There seems to be a hardship in obliging the proprietor to pay a tax for an untenanted house, from which he can derive no revenue, especially so very heavy a tax. In Holland, where the market rate of interest does not exceed three per cent. two and a half per cent. upon the whole value of the house, must, in most cases, amount to more than a third of the building-rent, perhaps of the whole rent. The valuation, indeed, according to which the houses are rated, though very unequal, is said to be always below the real value. When a house is rebuilt, improved or enlarged, there is a new valuation, and the tax is rated accordingly.

The contrivers of the several taxes which in England have at different times, been imposed upon houses, seem to have imagined that there was some great difficulty in ascertaining with tolerable exactness, what was the real rent of every house. They have regulated their taxes, therefore, according to some more obvious circumstance, such as they had probably imagined would, in most cases, bear some proportion to the rent.

The first tax of this kind was hearth-money; or a tax of two shillings upon every hearth. In order to ascertain how many hearths were in the house, it was necessary that the tax-gatherer should enter every room in it. This odious visit rendered the tax odious. Soon after the revolution, therefore, it was abolished as a badge of slavery.

The next tax of this kind was, a tax of two shillings upon every dwelling house inhabited. A house with ten windows to pay four shillings more. A house with twenty windows and upwards to pay eight shillings. This tax was afterwards so far altered, that houses with twenty windows, and with less than thirty, were ordered to pay ten shillings, and those with thirty windows and upwards to pay twenty shillings. The number of windows can, in most cases, be counted from the outside, and, in all cases, without entering every room in the house. The visit of the tax-gatherer, therefore, was less offensive in this tax than in the hearth-money.

This tax was afterwards repealed, and in the room of it was established the window-tax, which has undergone too several alterations and augmentations. The window-tax, as it stands at present (January, 1775), over and above the duty of three shillings upon every house in England, and of one shilling upon every house in Scotland, lays a duty upon every window, which, in England, augments gradually from two-pence, the lowest rate, upon houses with not more than seven windows; to two shillings, the highest rate, upon houses with twenty-five windows and upwards.

The principal objection to all such taxes is their inequality, an inequality of the worst kind, as they must frequently fall much heavier upon the poor than upon the rich. A house of ten pounds rent in a country town may sometimes have more windows than a house of five hundred pounds rent in London; and though the inhabitant of the former is likely to be a much poorer man than that of the latter, yet so far as his contribution is regulated by the window-tax, he must contribute more to the support of the state. Such taxes are, therefore, directly contrary to the first of the four maxims above mentioned. They do not seem to offend much against any of the other three.

The natural tendency of the window-tax, and of all other taxes upon houses, is to lower rents. The more a man pays for the tax, the less, it is evident, he can afford to pay for the rent. Since the imposition of the window-tax, however, the rents of houses have upon the whole risen, more or less, in almost every town and village of Great Britain, with which I am acquainted. Such has been almost everywhere the increase of the demand for houses, that it has raised the rents more than the window-tax could sink them; one of the many proofs of the great prosperity of the country, and of the increasing revenue of its inhabitants. Had it not been for the tax, rents would probably have risen still higher.

ARTICLE II

Taxes upon Profit, or upon the Revenue arising from Stock

The revenue or profit arising from stock naturally divides itself into two parts; that which pays the interest, and which belongs to the owner of the stock; and that surplus part which is over and above what is necessary for paying the interest.

This latter profit is evidently a subject not taxable directly. It is the compensation, and in most cases it is no more than a very moderate compensation, for the risk and trouble of employing the stock. The employer must have this compensation, otherwise he cannot, consistently with his own interest, continue the employment. If he was taxed directly, therefore, in proportion to the whole profit, he would be obliged either to raise the rate of his profit, or to charge the tax upon the interest of money; that is, to pay less interest If he raised the rate of his profit in proportion to the tax, the whole tax, though it might be advanced by him, would be finally paid by one or other of two different sets of people, according to the different ways in which he might employ the stock of which he had the management. If he employed it as a farming stock in the cultivation of land, he could raise the rate of his profit only by retaining a greater portion, or, what comes to the same thing, the price of a greater portion of the produce of the land; and as this could be done only by a reduction of rent, the final payment of the tax would fall upon the landlord. If he employed it as a mercantile or manufacturing stock, he could raise the rate of his profit only by raising the price of his goods; in which case the final payment of the tax would fall altogether upon the consumers of those goods. If he did not raise the rate of his profit, he would be obliged to charge the whole tax upon that part of it which was allotted for the interest of money. He could afford less interest for whatever stock he borrowed, and the whole weight of the tax would in this case fall ultimately upon the interest of money. So far as he could not relieve himself from the tax in the one way, he would be obliged to relieve himself in the other.

The interest of money seems at first sight a subject equally capable of being taxed directly as the rent of land. Like the rent of land, it is a neat produce which remains after completely compensating the whole risk and trouble of employing the stock. As a tax upon the rent of land cannot raise rents; because the neat produce which remains after replacing the stock of the farmer, together with his reasonable profit, cannot be greater after the tax than before it; so, for the same reason, a tax upon the interest of money could not raise the rate of interest; the quantity of stock or money in the country, like the quantity of land, being supposed to remain the same after the tax as before it. The ordinary rate of profit, it has been shewn in the first book, is every where regulated by the quantity of stock to be employed in proportion to the quantity of the employment, or of the business which must be done by it. But the quantity of the employment, or of the business to be done by stock, could neither be increased nor diminished by any tax upon the interest of money. If the quantity of the stock to be employed, therefore, was neither increased nor diminished by it, the ordinary rate of profit would necessarily remain the same. But the portion of this profit necessary for compensating the risk and trouble of the employer, would likewise remain the same; that risk and trouble being in no respect altered. The residue, therefore, that portion which belongs to the owner of the stock, and which pays the interest of money, would necessarily remain the same too. At first sight, therefore, the interest of money seems to be a subject as fit to be taxed directly as the rent of land.

There are, however, two different circumstances which render the interest of money a much less proper subject of direct taxation than the rent of land.

First, the quantity and value of the land which any man possesses can never be a secret, and can always be ascertained with great exactness. But the whole amount of the capital stock which he possesses is almost always a secret, and can scarce ever be ascertained with tolerable exactness. It is liable, besides, to almost continual variations. A year seldom passes away, frequently not a month, sometimes scarce a single day, in which it does not rise or fall more or less. An inquisition into every man's private circumstances, and an inquisition which, in order to accommodate the tax to them, watched over all the fluctuations of his fortune, would be a source of such continual and endless vexation as no people could support.

Secondly, land is a subject which cannot be removed, whereas stock easily may. The proprietor of land is necessarily a citizen of the particular country in which his estate lies. The proprietor of stock is properly a citizen of the world, and is not necessarily attached to any particular country. He would be apt to abandon the country in which he was exposed to a vexatious inquisition, in order to be assessed to a burdensome tax, and would remove his stock to some other country where he could either carry on his business, or enjoy his fortune more at his ease. By removing his stock he would put an end to all the industry which it had maintained in the country which he left. Stock cultivates land; stock employs labour. A tax which tended to drive away stock from any particular country, would so far tend to dry up every source of revenue, both to the sovereign and to the society. Not only the profits of stock, but the rent of land and the wages of labour, would necessarily be more or less diminished by its removal.

The nations, accordingly, who have attempted to tax the revenue arising from stock, instead of any severe inquisition of this kind, have been obliged to content themselves with some very loose, and, therefore, more or less arbitrary estimation. The extreme inequality and unc rtainty of a tax assessed in this manner, can be compensated only by its extreme moderation, in consequence of which every man finds himself rated so very much below his real revenue, that he gives himself little disturbance though his neighbour should be rated somewhat lower.

By what is called the land-tax in England, it was intended that stock should be taxed in the same proportion as land. When the tax upon land was at four shillings in the pound, or at one-fifth of the supposed rent, it was intended that stock should be taxed at one-fifth of the supposed interest. When the present annual land-tax was first imposed, the legal rate of interest was six per cent. Every hundred pounds stock, accordingly, was supposed to be taxed at twenty-four shillings, the fifth part of six pounds. Since the legal rate of interest has been reduced to five per cent. every hundred pounds stock is supposed to be taxed at twenty shillings only. The sum to be raised, by what is called the land-tax, was divided between the country and the principal towns. The greater part of it was laid upon the country; and of what was laid upon the towns, the greater part was assessed upon the houses. What remained to be assessed upon the stock or trade of the towns (for the stock upon the land was not meant to be taxed) was very much below the real value of that stock or trade. Whatever inequalities, therefore, there might be in the original assessment, gave little disturbance. Every parish and district still continues to be rated for its land, its houses, and its stock, according to the original assessment; and the almost universal prosperity of the country, which in most places has raised very much the value of all these, has rendered those inequalities of still less importance now. The rate too upon each district continuing always the same, the uncertainty of this tax, so far as it might be assessed upon the stock of any individual, has been very much diminished, as well as rendered of much less consequence. If the greater part of the lands of England are not rated to the land-tax at half their actual value, the greater part of the stock of England is, perhaps, scarce rated at the fiftieth part of its actual value. In some towns the whole land-tax is assessed upon houses; as in Westminster, where stock and trade are free. It is otherwise in London.

In all countries a severe inquisition into the circumstances of private persons has been carefully avoided.

At Hamburgh every inhabitant is obliged to pay to the state, one-fourth per cent. of all that he possesses; and as the wealth of the people of Hamburgh consists principally in stock, this tax may be considered as a tax upon stock. Every man assesses himself, and, in the presence of the magistrate, puts annually into the public coffer a certain sum of money, which he declares upon oath to be one-fourth per cent. of all that he possesses, but without declaring what it amounts to, or being liable to any examination upon that subject. This tax is generally supposed to be paid with great fidelity. In a small republic, where the people have entire confidence in their magistrates, are convinced of the necessity of the tax for the support of the state, and believe that it will be faithfully applied to that purpose, such conscientious and voluntary payment may sometimes be expected. It is not peculiar to the people of Hamburgh.

The canton of Underwald in Switzerland is frequently ravaged by storms and inundations, and is thereby exposed to extraordinary expences. Upon such occasions the people assemble, and every one is said to declare with the greatest frankness what he is worth, in order to be taxed accordingly. At Zurich the law orders, that, in cases of necessity, every one should be taxed in proportion to his revenue; the amount of which, he is obliged to declare upon oath. They have no suspicion, it is said, that any of their fellow-citizens will deceive them. At Basil the principal revenue of the state arises from a small custom upon goods exported. All the citizens make oath that they will pay every three months all the taxes imposed by the law. All merchants and even all inn-keepers are trusted with keeping themselves the account of the goods which they sell either within or without the territory. At the end of every three months they send this account to the treasurer, with the amount of the tax computed at the bottom of it. It is not suspected that the revenue suffers by this confidence.

To oblige every citizen to declare publicly upon oath the amount of his fortune, must not, it seems, in those Swiss cantons, be reckoned a hardship. At Hamburgh it would be reckoned the greatest. Merchants engaged in the hazardous projects of trade, all tremble at the thoughts of being obliged at all times to expose the real state of their circumstances. The ruin of their credit and the miscarriage of their projects, they foresee, would too often be the consequence. A sober and parsimonious people, who are strangers to all such projects, do not feel that they have occasion for any such concealment.

In Holland, soon after the exaltation of the late prince of Orange to the stadtholdership, a tax of two per cent. or the fiftieth penny, as it was called, was imposed upon the whole substance of every citizen. Every citizen assessed himself and paid his tax in the same manner as at Hamburgh; and it was in general supposed to have been paid with great fidelity. The people had at that time the greatest affection for their new government, which they had just established by a general insurrection. The tax was to be paid but once; in order to relieve the state in a particular exigency. It was, indeed, too heavy to be permanent. In a country where the market rate of interest seldom exceeds three per cent., a tax of two per cent. amounts to thirteen shillings and fourpence in the pound upon the highest neat revenue which is commonly drawn from stock. It is a tax which very few people could pay without encroaching more or less upon their capitals. In a particular exigency the people may, from great public zeal, make a great effort, and give up even a part of their capital, in order to relieve the state. But it is impossible that they should continue to do so for any considerable time; and if they did, the tax would soon ruin them so completely as to render them altogether incapable of supporting the state.

The tax upon stock imposed by the land-tax bill in England, though it is proportioned to the capital, is not intended to diminish or take away any part of that capital. It is meant only to be a tax upon the interest of money proportioned to that upon the rent of land; so that when the latter is at four shillings in the pound, the former may be at four shillings in the pound too. The tax at Hamburgh, and the still more moderate taxes of Underwald and Zurich, are meant, in the same manner, to be taxes, not upon the capital, but upon the interest or neat revenue of stock. That of Holland was meant to be a tax upon the capital.

TAXES UPON THE PROFIT OF PARTICULAR EMPLOYMENTS

In some countries extraordinary taxes are imposed upon the profits of stock; sometimes when employed in particular branches of trade, and sometimes when employed in agriculture.

Of the former kind are in England the tax upon hawkers and pedlars, that upon hackney coaches and chairs, and that which the keepers of ale-houses pay for a licence to retail ale and spirituous liquors. During the late war, another tax of the same kind was proposed upon shops. The war having been undertaken, it was said, in defence of the trade of the country, the merchants, who were to profit by it, ought to contribute towards the support of it.

A tax, however, upon the profits of stock employed in any particular branch of trade, can never fall finally upon the dealers (who must in all ordinary cases have their reasonable profit, and, where the competition is free, can seldom have more than that profit), but always upon the consumers, who must be obliged to pay in the price of the goods the tax which the dealer advances; and generally with some overcharge

A tax of this kind when it is proportioned to the trade of the dealer, is finally paid by the consumer, and occasions no oppression to the dealer. When it is not so proportioned, but is the same upon all dealers, though in this case too it is finally paid by the consumer, yet it favours the great, and occasions some oppression to the small dealer. The tax of five shillings a week upon every hackney coach, and that of ten shillings a year upon every hackney chair, so far as it is advanced by the different keepers of such coaches and chairs, is exactly enough proportioned to the extent of their respective dealings. It neither favours the great, nor oppresses the smaller dealer. The tax of twenty shillings a year for a license to sell ale; of forty shillings for a licence to sell spirituous liquors; and of forty shillings more for a licence to sell wine, being the same upon all retailers, must necessarily give some advantage to the great, and occasion some oppression to the small dealers. The former must find it more easy to get back the tax in the price of their goods than the latter. The moderation of the tax, however, renders this inequality of less importance, and it may to many people appear not improper to give some discouragement to the multiplication of little ale-houses. The tax upon shops, it was intended, should be the same upon all shops. It could not well have been otherwise. It would have been impossible to proportion with tolerable exactness the tax upon a shop to the extent of the trade carried on in it, without such an inquisition as would have been altogether insupportable in a free country. If the tax had been considerable, it would have oppressed the small, and forced almost the whole retail trade into the hands of the great dealers. The competition of the former being taken away, the latter would have enjoyed a monopoly of the trade; and like all other monopolists would soon have combined to raise their profits much beyond what was necessary for the payment of the tax. The final payment, instead of falling upon the shopkeeper, would have fallen upon the consumer, with a considerable overcharge to the profit of the shopkeeper. For these reasons, the project of a tax upon shops was laid aside, and in the room of it was substituted the subsidy 1759.

When a tax is imposed upon the profits of stock in a particular branch of trade, the traders are all careful to bring no more goods to market than what they can sell at a price sufficient to reimburse them for advancing the tax. Some of them withdraw a part of their stocks from the trade, and the market is more sparingly supplied than before. The price of the goods rises, and the final payment of the tax falls upon the consumer. But when a tax is imposed upon the profits of stock employed in agriculture, it is not the interest of the farmers to withdraw any part of their stock from that employment. Each farmer occupies a certain quantity of land, for which he pays rent. For the proper cultivation of this land a certain quantity of stock is necessary; and by withdrawing any part of this necessary quantity, the farmer is not likely to be more able to pay, either the rent or the tax. In order to pay the tax, it can never be his interest to diminish the quantity of his produce, nor consequently to supply the market more sparingly than before. The tax, therefore, will never enable him to raise the price of his produce, so as to reimburse himself by throwing the final payment upon the consumer. The farmer, however, must have his reasonable profit as well as every other dealer, otherwise he must give up the trade. After the imposition of a tax of this kind, he can get this reasonable profit only by paying less rent to the landlord. The more he is obliged to pay in the way of tax, the less he can afford to pay in the way of rent. A tax of this kind imposed during the currency of a lease may, no doubt, distress or ruin the farmer. Upon the renewal of the lease it must always fall upon the landlord.

What are called poll-taxes in the southern provinces of North America, and in the West Indian islands, annual taxes of so much a head upon every negroe, are properly taxes upon the profits of a certain species of stock employed in agriculture. As the planters are, the greater part of them, both farmers and landlords, the final payment of the tax falls upon them in their quality of landlords without any retribution.

Taxes of so much a head upon the bondmen employed in cultivation, seem anciently to have been common all over Europe. There subsists at present a tax of this kind in the empire of Russia. It is probably upon this account that poll-taxes of all kinds have often been represented as badges of slavery. Every tax, however, is to the person who pays it a badge, not of slavery, but of liberty. It denotes that he is subject to government, indeed, but that, as he has some property, he cannot himself be the property of a master. A poll-tax upon slaves is altogether different from a poll-tax upon freemen. The latter is paid by the persons upon whom it is imposed; the former by a different set of persons. The latter is either altogether arbitrary or altogether unequal, and in most cases is both the one and the other; the former, though in some respects unequal, different slaves being of different values, is in no respect arbitrary. Every master who knows the number of his own slaves, knows exactly what he has to pay. Those different taxes, however, being called by the same name, have been considered as of the same nature.

The taxes which in Holland are imposed upon men and maid servants, are taxes, not upon stock, but upon expence; and so far resemble the taxes upon consumable commodities. The tax of a guinea a head for every man servant, which has lately been imposed in Great Britain, is of the same kind. It falls heaviest upon the middling rank. A man of two hundred a year may keep a single man servant. A man of ten thousand a year will not keep fifty. It does not affect the poor.

Taxes upon the profits of stock in particular employments can never affect the interest of money. Nobody will lend his money for less interest to those who exercise the taxed, than to those who exercise the untaxed employments. Taxes upon the revenue arising from stock in all employments, where the government attempts to levy them with any degree of exactness, will, in many cases, fall upon the interest of money. The Vingtieme, or twentieth penny, in France, is a tax of the same kind with what is called the land-tax in England, and is assessed, in the same manner, upon the revenue arising from land, houses, and stock. So far as it affects stock it is assessed, though not with great rigour, yet with much more exactness than that part of the land-tax of England which is imposed upon the same fund. It, in many cases, falls altogether upon the interest of money. Money is frequently sunk in France upon what are called Contracts for the constitution of a rent; that is, perpetual annuities redeemable at any time by the debtor upon repayment of the sum originally advanced, but of which this redemption is not exigible by the creditor except in particular cases. The Vingtieme seems not to have raised the rate of those annuities, though it is exactly levied upon them all.

APPENDIX TO ARTICLES I AND II

Taxes upon the Capital Value of Land, Houses, and Stock

While property remains in the possession of the same person, whatever permanent taxes may have been imposed upon it, they have never been intended to diminish or take away any part of its capital value, but only some part of the revenue arising from it. But when property changes hands, when it is transmitted either from the dead to the living, or from the living to the living, such taxes have frequently been imposed upon it as necessarily take away some part of its capital value.

The transference of all sorts of property from the dead to the living, and that of immoveable property, of lands and houses, from the living to the living, are transactions which are in their nature either public and notorious, or such as cannot be long concealed. Such transactions, therefore, may be taxed directly. The transference of stock or moveable property, from the living to the living, by the lending of money, is frequently a secret transaction, and may always be made so. It cannot easily, therefore, be taxed directly. It has been taxed indirectly in two different ways; first, by requiring that the deed, containing the obligation to repay, should be written upon paper or parchment which had paid a certain stamp-duty, otherwise not to be valid; secondly, by requiring, under the like penalty of invalidity, that it should be recorded either in a public or secret register, and by imposing certain duties upon such registration. Stamp-duties and duties of registration have frequently been imposed likewise upon the deeds transferring property of all kinds from the dead to the living, and upon those transferring immoveable property from the living to the living, transactions which might easily have been taxed directly.

The Vicesima Hereditatum, the twentieth penny of inheritances, imposed by Augustus upon the ancient Romans, was a tax upon the transference of property from the dead to the living. Dion Cassius, the author who writes concerning it the least indistinctly, says, that it was imposed upon all successions, legacies, and donations, in case of death, except upon those to the nearest relations, and to the poor.

Of the same kind is the Dutch tax upon successions. Collateral successions are taxed, according to the degree of relation, from five to thirty per cent, upon the whole value of the succession. Testamentary donations, or legacies to collaterals, are subject to the like duties. Those from husband to wife, or from wife to husband, to the fifteenth penny. The Luctuosa Hereditas, the mournful succession of ascendents to descendents, to the twentieth penny only. Direct successions, or those of descendents to ascendents, pay no tax. The death of a father, to such of his children as live in the same house with him, is seldom attended with any increase, and frequently with a considerable diminution of revenue; by the loss of his industry, of his office, or of some life-rent estate, of which he may have been in possession. That tax would be cruel and oppressive which aggravated their loss by taking from them any part of his succession. It may, however, sometimes be otherwise with those children who, in the language of the Roman law, are said to be emancipated; in that of the Scotch law, to be foris-familiated; that is, who have received their portion, have got families of their own, and are supported by funds separate and independent of those of their father. Whatever part of his succession might come to such children, would be a real addition to their fortune, and might therefore, perhaps, without more inconveniency than what attends all duties of this kind, be liable to some tax.

The casualties of the feudal law were taxes upon the transference of land, both from the dead to the living, and from the living to the living. In ancient times they constituted in every part of Europe one of the principal branches of the revenue of the crown.

The heir of every immediate vassal of the crown paid a certain duty, generally a year's rent, upon receiving the investiture of the estate. If the heir was a minor, the whole rents of the estate, during the continuance of the minority, devolved to the superior without any other charge, besides the maintenance of the minor, and the payment of the widow's dower, when there happened to be a dowager upon the land. When the minor came to be of age, another tax, called Relief, was still due to the superior, which generally amounted likewise to a year's rent. A long minority, which in the present times so frequently disburdens a great estate of all its incumbrances, and restores the family to their ancient splendour, could in those times have no such effect. The waste, and not the disincumbrance of the estate, was the common effect of a long minority.

By the feudal law the vassal could not alienate without the consent of his superior, who generally extorted a fine or composition for granting it. This fine, which was at first arbitrary, came in many countries to be regulated at a certain portion of the price of the land. In some countries, where the greater part of the other feudal customs have gone into disuse, this tax upon the alienation of land still continues to make a very considerable branch of the revenue of the sovereign. In the canton of Berne it is so high as a sixth part of the price of all noble fiefs; and a tenth part of that of all ignoble ones. In the canton of Lucerne the tax upon the sale of lands is not universal, and takes place only in certain districts. But if any person sells his land, in order to remove out of the territory, he pays ten per cent. upon the whole price of the sale. Taxes of the same kind upon the sale either of all lands, or of lands held by certain tenures, take place in many other countries, and make a more or less considerable branch of the revenue of the sovereign.

Such transactions may be taxed indirectly, by means either of stamp-duties, or of duties upon registration; and those duties either may or may not be proportioned to the value of the subject which is transferred.

In Great Britain the stamp-duties are higher or lower, not so much according to the value of the property transferred (an eighteen penny or half crown stamp being sufficient upon a bond for the largest sum of money) as according to the nature of the deed. The highest do not exceed six pounds upon every sheet of paper, or skin of parchment; and these high duties fall chiefly upon grants from the crown, and upor certain law proceedings, without any regard to the value of the subject. There are in Great Britain no duties on the registration of deeds or writings, except the fees of the officers who keep the register; and these are seldom more than a reasonable recompence for their labour. The crown derives no revenue from them.

In Holland there are both stamp-duties and duties upon registration; which in somes cases are, and in some are not proportioned to the value of the property transferred. All testaments must be written upon stamped paper of which the price is proportioned to the property disposed of, so that there are stamps which cost from three pence, or three stivers a sheet, to three hundred florins, equal to about twenty-seven pounds ten shillings of our money. If the stamp is of an inferior price to what the testator ought to have made use of, his succession is confiscated. This is over and above all their other taxes on succession. Except bills of exchange, and some other mercantile bills, all other deeds, bonds, and contracts, are subject to a stamp-duty. This duty, however, does not rise in proportion to the value of the subject. All sales of land and of houses, and all mortgages upon either, must be registered, and, upon registration, pay a duty to the state of two and a half per cent. upon the amount of the price or of the mortgage. This duty is extended to the sale of all ships and vessels of more than two tons burthen, whether decked or undecked. These, it seems, are considered as a sort of houses upon the water. The sale of moveables, when it is ordered by a court of justice, is subject to the like duty of two and a half per cent.

In France there are both stamp-duties and duties upon registration. The former are considered as a branch of the aides or excise, and in the provinces where those duties take place, are levied by the excise officers. The latter are considered as a branch of the domain of the crown, and are levied by a different set of officers.

Those modes of taxation, by stamp-duties and by duties upon registration, are of very modern invention. In the course of little more than a century, however, stamp-duties have, in Europe, become almost universal, and duties upon registration extremely common. There is no art which one government sooner learns of another, than that of draining money from the pockets of the people.

Taxes upon the transference of property from the dead to the living, fall finally as well as immediately upon the person to whom the property is transferred. Taxes upon the sale of land fall altogether upon the seller. The seller is almost always under the necessity of selling, and must, therefore, take such a price as he can get. The buyer is scarce ever under the necessity of buying, and will, therefore, only give such a price as he likes. He considers what the land will cost him in tax and price together. The more he is obliged to pay in the way of tax, the less he will be disposed to give in the way of price. Such taxes, therefore, fall almost always upon a necessitous person, and must, therefore, be frequently very cruel and oppressive. Taxes upon the sale of new-built houses, where the building is sold without the ground, fall generally upon the buyer, because the builder must generally have his profit; otherwise he must give up the trade. If he advances the tax, therefore, the buyer must generally repay it to him. Taxes upon the sale of old houses, for the same reason as those upon the sale of land, fall generally upon the seller; whom in most cases either conveniency or necessity obliges to sell. The number of new-built houses that are annually brought to market, is more or less regulated by the demand. Unless the demand is such as to afford the builder his profit, after paying all expences, he will build no more houses. The number of old houses which happen at any time to come to market is regulated by accidents of which the greater part have no relation to the demand. Two or three great bankruptcies in a mercantile town, will bring many houses to sale, which must be sold for what can be got for them. Taxes upon the sale of ground rents fall altogether upon the seller; for the same reason as those upon the sale of land. Stamp-duties, and duties upon the registration of bonds and contracts for borrowed money, fall altogether upon the borrower, and, in fact, are always paid by him. Duties of the same kind upon law proceedings fall upon the suitors. They reduce to both the capital value of the subject in dispute. The more it costs to acquire any property, the less must be the neat value of it when acquired.

All taxes upon the transference of property of every kind, so far as they diminish the capital value of that property, tend to diminish the funds destined for the maintenance of productive labour. They are all more or less unthrifty taxes that increase the revenue of the sovereign, which seldom maintains any but unproductive labourers; at the expence of the capital of the people, which maintains none but productive.

Such taxes, even when they are proportioned to the value of the property transferred, are still unequal; the frequency of transference not being always equal in property of equal value. When they are not proportioned to this value, which is the case with the greater part of the stamp duties, and duties of registration, they are still more so. They are in no respect arbitrary, but are or may be in all cases perfectly clear and certain. Though they sometimes fall upon the person who is not very able to pay; the time of payment is in most cases sufficiently convenient for him. When the payment becomes due, he must in most cases have the money to pay. They are levied at very little expence, and in general subject the contributors to no other inconveniency besides always the unavoidable one of paying the tax.

In France the stamp-duties are not much complained of. Those of registration, which they call the Contrôle, are. They give occasion, it is pretended, to much extortion in the officers of the farmers-general who collect the tax, which is in a great measure arbitrary and uncertain. In the greater part of the libels which have been written against the present system of finances in France, the abuses of the Contrôle make a principal article. Uncertainty, however, does not seem to be necessarily inherent in the nature of such taxes. If the popular complaints are well founded, the abuse must arise, not so much from the nature of the tax, as from the want of precision and distinctness in the words of the edicts or laws which impose it.

The registration of mortgages, and in general of all rights upon immoveable property, as it gives great security both to creditors and purchasers, is extremely advantageous to the public. That of the greater part of deeds of other kinds is frequently inconvenient and even dangerous to individuals, without any advantage to the public. All registers which, it is acknowledged, ought to be kept secret, ought certainly never to exist. The credit of individuals ought certainly never to depend upon so very slender a security as the probity and religion of the inferior officers of revenue. But where the fees of registration have been made a source of revenue to the sovereign, register offices have commonly been multiplied without end, both for the deeds which ought to be registered, and for those which ought not. In France there are several different sorts of secret registers. This abuse, though not perhaps a necessary, it must be acknowledged, is a very natural effect of such taxes.

Such stamp-duties as those in England upon cards and dice, upon news-papers and periodical pamphlets, &c. are properly taxes upon consumption; the final payment falls upon the persons who use or consume such commodities. Such stamp-duties as those upon licences to retail ale, wine, and spirituous liquors, though intended, perhaps, to fall upon the profits of the retailers, are likewise finally paid by the consumers of those liquors. Such taxes, though called by the same name, and levied by the same officers and in the same manner with the stamp-duties above mentioned upon the transference of property, are however of a quite different nature, and fall upon quite different funds.

ARTICLE III

Taxes upon the Wages of Labour

The wages of the inferior classes of workmen, I have endeavoured to show in the first book, are every where necessarily regulated by two different circumstances; the demand for labour, and the ordinary or average price of provisions. The demand for labour, according as it happens to be either increasing, stationary, or declining; or to require an increasing, stationary, or declining population, regulates the subsistence of the labourer, and determines in what degree it shall be, either liberal, moderate, or scanty.

The ordinary or average price of provisions determines the quantity of money which must be paid to the workman in order to enable him, one year with another, to purchase this liberal, moderate, or scanty subsistence. While the demand for labour and the price of provisions, therefore, remain the same, a direct tax upon the wages of labour can have no other effect than to raise them somewhat higher than the tax. Let us suppose, for example, that in a particular place the demand for labour and the price of provisions were such, as to render ten shillings a week the ordinary wages of labour; and that a tax of one-fifth, or four shillings in the pound, was imposed upon wages. If the demand for labour and the price of provisions remained the same, it would still be necessary that the labourer should in that place earn such a subsistence as could be bought only for ten shillings a week, or that after paying the tax he should have ten shillings a week free wages. But in order to leave him such free wages after paying such a tax, the price of labour must in that place soon rise, not to twelve shillings a week only, but to twelve and sixpence; that is, in order to enable him to pay a tax of one-fifth, his wages must necessarily soon rise, not one-fifth part only, but one-fourth. Whatever was the proportion of the tax, the wages of labour must in all cases rise, not only in that proportion, but in a higher proportion. If the tax, for example, was one-tenth, the wages of labour must necessarily soon rise, not one-tenth part only, but one-eighth.

A direct tax upon the wages of labour, therefore, though the labourer might perhaps pay it out of his hand, could not properly be said to be even advanced by him; at least if the demand for labour and the average price of provisions remained the same after the tax as before it. In all such cases, not only the tax, but something more than the tax, would in reality be advanced by the person who immediately employed him. The final payment would in different cases fall upon different persons. The rise which such a tax might occasion in the wages of manufacturing labour would be advanced by the master manufacturer, who would both be entitled and obliged to charge it, with a profit, upon the price of his goods. The final payment of this rise of wages, therefore, together with the additional profit of the master manufacturer, would fall upon the consumer. The rise which such a tax might occasion in the wages of country labour would be advanced by the farmer, who, in order to maintain the same number of labourers as before, would be obliged to employ a greater capital. In order to get back this greater capital, together with the ordinary profits of stock, it would be necessary that he should retain a larger portion, or what comes to the same thing, the price of a larger portion, of the produce of the land, and consequently that he should pay less rent to the landlord. The final payment of this rise of wages, therefore, would in this case fall upon the landlord, together with the additional profit of the farmer who had advanced it. In all cases a direct tax upon the wages of labour must, in the long-run, occasion both a greater reduction in the rent of land, and a greater rise in the price of manufactured goods, than would have followed from the proper assessment of a sum equal to the produce of the tax, partly upon the rent of land, and partly upon consumable commodities.

If direct taxes upon the wages of labour have not always occasioned a proportionable rise in those wages, it is because they have generally occasioned a considerable fall in the demand for labour. The declension of industry, the decrease of employment for the poor, the diminution of the annual produce of the land and labour of the country, have generally been the effects of such taxes. In consequence of them, however, the price of labour must always be higher than it otherwise would have been in the actual state of the demand: and this enhancement of price, together with the profit of those who advance it, must always be finally paid by the landlords and consumers.

A tax upon the wages of country labour does not raise the price of the rude produce of land in proportion to the tax; for the same reason that a tax upon the farmer's profit does not raise that price in that proportion.

Absurd and destructive as such taxes are, however, they take place in many countries. In France that part of the taille which is charged upon the industry of workmen and day-labourers in country villages, is properly a tax of this kind. Their wages are computed according to the common rate of the district in which they reside, and that they may be as little liable as possible to any over-charge, their yearly gains are estimated at no more than two hundred working days in the year. The tax of each individual is varied from year to year according to different circumstances, of which the collector or the commissary, whom the intendant appoints to assist him, are the judges. In Bohemia, in consequence of the alteration in the system of finances which was begun in 1748, a very heavy tax is imposed upon the industry of artificers. They are divided into four classes. The highest class pay a hundred florins a year; which, at two-and-twenty-pence halfpenny a florin, amounts to *9l. 7s. 6d.* The second class are taxed at seventy; the third at fifty; and the fourth, comprehending artificers in villages, and the lowest class of those in towns, at twenty-five florins.

The recompence of ingenious artists and of men of liberal professions, I have endeavoured to show in the first book, necessarily keeps a certain proportion to the emoluments of inferior trades. A tax upon this recompence, therefore, could have no other effect than to raise it somewhat higher than in proportion to the tax. If it did not rise in this manner, the ingenious arts and the liberal professions, being no longer upon a level with other trades, would be so much deserted that they would soon return to that level.

The emoluments of offices are not, like those of trades and professions, regulated by the free competition of the market, and do not, therefore, always bear a just proportion to what the nature of the employment requires. They are perhaps, in most countries, higher than it requires; the persons who have the administration of government being generally disposed to reward both themselves and their immediate dependents rather more than enough. The emoluments of offices, therefore, can in most cases very well bear to be taxed. The persons, besides, who enjoy public offices, especially the more lucrative, are in all countries the objects of general envy; and a tax upon their emoluments, even though it should be somewhat higher than upon any other sort of revenue, is always a very popular tax. In England, for example, when by the land-tax every other sort of revenue was supposed to be assessed at four shillings in the pound, it was very popular to lay a real tax of five shillings and sixpence in the pound upon the salaries of offices which exceeded a hundred pounds a year; the pensions of the younger branches of the royal family, the pay of the officers of the army and navy, and a few others less obnoxious to envy excepted. There are in England no other direct taxes upon the wages of labour.

ARTICLE IV

Taxes which, it is intended, should fall indifferently upon every different Species of Revenue

The taxes which, it is intended, should fall indifferently upon every different species of revenue, are capitation taxes, and taxes upon consumable commodities. These must be paid indifferently from whatever revenue the contributors may possess; from the rent of their land, from the profits of their stock, or from the wages of their labour.

CAPITATION TAXES

Capitation taxes, if it is attempted to proportion them to the fortune or revenue of each contributor, become altogether arbitrary. The state of a man's fortune varies from day to day, and without an inquisition more intolerable than any tax, and renewed at least once every year, can only be guessed at. His assessment, therefore, must in most cases depend upon the good or bad humour of his assessors, and must, therefore, be altogether arbitrary and uncertain.

Capitation taxes, if they are proportioned not to the supposed fortune, but to the rank of each contributor, become altogether unequal; the degrees of fortune being frequently unequal in the same degree of rank.

Such taxes, therefore, if it is attempted to render them equal, become altogether arbitrary and uncertain; and if it is attempted to render them certain and not arbitrary, become altogether unequal. Let the tax be light or heavy, uncertainty is always a great grievance. In a light tax a considerable degree of inequality may be supported; in a heavy one it is altogether intolerable.

In the different poll-taxes which took place in England during the reign of William III. the contributors were, the greater part of them, assessed according to the degree of their rank; as dukes, marquisses, earls, viscounts, barons, esquires, gentlemen, the eldest and youngest sons of peers, &c. All shopkeepers and tradesmen worth more than three hundred pounds, that is, the better sort of them, were subject to the same assessment; how great soever might be the difference in their fortunes. Their rank was more considered than their fortune. Several of those who in the first poll-tax were rated according to their supposed fortune, were afterwards rated according to their rank. Serjeants, attornies, and proctors at law, who in the first poll-tax were assessed at three shillings in the pound of their supposed income, were afterwards assessed as gentlemen. In the assessment of a tax which was not very heavy, a considerable degree of inequality had been found less insupportable than any degree of uncertainty.

In the capitation which has been levied in France without any interruption since the beginning of the present century, the highest orders of people are rated according to their rank, by an invariable tariff; the lower orders of people, according to what is supposed to be their fortune, by an assessment which varies from year to year. The officers of the king's court, the judges and other officers in the superior courts of justice, the officers of the troops, &c. are assessed in the first manner. The inferior ranks of people in the provinces are assessed in the second. In France the great easily submit to a considerable degree of inequality in a tax which, so far as it affects them, is not a very heavy one; but could not brook the arbitrary assessment of an intendant. The inferior ranks of people must, in that country, suffer patiently the usage which their superiors think proper to give them.

In England the different poll-taxes never produced the sum which had been expected from them, or which, it was supposed, they might have produced, had they been exactly levied. In France the capitation always produces the sum expected from it. The mild government of England, when it assessed the different ranks of people to the poll-tax, contented itself with what that assessment happened to produce; and required no compensation for the loss which the state might sustain either by those who could not pay, or by those who would not pay (for there were many such), and who, by the indulgent execution of the law, were not forced to pay. The more severe government of France assesses upon each generality a certain sum, which the intendant must find as he can. If any province complains of being assessed too high, it may, in the assessment of next year, obtain an abatement proportioned to the over-charge of the year before. But it must pay in the mean time. The intendant, in order to be sure of finding the sum assessed upon his generality, was impowered to assess it in a larger sum, that the failure or inability of some of the contributors might be compensated by the over-charge of the rest; and till 1765, the fixation of this surplus assessment was left altogether to his discretion. In that year indeed the council assumed this power to itself. In the capitation of the provinces, it is observed by the perfectly well-informed author of the Memoirs upon the impositions in France, the proportion which falls upon the nobility, and upon those whose privileges exempt them from the taille, is the least considerable. The largest falls upon those subject to the taille, who are assessed to the capitation at so much a pound of what they pay to that other tax.

Capitation taxes, so far as they are levied upon the lower ranks of people, are direct taxes upon the wages of labour, and are attended with all the inconveniences of such taxes.

Capitation taxes are levied at little expence; and, where they are rigorously exacted, afford a very sure revenue to the state. It is upon this account that in countries where the ease, comfort, and security of the inferior ranks of people are little attended to, capitation taxes are very common. It is in general, however, but a small part of the public revenue, which, in a great empire, has ever been drawn from such taxes; and the greatest sum which they have ever afforded, might always have been found in some other way much more convenient to the people.

TAXES UPON CONSUMABLE COMMODITIES

The impossibility of taxing the people, in proportion to their revenue, by any capitation, seems to have given occasion to the invention of taxes upon consumable commodities. The state not knowing how to tax, directly and proportionably, the revenue of its subjects, endeavours to tax it indirectly by taxing their expence, which, it is supposed, will in most cases be nearly in proportion to their revenue. Their expence is taxed by taxing the consumable commodities upon which it is laid out.

Consumable commodities are either necessaries or luxuries.

By necessaries I understand, not only the commodities which are indispensably necessary for the support of life, but whatever the custom of the country renders it indecent for creditable people, even of the lowest order, to be without. A linen shirt, for example, is, strictly speaking, not a necessary of life. The Greeks and Romans lived, I suppose, very comfortably, though they had no linen. But in the present times, through the greater part of Europe, a creditable day-labourer would be ashamed to appear in public without a linen shirt, the want of which would be supposed to denote that disgraceful degree of poverty, which, it is presumed, no body can well fall into without extreme bad conduct. Custom, in the same manner, has rendered leather shoes a necessary of life in England. The poorest creditable person of either sex would be ashamed to appear in public without them. In Scotland, custom has rendered them a necessary of life to the lowest order of men; but not to the same order of women, who may, without any discredit, walk about bare-footed. In France, they are necessaries neither to men nor to women; the lowest rank of both sexes appearing there publicly, without any discredit, sometimes in wooden shoes, and sometimes bare-footed. Under necessaries therefore, I comprehend, not only those things which nature, but those things which the established rules of decency have rendered necessary to the lowest rank of people. All other things I call luxuries; without meaning by this appellation, to throw the smallest degree of reproach upon the temperate use of them. Beer and ale, for example, in Great Britain, and wine, even in the wine countries, I call luxuries. A man of any rank may, without any reproach, abstain totally from tasting such liquors. Nature does not render them necessary for the support of life; and custom nowhere renders it indecent to live without them.

As the wages of labour are every where regulated, partly by the demand for it, and partly by the average price of the necessary articles of subsistence; whatever raises this average price must necessarily raise those wages, so that the labourer may still be able to purchase that quantity of those necessary articles which the state of the demand for labour, whether increasing, stationary, or declining, requires that he should have. A tax upon those articles necessarily raises their price somewhat higher than the amount of the tax, because the dealer who advances the tax, must generally get it back with a profit. Such a tax must, therefore, occasion a rise in the wages of labour proportionable to this rise of price.

It is thus that a tax upon the necessaries of life, operates exactly in the same manner as a direct tax upon the wages of labour. The labourer, though he may pay it out of his hand, cannot, for any considerable time at least, be properly said even to advance it. It must always in the long-run be advanced to him by his immediate employer in the advanced rate of his wages. His employer, if he is a manufacturer, will charge upon the price of his goods this rise of wages, together with a profit; so that the final payment of the tax, together with this over-charge, will fall upon the consumer. If his employer is a farmer, the final payment, together with a like over-charge, will fall upon the rent of the landlord.

It is otherwise with taxes upon what I call luxuries; even upon those of the poor. The rise in the price of the taxed commodities, will not necessarily occasion any rise in the wages of labour. A tax upon tobacco, for example, though a luxury of the poor as well as of the rich, will not raise wages. Though it in taxed in England at three times, and in France at fifteen times its original price, those high duties seem to have no effect upon the wages of labour. The same thing may be said of the taxes upon tea and sugar; which in

England and Holland have become luxuries of the lowest ranks of people; and of those upon chocolate, which in Spain is said to have become so. The different taxes which in Great Britain have in the course of the present century been imposed upon spirituous liquors, are not supposed to have had any effect upon the wages of labour. The rise in the price of porter, occasioned by an additional tax of three shillings upon the barrel of strong beer, has not raised the wages of common labour in London. These were about eighteen pence and twenty-pence a day before the tax, and they are not more now.

The high price of such commodities does not necessarily diminish the ability of the inferior ranks of people to bring up families. Upon the sober and industrious poor, taxes upon such commodities act as sumptuary laws, and dispose them either to moderate, or to refrain altogether from the use of superfluities which they can no longer easily afford. Their ability to bring up families, in consequence of this forced frugality, instead of being diminished, is frequently, perhaps, increased by the tax. It is the sober and industrious poor who generally bring up the most numerous families, and who principally supply the demand for useful labour. All the poor indeed are not sober and industrious, and the dissolute and disorderly might continue to indulge themselves in the use of such commodities after this rise of price in the same manner as before; without regarding the distress which this indulgence might bring upon their families. Such disorderly persons, however, seldom rear up numerous families; their children generally perishing from neglect, mismanagement, and the scantiness or unwholesomeness of their food. If by the strength of their constitution they survive the hardships to which the bad conduct of their parents exposes them; yet the example of that bad conduct commonly corrupts their morals; so that, instead of being useful to society by their industry, they become public nuisances by their vices and disorders. Though the advanced price of the luxuries of the poor, therefore, might increase somewhat the distress of such disorderly families, and thereby diminish somewhat their ability to bring up children; it would not probably diminish much the useful population of the country.

Any rise in the average price of necessaries, unless it is compensated by a proportionable rise in the wages of labour, must necessarily diminish more or less the ability of the poor to bring up numerous families, and consequently to supply the demand for useful labour; whatever may be the state of that demand, whether increasing, stationary, or declining; or such as requires an increasing, stationary, or declining population.

Taxes upon luxuries have no tendency to raise the price of any other commodities except that of the commodities taxed. Taxes upon necessaries, by raising the wages of labour, necessarily tend to raise the price of all manufactures, and consequently to diminish the extent of their sale and consumption. Taxes upon luxuries are finally paid by the consumers of the commodities taxed, without any retribution. They fall indifferently upon every species of revenue, the wages of labour, the profits of stock, and the rent of land. Taxes upon necessaries, so far as they affect the labouring poor, are finally paid, partly by landlords in the diminished rent of their lands, and partly by rich consumers, whether landlords or others, in the advanced price of manufactured goods; and always with a considerable over-charge. The advanced price of such manufactures as are real necessaries of life, and are destined for the consumption of the poor, of coarse woollens, for example, must be compensated to the poor by a farther advancement of their wages. The middling and superior ranks of people, if they understood their own interest, ought always to oppose all taxes upon the necessaries of life, as well as all direct taxes upon the wages of labour. The final payment of both the one and the other falls altogether upon themselves, and always with a considerable over-charge. They fall heaviest upon the landlords, who always pay in a double capacity; in that of landlords, by the reduction of their rent; and in that of rich consumers, by the increase of their expence. The observation of Sir Matthew Decker, that certain taxes are, in the price of certain goods, sometimes repeated and accumulated four or five times, is perfectly just with regard to taxes upon the necessaries of life. In the price of leather, for example, you must pay, not only for the tax upon the leather of your own shoes, but for a part of that upon those of the shoemaker and the tanner. You must pay too for the tax upon the salt, upon the soap, and upon the candles which those workmen consume while employed in your service, and for the tax upon the leather, which the salt-maker, the soapmaker, and the candle-maker consume while employed in their service.

In Great Britain, the principal taxes upon the necessaries of life are those upon the four commodities just now mentioned, salt, leather, soap, and candles.

Salt is a very ancient and a very universal subject of taxation. It was taxed among the Romans, and it is so at present in, I believe, every part of Europe. The quantity annually consumed by any individual is so small, and may be purchased so gradually, that nobody, it seems to have been thought, could feel very sensibly even a pretty heavy tax upon it. It is in England taxed at three shillings and fourpence a bushel; about three times the original price of the commodity. In some other countries the tax is still higher. Leather is a real necessary of life. The use of linen renders soap such. In countries where the winter nights are long, candles are a necessary instrument of trade. Leather and soap are in Great Britain taxed at three halfpence a pound; candles at a penny; taxes which, upon the original price of leather, may amount to about eight or ten per cent.; upon that of soap about twenty or five and twenty per cent., and upon that of candles to about fourteen or fifteen per cent.; taxes which, though lighter than that upon salt, are still very heavy. As all those four commodities are real necessaries of life, such heavy taxes upon them must increase somewhat the expence of the sober and industrious poor, and must consequently raise more or less the wages of their labour.

In a country where the winters are so cold as in Great Britain, fuel is, during that season, in the strictest sense of the word, a necessary of life, not only for the purpose of dressing victuals, but for the comfortable subsistence of many different sorts of workmen who work within doors; and coals are the cheapest of all fuel. The price of fuel has so important an influence upon that of labour, that all over

Great Britain manufactures have confined themselves principally to the coal countries; other parts of the country, on account of the high price of this necessary article, not being able to work so cheap. In some manufactures, besides, coal is a necessary instrument of trade; as in those of glass, iron, and all other metals. If a bounty could in any case be reasonable, it might perhaps be so upon the transportation of coals from those parts of the country in which they abound, to those in which they are wanted. But the legislature, instead of a bounty, has imposed a tax of three shillings and three-pence a ton upon coal carried coastways; which upon most sorts of coal is more than sixty per cent. of the original price at the coal-pit. Coals carried either by land or by inland navigation pay no duty. Where they are naturally cheap, they are consumed duty free; where they are naturally dear, they are loaded with a heavy duty.

Such taxes, though they raise the price of subsistence, and consequently the wages of labour, yet they afford a considerable revenue to government, which it might not be easy to find in any other way. There may, therefore, be good reasons for continuing them. The bounty upon the exportation of corn, so far as it tends in the actual state of tillage to raise the price of that necessary article, produces all the like bad effects; and instead of affording any revenue, frequently occasions a very great expense to government. The high duties upon the importation of foreign corn, which in years of moderate plenty amount to a prohibition; and the absolute prohibition of the importation either of live cattle or of salt provisions, which takes place in the ordinary state of the law, and which, on account of the scarcity, is at present suspended for a limited time with regard to Ireland and the British plantations, have all the bad effects of taxes upon the necessaries of life, and produce no revenue to government. Nothing seems necessary for the repeal of such regulations, but to convince the public of the futility of that system in consequence of which they have been established.

Taxes upon the necessaries of life are much higher in many other countries than in Great Britain. Duties upon flour and meal when ground at the mill, and upon bread when baked at the oven, take place in many countries. In

Holland the money price of the bread consumed in towns is supposed to be doubled by means of such taxes. In lieu of a part of them, the people who live in the country pay every year so much a head, according to the sort of bread they are supposed to consume. Those who consume wheaten bread, pay three guilders fifteen stivers; about six shillings and ninepence halfpenny. These, and some other taxes of the same kind, by raising the price of labour, are said to have ruined the greater part of the manufactures of Holland. Similar taxes, though not quite so heavy, take place in the Milanese, in the states of Genoa, in the dutchy of Modena, in the dutchies of Parma, Placentia, and Guastalla, and in the ecclesiastical state. A French author of some note has proposed to reform the finances of his country, by substituting in the room of the greater part of other taxes, this most ruinous of all taxes. There is nothing so absurd, says Cicero, which has not sometimes been asserted by some philosophers.

Taxes upon butchers meat are still more common than those upon bread. It may indeed be doubted whether butchers meat is any where a necessary of life. Grain and other vegetables, with the help of milk, cheese, and butter, or oil, where butter is not to be had, it is known from experience, can, without any butchers meat, afford the most plentiful, the most wholesome, the most nourishing, and the most invigorating diet. Decency no where requires that any man should eat butchers meat, as it in most places requires that he should wear a linen shirt or a pair of leather shoes.

Consumable commodities, whether necessaries or luxuries, may be taxed in two different ways. The consumer may either pay an annual sum on account of his using or consuming goods of a certain kind; or the goods may be taxed while they remain in the hands of the dealer, and before they are delivered to the consumer. The consumable goods which last a considerable time before they are consumed altogether, are most properly taxed in the one way. Those of which the consumption is either immediate or more speedy, in the other. The coach-tax and plate-tax are examples of the former method of imposing: the greater part of the other duties of excise and customs, of the latter.

The duties of excise are imposed chiefly upon goods of home produce destined for home consumption. They are imposed only upon a few sorts of goods of the most general use. There can never be any doubt either concerning the goods which are subject to those duties, or concerning the particular duty which each species of goods is subject to. They fall almost altogether upon what I call luxuries, excepting always the four duties above mentioned, upon salt, soap, leather, candles, and, perhaps, that upon green glass.

The duties of customs are much more ancient than those of excise. They seem to have been called customs, as denoting customary payments which had been in use from time immemorial. They appear to have been originally considered as taxes upon the profits of merchants. During the barbarous times of feudal anarchy, merchants, like all the other inhabitants of burghs, were considered so little better than emancipated bondmen, whose persons were despised, and whose gains were envied. The great nobility, who had consented that the king should tallage the profits of their own tenants, were not unwilling that he should tallage likewise those of an order of men whom it was much less their interest to protect. In those ignorant times, it was not understood, that the profits of merchants are a subject not taxable directly; or that the final payment of all such taxes must fall, with a considerable over-charge, upon the consumers.

The gains of alien merchants were looked upon more unfavourably than those of English merchants. It was natural, therefore, that those of the former should be taxed more heavily than those of the latter. This distinction between the duties upon aliens and those upon English merchants, which was begun from ignorance, has been continued from the spirit of monopoly, or in order to give our own merchants an advantage both in the home and in the foreign market.

With this distinction, the ancient duties of customs were imposed equally upon all sorts of goods, necessaries as well as luxuries, goods exported as well as goods imported. Why should the dealers in one sort of goods, it seems to have been thought, be more favoured than those in another? or why should the merchant exporter be more favoured than the merchant importer?

The ancient customs were divided into three branches. The first, and perhaps the most ancient of all those duties, was that upon wool and leather. It seems to have been chiefly or altogether an exportation duty. When the woollen manufacture came to be established in England, lest the king should lose any part of his customs upon wool by the exportation of woollen cloths, a like duty was imposed upon them. The other two branches were, first, a duty upon wine, which, being imposed at so much a ton, was called a tonnage; and, secondly, a duty upon all other goods, which, being imposed at so much a pound of their supposed value, was called a poundage. In the forty-seventh year of Edward III. a duty of sixpence in the pound was imposed upon all goods exported and imported, except wools, wool-fells, leather, and wines, which were subject to particular duties. In the fourteenth of Richard II. this duty was raised to one shilling in the pound; but three years afterwards, it was again reduced to sixpence. It was raised to eight-pence in the second year of Henry IV.; and in the fourth year of the same prince, to one shilling. From this time to the ninth year of William III. this duty continued at one shilling in the pound. The duties of tonnage and poundage were generally granted to the king by one and the same act of parliament, and were called the Subsidy of Tonnage and Poundage. The subsidy of poundage having continued for so long a time at one shilling in the pound, or at five per cent.; a subsidy came, in the language of the customs, to denote a general duty of this kind of five per cent. The subsidy, which is now called the Old Subsidy, still continues to be levied according to the book of rates established in the twelfth of Charles II. The method of ascertaining, by a book of rates, the value of goods subject to this duty, is said to be older than the time of James I. The new subsidy imposed by the ninth and tenth of William III., was an additional five per cent. upon the greater part of goods. The one-third and the two-third subsidy made up between them another five per cent. of which they were proportionately parts. The subsidy of 1747 made a fourth five per cent. upon the greater part of goods; and that of 1759, a fifth upon some particular sorts of goods. Besides those five subsidies, a great variety of other duties have occasionally been imposed upon particular sorts of goods, in order sometimes to relieve the exigencies of the state, and sometimes to regulate the trade of the country, according to the principles of the mercantile system.

That system has come gradually more and more into fashion. The old subsidy was imposed indifferently upon exportation as well as importation. The four subsequent subsidies, as well as the other duties which have since been occasionally imposed upon particular sorts of goods, have, with a few exceptions, been laid altogether upon importation. The greater part of the ancient duties which had been imposed upon the exportation of the goods of home produce and manufacture, have either been lightened or taken away altogether. In most cases they have been taken away. Bounties have even been given upon the exportation of some of them. Drawbacks too, sometimes of the whole, and, in most cases, of a part of the duties which are paid upon the importation of foreign goods, have been granted upon their exportation. Only half the duties imposed by the old subsidy upon importation are drawn back upon exportation: but the whole of those imposed by the latter subsidies and other imposts are, upon the greater part of goods, drawn back in the same manner. This growing favour of exportation, and discouragement of importation, have suffered only a few exceptions, which chiefly concern the materials of some manufactures. These, our merchants and manufacturers are willing should come as cheap as possible to themselves, and as dear as possible to their rivals and competitors in other countries. Foreign materials are, upon this account, sometimes allowed to be imported duty free; Spanish wool, for example, flax, and raw linen yarn. The exportation of the materials of home produce, and of those which are the particular produce of our colonies, has sometimes been prohibited, and sometimes subjected to higher duties. The exportation of English wool has been prohibited. That of beaver skins, of beaver wool, and of gum Senega, has been subjected to higher duties; Great Britain, by the conquest of Canada and Senegal, having got almost the monopoly of those commodities.

That the mercantile system has not been very favourable

to the revenue of the great body of the people, to the annual produce of the land and labour of the country, I have endeavoured to shew in the fourth book of this Inquiry. It seems not to have been more favourable to the revenue of the sovereign; so far at least as that revenue depends upon the duties of customs.

In consequence of that system, the importation of several sorts of goods has been prohibited altogether. This prohibition has in some cases entirely prevented, and in others has very much diminished the importation of those commodities, by reducing the importers to the necessity of smuggling. It has entirely prevented the importation of foreign woollens; and it has very much diminished that of foreign silks and velvets. In both cases it has entirely annihilated the revenue of customs which might have been levied upon such importation.

The high duties which have been imposed upon the importation of many different sorts of foreign goods, in order to discourage their consumption in Great Britain, have in many cases served only to encourage smuggling; and in all cases have reduced the revenue of the customs below what more moderate duties would have afforded. The saying of Dr. Swift, that in the arithmetic of the customs two and two, instead of making four, make sometimes only one, holds perfectly true with regard to such heavy duties, which never could have been imposed, had not the mercantile system taught us, in many cases, to employ taxation as an instrument, not of revenue, but of monopoly.

In order that the greater part of the members of any society should contribute to the public revenue in proportion to their respective expence, it does not seem necessary that every single article of that expence should be taxed. The revenue, which is levied by the duties of excise, is supposed to fall as equally upon the contributors as that which is levied by the duties of customs; and the duties of excise are imposed upon a few articles only of the most general use and consumption. It has been the opinion of many people, that, by proper management, the duties of customs might likewise, without any loss to the public revenue, and with great advantage to foreign trade, be confined to a few articles only.

The foreign articles, of the most general use and consumption in Great Britain, seem at present to consist chiefly in foreign wines and brandies; in some of the productions of America and the West Indies, sugar, rum, tobacco, cocoanuts, &c. and in some of those of the East Indies, tea, coffee, china-ware, spiceries of all kinds, several sorts of piece-goods, &c. These different articles afford, perhaps, at present, the greater part of the revenue which is drawn from the duties of customs. The taxes which at present subsist upon foreign manufactures, if you except those upon the few contained in the foregoing enumeration, have the greater part of them been imposed for the purpose, not of revenue, but of monopoly, or to give our own merchants an advantage in the home market. By removing all prohibitions, and by subjecting all foreign manufactures to such moderate taxes, as it was found from experience afforded upon each article the greatest revenue to the public, our own workmen might still have a considerable advantage in the home market, and many articles, some of which at present afford no revenue to government, and others a very inconsiderable one, might afford a very great one.

High taxes, sometimes by diminishing the consumption of the taxed commodities, and sometimes by encouraging smuggling, frequently afford a smaller revenue to government than what might be drawn from more moderate taxes.

When the diminution of revenue is the effect of the diminution of consumption, there can be but one remedy, and that is the lowering of the tax.

When the diminution of the revenue is the effect of the encouragement given to smuggling, it may perhaps be remedied in two ways; either by diminishing the temptation to smuggle, or by increasing the difficulty of smuggling. The temptation to smuggle can be diminished only by the lowering of the tax; and the difficulty of smuggling can be increased only by establishing that system of administration which is most proper for preventing it.

The excise laws, it appears, I believe, from experience, obstruct and embarrass the operations of the smuggler much more effectually than those of the customs. By introducing into the customs a system of administration as similar to that of the excise as the nature of the different duties will admit, the difficulty of smuggling might be very much increased. This alteration, it has been supposed by many people, might very easily be brought about.

The importer of commodities liable to any duties of customs, it has been said, might at his option be allowed either to carry them to his own private warehouse, or to lodge them in a warehouse provided either at his own expence or at that of the public, but under the key of the customhouse officer, and never to be opened but in his presence. If the merchant carried them to his own private warehouse, the duties to be immediately paid, and never afterwards to be drawn back; and that warehouse to be at all times subject to the visit and examination of the customhouse officer, in order to ascertain how far the quantity contained in it corresponded with that for which the duty had been paid. If he carried them to the public warehouse, no duty to be paid till they were taken out for home consumption. If taken out for exportation, to be duty-free; proper security being always given that they should be so exported. The dealers in those particular commodities, either by wholesale or retail, to be at all times subject to the visit and examination of the customhouse officer; and to be obliged to justify by proper certificates the payment of the duty upon the whole quantity contained in their shops or warehouses. What are called the excise-duties upon rum imported are at present levied in this manner, and the same system of administration might perhaps be extended to all duties upon goods imported; provided always that those duties were, like the duties of excise, confined to a few sorts of goods of the most general use and consumption. If they were extended to almost all sorts of goods, as at present, public warehouses of sufficient extent could not easily be provided, and goods of a very delicate nature, or of which the preservation required much care and attention, could not safely be trusted by the merchant in any warehouse but his own.

If by such a system of administration smuggling, to any considerable extent, could be prevented even under pretty high duties; and if every duty was occasionally either heightened or lowered according as it was most likely, either the one way or the other, to afford the greatest revenue to the state; taxation being always employed as an instrument of revenue and never of monopoly; it seems not improbable that a revenue, at least equal to the present neat revenue of the customs, might be drawn from duties upon the importation of only a few sorts of goods of the most general use and consumption; and that the duties of customs might thus be brought to the same degree of simplicity, certainty, and precision, as those of excise. What the revenue at present loses, by drawbacks upon the re-exportation of foreign goods which are afterwards relanded and consumed at home, would under this system be saved altogether. If to this saving, which would alone be very considerable, were added the abolition of all bounties upon the exportation of home-produce; in all cases in which those bounties were not in reality drawbacks of some duties of excise which had before been advanced; it cannot well be doubted but that the neat revenue of customs might, after an alteration of this kind, be fully equal to what it had ever been before.

If by such a change of system the public revenue suffered no loss, the trade and manufactures of the country would certainly gain a very considerable advantage. The trade in the commodities not taxed, by far the greatest number, would be perfectly free, and might be carried on to and from all parts of the world with every possible advantage. Among those commodities would be comprehended all the necessaries of life, and all the materials of manufacture. So far as the free importation of the necessaries of life reduced their average money price in the home market, it would reduce the money price of labour, but without reducing in any respect its real recompence. The value of money is in proportion to the quantity of the necessaries of life which it will purchase. That of the necessaries of life is altogether independent of the quantity of money which can be had for them. The reduction in the money price of labour would necessarily be attended with a proportionable one in that of all home-manufactures, which would thereby gain some advantage in all foreign markets. The price of some manufactures would be reduced in a still greater proportion by the free importation of the raw materials. If raw silk could be imported from

China and Indostan duty-free, the silk manufacturers in England could greatly undersell those of both France and Italy. There would be no occasion to prohibit the importation of foreign silks and velvets. The cheapness of their goods would secure to our own workmen, not only the possession of the home, but a very great command of the foreign market. Even the trade in the commodities taxed would be carried on with much more advantage than at present. If those commodities were delivered out of the public warehouse for foreign exportation, being in this case exempted from all taxes, the trade in them would be perfectly free. The carrying trade in all sorts of goods would under this system enjoy every possible advantage. If those commodities were delivered out for home-consumption, the importer not being obliged to advance the tax till he had an opportunity of selling his goods, either to some dealer, or to some consumer, he could always afford to sell them cheaper than if he had been obliged to advance it at the moment of importation. Under the same taxes, the foreign trade of consumption even in the taxed commodities, might in this manner be carried on with much more advantage than it can at present.

It was the object of the famous excise scheme of Sir Robert Walpole to establish, with regard to wine and tobacco, a system not very unlike that which is here proposed. But though the bill which was then brought into parliament, comprehended those two commodities only; it was generally supposed to be meant as an introduction to a more extensive scheme of the same kind. Faction, combined with the interest of smuggling merchants, raised so violent, though so unjust, a clamour against that bill, that the minister thought proper to drop it; and from a dread of exciting a clamour of the same kind, none of his successors have dared to resume the project.

The duties upon foreign luxuries imported for home-consumption, though they sometimes fall upon the poor, fall principally upon people of middling or more than middling fortune. Such are, for example, the duties upon foreign wines, upon coffee, chocolate, tea, sugar, &c.

The duties upon the cheaper luxuries of home-produce destined for home-consumption, fall pretty equally upon people of all ranks in proportion to their respective expence. The poor pay the duties upon malt, hops, beer, and ale, upon their own consumption: The rich, upon both their own consumption and that of their servants.

The whole consumption of the inferior ranks of people, or of those below the middling rank, it must be observed, is in every country much greater, not only in quantity, but in value, than that of the middling and of those above the middling rank. The whole expence of the inferior is much greater than that of the superior ranks. In the first place, almost the whole capital of every country is annually distributed among the inferior ranks of people, as the wages of productive labour. Secondly, a great part of the revenue arising from both the rent of land and the profits of stock, is annually distributed among the same rank, in the wages and maintenance of menial servants, and other unproductive labourers. Thirdly, some part of the profits of stock belongs to the same rank, as a revenue arising from the employment of their small capitals. The amount of the profits annually made by small shopkeepers, tradesmen, and retailers of all kinds, is every where very considerable, and makes a very considerable portion of the annual produce. Fourthly, and lastly, some part even of the rent of land belongs to the same rank; a considerable part to those who are somewhat below the middling rank, and a small part even to the lowest rank; common labourers sometimes possessing in property an acre or two of land. Though the expence of those inferior ranks of people, therefore, taking them individually, is very small, yet the whole mass of it, taking them collectively, amounts always to by much the largest portion of the whole expence of the society; what remains, of the annual produce of the land and labour of the country for the consumption of the superior ranks, being always much less, not only in quantity but in value. The taxes upon expence, therefore, which fall chiefly upon that of the superior ranks of people, upon the smaller portion of the annual produce, are likely to be much less productive than either those which fall indifferently upon the expence of all ranks, or even those which fall chiefly upon that of the inferior ranks; than either those which fall indifferently upon the whole annual produce, or those which fall chiefly upon the larger portion of it. The excise upon the materials and manufacture of home-made fermented and spirituous liquors is accordingly, of all the different taxes upon expence, by far the most productive; and this branch of the excise falls very much, perhaps principally, upon the expence of the common people. In the year which ended on the 5th of July 1775, the gross produce of this branch of the excise amounted to 3,341,837*l.* 9*s.* 9*d.*

It must always be remembered, however, that it is the luxurious and not the necessary expence of the inferior ranks of people that ought ever to be taxed. The final payment of any tax upon their necessary expence would fall altogether upon the superior ranks of people; upon the smaller portion of the annual produce, and not upon the greater. Such a tax must in all cases either raise the wages of labour, or lessen the demand for it. It could not raise the wages of labour, without throwing the final payment of the tax upon the superior ranks of people. It could not lessen the demand for labour, without lessening the annual produce of the land and labour of the country, the fund from which all taxes must be finally paid. Whatever might be the state to which a tax of this kind reduced the demand for labour, it must always raise wages higher than they otherwise would be in that state; and the final payment of this enhancement of wages must in all cases fall upon the superior ranks of people.

Fermented liquors brewed, and spirituous liquors distilled, not for sale, but for private use, are not in Great Britain liable to any duties of excise. This exemption, of which the object is to save private families from the odious visit and examination of the tax-gatherer, occasions the burden of those duties to fall frequently much lighter upon the rich than upon the poor. It is not, indeed, very common to distil for private use, though it is done sometimes. But in the country, many middling and almost all rich and great families brew their own beer. Their strong beer, therefore, costs them eight shillings a barrel less than it costs the common brewer, who must have his profit upon the tax, as well as upon all the other expence which he advances. Such families, therefore, must drink their beer at least nine or ten shillings a barrel cheaper than any liquor of the same quality can be drunk by the common people, to whom it is every where more convenient to buy their beer, by little and little, from the brewery or the alehouse. Malt, in the same manner, that is made for the use of a private family, is not liable to the visit or examination of the tax-gatherer; but in this case the family must compound at seven shillings and sixpence a head for the tax. Seven shillings and sixpence are equal to the excise upon ten bushels of malt; a quantity fully equal to what all the different members of any sober family, men, women, and children, are at an average likely to consume. But in rich and great families, where country hospitality is much practised, the malt liquors consumed by the members of the family make but a small part of the consumption of the house. Either on account of this composition, however, or for other reasons, it is not near so common to malt as to brew for private use. It is difficult to imagine any equitable reason why those who either brew or distil for private use, should not be subject to a composition of the same kind.

A greater revenue than what is at present drawn from all the heavy taxes upon malt, beer, and ale, might be raised, it has frequently been said, by a much lighter tax upon malt; the opportunities of defrauding the revenue being much greater in a brewery than in a malt-house; and those who brew for private use being exempted from all duties or composition for duties, which is not the case with those who malt for private use

* * * * * * * * * * *

Besides such duties as those of customs and excise abovementioned, there are several others which affect the price of goods more unequally and more indirectly. Of this kind are the duties which in French are called Péages, which in old Saxon times were called Duties of Passage, and which seem to have been originally established for the same purpose as our turnpike tolls, or the tolls upon our canals and navigable rivers, for the maintenance of the road or of the navigation. Those duties, when applied to such purposes, are most properly imposed according to the bulk of weight of the goods. As they were originally local and provincial duties, applicable to local and provincial purposes, the administration of them was in most cases entrusted to the particular town, parish, or lordship, in which they were levied; such communities being in some way or other supposed to be accountable for the application. The sovereign, who is altogether unaccountable, has in many countries assumed to himself the administration of those duties; and though he has in most cases enhanced very much the duty, he has in many entirely neglected the application. If the turnpike tolls of Great Britain should ever become one of the resources of government, we may learn, by the example of many other nations, what would probably be the consequence. Such tolls are no doubt finally paid by the consumer; but the consumer is not taxed in proportion to his expence when he pays, not according to the value, but according to the bulk or weight of what he consumes. When such duties are imposed, not according to the bulk or weight, but according to the supposed value of the goods, they become properly a sort of inland customs or excises, which obstruct very much the most important of all branches of commerce, the interior commerce of the country.

In some small states duties similar to those passage duties are imposed upon goods carried across the territory, either by land or by water, from one foreign country to another. These are in some countries called transit-duties. Some of the little Italian states, which are situated upon the Po, and the rivers which run into it, derive some revenue from duties of this kind, which are paid altogether by foreigners, and which, perhaps, are the only duties that one state can impose upon the subjects of another, without obstructing in any respect the industry or commerce of its own. The most important transit-duty in the world is that levied by the king of Denmark upon all merchant ships which pass through the Sound.

Such taxes upon luxuries as the greater part of the duties of customs and excise, though they all fall indifferently upon every different species of revenue, and are paid finally, or without any retribution, by whoever consumes the commodities upon which they are imposed, yet they do not always fall equally or proportionably upon the revenue of every individual. As every man's humour regulates the degree of his consumption, every man contributes rather according to his humour than in proportion to his revenue; the profuse contribute more, the parsimonious less, than their proper proportion. During the minority of a man of great fortune, he contributes commonly very little, by his consumption, towards the support of that state from whose protection he derives a great revenue. Those who live in another country contribute nothing, by their consumption, towards the support of the government of that country, in which is situated the source of their revenue. If in this latter country there should be no land-tax, nor any considerable duty upon the transference either of moveable or of immoveable property, as is the case in Ireland, such absentees may derive a great revenue from the protection of a government to the support of which they do not contribute a single shilling. This inequality is likely to be greatest in a country of which the government is in some respects subordinate and dependent upon that of some other. The people who possess the most extensive property in the dependent, will in this case generally chuse to live in the governing country. Ireland is precisely in this situation, and we cannot therefore wonder that the proposal of a tax upon absentees should be so very popular in that country. It might, perhaps, be a little difficult to ascertain either what sort, or what degree of absence would subject a man to be taxed as an absentee, or at what precise time the tax should either begin or end. If you except, however, this very particular situation, any inequality in the contribution of individuals, which can arise from such taxes, is much more than compensated by the very circumstance which occasions that inequality; the circumstance that every man's contribution is altogether voluntary; it being altogether in his power either to consume or not to consume the commodity taxed. Where such taxes, therefore, are properly assessed and upon proper commodities, they are paid with less grumbling than any other. When they are advanced by the merchant or manufacturer, the consumer, who finally pays them, soon comes to confound them with the price of the commodities, and almost forgets that he pays any tax.

Such taxes are or may be perfectly certain, or may be assessed so as to leave no doubt concerning either what ought to be paid, or when it ought to be paid; concerning either the quantity or the time of payment. Whatever uncertainty there may sometimes be, either in the duties of customs in Great Britain, or in other duties of the same kind in other countries, it cannot arise from the nature of those duties, but from the inaccurate or unskilful manner in which the law that imposes them is expressed.

Taxes upon luxuries generally are, and always may be, paid piecemeal, or in proportion as the contributors have occasion to purchase the goods upon which they are imposed. In the time and mode of payment they are, or may be, of all taxes the most convenient. Upon the whole, such taxes, therefore, are, perhaps, as agreeable to the three first of the four general maxims concerning taxation, as any other. They offend in every respect against the fourth.

Such taxes, in proportion to what they bring into the public treasury of the state, always take out or keep out of the pockets of the people more than almost any other taxes. They seem to do this in all the four different ways in which it is possible to do it.

First, the levying of such taxes, even when imposed in the most judicious manner, requires a great number of customhouse and excise officers, whose salaries and perquisites are a real tax upon the people, which brings nothing into the treasury of the state. This expence, however, it must be acknowledged, is more moderate in Great Britain than in most other countries. In the year which ended on the fifth of July 1775, the gross produce of the different duties, under the management of the commissioners of excise in England, amounted to 5,507,308*l.* 18*s.* 8¼*d.* which was levied at an expence of little more than five and a half per cent. From this gross produce, however, there must be deducted what was paid away in bounties and drawbacks upon the exportation of exciseable goods, which will reduce the neat produce below five millions. The levying of the salt duty, an excise duty, but under a different management, is much more expensive. The neat revenue of the customs does not amount to two millions and a half, which is levied at an expense of more than ten per cent. in the salaries of officers, and other incidents. But the perquisites of customhouse officers are every where much greater than their salaries; at some ports more than double or triple those salaries. If the salaries of officers, and other incidents, therefore, amount to more than ten per cent. upon the neat revenue of the customs; the whole expense of levying that revenue may amount, in salaries and perquisites together, to more than twenty or thirty per cent. The officers of excise receive few or no perquisites: and the administration of that branch of the revenue being of more recent establishment, is in general less corrupted than that of the customs, into which length of time has introduced and authorized many abuses. By charging upon malt the whole revenue which is at present levied by the different duties upon malt and malt liquors, a saving, it is supposed, of more than fifty thousand pounds might be made in the annual expence of the excise. By confining the duties of customs to a few sorts of goods, and by levying those duties according to the excise laws, a much greater saving might probably be made in the annual expence of the customs.

Secondly, such taxes necessarily occasion some obstruction or discouragement to certain branches of industry. As they always raise the price of the commodity taxed, they so far discourage its consumption, and consequently its production. If it is a commodity of home growth or manufacture, less labour comes to be employed in raising and producing it. If it is a foreign commodity of which the tax increases in this manner, the price, the commodities of the same kind which are made at home may thereby, indeed, gain some advantage in the home market, and a greater quantity of domestic industry may thereby be turned toward preparing them. But though this rise of price in a foreign commodity may encourage domestic industry in one particular branch, it necessarily discourages that industry in almost every other. The dearer the Birmingham manufacturer buys his foreign wine, the cheaper he necessarily sells that part of his hardware with which, or, what comes to the same thing, with the price of which he buys it. That part of his hardware, therefore, becomes of less value to him, and he has less encouragement to work at it. The dearer the consumers in one country pay for the surplus produce of another, the cheaper they necessarily sell that part of their own surplus produce with which, or, what comes to the same thing, with the price of which they buy it. That part of their own surplus produce becomes of less value to them, and they have less encouragement to increase its quantity. All taxes upon consumable commodities, therefore, tend to reduce the quantity of productive labour below what it otherwise would be, either in preparing the commodities taxed, if they are home commodities; or in preparing those with which they are purchased, if they are foreign commodities. Such taxes too always alter, more or less, the natural direction of national industry, and turn it into a channel always different from, and always less advantageous than that in which it would have run of its own accord.

Thirdly, the hope of evading such taxes by smuggling gives frequent occasion to forfeitures and other penalties, which entirely ruin the smuggler; a person who, though no doubt highly blameable for violating the laws of his country, is frequently incapable of violating those of natural justice, and would have been, in every respect, an excellent citizen, had not the laws of his country made that a crime which nature never meant to be so. In those corrupted governments where there is at least a general suspicion of much unnecessary expence, and great misapplication of the public revenue, the laws which guard it are little respected. Not many people are scrupulous about smuggling, when, without perjury, they can find easy and safe opportunity of doing so. To pretend to have any scruple about buying smuggled goods, though a manifest encouragement to the violation of the revenue laws, and to the perjury which almost always attends it, would in most countries be regarded as one of those pedantic pieces of hypocrisy which, instead of gaining credit with any body, serve only to expose the person who affects to practise them, to the suspicion of being a greater knave than most of his neighbours. By this indulgence of the public, the smuggler is often encouraged to continue a trade which he is thus taught to consider as in some measure innocent; and when the severity of the revenue laws is ready to fall upon him, he is frequently disposed to defend with violence, what he has been accustomed to regard as his just property. From being at first, perhaps, rather imprudent than criminal, he at last too often becomes one of the hardiest and most determined violators of the laws of society. By the ruin of the smuggler, his capital, which had before been employed in maintaining productive labour, is absorbed either in the revenue of the state or in that of the revenue-officer, and is employed in maintaining unproductive, to the diminution of the general capital of the society, and of the useful industry which it might otherwise have maintained.

Fourthly, such taxes, by subjecting at least the dealers in the taxed commodities to the frequent visits and odious examination of the tax-gatherers, expose them sometimes, no doubt, to some degree of oppression, and always to much trouble and vexation; and though vexation, as has already been said, is not strictly speaking expence, it is certainly equivalent to the expence at which every man would be willing to redeem himself from it. The laws of excise, though more effectual for the purpose for which they were instituted, are, in this respect, more vexatious than those of the customs. When a merchant has imported goods subject to certain duties of customs, when he has paid those duties, and lodged the goods in his warehouse, he is not in most cases liable to any further trouble or vexation from the customhouse officer. It is otherwise with goods subject to duties of excise. The dealers have no respite from the continual visits and examination of the excise officers. The duties of excise are, upon this account, more unpopular than those of the customs; and so are the officers who levy them. Those officers, it is pretended, though in general, perhaps, they do their duty fully as well as those of the customs; yet, as that duty obliges them to be frequently very troublesome to some of their neighbours, commonly contract a certain hardness of character which the others frequently have not. This observation, however, may very probably be the mere suggestion of fraudulent dealers, whose smuggling is either prevented or detected by their diligence.

The inconveniencies, however, which are, perhaps, in some degree inseparable from taxes upon consumable commodities, fall as light upon the people of Great Britain as upon those of any other country of which the government is nearly as expensive. Our state is not perfect, and might be mended; but it is as good or better than that of most of our neighbours.

In consequence of the notion that duties upon consumable goods were taxes upon the profits of merchants, those duties have, in some countries, been repeated upon every successive sale of the goods. If the profits of the merchant importer or merchant manufacturer were taxed, equality seemed to require that those of all the middle buyers, who intervened between either of them and the consumer, should likewise be taxed. The famous Alcavala of Spain seems to have been established upon this principle. It was at first a tax of ten per cent., afterwards of fourteen per cent., and is at present of only six per cent. upon the sale of every sort of property, whether moveable or immoveable; and it is repeated every time the property is sold. The levying of this tax requires a multitude of revenue officers sufficient to guard the transportation of goods, not only from one province to another, but from one shop to another. It subjects, not only the dealers in some sorts of goods, but those in all sorts, every farmer, every manufacturer, every merchant and shop-keeper, to the continual visits and examination of the tax-gatherers. Through the greater part of a country in which a tax of this kind is established, nothing can be produced for distant sale. The produce of every part of the country must be proportioned to the consumption of the neighbourhood. It is to the Alcavala, accordingly, that Ustaritz imputes the ruin of the manufactures of Spain. He might have imputed to it likewise the declension of agriculture, it being imposed not only upon manufactures, but upon the rude produce of the land.

In the kingdom of Naples there is a similar tax of three per cent. upon the value of all contracts, and consequently upon that of all contracts of sale. It is both lighter than the Spanish tax, and the greater part of towns and parishes are allowed to pay a composition in lieu of it. They levy this composition in what manner they please, generally in a way that gives no interruption to the interior commerce of the place. The Neapolitan tax, therefore, is not near so ruinous as the Spanish one.

The uniform system of taxation, which, with a few exceptions of no great consequence, takes place in all the different parts of the united kingdom of Great Britain, leaves the interior commerce of the country, the inland and coasting trade, almost entirely free. The inland trade is almost perfectly free, and the greater part of goods may be carried from one end of the kingdom to the other, without requiring any permit or let-pass, without being subject to question, visit, or examination from the revenue officers. There are a few exceptions, but they are such as can give no interruption to any important branch of the inland commerce of the country. Goods carried coastwise, indeed, require certificates or coast cockets. If you except coals, however, the rest are almost all duty-free. This freedom of interior commerce, the effect of the uniformity of the system of taxation, is perhaps one of the principal causes of the prosperity of Great Britain; every great country being necessarily the best and most extensive market for the greater part of the productions of its own industry. If the same freedom, in consequence of the same uniformity, could be extended to Ireland and the plantations, both the grandeur of the state and the prosperity of every part of the empire, would probably be still greater than at present.

In France, the different revenue laws which take place in the different provinces, require a multitude of revenue-officers to surround, not only the frontiers of the kingdom, but those of almost each particular province, in order either to prevent the importation of certain goods, or to subject it to the payment of certain duties, to the no small interruption of the interior commerce of the country. Some provinces are allowed to compound for the gabelle or salt-tax. Others are exempted from it altogether. Some provinces are exempted from the exclusive sale of tobacco, which the farmers-general enjoy through the greater part of the kingdom. The aids, which correspond to the excise in England, are very different in different provinces. Some provinces are exempted from them, and pay a composition or equivalent. In those in which they take place and are in farm, there are many local duties which do not extend beyond a particular town or district. The Traites, which correspond to our customs, divide the kingdom into three great parts; first, the provinces subject to the tarif of 1664, which are called the provinces of the five great farms, and under which are comprehended Picardy, Normandy, and the greater part of the interior provinces of the kingdom; secondly, the provinces subject to the tarif of 1667, which are called the provinces reckoned foreign, and under which are comprehended the greater part of the frontier provinces; and, thirdly, those provinces which are said to be treated as foreign, or which, because they are allowed a free commerce with foreign countries, are in their commerce with the other provinces of France subjected to the same duties as other foreign countries. These are Alsace, the three bishopricks of Metz, Toul, and Verdun, and the three cities of Dunkirk, Bayonne, and Marseilles. Both in the provinces of the five great farms (called so on account of an ancient division of the duties of customs into five great branches, each of which was originally the subject of a particular farm, though they are now all united into one), and in those which are said to be reckoned foreign, there are many local duties which do not extend beyond a particular town or district. There are some such even in the provinces which are said to be treated as foreign, particularly in the city of Marseilles. It is unnecessary to observe how much, both the restraints upon the interior commerce of the country, and the number of the revenue officers must be multiplied, in order to guard the frontiers of those different provinces and districts, which are subject to such different systems of taxation.

Over and above the general restraints arising from this complicated system of revenue laws, the commerce of wine, after corn perhaps the most important production of France, is in the greater part of the provinces subject to particular restraints, arising from the favour which has been shewn to the vineyards of particular provinces and districts, above those of others. The provinces most famous for their wines, it will be found, I believe, are those in which the trade in that article is subject to the fewest restraints of this kind. The extensive market which such provinces enjoy, encourages good management both in the cultivation of their vineyards, and in the subsequent preparation of their wines.

Such various and complicated revenue laws are not peculiar to France. The little dutchy of Milan is divided into six provinces, in each of which there is a different system of taxation with regard to several different sorts of consumable goods. The still smaller territories of the duke of Parma are divided into three or four, each of which has, in the same manner, a system of its own. Under such absurd management, nothing, but the great fertility of the soil and happiness of the climate, could preserve such countries from soon relapsing into the lowest state of poverty and barbarism.

Taxes upon consumable commodities may either be levied by an administration of which the officers are appointed by government and are immediately accountable to government, of which the revenue must in this case vary from year to year, according to the occasional variations in the produce of the tax; or they may be let in farm for a rent certain, the farmer being allowed to appoint his own officers, who, though obliged to levy the tax in the manner directed by the law, are under his immediate inspection, and are immediately accountable to him. The best and most frugal way of levying a tax can never be by farm. Over and above what is necessary for paying the stipulated rent, the salaries of the officers, and the whole expence of administration, the farmer must always draw from the produce of the tax a certain profit proportioned at least to the advance which he makes, to the risk which he runs, to the trouble which he is at, and to the knowledge and skill which it requires to manage so very complicated a concern. Government, by establishing an administration under their own immediate inspection, of the same kind with that which the farmer establishes, might at least save this profit, which is almost always exorbitant. To farm any considerable branch of the public revenue, requires either a great capital or a great credit; circumstances which would alone restrain the competition for such an undertaking to a very small number of people. Of the few who have this capital or credit, a still smaller number have the necessary knowledge or experience; another circumstance which restrains the competition still further. The very few, who are in condition to become competitors, find it more for their interest to combine together; to become co-partners instead of competitors, and when the farm is set up to auction, to offer no rent, but what is much below the real value. In countries where the public revenues are in farm, the farmers are generally the most opulent people. Their wealth would alone excite the public indignation, and the vanity which almost always accompanies such upstart fortunes, the foolish ostentation with which they commonly display that wealth, excites that indignation still more.

The farmers of the public revenue never find the laws too severe, which punish any attempt to evade the payment of a tax. They have no bowels for the contributors, who are not their subjects, and whose universal bankruptcy, if it should happen the day after their farm is expired, would not much affect their interest. In the greatest exigencies of the state, when the anxiety of the sovereign for the exact payment of his revenue is necessarily the greatest, they seldom fail to complain that without laws more rigorous than those which actually take place, it will be impossible for them to pay even the usual rent. In those moments of public distress their demands cannot be disputed. The revenue laws, therefore, become gradually more and more severe. The most sanguinary are always to be found in countries where the greater part of the public revenue is in farm. The mildest, in countries where it is levied under the immediate inspection of the sovereign. Even a bad sovereign feels more compassion for his people than can be expected from the farmers of his revenue. He knows that the permanent grandeur of his family depends upon the prosperity of his people, and he will never knowingly ruin that prosperity for the sake of any momentary interest of his own. It is otherwise with the farmers of his revenue, whose grandeur may frequently be the effect of the ruin, and not of the prosperity of his people.

A tax is sometimes, not only farmed for a certain rent, but the farmer has, besides, the monopoly of the commodity taxed. In France, the duties upon tobacco and salt are levied in this manner. In such cases the farmer, instead of one, levies two exorbitant profits upon the people; the profit of the farmer, and the still more exorbitant one of the monopolist. Tobacco being a luxury, every man is allowed to buy or not to buy as he chuses. But salt being a necessary, every man is obliged to buy of the farmer a certain quantity of it; because, if he did not buy this quantity of the farmer, he would, it is presumed, buy it of some smuggler. The taxes upon both commodities are exorbitant. The temptation to smuggle consequently is to many people irresistible, while at the same time the rigour of the law, and the vigilance of the farmer's officers, render the yielding to that temptation almost certainly ruinous. The smuggling of salt and tobacco sends every year several hundred people to the gallies, besides a very considerable number whom it sends to the gibbet. Those taxes levied in this manner yield a very considerable revenue to government. In 1767, the farm of tobacco was let for twenty-two millions five hundred and forty-one thousand two hundred and seventy-eight livres a year. That of salt, for thirty-six millions four hundred and nine-two thousand four hundred and four livres. The farm in both cases was to commence in 1768, and to last for six years. Those who consider the blood of the people as nothing in comparison with the revenue of the prince, may perhaps approve of this method of levying taxes. Similar taxes and monopolies of salt and tobacco have been established in many other countries; particularly in the Austrian and Prussian dominions, and in the greater part of the states of Italy.

In France, the greater part of the actual revenue of the crown is derived from eight different sources; the taille, the capitation, the two vingtiemes, the gabelles, the aides, the traites, the domaine, and the farm of tobacco. The five last are, in the greater part of the provinces, under farm. The three first are every where levied by an administration under the immediate inspection and direction of government, and it is universally acknowledged that, in proportion to what they take out of the pockets of the people, they bring more into the treasury of the prince than the other five, of which the administration is much more wasteful and expensive.

The finances of France seem, in their present state, to admit of three very obvious reformations. First, by abolishing the taille and the capitation, and by encreasing the number of vingtiemes, so as to produce an additional revenue equal to the amount of those other taxes, the revenue of the crown might be preserved; the expence of collection might be much diminished; the vexation of the inferior ranks of people, which the taille and capitation occasion, might be entirely prevented; and the superior ranks might not be more burdened than the greater part of them are at present. The vingtieme, I have already observed, is a tax very nearly of the same kind with what is called the land-tax of England. The burden of the taille, it is acknowledged, falls finally upon the proprietors of land, and as the greater part of the capitation is assessed upon those who are subject to the taille at so much a pound of that other tax, the final payment of the greater part of it must likewise fall upon the same order of people. Though the number of the vingtiemes, therefore, was increased so as to produce an additional revenue equal to the amount of both those taxes, the superior ranks of people might not be more burdened than they are at present. Many individuals no doubt would, on account of the great inequalities with which the taille is commonly assessed upon the estates and tenants of different individuals. The interest and opposition of such favoured subjects are the obstacles most likely to prevent this or any other reformation of the same kind. Secondly, by rendering the gabelle, the aides, the traites, the taxes upon tobacco, all the different customs and excises, uniform in all the different parts of the kingdom, those taxes might be levied at much less expence, and the interior commerce of the kingdom might be rendered as free as that of England. Thirdly, and lastly, by subjecting all those taxes to an administration under the immediate inspection and direction of government, the exorbitant profits of the farmers general might be added to the revenue of the state. The opposition arising from the private interest of individuals, is likely to be as effectual for preventing the two last as the first mentioned scheme of reformation.

The French system of taxation seems, in every respect, inferior to the British. In Great Britain ten million sterling are annually levied upon less than eight millions of people, without its being possible to say that any particular order is oppressed. From the collections of the Abbé Expilly, and the observations of the author of the Essay upon the legislation and commerce of corn, it appears probable, that France, including the provinces of Lorraine and Bar, contains about twenty-three or twenty-four millions of people; three times the number perhaps contained in Great Britain. The soil and climate of France are better than those of Great Britain. The country has been much longer in a state of improvement and cultivation, and is, upon that account, better stocked with all those things which it requires a long time to raise up and accumulate, such as great towns, and convenient and well-built houses, both in town and country. With these advantages, it might be expected that in France a revenue of thirty millions might be levied for the support of the state, with as little inconveniency as a revenue of ten millions is in Great Britain. In 1765 and 1766, the whole revenue paid into the treasury of France, according to the best, though, I acknowledge, very imperfect, accounts which I could get of it, usually run between 308 and 325 millions of livres; that is, it did not amount to fifteen millions sterling; not the half of what might have been expected, had the people contributed in the same proportion to their numbers as the people of Great Britain. The people of France, however, it is generally acknowledged, are much more oppressed by taxes than the people of Great Britain. France, however, is certainly the great empire in Europe which, after that of Great Britain, enjoys the mildest and most indulgent government.

In Holland the heavy taxes upon the necessaries of life have ruined, it is said, their principal manufactures, and are likely to discourage gradually even their fisheries and their trade in ship-building. The taxes upon the necessaries of life are inconsiderable in Great Britain, and no manufacture has hitherto been ruined by them. The British taxes which bear hardest on manufactures are some duties upon the importation of raw materials, particularly upon that of raw silk. The revenue of the states general and of the different cities, however, is said to amount to more than five millions two hundred and fifty thousand pounds sterling; and as the inhabitants of the United Provinces cannot well be supposed to amount to more than a third part of those of Great Britain, they must, in proportion to their number, be much more heavily taxed.

After all the proper subjects of taxation have been exhausted, if the exigencies of the state still continue to require new taxes, they must be imposed upon improper ones. The taxes upon the necessaries of life, therefore, may be no impeachment of the wisdom of that republic, which, in order to acquire and to maintain its independency, has, in spite of its great frugality, been involved in such expensive wars as have obliged it to contract great debts. The singular countries of Holland and Zealand, besides, require a considerable expence even to preserve their existence, or to prevent their being swallowed up by the sea, which must have contributed to increase considerably the load of taxes in those two provinces. The republican form of government seems to be the principal support of the present grandeur of Holland. The owners of great capitals, the great mercantile families, have generally either some direct share, or some indirect influence, in the administration of that government. For the sake of the respect and authority which they derive from this situation, they are willing to live in a country where their capital, if they employ it themselves, will bring them less profit, and if they lend it to another, less interest; and where the very moderate revenue which they can draw from it will purchase less of the necessaries and conveniences of life than in any other part of Europe. The residence of such wealthy people necessarily keeps alive, in spite of all disadvantages, a certain degree of industry in the country. Any public calamity which should destroy the republican form of government, which should throw the whole administration into the hands of nobles and of soldiers, which should annihilate altogether the importance of those wealthy merchants, would soon render it disagreeable to them to live in a country where they were no longer likely to be much respected. They would remove both their residence and their capital to some other country, and the industry and commerce of Holland would soon follow the capitals which supported them.

CHAPTER III

Of Public Debts

IN that rude state of society which precedes the extension of commerce and the improvement of manufactures, when those expensive luxuries which commerce and manufactures can alone introduce, are altogether unknown, the person who possesses a large revenue, I have endeavoured to show in the third book of this Inquiry, can spend or enjoy that revenue in no other way than by maintaining nearly as many people as it can maintain. A large revenue may at all times be said to consist in the command of a large quantity of the necessaries of life. In that rude state of things it is commonly paid in a large quantity of those necessaries, in the materials of plain food and coarse clothing, in corn and cattle, in wool and raw hides. When neither commerce nor manufactures furnish any thing for which the owner can exchange the greater part of those materials which are over and above his own consumption, he can do nothing with the surplus but feed and clothe nearly as many people as it will feed and clothe. A hospitality in which there is no luxury, and a liberality in which there is no ostentation, occasion, in this situation of things, the principal expences of the rich and the great. But these, I have likewise endeavoured to show in the same book, are expences by which people are not very apt to ruin themselves. There is not, perhaps, any selfish pleasure so frivolous, of which the pursuit has not sometimes ruined even sensible men. A passion for cock-fighting has ruined many. But the instances, I believe, are not very numerous of people who have been ruined by a hospitality or liberality of this kind; though the hospitality of luxury and the liberality of ostentation have ruined many. Among our feudal ancestors, the long time during which estates used to continue in the same family, sufficiently demonstrates the general disposition of people to live within their income. Though the rustic hospitality, constantly exercised by the great land-holders, may not, to us in the present times, seem consistent with that order, which we are apt to consider as inseparably connected with good œconomy, yet we must certainly allow them to have been at least so far frugal as not commonly to have spent their whole income. A part of their wool and raw hides they had generally an opportunity of selling for money. Some part of this money, perhaps, they spent in purchasing the few objects of vanity and luxury, with which the circumstances of the times could furnish them; but some part of it they seem commonly to have hoarded. They could not well indeed do any thing else but hoard whatever money they saved. To trade was disgraceful to a gentleman, and to lend money at interest, which at that time was considered as usury and prohibited by law, would have been still more so. In those times of violence and disorder, besides, it was convenient to have a hoard of money at hand, that in case they should be driven from their own home, they might have something of known value to carry with them to some place of safety. The same violence, which made it convenient to hoard, made it equally convenient to conceal the hoard. The frequency of treasure-trove, or of treasure found of which no owner was known, sufficiently demonstrates the frequency in those times both of hoarding and of concealing the hoard. Treasure-trove was then considered as an important branch of the revenue of the sovereign. All the treasure-trove of the kingdom would scarce perhaps in the present times make an important branch of the revenue of a private gentleman of a good estate.

The same disposition to save and to hoard prevailed in the sovereign, as well as in the subjects. Among nations to whom commerce and manufactures are little known, the sovereign, it has already been observed in the fourth book, is in a situation which naturally disposes him to the parsimony requisite for accumulation. In that situation the expence even of a sovereign cannot be directed by that vanity which delights in the gaudy finery of a court. The ignorance of the times affords but few of the trinkets in which that finery consists.

Standing armies are not then necessary, so that the expence even of a sovereign, like that of any other great lord, can be employed in scarce any thing but bounty to his tenants, and hospitality to his retainers. But bounty and hospitality very seldom lead to extravagance; though vanity almost always does. All the ancient sovereigns of Europe accordingly, it has already been observed, had treasures. Every Tartar chief in the present times is said to have one.

In a commercial country abounding with every sort of expensive luxury, the sovereign, in the same manner as almost all the great proprietors in his dominions, naturally spends a great part of his revenue in purchasing those luxuries. His own and the neighbouring countries supply him abundantly with all the costly trinkets which compose the splendid, but insignificant pageantry of a court. For the sake of an inferior pageantry of the same kind, his nobles dismiss their retainers, make their tenants independent, and become gradually themselves as insignificant as the greater part of the wealthy burghers in his dominions. The same frivolous passions, which influence their conduct, influence his. How can it be supposed that he should be the only rich man in his dominions who is insensible to pleasures of this kind? If he does not, what he is very likely to do, spend upon those pleasures so great a part of his revenue as to debilitate very much the defensive power of the state, it cannot well be expected that he should not spend upon them all that part of it which is over and above what is necessary for supporting that defensive power. His ordinary expence becomes equal to his ordinary revenue, and it is well if it does not frequently exceed it. The amassing of treasure can no longer be expected, and when extraordinary exigencies require extraordinary expences, he must necessarily call upon his subjects for an extraordinary aid. The present and the late king of Prussia are the only great princes of Europe, who, since the death of Henry IV. of France in 1610, are supposed to have amassed any considerable treasure. The parsimony which leads to accumulation has become almost as rare in republican as in monarchial governments. The Italian republics, the United Provinces of the Netherlands, are all in debt. The canton of Berne is the single republic in Europe which has amassed any considerable treasure. The other Swiss republics have not. The taste for some sort of pageantry, for splendid buildings, at least, and other public ornaments, frequently prevails as much in the apparently sober senate-house of a little republic, as in the dissipated court of the greatest king.

The want of parsimony in time of peace, imposes the necessity of contracting debt in time of war. When war comes, there is no money in the treasury but what is necessary for carrying on the ordinary expence of the peace establishment. In war an establishment of three or four times that expence becomes necessary for the defence of the state, and consequently a revenue three or four times greater than the peace revenue. Supposing that the sovereign should have, what he scarce ever has, the immediate means of augmenting his revenue in proportion to the augmentation of his expence, yet still the produce of the taxes, from which this increase of revenue must be drawn, will not begin to come into the treasury till perhaps ten or twelve months after they are imposed. But the moment in which war begins, or rather the moment in which it appears likely to begin, the army must be augmented, the fleet must be fitted out, the garrisoned towns must be put into a posture of defence; that army, that fleet, those garrisoned towns must be furnished with arms, ammunition, and provisions. An immediate and great expence must be incurred in that moment of immediate danger, which will not wait for the gradual and slow returns of the new taxes. In this exigency government can have no other resource but in borrowing.

The same commercial state of society which, by the operation of moral causes, brings government in this manner into the necessity of borrowing, produces in the subjects both an ability and an inclination to lend. If it commonly brings along with it the necessity of borrowing, it likewise brings along with it the facility of doing so.

A country abounding with merchants and manufacturers, necessarily abounds with a set of people through whose hands not only their own capitals, but the capitals of all those who either lend them money, or trust them with goods, pass as frequently, or more frequently, than the revenue of a private man, who, without trade or business, lives upon his income, passes through his hands. The revenue of such a man can regularly pass through his hands only once in a year. But the whole amount of the capital and credit of a merchant, who deals in a trade in which the returns are very quick, may sometimes pass through his hands two, three, or four times in a year. A country abounding with merchants and manufacturers, therefore, necessarily abounds with a set of people who have at all times in their power to advance, if they chuse to do so, a very large sum of money to government. Hence the ability in the subjects of a commercial state to lend.

Commerce and manufactures can seldom flourish long in any state which does not enjoy a regular administration of justice, in which the people do not feel themselves secure in the possession of their property, in which the faith of contracts is not supported by law, and in which the authority of the state is not supposed to be regularly employed in enforcing the payment of debts from all those who are able to pay. Commerce and manufactures, in short, can seldom flourish in any state in which there is not a certain degree of confidence in the justice of government. The same confidence which disposes great merchants and manufacturers, upon ordinary occasions, to trust their property to the protection of a particular government; disposes them, upon extraordinary occasions, to trust that government with the use of their property. By lending money to government, they do not even for a moment diminish their ability to carry on their trade and manufactures. On the contrary, they commonly augment it. The necessities of the state render government upon most occasions willing to borrow upon terms extremely advantageous to the lender. The security which it grants to the original creditor, is made transferable to any other creditor, and, from the universal confidence in the justice of the state, generally sells in the market for more than was originally paid for it. The merchant or monied man makes money by lending money to government, and instead of diminishing, increases his trading capital. He generally considers it as a favour, therefore, when the administration admits him to a share in the first subscription for a new loan. Hence the inclination or willingness in the subjects of a commercial state to lend.

The government of such a state is very apt to repose itself upon this ability and willingness of its subjects to lend it their money on extraordinary occasions. It foresees the facility of borrowing, and therefore dispenses itself from the duty of saving.

In a rude state of society there are no great mercantile or manufacturing capitals. The individuals, who hoard whatever money they can save, and who conceal their hoard, do so from a distrust of the justice of government, from a fear that if it was known that they had a hoard, and where that hoard was to be found, they would quickly be plundered. In such a state of things few people would be able, and no body would be willing, to lend their money to government on extraordinary exigencies. The sovereign feels that he must provide for such exigencies by saving, because he foresees the absolute impossibility of borrowing. This foresight increases still further his natural disposition to save.

The progress of the enormous debts which at present oppress, and will in the long-run probably ruin, all the great nations of Europe, has been pretty uniform. Nations, like private men, have generally begun to borrow upon what may be called personal credit, without assigning or mortgaging any particular fund for the payment of the debt; and when this resource has failed them, they have gone on to borrow upon assignments or mortgages of particular funds.

What is called the unfunded debt of Great Britain, is contracted in the former of those two ways. It consists partly in a debt which bears, or is supposed to bear, no interest, and which resembles the debts that a private man contracts upon account; and partly in a debt which bears interest, and which resembles what a private man contracts upon his bill or promissory note. The debts which are due either for extraordinary services, or for services either not provided for, or not paid at the time when they are performed; part of the extraordinaries of the army, navy, and ordnance, the arrears of subsidies to foreign princes, those of seamen's wages, &c. usually constitute a debt of the first kind. Navy and Exchequer bills, which are issued sometimes in payment of a part of such debts and sometimes for other purposes, constitute a debt of the second kind; Exchequer bills bearing interest from the day on which they are issued, and navy bills six months after they are issued. The bank of England, either by voluntarily discounting those bills at their current value, or by agreeing with government for certain considerations to circulate Exchequer bills, that is, to receive them at par, paying the interest which happens to be due upon them, keeps up their value and facilitates their circulation, and thereby frequently enables government to contract a very large debt of this kind. In France, where there is no bank, the state bills (billets d'état) have sometimes sold at sixty and seventy per cent. discount. During the great re-coinage in King William's time, when the bank of England thought proper to put a stop to its usual transactions, Exchequer bills and tallies are said to have sold from twenty-five to sixty per cent. discount; owing partly, no doubt, to the supposed instability of the new government established by the Revolution, but partly too to the want of the support of the bank of England.

When this resource is exhausted, and it becomes necessary, in order to raise money, to assign or mortgage some particular branch of the public revenue for the payment of the debt, government has upon different occasions done this in two different ways. Sometimes it has made this assignment or mortgage for a short period of time only, a year, or a few years, for example; and sometimes for perpetuity. In the one case, the fund was supposed sufficient to pay, within the limited time, both principal and interest of the money borrowed. In the other, it was supposed sufficient to pay the interest only, or a perpetual annuity equivalent to the interest, government being at liberty to redeem at any time this annuity, upon paying back the principal sum borrowed. When money was raised in the one way, it was said to be raised by anticipation; when in the other, by perpetual funding, or, more shortly, by funding.

* * * * * * * *

The ordinary expence of the greater part of modern governments in time of peace being equal or nearly equal to their ordinary revenue, when war comes, they are both unwilling and unable to increase their revenue in proportion to the increase of their expence. They are unwilling, for fear of offending the people, who by so great and so sudden an increase of taxes, would soon be disgusted with the war; and they are unable, from not well knowing what taxes would be sufficient to produce the revenue wanted. The facility of borrowing delivers them from the embarrassment which this fear and inability would otherwise occasion. By means of borrowing they are enabled, with a very moderate increase of taxes, to raise, from year to year, money sufficient for carrying on the war, and by the practice of perpetual funding they are enabled, with the smallest possible increase of taxes, to raise annually the largest possible sum of money. In great empires the people who live in the capital, and in the provinces remote from the scene of action, feel, many of them, scarce any inconveniency from the war; but enjoy, at their ease, the amusement of reading in the newspapers the exploits of their own fleets and armies. To them this amusement compensates the small difference between the taxes which they pay on account of the war, and those which they had been accustomed to pay in time of peace. They are commonly dissatisfied with the return of peace, which puts an end to their amusement, and to a thousand visionary hopes of conquest and national glory, from a longer continuance of the war.

The return of peace, indeed, seldom relieves them from the greater part of the taxes imposed during the war. These are mortgaged for the interest of the debt contracted in order to carry it on. If, over and above paying the interest of this debt, and defraying the ordinary expence of government, the old revenue, together with the new taxes, produce some surplus revenue, it may perhaps be converted into a sinking fund for paying off the debt. But, in the first place, this sinking fund, even supposing it should be applied to no other purpose, is generally altogether inadequate for paying, in the course of any period during which it can reasonably be expected that peace should continue, the whole debt contracted during the war; and, in the second place, this fund is almost always applied to other purposes.

The new taxes were imposed for the sole purpose of paying the interest of the money borrowed upon them. If they produce more, it is generally something which was neither intended nor expected, and is therefore seldom very considerable. Sinking funds have generally arisen, not so much from any surplus of the taxes which was over and above what was necessary for paying the interest or annuity originally charged upon them, as from a subsequent reduction of that interest. That of Holland in 1655, and that of the ecclesiastical state in 1685, were both formed in this manner. Hence the usual insufficiency of such funds.

During the most profound peace, various events occur which require an extraordinary expence, and government finds it always more convenient to defray this expence by misapplying the sinking fund than by imposing a new tax. Every new tax is immediately felt more or less by the people. It occasions always some murmur, and meets with some opposition. The more taxes may have been multiplied, the higher they may have been raised upon every different subject of taxation; the more loudly the people complain of every new tax, the more difficult it becomes too either to find out new subjects of taxation, or to raise much higher the taxes already imposed upon the old. A momentary suspension of the payment of debt is not immediately felt by the people, and occasions neither murmur nor complaint. To borrow of the sinking fund is always an obvious and easy expedient for getting out of the present difficulty. The more the public debts may have been accumulated, the more necessary it may have become to study to reduce them, the more dangerous, the more ruinous it may be to misapply any part of the sinking fund; the less likely is the public debt to be reduced to any considerable degree, the more likely, the more certainly is the sinking fund to be misapplied towards defraying all the extraordinary expences which occur in time of peace. When a nation is already overburdened with taxes, nothing but the necessities of a new war, nothing but either the animosity of national vengeance, or the anxiety for national security, can induce the people to submit, with tolerable patience, to a new tax. Hence the usual misapplication of the sinking fund.

* * * * * * * * * *

The public funds of the different indebted nations of Europe, particularly those of England, have by one author been represented as the accumulation of a great capital superadded to the other capital of the country, by means of which its trade is extended, its manufactures multiplied, and its lands cultivated and improved much beyond what they could have been by means of that other capital only. He does not consider that the capital which the first creditors of the public advanced to government, was, from the moment in which they advanced it, a certain portion of the annual produce turned away from serving in the function of a capital, to serve in that of a revenue; from maintaining productive labourers to maintain unproductive ones, and to be spent and wasted, generally in the course of the year, without even the hope of any future reproduction. In return for the capital which they advanced they obtained, indeed, an annuity in the public funds in most cases of more than equal value. This annuity, no doubt, replaced to them their capital, and enabled them to carry on their trade and business to the same or perhaps to a greater extent than before; that is, they were enabled either to borrow of other people a new capital upon the credit of this annuity, or by selling it to get from other people a new capital of their own, equal or superior to that which they had advanced to government. This new capital, however, which they in this manner either bought or borrowed of other people, must have existed in the country before, and must have been employed as all capitals are, in maintaining productive labour. When it came into the hands of those who had advanced their money to government, though it was in some respects a new capital to them, it was not so to the country; but was only a capital withdrawn from certain employments in order to be turned towards others. Though it replaced to them what they had advanced to government, it did not replace it to the country. Had they not advanced this capital to government, there would have been in the country two capitals, two portions of the annual produce, instead of one, employed in maintaining productive labour.

When for defraying the expence of government a revenue is raised within the year from the produce of free or unmortgaged taxes, a certain portion of the revenue of private people is only turned away from maintaining one species of unproductive labour, towards maintaining another. Some part of what they pay in those taxes might no doubt have been accumulated into capital, and consequently employed in maintaining productive labour; but the greater part would probably have been spent and consequently employed in maintaining unproductive labour. The public expence, however, when defrayed in this manner, no doubt hinders more or less the further accumulation of new capital; but it does not necessarily occasion the destruction of any actually existing capital.

When the public expence is defrayed by funding, it is defrayed by the annual destruction of some capital which had before existed in the country; by the perversion of some portion of the annual produce which had before been destined for the maintenance of productive labour, towards that of unproductive labour. As in this case, however, the taxes are lighter than they would have been, had a revenue sufficient for defraying the same expence been raised within the year; the private revenue of individuals is necessarily less burdened, and consequently their ability to save and accumulate some part of that revenue into capital is a good deal less impaired. If the method of funding destroy more old capital, it at the same time hinders less the accumulation or acquisition of new capital, than that of defraying the public expence by a revenue raised within the year. Under the system of funding, the frugality and industry of private people can more easily repair the breaches which the waste and extravagance of government may occasionally make in the general capital of the society.

It is only during the continuance of war, however, that the system of funding has this advantage over the other system. Were the expence of war to be defrayed always by a revenue raised within the year, the taxes from which that extraordinary revenue was drawn would last no longer than the war. The ability of private people to accumulate, though less during the war, would have been greater during the peace than under the system of funding. War would not necessarily have occasioned the destruction of any old capitals, and peace would have occasioned the accumulation of many more new. Wars would in general be more speedily concluded, and less wantonly undertaken. The people feeling, during the continuance of the war, the complete burden of it, would soon grow weary of it, and government, in order to humour them, would not be under the necessity of carrying it on longer than it was necessary to do so. The foresight of the heavy and unavoidable burdens of war would hinder the people from wantonly calling for it when there was no real or solid interest to fight for. The seasons during which the ability of private people to accumulate was somewhat impaired, would occur more rarely, and be of shorter continuance. Those on the contrary, during which that ability was in the highest vigour, would be of much longer duration than they can well be under the system of funding.

When funding, besides, has made a certain progress, the multiplication of taxes which it brings along with it sometimes impairs as much the ability of private people to accumulate even in time of peace, as the other system would in time of war. The peace revenue of Great Britain amounts at present to more than ten millions a year. If free and unmortgaged, it might be sufficient, with proper management and without contracting a shilling of new debt, to carry on the most vigorous war. The private revenue of the inhabitants of Great Britain is at present as much encumbered in time of peace, their ability to accumulate is as much impaired as it would have been in the time of the most expensive war, had the pernicious system of funding never been adopted.

In the payment of the interest of the public debt, it has been said, it is the right hand which pays the left. The money does not go out of the country. It is only a part of the revenue of one set of the inhabitants which is transferred to another; and the nation is not a farthing the poorer. This apology is founded altogether in the sophistry of the mercantile system, and after the long examination which I have already bestowed upon that system, it may perhaps be unnecessary to say any thing further about it. It supposes, besides, that the whole public debt is owing to the inhabitants of the country, which happens not to be true; the Dutch, as well as several other foreign nations, having a very considerable share in our public funds. But though the whole debt were owing to the inhabitants of the country, it would not upon that account be less pernicious.

Land and capital stock are the two original sources of all revenue both private and public. Capital stock pays the wages of productive labour, whether employed in agriculture, manufactures, or commerce. The management of those two original sources of revenue belongs to two different sets of people; the proprietors of land, and the owners or employers of capital stock.

The proprietor of land is interested for the sake of his own revenue to keep his estate in as good condition as he can, by building and repairing his tenants houses, by making and maintaining the necessary drains and enclosures, and all those other expensive improvements which it properly belongs to the landlord to make and maintain. But by different land-taxes the revenue of the landlord may be so much diminished; and by different duties upon the necessaries and conveniences of life, that diminished revenue may be rendered of so little real value, that he may find himself altogether unable to make or maintain those expensive improvements. When the landlord, however, ceases to do his part, it is altogether impossible that the tenant should continue to do his. As the distress of the landlord increases, the agriculture of the country must necessarily decline.

When, by different taxes upon the necessaries and conveniences of life, the owners and employers of capital stock find, that whatever revenue they derive from it, will not, in a particular country, purchase the same quantity of those necessaries and conveniences which an equal revenue would in almost any other, they will be disposed to remove to some other. And when, in order to raise those taxes, all or the greater part of merchants and manufacturers, that is, all or the greater part of the employers of great capitals, come to be continually exposed to the mortifying and vexatious visits of the tax-gatherers, this disposition to remove will soon be changed into an actual removal. The industry of the country will necessarily fall with the removal of the capital which supported it, and the ruin of trade and manufactures will follow the declension of agriculture.

To transfer from the owners of those two great sources of revenue, land and capital stock, from the persons immediately interested in the good condition of every particular portion of land, and in the good management of every particular portion of capital stock, to another set of persons (the creditors of the public, who have no such particular interest), the greater part of the revenue arising from either, must, in the long-run, occasion both the neglect of land, and the waste or removal of capital stock. A creditor of the public has no doubt a general interest in the prosperity of the agriculture, manufactures, and commerce of the country; and consequently in the good condition of its lands, and in the good management of its capital stock. Should there be any general failure or declension in any of these things, the produce of the different taxes might no longer be sufficient to pay him the annuity or interest which is due him. But a creditor of the public, considered merely as such, has no interest in the good condition of any particular portion of land, or in the good management of any particular portion of capital stock. As a creditor of the public he has no knowledge of any such particular portion. He has no inspection of it. He can have no care about it. Its ruin may in some cases be unknown to him, and cannot directly affect him.

The practice of funding has gradually enfeebled every state which has adopted it. The Italian republics seem to have begun it. Genoa and Venice, the only two remaining which can pretend to an independent existence, have both been enfeebled by it. Spain seems to have learned the practice from the Italian republics, and (its taxes being probably less judicious than theirs) it has, in proportion to its natural strength, been still more enfeebled. The debts of Spain are of very old standing. It was deeply in debt before the end of the sixteenth century, about a hundred years before England owed a shilling. France, notwithstanding all its natural resources, languishes under an oppressive load of the same kind. The republic of the United Provinces is as much enfeebled by its debts as either Genoa or Venice. Is it likely that in Great Britain alone a practice, which has brought either weakness or desolation into every other country, should prove altogether innocent?

The system of taxation established in those different countries, it may be said, is inferior to that of England. I believe it is so. But it ought to be remembered, that when the wisest government has exhausted all the proper subjects of taxation, it must, in cases of urgent necessity, have recourse to improper ones. The wise republic of Holland has upon some occasions been obliged to have recourse to taxes as inconvenient as the greater part of those of Spain. Another war begun before any considerable liberation of the public revenue had been brought about, and growing in its progress as expensive as the last war, may, from irresistible necessity, render the British system of taxation as oppressive as that of Holland, or even as that of Spain. To the honour of our present system of taxation, indeed, it has hitherto given so little embarrassment to industry, that, during the course even of the most expensive wars, the frugality and good conduct of individuals seem to have been able, by saving and accumulation, to repair all the breaches which the waste and extravagance of government had made in the general capital of the society. At the conclusion of the late war, the most expensive that Great Britain ever waged, her agriculture was as flourishing, her manufacturers as numerous and as fully employed, and her commerce as extensive, as they had ever been before. The capital, therefore, which supported all those different branches of industry, must have been equal to what it had ever been before. Since the peace, agriculture has been still further improved, the rents of houses have risen in every town and village of the country, a proof of the increasing wealth and revenue of the people; and the annual amount of the greater part of the old taxes, of the principal branches of the excise and customs in particular, has been continually increasing, an equally clear proof of an increasing consumption, and consequently of an increasing produce, which could alone support that consumption. Great Britain seems to support with ease a burden which, half a century ago, nobody believed her capable of supporting. Let us not, however, upon this account rashly conclude that she is capable of supporting any burden; nor even be too confident that she could support, without great distress, a burden a little greater than what has already been laid upon her.

When national debts have once been accumulated to a certain degree, there is scarce, I believe, a single instance of their having been fairly and completely paid. The liberation of the public revenue, if it has ever been brought about at all, has always been brought about by a bankruptcy; sometimes by an avowed one, but always by a real one, though frequently by a pretended payment.

The raising of the denomination of the coin has been the most usual expedient by which a real public bankruptcy has been disguised under the appearance of a pretended payment. If a sixpence, for example, should either by act of parliament or royal proclamation be raised to the denomination of a shilling, and twenty sixpences to that of a pound sterling; the person who under the old denomination had borrowed twenty shillings, or near four ounces of silver, would, under the new, pay with twenty sixpences, or with something less than two ounces. A national debt of about a hundred and twenty-eight millions, nearly the capital of the funded and unfunded debt of Great Britain, might in this manner be paid with about sixty-four millions of our present money. It would indeed be a pretended payment only, and the creditors of the public would really be defrauded of ten shillings in the pound of what was due to them. The calamity, too, would extend much further than to the creditors of the public, and those of every private person would suffer a proportionable loss; and this without any advantage, but in most cases with a great additional loss, to the creditors of the public. If the creditors of the public indeed were generally much in debt to other people, they might in some measure compensate their loss by paying their creditors in the same coin in which the public had paid them. But in most countries the creditors of the public are, the greater part of them, wealthy people, who stand more in the relation of creditors than in that of debtors towards the rest of their fellow-citizens. A pretended payment of this kind, therefore, instead of alleviating, aggravates in most cases the loss of the creditors of the public; and without any advantage to the public, extends the calamity to a great number of other innocent people. It occasions a general and most pernicious subversion of the fortunes of private people; enriching in most cases the idle and profuse debtor at the expense of the industrious and frugal creditor, and transporting a great part of the national capital from the hands which were likely to increase and improve it, to those which are likely to dissipate and destroy it. When it becomes necessary for a state to declare itself bankrupt, in the same manner as when it becomes necessary for an individual to do so, a fair, open, and avowed bankruptcy is always the measure which is both least dishonourable to the debtor, and least hurtful to the creditor. The honour of a state is surely very poorly provided for, when, in order to cover the disgrace of a real bankruptcy, it has recourse to a juggling trick of this kind, so easily seen through, and at the same time so extremely pernicious.

GREAT BOOKS IN PHILOSOPHY PAPERBACK SERIES

ESTHETICS

- ❑ Aristotle—*The Poetics*
- ❑ Aristotle—*Treatise on Rhetoric*

ETHICS

- ❑ Aristotle—*The Nicomachean Ethics*
- ❑ Marcus Aurelius—*Meditations*
- ❑ Jeremy Bentham—*The Principles of Morals and Legislation*
- ❑ John Dewey—*Human Nature and Conduct*
- ❑ John Dewey—*The Moral Writings of John Dewey, Revised Edition*
- ❑ Epictetus—*Enchiridion*
- ❑ David Hume—*An Enquiry Concerning the Principles of Morals*
- ❑ Immanuel Kant—*Fundamental Principles of the Metaphysic of Morals*
- ❑ John Stuart Mill—*Utilitarianism*
- ❑ George Edward Moore—*Principia Ethica*
- ❑ Friedrich Nietzsche—*Beyond Good and Evil*
- ❑ Plato—*Protagoras, Philebus, and Gorgias*
- ❑ Bertrand Russell—*Bertrand Russell On Ethics, Sex, and Marriage*
- ❑ Arthur Schopenhauer—*The Wisdom of Life* and *Counsels and Maxims*
- ❑ Adam Smith—*The Theory of Moral Sentiments*
- ❑ Benedict de Spinoza—*Ethics* and *The Improvement of the Understanding*

LOGIC

- ❑ George Boole—*The Laws of Thought*

METAPHYSICS/EPISTEMOLOGY

- ❑ Aristotle—*De Anima*
- ❑ Aristotle—*The Metaphysics*
- ❑ Francis Bacon—*Essays*
- ❑ George Berkeley—*Three Dialogues Between Hylas and Philonous*
- ❑ W. K. Clifford—*The Ethics of Belief and Other Essays*
- ❑ René Descartes—*Discourse on Method* and *The Meditations*
- ❑ John Dewey—*How We Think*
- ❑ John Dewey—*The Influence of Darwin on Philosophy and Other Essays*
- ❑ Epicurus—*The Essential Epicurus: Letters, Principal Doctrines, Vatican Sayings, and Fragments*
- ❑ Sidney Hook—*The Quest for Being*
- ❑ David Hume—*An Enquiry Concerning Human Understanding*
- ❑ David Hume—*A Treatise on Human Nature*
- ❑ William James—*The Meaning of Truth*
- ❑ William James—*Pragmatism*
- ❑ Immanuel Kant—*The Critique of Judgment*
- ❑ Immanuel Kant—*Critique of Practical Reason*
- ❑ Immanuel Kant—*Critique of Pure Reason*
- ❑ Gottfried Wilhelm Leibniz—*Discourse on Metaphysics* and *The Monadology*
- ❑ John Locke—*An Essay Concerning Human Understanding*
- ❑ George Herbert Mead—*The Philosophy of the Present*

- ❑ Charles S. Peirce—*The Essential Writings*
- ❑ Plato—*The Euthyphro, Apology, Crito,* and *Phaedo*
- ❑ Plato—*Lysis, Phaedrus, and Symposium*
- ❑ Bertrand Russell—*The Problems of Philosophy*
- ❑ George Santayana—*The Life of Reason*
- ❑ Sextus Empiricus—*Outlines of Pyrrhonism*
- ❑ Ludwig Wittgenstein—*Wittgenstein's Lectures: Cambridge, 1932–1935*

PHILOSOPHY OF RELIGION

- ❑ Jeremy Bentham—*The Influence of Natural Religion on the Temporal Happiness of Mankind*
- ❑ Marcus Tullius Cicero—*The Nature of the Gods* and *On Divination*
- ❑ Ludwig Feuerbach—*The Essence of Christianity*
- ❑ Paul Henri Thiry, Baron d'Holbach—*Good Sense*
- ❑ David Hume—*Dialogues Concerning Natural Religion*
- ❑ William James—*The Varieties of Religious Experience*
- ❑ John Locke—*A Letter Concerning Toleration*
- ❑ Lucretius—*On the Nature of Things*
- ❑ John Stuart Mill—*Three Essays on Religion*
- ❑ Friedrich Nietzsche—*The Antichrist*
- ❑ Thomas Paine—*The Age of Reason*
- ❑ Bertrand Russell—*Bertrand Russell On God and Religion*

SOCIAL AND POLITICAL PHILOSOPHY

- ❑ Aristotle—*The Politics*
- ❑ Mikhail Bakunin—*The Basic Bakunin: Writings, 1869–1871*
- ❑ Edmund Burke—*Reflections on the Revolution in France*
- ❑ John Dewey—*Freedom and Culture*
- ❑ John Dewey—*Individualism Old and New*
- ❑ John Dewey—*Liberalism and Social Action*
- ❑ G. W. F. Hegel—*The Philosophy of History*
- ❑ G. W. F. Hegel—*Philosophy of Right*
- ❑ Thomas Hobbes—*The Leviathan*
- ❑ Sidney Hook—*Paradoxes of Freedom*
- ❑ Sidney Hook—*Reason, Social Myths, and Democracy*
- ❑ John Locke—*The Second Treatise on Civil Government*
- ❑ Niccolo Machiavelli—*The Prince*
- ❑ Karl Marx (with Friedrich Engels)—*The Economic and Philosophic Manuscripts of 1844* and *The Communist Manifesto*
- ❑ Karl Marx (with Friedrich Engels)—*The German Ideology,* including *Theses on Feuerbach* and *Introduction to the Critique of Political Economy*
- ❑ Karl Marx—*The Poverty of Philosophy*
- ❑ John Stuart Mill—*Considerations on Representative Government*
- ❑ John Stuart Mill—*On Liberty*
- ❑ John Stuart Mill—*On Socialism*
- ❑ John Stuart Mill—*The Subjection of Women*
- ❑ Montesquieu, Charles de Secondat—*The Spirit of Laws*
- ❑ Friedrich Nietzsche—*Thus Spake Zarathustra*

PSYCHOLOGY

- ❑ Sigmund Freud—*Totem and Taboo*

RELIGION/FREETHOUGHT

- ❑ Desiderius Erasmus—*The Praise of Folly*
- ❑ Thomas Henry Huxley—*Agnosticism and Christianity and Other Essays*
- ❑ Ernest Renan—*The Life of Jesus*
- ❑ Upton Sinclair—*The Profits of Religion*
- ❑ Elizabeth Cady Stanton—*The Woman's Bible*
- ❑ Voltaire—*A Treatise on Toleration and Other Essays*
- ❑ Andrew D. White—*A History of the Warfare of Science with Theology in Christendom*

SCIENCE

- ❑ Jacob Bronowski—*The Identity of Man*
- ❑ Nicolaus Copernicus—*On the Revolutions of Heavenly Spheres*
- ❑ Marie Curie—*Radioactive Substances*
- ❑ Charles Darwin—*The Autobiography of Charles Darwin*
- ❑ Charles Darwin—*The Descent of Man*
- ❑ Charles Darwin—*The Origin of Species*
- ❑ Charles Darwin—*The Voyage of the* Beagle
- ❑ René Descartes—*Treatise of Man*
- ❑ Albert Einstein—*Relativity*
- ❑ Michael Faraday—*The Forces of Matter*
- ❑ Galileo Galilei—*Dialogues Concerning Two New Sciences*
- ❑ Ernst Haeckel—*The Riddle of the Universe*
- ❑ William Harvey—*On the Motion of the Heart and Blood in Animals*
- ❑ Werner Heisenberg—*Physics and Philosophy*
- ❑ Julian Huxley—*Evolutionary Humanism*
- ❑ Thomas H. Huxley—*Evolution and Ethics* and *Science and Morals*
- ❑ Edward Jenner—*Vaccination against Smallpox*
- ❑ Johannes Kepler—*Epitome of Copernican Astronomy* and *Harmonies of the World*
- ❑ James Clerk Maxwell—*Matter and Motion*
- ❑ Isaac Newton—*Opticks, Or Treatise of the Reflections, Inflections, and Colours of Light*
- ❑ Isaac Newton—*The Principia*
- ❑ Louis Pasteur and Joseph Lister—*Germ Theory and Its Application to Medicine* and *On the Antiseptic Principle of the Practice of Surgery*
- ❑ William Thomson (Lord Kelvin) and Peter Guthrie Tait—*The Elements of Natural Philosophy*
- ❑ Alfred Russel Wallace—*Island Life*

SOCIOLOGY

- ❑ Emile Durkheim—*Ethics and the Sociology of Morals*